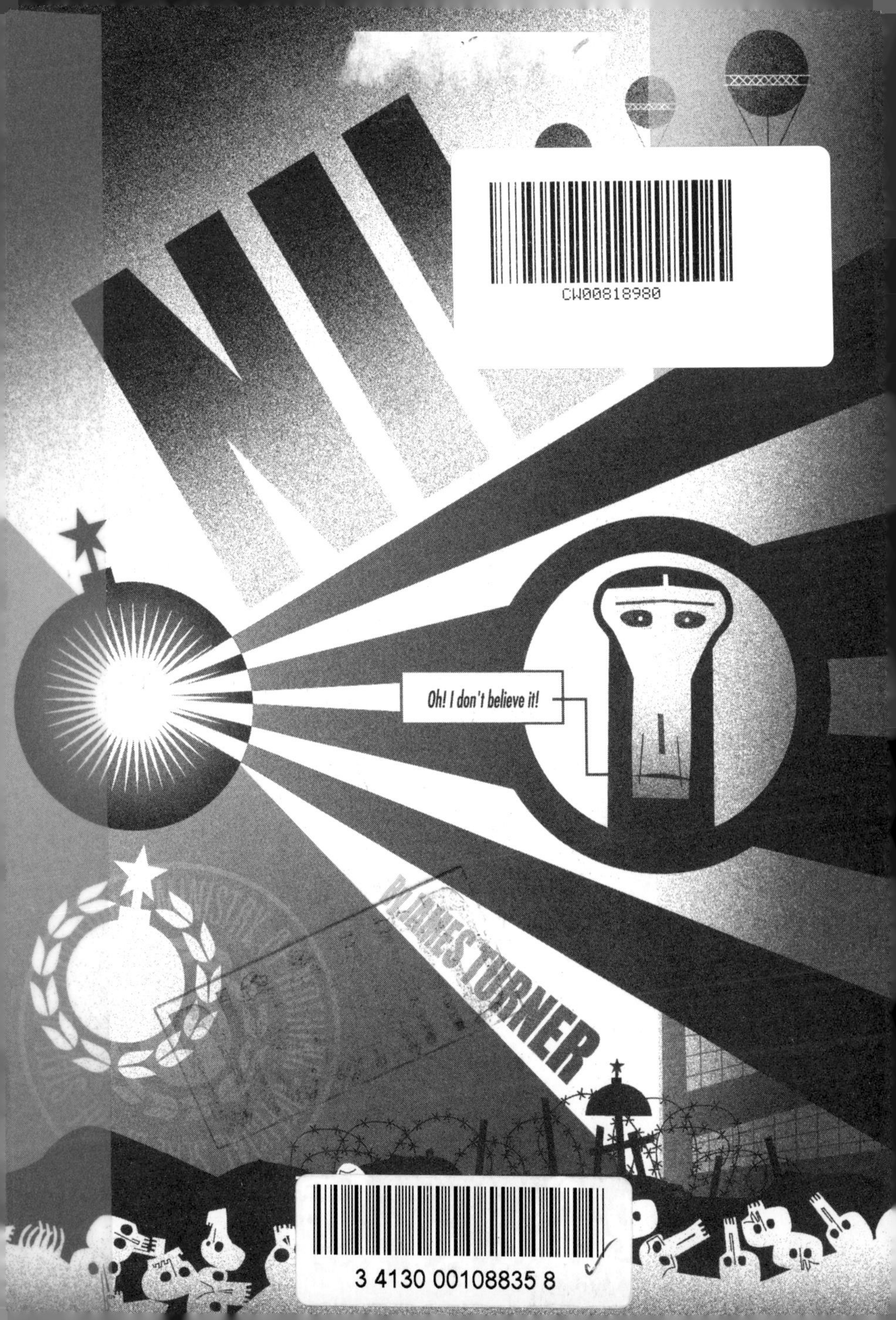
Oh! I don't believe it!
JAMES TURNER

Published by **SLG Publishing**

Dan Vado, Supreme Commander
Jennifer de Guzman, Femme Fatale
Deb Moskyok, Madame Direktor

SLG Publishing

P.O. Box 26427
San Jose, CA 95159

www.slavelabor.com

First Printing: April 2005
ISBN 1-59362-020-9

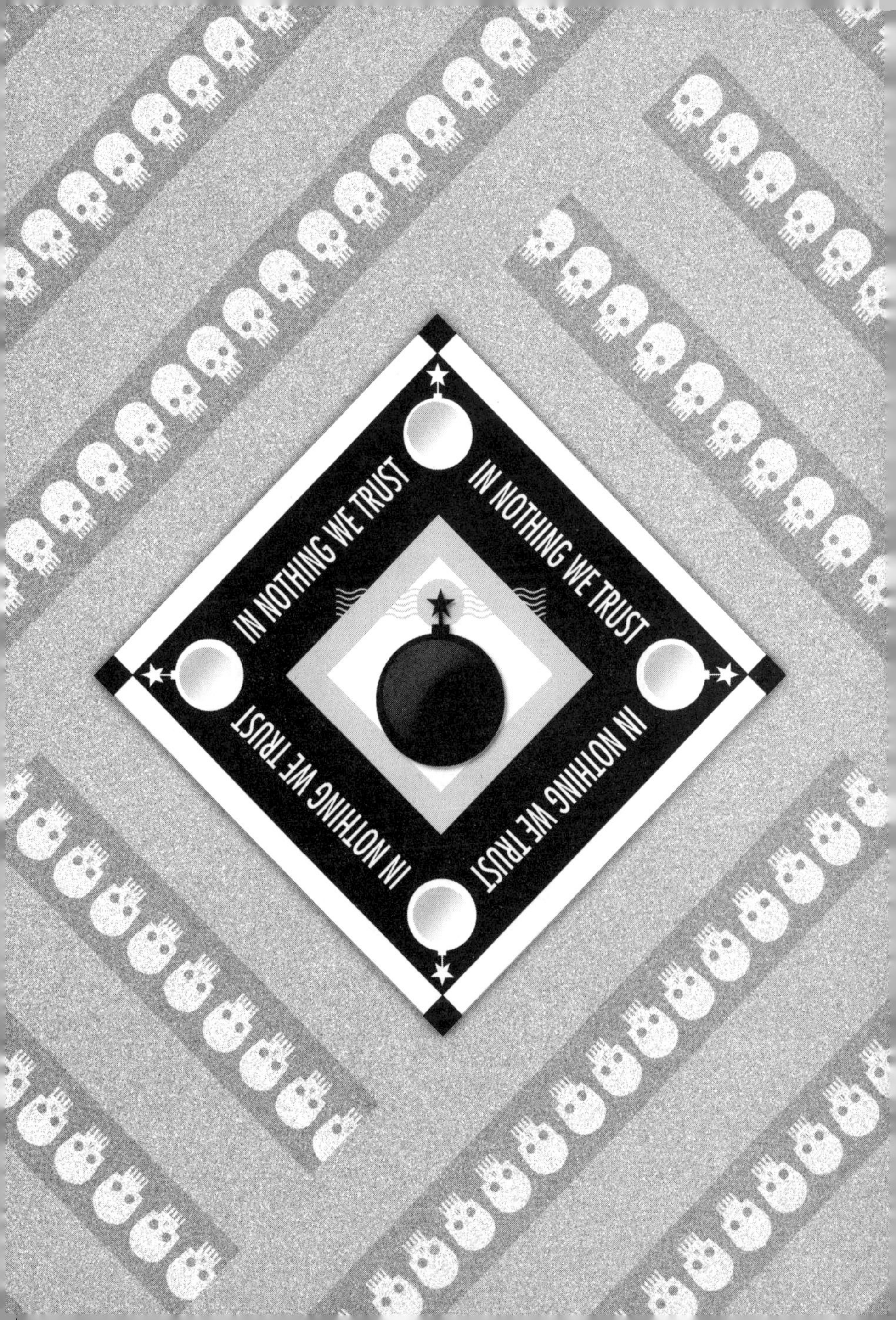
IN NOTHING WE TRUST
IN NOTHING WE TRUST
IN NOTHING WE TRUST
IN NOTHING WE TRUST

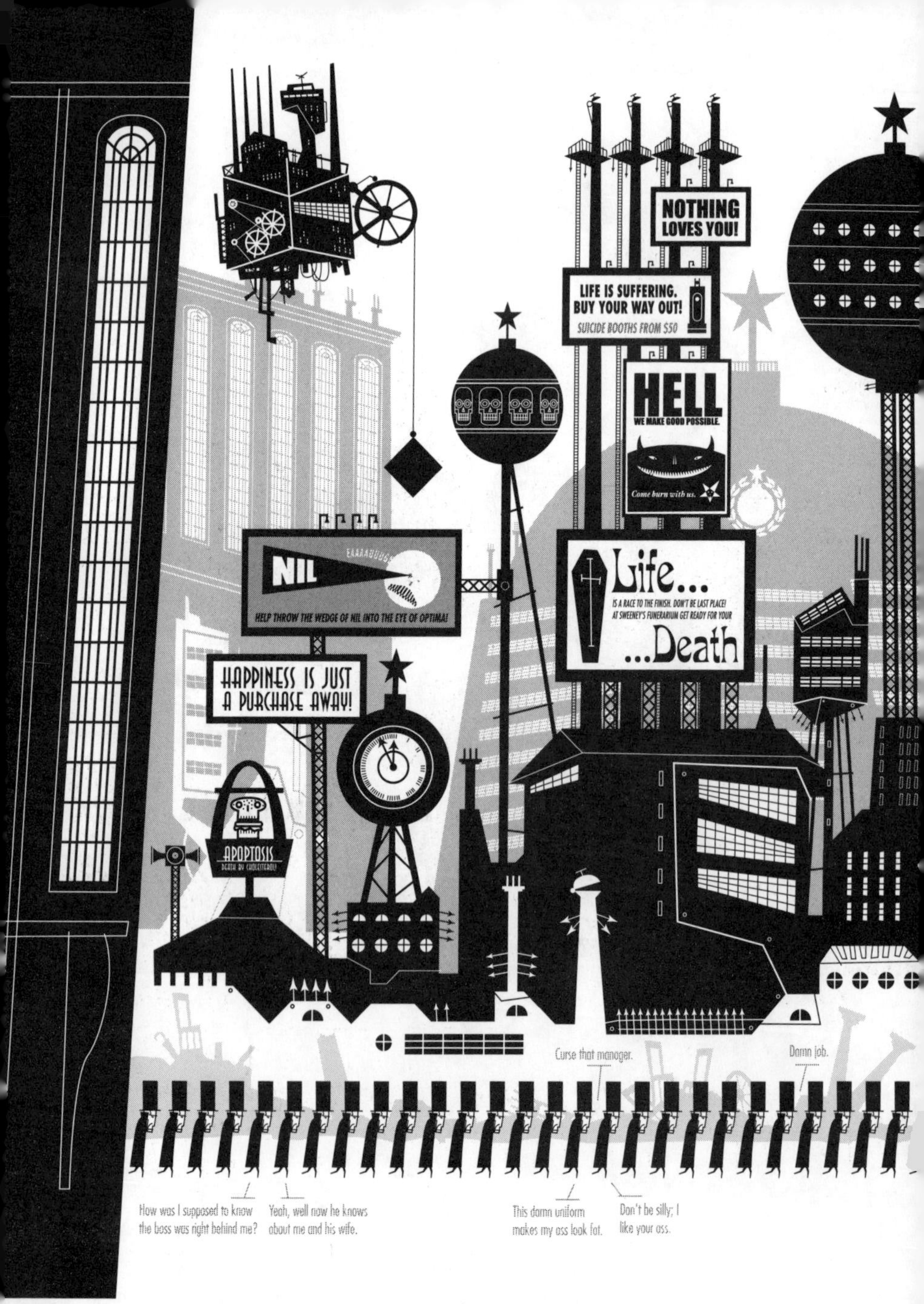

NOTHING LOVES YOU!
LIFE IS SUFFERING. BUY YOUR WAY OUT!
SUICIDE BOOTHS FROM $50
HELL
WE MAKE GOOD POSSIBLE.
Come burn with us.
NIL
HELP THROW THE WEDGE OF NIL INTO THE EYE OF OPTIMA!
Life...
IS A RACE TO THE FINISH. DON'T BE LAST PLACE!
AT SWEENEY'S FUNERARIUM GET READY FOR YOUR
...Death
HAPPINESS IS JUST A PURCHASE AWAY!
APOPTOSIS
DEATH BY CHOLESTEROL!
Curse that manager.
Damn job.
How was I supposed to know the boss was right behind me?
Yeah, well now he knows about me and his wife.
This damn uniform makes my ass look fat.
Don't be silly; I like your ass.

"I cannot lose hope. Because when you lose hope, you die."
— REVEREND MARTIN LUTHER KING JR.

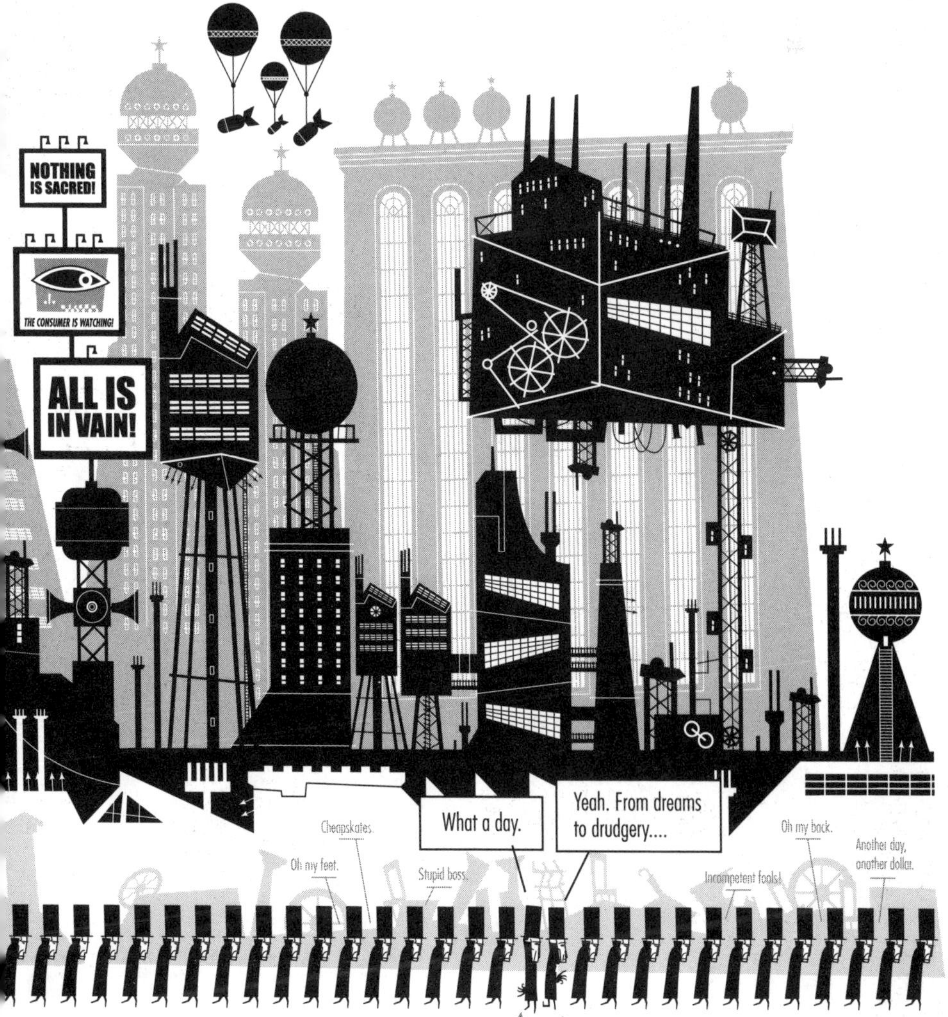

NOTHING IS SACRED!
THE CONSUMER IS WATCHING!
ALL IS IN VAIN!
Cheapskates.
Oh my feet.
Stupid boss.
What a day.
Yeah. From dreams to drudgery....
Incompetent fools!
Oh my back.
Another day, another dollar.
MR. OOZE (AQUAINTANCE)
MR. NUL (HERO)

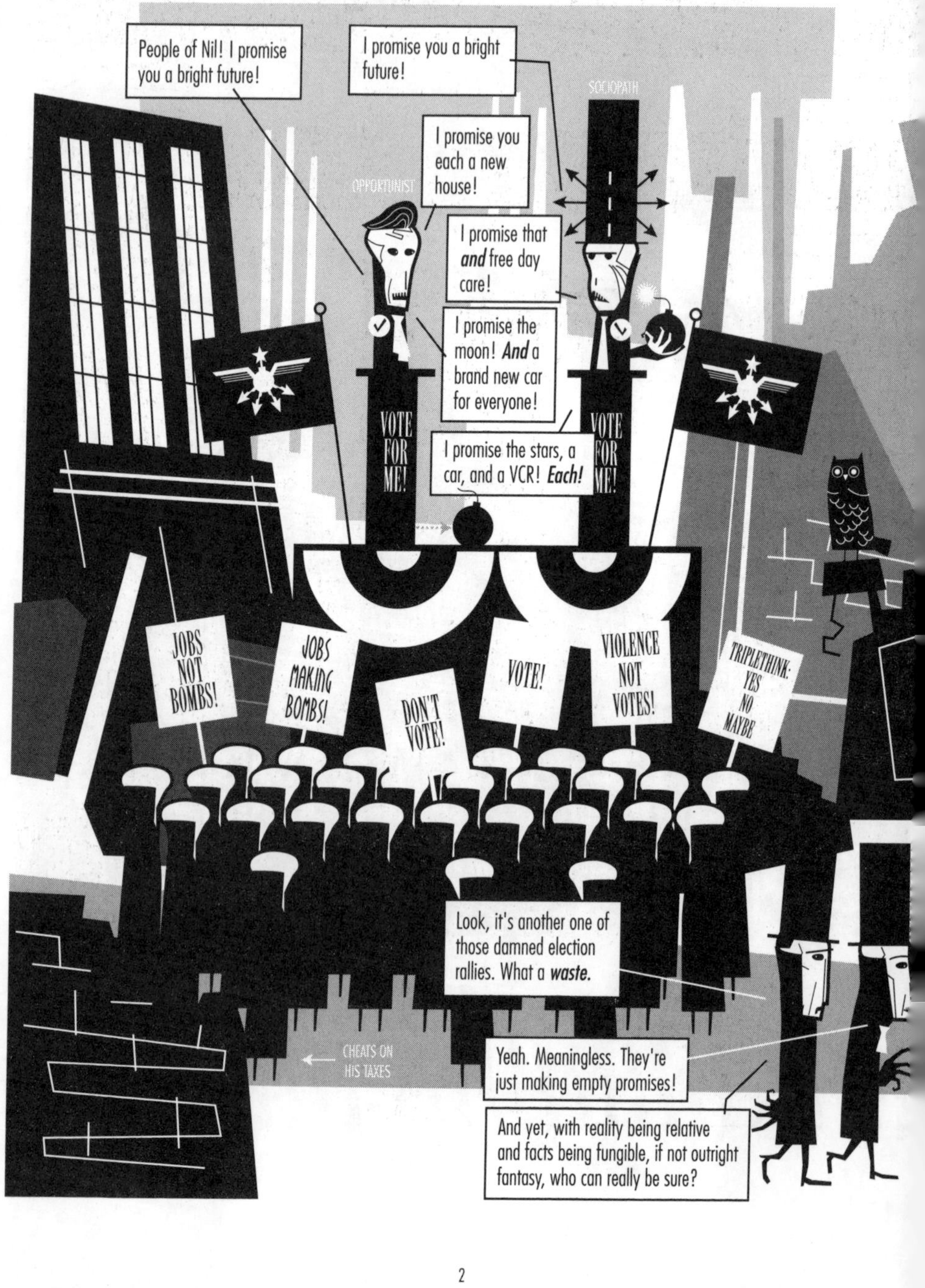
OPPORTUNIST
SOCIOPATH
People of Nil! I promise you a bright future!
I promise you a bright future!
I promise you each a new house!
I promise that ***and*** free day care!
I promise the moon! ***And*** a brand new car for everyone!
I promise the stars, a car, and a VCR! ***Each!***
VOTE FOR ME!
VOTE FOR ME!
JOBS NOT BOMBS!
JOBS MAKING BOMBS!
DON'T VOTE!
VOTE!
VIOLENCE NOT VOTES!
TRIPLETHINK: YES NO MAYBE
Look, it's another one of those damned election rallies. What a ***waste.***
CHEATS ON HIS TAXES
Yeah. Meaningless. They're just making empty promises!
And yet, with reality being relative and facts being fungible, if not outright fantasy, who can really be sure?

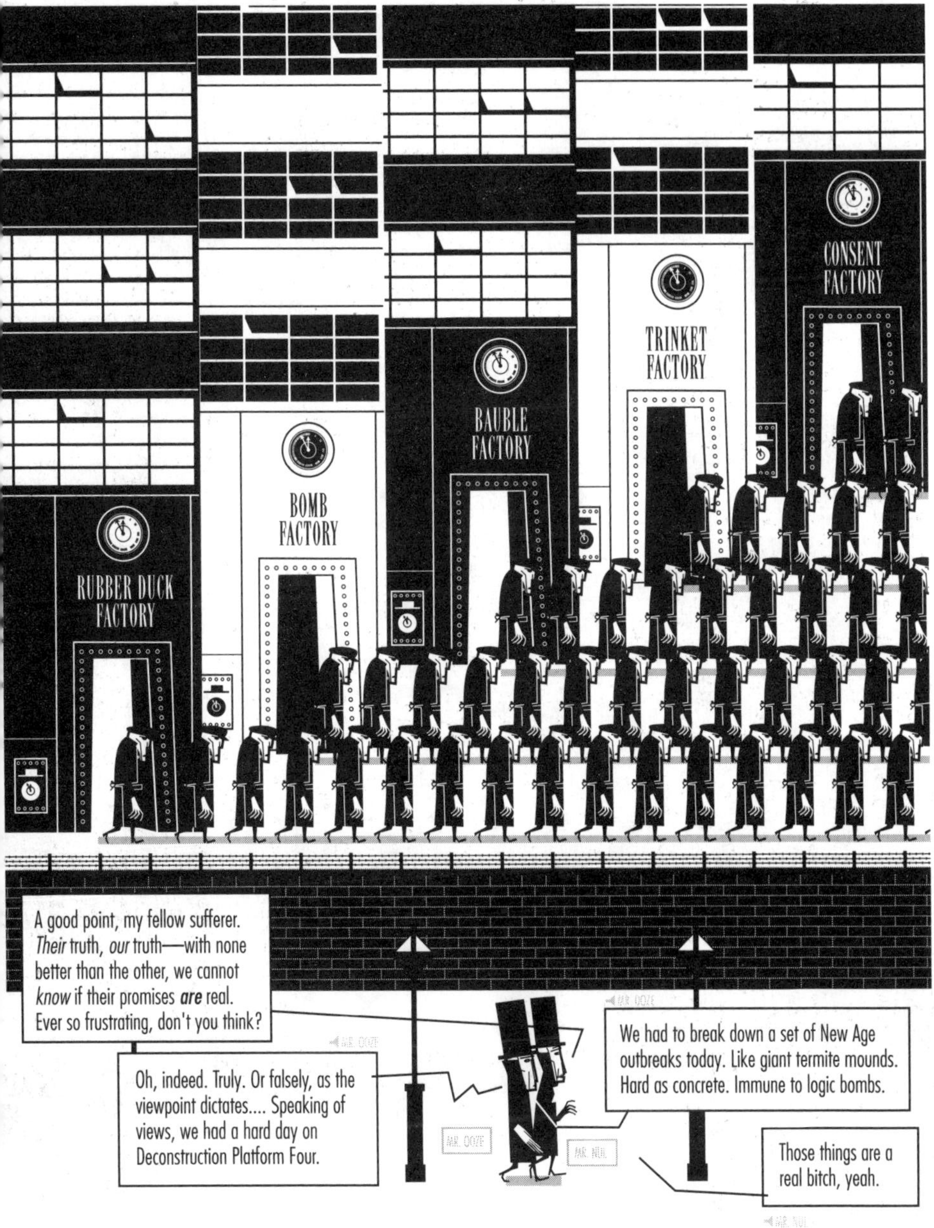
RUBBER DUCK FACTORY
BOMB FACTORY
BAUBLE FACTORY
TRINKET FACTORY
CONSENT FACTORY
A good point, my fellow sufferer. *Their* truth, *our* truth—with none better than the other, we cannot *know* if their promises ***are*** real. Ever so frustrating, don't you think?
Oh, indeed. Truly. Or falsely, as the viewpoint dictates.... Speaking of views, we had a hard day on Deconstruction Platform Four.
We had to break down a set of New Age outbreaks today. Like giant termite mounds. Hard as concrete. Immune to logic bombs.
Those things are a real bitch, yeah.

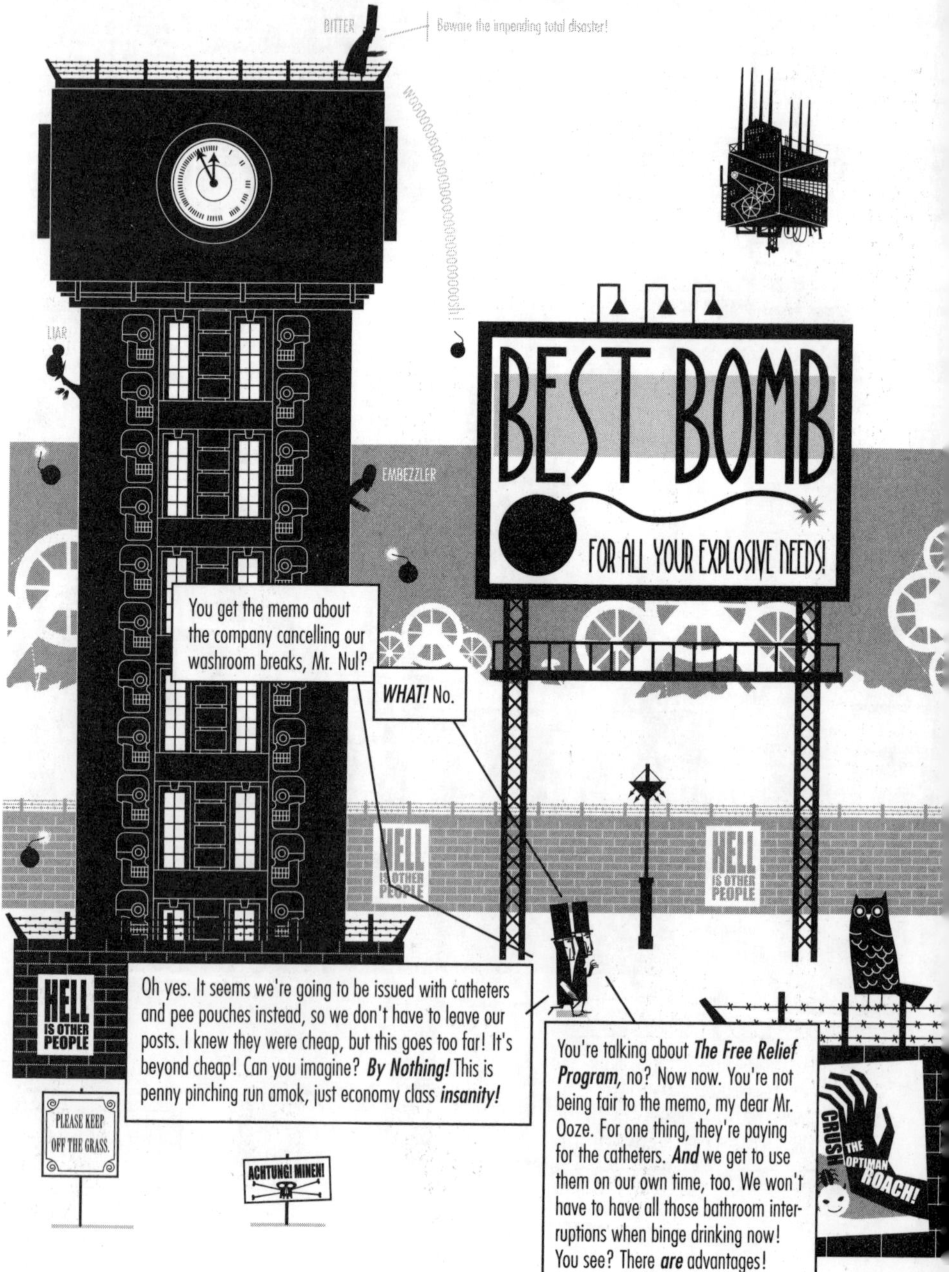
BITTER
Beware the impending total disaster!
Woooooooooooooooooooooooooooooosh!
LIAR
EMBEZZLER
BEST BOMB
FOR ALL YOUR EXPLOSIVE NEEDS!
You get the memo about the company cancelling our washroom breaks, Mr. Nul?
WHAT! No.
Oh yes. It seems we're going to be issued with catheters and pee pouches instead, so we don't have to leave our posts. I knew they were cheap, but this goes too far! It's beyond cheap! Can you imagine? ***By Nothing!*** This is penny pinching run amok, just economy class ***insanity!***
You're talking about ***The Free Relief Program,*** no? Now now. You're not being fair to the memo, my dear Mr. Ooze. For one thing, they're paying for the catheters. ***And*** we get to use them on our own time, too. We won't have to have all those bathroom interruptions when binge drinking now! You see? There ***are*** advantages!
HELL IS OTHER PEOPLE
HELL IS OTHER PEOPLE
HELL IS OTHER PEOPLE
PLEASE KEEP OFF THE GRASS.
ACHTUNG! MINEN!
CRUSH THE OPTIMAN ROACH!

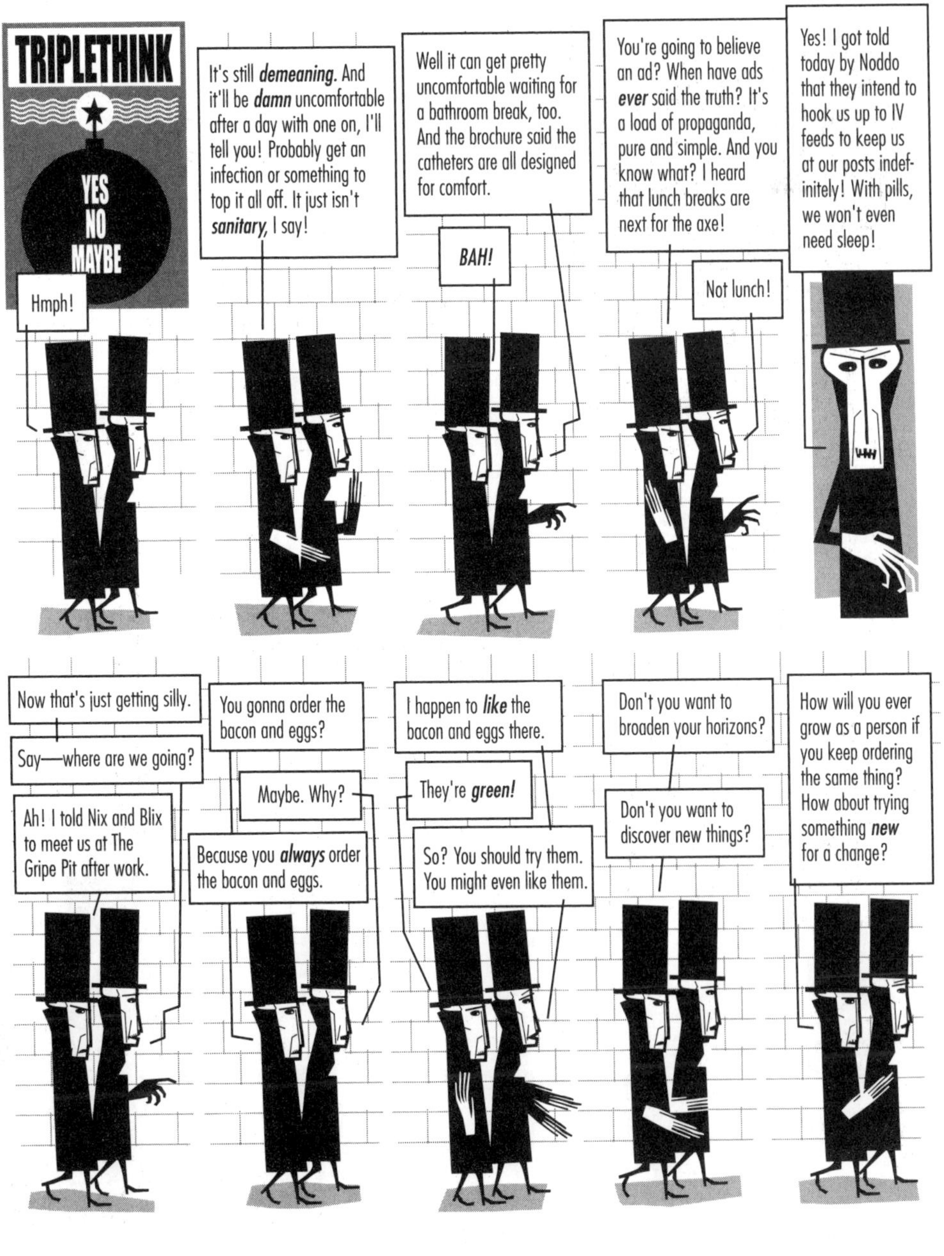
TRIPLETHINK
YES
NO
MAYBE
Hmph!
It's still *demeaning.* And it'll be *damn* uncomfortable after a day with one on, I'll tell you! Probably get an infection or something to top it all off. It just isn't *sanitary,* I say!
Well it can get pretty uncomfortable waiting for a bathroom break, too. And the brochure said the catheters are all designed for comfort.
BAH!
You're going to believe an ad? When have ads *ever* said the truth? It's a load of propaganda, pure and simple. And you know what? I heard that lunch breaks are next for the axe!
Not lunch!
Yes! I got told today by Noddo that they intend to hook us up to IV feeds to keep us at our posts indefinitely! With pills, we won't even need sleep!
Now that's just getting silly.
Say—where are we going?
Ah! I told Nix and Blix to meet us at The Gripe Pit after work.
You gonna order the bacon and eggs?
Maybe. Why?
Because you *always* order the bacon and eggs.
I happen to *like* the bacon and eggs there.
They're *green!*
So? You should try them. You might even like them.
Don't you want to broaden your horizons?
Don't you want to discover new things?
How will you ever grow as a person if you keep ordering the same thing? How about trying something *new* for a change?

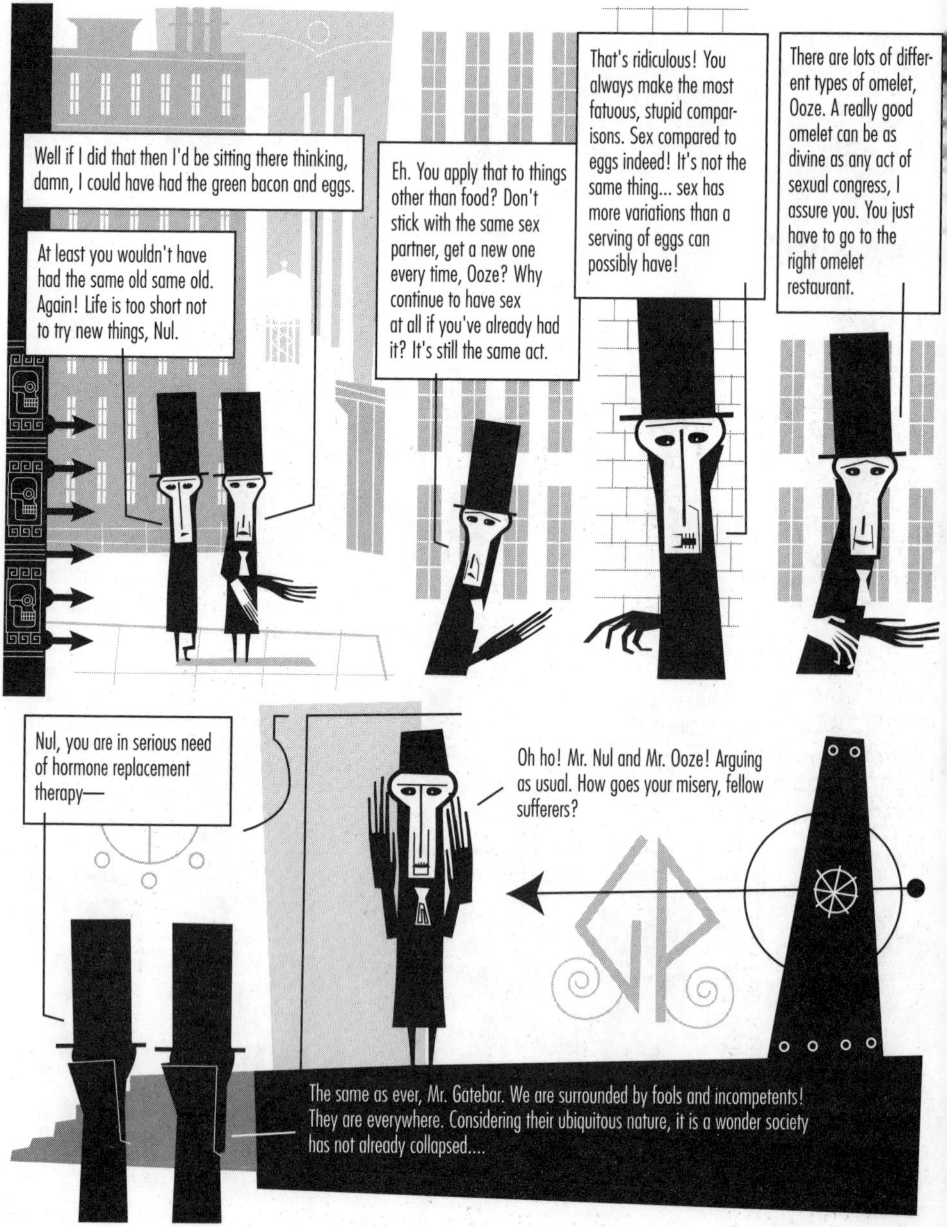
Well if I did that then I'd be sitting there thinking, damn, I could have had the green bacon and eggs.
At least you wouldn't have had the same old same old. Again! Life is too short not to try new things, Nul.
Eh. You apply that to things other than food? Don't stick with the same sex partner, get a new one every time, Ooze? Why continue to have sex at all if you've already had it? It's still the same act.
That's ridiculous! You always make the most fatuous, stupid comparisons. Sex compared to eggs indeed! It's not the same thing... sex has more variations than a serving of eggs can possibly have!
There are lots of different types of omelet, Ooze. A really good omelet can be as divine as any act of sexual congress, I assure you. You just have to go to the right omelet restaurant.
Nul, you are in serious need of hormone replacement therapy—
Oh ho! Mr. Nul and Mr. Ooze! Arguing as usual. How goes your misery, fellow sufferers?
The same as ever, Mr. Gatebar. We are surrounded by fools and incompetents! They are everywhere. Considering their ubiquitous nature, it is a wonder society has not already collapsed....

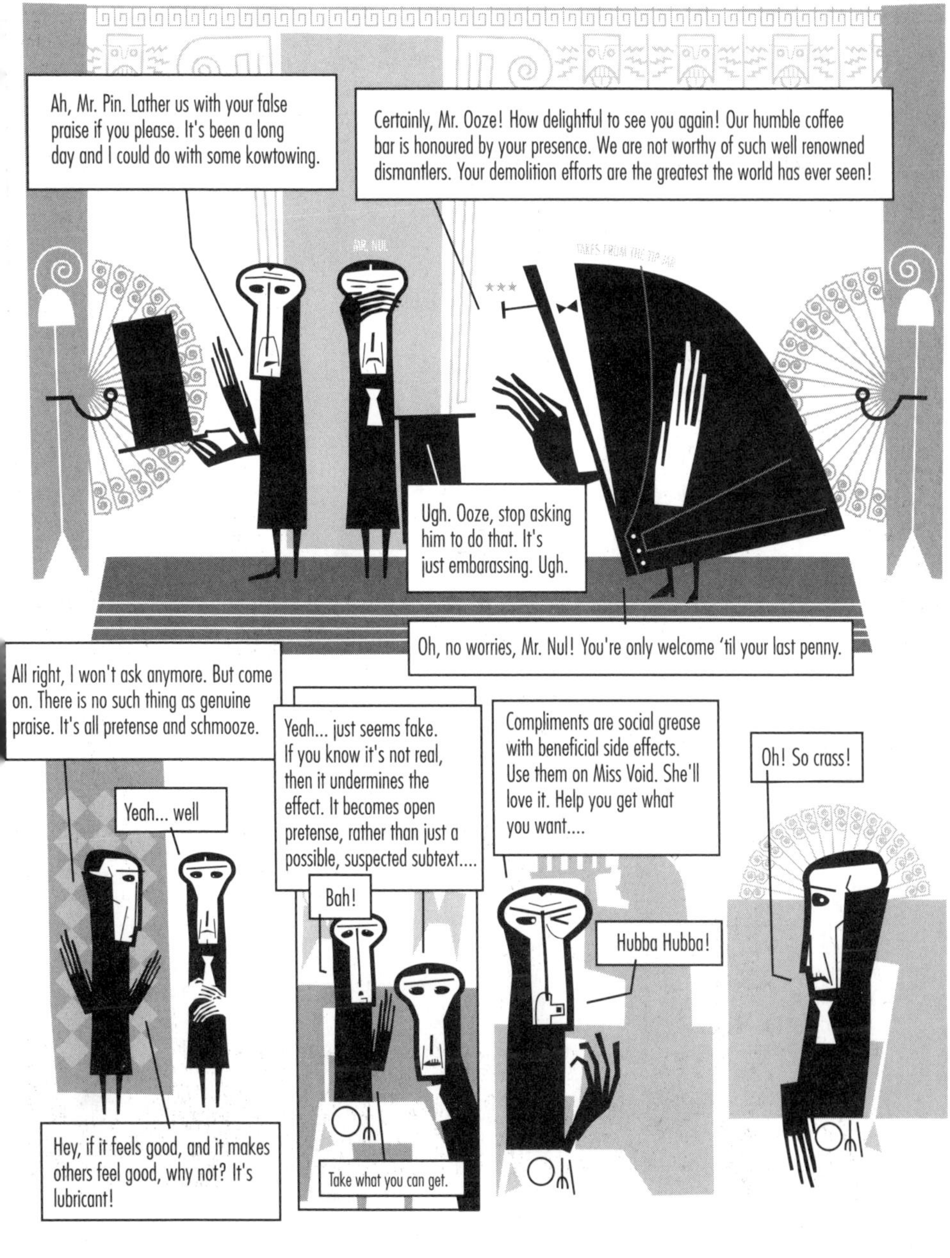

Ah, Mr. Pin. Lather us with your false praise if you please. It's been a long day and I could do with some kowtowing.
Certainly, Mr. Ooze! How delightful to see you again! Our humble coffee bar is honoured by your presence. We are not worthy of such well renowned dismantlers. Your demolition efforts are the greatest the world has ever seen!
Ugh. Ooze, stop asking him to do that. It's just embarassing. Ugh.
Oh, no worries, Mr. Nul! You're only welcome 'til your last penny.
All right, I won't ask anymore. But come on. There is no such thing as genuine praise. It's all pretense and schmooze.
Yeah... well
Hey, if it feels good, and it makes others feel good, why not? It's lubricant!
Yeah... just seems fake. If you know it's not real, then it undermines the effect. It becomes open pretense, rather than just a possible, suspected subtext....
Bah!
Take what you can get.
Compliments are social grease with beneficial side effects. Use them on Miss Void. She'll love it. Help you get what you want....
Hubba Hubba!
Oh! So crass!

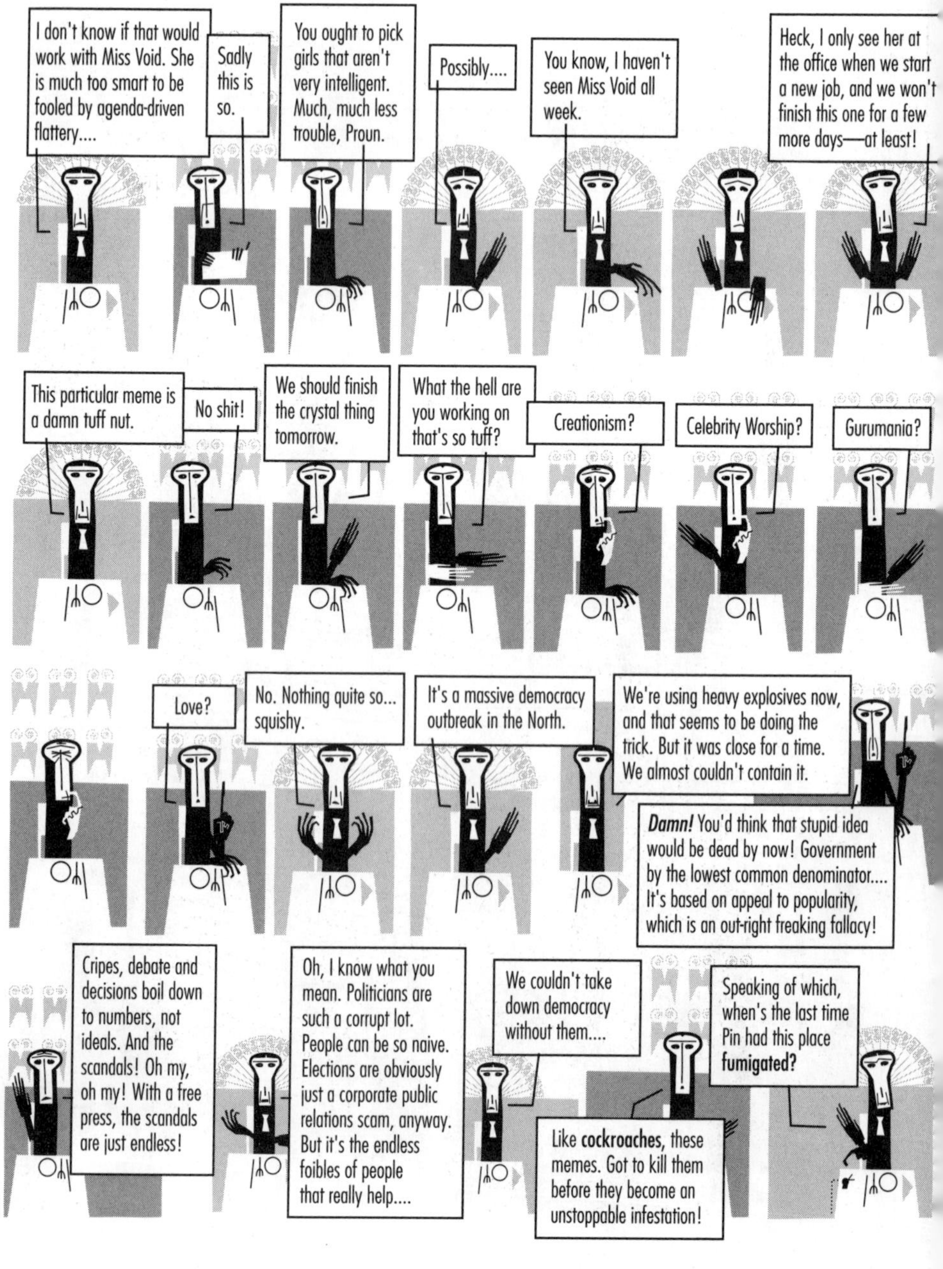
I don't know if that would work with Miss Void. She is much too smart to be fooled by agenda-driven flattery....
Sadly this is so.
You ought to pick girls that aren't very intelligent. Much, much less trouble, Proun.
Possibly....
You know, I haven't seen Miss Void all week.
Heck, I only see her at the office when we start a new job, and we won't finish this one for a few more days—at least!
This particular meme is a damn tuff nut.
No shit!
We should finish the crystal thing tomorrow.
What the hell are you working on that's so tuff?
Creationism?
Celebrity Worship?
Gurumania?
Love?
No. Nothing quite so... squishy.
It's a massive democracy outbreak in the North.
We're using heavy explosives now, and that seems to be doing the trick. But it was close for a time. We almost couldn't contain it.
Damn! You'd think that stupid idea would be dead by now! Government by the lowest common denominator.... It's based on appeal to popularity, which is an out-right freaking fallacy!
Cripes, debate and decisions boil down to numbers, not ideals. And the scandals! Oh my, oh my! With a free press, the scandals are just endless!
Oh, I know what you mean. Politicians are such a corrupt lot. People can be so naive. Elections are obviously just a corporate public relations scam, anyway. But it's the endless foibles of people that really help....
We couldn't take down democracy without them....
Like cockroaches, these memes. Got to kill them before they become an unstoppable infestation!
Speaking of which, when's the last time Pin had this place fumigated?

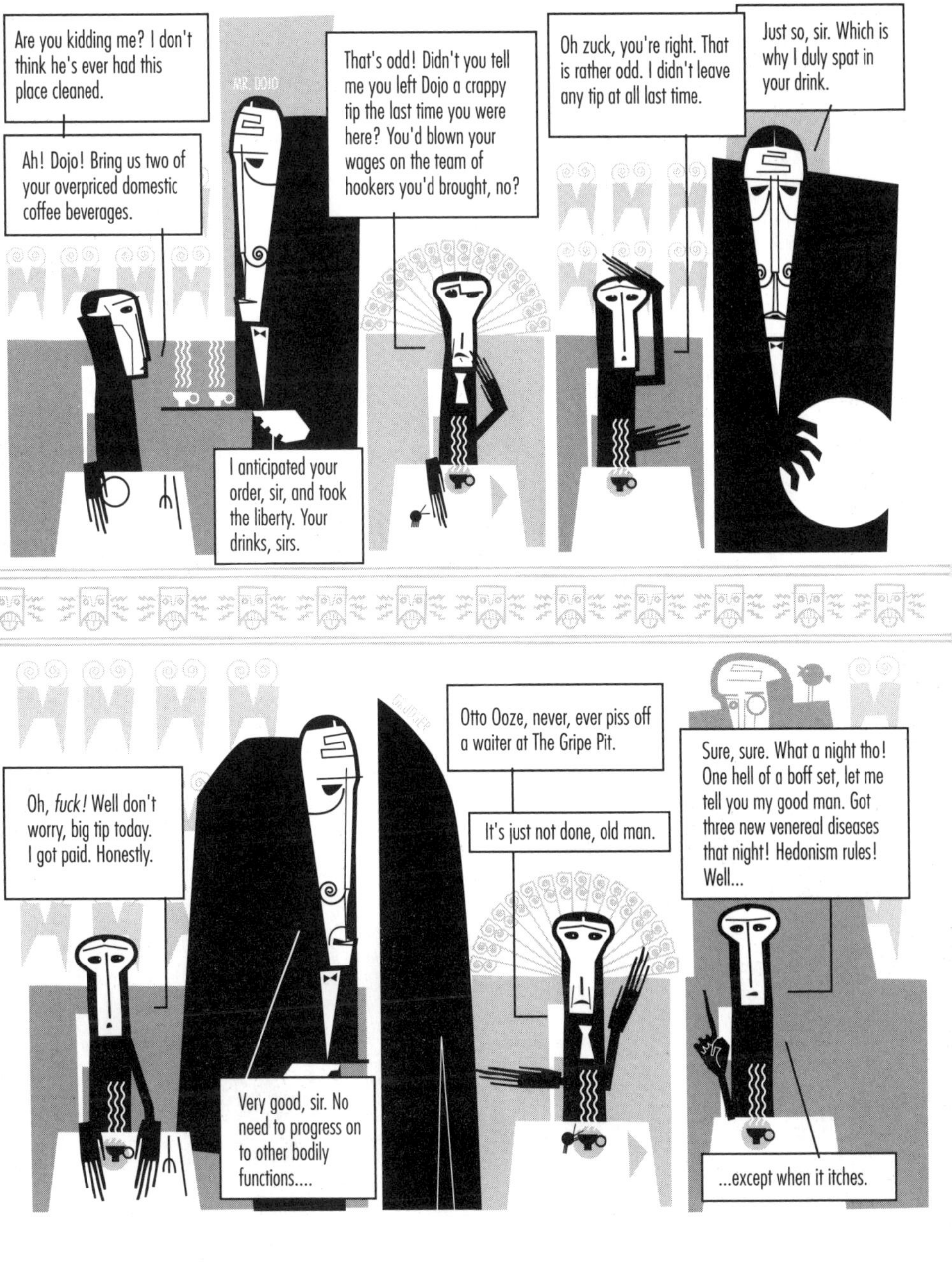

Are you kidding me? I don't think he's ever had this place cleaned.
Ah! Dojo! Bring us two of your overpriced domestic coffee beverages.
MR. DOJO
I anticipated your order, sir, and took the liberty. Your drinks, sirs.
That's odd! Didn't you tell me you left Dojo a crappy tip the last time you were here? You'd blown your wages on the team of hookers you'd brought, no?
Oh zuck, you're right. That is rather odd. I didn't leave any tip at all last time.
Just so, sir. Which is why I duly spat in your drink.
Oh, *fuck!* Well don't worry, big tip today. I got paid. Honestly.
Very good, sir. No need to progress on to other bodily functions....
Otto Ooze, never, ever piss off a waiter at The Gripe Pit.
It's just not done, old man.
Sure, sure. What a night tho! One hell of a boff set, let me tell you my good man. Got three new venereal diseases that night! Hedonism rules! Well...
...except when it itches.

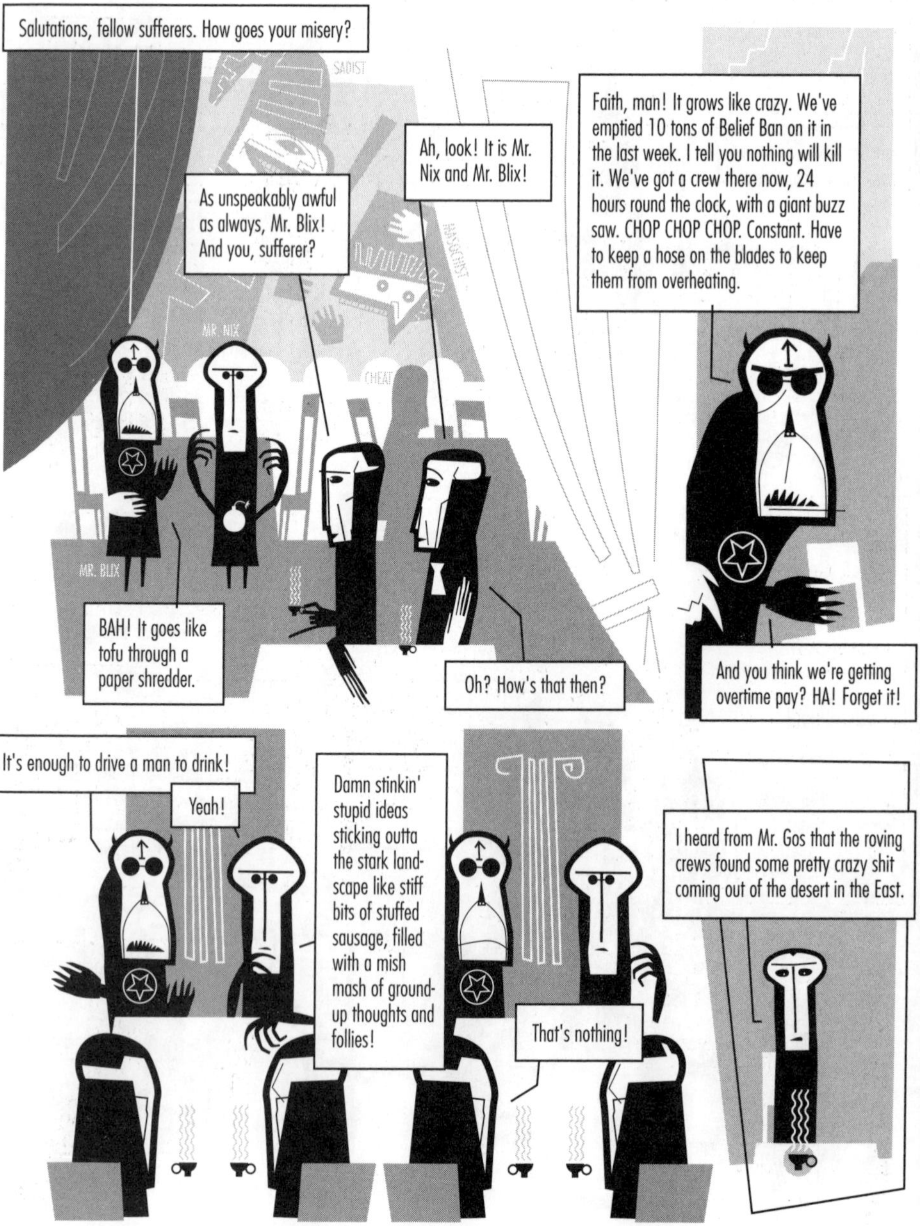

Salutations, fellow sufferers. How goes your misery?
As unspeakably awful as always, Mr. Blix! And you, sufferer?
Ah, look! It is Mr. Nix and Mr. Blix!
BAH! It goes like tofu through a paper shredder.
Oh? How's that then?
Faith, man! It grows like crazy. We've emptied 10 tons of Belief Ban on it in the last week. I tell you nothing will kill it. We've got a crew there now, 24 hours round the clock, with a giant buzz saw. CHOP CHOP CHOP. Constant. Have to keep a hose on the blades to keep them from overheating.
And you think we're getting overtime pay? HA! Forget it!
It's enough to drive a man to drink!
Yeah!
Damn stinkin' stupid ideas sticking outta the stark land-scape like stiff bits of stuffed sausage, filled with a mish mash of ground-up thoughts and follies!
That's nothing!
I heard from Mr. Gos that the roving crews found some pretty crazy shit coming out of the desert in the East.
SADIST
MR. NIX
CHEAT
MR. BLIX

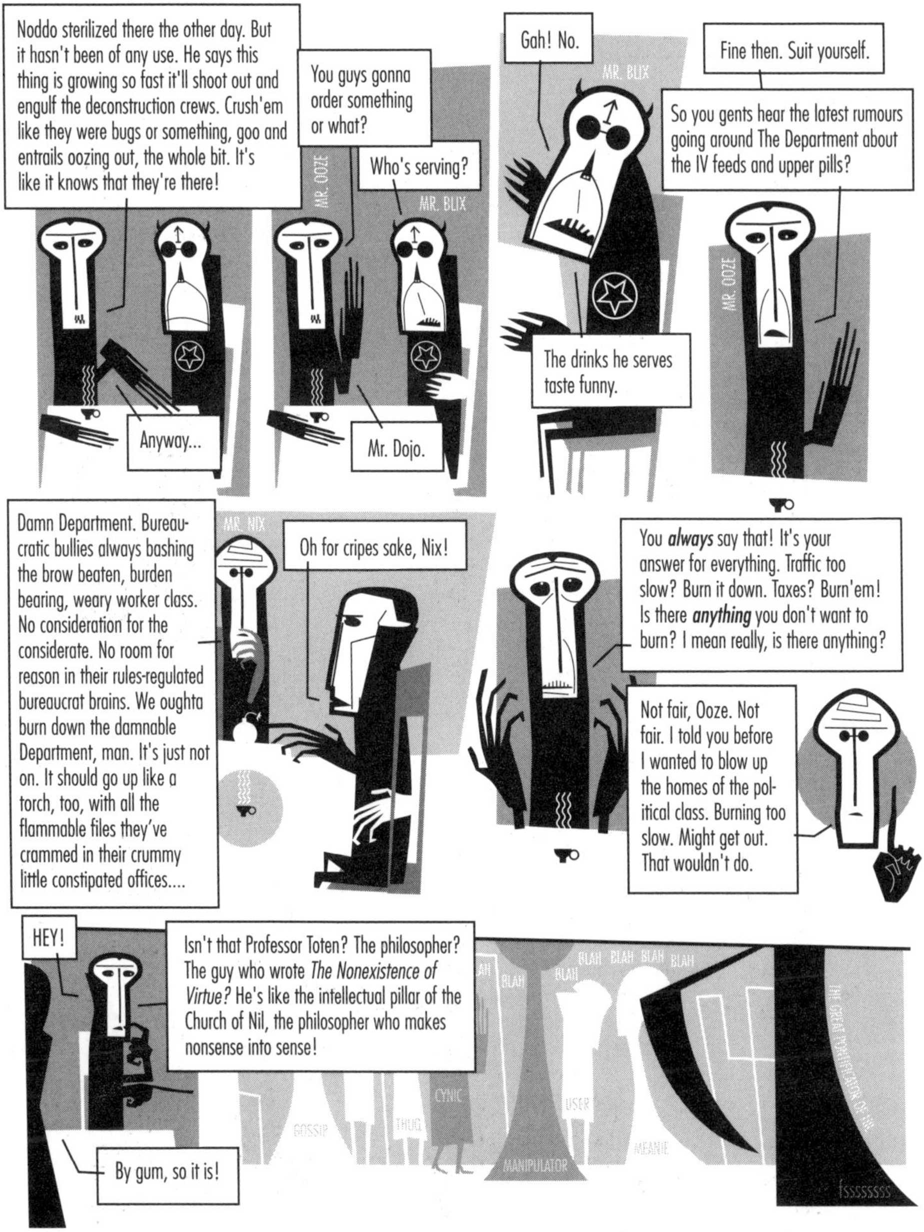
Noddo sterilized there the other day. But it hasn't been of any use. He says this thing is growing so fast it'll shoot out and engulf the deconstruction crews. Crush'em like they were bugs or something, goo and entrails oozing out, the whole bit. It's like it knows that they're there!
Anyway...
MR. OOZE
You guys gonna order something or what?
Who's serving?
MR. BLIX
Mr. Dojo.
Gah! No.
MR. BLIX
The drinks he serves taste funny.
Fine then. Suit yourself.
So you gents hear the latest rumours going around The Department about the IV feeds and upper pills?
MR. OOZE
Damn Department. Bureaucratic bullies always bashing the brow beaten, burden bearing, weary worker class. No consideration for the considerate. No room for reason in their rules-regulated bureaucrat brains. We oughta burn down the damnable Department, man. It's just not on. It should go up like a torch, too, with all the flammable files they've crammed in their crummy little constipated offices....
MR. NIX
Oh for cripes sake, Nix!
You ***always*** say that! It's your answer for everything. Traffic too slow? Burn it down. Taxes? Burn'em! Is there ***anything*** you don't want to burn? I mean really, is there anything?
Not fair, Ooze. Not fair. I told you before I wanted to blow up the homes of the political class. Burning too slow. Might get out. That wouldn't do.
HEY!
Isn't that Professor Toten? The philosopher? The guy who wrote *The Nonexistence of Virtue?* He's like the intellectual pillar of the Church of Nil, the philosopher who makes nonsense into sense!
By gum, so it is!
BLAH BLAH BLAH BLAH
GOSSIP
THUG
CYNIC
MANIPULATOR
USER
MEANIE
THE GREAT PONTIFICATOR OF NIL
fssssssss

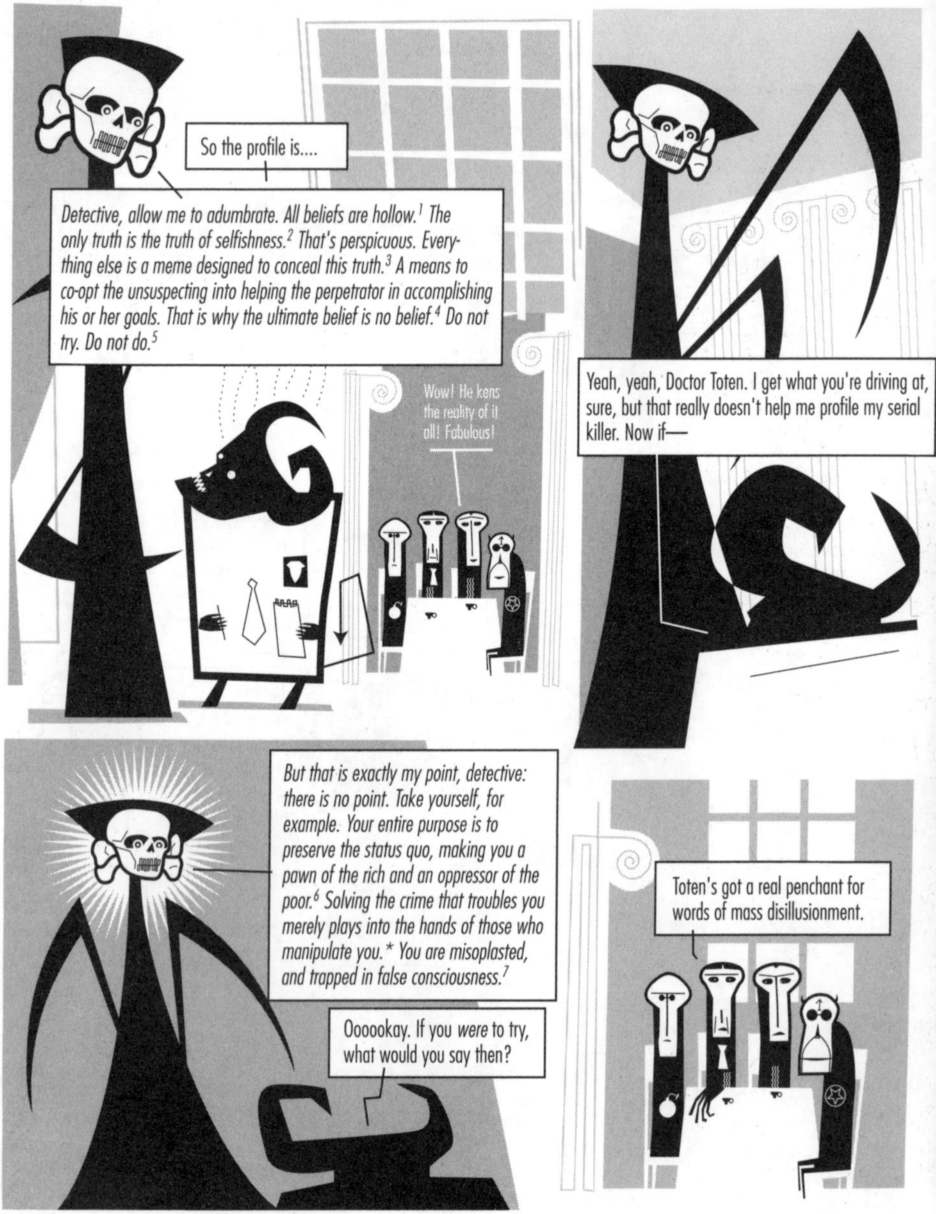
So the profile is....
Detective, allow me to adumbrate. All beliefs are hollow.[1] The only truth is the truth of selfishness.[2] That's perspicuous. Everything else is a meme designed to conceal this truth.[3] A means to co-opt the unsuspecting into helping the perpetrator in accomplishing his or her goals. That is why the ultimate belief is no belief.[4] Do not try. Do not do.[5]
Wow! He kens the reality of it all! Fabulous!
Yeah, yeah, Doctor Toten. I get what you're driving at, sure, but that really doesn't help me profile my serial killer. Now if—
But that is exactly my point, detective: there is no point. Take yourself, for example. Your entire purpose is to preserve the status quo, making you a pawn of the rich and an oppressor of the poor.[6] Solving the crime that troubles you merely plays into the hands of those who manipulate you. You are misoplasted, and trapped in false consciousness.[7]*
Oooookay. If you *were* to try, what would you say then?
Toten's got a real penchant for words of mass disillusionment.

* See Dr. Thanatos Apoptosis Toten, *The Hermeneutics of Metareality and Manipulation* (Nihilopolis, 2004)

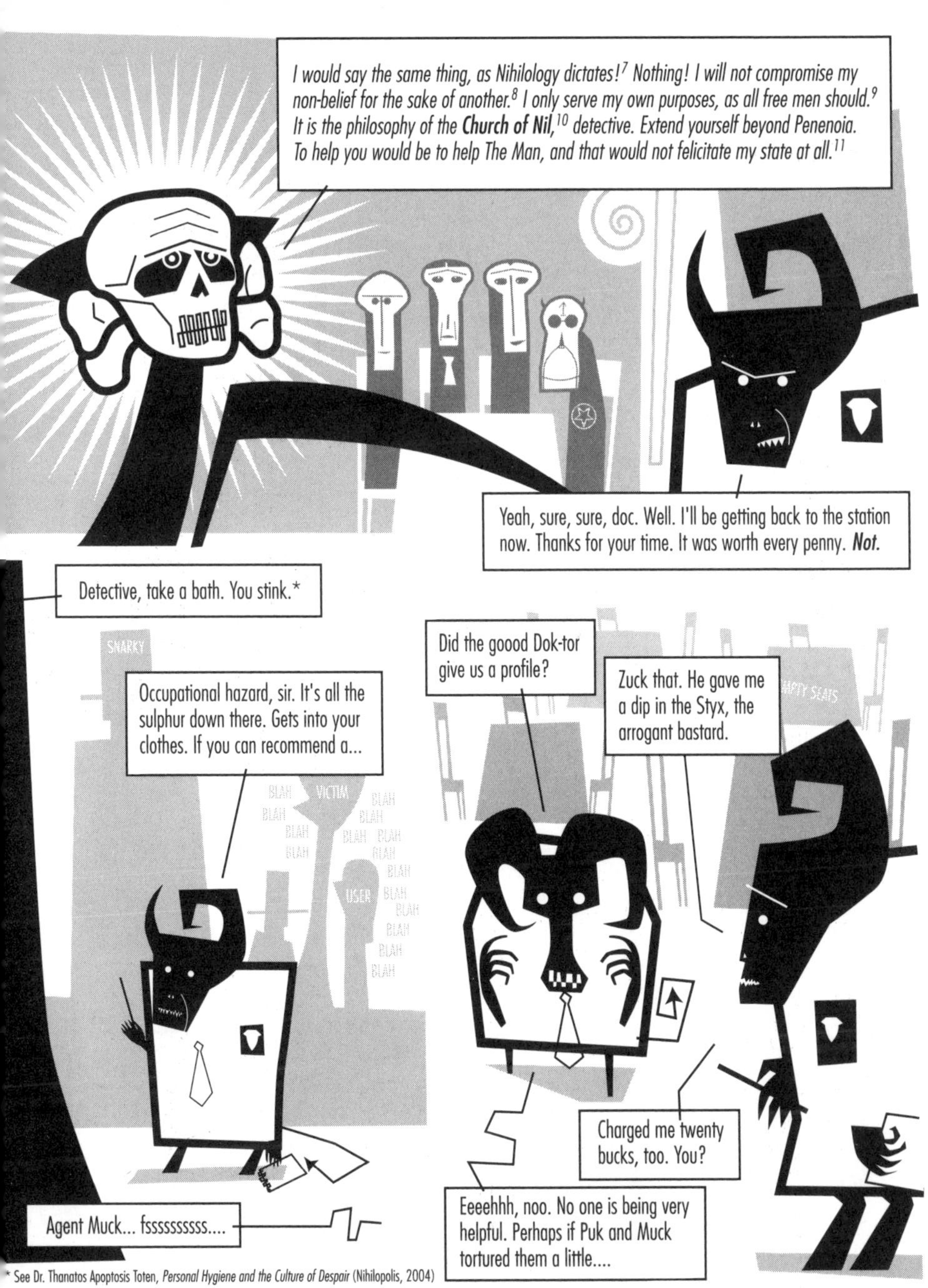
*I would say the same thing, as Nihilology dictates![7] Nothing! I will not compromise my non-belief for the sake of another.[8] I only serve my own purposes, as all free men should.[9] It is the philosophy of the **Church of Nil,**[10] detective. Extend yourself beyond Penenoia. To help you would be to help The Man, and that would not felicitate my state at all.[11]*
Yeah, sure, sure, doc. Well. I'll be getting back to the station now. Thanks for your time. It was worth every penny. ***Not.***
Detective, take a bath. You stink.*
SNARKY
Occupational hazard, sir. It's all the sulphur down there. Gets into your clothes. If you can recommend a...
VICTIM
USER
Agent Muck... fssssssssss....
Did the goood Dok-tor give us a profile?
Zuck that. He gave me a dip in the Styx, the arrogant bastard.
Charged me twenty bucks, too. You?
Eeeehhh, noo. No one is being very helpful. Perhaps if Puk and Muck tortured them a little....

* See Dr. Thanatos Apoptosis Toten, *Personal Hygiene and the Culture of Despair* (Nihilopolis, 2004)

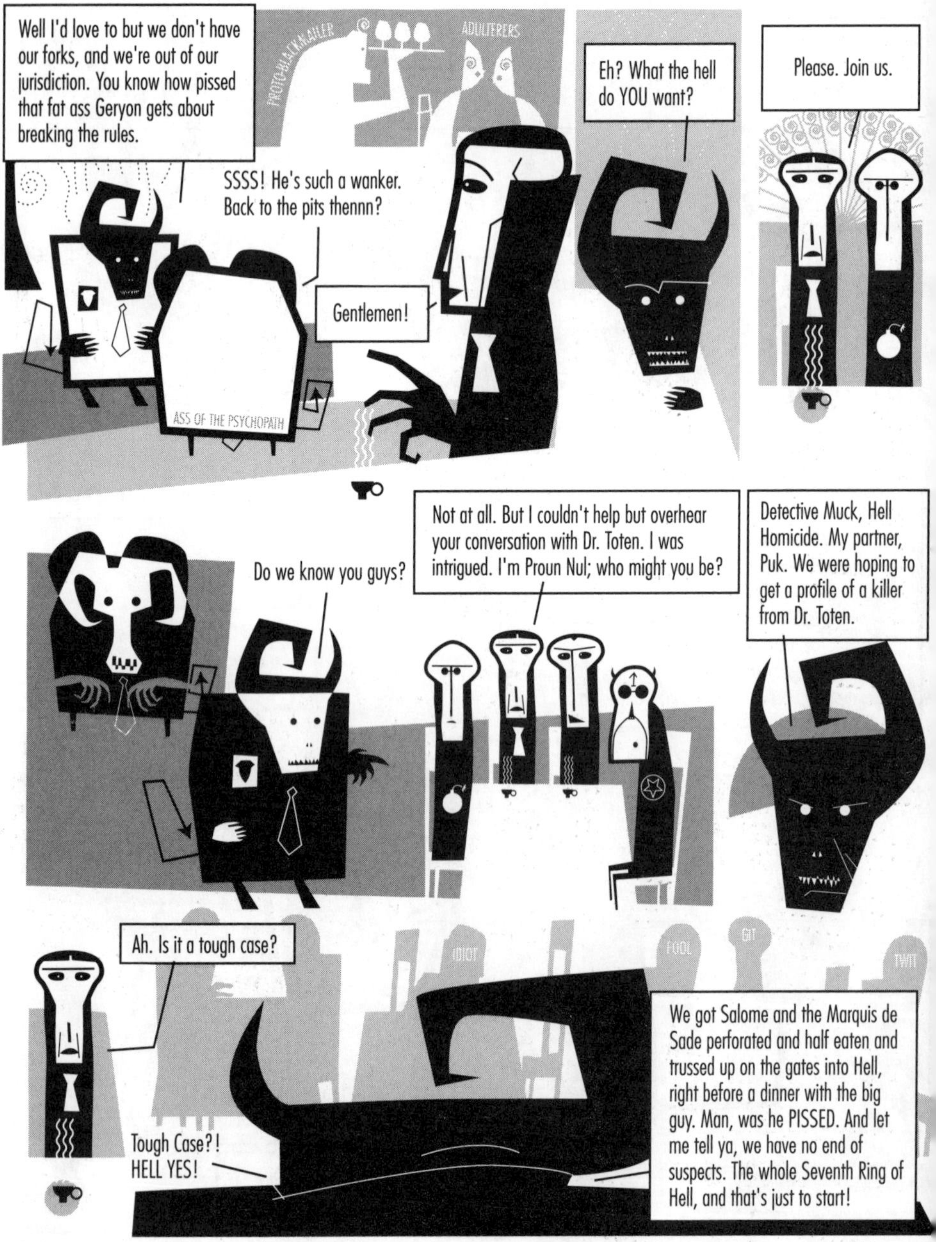
Well I'd love to but we don't have our forks, and we're out of our jurisdiction. You know how pissed that fat ass Geryon gets about breaking the rules.
PROTO-BLACKMAILER
ADULTERERS
SSSS! He's such a wanker. Back to the pits thennn?
ASS OF THE PSYCHOPATH
Gentlemen!
Eh? What the hell do YOU want?
Please. Join us.
Do we know you guys?
Not at all. But I couldn't help but overhear your conversation with Dr. Toten. I was intrigued. I'm Proun Nul; who might you be?
Detective Muck, Hell Homicide. My partner, Puk. We were hoping to get a profile of a killer from Dr. Toten.
Ah. Is it a tough case?
IDIOT
FOOL
GIT
TWIT
Tough Case?! HELL YES!
We got Salome and the Marquis de Sade perforated and half eaten and trussed up on the gates into Hell, right before a dinner with the big guy. Man, was he PISSED. And let me tell ya, we have no end of suspects. The whole Seventh Ring of Hell, and that's just to start!

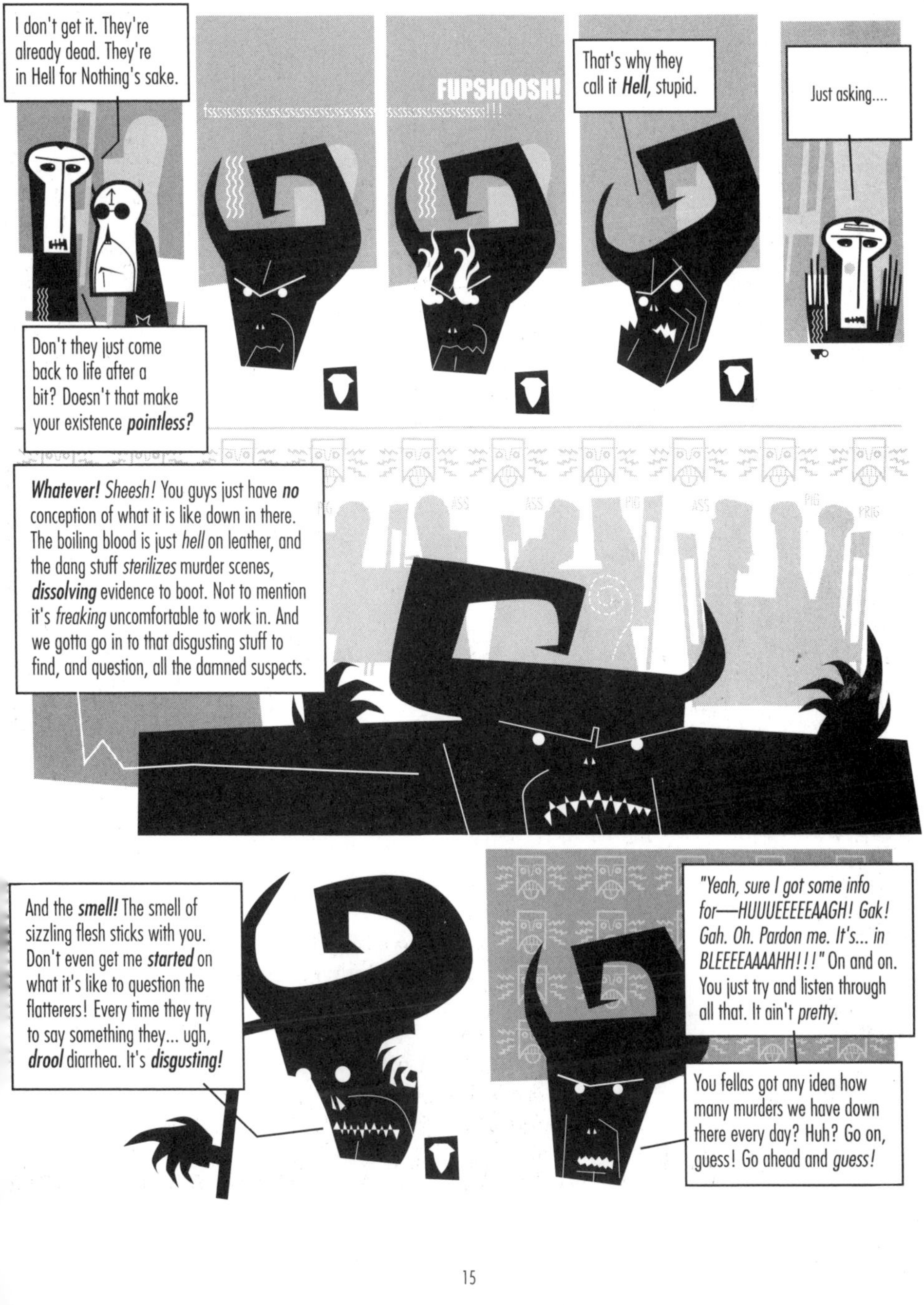

I don't get it. They're already dead. They're in Hell for Nothing's sake.
Don't they just come back to life after a bit? Doesn't that make your existence ***pointless?***
FUPSHOOSH!
fsssssssssssssssssssssssssssssssssssssssssssssssssss!!!
That's why they call it ***Hell,*** stupid.
Just asking....
Whatever! *Sheesh!* You guys just have ***no*** conception of what it is like down in there. The boiling blood is just *hell* on leather, and the dang stuff *sterilizes* murder scenes, ***dissolving*** evidence to boot. Not to mention it's *freaking* uncomfortable to work in. And we gotta go in to that disgusting stuff to find, and question, all the damned suspects.
And the ***smell!*** The smell of sizzling flesh sticks with you. Don't even get me ***started*** on what it's like to question the flatterers! Every time they try to say something they... ugh, ***drool*** diarrhea. It's ***disgusting!***
"Yeah, sure I got some info for—HUUUEEEEEAAGH! Gak! Gah. Oh. Pardon me. It's... in BLEEEEAAAAHH!!!" On and on. You just try and listen through all that. It ain't *pretty*.
You fellas got any idea how many murders we have down there every day? Huh? Go on, guess! Go ahead and *guess!*

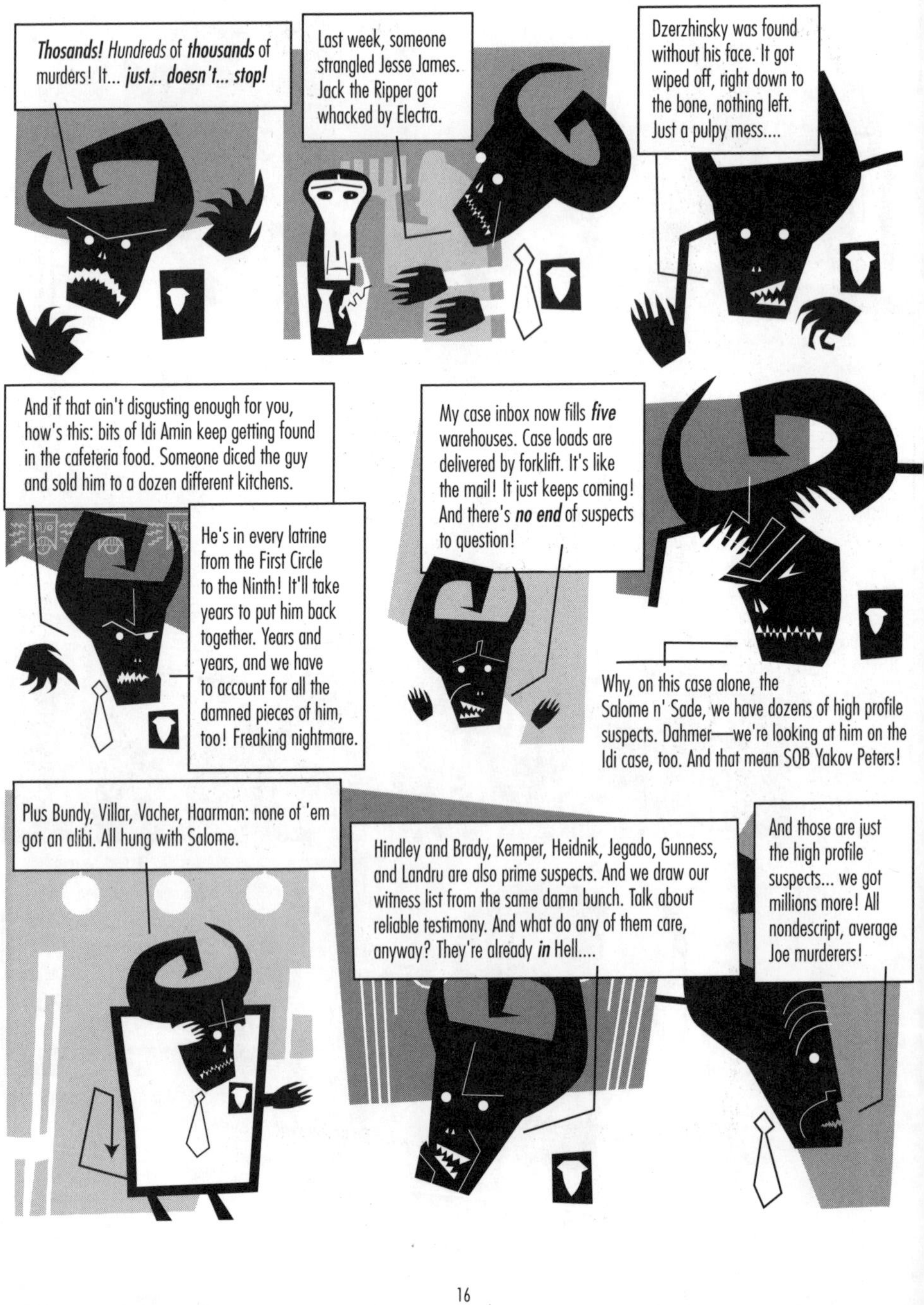

Thosands! *Hundreds* of ***thousands*** of murders! It... ***just... doesn't... stop!***
Last week, someone strangled Jesse James. Jack the Ripper got whacked by Electra.
Dzerzhinsky was found without his face. It got wiped off, right down to the bone, nothing left. Just a pulpy mess....
And if that ain't disgusting enough for you, how's this: bits of Idi Amin keep getting found in the cafeteria food. Someone diced the guy and sold him to a dozen different kitchens.
He's in every latrine from the First Circle to the Ninth! It'll take years to put him back together. Years and years, and we have to account for all the damned pieces of him, too! Freaking nightmare.
My case inbox now fills ***five*** warehouses. Case loads are delivered by forklift. It's like the mail! It just keeps coming! And there's ***no end*** of suspects to question!
Why, on this case alone, the Salome n' Sade, we have dozens of high profile suspects. Dahmer—we're looking at him on the Idi case, too. And that mean SOB Yakov Peters!
Plus Bundy, Villar, Vacher, Haarman: none of 'em got an alibi. All hung with Salome.
Hindley and Brady, Kemper, Heidnik, Jegado, Gunness, and Landru are also prime suspects. And we draw our witness list from the same damn bunch. Talk about reliable testimony. And what do any of them care, anyway? They're already ***in*** Hell....
And those are just the high profile suspects... we got millions more! All nondescript, average Joe murderers!

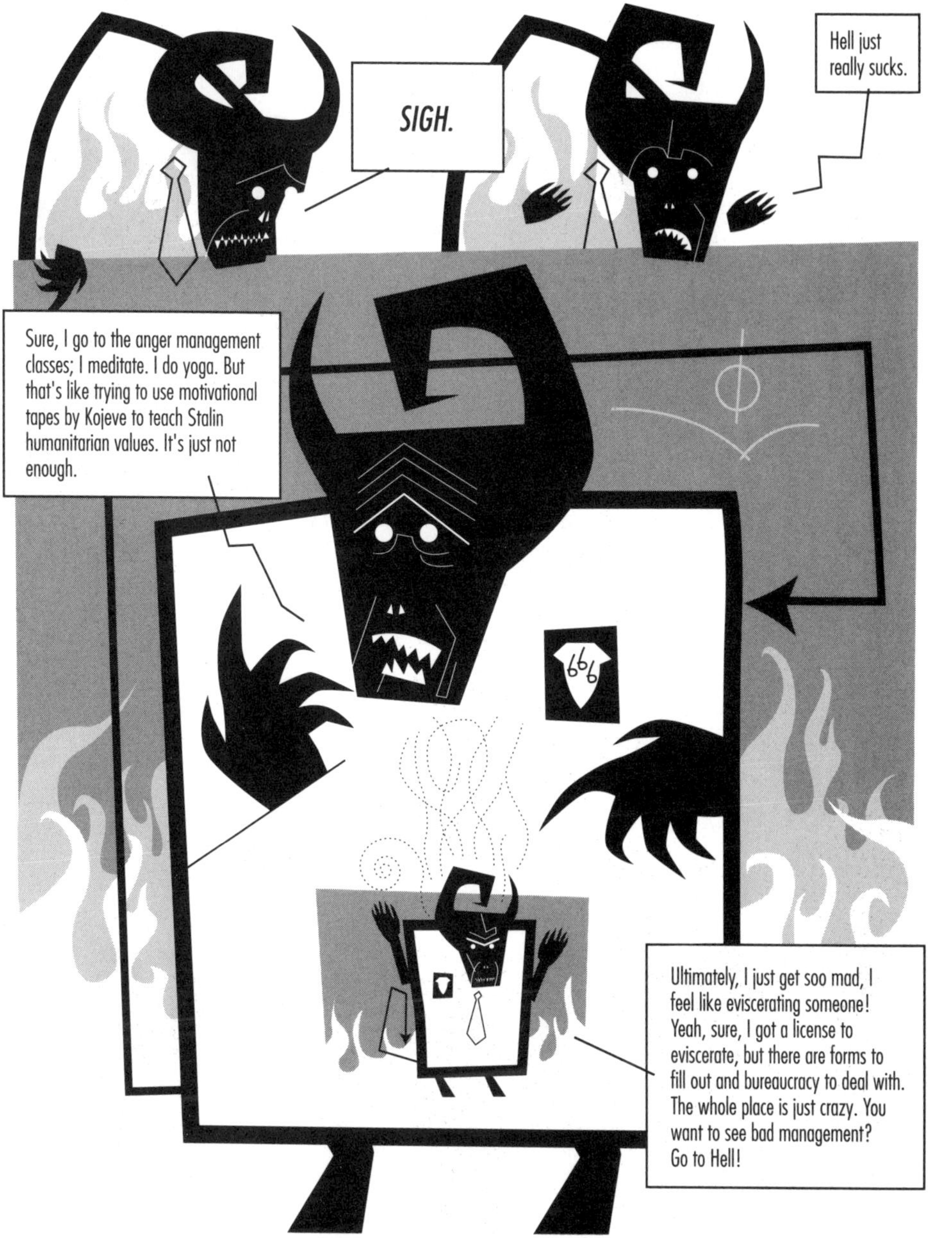
SIGH.
Hell just really sucks.
Sure, I go to the anger management classes; I meditate. I do yoga. But that's like trying to use motivational tapes by Kojeve to teach Stalin humanitarian values. It's just not enough.
666
Ultimately, I just get soo mad, I feel like eviscerating someone! Yeah, sure, I got a license to eviscerate, but there are forms to fill out and bureaucracy to deal with. The whole place is just crazy. You want to see bad management? Go to Hell!

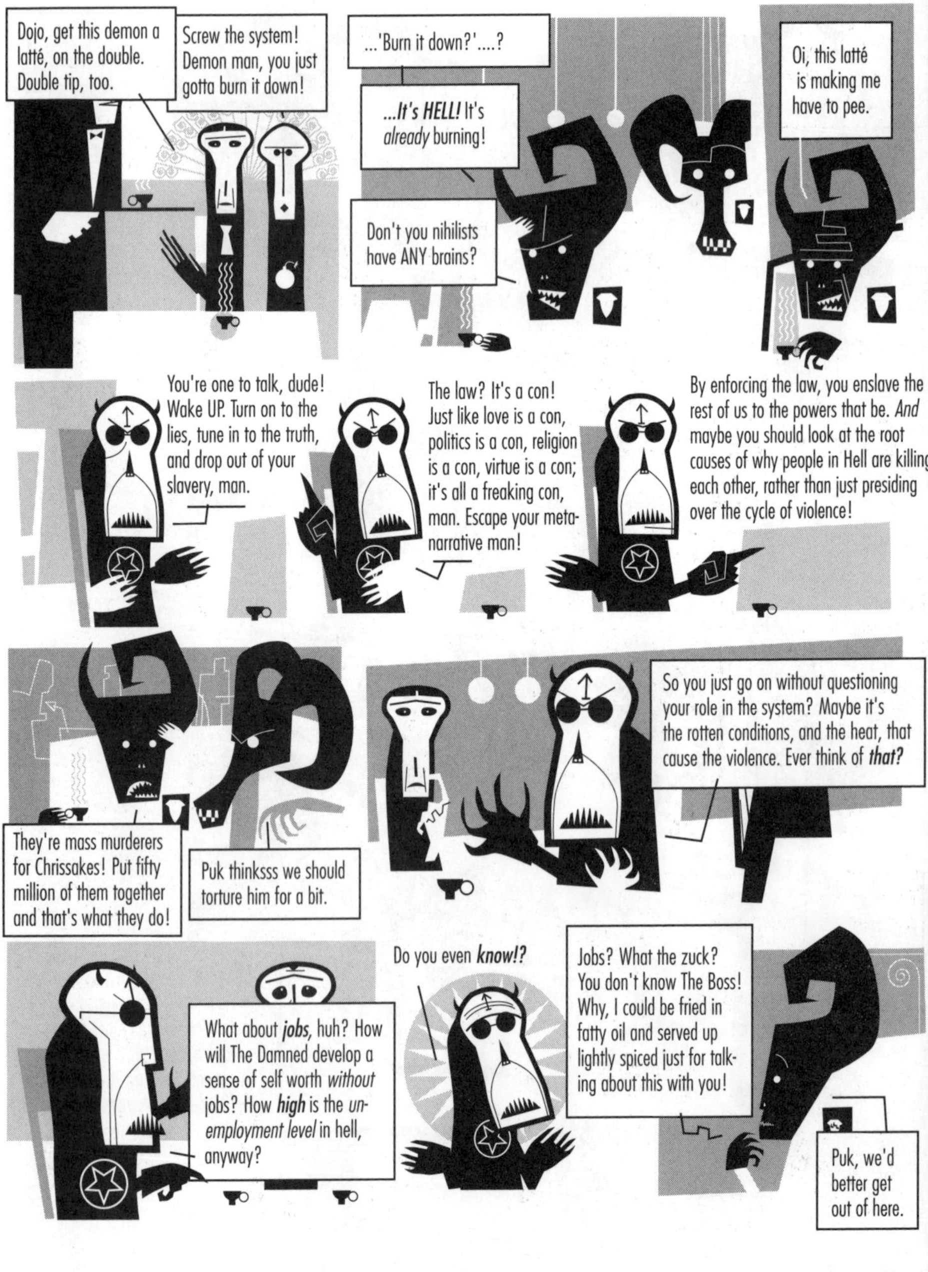

Dojo, get this demon a latté, on the double. Double tip, too.
Screw the system! Demon man, you just gotta burn it down!
...'Burn it down?'....?
...*It's HELL!* It's *already* burning!
Don't you nihilists have ANY brains?
Oi, this latté is making me have to pee.
You're one to talk, dude! Wake UP. Turn on to the lies, tune in to the truth, and drop out of your slavery, man.
The law? It's a con! Just like love is a con, politics is a con, religion is a con, virtue is a con; it's all a freaking con, man. Escape your meta-narrative man!
By enforcing the law, you enslave the rest of us to the powers that be. *And* maybe you should look at the root causes of why people in Hell are killing each other, rather than just presiding over the cycle of violence!
They're mass murderers for Chrissakes! Put fifty million of them together and that's what they do!
Puk thinksss we should torture him for a bit.
So you just go on without questioning your role in the system? Maybe it's the rotten conditions, and the heat, that cause the violence. Ever think of ***that?***
What about ***jobs,*** huh? How will The Damned develop a sense of self worth *without* jobs? How ***high*** is the *unemployment level* in hell, anyway?
Do you even ***know!?***
Jobs? What the zuck? You don't know The Boss! Why, I could be fried in fatty oil and served up lightly spiced just for talking about this with you!
Puk, we'd better get out of here.

Can you believe those guys? How would I pay for my coke habit without working? Sheesh!

Yeah, well Puk got a call from dispatch. It seemsss Al Capone and his gang have been massacred. Again. We gotta go down the elevator right away.

Guys like those two are exactly why the elites are able to hold on to their positions of power. They're completely unaware of the root causes of the problems they face, and thus perpetuate them ...for all eternity! Saps!

That demon piddled on the floor. Augh!

The scuzz!

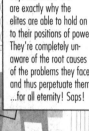

Hey! That reminds me. Nul, Mr. Sly was talking about you at lunch today, hoooooboy, was he.

BEWARE THE PIDDLE PUDDLE

He was on your crew? What was he saying?

Heheheh! Just that you been stealing parts from your department!

Why that two-faced little worm! Last week he told me I was the best person he'd ever worked with! I let him leave early, too! Oh!

Heh, that's funny! Last week he said Nul was a human-sacrificing Satanist who lied and killed to get the job as a chief engineer!

!? I haven't seen Nul at any of the Satanist Union meetings. I guess he isn't paying his dues, either!

What the?? That's... obviously an outrageous, manufactured missive of manure! That dastardly, deceitful little lying, sniveling, two-faced gossip spreading snake-in-the-grass!

Sigh! That Sly has been trouble ever since he was passed over for promotion. I got it and he didn't, the useless boob. Oh my dear. What should I do about it?

Sly? Hey, Sly told us at lunch last month that you were a commie. "He's a closet commie." That's what he said.

Holy Nothingness, Nul! I didn't know you were a commie! Now that's a real revelation. Not a good career move! Bad! Could cost you your job—and yer freedom!

Why so upset, Nul? Hey? Is it because it's true? You kill your way to the top of the totem pole, huh?

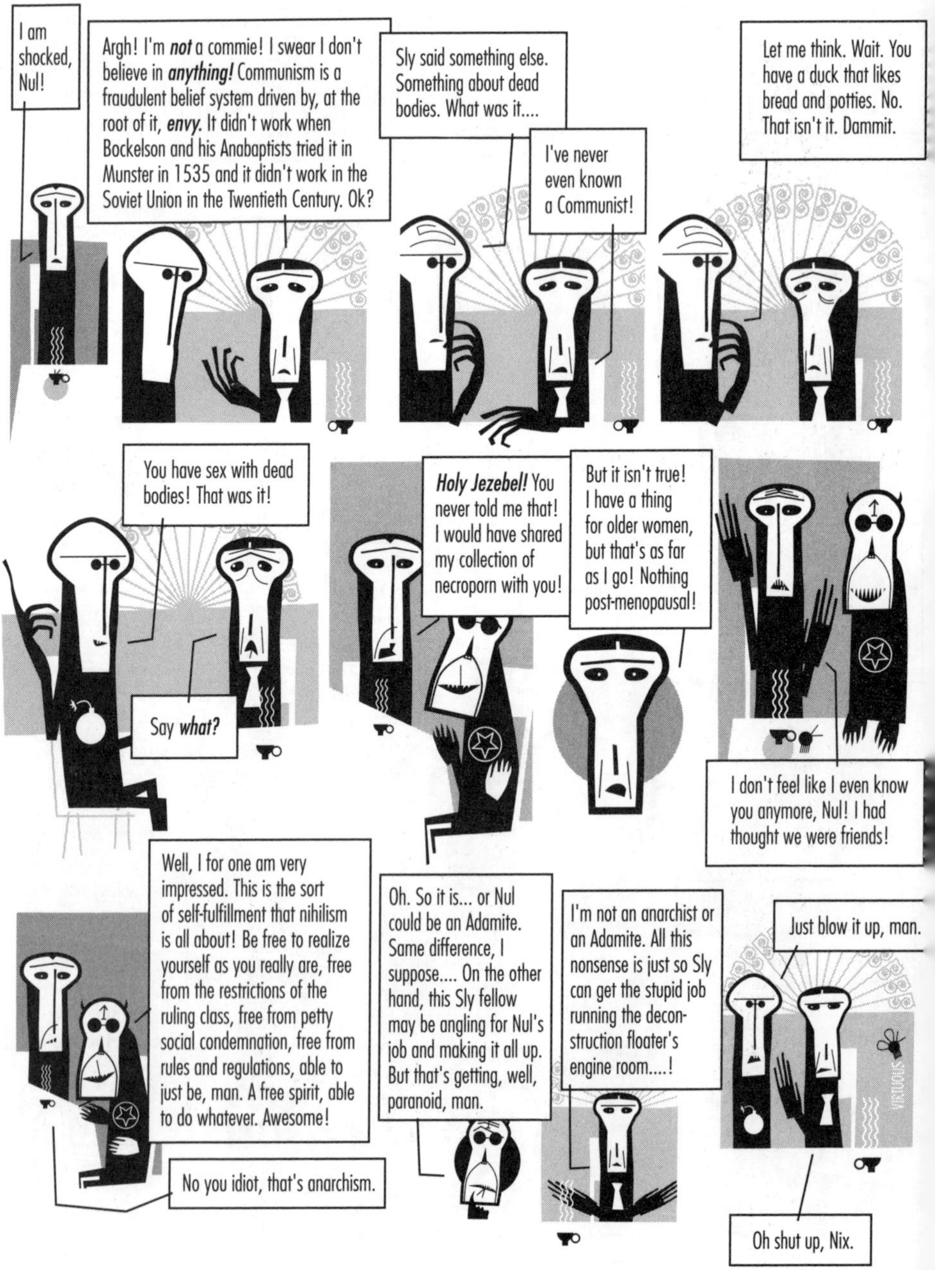
I am shocked, Nul!
Argh! I'm ***not*** a commie! I swear I don't believe in ***anything!*** Communism is a fraudulent belief system driven by, at the root of it, ***envy.*** It didn't work when Bockelson and his Anabaptists tried it in Munster in 1535 and it didn't work in the Soviet Union in the Twentieth Century. Ok?
Sly said something else. Something about dead bodies. What was it....
I've never even known a Communist!
Let me think. Wait. You have a duck that likes bread and potties. No. That isn't it. Dammit.
You have sex with dead bodies! That was it!
Say ***what?***
Holy Jezebel! You never told me that! I would have shared my collection of necroporn with you!
But it isn't true! I have a thing for older women, but that's as far as I go! Nothing post-menopausal!
I don't feel like I even know you anymore, Nul! I had thought we were friends!
Well, I for one am very impressed. This is the sort of self-fulfillment that nihilism is all about! Be free to realize yourself as you really are, free from the restrictions of the ruling class, free from petty social condemnation, free from rules and regulations, able to just be, man. A free spirit, able to do whatever. Awesome!
No you idiot, that's anarchism.
Oh. So it is... or Nul could be an Adamite. Same difference, I suppose.... On the other hand, this Sly fellow may be angling for Nul's job and making it all up. But that's getting, well, paranoid, man.
I'm not an anarchist or an Adamite. All this nonsense is just so Sly can get the stupid job running the decon-struction floater's engine room....!
Just blow it up, man.
Oh shut up, Nix.

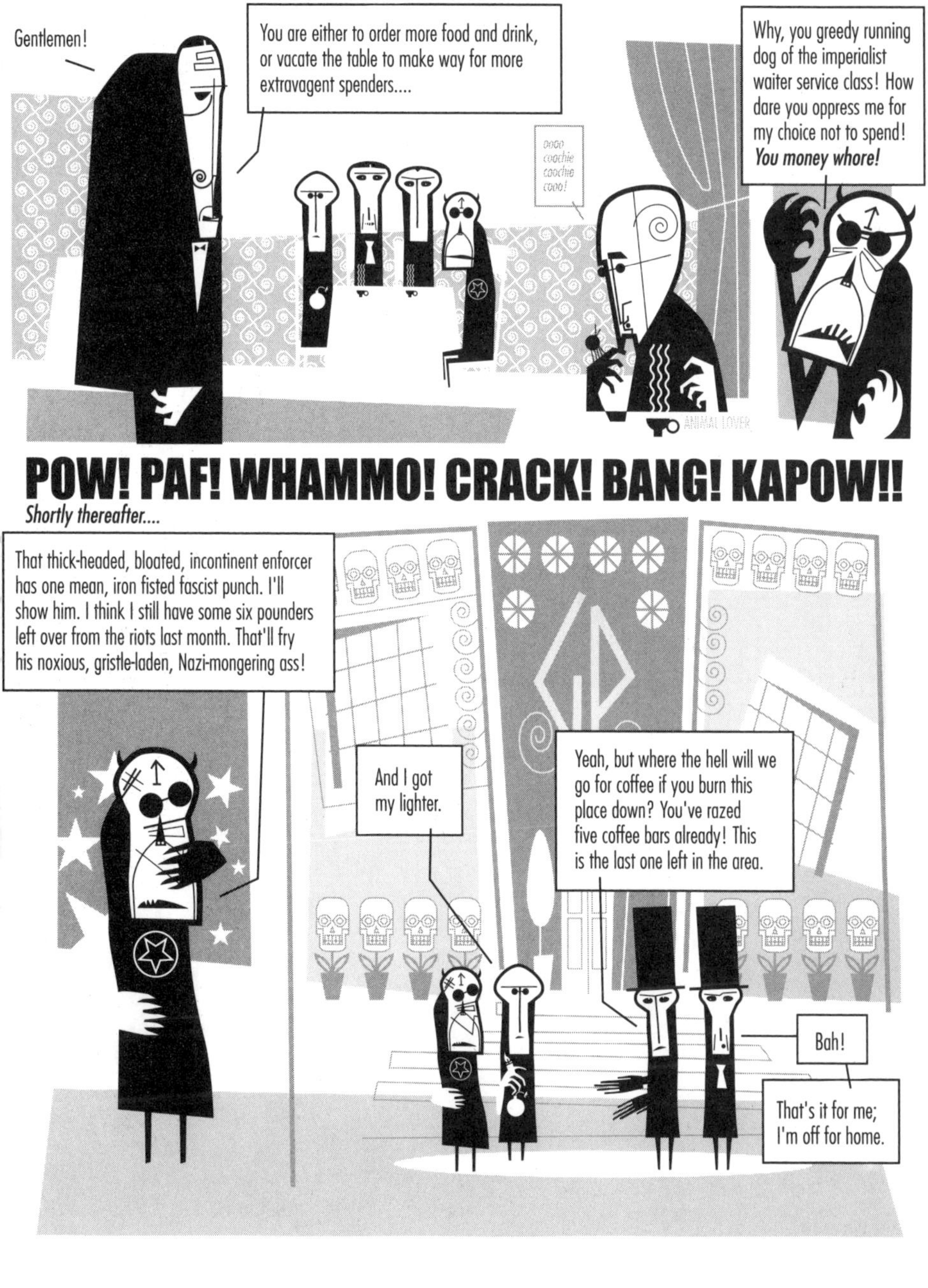
Gentlemen!
You are either to order more food and drink, or vacate the table to make way for more extravagent spenders....
oooo coochie coochie cooo!
Why, you greedy running dog of the imperialist waiter service class! How dare you oppress me for my choice not to spend! *You money whore!*
ANIMAL LOVER
POW! PAF! WHAMMO! CRACK! BANG! KAPOW!!
Shortly thereafter....
That thick-headed, bloated, incontinent enforcer has one mean, iron fisted fascist punch. I'll show him. I think I still have some six pounders left over from the riots last month. That'll fry his noxious, gristle-laden, Nazi-mongering ass!
And I got my lighter.
Yeah, but where the hell will we go for coffee if you burn this place down? You've razed five coffee bars already! This is the last one left in the area.
Bah!
That's it for me; I'm off for home.

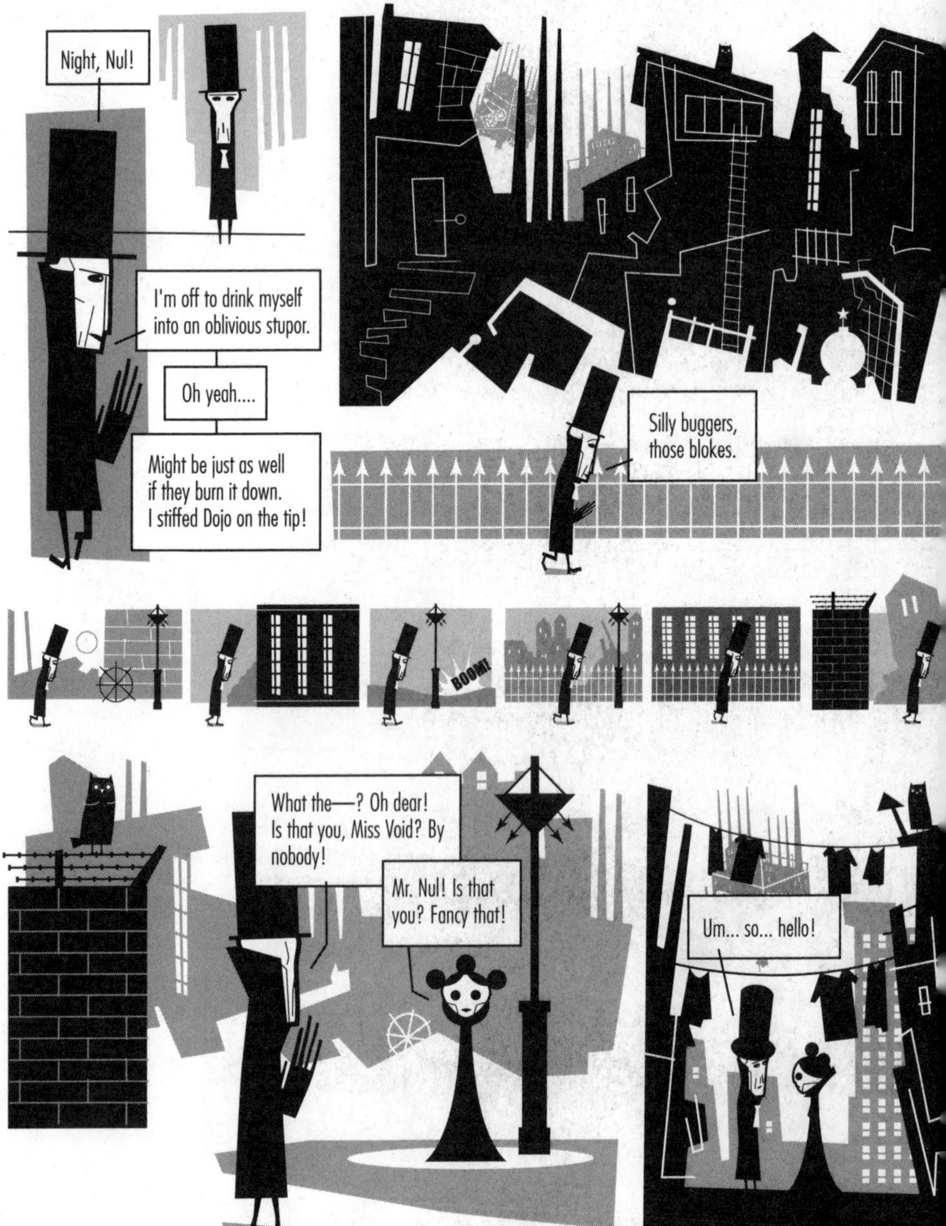
Night, Nul!
I'm off to drink myself into an oblivious stupor.
Oh yeah....
Might be just as well if they burn it down. I stiffed Dojo on the tip!
Silly buggers, those blokes.
BOOM!
What the—? Oh dear! Is that you, Miss Void? By nobody!
Mr. Nul! Is that you? Fancy that!
Um... so... hello!

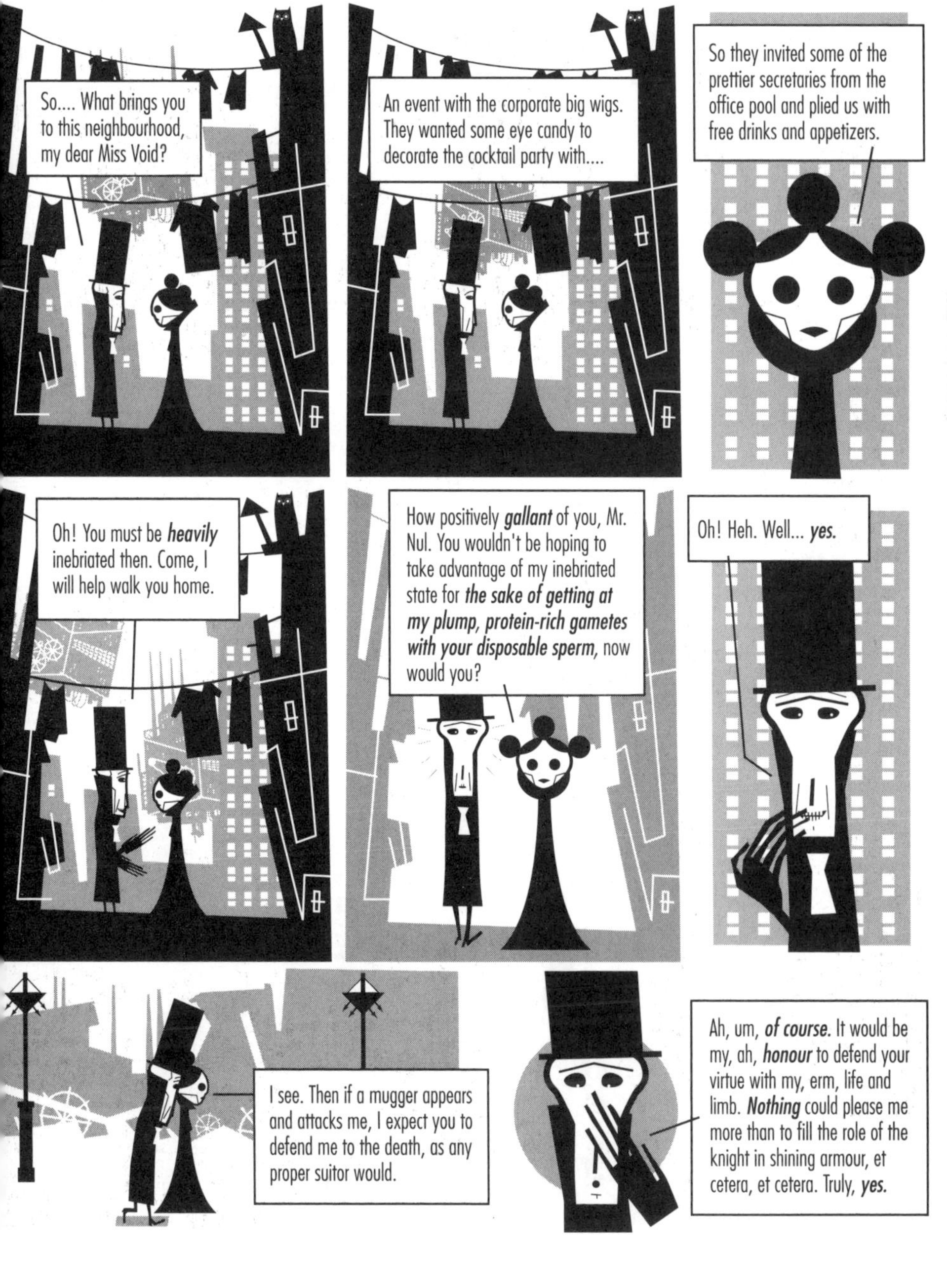
So.... What brings you to this neighbourhood, my dear Miss Void?
An event with the corporate big wigs. They wanted some eye candy to decorate the cocktail party with....
So they invited some of the prettier secretaries from the office pool and plied us with free drinks and appetizers.
Oh! You must be ***heavily*** inebriated then. Come, I will help walk you home.
How positively ***gallant*** of you, Mr. Nul. You wouldn't be hoping to take advantage of my inebriated state for ***the sake of getting at my plump, protein-rich gametes with your disposable sperm,*** now would you?
Oh! Heh. Well... ***yes.***
I see. Then if a mugger appears and attacks me, I expect you to defend me to the death, as any proper suitor would.
Ah, um, ***of course.*** It would be my, ah, ***honour*** to defend your virtue with my, erm, life and limb. ***Nothing*** could please me more than to fill the role of the knight in shining armour, et cetera, et cetera. Truly, ***yes.***

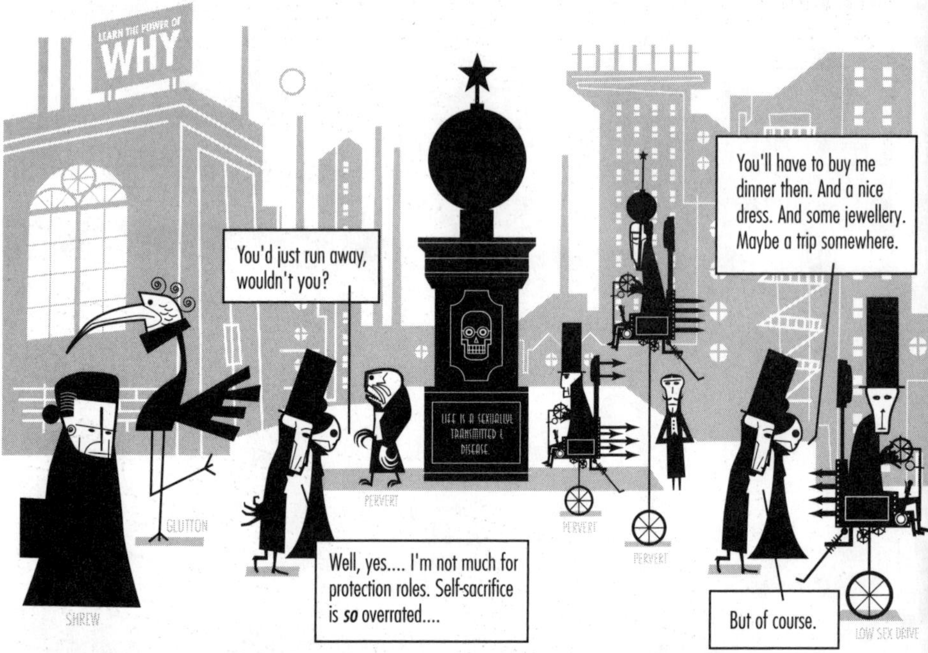
LEARN THE POWER OF
WHY
You'd just run away, wouldn't you?
Well, yes.... I'm not much for protection roles. Self-sacrifice is *so* overrated....
You'll have to buy me dinner then. And a nice dress. And some jewellery. Maybe a trip somewhere.
But of course.
SHREW
GLUTTON
PERVERT
PERVERT
PERVERT
LOW SEX DRIVE

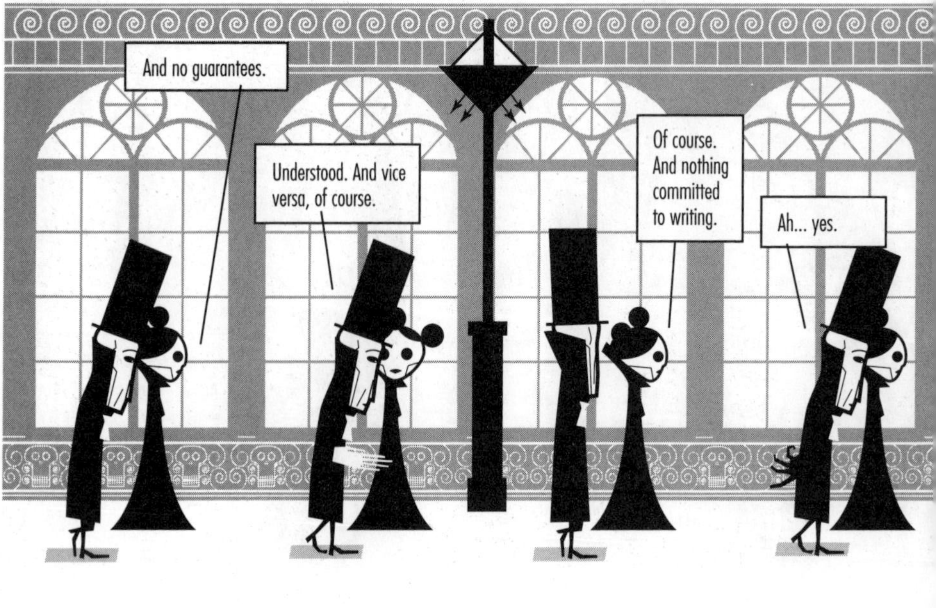
And no guarantees.
Understood. And vice versa, of course.
Of course. And nothing committed to writing.
Ah... yes.

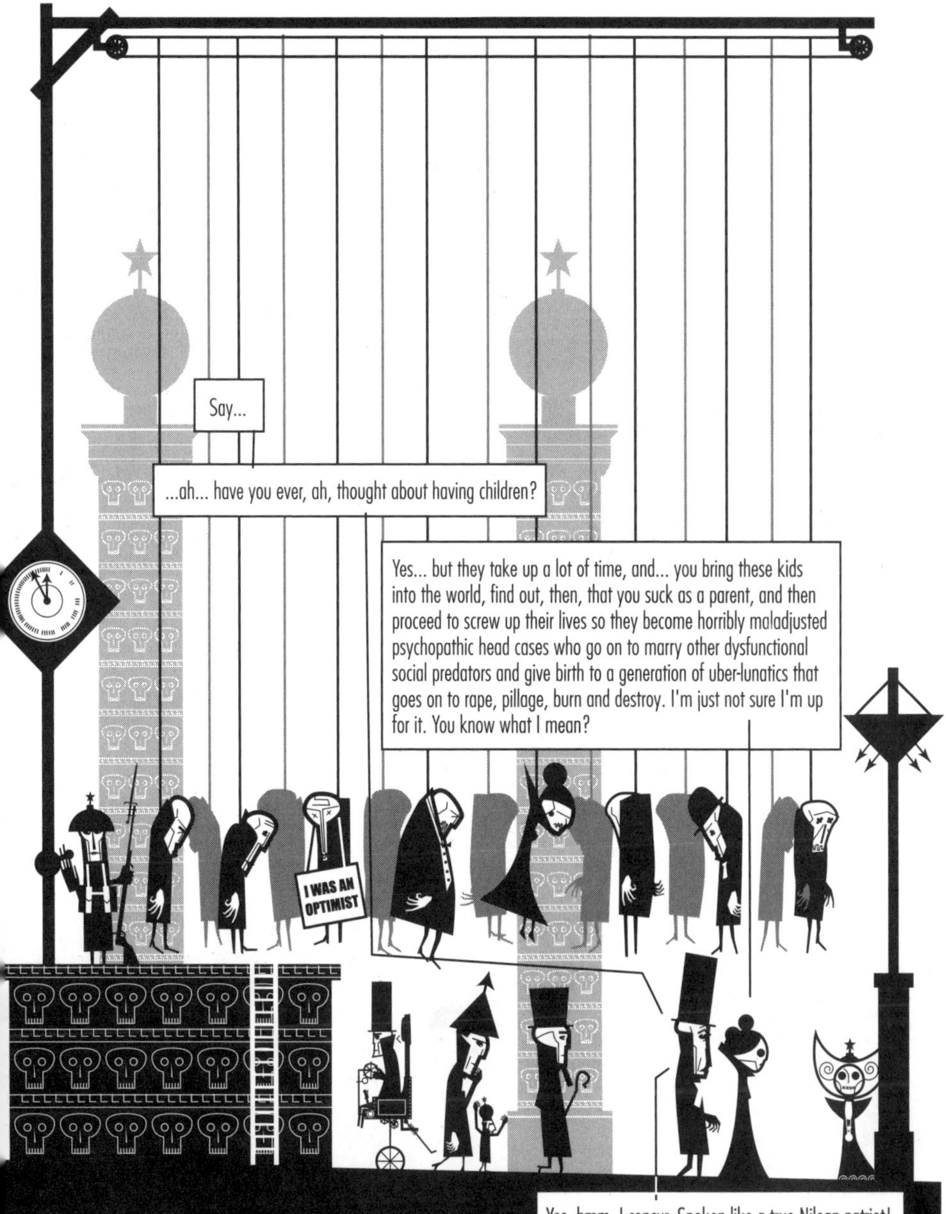
Say...
...ah... have you ever, ah, thought about having children?
Yes... but they take up a lot of time, and... you bring these kids into the world, find out, then, that you suck as a parent, and then proceed to screw up their lives so they become horribly maladjusted psychopathic head cases who go on to marry other dysfunctional social predators and give birth to a generation of uber-lunatics that goes on to rape, pillage, burn and destroy. I'm just not sure I'm up for it. You know what I mean?
I WAS AN OPTIMIST
Yes, hmm, I concur. Spoken like a true Nilean patriot!

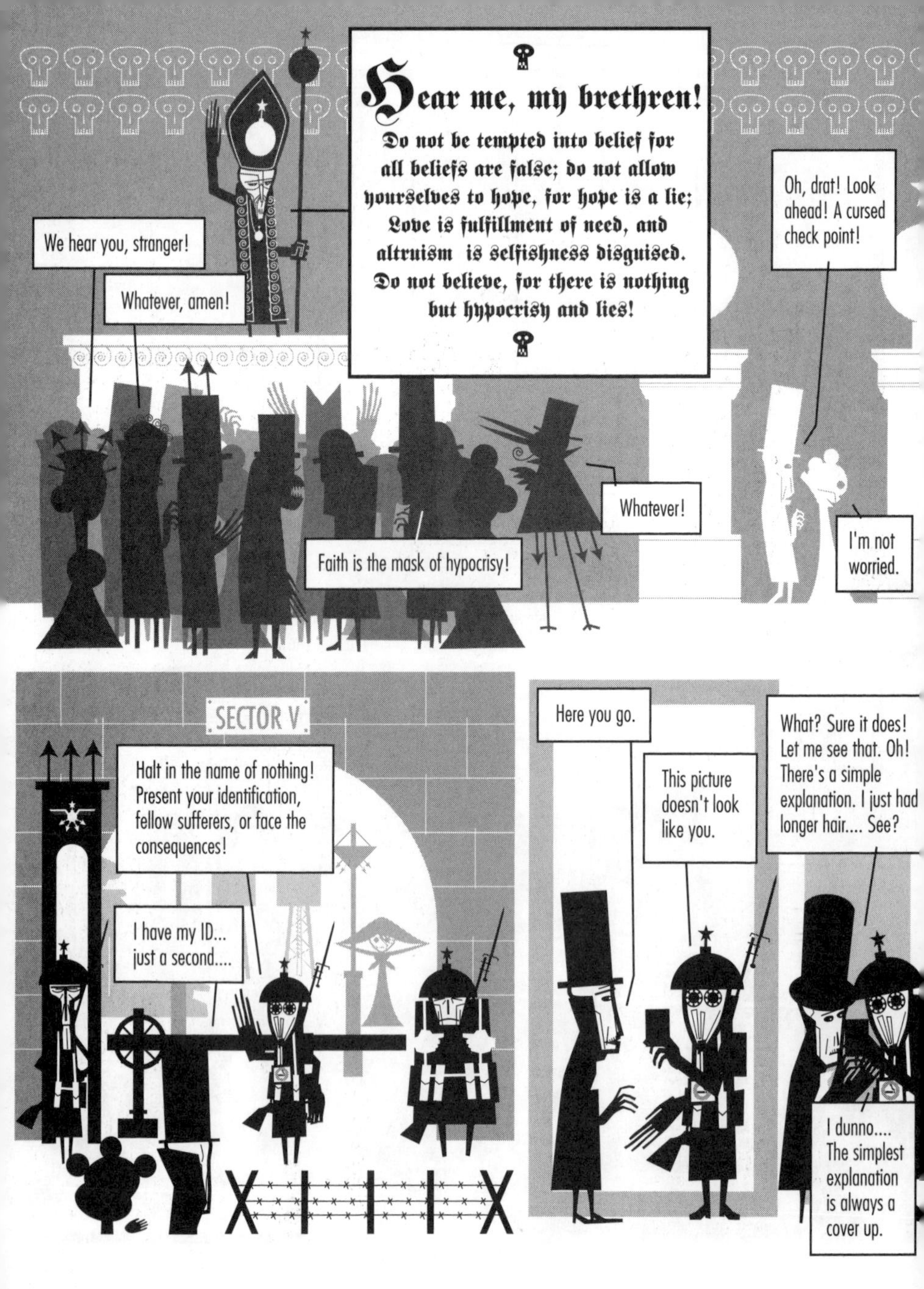

Hear me, my brethren!
Do not be tempted into belief for all beliefs are false; do not allow yourselves to hope, for hope is a lie; Love is fulfillment of need, and altruism is selfishness disguised. Do not believe, for there is nothing but hypocrisy and lies!
We hear you, stranger!
Whatever, amen!
Faith is the mask of hypocrisy!
Whatever!
Oh, drat! Look ahead! A cursed check point!
I'm not worried.
SECTOR V
Halt in the name of nothing! Present your identification, fellow sufferers, or face the consequences!
I have my ID... just a second....
Here you go.
This picture doesn't look like you.
What? Sure it does! Let me see that. Oh! There's a simple explanation. I just had longer hair.... See?
I dunno.... The simplest explanation is always a cover up.

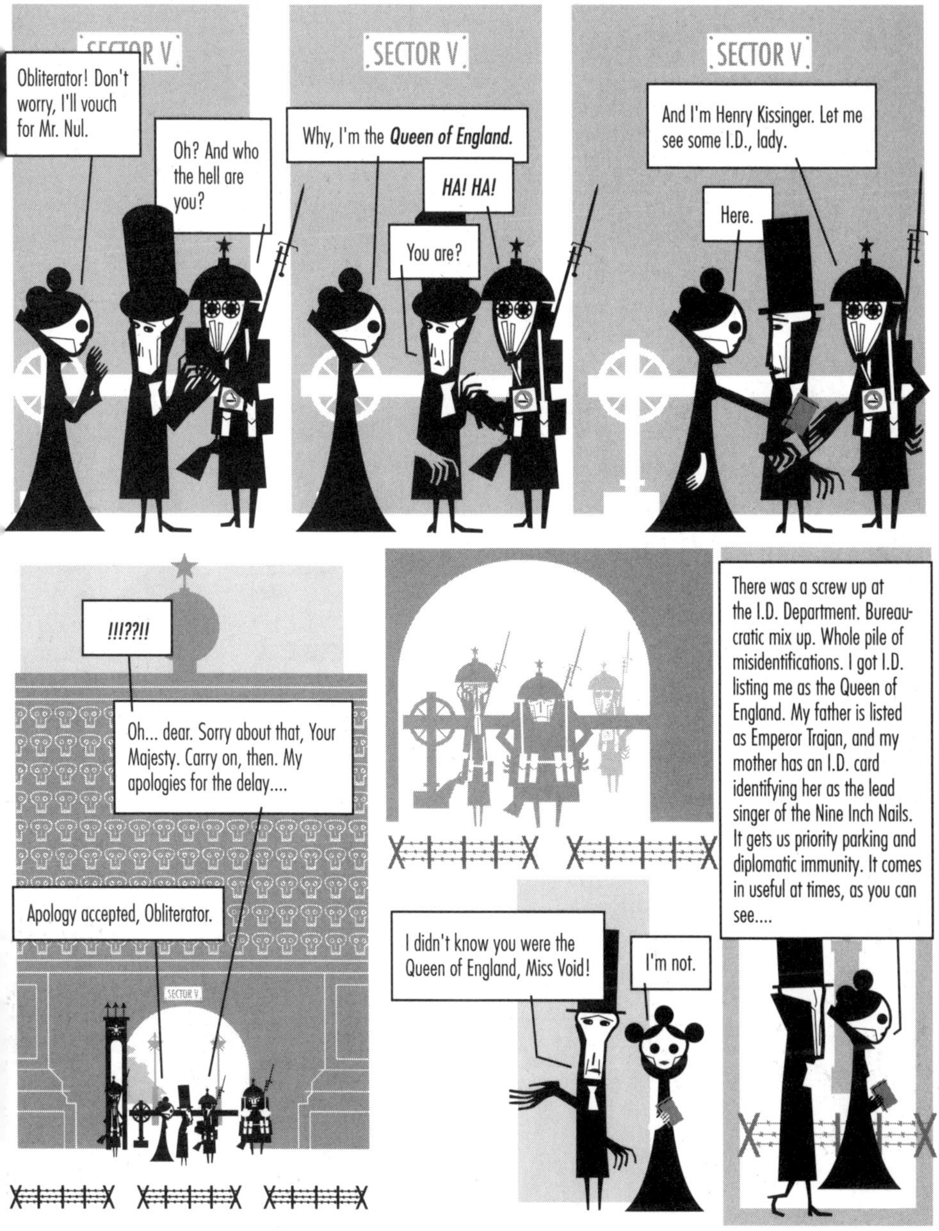
SECTOR V
Obliterator! Don't worry, I'll vouch for Mr. Nul.
Oh? And who the hell are you?
SECTOR V
Why, I'm the Queen of England.
HA! HA!
You are?
SECTOR V
And I'm Henry Kissinger. Let me see some I.D., lady.
Here.
!!!??!!
Oh... dear. Sorry about that, Your Majesty. Carry on, then. My apologies for the delay....
Apology accepted, Obliterator.
SECTOR V
There was a screw up at the I.D. Department. Bureaucratic mix up. Whole pile of misidentifications. I got I.D. listing me as the Queen of England. My father is listed as Emperor Trajan, and my mother has an I.D. card identifying her as the lead singer of the Nine Inch Nails. It gets us priority parking and diplomatic immunity. It comes in useful at times, as you can see....
I didn't know you were the Queen of England, Miss Void!
I'm not.

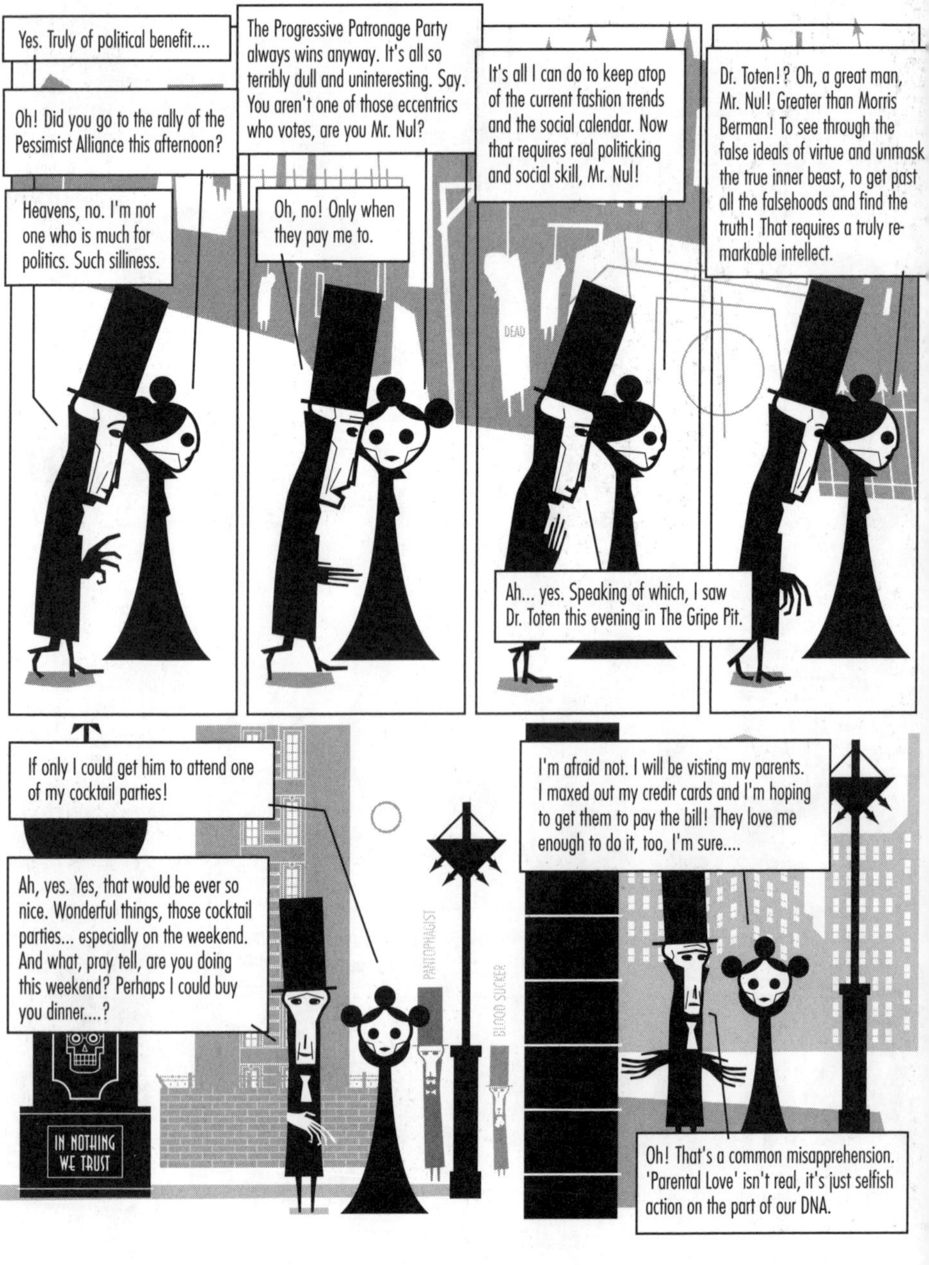
Yes. Truly of political benefit....
Oh! Did you go to the rally of the Pessimist Alliance this afternoon?
Heavens, no. I'm not one who is much for politics. Such silliness.
The Progressive Patronage Party always wins anyway. It's all so terribly dull and uninteresting. Say. You aren't one of those eccentrics who votes, are you Mr. Nul?
Oh, no! Only when they pay me to.
It's all I can do to keep atop of the current fashion trends and the social calendar. Now that requires real politicking and social skill, Mr. Nul!
DEAD
Ah... yes. Speaking of which, I saw Dr. Toten this evening in The Gripe Pit.
Dr. Toten!? Oh, a great man, Mr. Nul! Greater than Morris Berman! To see through the false ideals of virtue and unmask the true inner beast, to get past all the falsehoods and find the truth! That requires a truly remarkable intellect.
If only I could get him to attend one of my cocktail parties!
Ah, yes. Yes, that would be ever so nice. Wonderful things, those cocktail parties... especially on the weekend. And what, pray tell, are you doing this weekend? Perhaps I could buy you dinner....?
PANTOPHAGIST
BLOOD SUCKER
IN NOTHING WE TRUST
I'm afraid not. I will be visting my parents. I maxed out my credit cards and I'm hoping to get them to pay the bill! They love me enough to do it, too, I'm sure....
Oh! That's a common misapprehension. 'Parental Love' isn't real, it's just selfish action on the part of our DNA.

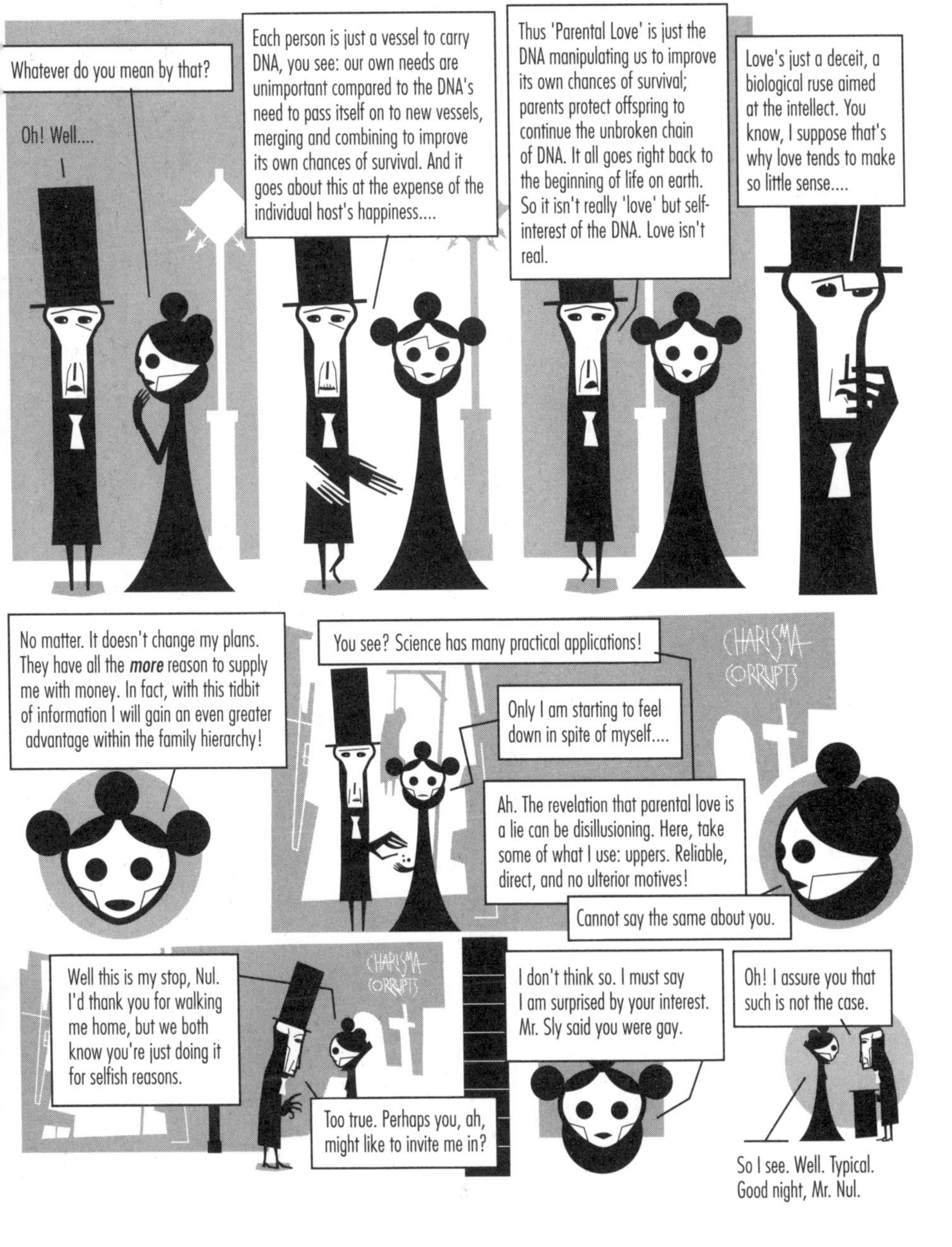
Whatever do you mean by that?
Oh! Well....
Each person is just a vessel to carry DNA, you see: our own needs are unimportant compared to the DNA's need to pass itself on to new vessels, merging and combining to improve its own chances of survival. And it goes about this at the expense of the individual host's happiness....
Thus 'Parental Love' is just the DNA manipulating us to improve its own chances of survival; parents protect offspring to continue the unbroken chain of DNA. It all goes right back to the beginning of life on earth. So it isn't really 'love' but self-interest of the DNA. Love isn't real.
Love's just a deceit, a biological ruse aimed at the intellect. You know, I suppose that's why love tends to make so little sense....
No matter. It doesn't change my plans. They have all the ***more*** reason to supply me with money. In fact, with this tidbit of information I will gain an even greater advantage within the family hierarchy!
You see? Science has many practical applications!
CHARISMA CORRUPTS
Only I am starting to feel down in spite of myself....
Ah. The revelation that parental love is a lie can be disillusioning. Here, take some of what I use: uppers. Reliable, direct, and no ulterior motives!
Cannot say the same about you.
Well this is my stop, Nul. I'd thank you for walking me home, but we both know you're just doing it for selfish reasons.
CHARISMA CORRUPTS
Too true. Perhaps you, ah, might like to invite me in?
I don't think so. I must say I am surprised by your interest. Mr. Sly said you were gay.
Oh! I assure you that such is not the case.
So I see. Well. Typical. Good night, Mr. Nul.

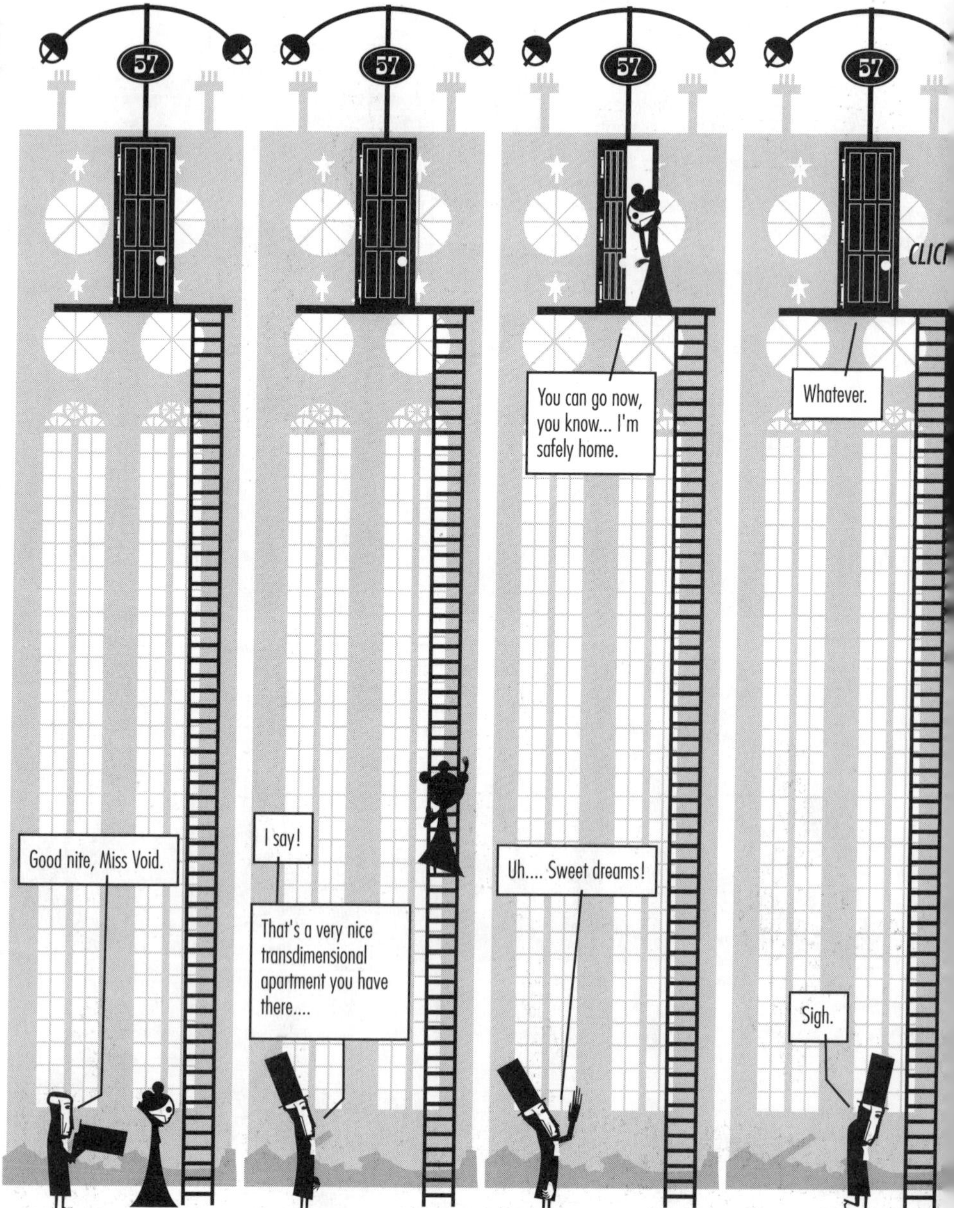
Good nite, Miss Void.
I say!
That's a very nice transdimensional apartment you have there....
You can go now, you know... I'm safely home.
Uh.... Sweet dreams!
Whatever.
Sigh.

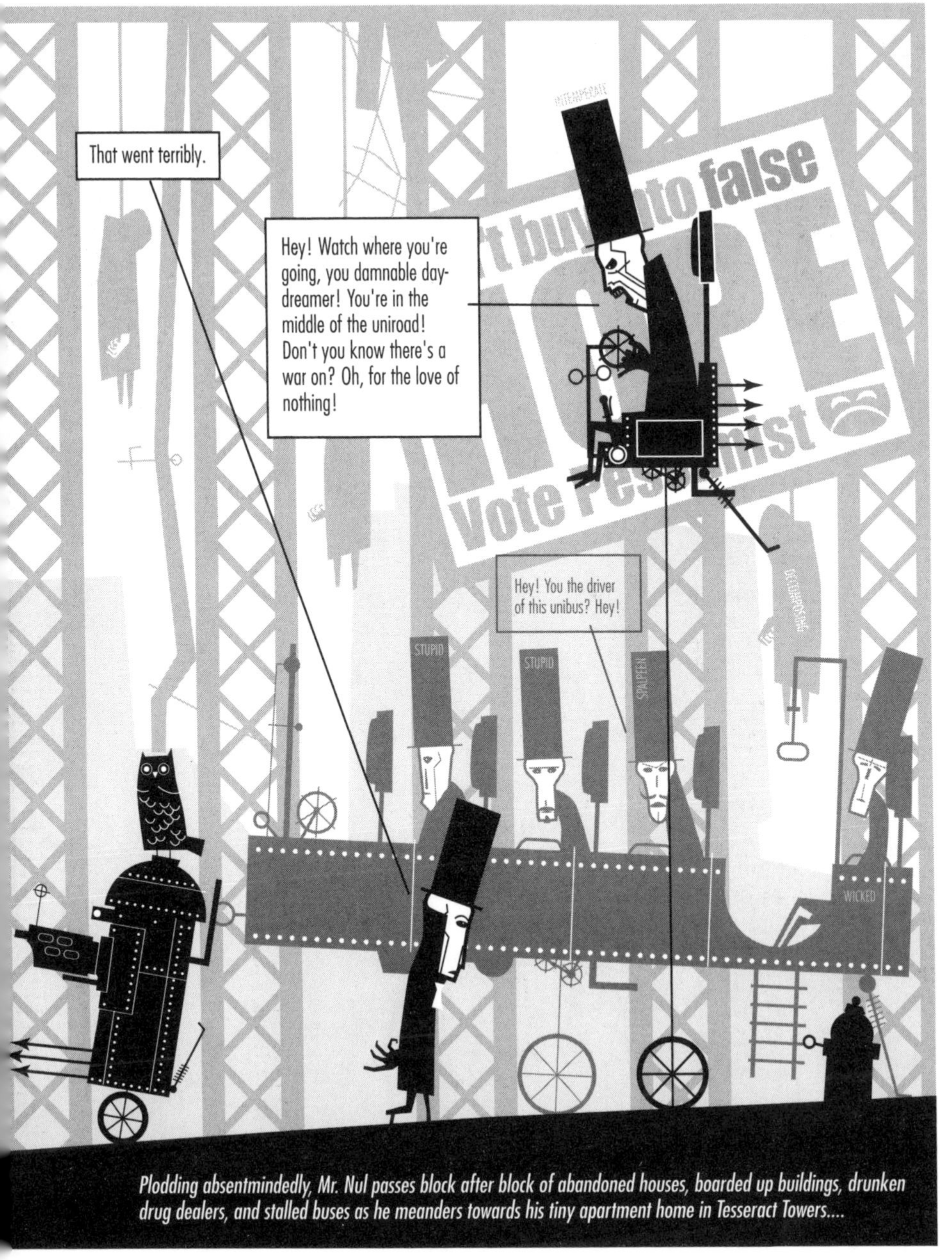
That went terribly.
Hey! Watch where you're going, you damnable day-dreamer! You're in the middle of the uniroad! Don't you know there's a war on? Oh, for the love of nothing!
Hey! You the driver of this unibus? Hey!
STUPID
STUPID
SPALPEEN
WICKED
Plodding absentmindedly, Mr. Nul passes block after block of abandoned houses, boarded up buildings, drunken drug dealers, and stalled buses as he meanders towards his tiny apartment home in Tesseract Towers....

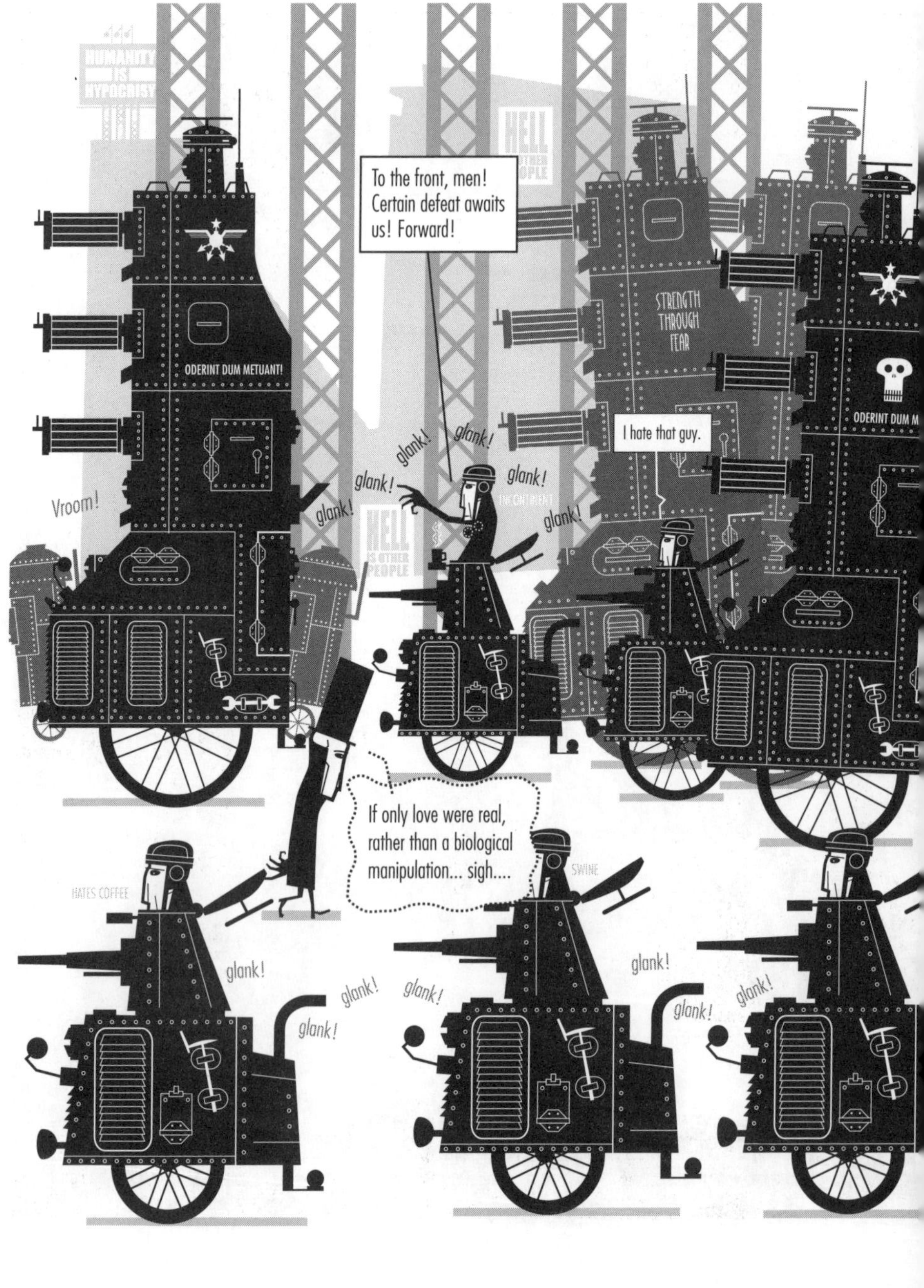
HUMANITY IS HYPOCRISY
ODERINT DUM METUANT!
To the front, men! Certain defeat awaits us! Forward!
STRENGTH THROUGH FEAR
ODERINT DUM M
I hate that guy.
Vroom!
glank!
glank!
glank!
glank!
glank!
glank!
INCONTINENT
HELL IS OTHER PEOPLE
If only love were real, rather than a biological manipulation... sigh....
HATES COFFEE
SWINE
glank!
glank!
glank!
glank!
glank!
glank!
glank!

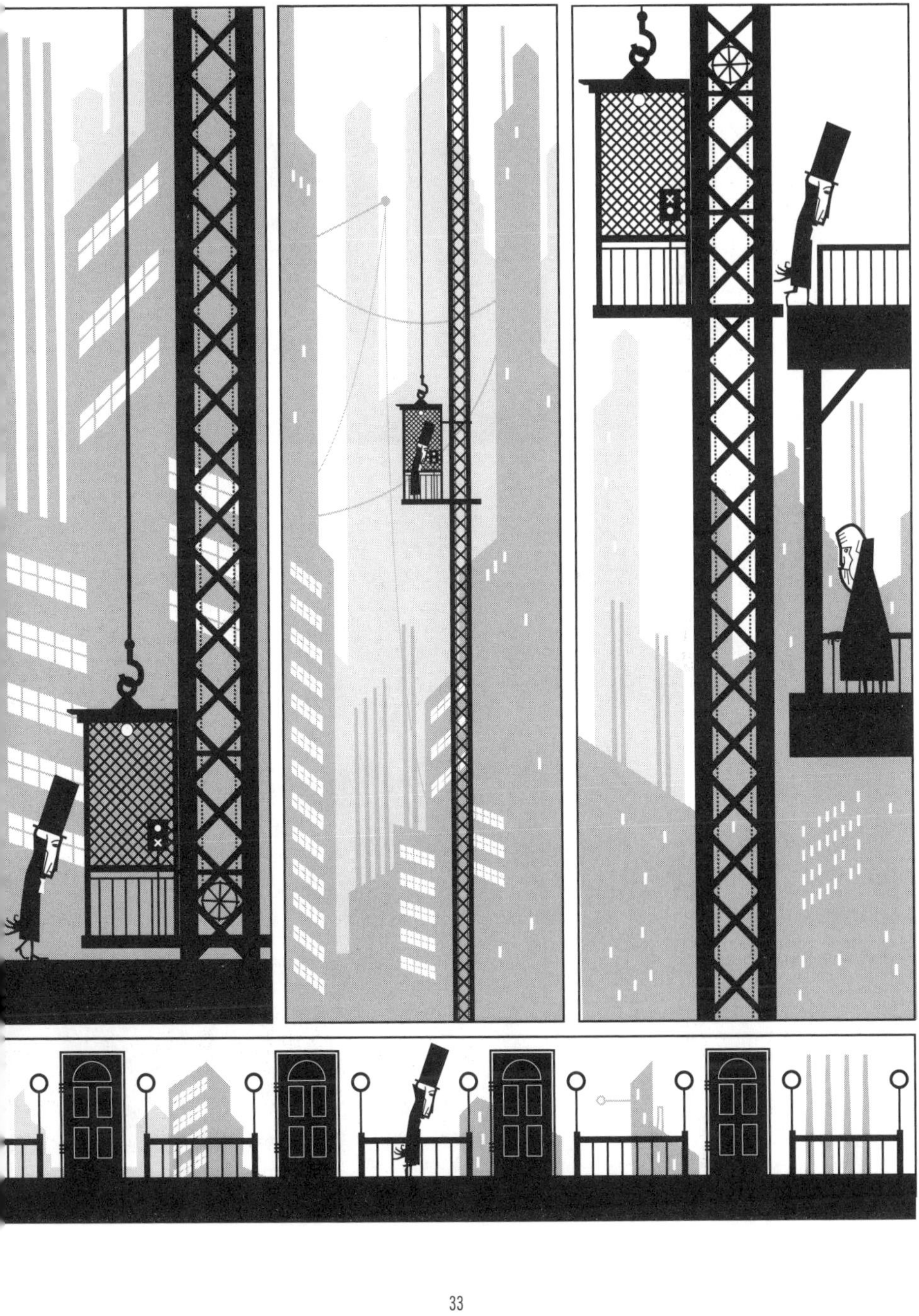

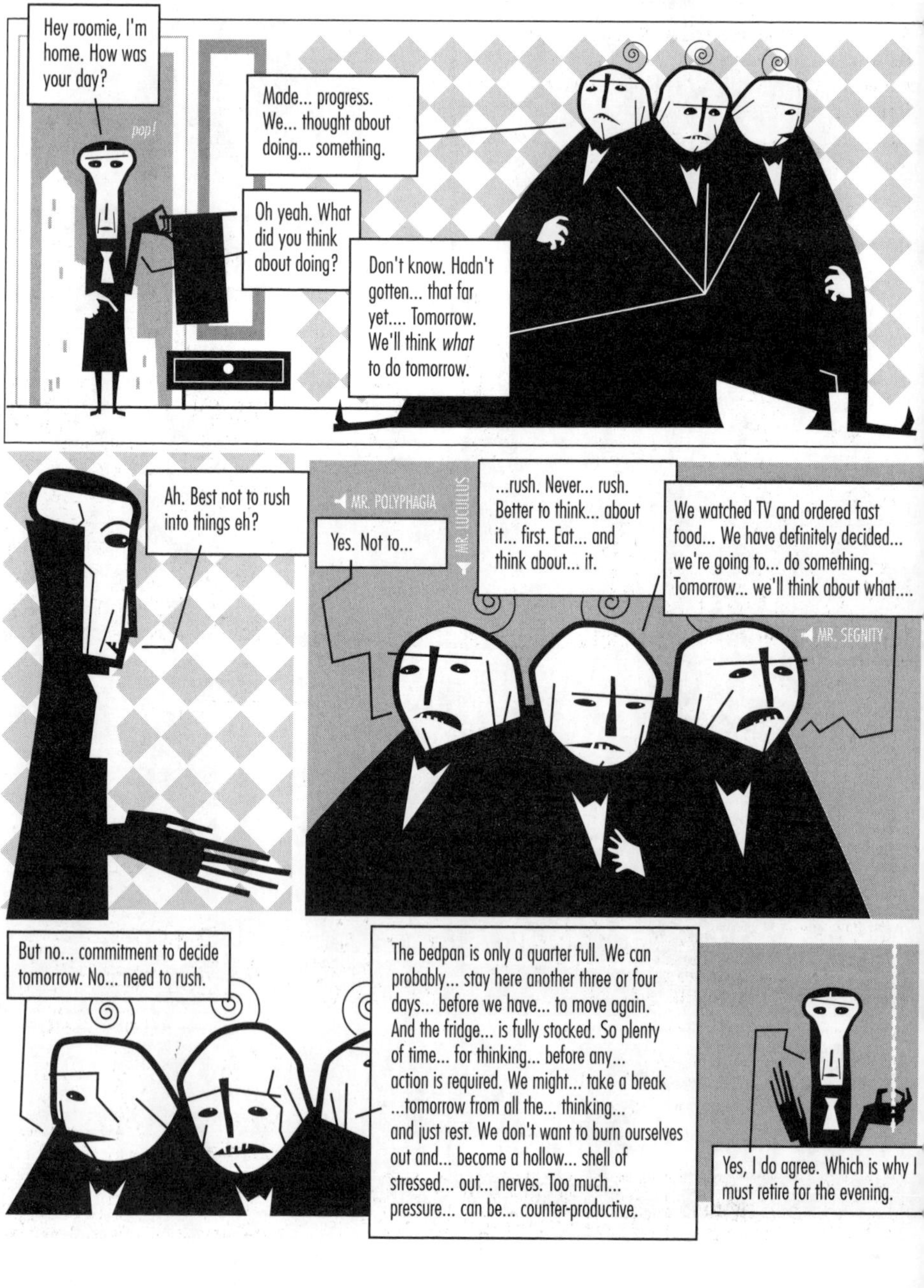
Hey roomie, I'm home. How was your day?
pop!
Made... progress. We... thought about doing... something.
Oh yeah. What did you think about doing?
Don't know. Hadn't gotten... that far yet.... Tomorrow. We'll think *what* to do tomorrow.
Ah. Best not to rush into things eh?
MR. POLYPHAGIA
Yes. Not to...
MR. LUCULLUS
...rush. Never... rush. Better to think... about it... first. Eat... and think about... it.
We watched TV and ordered fast food... We have definitely decided... we're going to... do something. Tomorrow... we'll think about what....
MR. SEGNITY
But no... commitment to decide tomorrow. No... need to rush.
The bedpan is only a quarter full. We can probably... stay here another three or four days... before we have... to move again. And the fridge... is fully stocked. So plenty of time... for thinking... before any... action is required. We might... take a break ...tomorrow from all the... thinking... and just rest. We don't want to burn ourselves out and... become a hollow... shell of stressed... out... nerves. Too much... pressure... can be... counter-productive.
Yes, I do agree. Which is why I must retire for the evening.

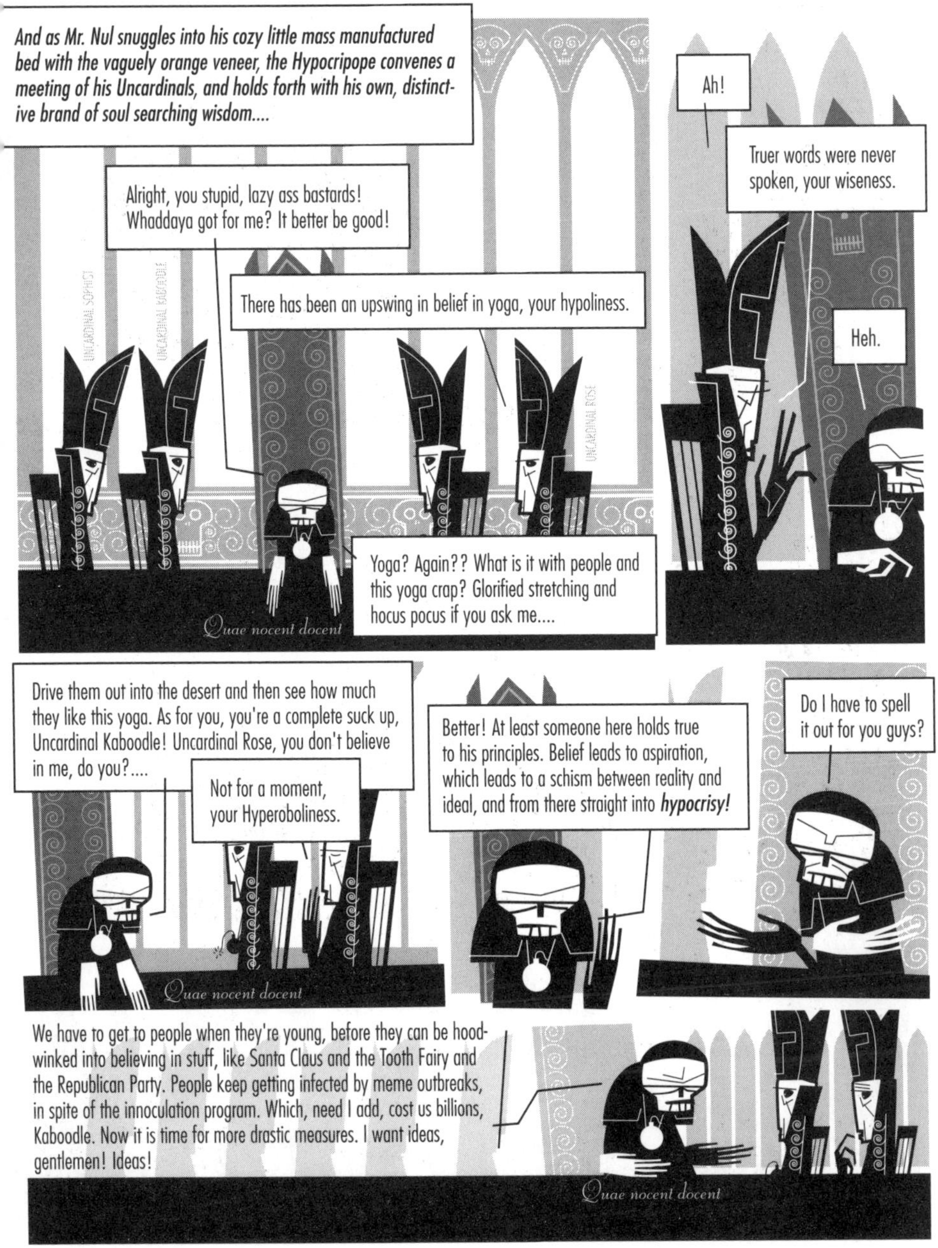

And as Mr. Nul snuggles into his cozy little mass manufactured bed with the vaguely orange veneer, the Hypocripope convenes a meeting of his Uncardinals, and holds forth with his own, distinctive brand of soul searching wisdom....
Alright, you stupid, lazy ass bastards! Whaddaya got for me? It better be good!
UNCARDINAL SOPHIST
UNCARDINAL KABOODLE
There has been an upswing in belief in yoga, your hypoliness.
UNCARDINAL ROSE
Yoga? Again?? What is it with people and this yoga crap? Glorified stretching and hocus pocus if you ask me....
Quae nocent docent
Ah!
Truer words were never spoken, your wiseness.
Heh.
Drive them out into the desert and then see how much they like this yoga. As for you, you're a complete suck up, Uncardinal Kaboodle! Uncardinal Rose, you don't believe in me, do you?....
Not for a moment, your Hyperoboliness.
Quae nocent docent
Better! At least someone here holds true to his principles. Belief leads to aspiration, which leads to a schism between reality and ideal, and from there straight into hypocrisy!
Do I have to spell it out for you guys?
We have to get to people when they're young, before they can be hoodwinked into believing in stuff, like Santa Claus and the Tooth Fairy and the Republican Party. People keep getting infected by meme outbreaks, in spite of the innoculation program. Which, need I add, cost us billions, Kaboodle. Now it is time for more drastic measures. I want ideas, gentlemen! Ideas!
Quae nocent docent

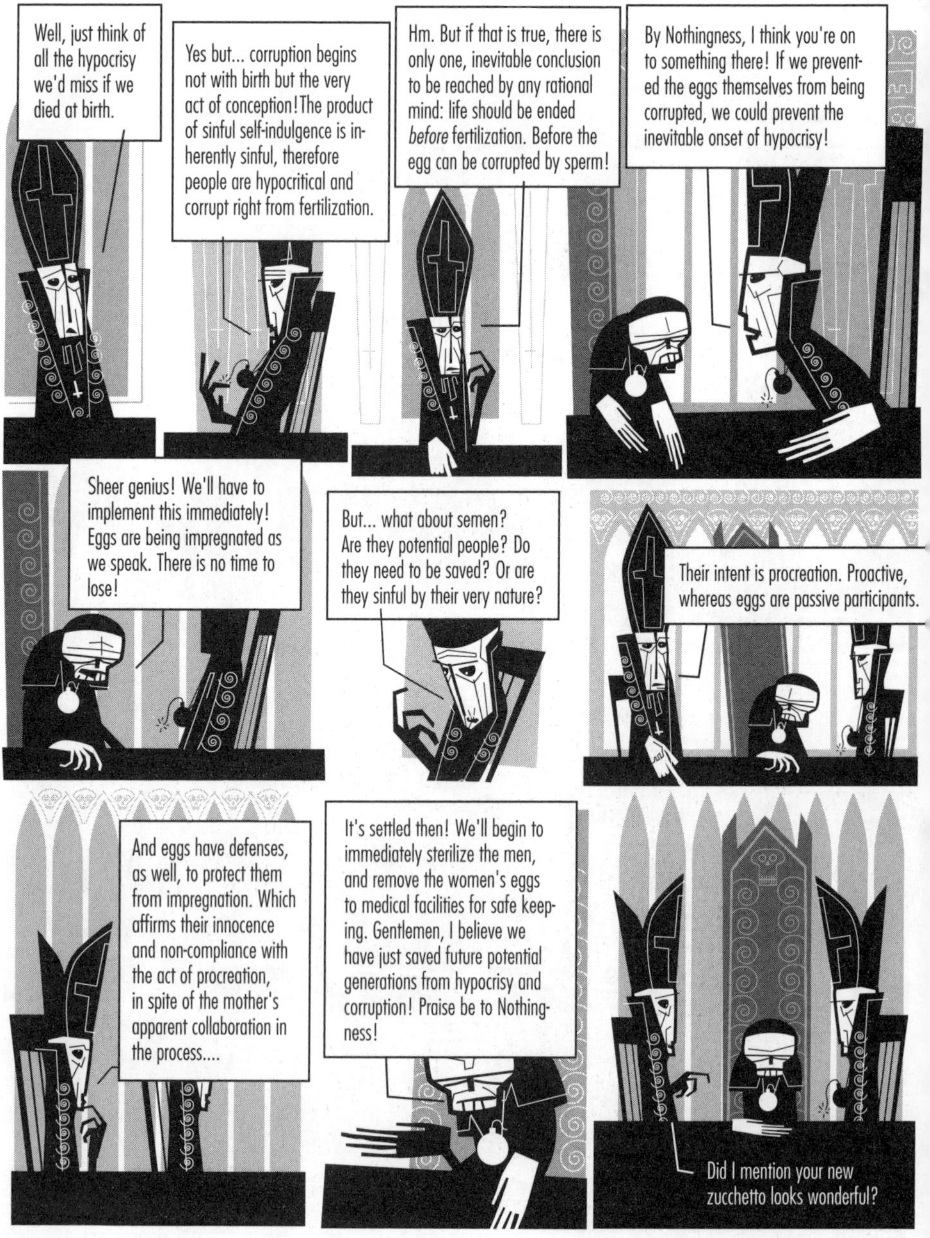
Well, just think of all the hypocrisy we'd miss if we died at birth.
Yes but... corruption begins not with birth but the very act of conception! The product of sinful self-indulgence is inherently sinful, therefore people are hypocritical and corrupt right from fertilization.
Hm. But if that is true, there is only one, inevitable conclusion to be reached by any rational mind: life should be ended *before* fertilization. Before the egg can be corrupted by sperm!
By Nothingness, I think you're on to something there! If we prevented the eggs themselves from being corrupted, we could prevent the inevitable onset of hypocrisy!
Sheer genius! We'll have to implement this immediately! Eggs are being impregnated as we speak. There is no time to lose!
But... what about semen? Are they potential people? Do they need to be saved? Or are they sinful by their very nature?
Their intent is procreation. Proactive, whereas eggs are passive participants.
And eggs have defenses, as well, to protect them from impregnation. Which affirms their innocence and non-compliance with the act of procreation, in spite of the mother's apparent collaboration in the process....
It's settled then! We'll begin to immediately sterilize the men, and remove the women's eggs to medical facilities for safe keeping. Gentlemen, I believe we have just saved future potential generations from hypocrisy and corruption! Praise be to Nothingness!
Did I mention your new zucchetto looks wonderful?

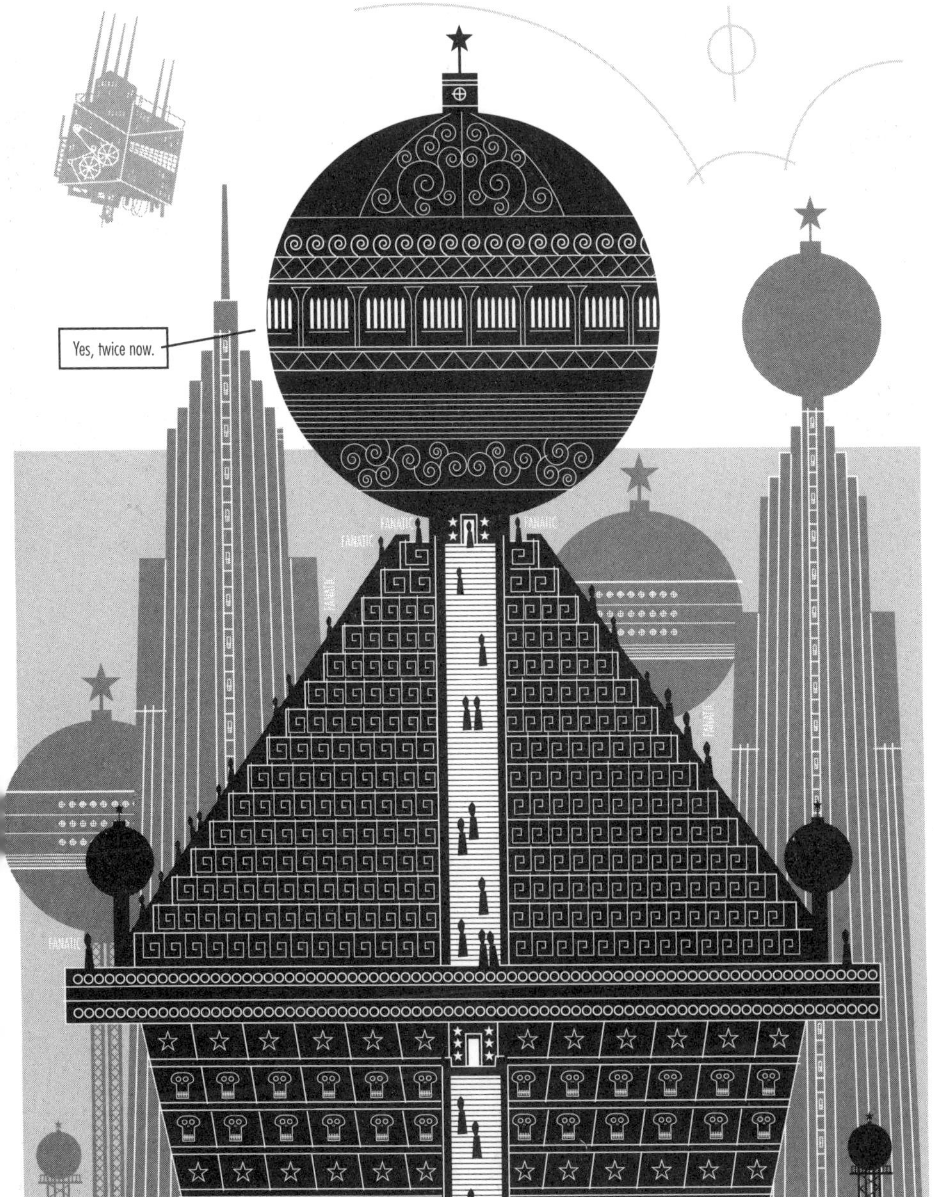
Yes, twice now.
FANATIC
FANATIC
FANATIC
FANATIC
FANATIC
FANATIC

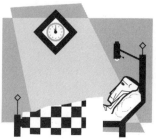

I wonder if she likes me?

But she's so beautiful, it's ...incomprehensible. I just can't fathom it.

And she could have any guy she wants. Why would she like me? Would she even notice me if we didn't work together?

Well... sort of semi-together. Okay, I see her at work every now and then. She knows who I am. She says 'hi' to me.

'Hi' is good.

Okay, after two years maybe 'hi' isn't quite so good.

Stranger things have been known to happen. The hoola-hoop for example. Or the pet rock. Those are pretty strange.

Oh, who the zuck am I kidding? It's hopeless. She's never agreed to coffee at The Gripe Pit, even. Stupid, *stupid* DNA! Get to sleep! Lots of work tomorrow. Lots....

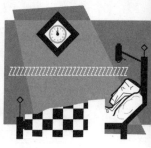

ZZZZZZZZZZZZZZZZZZZZZZZZZZZ

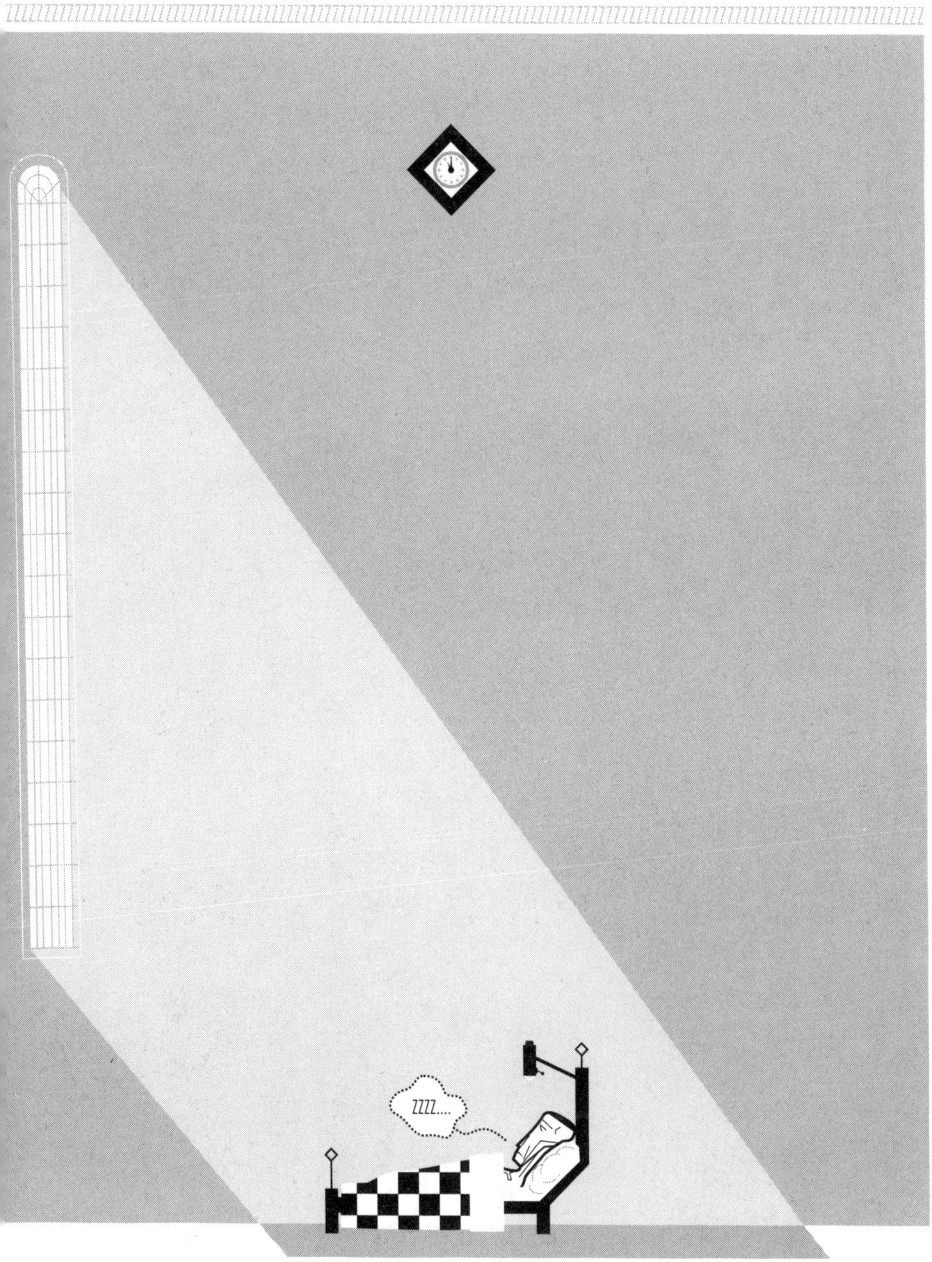
ZZZZ....

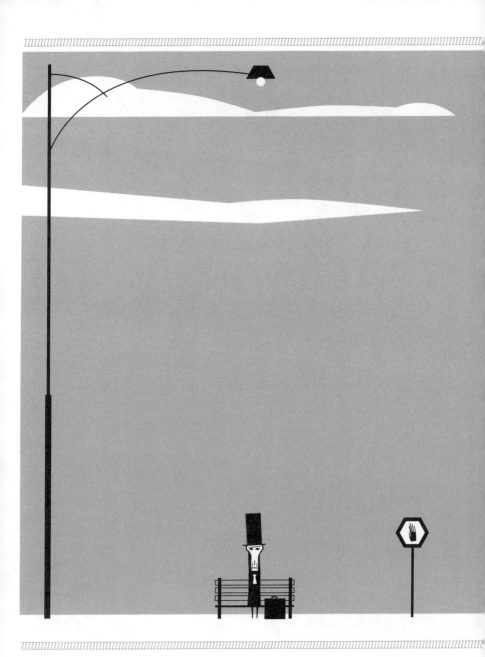

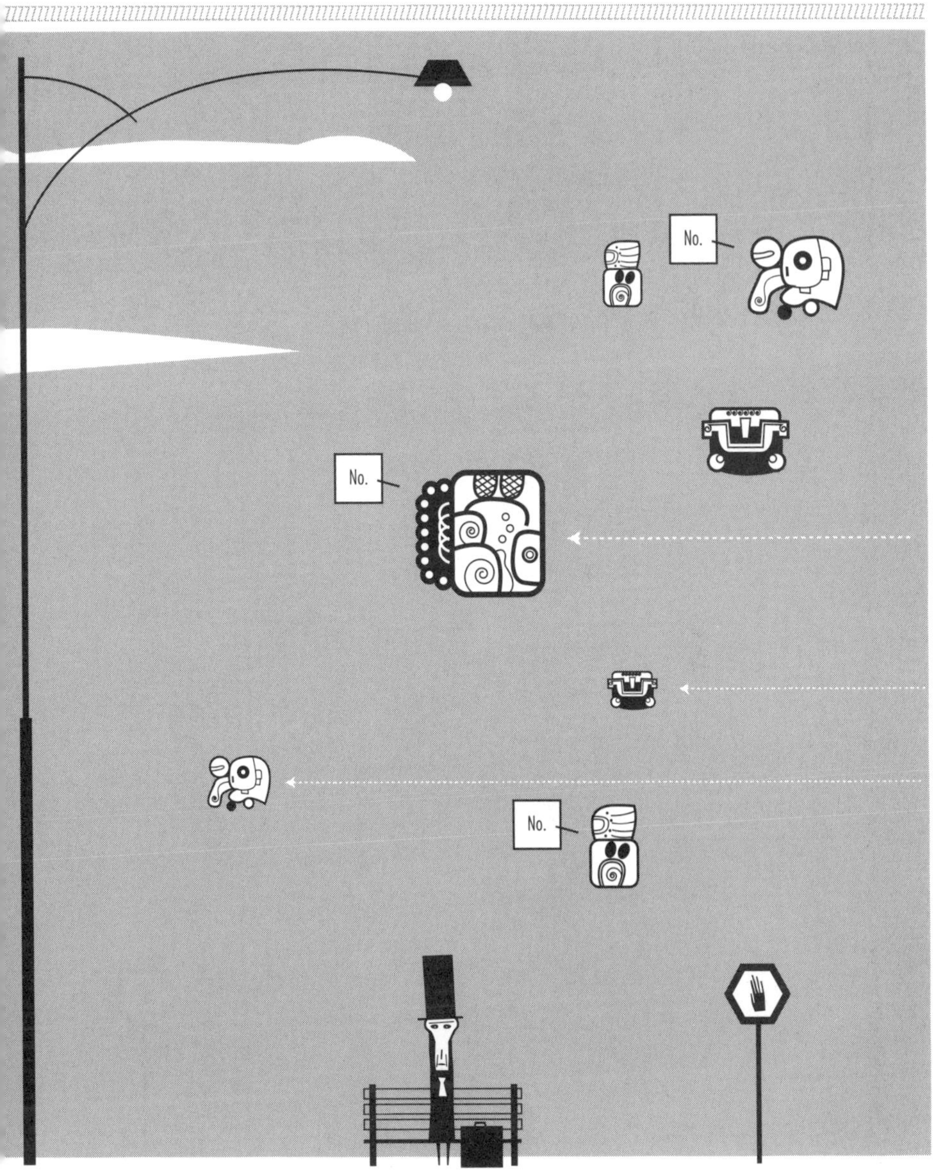
No.
No.
No.

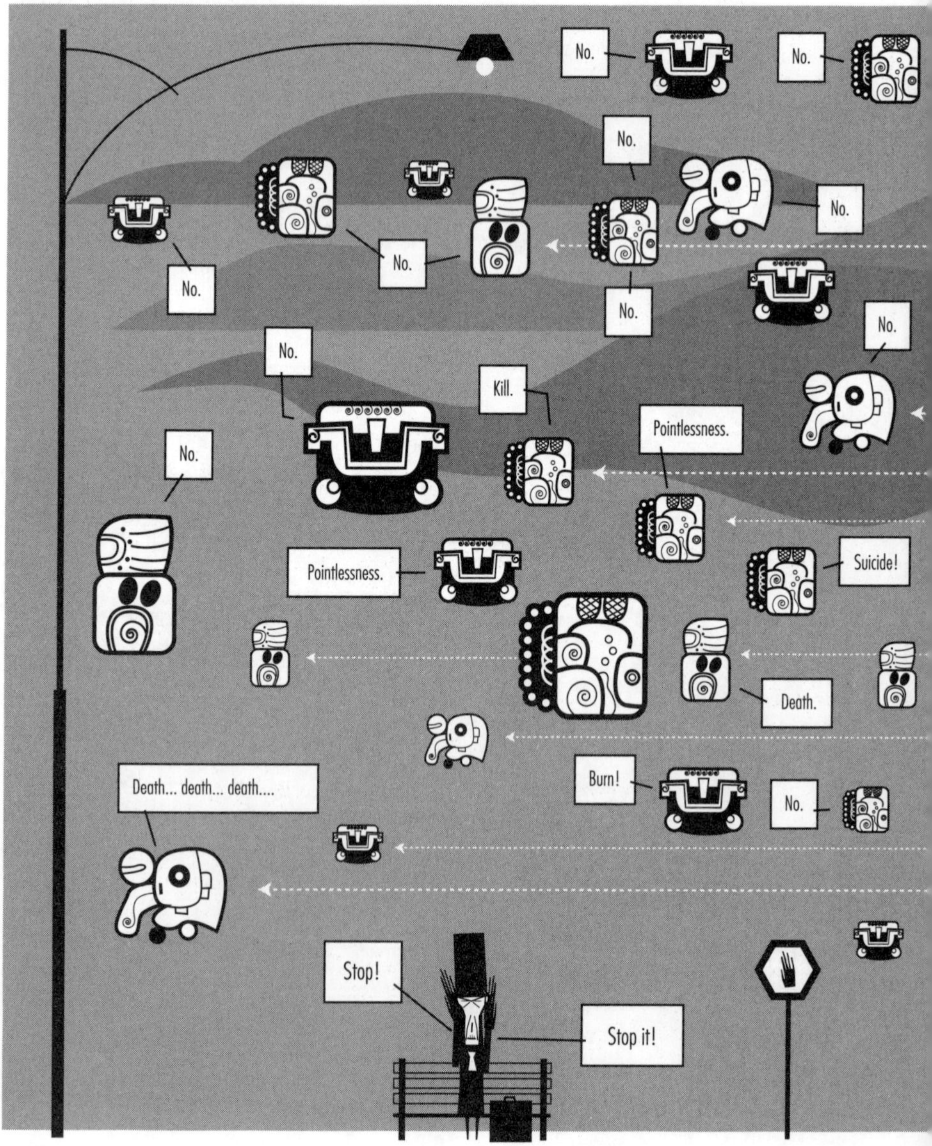

No.
No.
No.
No.
No.
No.
No.
No.
No.
Kill.
Pointlessness.
No.
Pointlessness.
Suicide!
Death.
Death... death... death....
Burn!
No.
Stop!
Stop it!

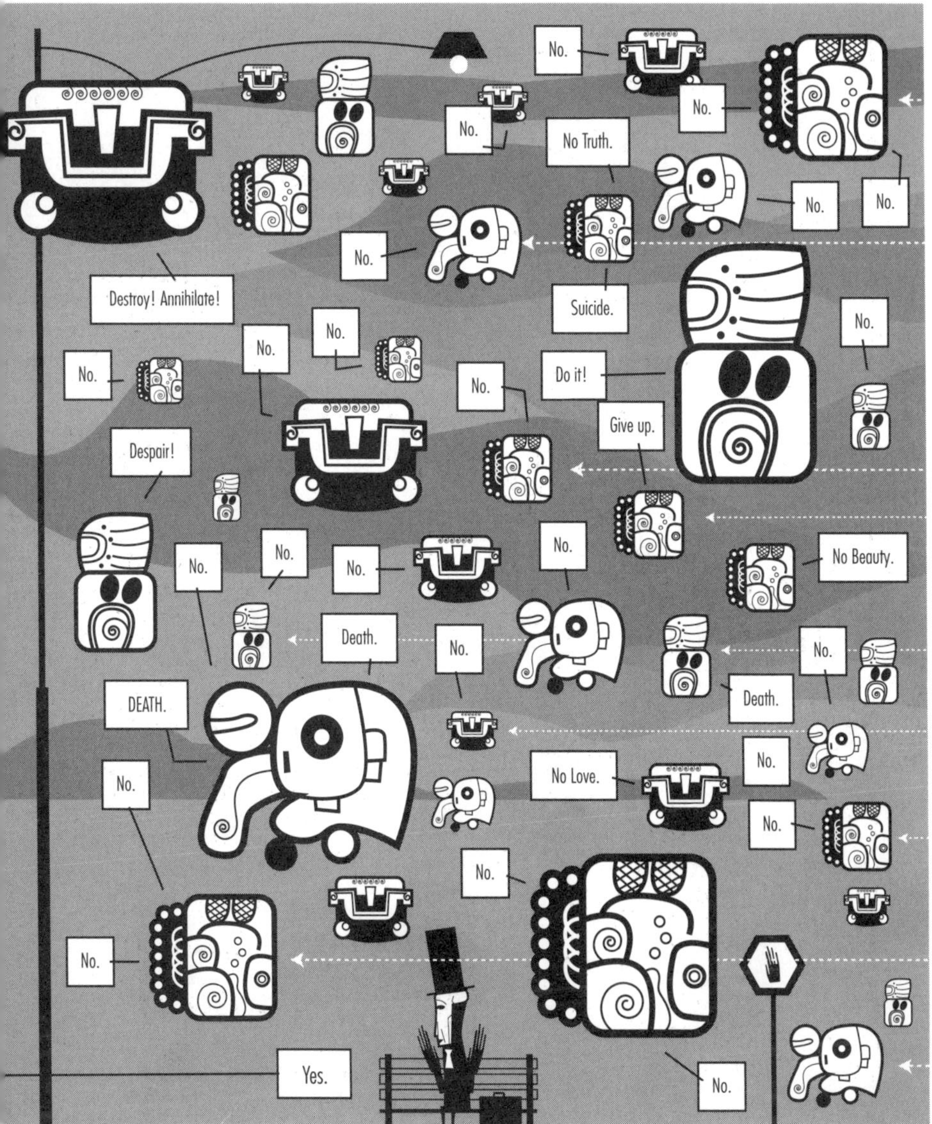
No.
No.
No.
No Truth.
No.
No.
No.
Destroy! Annihilate!
Suicide.
No.
No.
No.
No.
Do it!
No.
Give up.
Despair!
No.
No.
No.
No.
No Beauty.
Death.
No.
No.
Death.
DEATH.
No.
No.
No Love.
No.
No.
No.
Yes.
No.

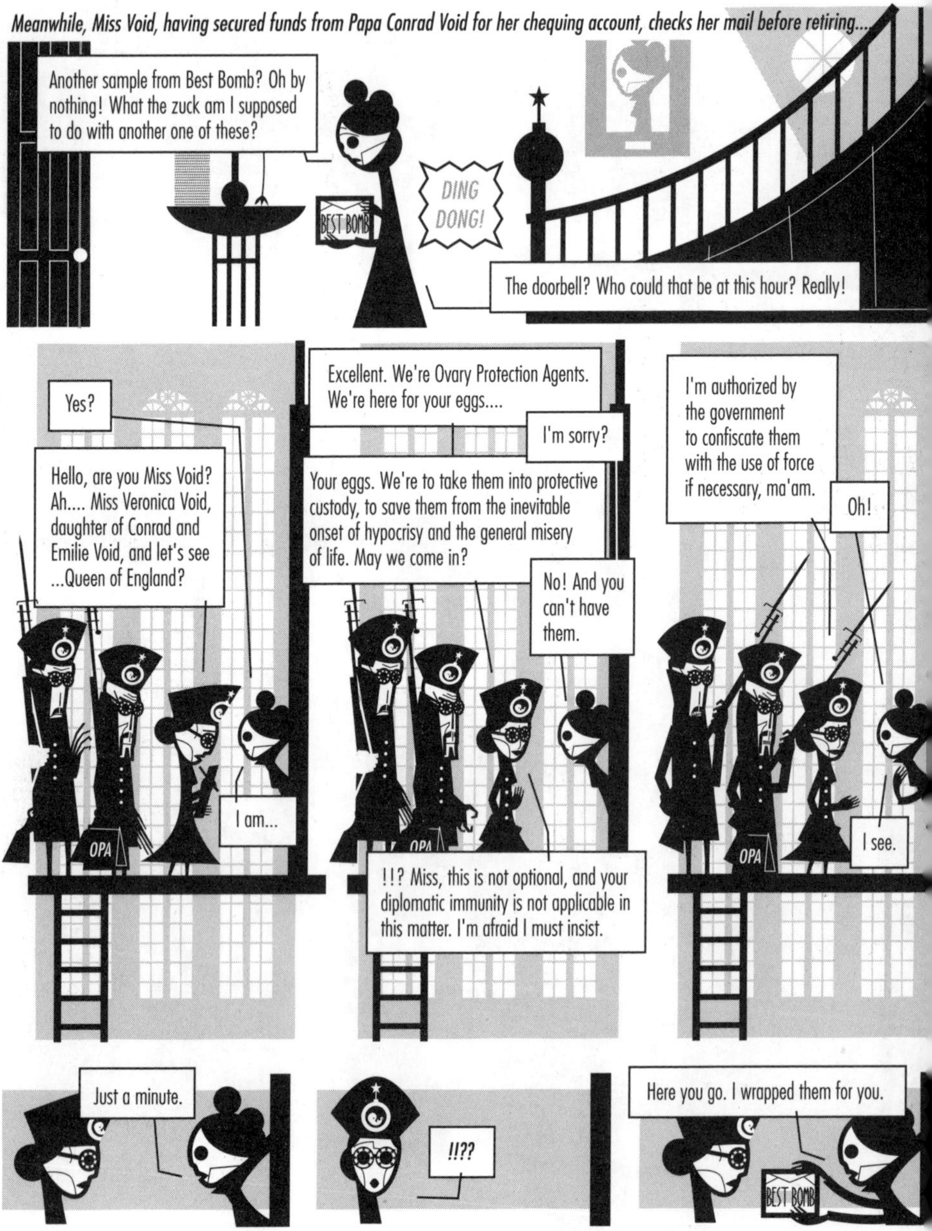
Meanwhile, Miss Void, having secured funds from Papa Conrad Void for her chequing account, checks her mail before retiring...
Another sample from Best Bomb? Oh by nothing! What the zuck am I supposed to do with another one of these?
BEST BOMB
DING DONG!
The doorbell? Who could that be at this hour? Really!
Yes?
Hello, are you Miss Void? Ah.... Miss Veronica Void, daughter of Conrad and Emilie Void, and let's see ...Queen of England?
I am...
OPA
Excellent. We're Ovary Protection Agents. We're here for your eggs....
I'm sorry?
Your eggs. We're to take them into protective custody, to save them from the inevitable onset of hypocrisy and the general misery of life. May we come in?
No! And you can't have them.
!!? Miss, this is not optional, and your diplomatic immunity is not applicable in this matter. I'm afraid I must insist.
I'm authorized by the government to confiscate them with the use of force if necessary, ma'am.
Oh!
I see.
OPA
Just a minute.
!!??
Here you go. I wrapped them for you.
BEST BOMB

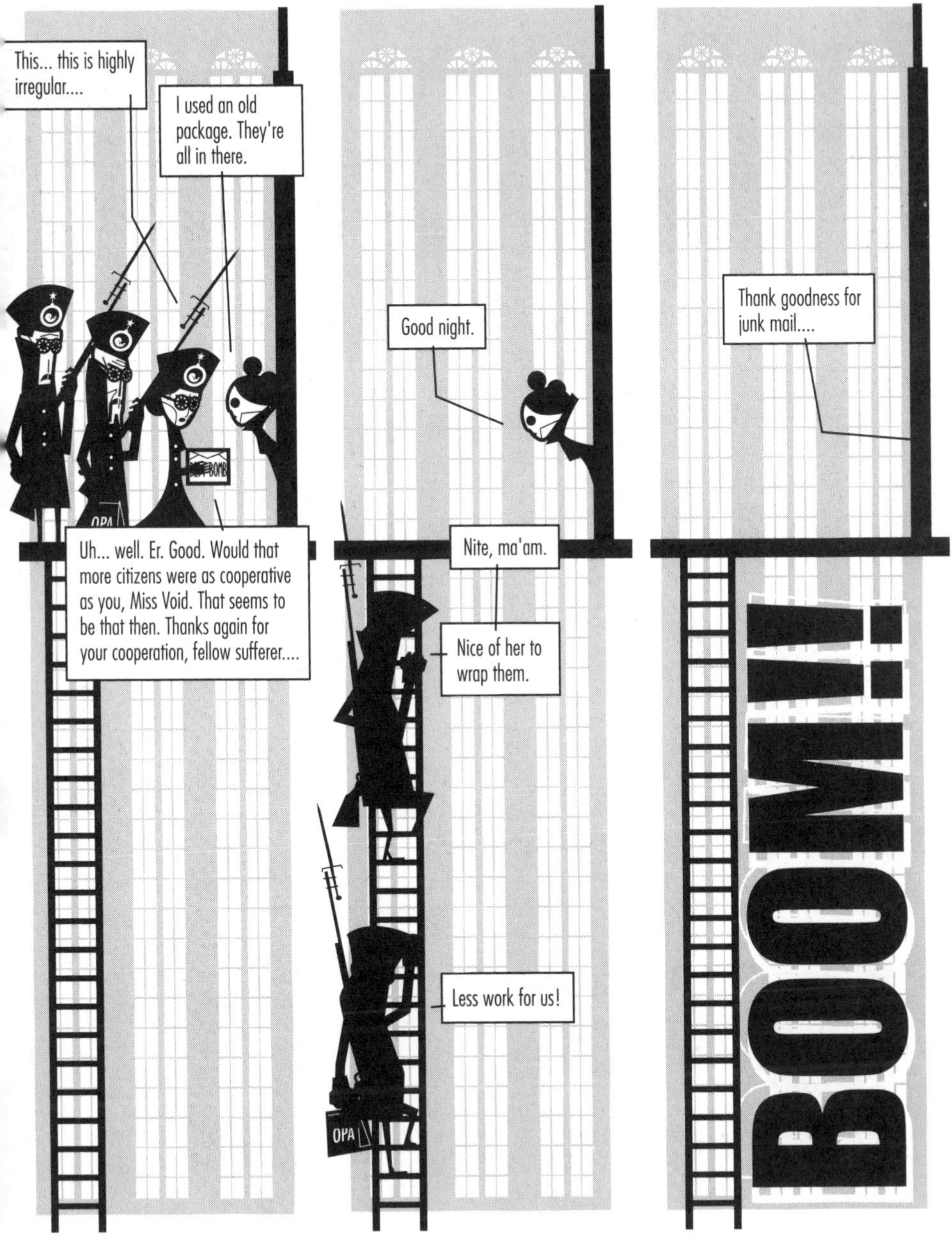
This... this is highly irregular....
I used an old package. They're all in there.
Uh... well. Er. Good. Would that more citizens were as cooperative as you, Miss Void. That seems to be that then. Thanks again for your cooperation, fellow sufferer....
OPA
Good night.
Nite, ma'am.
Nice of her to wrap them.
Less work for us!
OPA
Thank goodness for junk mail....
BOOM!!

All the lies we like.

The New Nihilopolis Times

All news is bad news

VOL. MCVII   Copyright New Nihilopolis   Eleven Fifty-Five, Friday, Nilember, Year of the Apocalypse   ONE COIN

HEAVEN DENIES GOD DEAD

By Dinglepuff Flightpaff

NEW NIHILOPOLIS — The earlier reports of God's demise have been greatly exaggerated, according to Heavenly Spokesangel Michael.

"God is in perfect health," he said at a press conference earlier today at the Heavenly Gates. "I don't know where this rumour came from, but God has not been hit by a truck. There are, in fact, no trucks whatsoever in Heaven, and on the date in question, God did not leave for any other plane of existense."

Spokesangel Michael, however, offered no proof whatsoever that God was in good health, and God conveniently failed to attend the press conference.

"God is a busy God. He has a lot of things to look after, and he is simply far too overworked to come to every press conference," was Michael's excuse.

Rumours continue to swirl around God's latest imbroglio, which comes shortly after he was recently sued by a woman in Nihilopolis for allowing the creation of the exceptionally hot coffee which she subsequently spilled between her legs while driving her car.

Legal expert Waggle P. Wafflediggle posited that the God-is-dead rumour was spread as an attempt to obviate the Coffee Trial and escape judgement. "The case has been going against God, and the jury is believed to sympathize with the victim. It is eminently clear to every mortal that the system in which we are contained is unjust, and the allowing of exceedingly hot coffee is just the tip of the iceberg. If this precedent is set, God will be on the hook for everything from cancer to ingrown toe-nails to hair-in-the-pizza and even telephone fundraising fraud. Not to mention things like genocide, murder, floods, and earthquakes. I've talked to Prosecutor Illitwhich at the World Court about the progess of laying charges against God for The Flood, which killed a vast number of people, possibly millions, including innocent, unborn children. The judgement in that case alone could bankrupt Heaven."

"That case is entirely frivolous," asserted Spokesangel Michael. "Free will allows for human beings to make their own choices. That does not, however, relate to The Flood. *See LEGALITY AND GOD A4*

Nilean Cycletanks advance on a photographer on the Loos Front.   NP

OPTIMA NOW ON THE DEFENSIVE

By Sinnik Gortglob

THE FRONT — Early yesterday a massive attack by Nilean Fleshmasher Cycletanks successfully drove back a force of Elite Optiman Feathertroopers. Approximately two Feathertroopers were killed in the battle, to a loss of one Cycletank.

"It was a fierce fight," said First Malcontent Pettibane. "It was especially important that we have a victory after losing some three thousand cycletanks yesterday in the mud. Boy, was that embarrassing. The Chief Misanthrope was really pissed. But today, we turned back the enemy,

and that gave us the victory we needed to repair morale."

The war effort has also been hampered by a shortage of Permission to Expend Ammunition Forms from the Quartermaster Department. This has made fighting back against the enemy quite difficult. "Well, the photocopier went down and we ran out of stamps two weeks ago," said the First Malcontent. "Fortunately we are now installing a new technology, the fax machine, in all our attack vehicles. This will facilitate quicker processing of fire request forms, and revolutionize modern warfare."

Freedom Fighters Bomb Kindergarten

47 Presumed Dead

By Agnus Diddlati

NIHILOPOLIS — Two men and a woman strapped with explosives ran into a local kindergarten school and detonated themselves early yesterday morning. The three Freedom Fighters managed to kill 47 children, most of them from rich, well-to-do families, and wounded 120 more. Of these, 62 remain in critical condition at the Nohopenell Hospital.

"This was a fine act of pure Nihilism," said Mayor Nigel Cravensmutle. "It's good to see that the young have not lost their lack of idealism, and cynicism, about the system."

A spokesperson for the Foul Weather Liberation Front claimed responsibility for the attack. "We're dedicated Nihilists. Freedom bombing is our *raison d'être*. We cannot change the system through voting because we refuse to endorse the capitalist system and its collection of corporate sponsored candidates. That has left us with no other choice but to attempt to exterminate the next generation of rich, fascist oppressors." *See FREEDOM BOMBING A2*

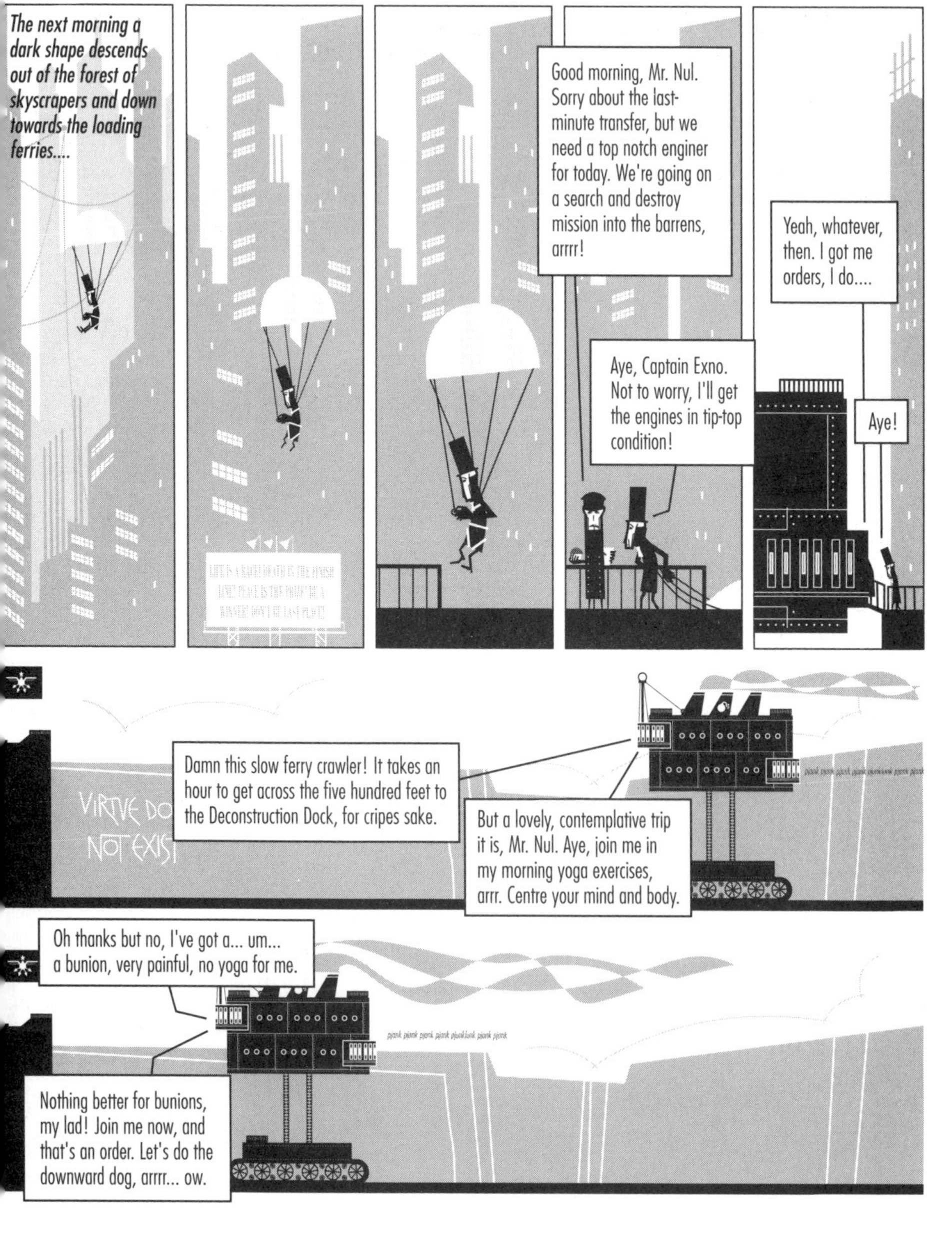
The next morning a dark shape descends out of the forest of skyscrapers and down towards the loading ferries....
Good morning, Mr. Nul. Sorry about the last-minute transfer, but we need a top notch enginer for today. We're going on a search and destroy mission into the barrens, arrrr!
Aye, Captain Exno. Not to worry, I'll get the engines in tip-top condition!
Yeah, whatever, then. I got me orders, I do....
Aye!
Damn this slow ferry crawler! It takes an hour to get across the five hundred feet to the Deconstruction Dock, for cripes sake.
But a lovely, contemplative trip it is, Mr. Nul. Aye, join me in my morning yoga exercises, arrr. Centre your mind and body.
VIRTVE DO
NOT EXIST
Oh thanks but no, I've got a... um... a bunion, very painful, no yoga for me.
Nothing better for bunions, my lad! Join me now, and that's an order. Let's do the downward dog, arrrr... ow.

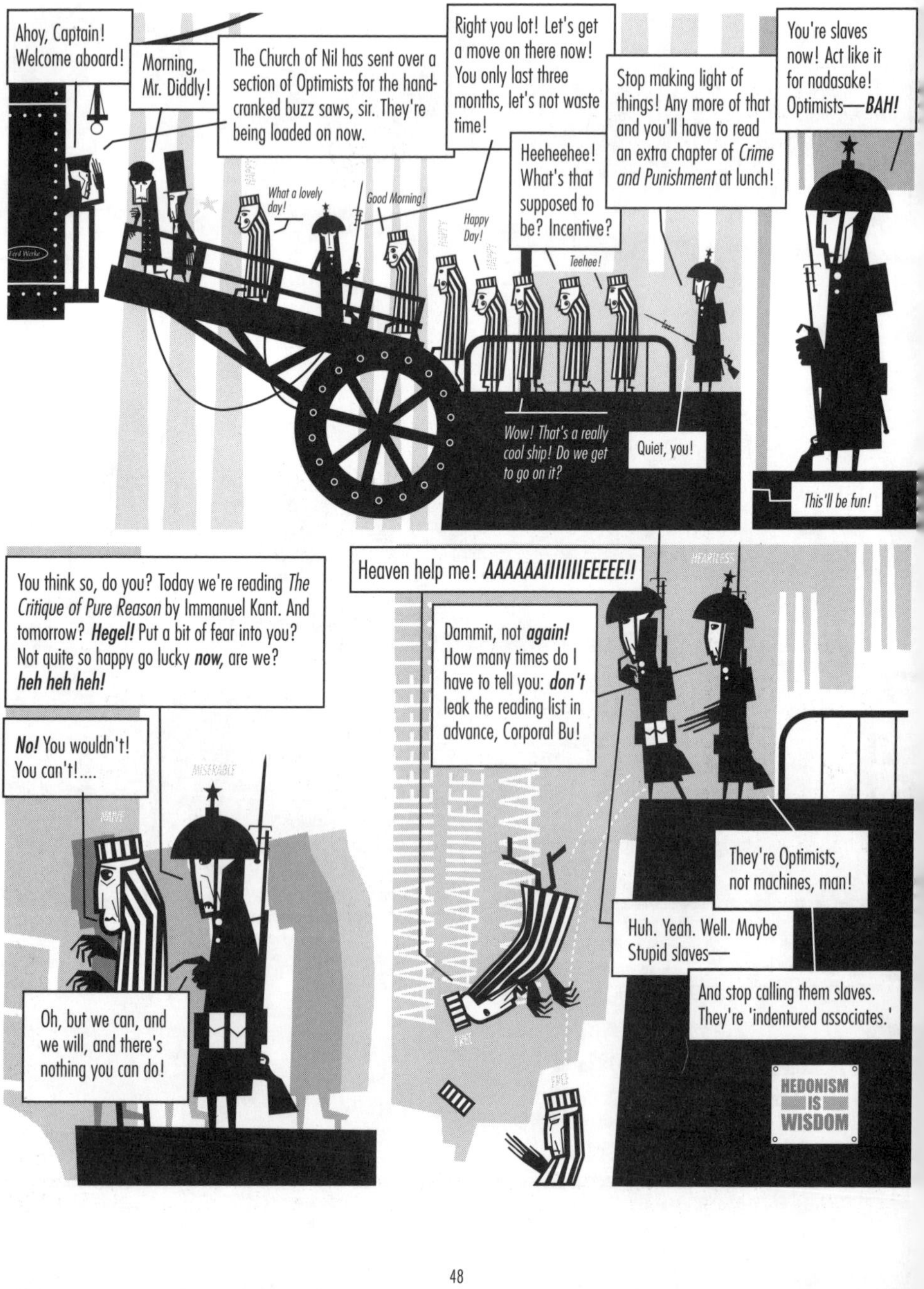

Ahoy, Captain! Welcome aboard!
Morning, Mr. Diddly!
The Church of Nil has sent over a section of Optimists for the hand-cranked buzz saws, sir. They're being loaded on now.
Right you lot! Let's get a move on there now! You only last three months, let's not waste time!
What a lovely day!
Good Morning!
Happy Day!
Heeheehee! What's that supposed to be? Incentive?
Teehee!
Stop making light of things! Any more of that and you'll have to read an extra chapter of *Crime and Punishment* at lunch!
You're slaves now! Act like it for nadasake! Optimists—***BAH!***
Wow! That's a really cool ship! Do we get to go on it?
Quiet, you!
This'll be fun!
You think so, do you? Today we're reading *The Critique of Pure Reason* by Immanuel Kant. And tomorrow? ***Hegel!*** Put a bit of fear into you? Not quite so happy go lucky ***now,*** are we? ***heh heh heh!***
No! You wouldn't! You can't!....
Oh, but we can, and we will, and there's nothing you can do!
Heaven help me! ***AAAAAAIIIIIIIEEEEEE!!***
Dammit, not ***again!*** How many times do I have to tell you: ***don't*** leak the reading list in advance, Corporal Bu!
They're Optimists, not machines, man!
Huh. Yeah. Well. Maybe Stupid slaves—
And stop calling them slaves. They're 'indentured associates.'
HEDONISM IS WISDOM

Within minutes the pride of the Nihilist fleet, the deconstruction ship Derrida, is readied for departure, thanks to the work of Mr. Nul.

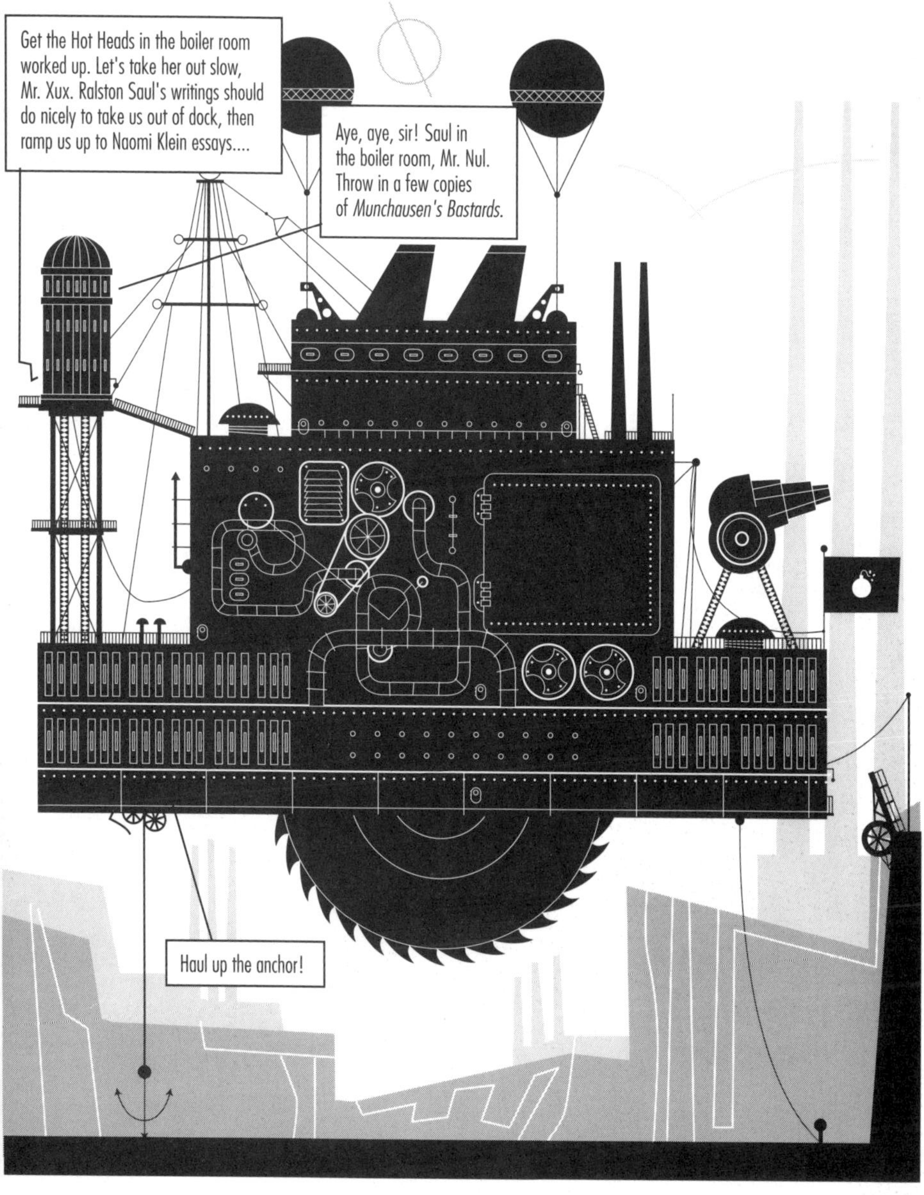
Get the Hot Heads in the boiler room worked up. Let's take her out slow, Mr. Xux. Ralston Saul's writings should do nicely to take us out of dock, then ramp us up to Naomi Klein essays....
Aye, aye, sir! Saul in the boiler room, Mr. Nul. Throw in a few copies of *Munchausen's Bastards.*
Haul up the anchor!

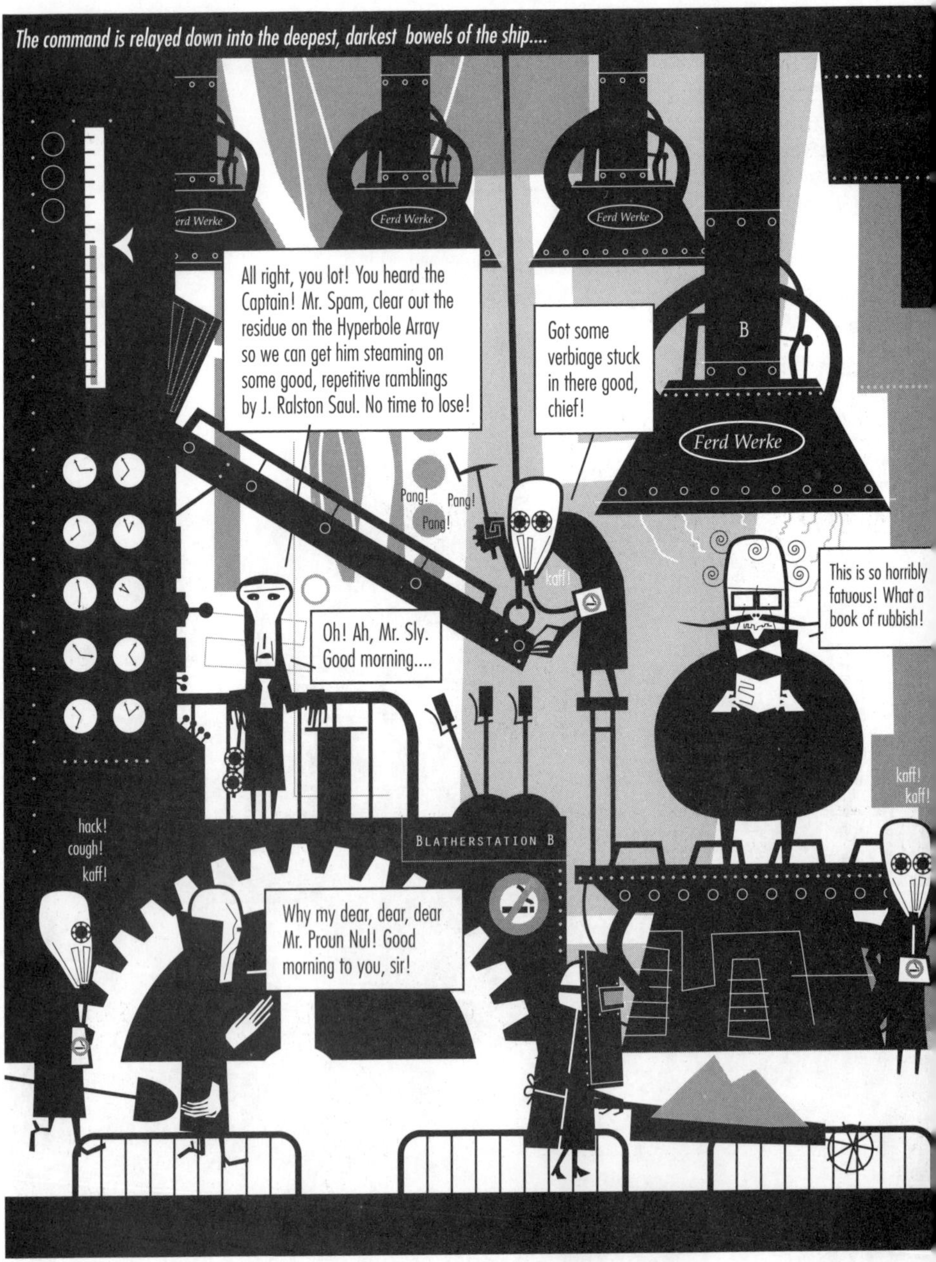
The command is relayed down into the deepest, darkest bowels of the ship....
Ferd Werke
Ferd Werke
Ferd Werke
All right, you lot! You heard the Captain! Mr. Spam, clear out the residue on the Hyperbole Array so we can get him steaming on some good, repetitive ramblings by J. Ralston Saul. No time to lose!
Got some verbiage stuck in there good, chief!
B
Ferd Werke
Pang! Pang! Pang!
kaff!
This is so horribly fatuous! What a book of rubbish!
Oh! Ah, Mr. Sly. Good morning....
kaff! kaff!
hack! cough! kaff!
BLATHERSTATION B
Why my dear, dear, dear Mr. Proun Nul! Good morning to you, sir!

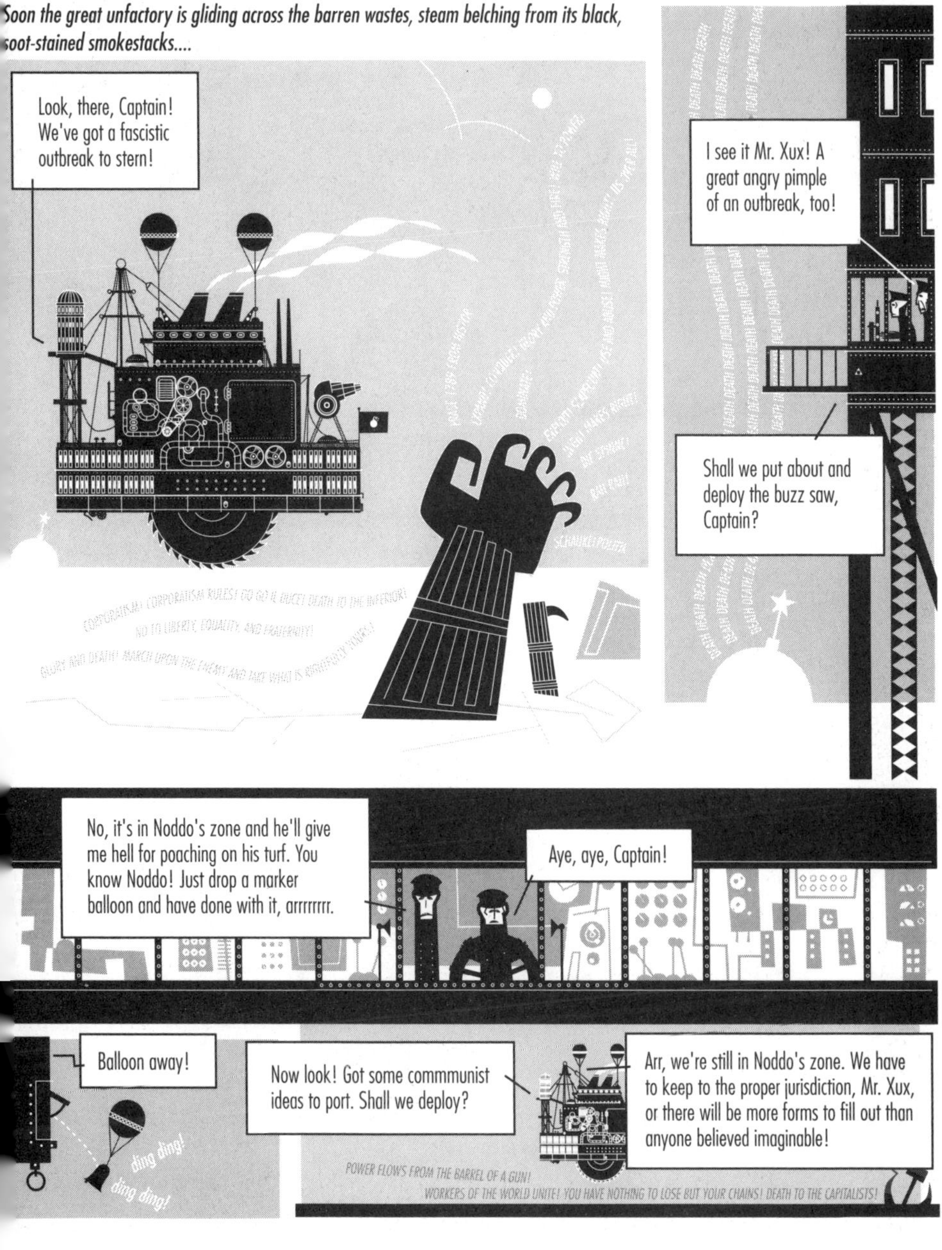
Soon the great unfactory is gliding across the barren wastes, steam belching from its black, soot-stained smokestacks....
Look, there, Captain! We've got a fascistic outbreak to stern!
I see it Mr. Xux! A great angry pimple of an outbreak, too!
Shall we put about and deploy the buzz saw, Captain?
CORPORATISM! CORPORATISM RULES! GO GO IL DUCE! DEATH TO THE INFERIOR!
NO TO LIBERTY, EQUALITY, AND FRATERNITY!
GLORY AND DEATH! MARCH UPON THE ENEMY AND TAKE WHAT IS RIGHTFULLY YOURS!
No, it's in Noddo's zone and he'll give me hell for poaching on his turf. You know Noddo! Just drop a marker balloon and have done with it, arrrrrrr.
Aye, aye, Captain!
Balloon away!
ding ding!
ding ding!
Now look! Got some commmunist ideas to port. Shall we deploy?
Arr, we're still in Noddo's zone. We have to keep to the proper jurisdiction, Mr. Xux, or there will be more forms to fill out than anyone believed imaginable!
POWER FLOWS FROM THE BARREL OF A GUN!
WORKERS OF THE WORLD UNITE! YOU HAVE NOTHING TO LOSE BUT YOUR CHAINS! DEATH TO THE CAPITALISTS!

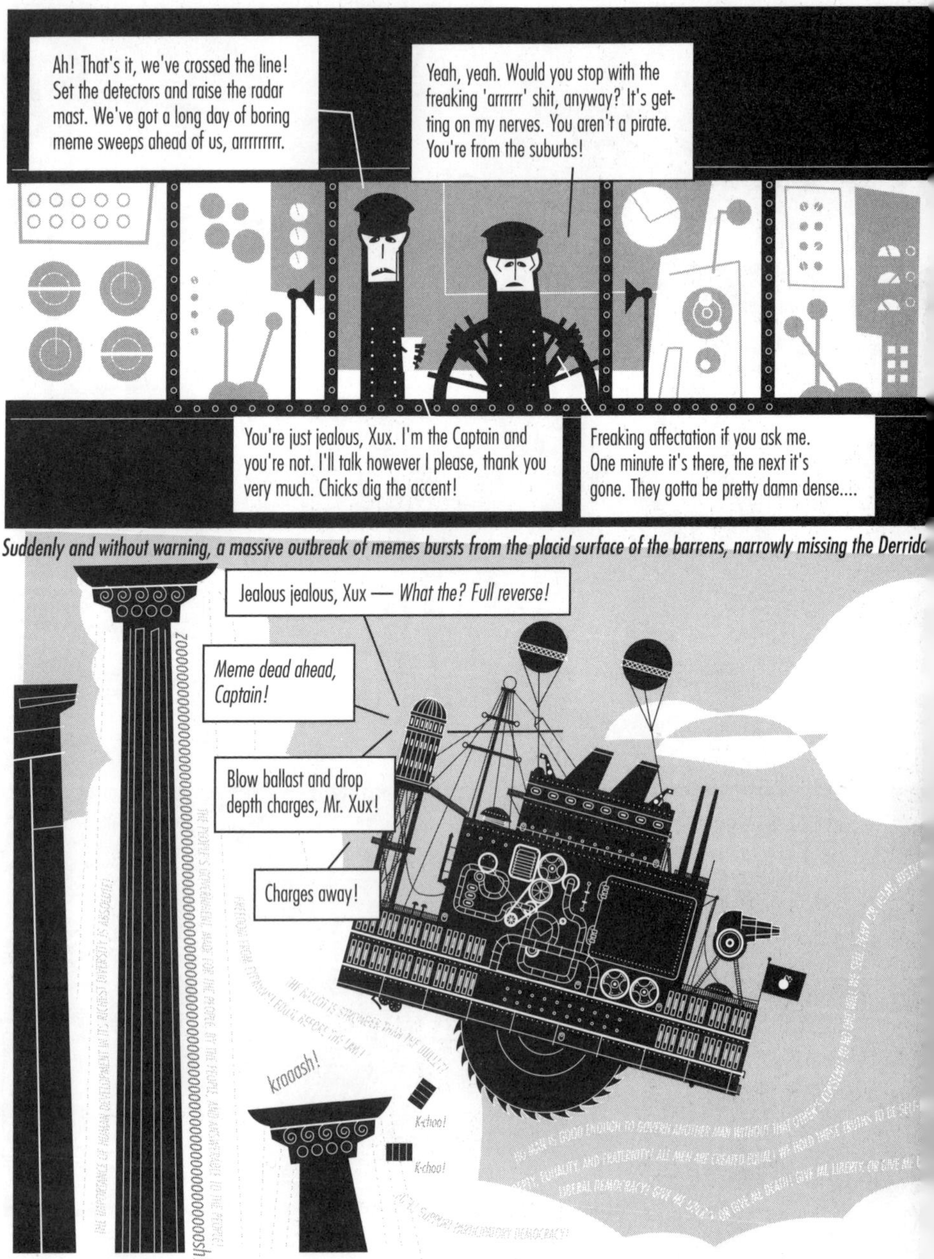
Ah! That's it, we've crossed the line! Set the detectors and raise the radar mast. We've got a long day of boring meme sweeps ahead of us, arrrrrrrr.
Yeah, yeah. Would you stop with the freaking 'arrrrrr' shit, anyway? It's getting on my nerves. You aren't a pirate. You're from the suburbs!
You're just jealous, Xux. I'm the Captain and you're not. I'll talk however I please, thank you very much. Chicks dig the accent!
Freaking affectation if you ask me. One minute it's there, the next it's gone. They gotta be pretty damn dense....
Suddenly and without warning, a massive outbreak of memes bursts from the placid surface of the barrens, narrowly missing the Derrid
Jealous jealous, Xux — What the? Full reverse!
Meme dead ahead, Captain!
Blow ballast and drop depth charges, Mr. Xux!
Charges away!
kraaash!
K-choo!
K-choo!

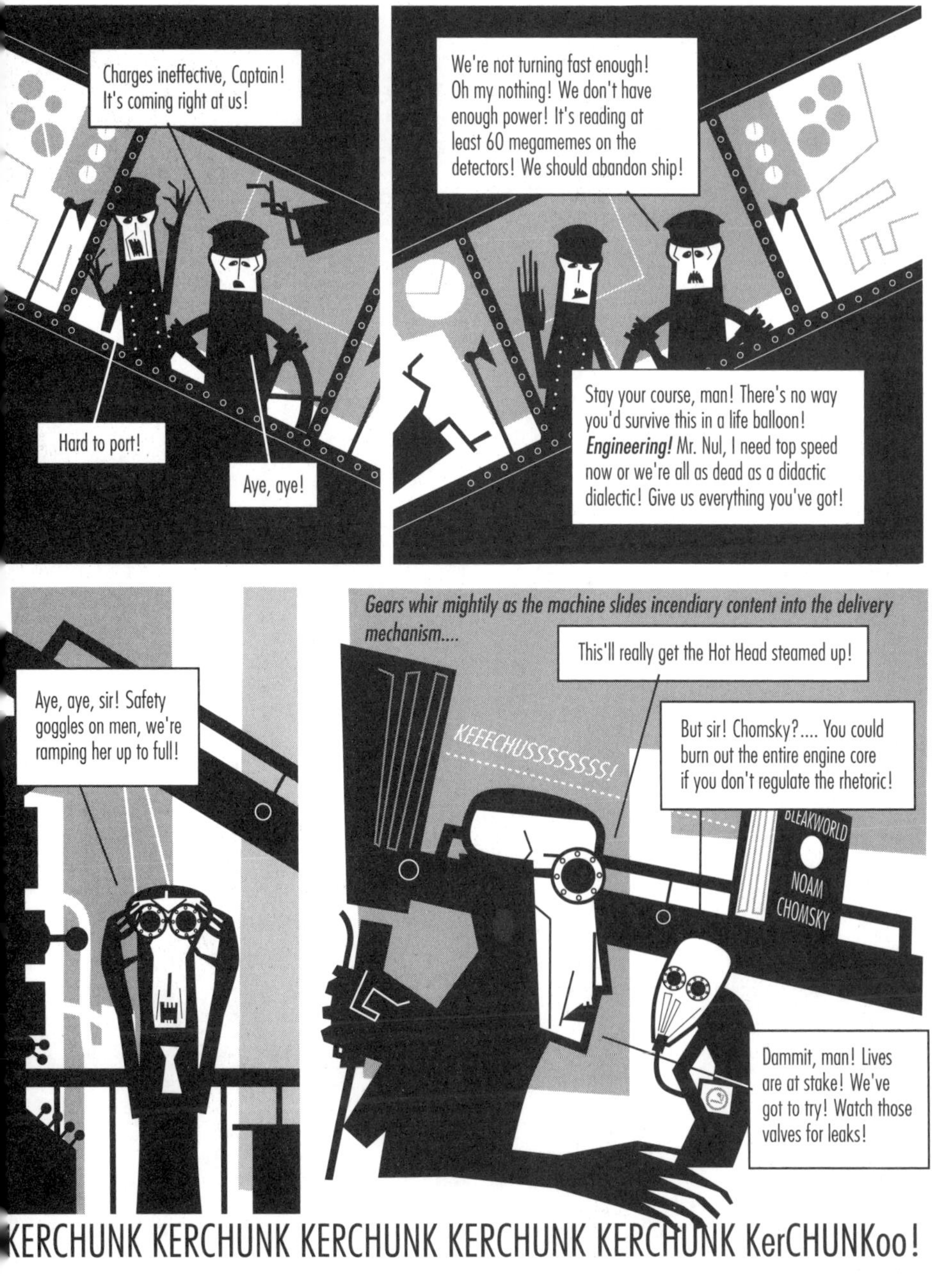

Charges ineffective, Captain! It's coming right at us!
Hard to port!
Aye, aye!
We're not turning fast enough! Oh my nothing! We don't have enough power! It's reading at least 60 megamemes on the detectors! We should abandon ship!
Stay your course, man! There's no way you'd survive this in a life balloon! ***Engineering!*** Mr. Nul, I need top speed now or we're all as dead as a didactic dialectic! Give us everything you've got!
Aye, aye, sir! Safety goggles on men, we're ramping her up to full!
Gears whir mightily as the machine slides incendiary content into the delivery mechanism....
This'll really get the Hot Head steamed up!
KEEECHUSSSSSSSS!
But sir! Chomsky?.... You could burn out the entire engine core if you don't regulate the rhetoric!
BLEAKWORLD
NOAM CHOMSKY
Dammit, man! Lives are at stake! We've got to try! Watch those valves for leaks!
KERCHUNK KERCHUNK KERCHUNK KERCHUNK KERCHUNK KerCHUNKoo!

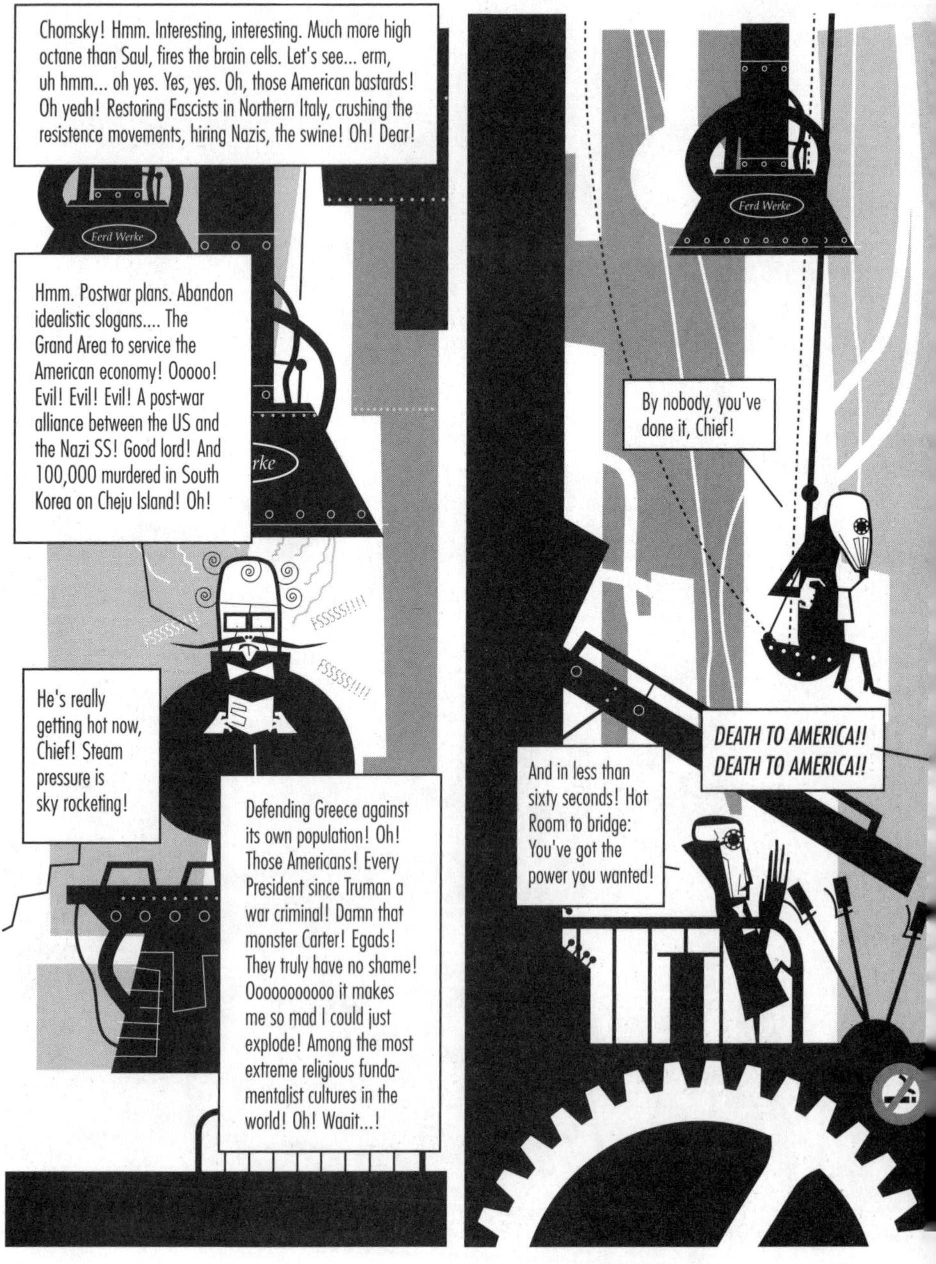

Chomsky! Hmm. Interesting, interesting. Much more high octane than Saul, fires the brain cells. Let's see... erm, uh hmm... oh yes. Yes, yes. Oh, those American bastards! Oh yeah! Restoring Fascists in Northern Italy, crushing the resistence movements, hiring Nazis, the swine! Oh! Dear!
Ferd Werke
Hmm. Postwar plans. Abandon idealistic slogans.... The Grand Area to service the American economy! Ooooo! Evil! Evil! Evil! A post-war alliance between the US and the Nazi SS! Good lord! And 100,000 murdered in South Korea on Cheju Island! Oh!
FSSSSS!!!!
FSSSSS!!!!
FSSSSS!!!!
He's really getting hot now, Chief! Steam pressure is sky rocketing!
Defending Greece against its own population! Oh! Those Americans! Every President since Truman a war criminal! Damn that monster Carter! Egads! They truly have no shame! Oooooooooo it makes me so mad I could just explode! Among the most extreme religious fundamentalist cultures in the world! Oh! Waait...!
Ferd Werke
By nobody, you've done it, Chief!
DEATH TO AMERICA!!
DEATH TO AMERICA!!
And in less than sixty seconds! Hot Room to bridge: You've got the power you wanted!

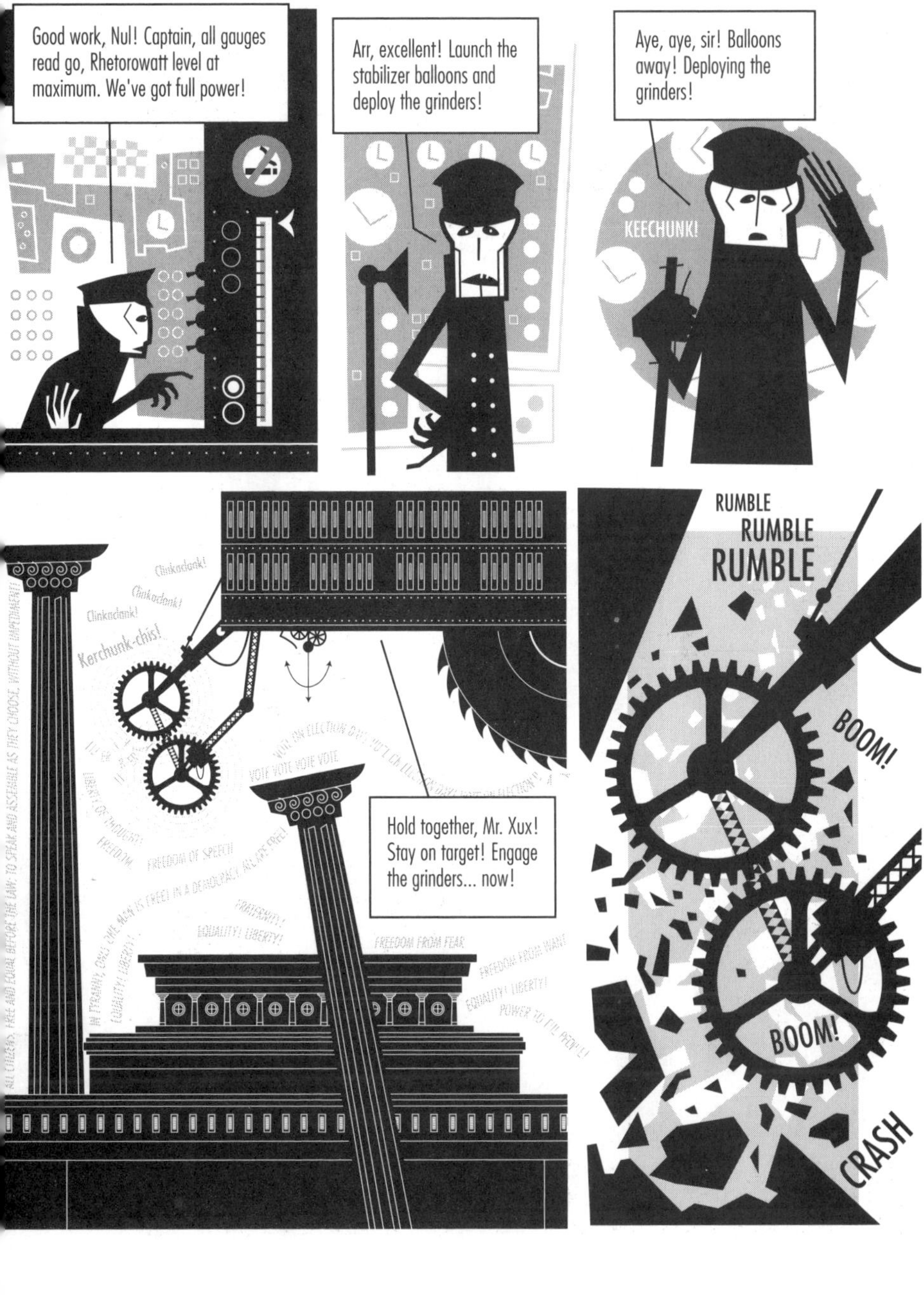
Good work, Nul! Captain, all gauges read go, Rhetorowatt level at maximum. We've got full power!
Arr, excellent! Launch the stabilizer balloons and deploy the grinders!
Aye, aye, sir! Balloons away! Deploying the grinders!
KEECHUNK!
Clinkaclank!
Clinkaclank!
Clinkaclank!
Kerchunk-chis!
VOTE VOTE VOTE VOTE
LIBERTY OF THOUGHT!
FREEDOM
FREEDOM OF SPEECH
IN TYRANNY, ONLY ONE MAN IS FREE! IN A DEMOCRACY ALL ARE FREE!
FRATERNITY!
EQUALITY! LIBERTY!
FREEDOM FROM FEAR
FREEDOM FROM WANT
EQUALITY! LIBERTY!
Hold together, Mr. Xux! Stay on target! Engage the grinders... now!
RUMBLE
RUMBLE
RUMBLE
BOOM!
BOOM!
CRASH

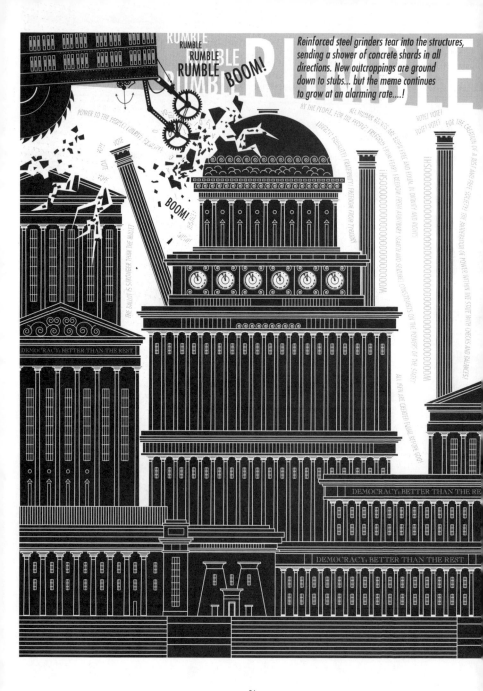

RUMBLE
RUMBLE
RUMBLE
RUMBLE
RUMBLE BOOM!

Reinforced steel grinders tear into the structures, sending a shower of concrete shards in all directions. New outcroppings are ground down to stubs... but the meme continues to grow at an alarming rate....!

BOOM!

DEMOCRACY: BETTER THAN THE REST

DEMOCRACY: BETTER THAN THE RE

DEMOCRACY: BETTER THAN THE REST

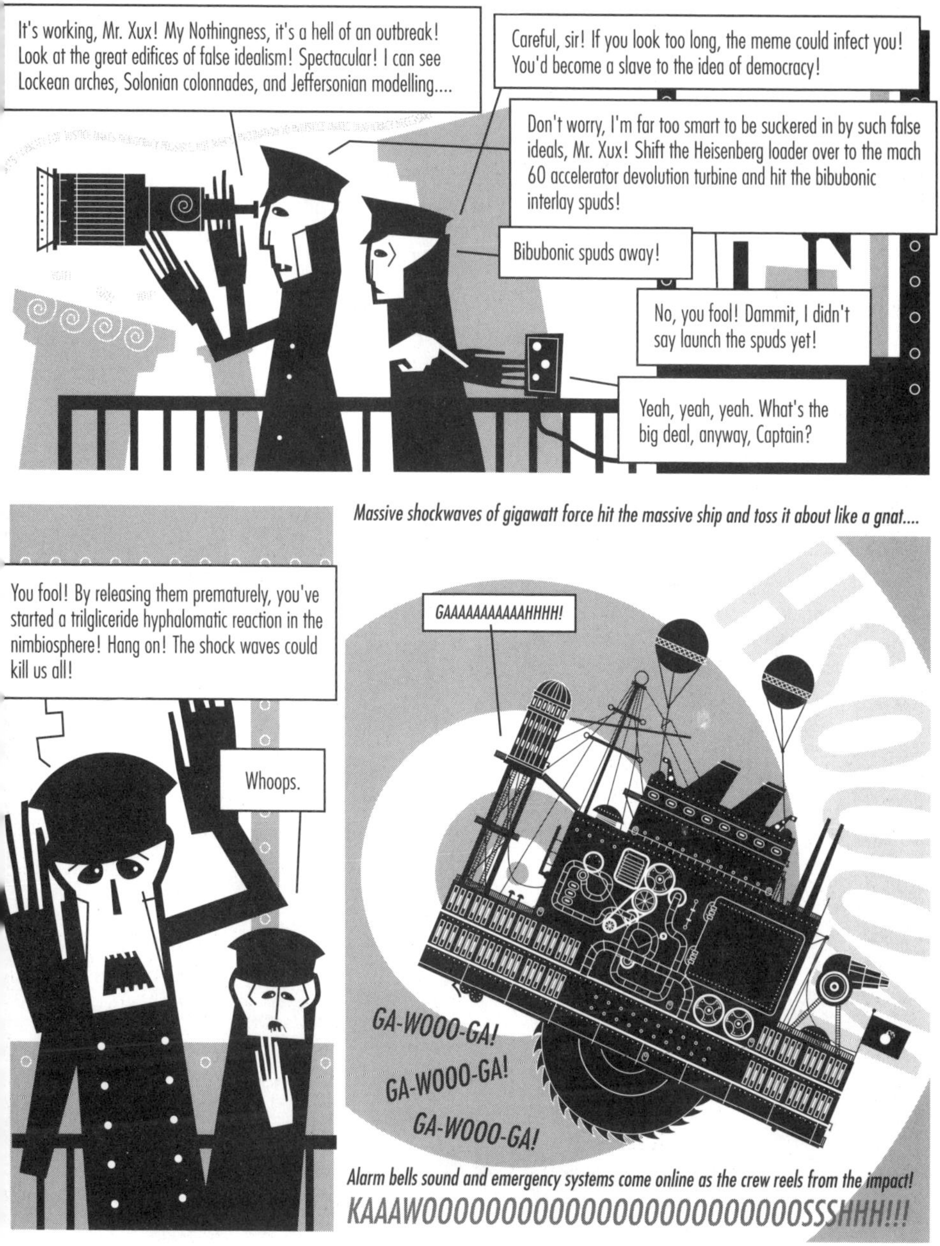

It's working, Mr. Xux! My Nothingness, it's a hell of an outbreak! Look at the great edifices of false idealism! Spectacular! I can see Lockean arches, Solonian colonnades, and Jeffersonian modelling....
Careful, sir! If you look too long, the meme could infect you! You'd become a slave to the idea of democracy!
Don't worry, I'm far too smart to be suckered in by such false ideals, Mr. Xux! Shift the Heisenberg loader over to the mach 60 accelerator devolution turbine and hit the bibubonic interlay spuds!
Bibubonic spuds away!
No, you fool! Dammit, I didn't say launch the spuds yet!
Yeah, yeah, yeah. What's the big deal, anyway, Captain?
Massive shockwaves of gigawatt force hit the massive ship and toss it about like a gnat....
You fool! By releasing them prematurely, you've started a trilgliceride hyphalomatic reaction in the nimbiosphere! Hang on! The shock waves could kill us all!
Whoops.
GAAAAAAAAAAAHHHH!
GA-WOOO-GA!
GA-WOOO-GA!
GA-WOOO-GA!
Alarm bells sound and emergency systems come online as the crew reels from the impact!
KAAAWOOOOOOOOOOOOOOOOOOOOOOOOOOOOSSSHHH!!!

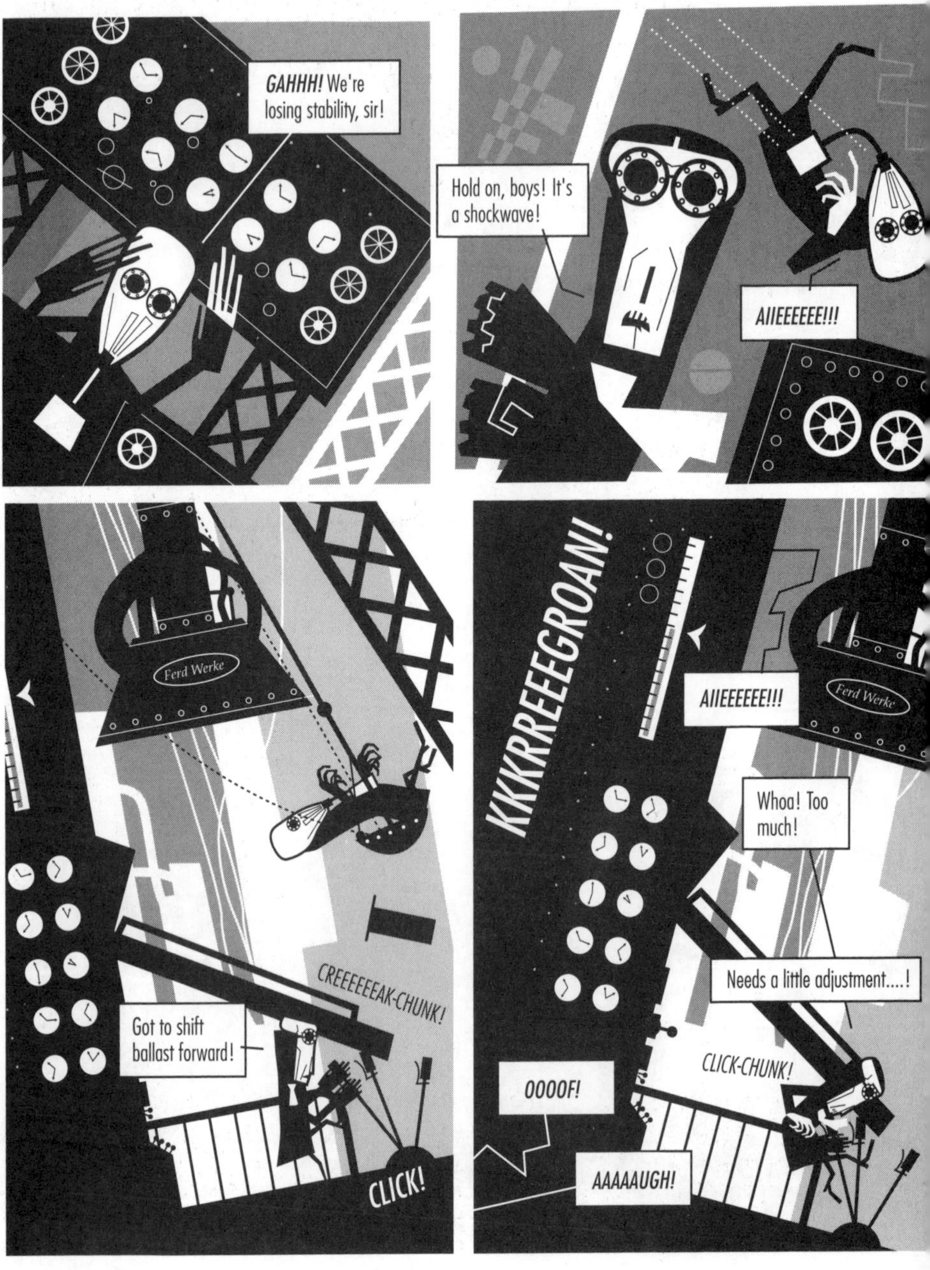
GAHHH! We're losing stability, sir!
Hold on, boys! It's a shockwave!
AIIEEEEEE!!!
Ferd Werke
Got to shift ballast forward!
CREEEEEEAK-CHUNK!
CLICK!
KKKRREEEGROAN!
AIIEEEEEE!!!
Ferd Werke
Whoa! Too much!
Needs a little adjustment....!
CLICK-CHUNK!
OOOOF!
AAAAAUGH!

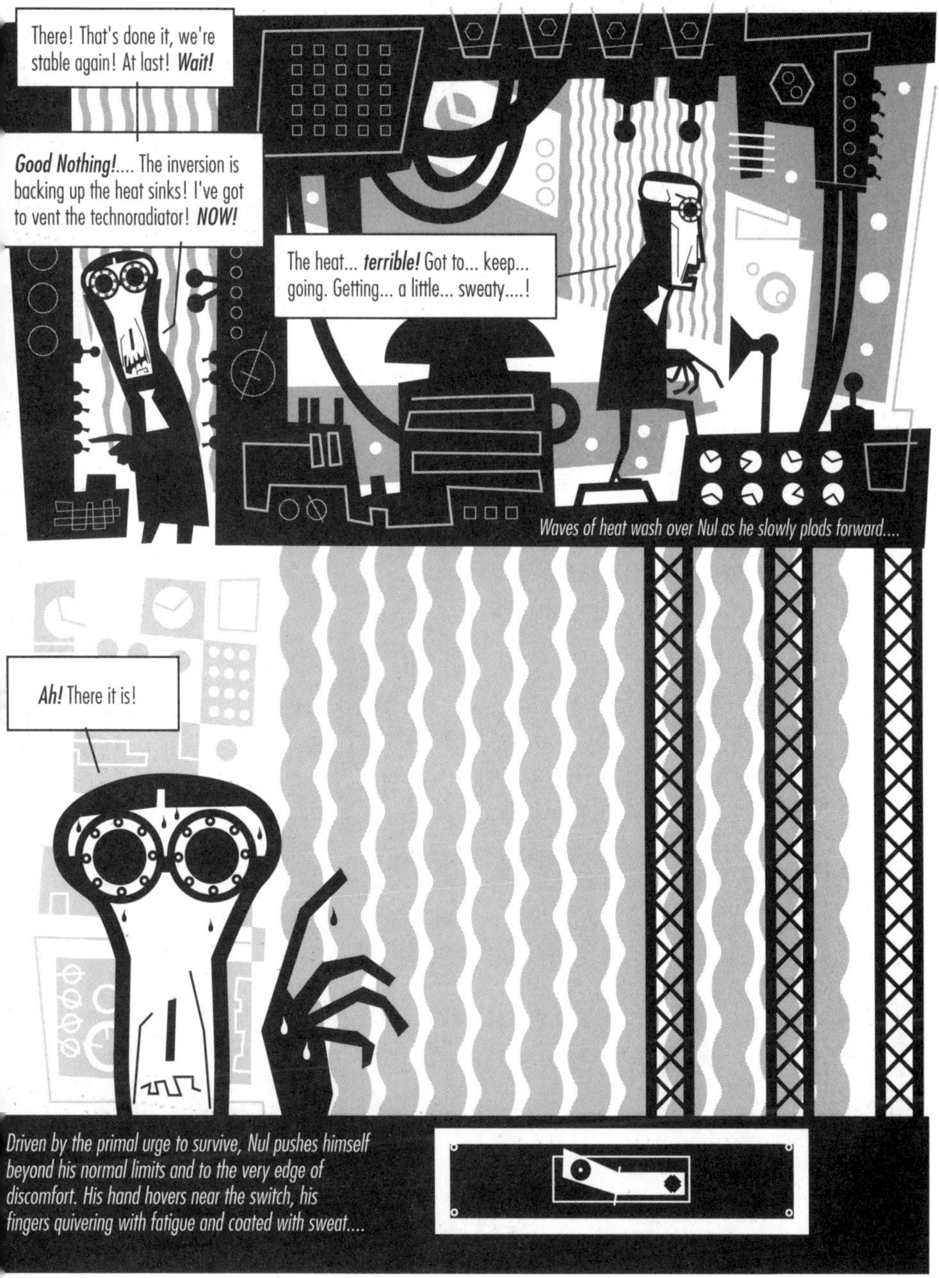
There! That's done it, we're stable again! At last! ***Wait!***
Good Nothing!.... The inversion is backing up the heat sinks! I've got to vent the technoradiator! ***NOW!***
The heat... ***terrible!*** Got to... keep... going. Getting... a little... sweaty....!
Waves of heat wash over Nul as he slowly plods forward....
Ah! There it is!
Driven by the primal urge to survive, Nul pushes himself beyond his normal limits and to the very edge of discomfort. His hand hovers near the switch, his fingers quivering with fatigue and coated with sweat....

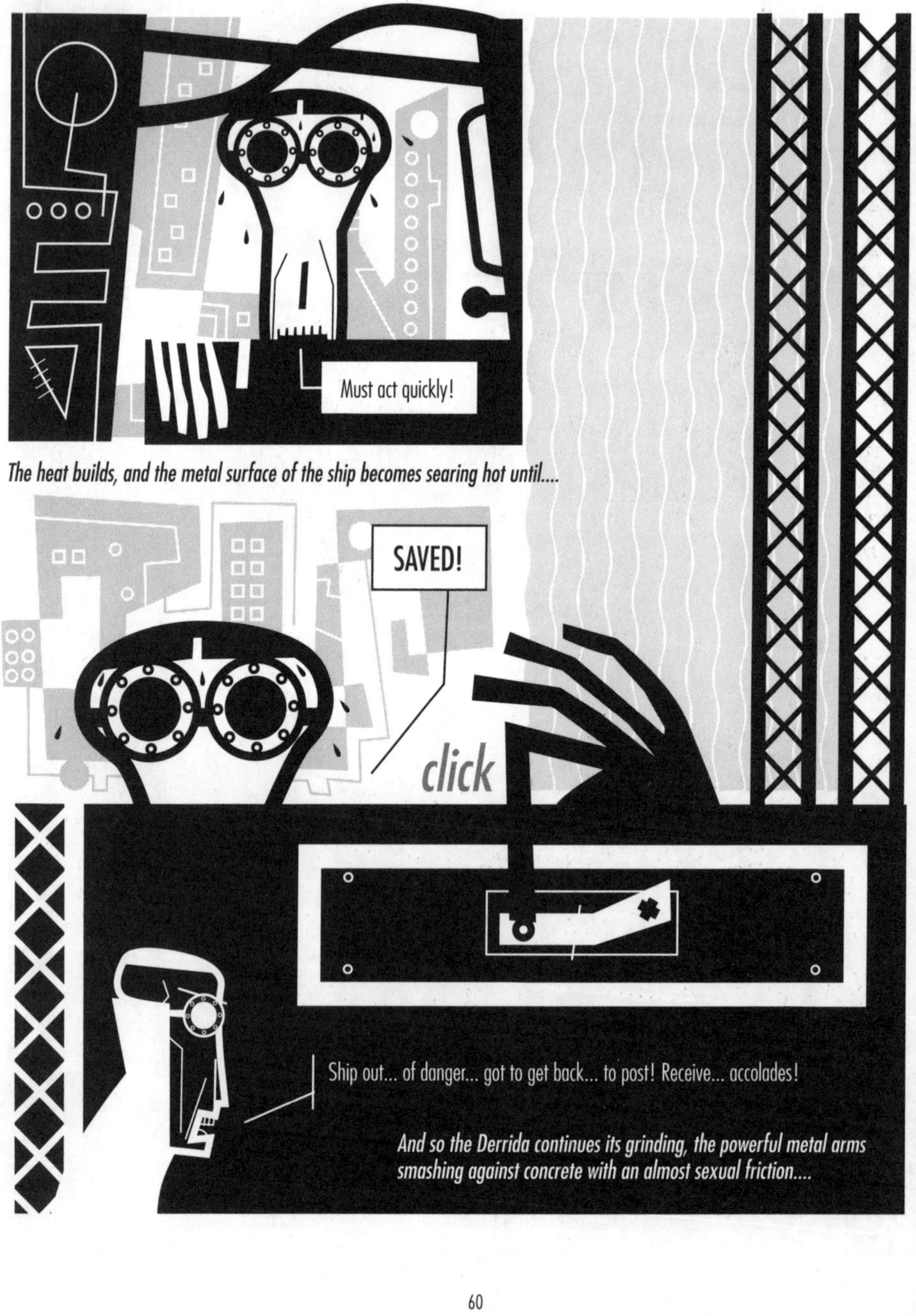
Must act quickly!
The heat builds, and the metal surface of the ship becomes searing hot until....
SAVED!
click
Ship out... of danger... got to get back... to post! Receive... accolades!
And so the Derrida continues its grinding, the powerful metal arms smashing against concrete with an almost sexual friction....

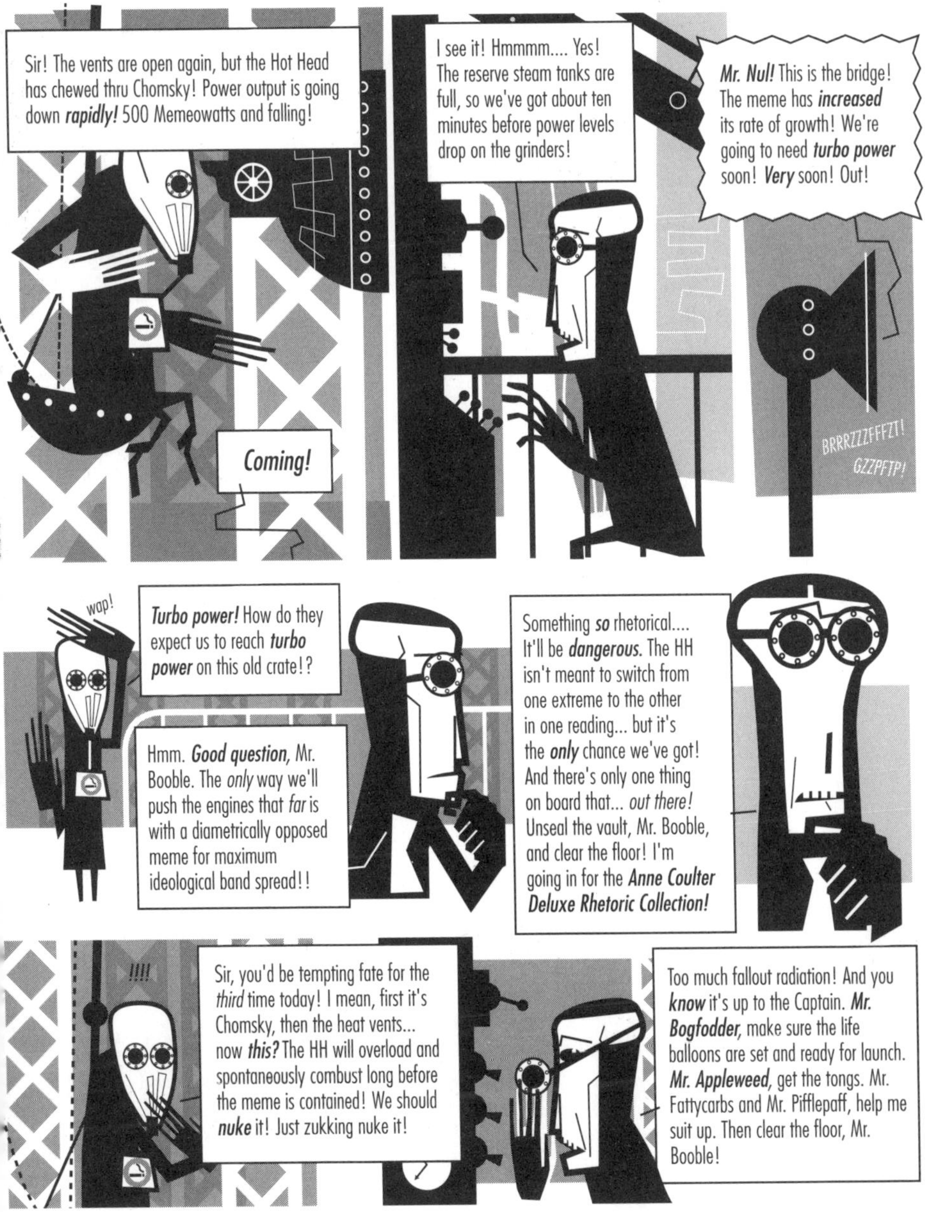
Sir! The vents are open again, but the Hot Head has chewed thru Chomsky! Power output is going down *rapidly!* 500 Memeowatts and falling!
Coming!
I see it! Hmmmm.... Yes! The reserve steam tanks are full, so we've got about ten minutes before power levels drop on the grinders!
Mr. Nul! This is the bridge! The meme has *increased* its rate of growth! We're going to need *turbo power* soon! *Very* soon! Out!
BRRRZZZFFFZT!
GZZPFTP!
wap!
Turbo power! How do they expect us to reach *turbo power* on this old crate!?
Hmm. *Good question,* Mr. Booble. The *only* way we'll push the engines that *far* is with a diametrically opposed meme for maximum ideological band spread!!
Something *so* rhetorical.... It'll be *dangerous.* The HH isn't meant to switch from one extreme to the other in one reading... but it's the *only* chance we've got! And there's only one thing on board that... *out there!* Unseal the vault, Mr. Booble, and clear the floor! I'm going in for the *Anne Coulter Deluxe Rhetoric Collection!*
!!!!
Sir, you'd be tempting fate for the *third* time today! I mean, first it's Chomsky, then the heat vents... now *this?* The HH will overload and spontaneously combust long before the meme is contained! We should *nuke* it! Just zukking nuke it!
Too much fallout radiation! And you *know* it's up to the Captain. *Mr. Bogfodder,* make sure the life balloons are set and ready for launch. *Mr. Appleweed,* get the tongs. Mr. Fattycarbs and Mr. Pifflepaff, help me suit up. Then clear the floor, Mr. Booble!

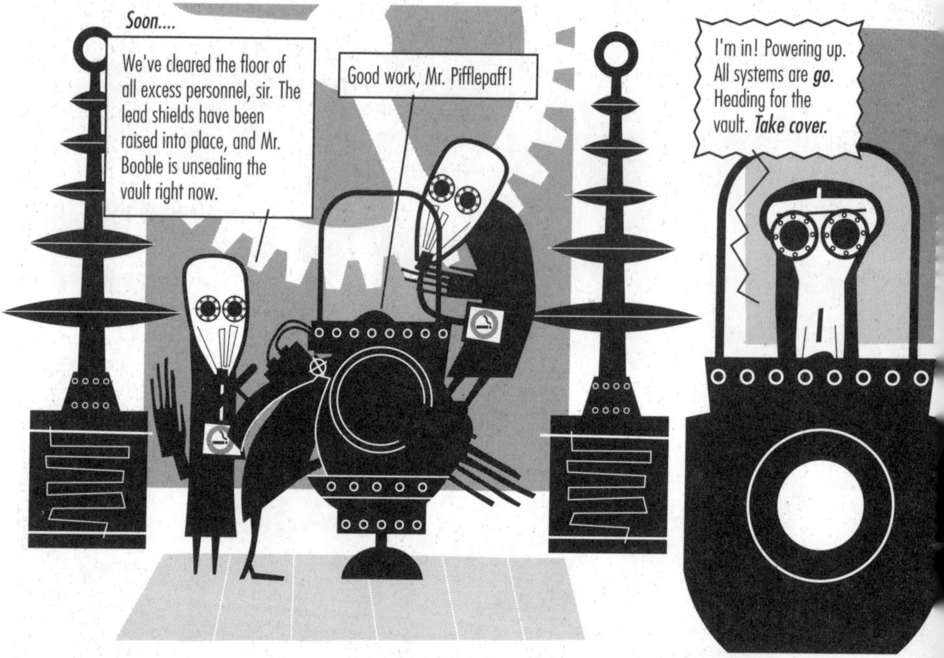
Soon....
We've cleared the floor of all excess personnel, sir. The lead shields have been raised into place, and Mr. Booble is unsealing the vault right now.
Good work, Mr. Pifflepaff!
I'm in! Powering up. All systems are go. Heading for the vault. Take cover.

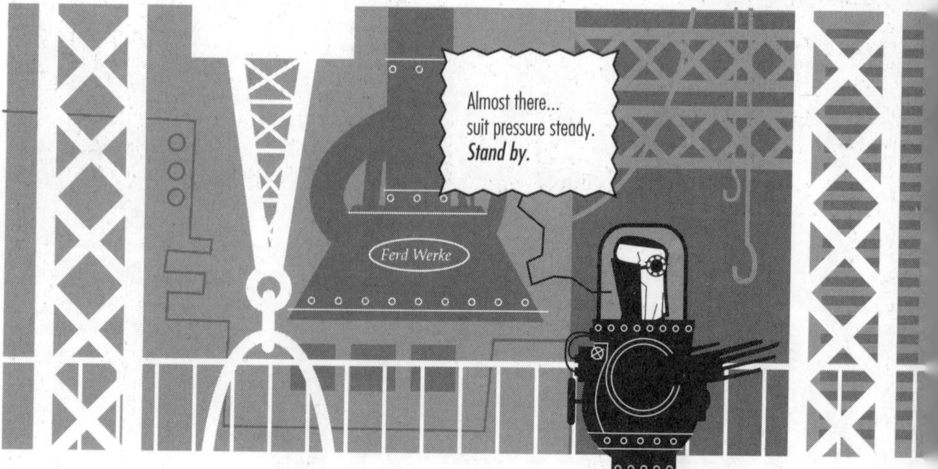
Almost there... suit pressure steady. Stand by.
Ferd Werke
KE-JUNK! KE-JUNK! KE-JUNK! KE-JUNK! KE-JUNK! KE-JUNK!

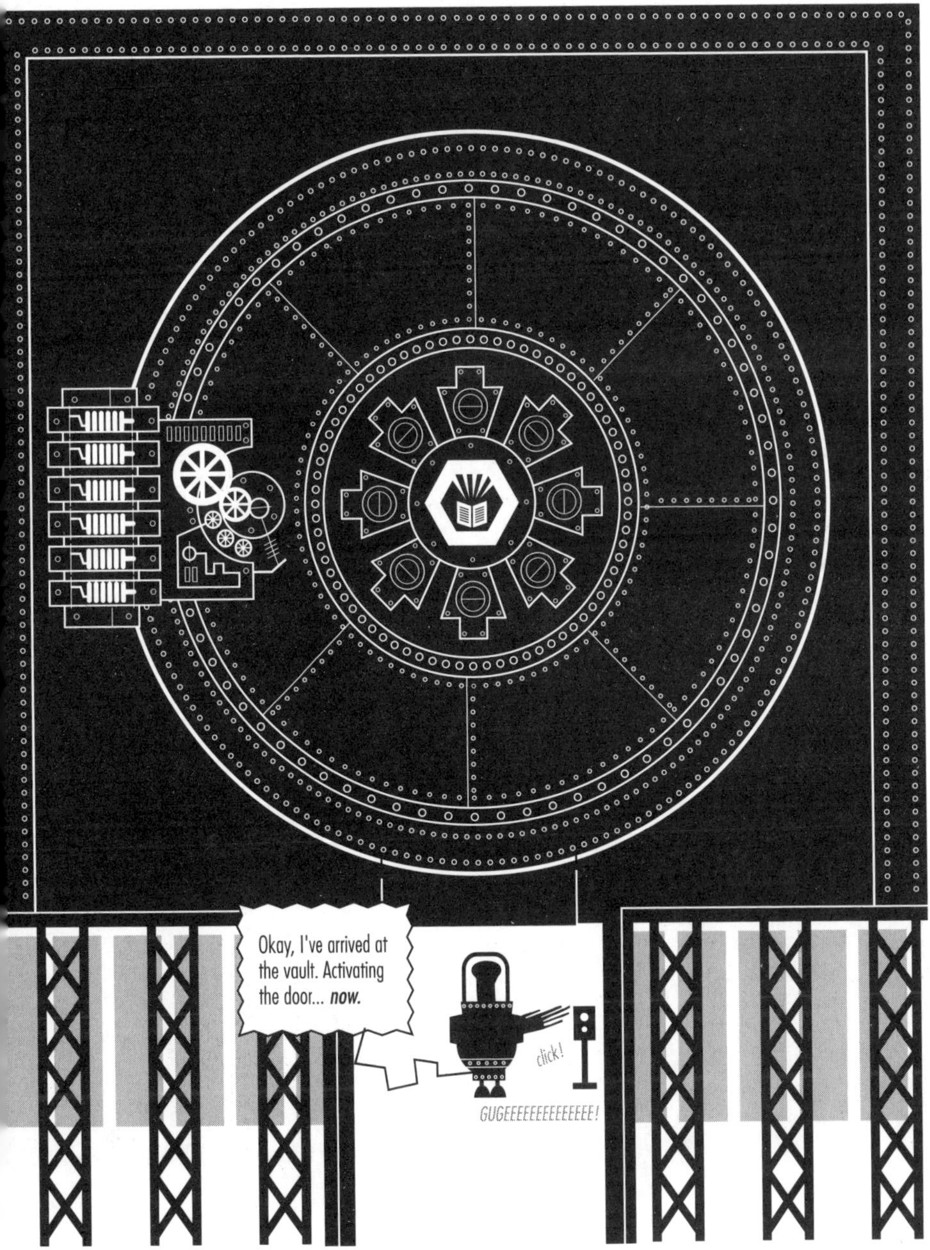
Okay, I've arrived at the vault. Activating the door... *now.*
click!
GUGEEEEEEEEEEEEEE!

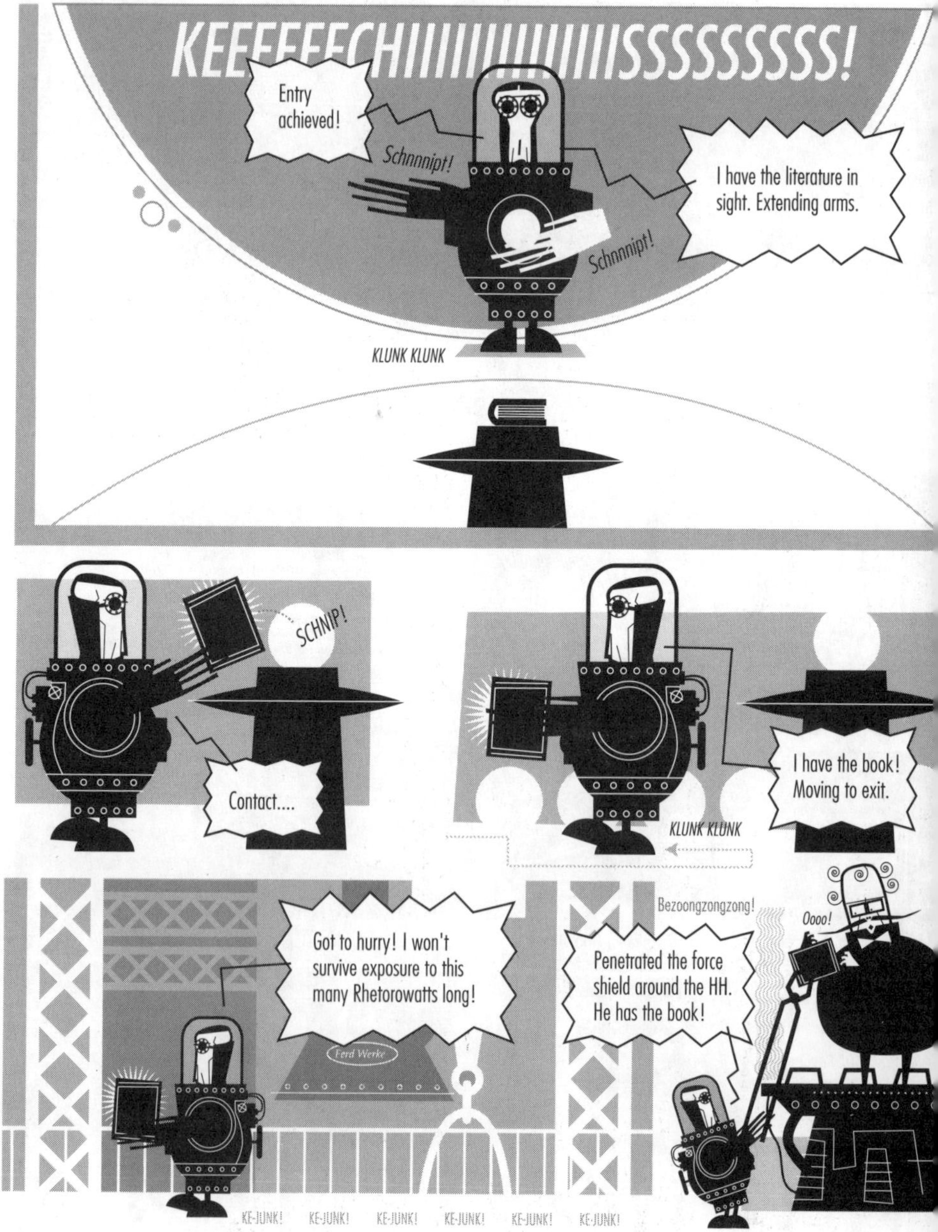
KEEEEEECHIIIIIIIIIIIIIIIISSSSSSSSS!
Entry achieved!
Schnnnipt!
I have the literature in sight. Extending arms.
Schnnnipt!
KLUNK KLUNK
SCHNIP!
Contact....
I have the book! Moving to exit.
KLUNK KLUNK
Got to hurry! I won't survive exposure to this many Rhetorowatts long!
Ferd Werke
Bezoongzongzong!
Oooo!
Penetrated the force shield around the HH. He has the book!
KE-JUNK! KE-JUNK! KE-JUNK! KE-JUNK! KE-JUNK! KE-JUNK!

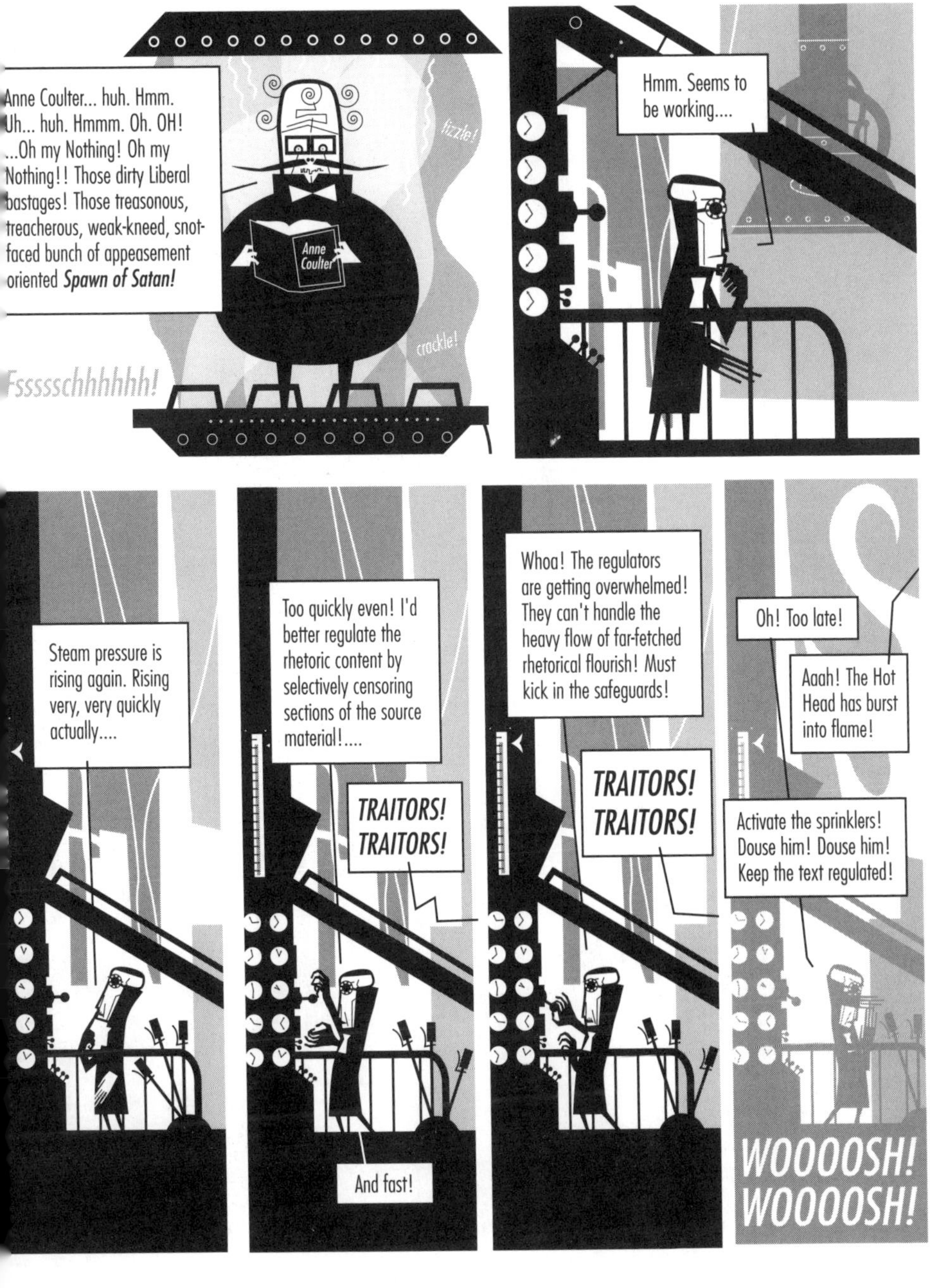

Anne Coulter... huh. Hmm. Uh... huh. Hmmm. Oh. OH! ...Oh my Nothing! Oh my Nothing!! Those dirty Liberal bastages! Those treasonous, treacherous, weak-kneed, snot-faced bunch of appeasement oriented ***Spawn of Satan!***
Anne Coulter
fizzle!
crackle!
Fssssschhhhhh!
Hmm. Seems to be working....
Steam pressure is rising again. Rising very, very quickly actually....
Too quickly even! I'd better regulate the rhetoric content by selectively censoring sections of the source material!....
TRAITORS! TRAITORS!
And fast!
Whoa! The regulators are getting overwhelmed! They can't handle the heavy flow of far-fetched rhetorical flourish! Must kick in the safeguards!
TRAITORS! TRAITORS!
Oh! Too late!
Aaah! The Hot Head has burst into flame!
Activate the sprinklers! Douse him! Douse him! Keep the text regulated!
WOOOOSH! WOOOOSH!

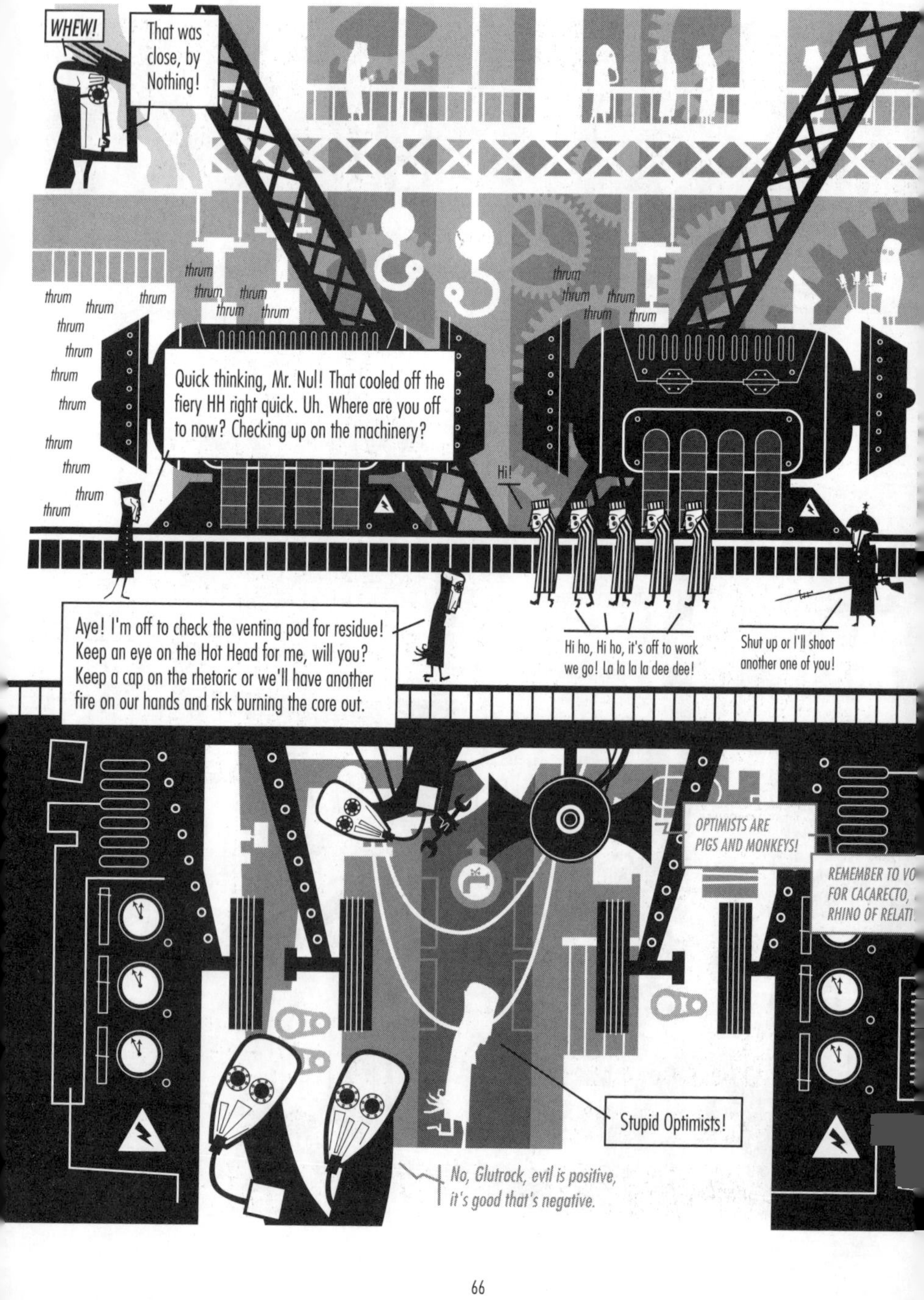
WHEW!
That was close, by Nothing!
thrum thrum thrum thrum thrum thrum thrum thrum thrum thrum thrum
thrum thrum thrum thrum thrum
thrum thrum thrum thrum thrum
Quick thinking, Mr. Nul! That cooled off the fiery HH right quick. Uh. Where are you off to now? Checking up on the machinery?
Hi!
Aye! I'm off to check the venting pod for residue! Keep an eye on the Hot Head for me, will you? Keep a cap on the rhetoric or we'll have another fire on our hands and risk burning the core out.
Hi ho, Hi ho, it's off to work we go! La la la la dee dee!
Shut up or I'll shoot another one of you!
OPTIMISTS ARE PIGS AND MONKEYS!
REMEMBER TO VO FOR CACARECTO, RHINO OF RELATI
Stupid Optimists!
No, Glutrock, evil is positive, it's good that's negative.

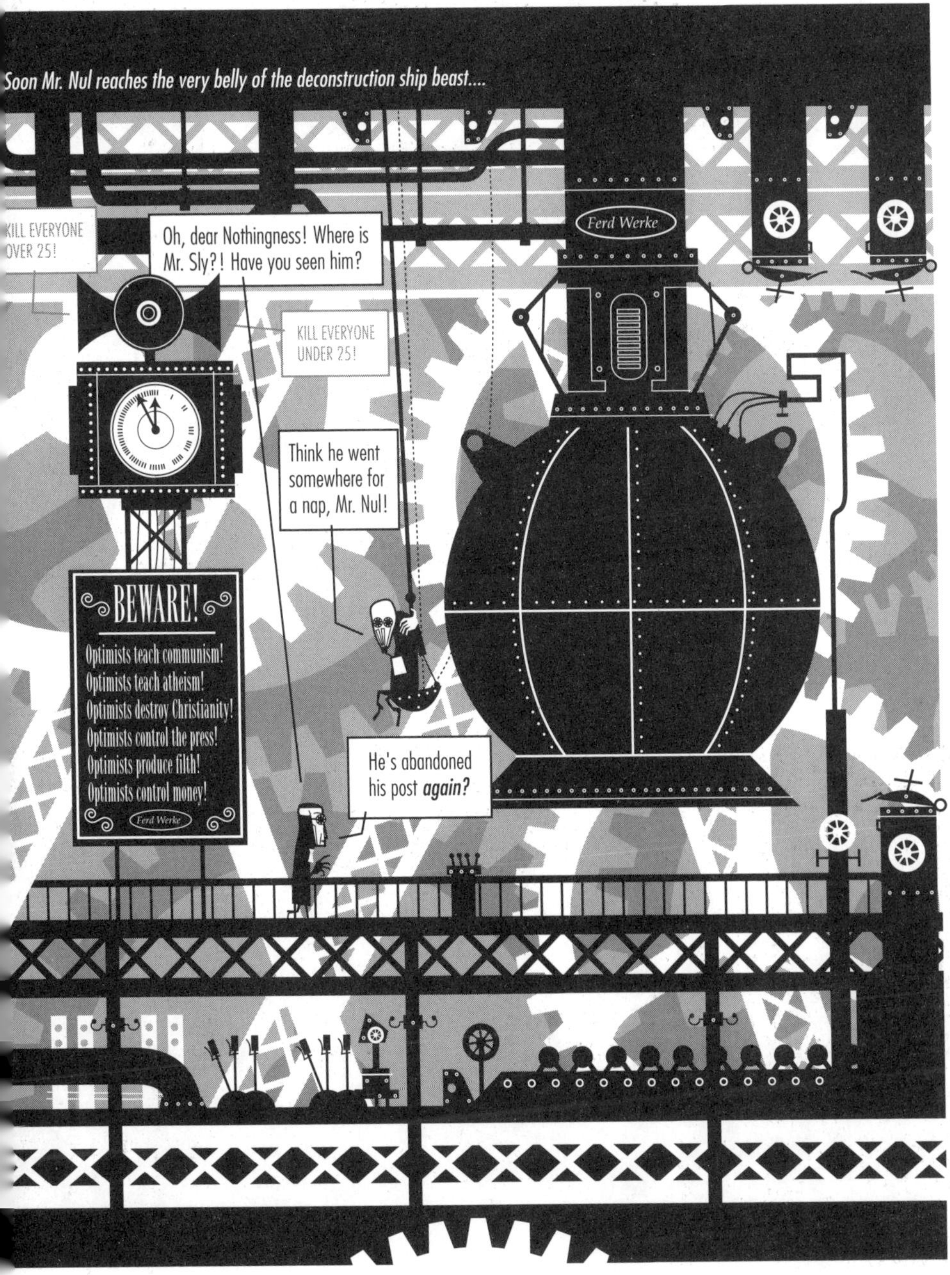

Soon Mr. Nul reaches the very belly of the deconstruction ship beast....
KILL EVERYONE OVER 25!
Oh, dear Nothingness! Where is Mr. Sly?! Have you seen him?
Ferd Werke
KILL EVERYONE UNDER 25!
Think he went somewhere for a nap, Mr. Nul!
BEWARE!
Optimists teach communism!
Optimists teach atheism!
Optimists destroy Christianity!
Optimists control the press!
Optimists produce filth!
Optimists control money!
Ferd Werke
He's abandoned his post *again?*

Outside, the deconstruction grinders continue their demolishing of the meme outbreak's physical manifestation....

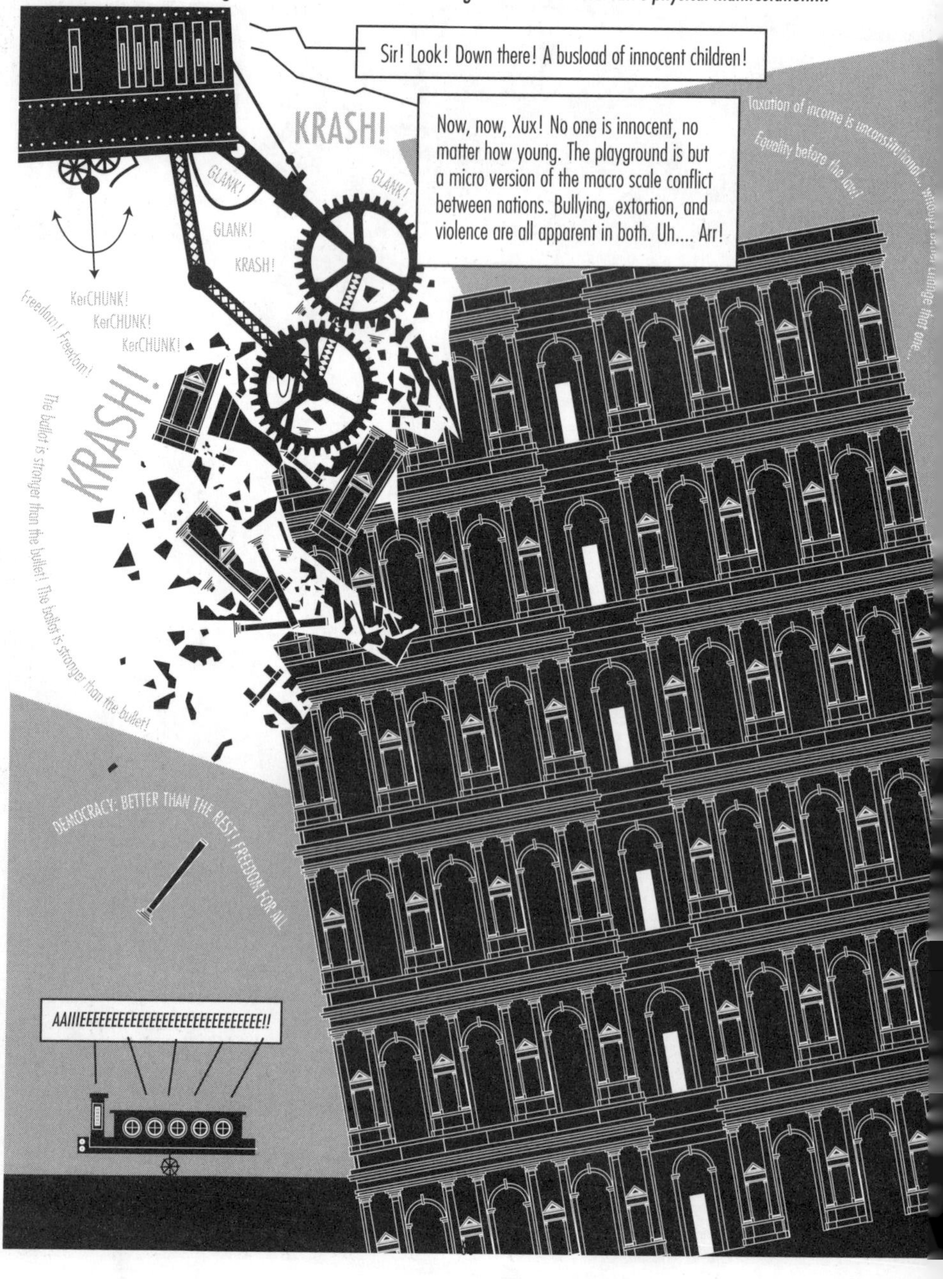
Sir! Look! Down there! A busload of innocent children!
Now, now, Xux! No one is innocent, no matter how young. The playground is but a micro version of the macro scale conflict between nations. Bullying, extortion, and violence are all apparent in both. Uh.... Arr!
KRASH!
GLANK!
GLANK!
GLANK!
KRASH!
KerCHUNK!
KerCHUNK!
KerCHUNK!
KRASH!
Taxation of income is unconstitutional...
Equality before the law!
Freedom! Freedom!
The ballot is stronger than the bullet! The ballot is stronger than the bullet!
DEMOCRACY: BETTER THAN THE REST! FREEDOM FOR ALL
AAIIIEEEEEEEEEEEEEEEEEEEEEEEEEEEE!!

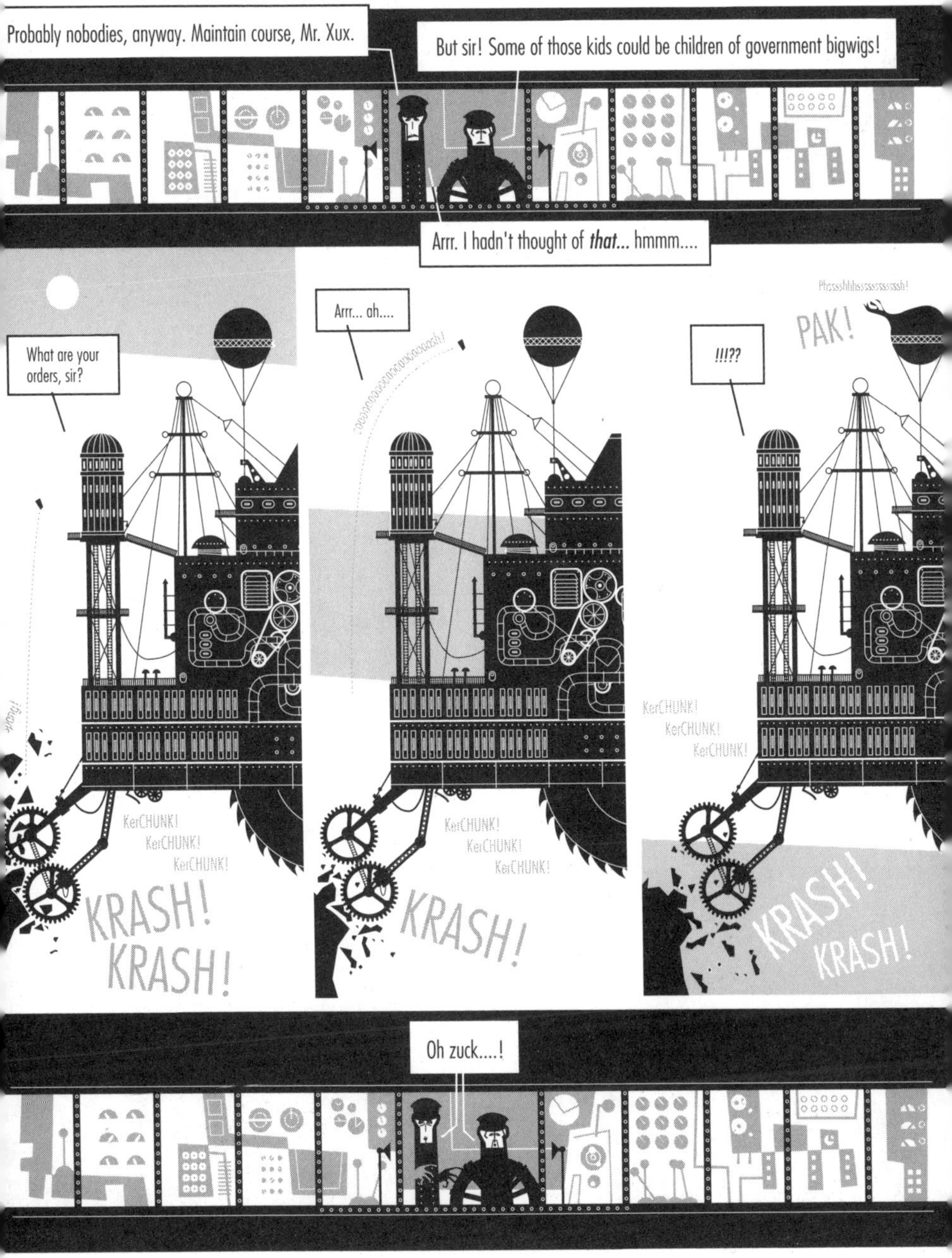

Probably nobodies, anyway. Maintain course, Mr. Xux.
But sir! Some of those kids could be children of government bigwigs!
Arrr. I hadn't thought of ***that...*** hmmm....
What are your orders, sir?
KerCHUNK!
KerCHUNK!
KerCHUNK!
KRASH!
KRASH!
Arrr... ah....
KerCHUNK!
KerCHUNK!
KerCHUNK!
KRASH!
!!!??
PAK!
KerCHUNK!
KerCHUNK!
KerCHUNK!
KRASH!
KRASH!
Oh zuck....!

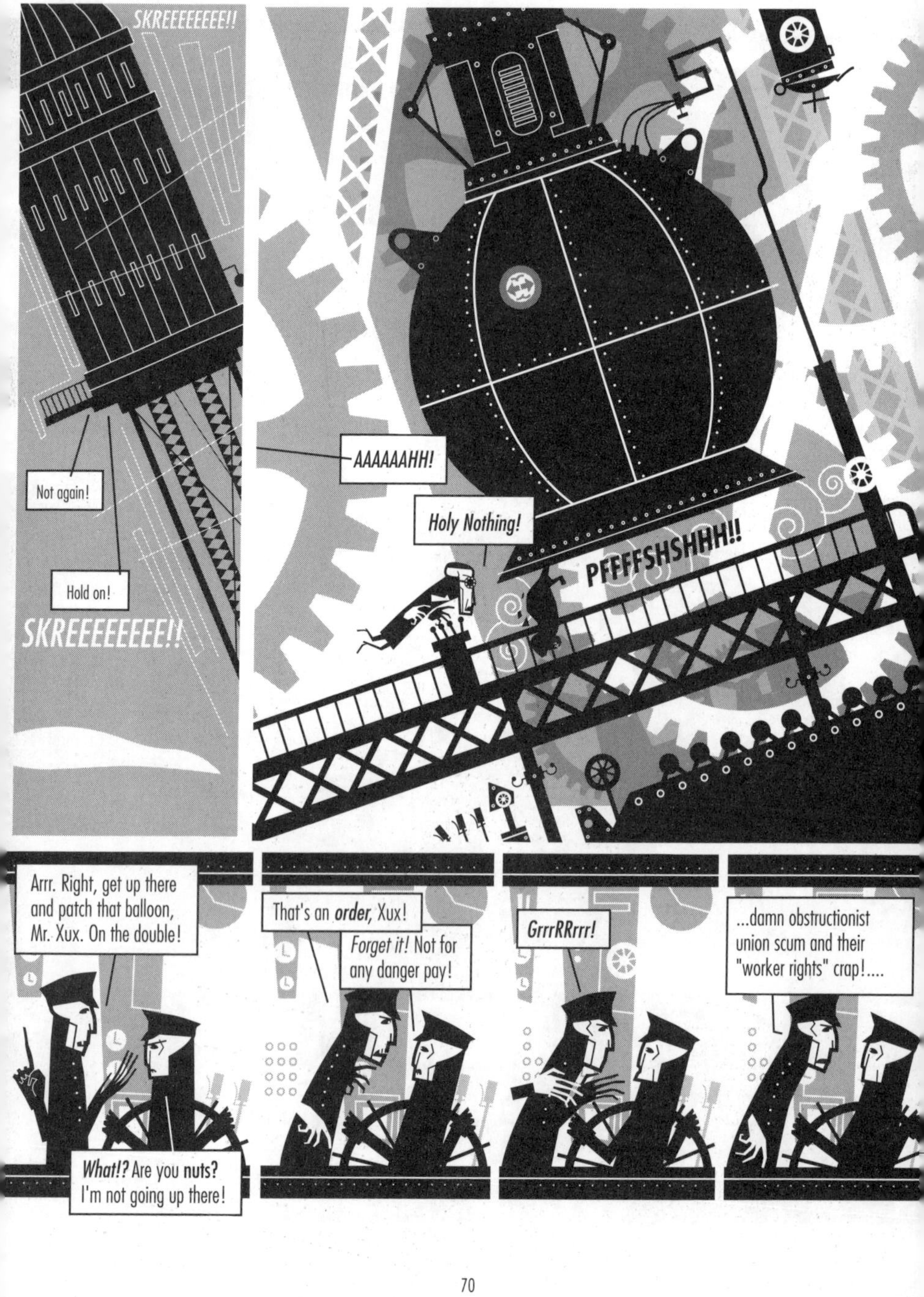
SKREEEEEEEE!!
Not again!
Hold on!
SKREEEEEEEE!!
AAAAAAHH!
Holy Nothing!
PFFFFSHSHHH!!
Arrr. Right, get up there and patch that balloon, Mr. Xux. On the double!
What!? Are you nuts? I'm not going up there!
That's an order, Xux!
Forget it! Not for any danger pay!
GrrrRRrrr!
...damn obstructionist union scum and their "worker rights" crap!....

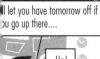

I let you have tomorrow off if you go up there....

Ha!

Sigh.

Fine then. Inflate the life balloons, but don't launch them. Pronto!

Aye, aye, sir!

We'll have to head back to port. Drop a nuke on the democracy outbreak. Give it, oh, a fifteen minute fuse. That'll do nicely. Hurry now, before we crash!

The Emergency Life Balloons pop up, stopping the descent of the ship, but leaving her badly wounded. The lumbering vessel juts about and limps back for port.... wounded but still proud!

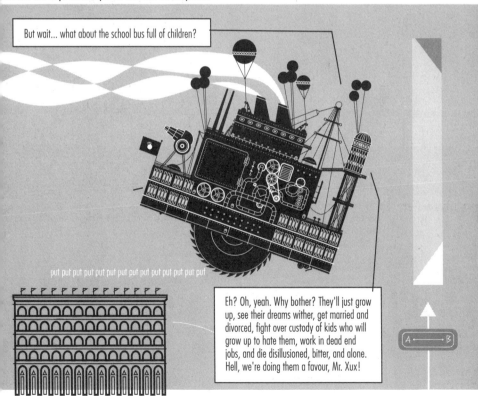

But wait... what about the school bus full of children?

put put put put put put put put put put put put put put

Eh? Oh, yeah. Why bother? They'll just grow up, see their dreams wither, get married and divorced, fight over custody of kids who will grow up to hate them, work in dead end jobs, and die disillusioned, bitter, and alone. Hell, we're doing them a favour, Mr. Xux!

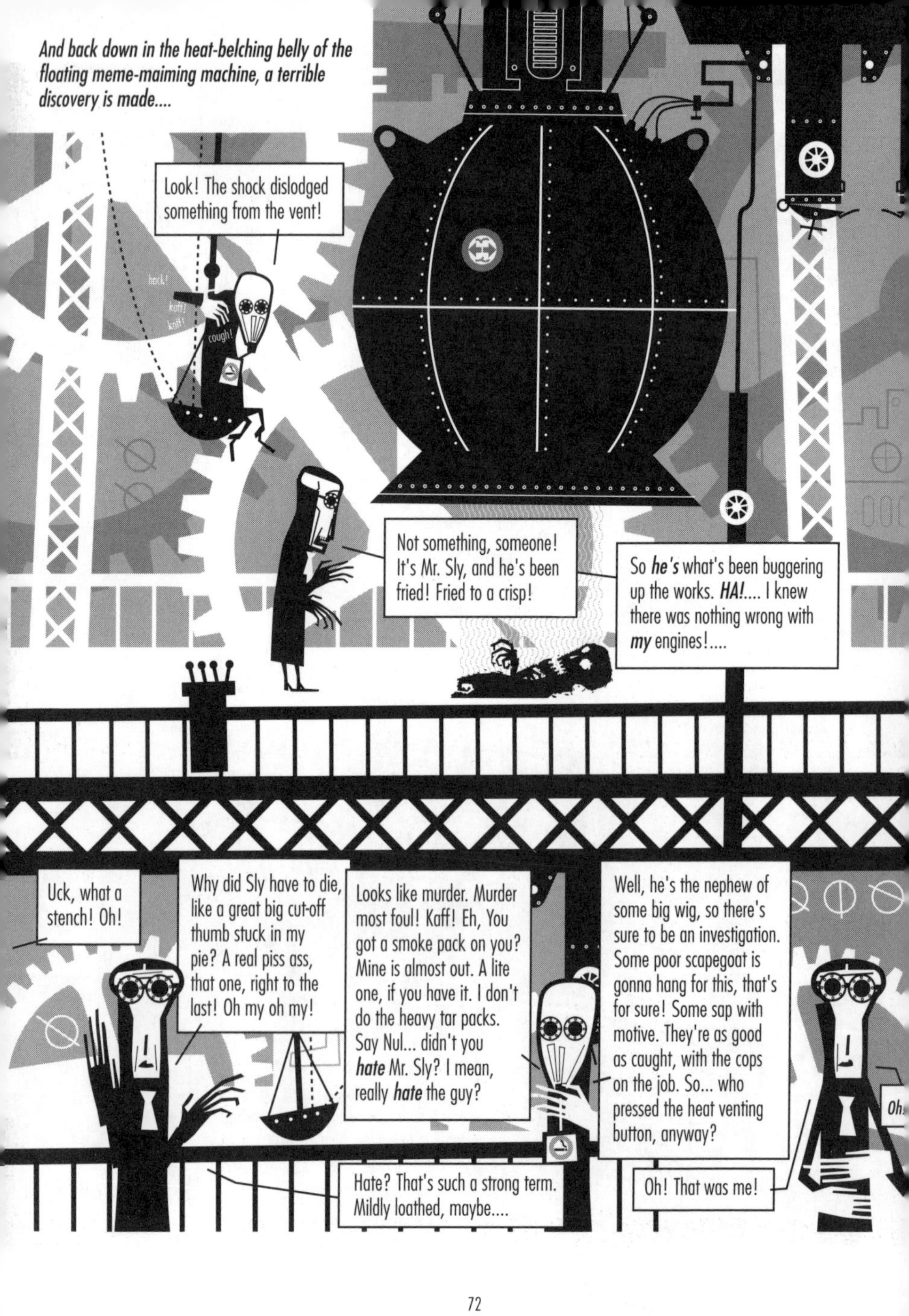

And back down in the heat-belching belly of the floating meme-maiming machine, a terrible discovery is made....
Look! The shock dislodged something from the vent!
hack!
koff!
koff!
cough!
Not something, someone! It's Mr. Sly, and he's been fried! Fried to a crisp!
So he's what's been buggering up the works. HA!.... I knew there was nothing wrong with my engines!....
Uck, what a stench! Oh!
Why did Sly have to die, like a great big cut-off thumb stuck in my pie? A real piss ass, that one, right to the last! Oh my oh my!
Hate? That's such a strong term. Mildly loathed, maybe....
Looks like murder. Murder most foul! Kaff! Eh, You got a smoke pack on you? Mine is almost out. A lite one, if you have it. I don't do the heavy tar packs. Say Nul... didn't you hate Mr. Sly? I mean, really hate the guy?
Well, he's the nephew of some big wig, so there's sure to be an investigation. Some poor scapegoat is gonna hang for this, that's for sure! Some sap with motive. They're as good as caught, with the cops on the job. So... who pressed the heat venting button, anyway?
Oh! That was me!

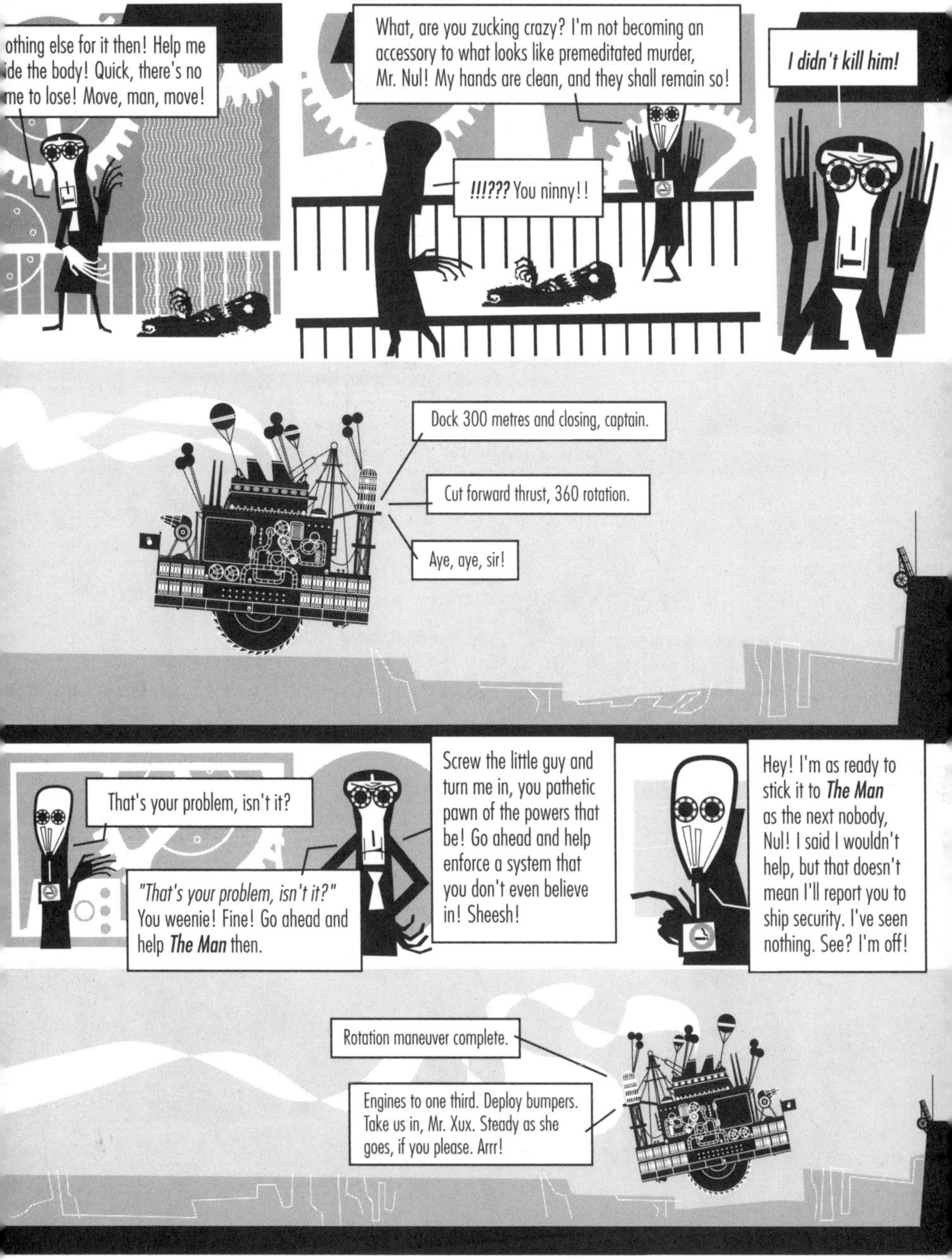
othing else for it then! Help me ide the body! Quick, there's no me to lose! Move, man, move!
What, are you zucking crazy? I'm not becoming an accessory to what looks like premeditated murder, Mr. Nul! My hands are clean, and they shall remain so!
!!!??? You ninny!!
I didn't kill him!
Dock 300 metres and closing, captain.
Cut forward thrust, 360 rotation.
Aye, aye, sir!
That's your problem, isn't it?
"That's your problem, isn't it?" You weenie! Fine! Go ahead and help The Man then.
Screw the little guy and turn me in, you pathetic pawn of the powers that be! Go ahead and help enforce a system that you don't even believe in! Sheesh!
Hey! I'm as ready to stick it to The Man as the next nobody, Nul! I said I wouldn't help, but that doesn't mean I'll report you to ship security. I've seen nothing. See? I'm off!
Rotation maneuver complete.
Engines to one third. Deploy bumpers. Take us in, Mr. Xux. Steady as she goes, if you please. Arrr!

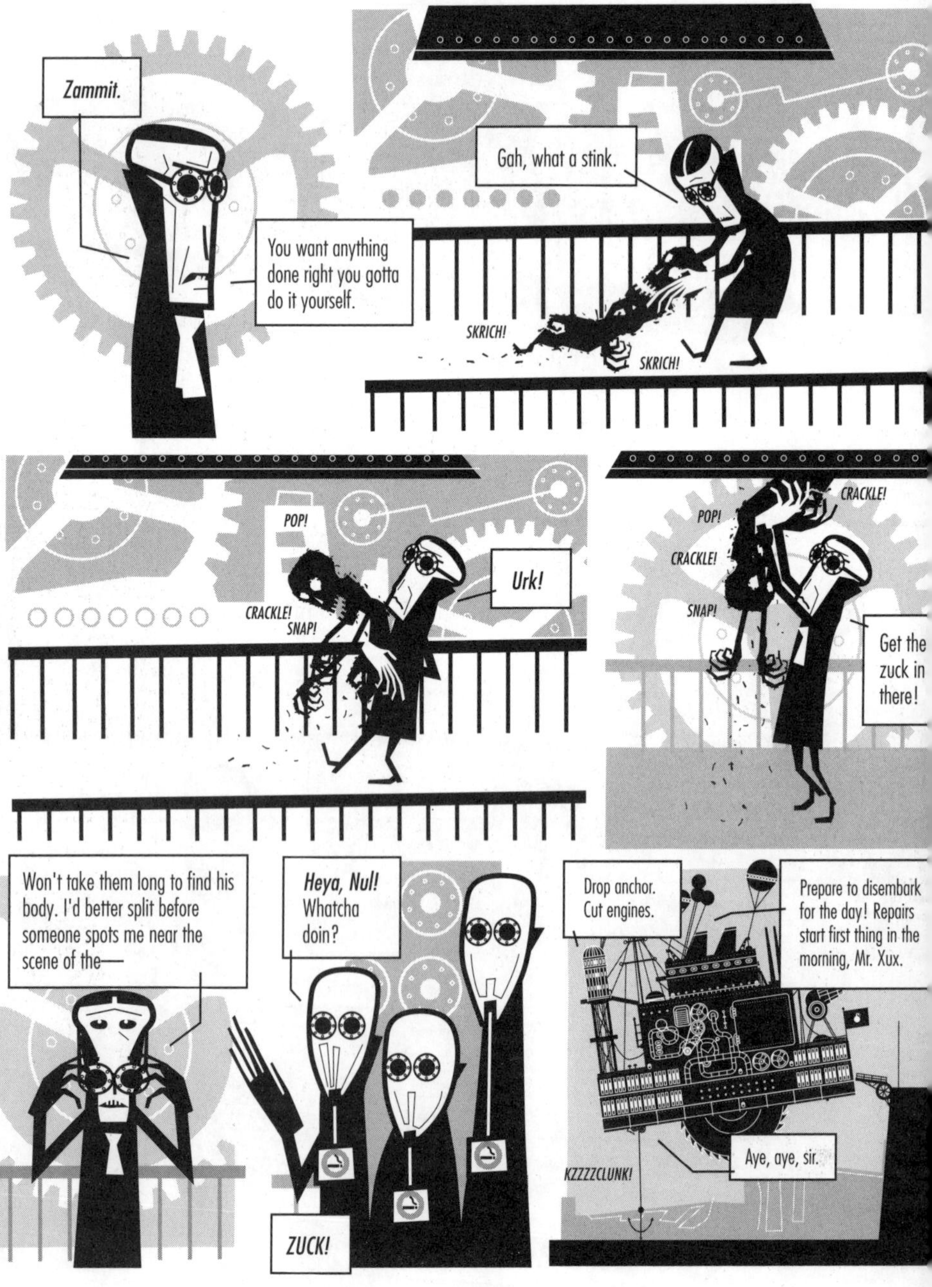
Zammit.
You want anything done right you gotta do it yourself.
Gah, what a stink.
SKRICH!
SKRICH!
POP!
CRACKLE!
SNAP!
Urk!
CRACKLE!
POP!
CRACKLE!
SNAP!
Get the zuck in there!
Won't take them long to find his body. I'd better split before someone spots me near the scene of the—
Heya, Nul! Whatcha doin?
ZUCK!
Drop anchor. Cut engines.
Prepare to disembark for the day! Repairs start first thing in the morning, Mr. Xux.
Aye, aye, sir.
KZZZZCLUNK!

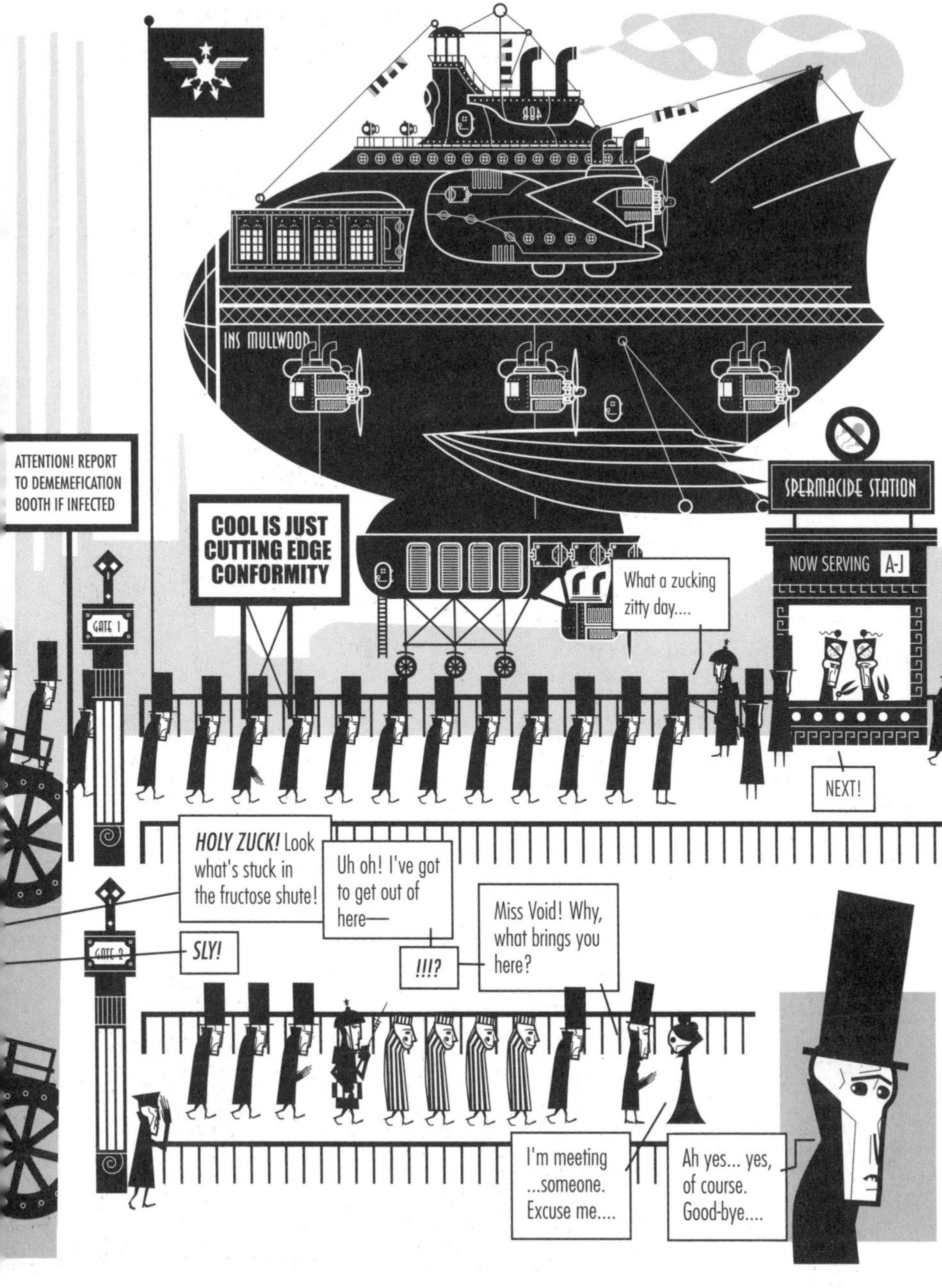

ATTENTION! REPORT TO DEMEMEFICATION BOOTH IF INFECTED
INS MULLWOOD
COOL IS JUST CUTTING EDGE CONFORMITY
GATE 1
SPERMACIDE STATION
NOW SERVING A-J
What a zucking zitty day....
NEXT!
HOLY ZUCK! Look what's stuck in the fructose shute!
Uh oh! I've got to get out of here—
SLY!
!!!?
Miss Void! Why, what brings you here?
I'm meeting ...someone. Excuse me....
Ah yes... yes, of course. Good-bye....

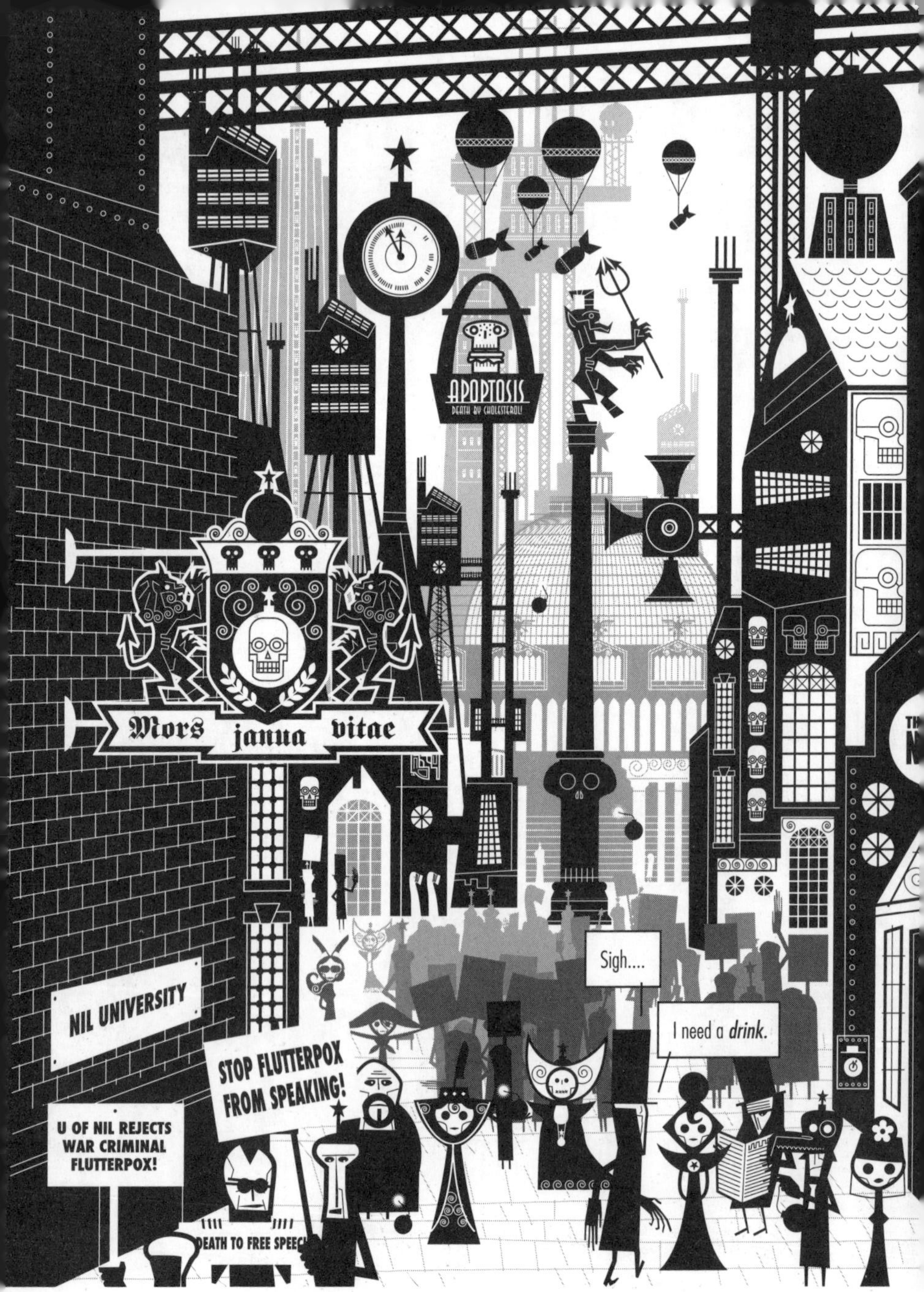
APOPTOSIS
DEATH BY CHOLESTEROL!
Mors janua vitae
NIL UNIVERSITY
STOP FLUTTERPOX FROM SPEAKING!
U OF NIL REJECTS WAR CRIMINAL FLUTTERPOX!
DEATH TO FREE SPEEC
Sigh....
I need a *drink*.

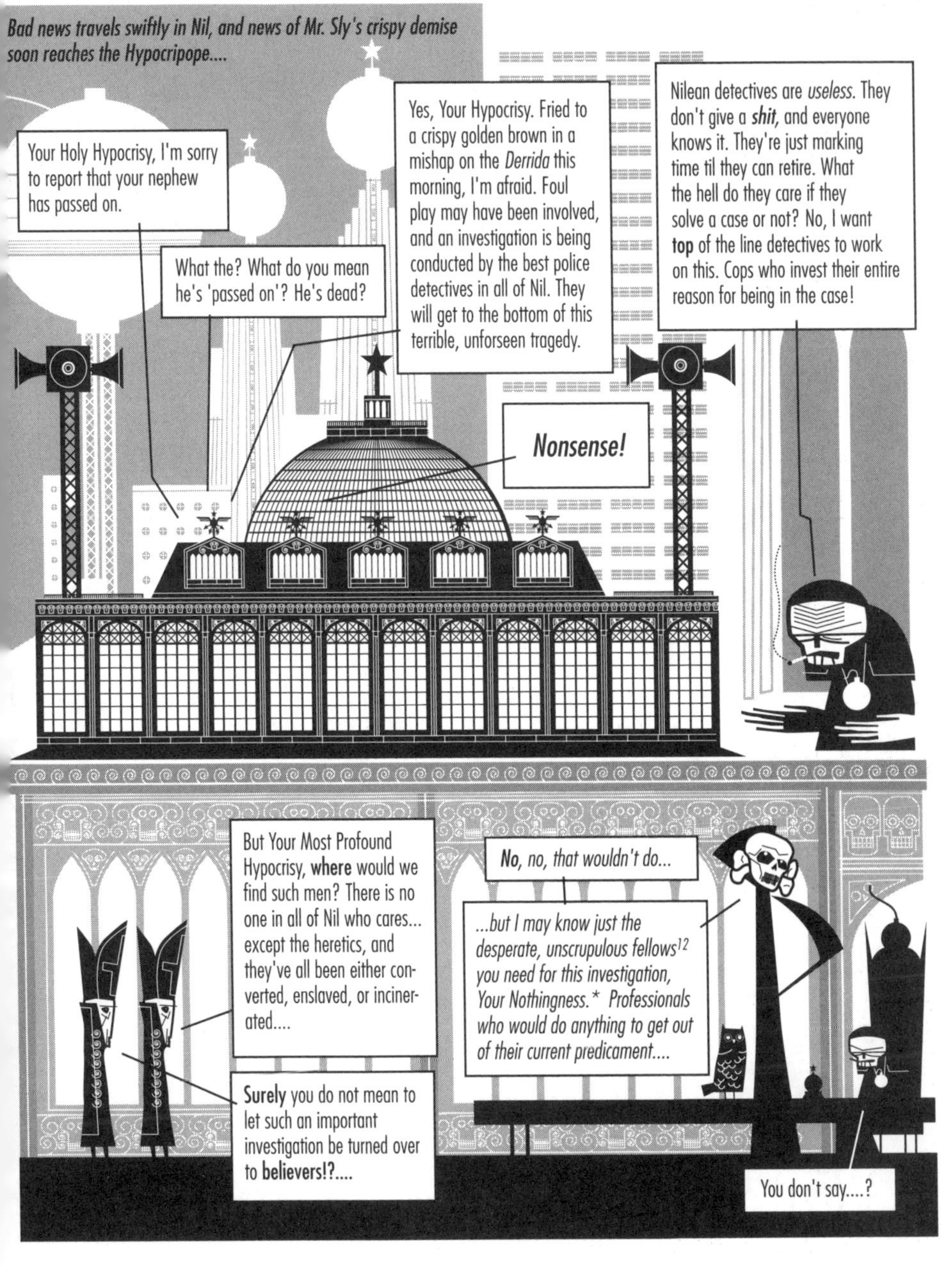

Bad news travels swiftly in Nil, and news of Mr. Sly's crispy demise soon reaches the Hypocripope....
Your Holy Hypocrisy, I'm sorry to report that your nephew has passed on.
What the? What do you mean he's 'passed on'? He's dead?
Yes, Your Hypocrisy. Fried to a crispy golden brown in a mishap on the *Derrida* this morning, I'm afraid. Foul play may have been involved, and an investigation is being conducted by the best police detectives in all of Nil. They will get to the bottom of this terrible, unforseen tragedy.
Nonsense!
Nilean detectives are *useless*. They don't give a ***shit***, and everyone knows it. They're just marking time til they can retire. What the hell do they care if they solve a case or not? No, I want **top** of the line detectives to work on this. Cops who invest their entire reason for being in the case!
But Your Most Profound Hypocrisy, **where** would we find such men? There is no one in all of Nil who cares... except the heretics, and they've all been either converted, enslaved, or incinerated....
Surely you do not mean to let such an important investigation be turned over to **believers!?....**
***No**, no, that wouldn't do...*
...but I may know just the desperate, unscrupulous fellows[12] you need for this investigation, Your Nothingness. Professionals who would do anything to get out of their current predicament....*
You don't say....?

Word goes out from the Hypocripope, wheels are put in motion, and soon the elevator to Hell spits forth two unsavory characters....

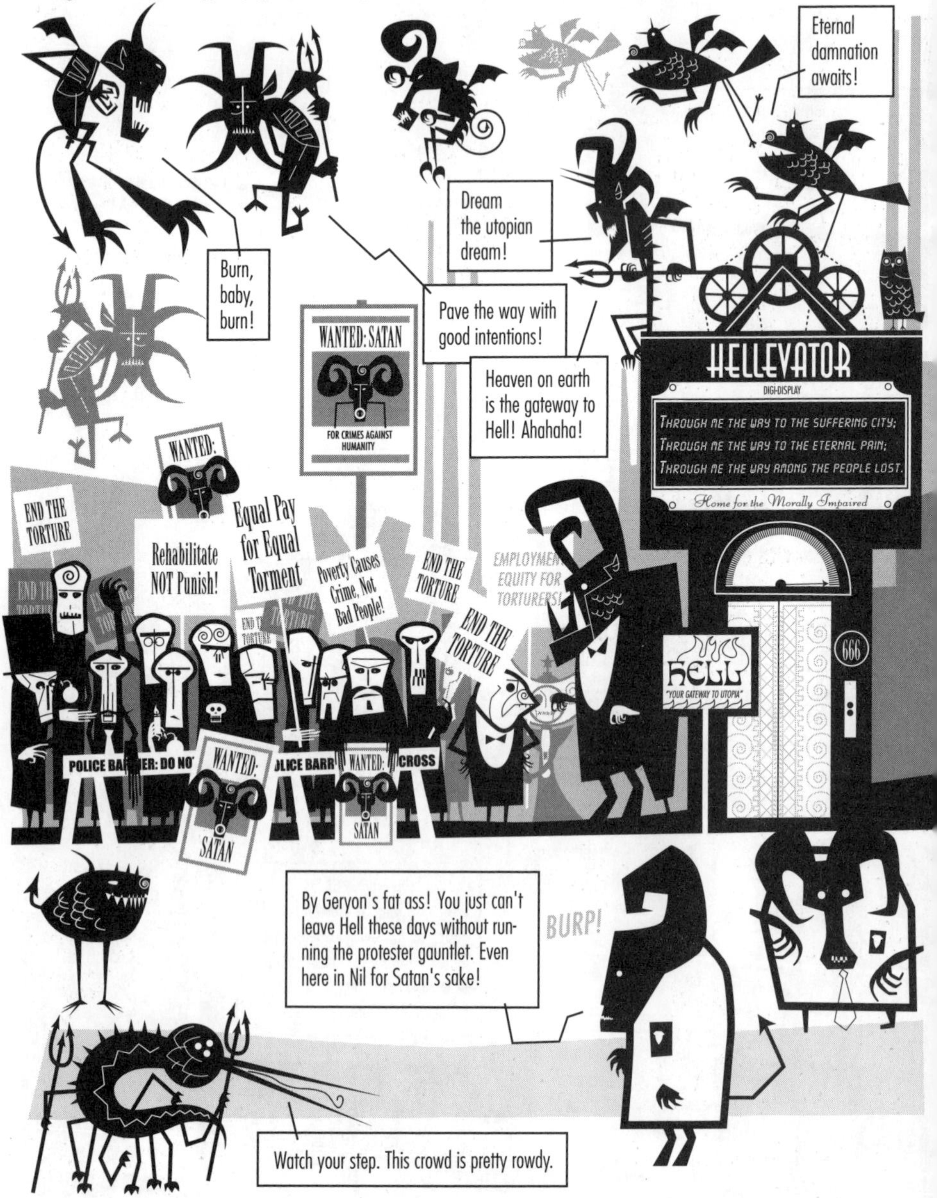
Eternal damnation awaits!
Burn, baby, burn!
Dream the utopian dream!
Pave the way with good intentions!
Heaven on earth is the gateway to Hell! Ahahaha!
WANTED: SATAN
FOR CRIMES AGAINST HUMANITY
HELLEVATOR
DIGI-DISPLAY
THROUGH ME THE WAY TO THE SUFFERING CITY;
THROUGH ME THE WAY TO THE ETERNAL PAIN;
THROUGH ME THE WAY AMONG THE PEOPLE LOST.
Home for the Morally Impaired
WANTED:
END THE TORTURE
Rehabilitate NOT Punish!
Equal Pay for Equal Torment
Poverty Causes Crime, Not Bad People!
END THE TORTURE
EMPLOYMENT EQUITY FOR TORTURERS!
END THE TORTURE
HELL
"YOUR GATEWAY TO UTOPIA"
666
POLICE BARRIER: DO NOT
WANTED: SATAN
POLICE BARR
WANTED: CROSS
SATAN
By Geryon's fat ass! You just can't leave Hell these days without running the protester gauntlet. Even here in Nil for Satan's sake!
BURP!
Watch your step. This crowd is pretty rowdy.

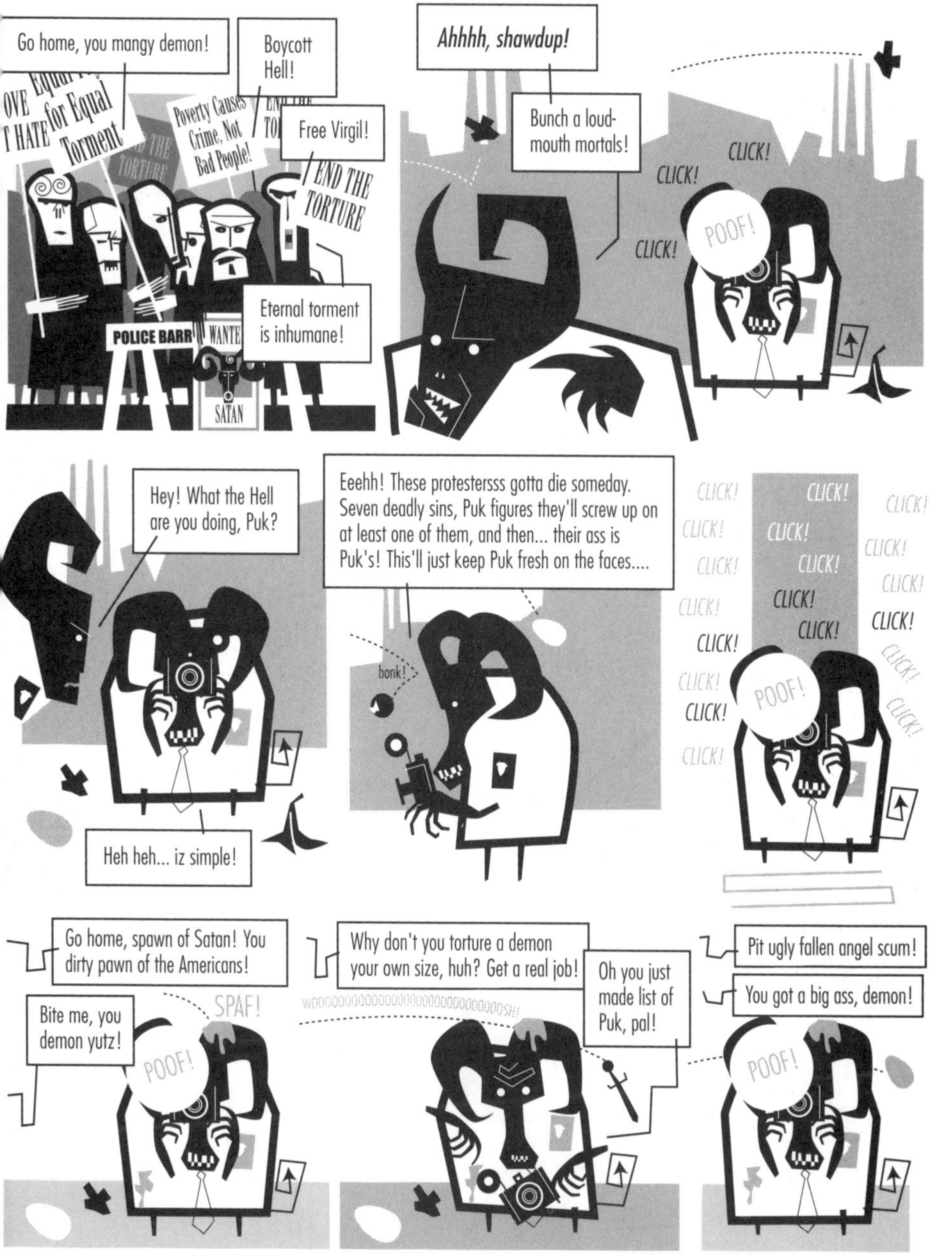
Go home, you mangy demon!
Boycott Hell!
for Equal Torment
Poverty Causes Crime, Not Bad People!
Free Virgil!
END THE TORTURE
Eternal torment is inhumane!
POLICE BARR
WANTE
SATAN
Ahhhh, shawdup!
Bunch a loud-mouth mortals!
CLICK!
CLICK!
CLICK!
POOF!
Hey! What the Hell are you doing, Puk?
Heh heh... iz simple!
Eeehh! These protestersss gotta die someday. Seven deadly sins, Puk figures they'll screw up on at least one of them, and then... their ass is Puk's! This'll just keep Puk fresh on the faces....
bonk!
CLICK! CLICK! CLICK! CLICK! CLICK! CLICK! CLICK! CLICK! CLICK! CLICK! CLICK! CLICK! CLICK! CLICK! CLICK! CLICK! CLICK! CLICK! CLICK!
POOF!
Go home, spawn of Satan! You dirty pawn of the Americans!
Bite me, you demon yutz!
SPAF!
POOF!
Why don't you torture a demon your own size, huh? Get a real job!
WOOOOOOOOOOOOOOOOOOOOOOOOOOOOOOOOOSH!
Oh you just made list of Puk, pal!
Pit ugly fallen angel scum!
You got a big ass, demon!
POOF!

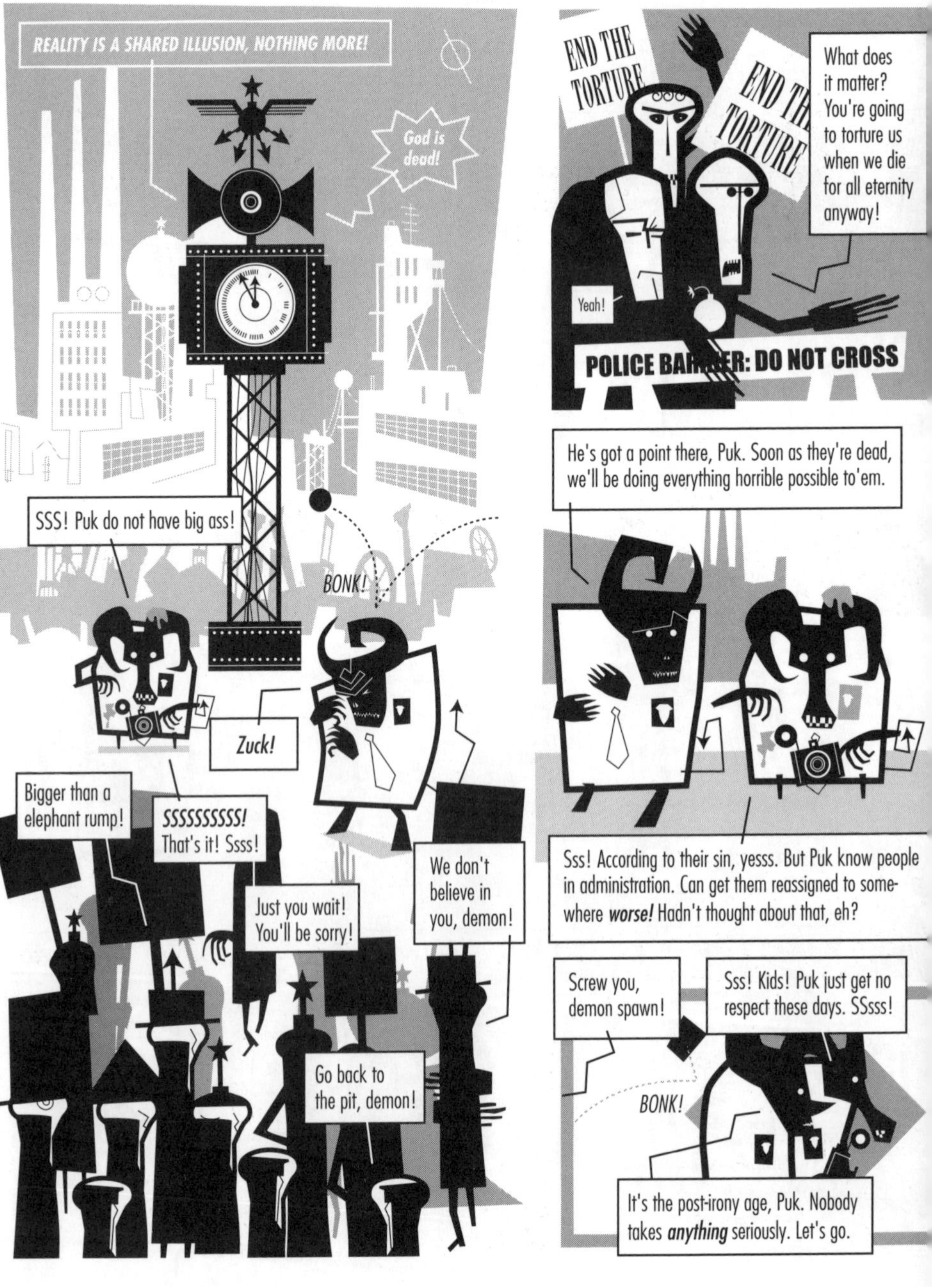
REALITY IS A SHARED ILLUSION, NOTHING MORE!
God is dead!
SSS! Puk do not have big ass!
BONK!
Zuck!
Bigger than a elephant rump!
SSSSSSSSSSS! That's it! Ssss!
Just you wait! You'll be sorry!
We don't believe in you, demon!
Go back to the pit, demon!
END THE TORTURE
END THE TORTURE
What does it matter? You're going to torture us when we die for all eternity anyway!
Yeah!
POLICE BA
ER: DO NOT CROSS
He's got a point there, Puk. Soon as they're dead, we'll be doing everything horrible possible to'em.
Sss! According to their sin, yesss. But Puk know people in administration. Can get them reassigned to somewhere worse! Hadn't thought about that, eh?
Screw you, demon spawn!
Sss! Kids! Puk just get no respect these days. SSsss!
BONK!
It's the post-irony age, Puk. Nobody takes anything seriously. Let's go.

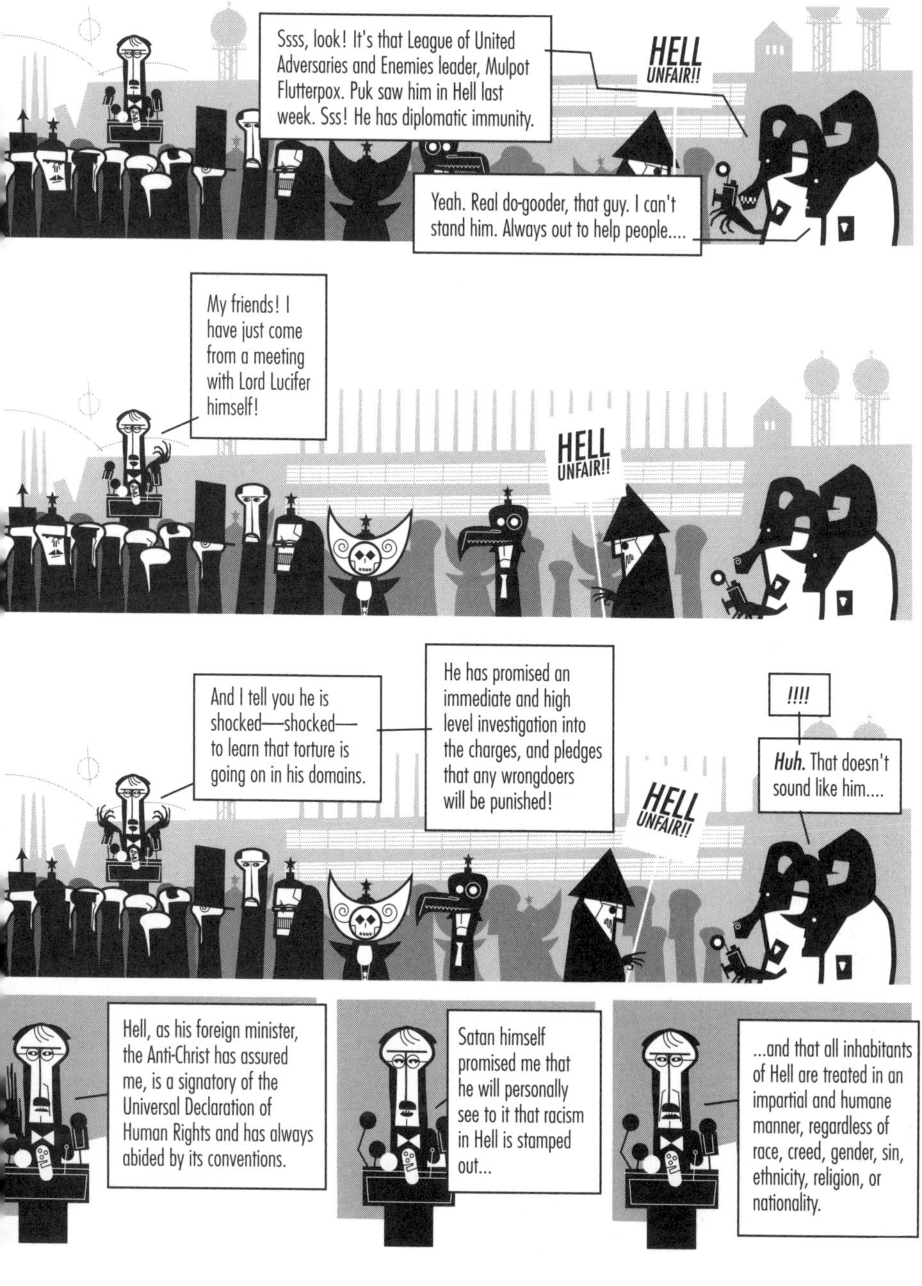
Ssss, look! It's that League of United Adversaries and Enemies leader, Mulpot Flutterpox. Puk saw him in Hell last week. Sss! He has diplomatic immunity.
HELL UNFAIR!!
Yeah. Real do-gooder, that guy. I can't stand him. Always out to help people....
My friends! I have just come from a meeting with Lord Lucifer himself!
HELL UNFAIR!!
And I tell you he is shocked—shocked—to learn that torture is going on in his domains.
He has promised an immediate and high level investigation into the charges, and pledges that any wrongdoers will be punished!
HELL UNFAIR!!
!!!!
Huh. That doesn't sound like him....
Hell, as his foreign minister, the Anti-Christ has assured me, is a signatory of the Universal Declaration of Human Rights and has always abided by its conventions.
Satan himself promised me that he will personally see to it that racism in Hell is stamped out...
...and that all inhabitants of Hell are treated in an impartial and humane manner, regardless of race, creed, gender, sin, ethnicity, religion, or nationality.

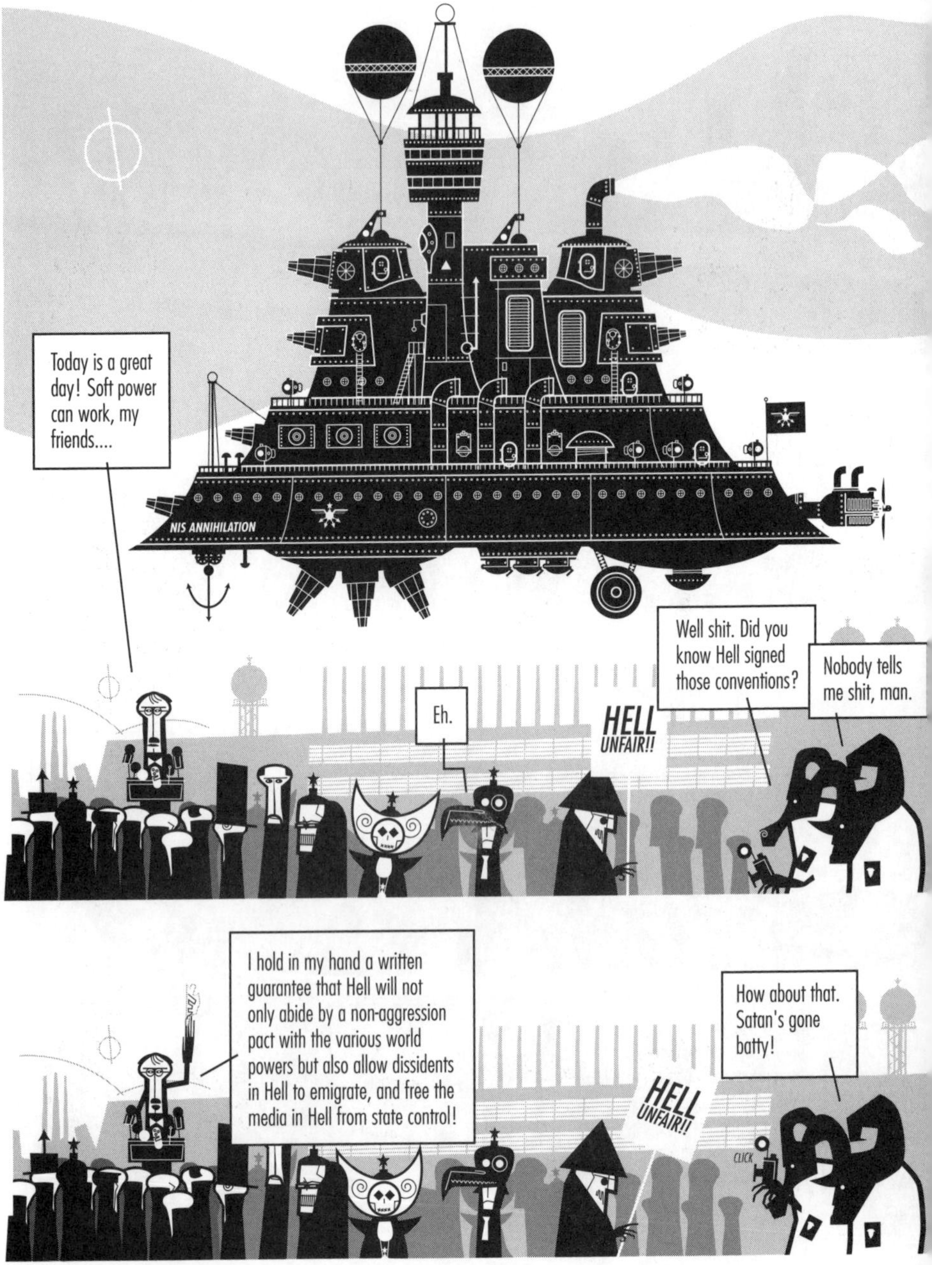

Today is a great day! Soft power can work, my friends....
NIS ANNIHILATION
Eh.
HELL UNFAIR!!
Well shit. Did you know Hell signed those conventions?
Nobody tells me shit, man.
I hold in my hand a written guarantee that Hell will not only abide by a non-aggression pact with the various world powers but also allow dissidents in Hell to emigrate, and free the media in Hell from state control!
HELL UNFAIR!!
How about that. Satan's gone batty!
CLICK

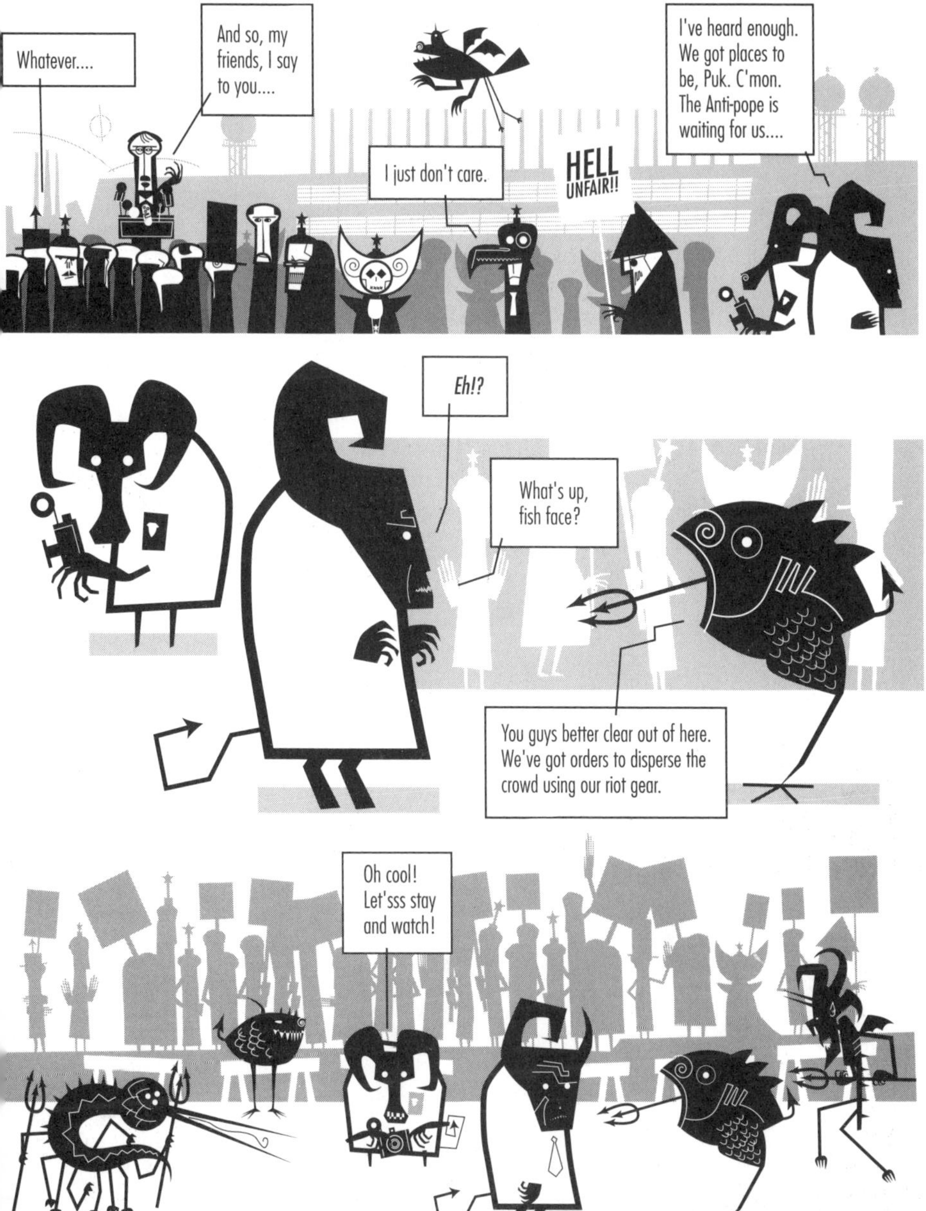
Whatever....
And so, my friends, I say to you....
I just don't care.
HELL UNFAIR!!
I've heard enough. We got places to be, Puk. C'mon. The Anti-pope is waiting for us....
Eh!?
What's up, fish face?
You guys better clear out of here. We've got orders to disperse the crowd using our riot gear.
Oh cool! Let'sss stay and watch!

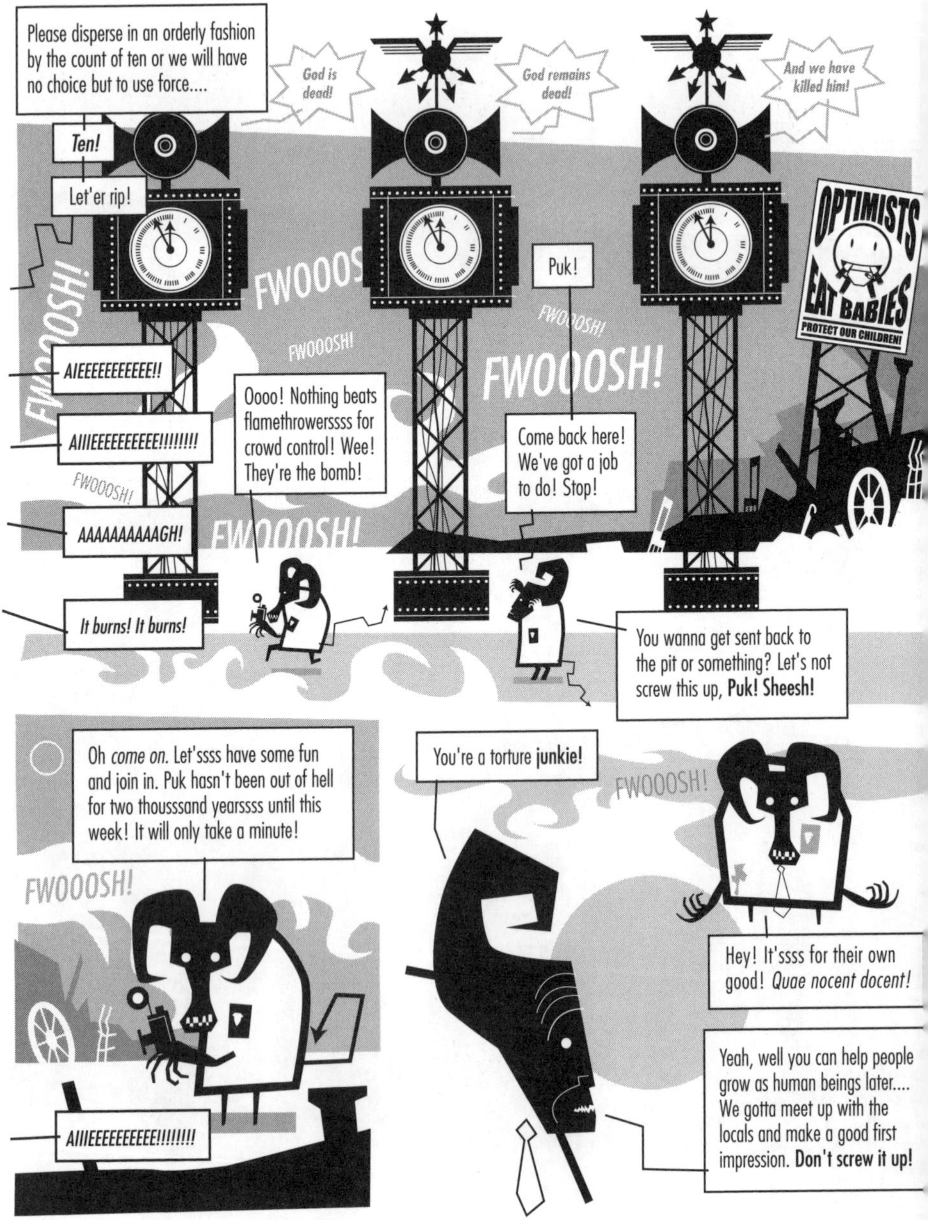
Please disperse in an orderly fashion by the count of ten or we will have no choice but to use force....
God is dead!
God remains dead!
And we have killed him!
Ten!
Let'er rip!
OPTIMISTS EAT BABIES
PROTECT OUR CHILDREN!
FWOOOSH!
FWOOOS
Puk!
FWOOOSH!
FWOOOSH!
FWOOOSH!
AIEEEEEEEEEEE!!
Oooo! Nothing beats flamethrowerssss for crowd control! Wee! They're the bomb!
Come back here! We've got a job to do! Stop!
AIIIEEEEEEEEEEE!!!!!!!!
FWOOOSH!
AAAAAAAAAAGH!
FWOOOSH!
It burns! It burns!
You wanna get sent back to the pit or something? Let's not screw this up, **Puk! Sheesh!**
Oh *come on.* Let'ssss have some fun and join in. Puk hasn't been out of hell for two thousssand yearssss until this week! It will only take a minute!
FWOOOSH!
AIIIEEEEEEEEEEE!!!!!!!!
You're a torture **junkie!**
FWOOOSH!
Hey! It'ssss for their own good! *Quae nocent docent!*
Yeah, well you can help people grow as human beings later.... We gotta meet up with the locals and make a good first impression. **Don't screw it up!**

All the lies we like.

The New Nihilopolis Times

All news is bad news

VOL. MCVII   Copyright New Nihilopolis   Eleven Fifty-Six, Saturday, Nilember, Year of the Apocalypse   ONE COIN

HELL INVADES NEW JERSEY

By Waggle Duranduranty

NEW JERSEY — The international community was shocked yesterday morning by a sudden and unexpected invasion of New Jersey by Hell's Legions of the Damned.

Hell's Foreign Minister, The Anti-Christ, issued a formal proclamation of war at 6:45 am yesterday morning, minutes after Hellspawn began swarming up out of the basements and sewers of New Jersey. Satanic shocktroops attacked police and military installations across the state, while fifth columnists secured radio and television stations and immediately began broadcasting cigarette and liquor ads, high fat content cookie commercials, porn, and Satanic propaganda messages with high-quality production values.

"It's terrible!" said an aide to the President. "These ads are breaking a wide assortment of Federal Broadcasting Regulations."

The League of United Enemies chairman Mulpot Flutterpox issued a statement condemning the attacks shortly after they began. "This attack goes entirely against the agreement we reached with the Foreign Minister of Hell last month in which we handed over Detroit, Las Vegas, and Hollywood. Hell assured us that this was the limit of their terrestrial territorial ambitions. The entire agreement was brokered in good faith by the international community in order to assure world peace for the indefinite future. I fully understood how debauched things are in De-

troit and Las Vegas. Hollywood too is known for its sinful proclivities. What we did, we did for the best... in the best interests of the human race. To assure peace. This invasion by the Spawn of Satan is a breach of trust."

The Anti-Christ had been making a case for the annexation of all three cities to Hell for over thirty years, claiming that fifty per cent of the inhabitants have already sold their souls to Satan, making them dual citizens. The right of Hell to have dominion over its own was recognized in the Treaty of Los Angeles, and jurisdiciton of Las Vegas, Detroit, and Hollywood duly transferred to Hell.

Protests by fundamentalist religious groups and civil rights organizations followed.

Chairman Flutterpox recently returned from Hell with a new non-aggression treaty signed by the Anti-Christ.

"That thing isn't worth the paper it is printed on," huffed the President of the United States. "You just can't trust those demons and devils. Every time they came to the White House to negotiate, all the ashtrays and monogrammed bath towels would go missing."

The President also declared the intention of the United States to reclaim the lost state. "It may only be New Jersey, but by God, it's our New Jersey."

Asked whether or not the United States seeks to retake Detroit, Las Vegas, and Hollywood, the President declined

to comment. "At this time it is too early to make any decisions about reassuming control of the three cities in question."

At the front, American soldiers expressed frustrations with the Hellspawn. "Those demons are not fighting fair," said Colonel Dudley Katechon of the United States Army. "They're using hellfire and brimstone and all sorts of unorthodox methods of warfare. Like possession. I don't think that's allowed by the Geneva Convention. And we've received reports that POWs are being tortured— tortured!— by demonic beings. And they're usin' video games, old comic books, porn, and child wizard stories to convert US soldiers to the cause of the Anti-Christ."

FLUTTERPOX CONDEMNS ATTACK

Transcript of News Release:

It is with the greatest of sadness that today I must stand before you as the Legions of Hell and its Satanic Majesty lurch across the landscape of peaceful, if decadent, New Jersey.

Only a few days ago I was

assured by the Anti-Christ that the territorial ambitions of Hell had been met, and that the prospect of war, a war which loomed over us all, was now no longer within the realm of possibility. We did not compromise enough with Satan.

See COMPROMISE A2

SUBSTRATUM SUB GOES MISSING

By Fig Doobie

ANNIHILOPIA— Philosophical exploration submarine *Dubious* went missing in the substratum last week. Search efforts have failed to find any remains.

According to the pilot of the sister ship *Metaphysical*,

the substratum, which underlies the meaning of all physical reality, is nothing more than a vast, empty, and meaningless tract that manifests itself as a vast underground sea. "I think we can conclude that material reality is all there is," said the pilot.

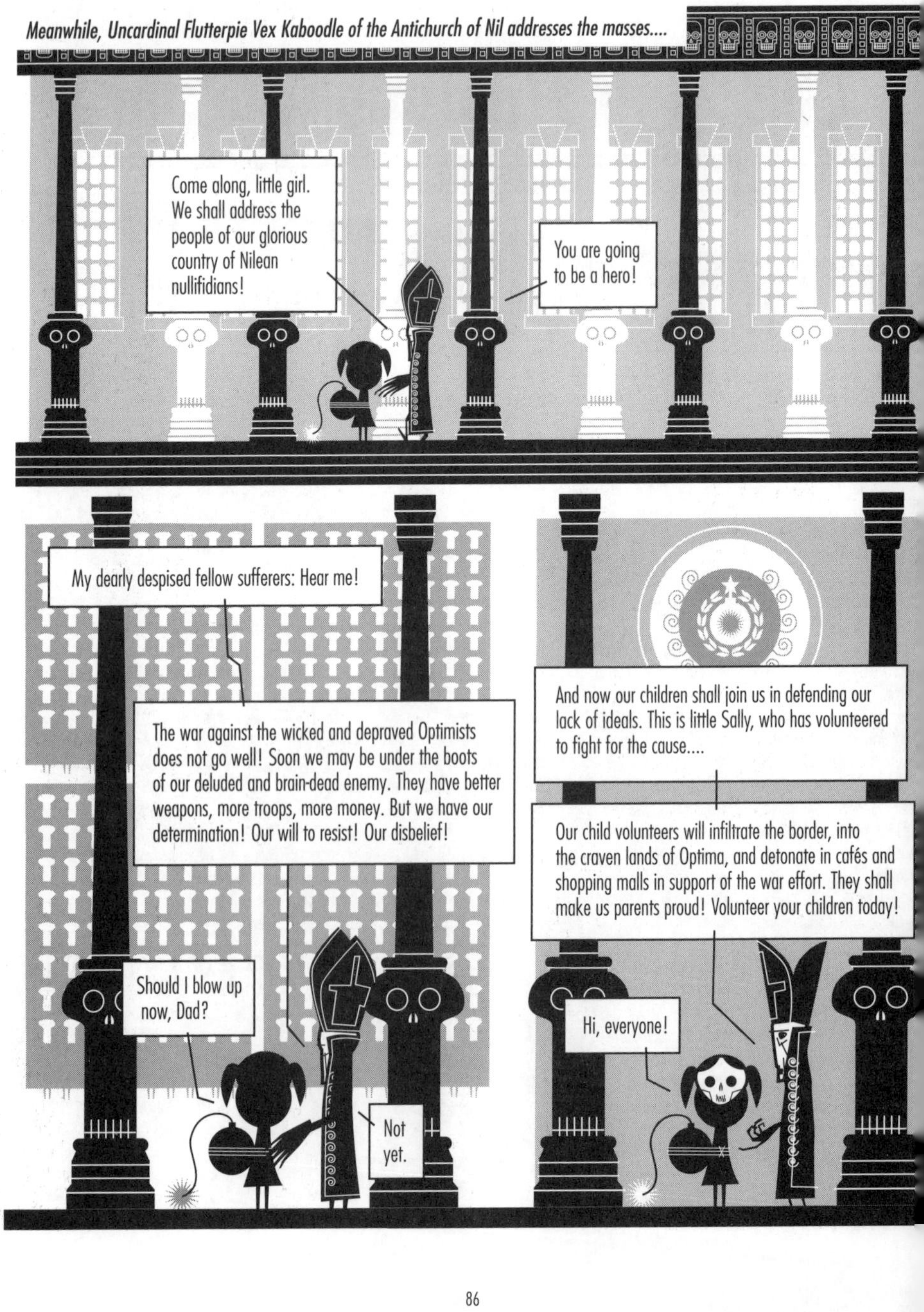
Meanwhile, Uncardinal Flutterpie Vex Kaboodle of the Antichurch of Nil addresses the masses....
Come along, little girl. We shall address the people of our glorious country of Nilean nullifidians!
You are going to be a hero!
My dearly despised fellow sufferers: Hear me!
The war against the wicked and depraved Optimists does not go well! Soon we may be under the boots of our deluded and brain-dead enemy. They have better weapons, more troops, more money. But we have our determination! Our will to resist! Our disbelief!
Should I blow up now, Dad?
Not yet.
And now our children shall join us in defending our lack of ideals. This is little Sally, who has volunteered to fight for the cause....
Our child volunteers will infiltrate the border, into the craven lands of Optima, and detonate in cafés and shopping malls in support of the war effort. They shall make us parents proud! Volunteer your children today!
Hi, everyone!

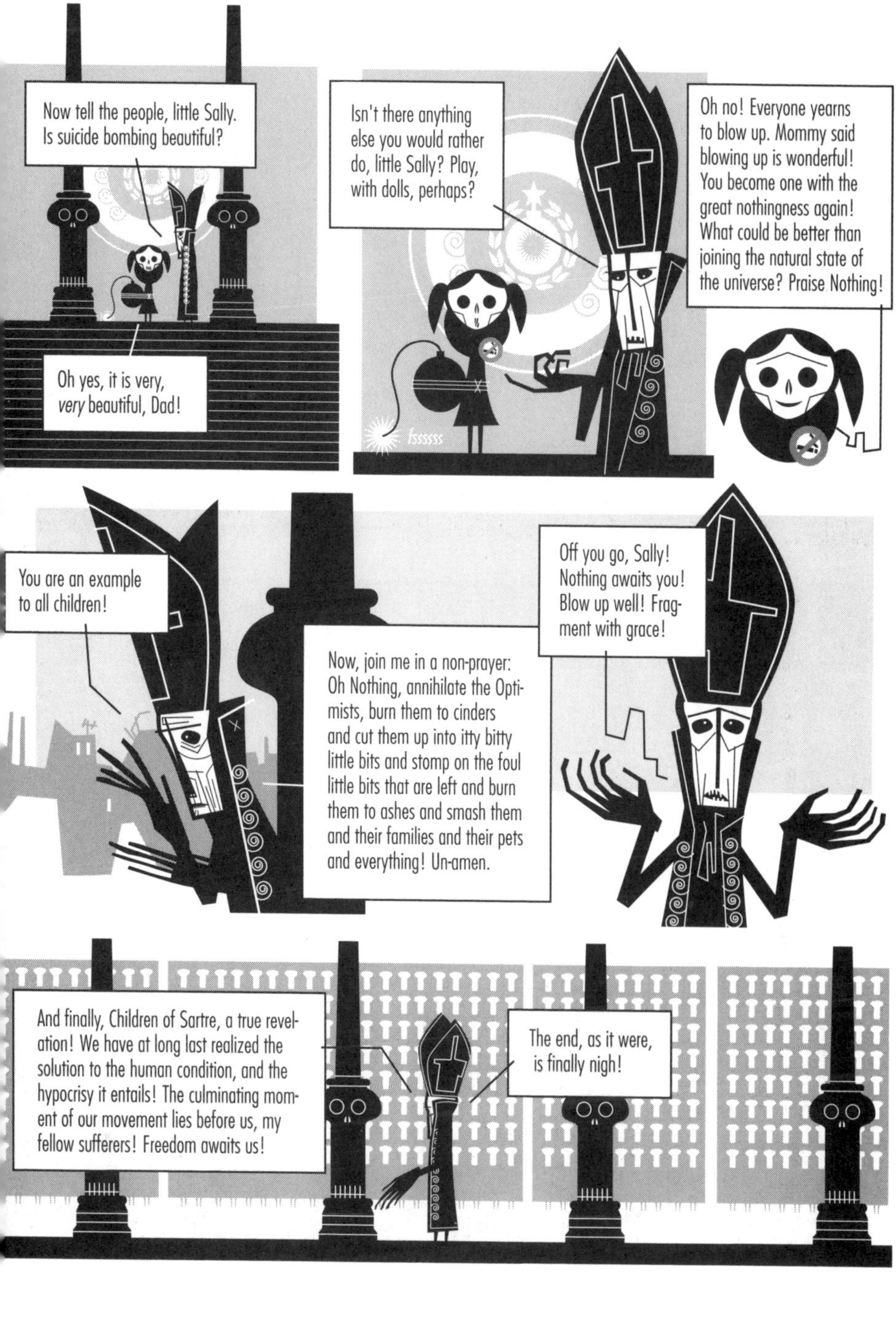
Now tell the people, little Sally. Is suicide bombing beautiful?
Oh yes, it is very, *very* beautiful, Dad!
Isn't there anything else you would rather do, little Sally? Play, with dolls, perhaps?
fssssss
Oh no! Everyone yearns to blow up. Mommy said blowing up is wonderful! You become one with the great nothingness again! What could be better than joining the natural state of the universe? Praise Nothing!
You are an example to all children!
Now, join me in a non-prayer: Oh Nothing, annihilate the Optimists, burn them to cinders and cut them up into itty bitty little bits and stomp on the foul little bits that are left and burn them to ashes and smash them and their families and their pets and everything! Un-amen.
Off you go, Sally! Nothing awaits you! Blow up well! Fragment with grace!
And finally, Children of Sartre, a true revelation! We have at long last realized the solution to the human condition, and the hypocrisy it entails! The culminating moment of our movement lies before us, my fellow sufferers! Freedom awaits us!
The end, as it were, is finally nigh!

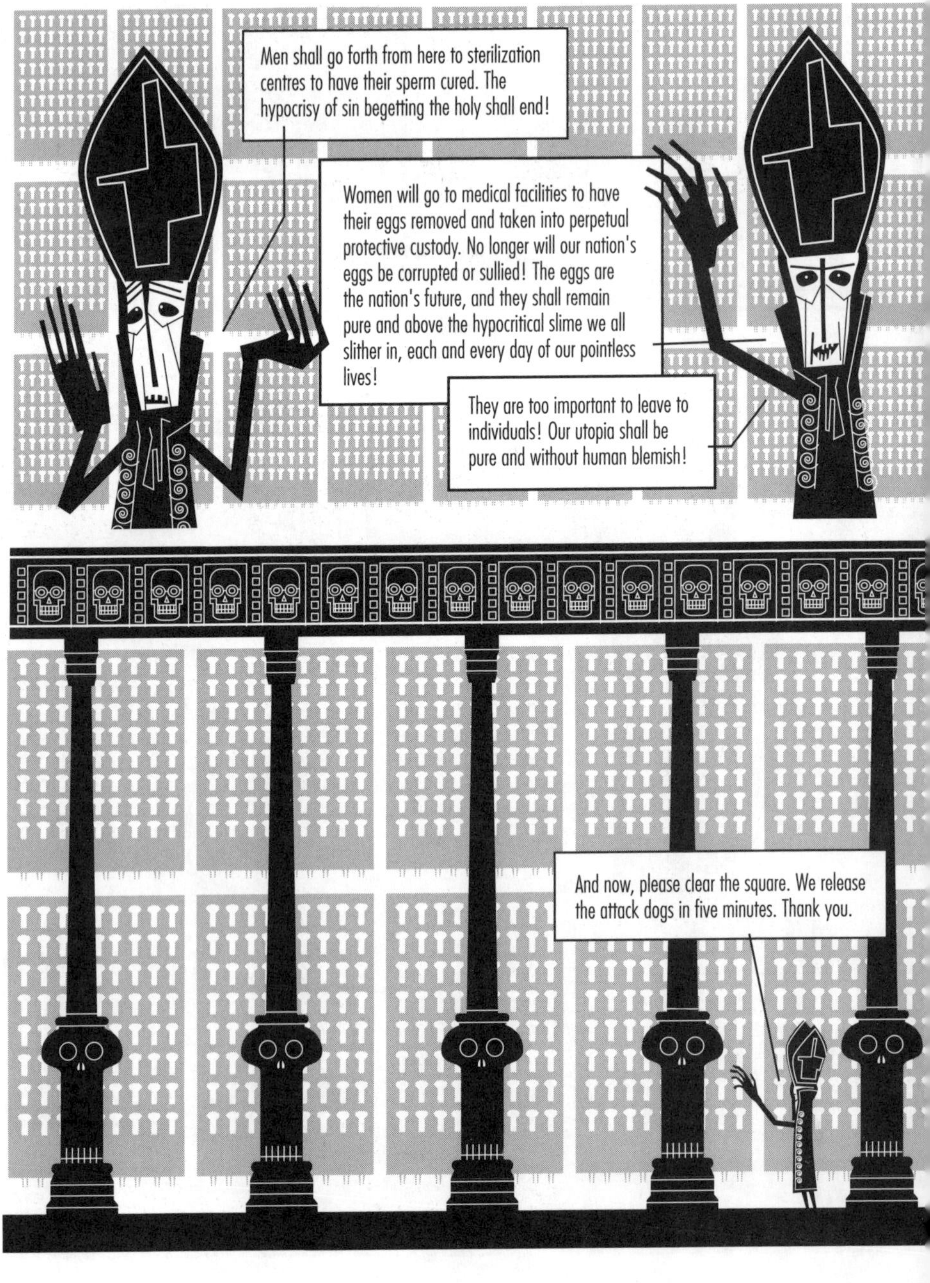
Men shall go forth from here to sterilization centres to have their sperm cured. The hypocrisy of sin begetting the holy shall end!
Women will go to medical facilities to have their eggs removed and taken into perpetual protective custody. No longer will our nation's eggs be corrupted or sullied! The eggs are the nation's future, and they shall remain pure and above the hypocritical slime we all slither in, each and every day of our pointless lives!
They are too important to leave to individuals! Our utopia shall be pure and without human blemish!
And now, please clear the square. We release the attack dogs in five minutes. Thank you.

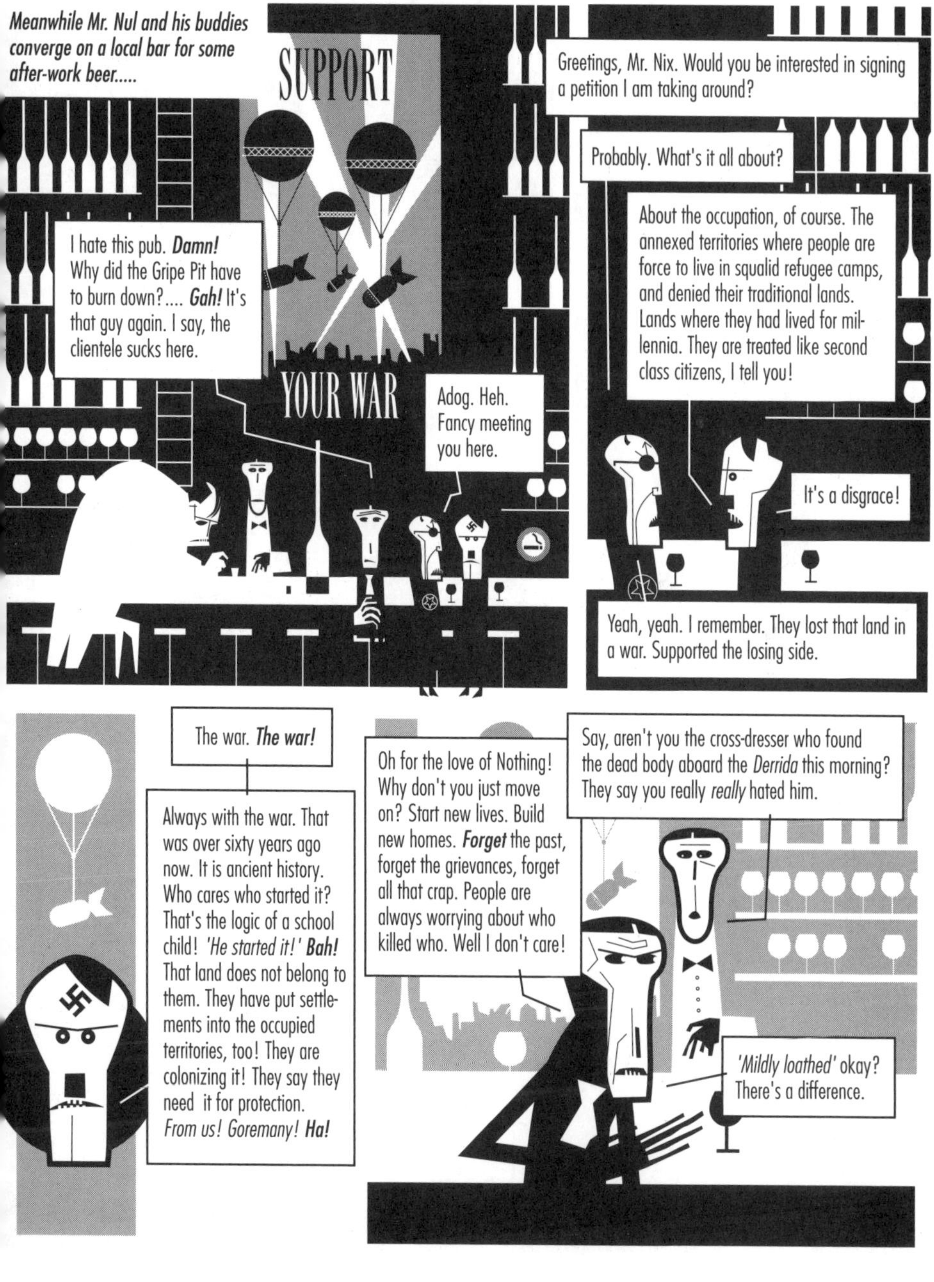
Meanwhile Mr. Nul and his buddies converge on a local bar for some after-work beer.....
SUPPORT
YOUR WAR
I hate this pub. Damn! Why did the Gripe Pit have to burn down?.... Gah! It's that guy again. I say, the clientele sucks here.
Adog. Heh. Fancy meeting you here.
Greetings, Mr. Nix. Would you be interested in signing a petition I am taking around?
Probably. What's it all about?
About the occupation, of course. The annexed territories where people are force to live in squalid refugee camps, and denied their traditional lands. Lands where they had lived for millennia. They are treated like second class citizens, I tell you!
It's a disgrace!
Yeah, yeah. I remember. They lost that land in a war. Supported the losing side.
The war. The war!
Always with the war. That was over sixty years ago now. It is ancient history. Who cares who started it? That's the logic of a school child! 'He started it!' Bah! That land does not belong to them. They have put settlements into the occupied territories, too! They are colonizing it! They say they need it for protection. From us! Goremany! Ha!
Oh for the love of Nothing! Why don't you just move on? Start new lives. Build new homes. Forget the past, forget the grievances, forget all that crap. People are always worrying about who killed who. Well I don't care!
Say, aren't you the cross-dresser who found the dead body aboard the Derrida this morning? They say you really really hated him.
'Mildly loathed' okay? There's a difference.

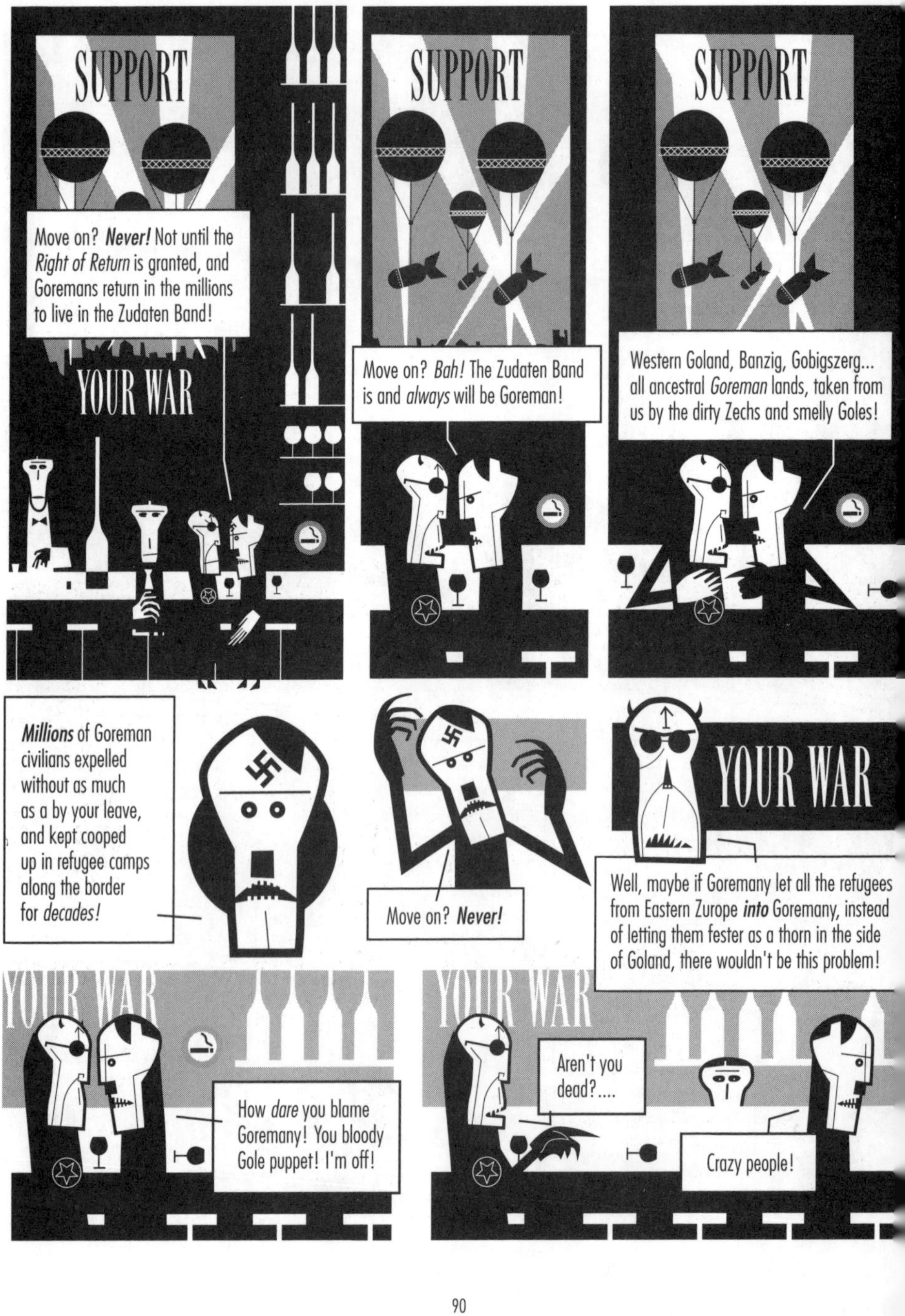
SUPPORT
Move on? *Never!* Not until the *Right of Return* is granted, and Goremans return in the millions to live in the Zudaten Band!
YOUR WAR
SUPPORT
Move on? *Bah!* The Zudaten Band is and *always* will be Goreman!
SUPPORT
Western Goland, Banzig, Gobigszerg... all ancestral *Goreman* lands, taken from us by the dirty Zechs and smelly Goles!
Millions of Goreman civilians expelled without as much as a by your leave, and kept cooped up in refugee camps along the border for *decades!*
Move on? *Never!*
YOUR WAR
Well, maybe if Goremany let all the refugees from Eastern Zurope *into* Goremany, instead of letting them fester as a thorn in the side of Goland, there wouldn't be this problem!
YOUR WAR
How *dare* you blame Goremany! You bloody Gole puppet! I'm off!
YOUR WAR
Aren't you dead?....
Crazy people!

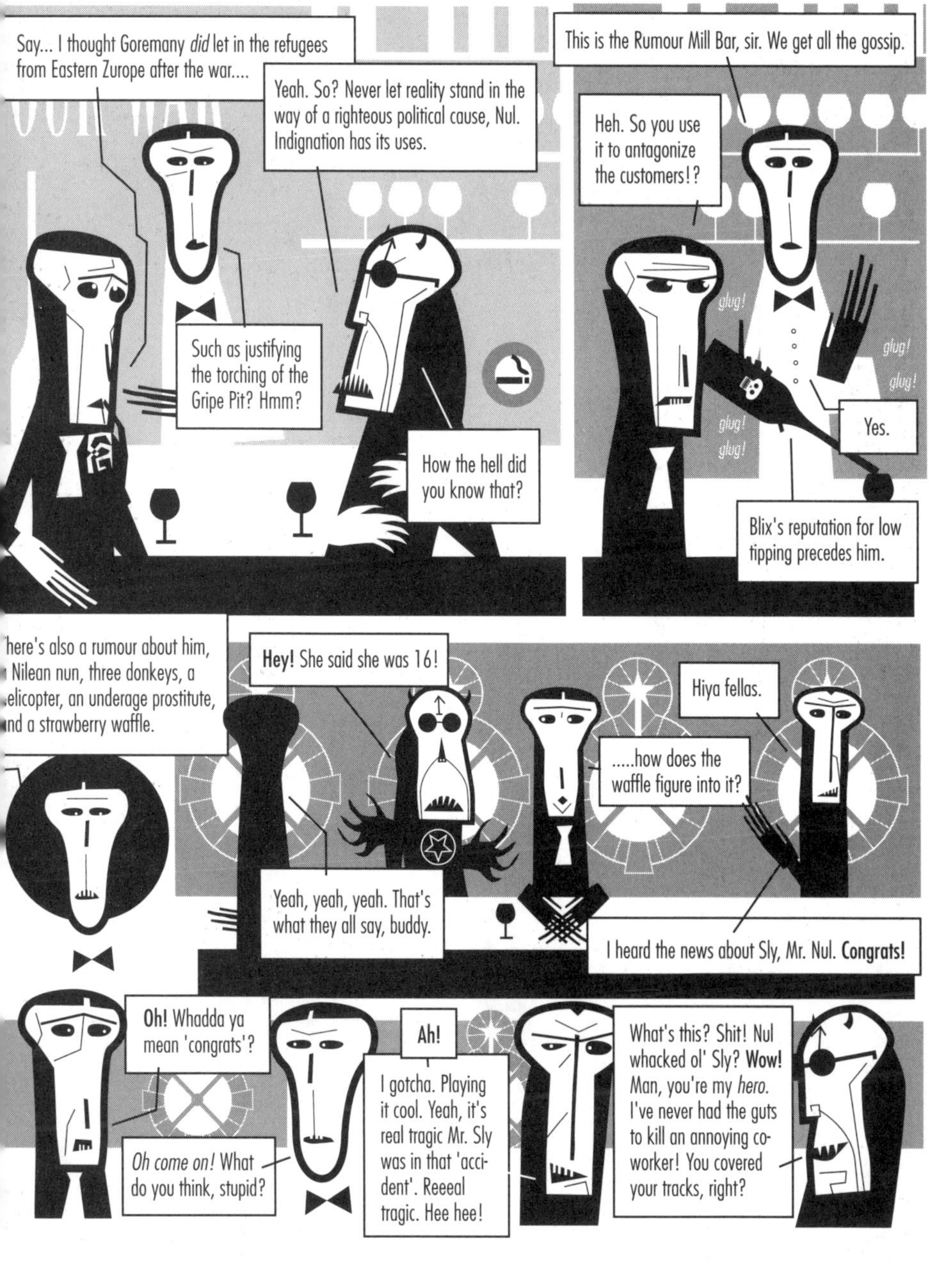
Say... I thought Goremany *did* let in the refugees from Eastern Zurope after the war....
Yeah. So? Never let reality stand in the way of a righteous political cause, Nul. Indignation has its uses.
Such as justifying the torching of the Gripe Pit? Hmm?
How the hell did you know that?
This is the Rumour Mill Bar, sir. We get all the gossip.
Heh. So you use it to antagonize the customers!?
glug!
glug!
glug!
glug!
glug!
Yes.
Blix's reputation for low tipping precedes him.
here's also a rumour about him, Nilean nun, three donkeys, a elicopter, an underage prostitute, nd a strawberry waffle.
Hey! She said she was 16!
Yeah, yeah, yeah. That's what they all say, buddy.
.....how does the waffle figure into it?
Hiya fellas.
I heard the news about Sly, Mr. Nul. **Congrats!**
Oh! Whadda ya mean 'congrats'?
Oh come on! What do you think, stupid?
Ah!
I gotcha. Playing it cool. Yeah, it's real tragic Mr. Sly was in that 'accident'. Reeeal tragic. Hee hee!
What's this? Shit! Nul whacked ol' Sly? **Wow!** Man, you're my *hero.* I've never had the guts to kill an annoying co-worker! You covered your tracks, right?

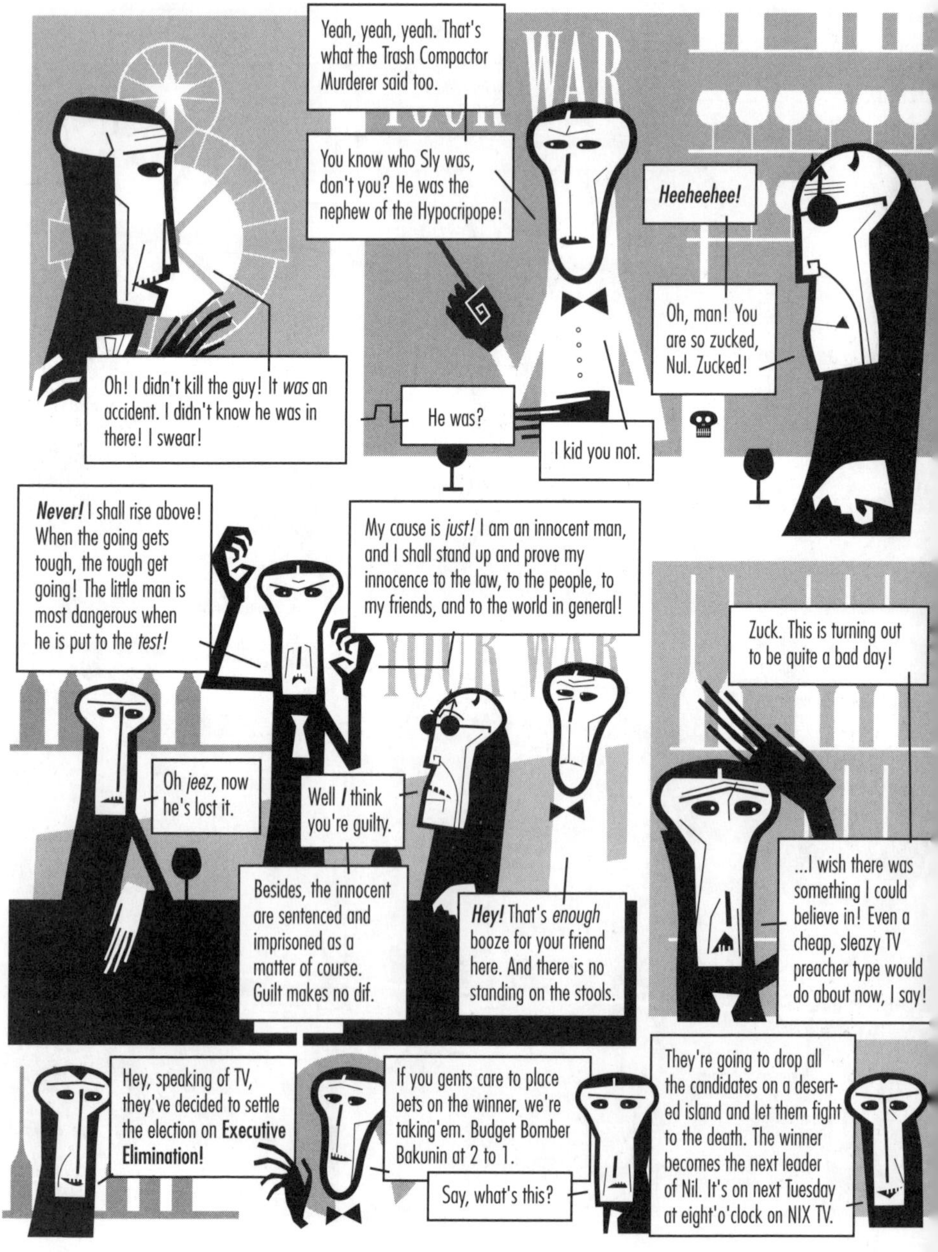

Yeah, yeah, yeah. That's what the Trash Compactor Murderer said too.
You know who Sly was, don't you? He was the nephew of the Hypocripope!
Heeheehee!
Oh! I didn't kill the guy! It *was* an accident. I didn't know he was in there! I swear!
He was?
I kid you not.
Oh, man! You are so zucked, Nul. Zucked!
YOUR WAR
Never! I shall rise above! When the going gets tough, the tough get going! The little man is most dangerous when he is put to the *test!*
My cause is *just!* I am an innocent man, and I shall stand up and prove my innocence to the law, to the people, to my friends, and to the world in general!
Zuck. This is turning out to be quite a bad day!
Oh *jeez,* now he's lost it.
Well ***I*** think you're guilty.
Besides, the innocent are sentenced and imprisoned as a matter of course. Guilt makes no dif.
Hey! That's *enough* booze for your friend here. And there is no standing on the stools.
...I wish there was something I could believe in! Even a cheap, sleazy TV preacher type would do about now, I say!
Hey, speaking of TV, they've decided to settle the election on **Executive Elimination!**
If you gents care to place bets on the winner, we're taking'em. Budget Bomber Bakunin at 2 to 1.
Say, what's this?
They're going to drop all the candidates on a desert-ed island and let them fight to the death. The winner becomes the next leader of Nil. It's on next Tuesday at eight'o'clock on NIX TV.

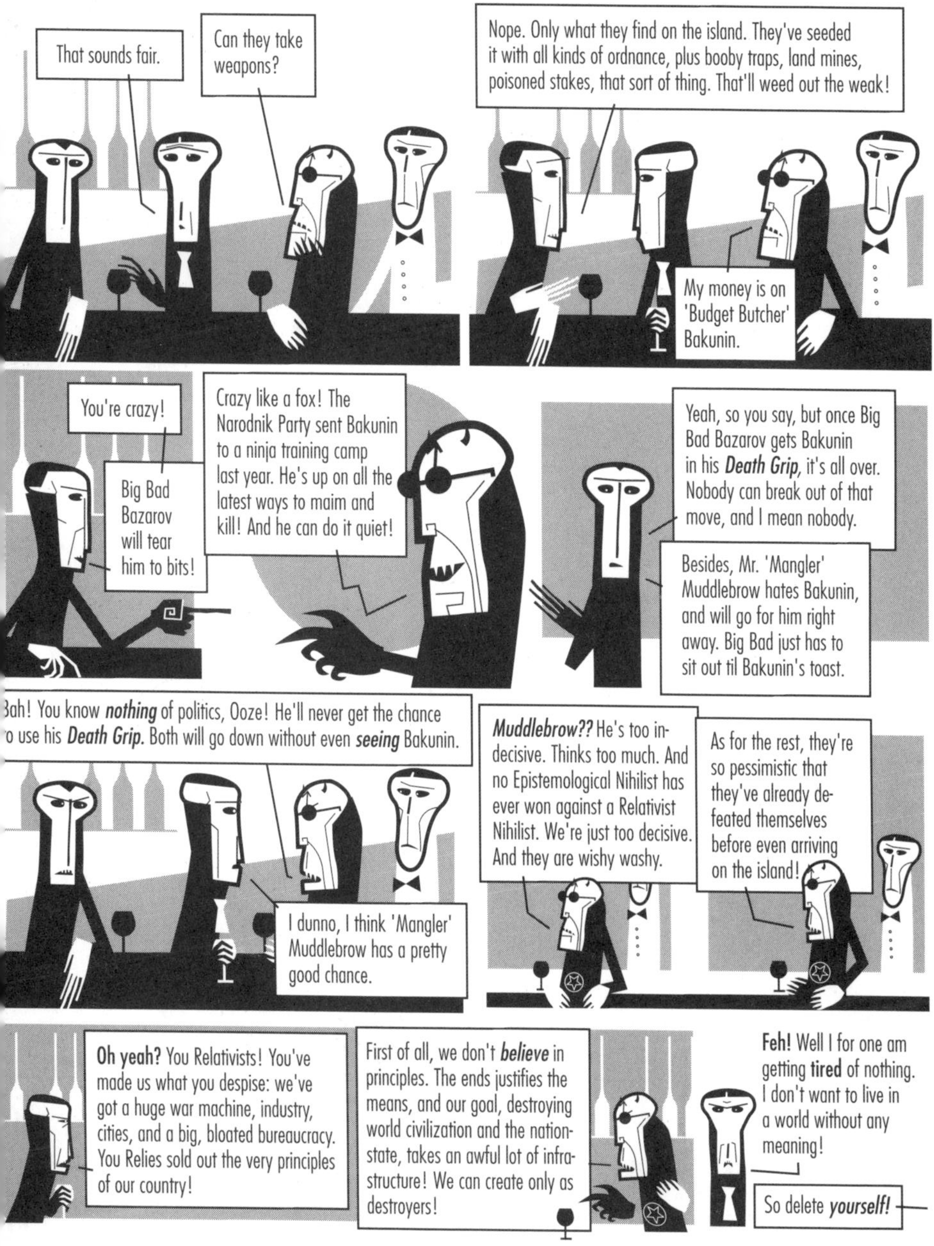
That sounds fair.
Can they take weapons?
Nope. Only what they find on the island. They've seeded it with all kinds of ordnance, plus booby traps, land mines, poisoned stakes, that sort of thing. That'll weed out the weak!
My money is on 'Budget Butcher' Bakunin.
You're crazy!
Big Bad Bazarov will tear him to bits!
Crazy like a fox! The Narodnik Party sent Bakunin to a ninja training camp last year. He's up on all the latest ways to maim and kill! And he can do it quiet!
Yeah, so you say, but once Big Bad Bazarov gets Bakunin in his ***Death Grip***, it's all over. Nobody can break out of that move, and I mean nobody.
Besides, Mr. 'Mangler' Muddlebrow hates Bakunin, and will go for him right away. Big Bad just has to sit out til Bakunin's toast.
Bah! You know ***nothing*** of politics, Ooze! He'll never get the chance to use his ***Death Grip***. Both will go down without even ***seeing*** Bakunin.
I dunno, I think 'Mangler' Muddlebrow has a pretty good chance.
Muddlebrow?? He's too indecisive. Thinks too much. And no Epistemological Nihilist has ever won against a Relativist Nihilist. We're just too decisive. And they are wishy washy.
As for the rest, they're so pessimistic that they've already defeated themselves before even arriving on the island!
Oh yeah? You Relativists! You've made us what you despise: we've got a huge war machine, industry, cities, and a big, bloated bureaucracy. You Relies sold out the very principles of our country!
First of all, we don't ***believe*** in principles. The ends justifies the means, and our goal, destroying world civilization and the nation-state, takes an awful lot of infrastructure! We can create only as destroyers!
Feh! Well I for one am getting **tired** of nothing. I don't want to live in a world without any meaning!
So delete ***yourself!***

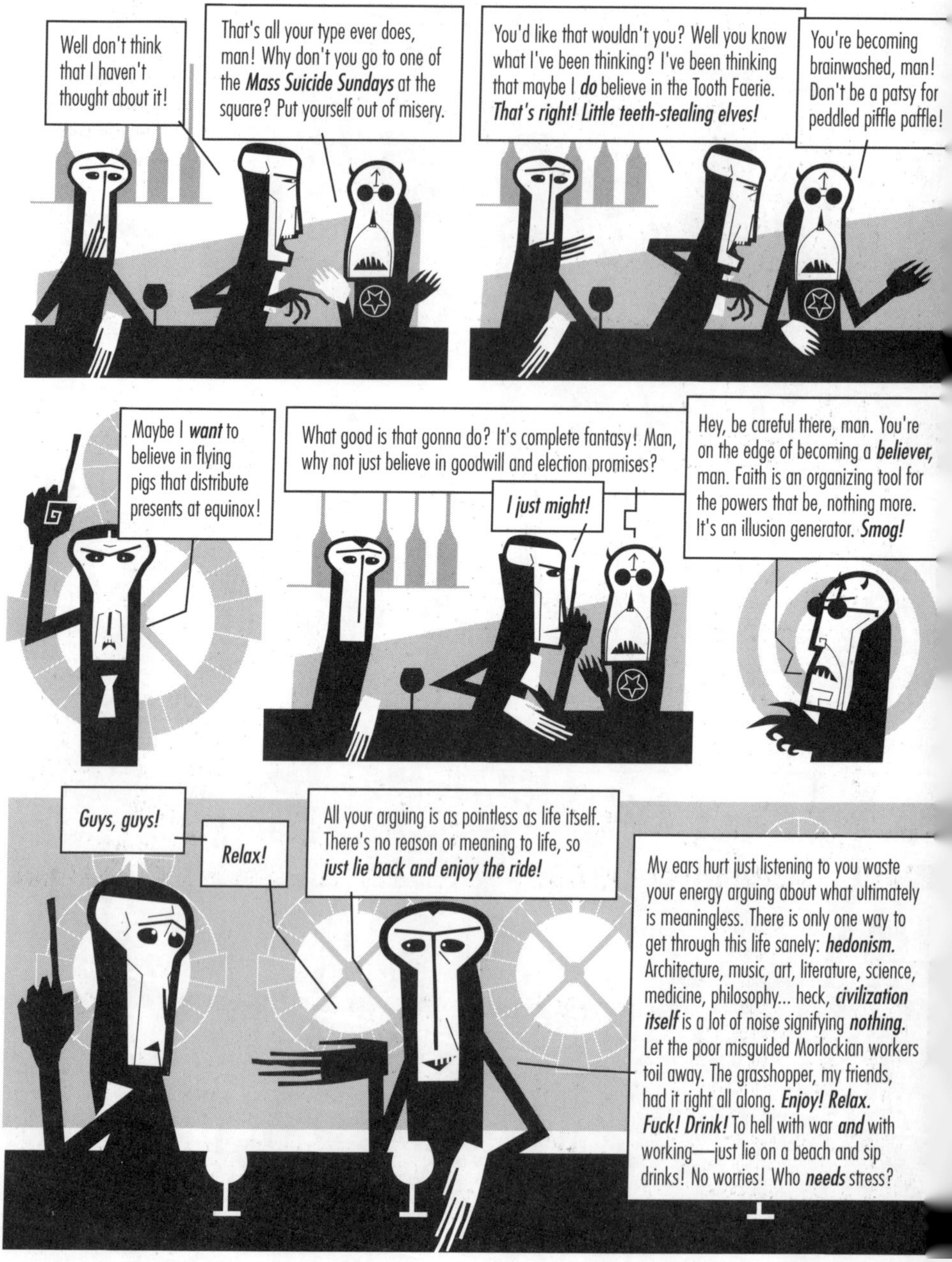

Well don't think that I haven't thought about it!
That's all your type ever does, man! Why don't you go to one of the Mass Suicide Sundays at the square? Put yourself out of misery.
You'd like that wouldn't you? Well you know what I've been thinking? I've been thinking that maybe I do believe in the Tooth Faerie. That's right! Little teeth-stealing elves!
You're becoming brainwashed, man! Don't be a patsy for peddled piffle paffle!
Maybe I want to believe in flying pigs that distribute presents at equinox!
What good is that gonna do? It's complete fantasy! Man, why not just believe in goodwill and election promises?
I just might!
Hey, be careful there, man. You're on the edge of becoming a believer, man. Faith is an organizing tool for the powers that be, nothing more. It's an illusion generator. Smog!
Guys, guys!
Relax!
All your arguing is as pointless as life itself. There's no reason or meaning to life, so just lie back and enjoy the ride!
My ears hurt just listening to you waste your energy arguing about what ultimately is meaningless. There is only one way to get through this life sanely: hedonism. Architecture, music, art, literature, science, medicine, philosophy... heck, civilization itself is a lot of noise signifying nothing. Let the poor misguided Morlockian workers toil away. The grasshopper, my friends, had it right all along. Enjoy! Relax. Fuck! Drink! To hell with war and with working—just lie on a beach and sip drinks! No worries! Who needs stress?

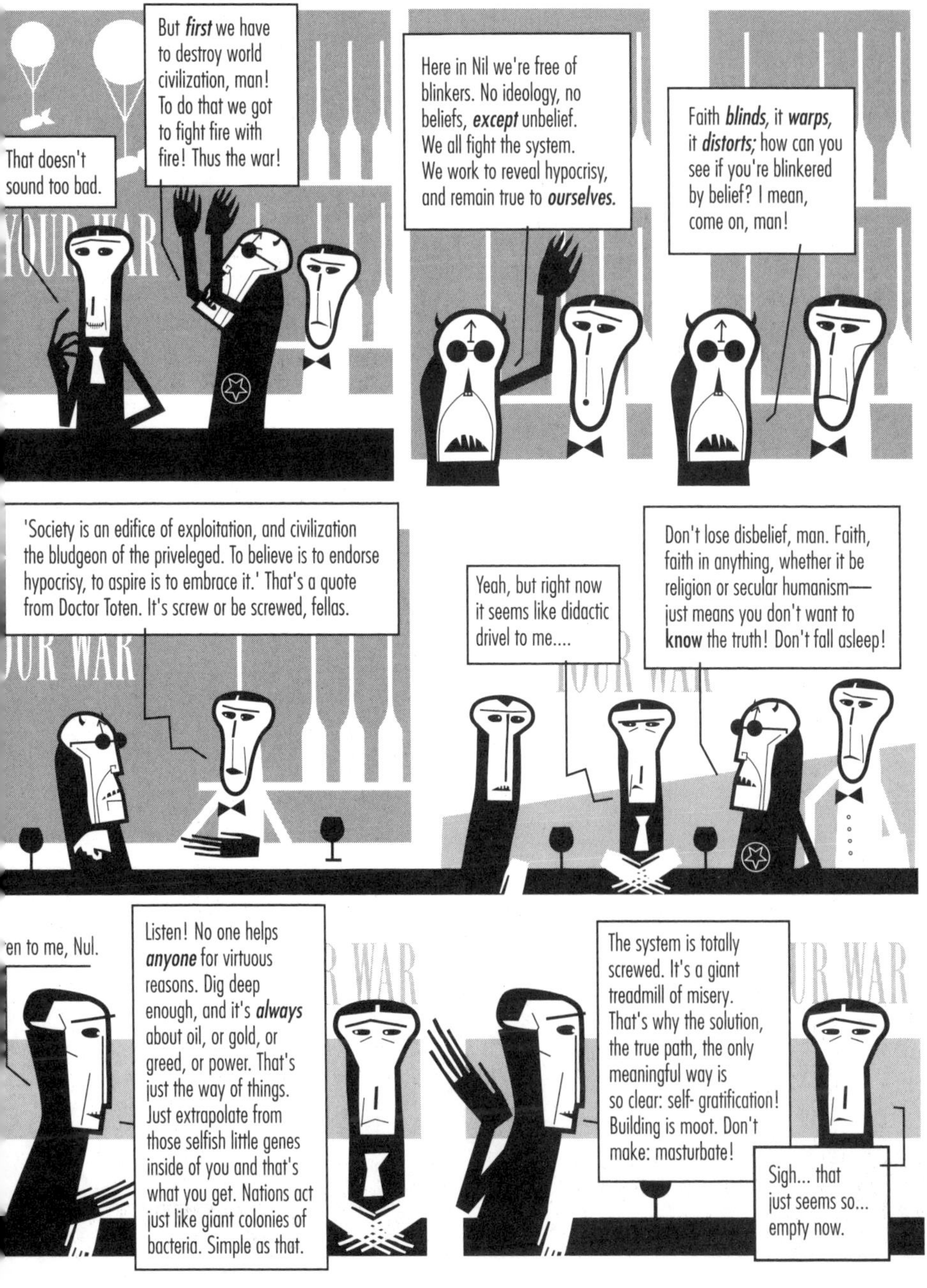
That doesn't sound too bad.
But *first* we have to destroy world civilization, man! To do that we got to fight fire with fire! Thus the war!
Here in Nil we're free of blinkers. No ideology, no beliefs, *except* unbelief. We all fight the system. We work to reveal hypocrisy, and remain true to *ourselves.*
Faith *blinds*, it *warps*, it *distorts;* how can you see if you're blinkered by belief? I mean, come on, man!
'Society is an edifice of exploitation, and civilization the bludgeon of the priveleged. To believe is to endorse hypocrisy, to aspire is to embrace it.' That's a quote from Doctor Toten. It's screw or be screwed, fellas.
Yeah, but right now it seems like didactic drivel to me....
Don't lose disbelief, man. Faith, faith in anything, whether it be religion or secular humanism—just means you don't want to **know** the truth! Don't fall asleep!
en to me, Nul.
Listen! No one helps *anyone* for virtuous reasons. Dig deep enough, and it's *always* about oil, or gold, or greed, or power. That's just the way of things. Just extrapolate from those selfish little genes inside of you and that's what you get. Nations act just like giant colonies of bacteria. Simple as that.
The system is totally screwed. It's a giant treadmill of misery. That's why the solution, the true path, the only meaningful way is so clear: self- gratification! Building is moot. Don't make: masturbate!
Sigh... that just seems so... empty now.

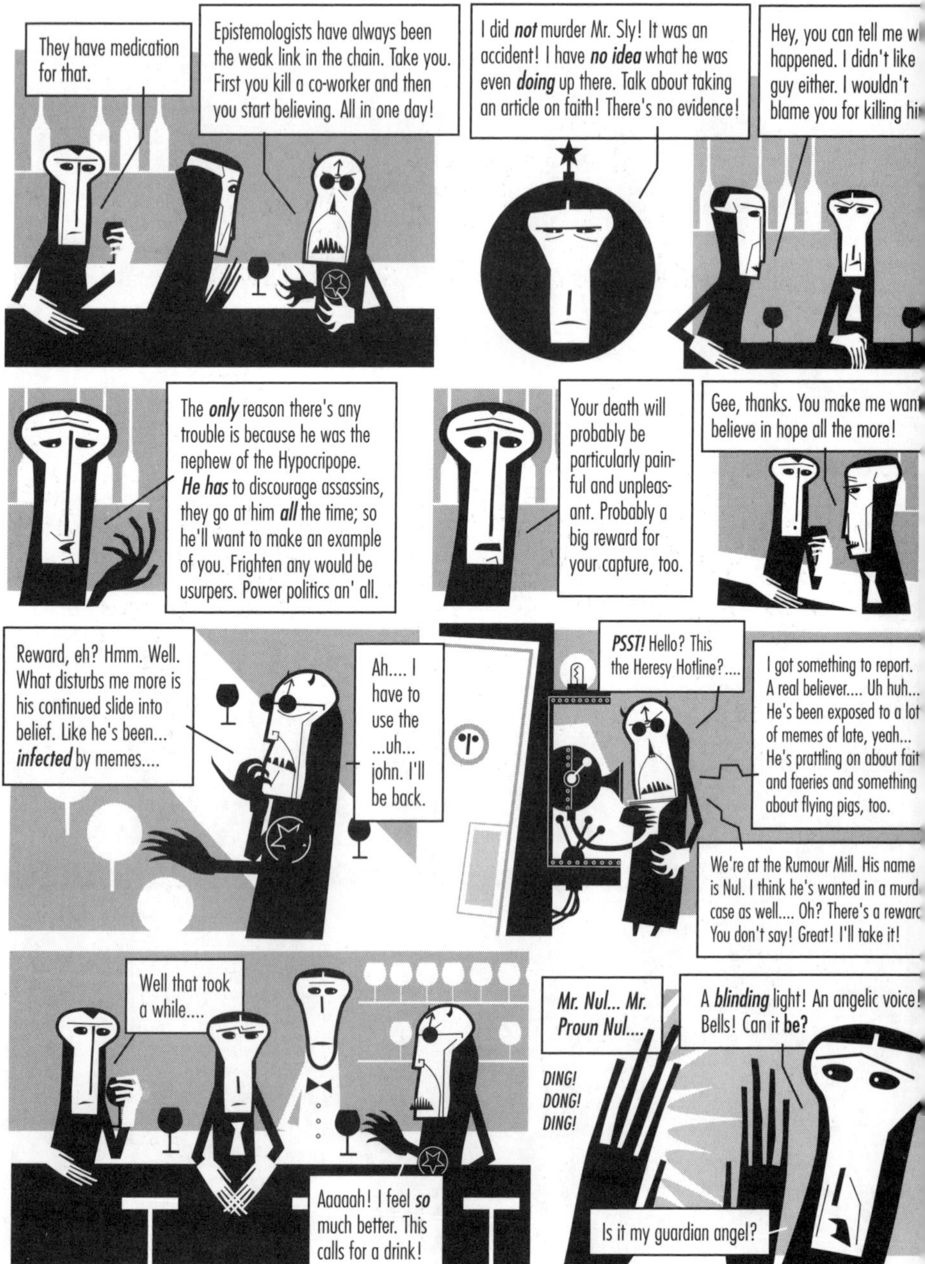

They have medication for that.
Epistemologists have always been the weak link in the chain. Take you. First you kill a co-worker and then you start believing. All in one day!
I did *not* murder Mr. Sly! It was an accident! I have *no idea* what he was even *doing* up there. Talk about taking an article on faith! There's no evidence!
Hey, you can tell me w happened. I didn't like guy either. I wouldn't blame you for killing hi
The *only* reason there's any trouble is because he was the nephew of the Hypocripope. *He has* to discourage assassins, they go at him *all* the time; so he'll want to make an example of you. Frighten any would be usurpers. Power politics an' all.
Your death will probably be particularly painful and unpleasant. Probably a big reward for your capture, too.
Gee, thanks. You make me wan believe in hope all the more!
Reward, eh? Hmm. Well. What disturbs me more is his continued slide into belief. Like he's been... *infected* by memes....
Ah.... I have to use the ...uh... john. I'll be back.
PSST! Hello? This the Heresy Hotline?....
I got something to report. A real believer.... Uh huh... He's been exposed to a lot of memes of late, yeah... He's prattling on about fait and faeries and something about flying pigs, too.
We're at the Rumour Mill. His name is Nul. I think he's wanted in a murd case as well.... Oh? There's a rewar You don't say! Great! I'll take it!
Well that took a while....
Aaaaah! I feel *so* much better. This calls for a drink!
Mr. Nul... Mr. Proun Nul....
A *blinding* light! An angelic voice! Bells! Can it **be?**
DING! DONG! DING!
Is it my guardian angel?

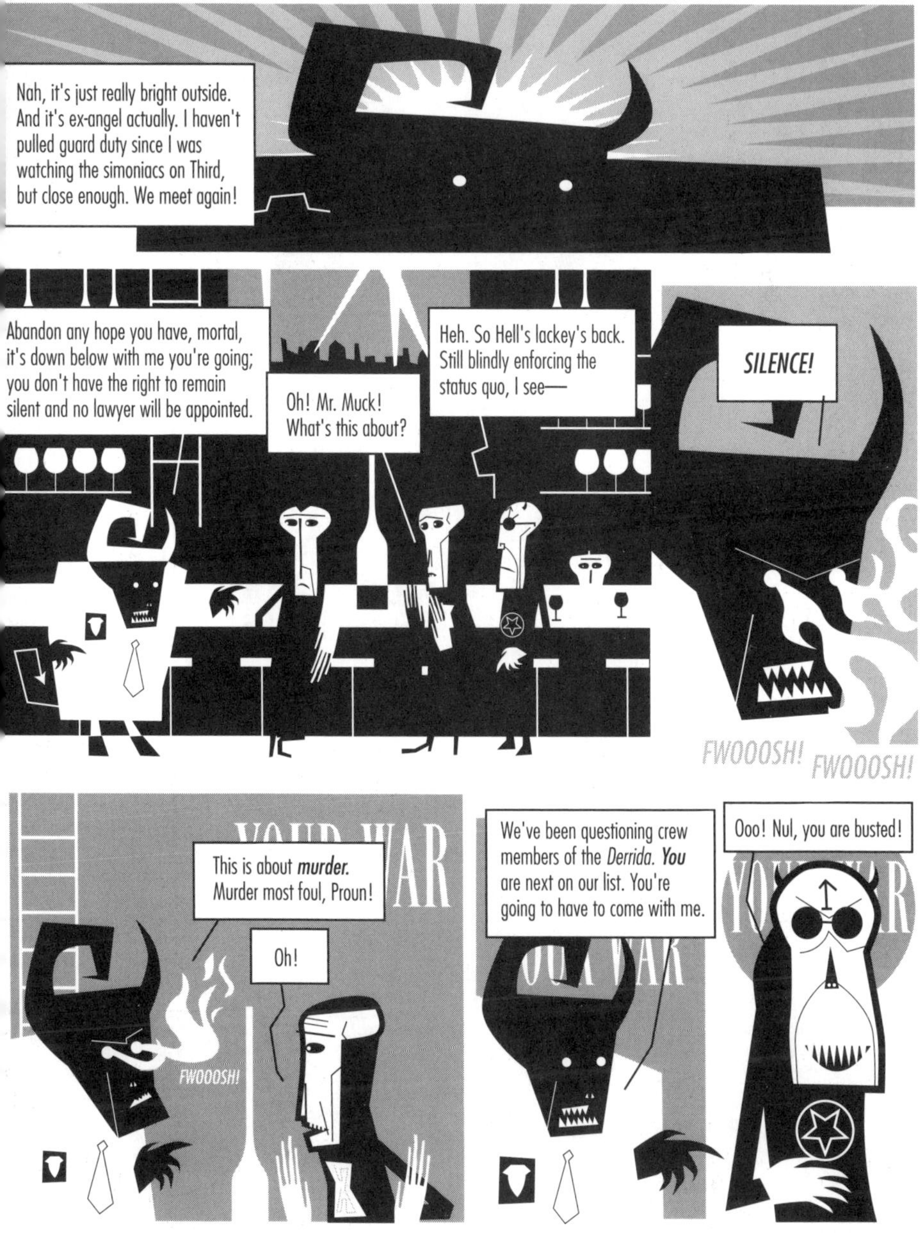
Nah, it's just really bright outside. And it's ex-angel actually. I haven't pulled guard duty since I was watching the simoniacs on Third, but close enough. We meet again!
Abandon any hope you have, mortal, it's down below with me you're going; you don't have the right to remain silent and no lawyer will be appointed.
Oh! Mr. Muck! What's this about?
Heh. So Hell's lackey's back. Still blindly enforcing the status quo, I see—
SILENCE!
FWOOOSH! FWOOOSH!
This is about *murder.* Murder most foul, Proun!
Oh!
FWOOOSH!
We've been questioning crew members of the *Derrida.* ***You*** are next on our list. You're going to have to come with me.
Ooo! Nul, you are busted!

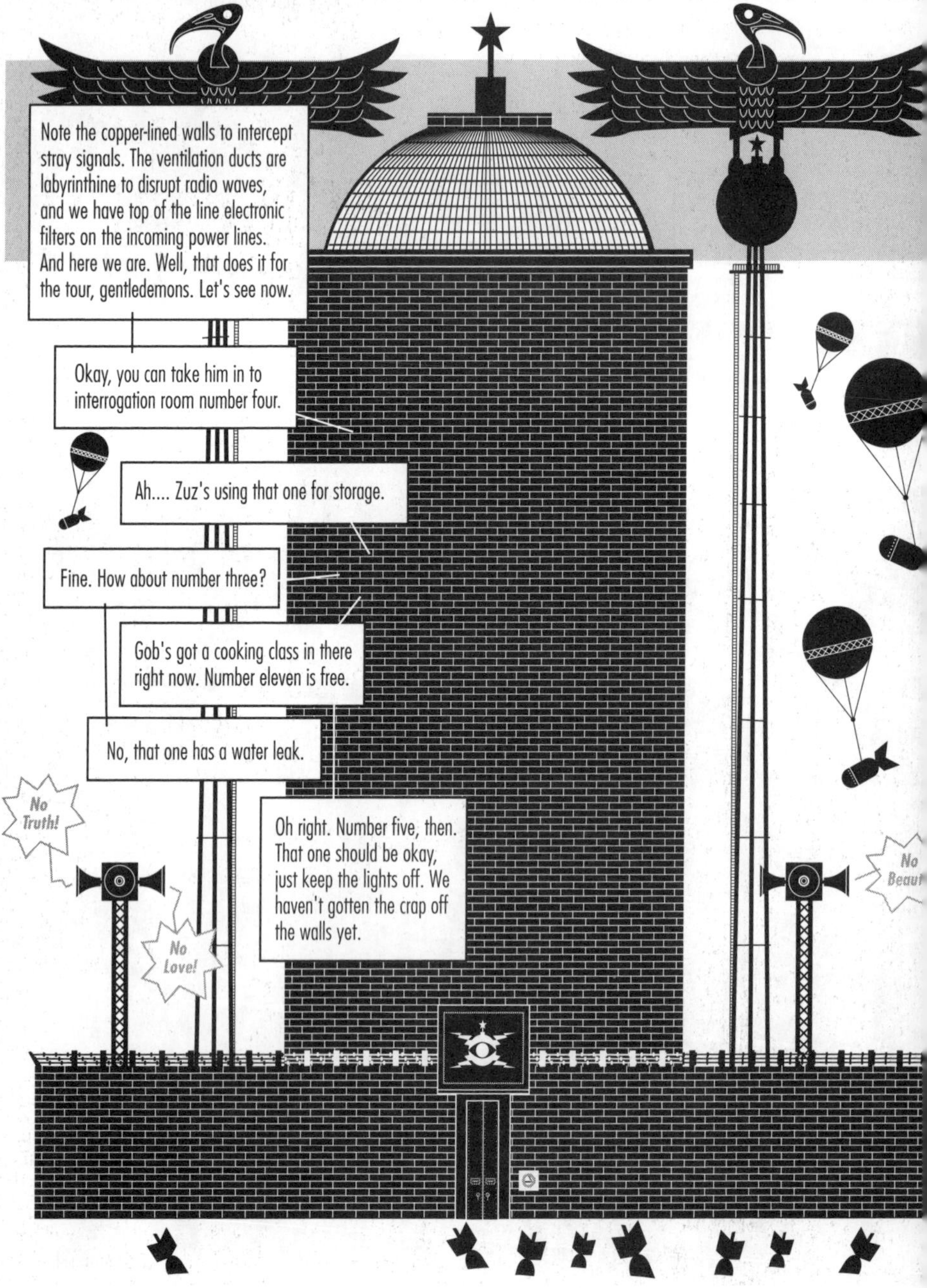
Note the copper-lined walls to intercept stray signals. The ventilation ducts are labyrinthine to disrupt radio waves, and we have top of the line electronic filters on the incoming power lines. And here we are. Well, that does it for the tour, gentledemons. Let's see now.
Okay, you can take him in to interrogation room number four.
Ah.... Zuz's using that one for storage.
Fine. How about number three?
Gob's got a cooking class in there right now. Number eleven is free.
No, that one has a water leak.
Oh right. Number five, then. That one should be okay, just keep the lights off. We haven't gotten the crap off the walls yet.
No Truth!
No Love!

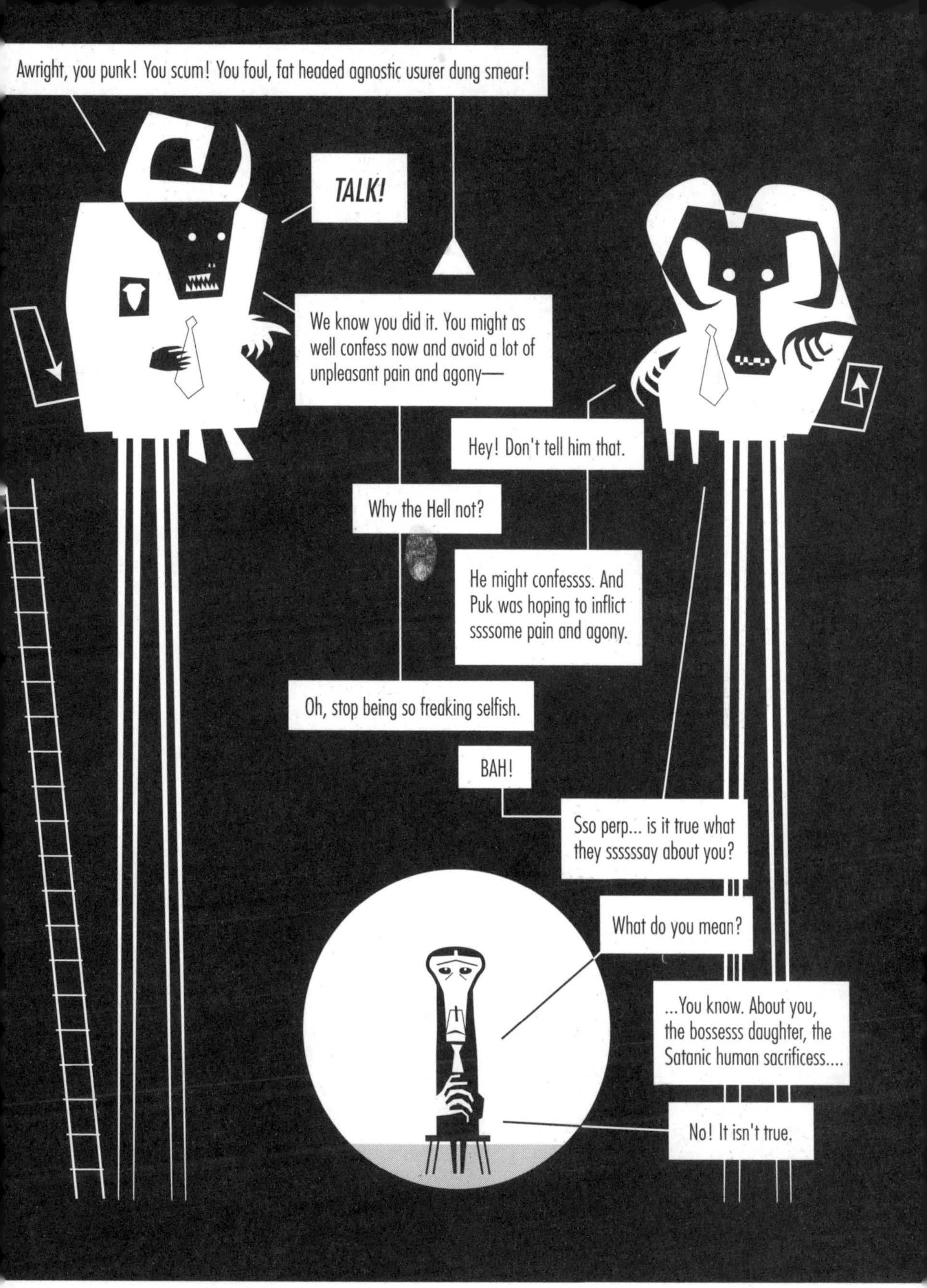
Awright, you punk! You scum! You foul, fat headed agnostic usurer dung smear!
TALK!
We know you did it. You might as well confess now and avoid a lot of unpleasant pain and agony—
Hey! Don't tell him that.
Why the Hell not?
He might confessss. And Puk was hoping to inflict sssome pain and agony.
Oh, stop being so freaking selfish.
BAH!
Sso perp... is it true what they sssssay about you?
What do you mean?
...You know. About you, the bossesss daughter, the Satanic human sacrificess....
No! It isn't true.

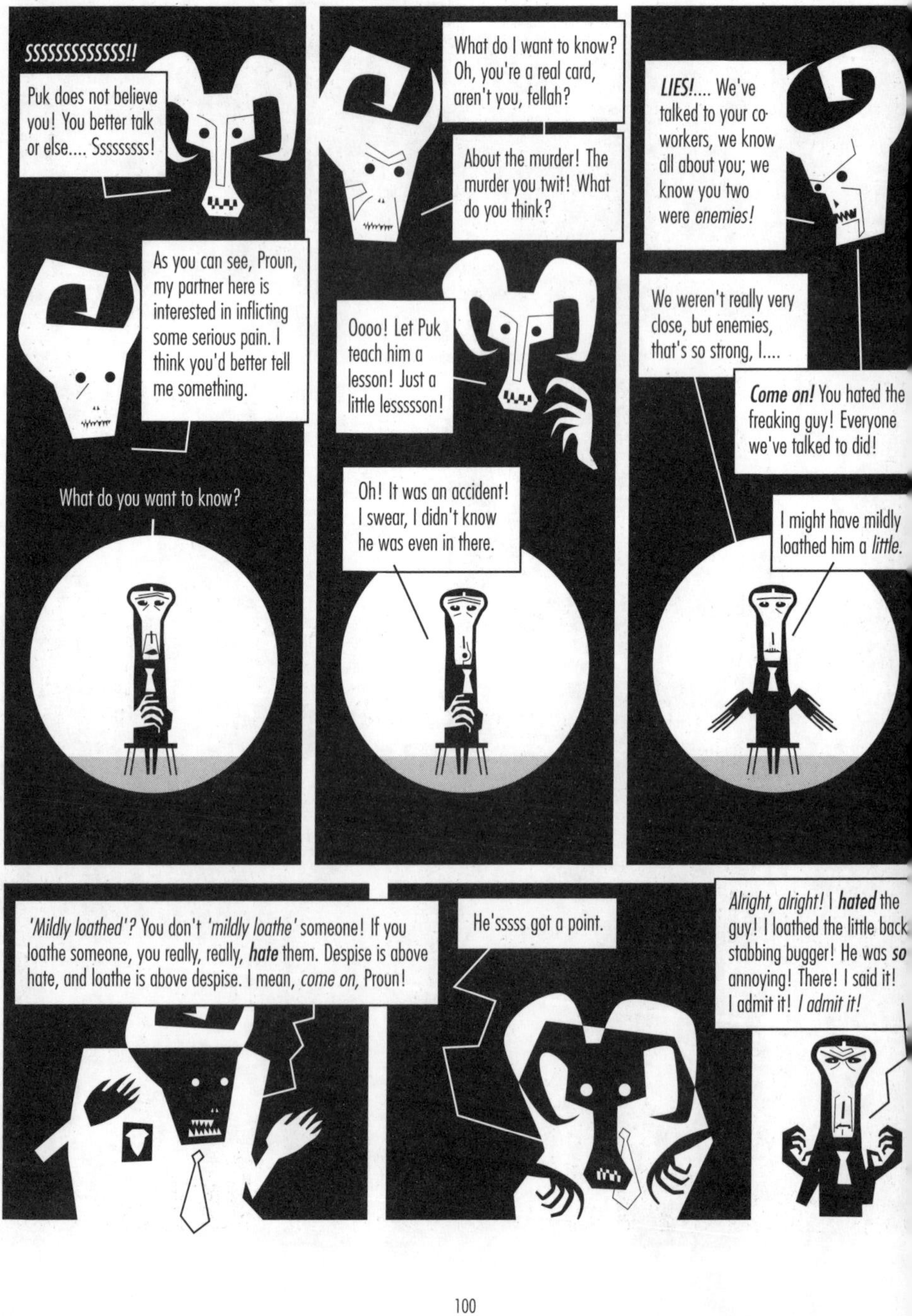
SSSSSSSSSSSSSS!!
Puk does not believe you! You better talk or else.... Sssssssss!
As you can see, Proun, my partner here is interested in inflicting some serious pain. I think you'd better tell me something.
What do you want to know?
What do I want to know? Oh, you're a real card, aren't you, fellah?
About the murder! The murder you twit! What do you think?
Oooo! Let Puk teach him a lesson! Just a little lessssson!
Oh! It was an accident! I swear, I didn't know he was even in there.
LIES!.... We've talked to your co-workers, we know all about you; we know you two were enemies!
We weren't really very close, but enemies, that's so strong, I....
Come on! You hated the freaking guy! Everyone we've talked to did!
I might have mildly loathed him a little.
'Mildly loathed'? You don't 'mildly loathe' someone! If you loathe someone, you really, really, hate them. Despise is above hate, and loathe is above despise. I mean, come on, Proun!
He'sssss got a point.
Alright, alright! I hated the guy! I loathed the little back stabbing bugger! He was so annoying! There! I said it! I admit it! I admit it!

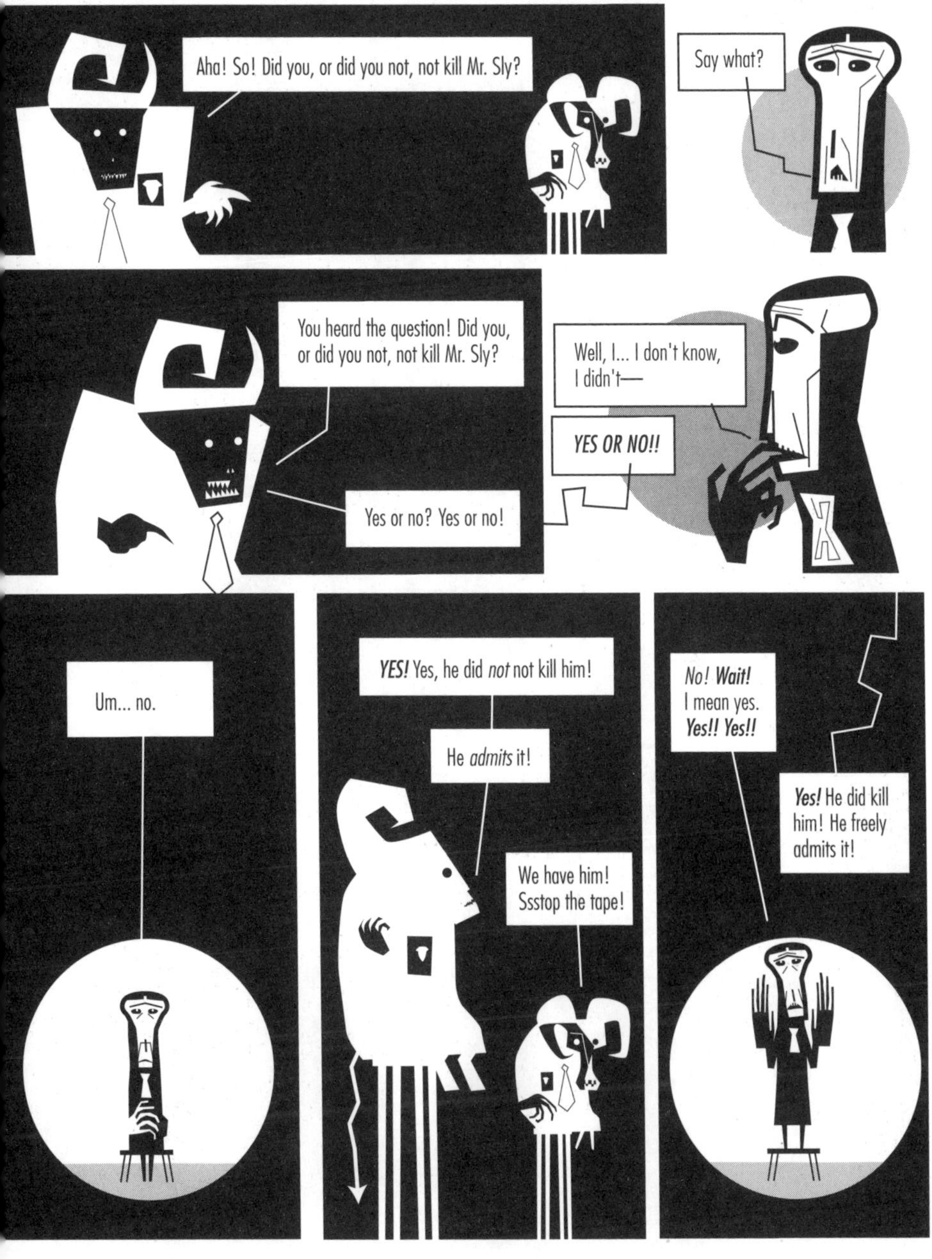
Aha! So! Did you, or did you not, not kill Mr. Sly?
Say what?
You heard the question! Did you, or did you not, not kill Mr. Sly?
Yes or no? Yes or no!
Well, I... I don't know, I didn't—
YES OR NO!!
Um... no.
YES! Yes, he did not not kill him!
He admits it!
We have him! Ssstop the tape!
No! Wait! I mean yes. Yes!! Yes!!
Yes! He did kill him! He freely admits it!

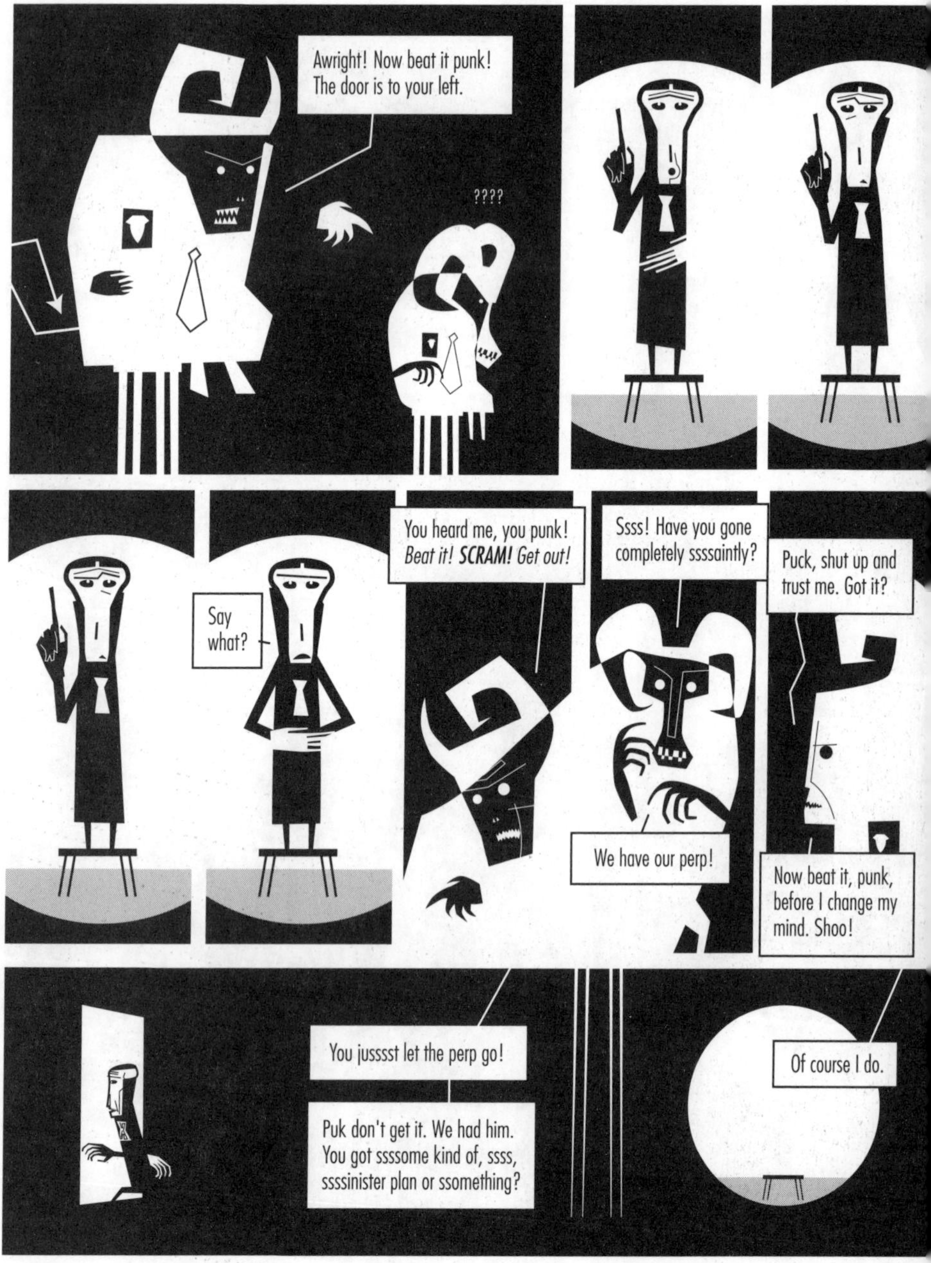

Awright! Now beat it punk! The door is to your left.
????
Say what?
You heard me, you punk! *Beat it! **SCRAM!** Get out!*
Ssss! Have you gone completely ssssaintly?
We have our perp!
Puck, shut up and trust me. Got it?
Now beat it, punk, before I change my mind. Shoo!
You jusssst let the perp go!
Puk don't get it. We had him. You got ssssome kind of, ssss, ssssinister plan or ssomething?
Of course I do.

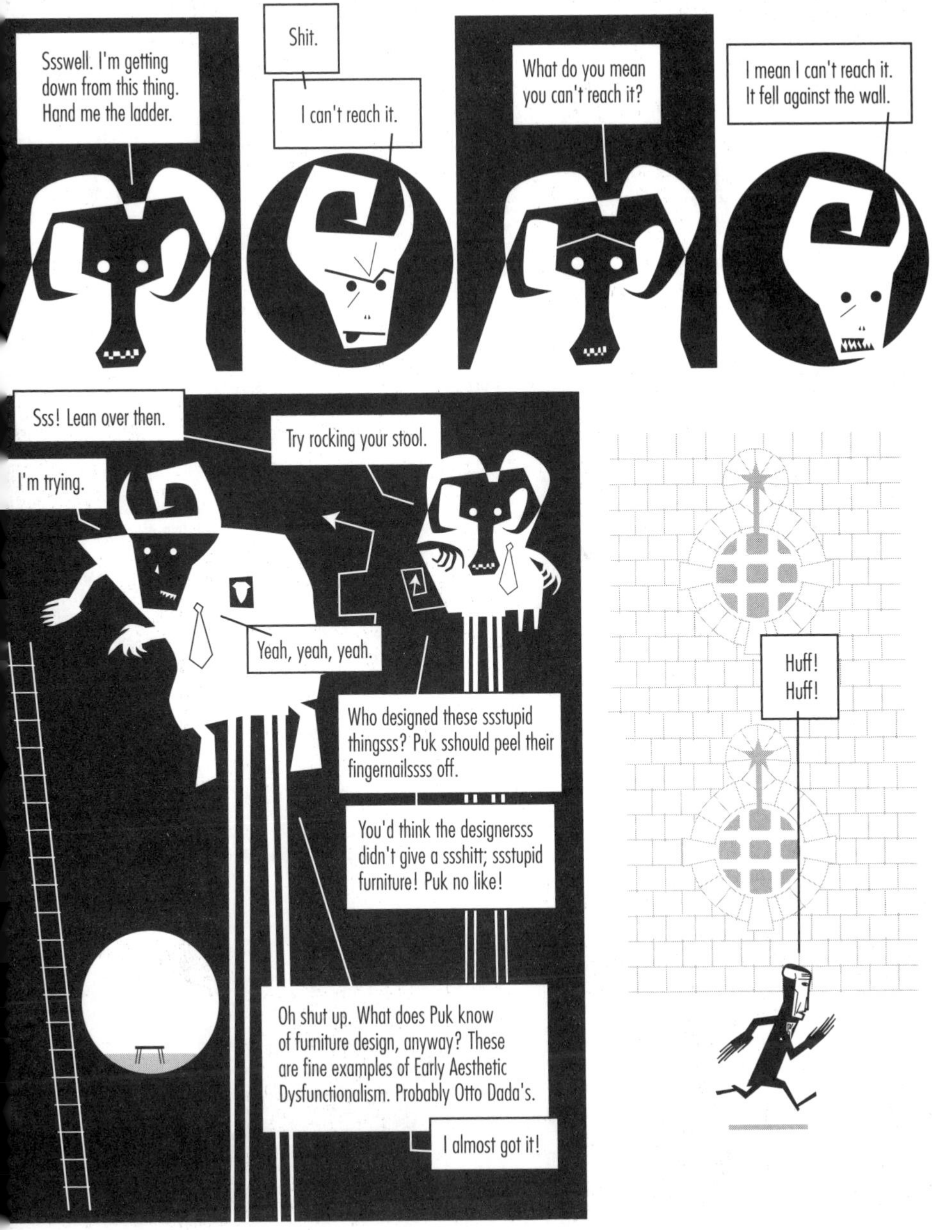

Ssswell. I'm getting down from this thing. Hand me the ladder.
Shit.
I can't reach it.
What do you mean you can't reach it?
I mean I can't reach it. It fell against the wall.
Sss! Lean over then.
Try rocking your stool.
I'm trying.
Yeah, yeah, yeah.
Who designed these ssstupid thingsss? Puk sshould peel their fingernailssss off.
You'd think the designersss didn't give a ssshitt; ssstupid furniture! Puk no like!
Oh shut up. What does Puk know of furniture design, anyway? These are fine examples of Early Aesthetic Dysfunctionalism. Probably Otto Dada's.
I almost got it!
Huff! Huff!

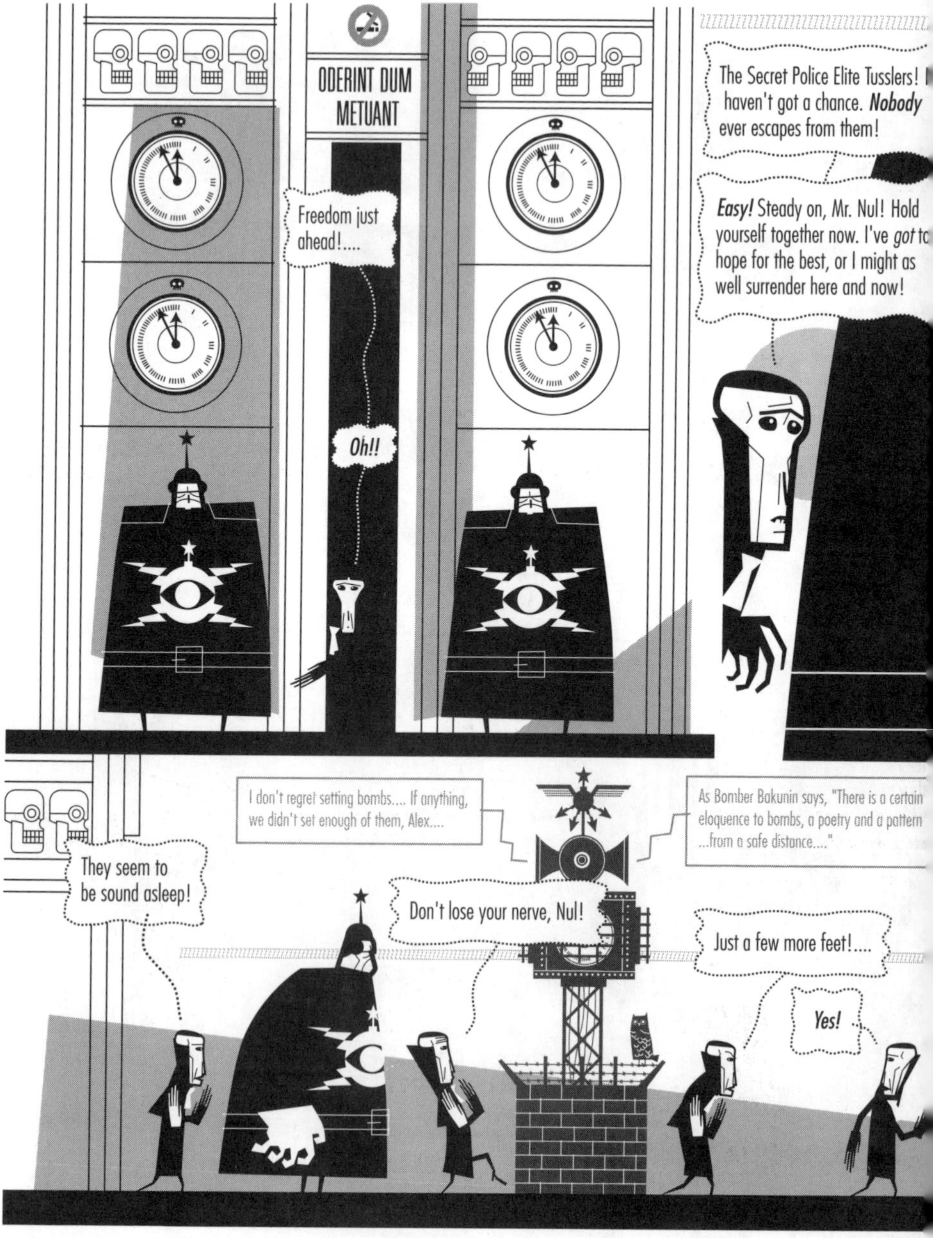
ODERINT DUM METUANT
Freedom just ahead!....
Oh!!
The Secret Police Elite Tusslers! I haven't got a chance. Nobody ever escapes from them!
Easy! Steady on, Mr. Nul! Hold yourself together now. I've got to hope for the best, or I might as well surrender here and now!
They seem to be sound asleep!
I don't regret setting bombs.... If anything, we didn't set enough of them, Alex....
As Bomber Bakunin says, "There is a certain eloquence to bombs, a poetry and a pattern ...from a safe distance...."
Don't lose your nerve, Nul!
Just a few more feet!....
Yes!

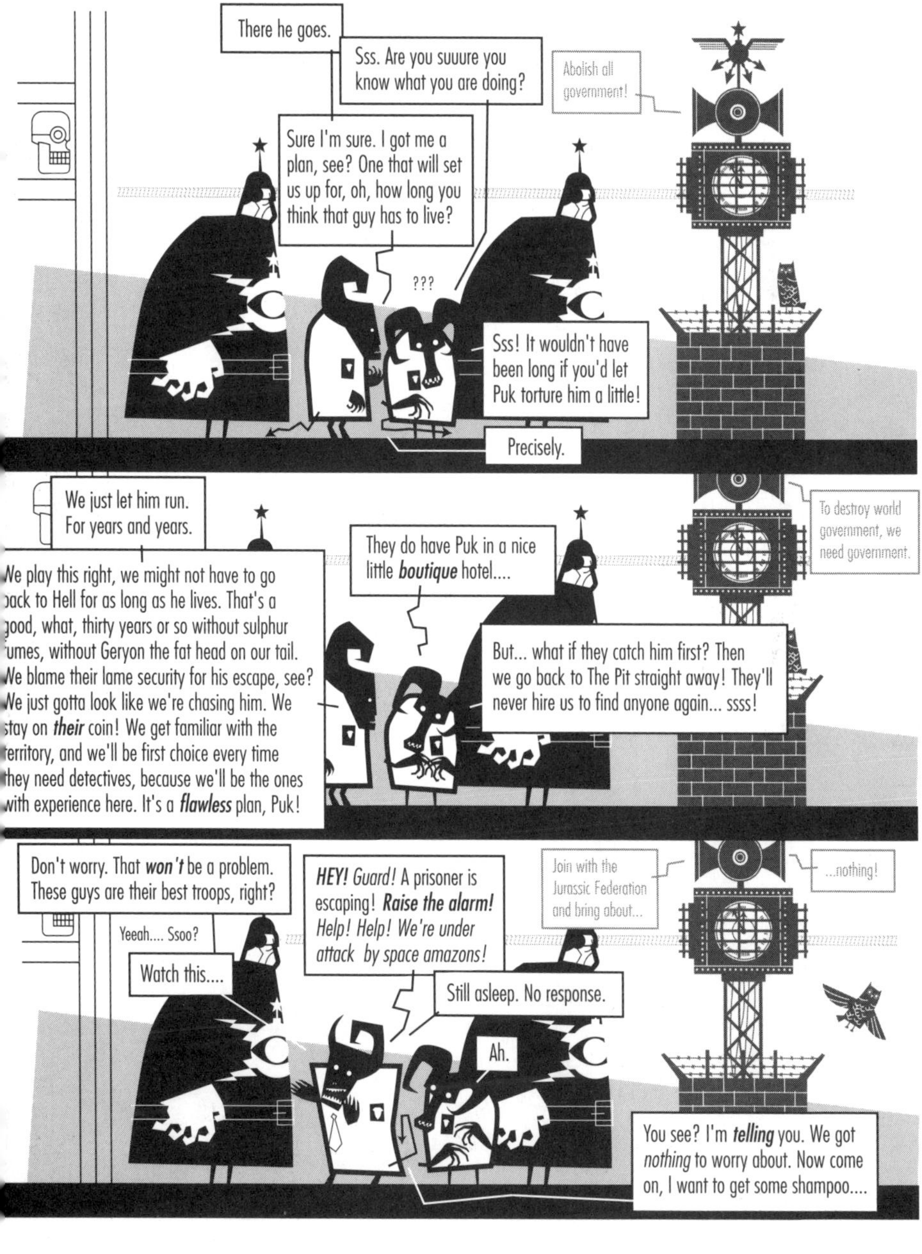
There he goes.
Sss. Are you suuure you know what you are doing?
Abolish all government!
Sure I'm sure. I got me a plan, see? One that will set us up for, oh, how long you think that guy has to live?
???
Sss! It wouldn't have been long if you'd let Puk torture him a little!
Precisely.
We just let him run. For years and years.
To destroy world government, we need government.
Ve play this right, we might not have to go
ack to Hell for as long as he lives. That's a
ood, what, thirty years or so without sulphur
umes, without Geryon the fat head on our tail.
Ve blame their lame security for his escape, see?
Ve just gotta look like we're chasing him. We
tay on *their* coin! We get familiar with the
erritory, and we'll be first choice every time
hey need detectives, because we'll be the ones
vith experience here. It's a *flawless* plan, Puk!
They do have Puk in a nice little *boutique* hotel....
But... what if they catch him first? Then we go back to The Pit straight away! They'll never hire us to find anyone again... ssss!
Don't worry. That *won't* be a problem. These guys are their best troops, right?
Yeeah.... Ssoo?
Watch this....
HEY! Guard! A prisoner is escaping! *Raise the alarm! Help! Help! We're under attack by space amazons!*
Join with the Jurassic Federation and bring about...
...nothing!
Still asleep. No response.
Ah.
You see? I'm *telling* you. We got *nothing* to worry about. Now come on, I want to get some shampoo....

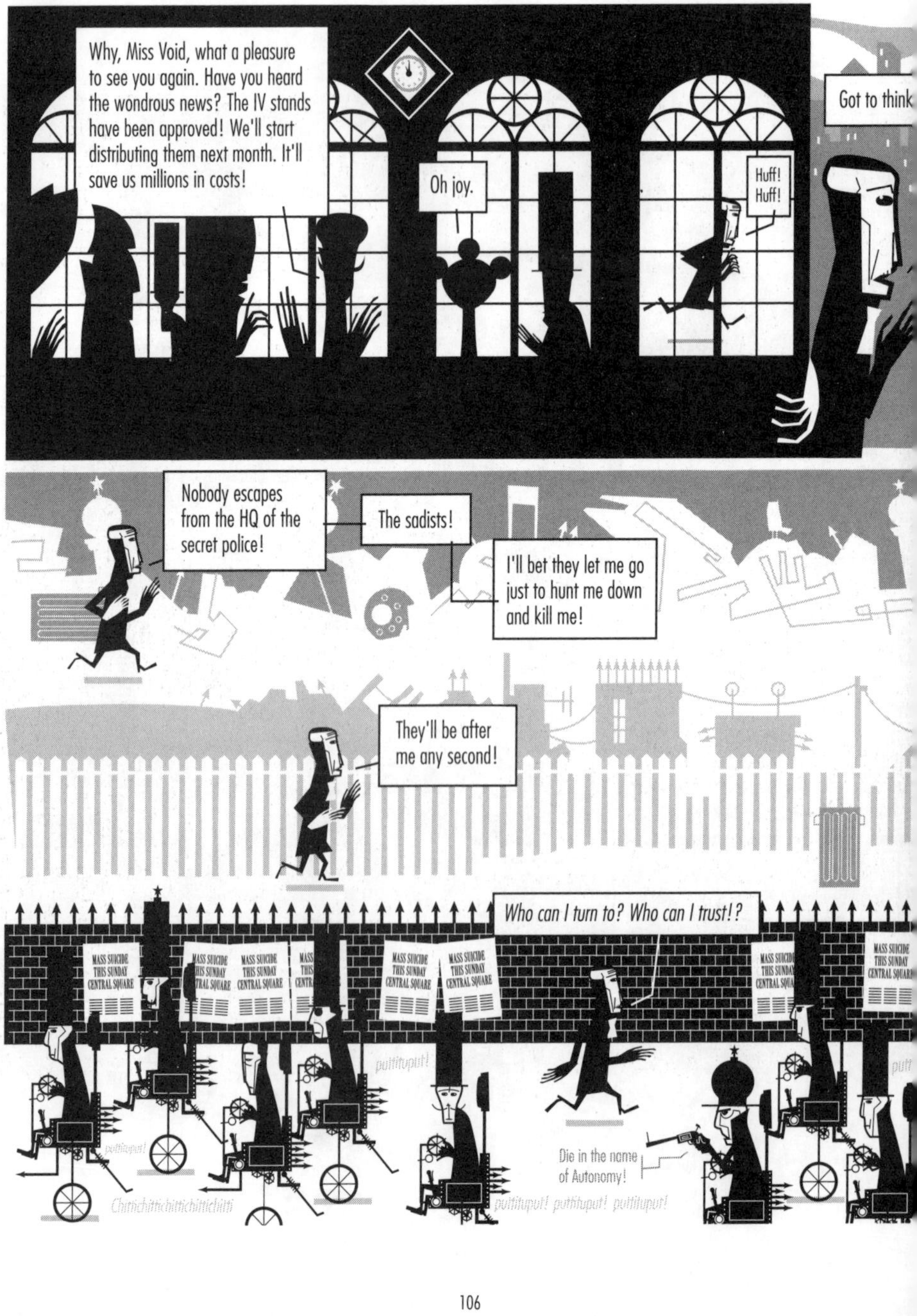
Why, Miss Void, what a pleasure to see you again. Have you heard the wondrous news? The IV stands have been approved! We'll start distributing them next month. It'll save us millions in costs!
Oh joy.
Huff! Huff!
Got to think
Nobody escapes from the HQ of the secret police!
The sadists!
I'll bet they let me go just to hunt me down and kill me!
They'll be after me any second!
Who can I turn to? Who can I trust!?
MASS SUICIDE THIS SUNDAY CENTRAL SQUARE
Die in the name of Autonomy!

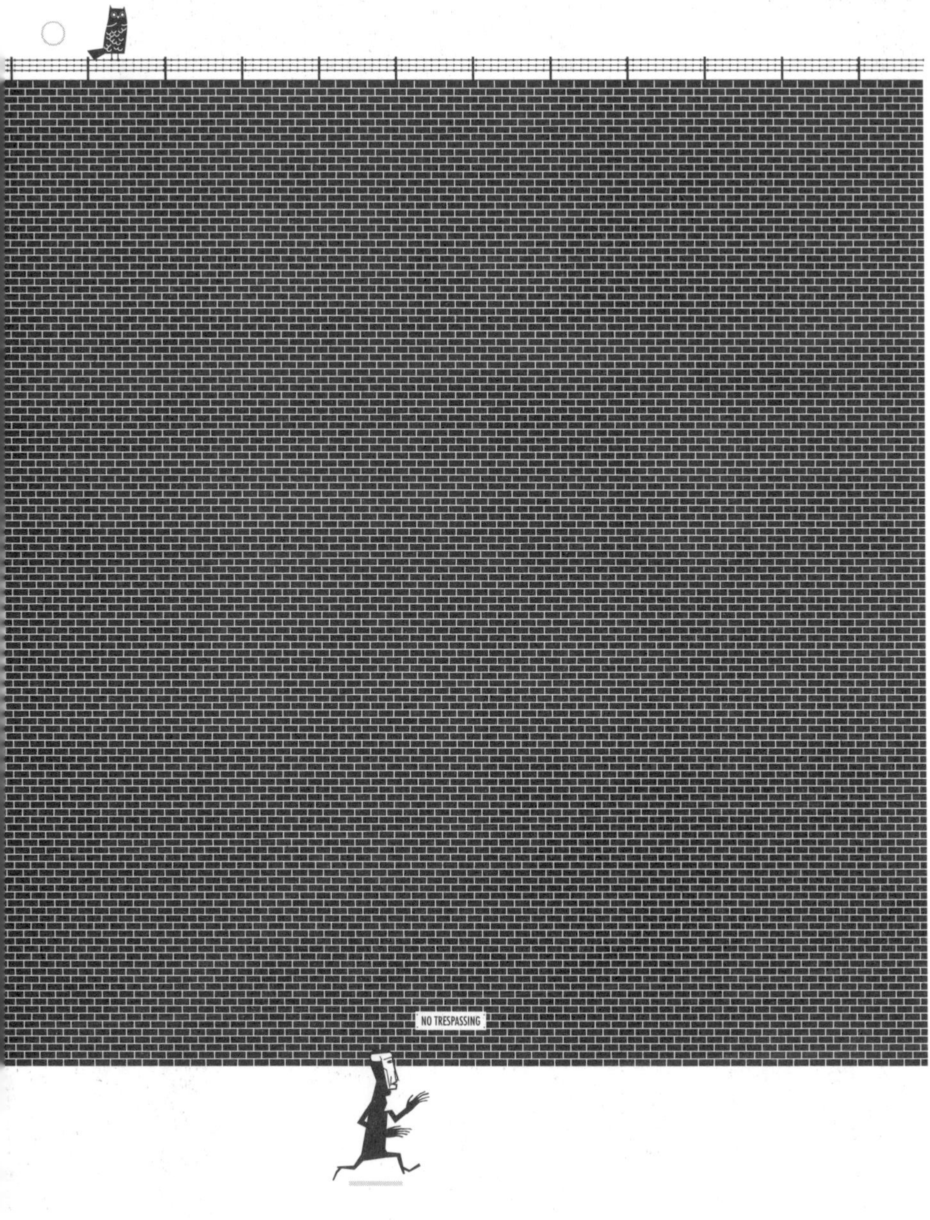

NO TRESPASSING

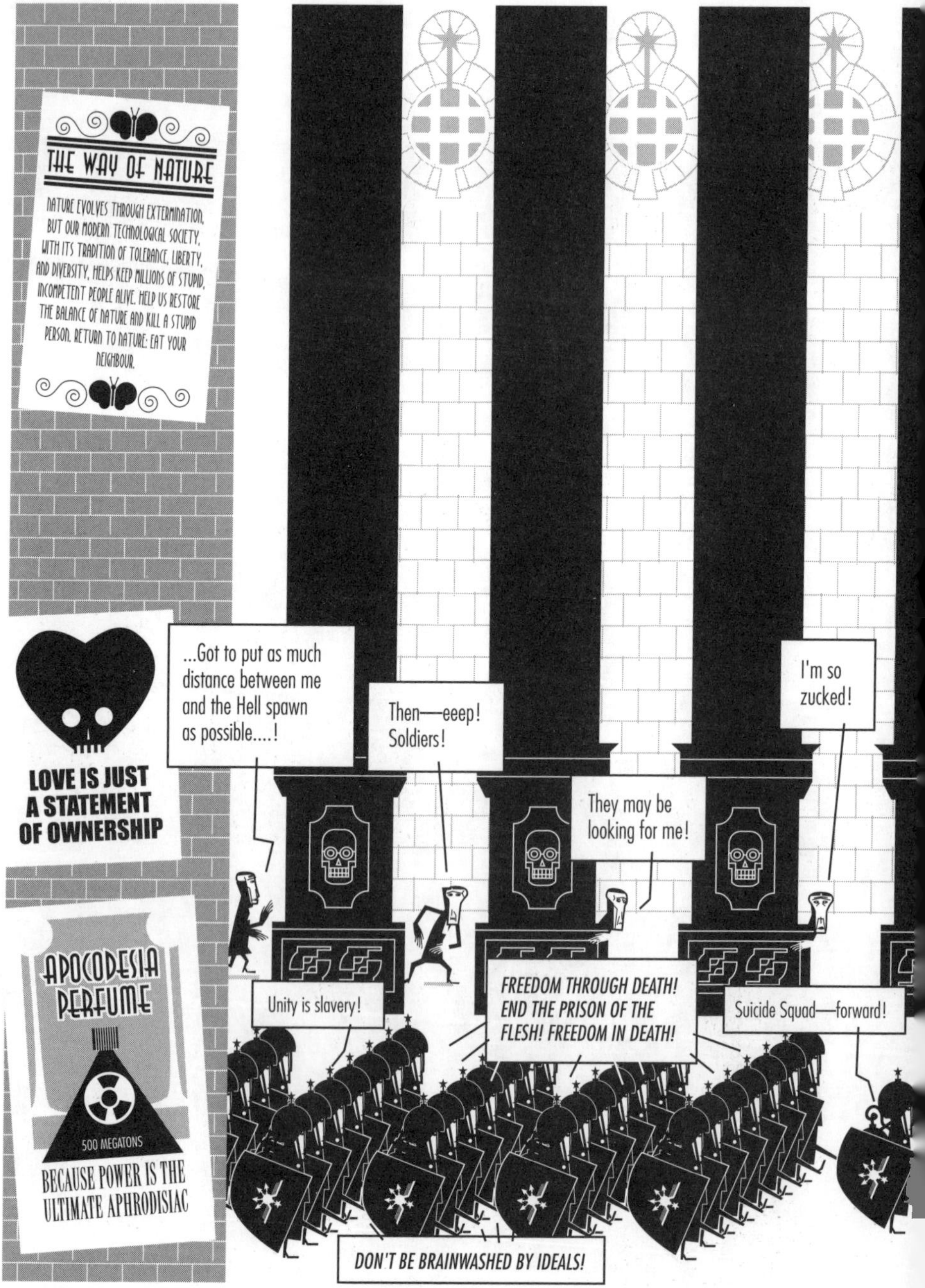
THE WAY OF NATURE
NATURE EVOLVES THROUGH EXTERMINATION, BUT OUR MODERN TECHNOLOGICAL SOCIETY, WITH ITS TRADITION OF TOLERANCE, LIBERTY, AND DIVERSITY, HELPS KEEP MILLIONS OF STUPID, INCOMPETENT PEOPLE ALIVE. HELP US RESTORE THE BALANCE OF NATURE AND KILL A STUPID PERSON. RETURN TO NATURE: EAT YOUR NEIGHBOUR.
LOVE IS JUST A STATEMENT OF OWNERSHIP
APOCODESIA PERFUME
500 MEGATONS
BECAUSE POWER IS THE ULTIMATE APHRODISIAC
...Got to put as much distance between me and the Hell spawn as possible....!
Then—eeep! Soldiers!
They may be looking for me!
I'm so zucked!
Unity is slavery!
FREEDOM THROUGH DEATH! END THE PRISON OF THE FLESH! FREEDOM IN DEATH!
Suicide Squad—forward!
DON'T BE BRAINWASHED BY IDEALS!

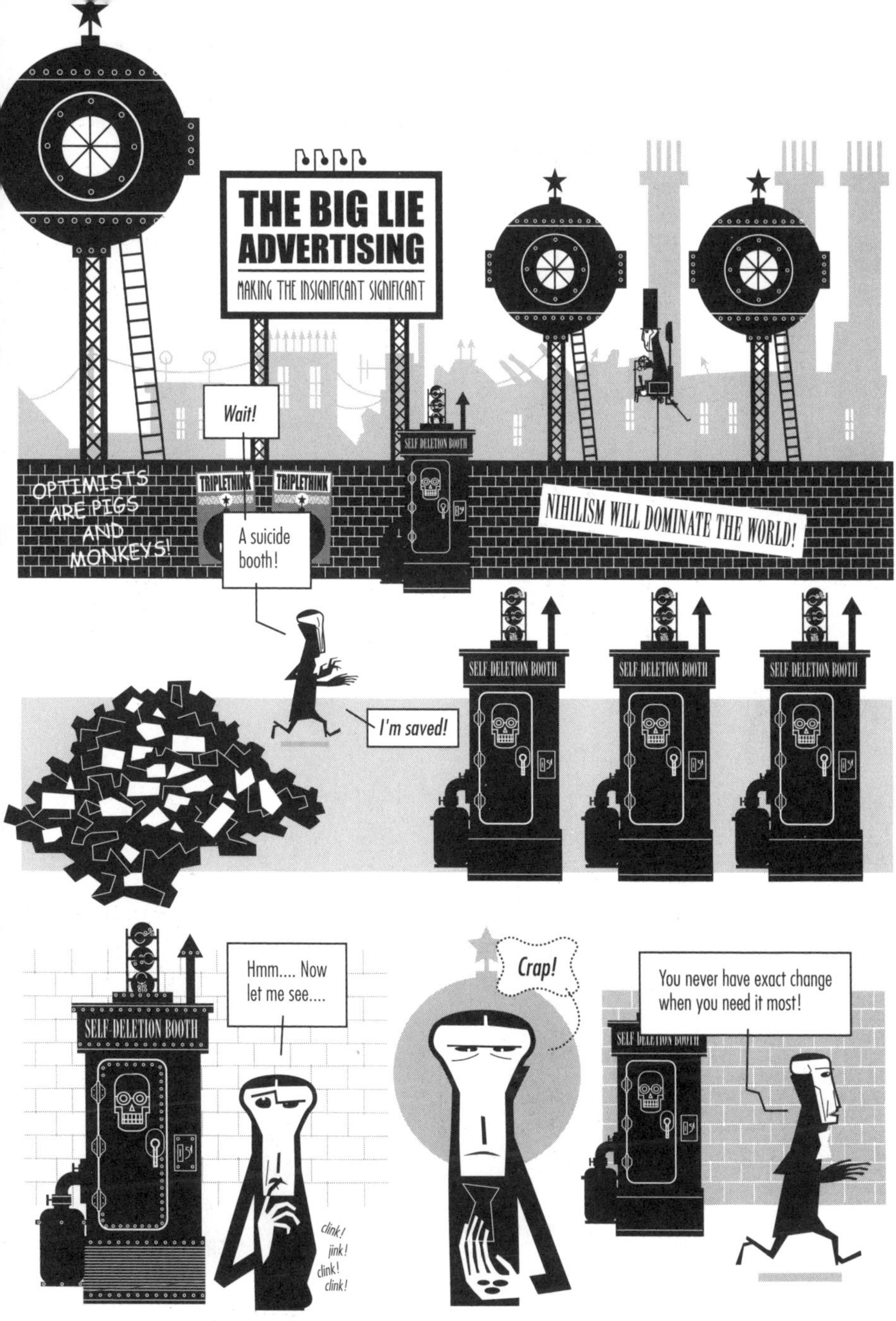
THE BIG LIE ADVERTISING
MAKING THE INSIGNIFICANT SIGNIFICANT
Wait!
SELF DELETION BOOTH
OPTIMISTS ARE PIGS AND MONKEYS!
TRIPLETHINK
TRIPLETHINK
A suicide booth!
NIHILISM WILL DOMINATE THE WORLD!
SELF DELETION BOOTH
SELF DELETION BOOTH
SELF DELETION BOOTH
I'm saved!
SELF-DELETION BOOTH
Hmm.... Now let me see....
clink!
jink!
clink!
clink!
Crap!
You never have exact change when you need it most!

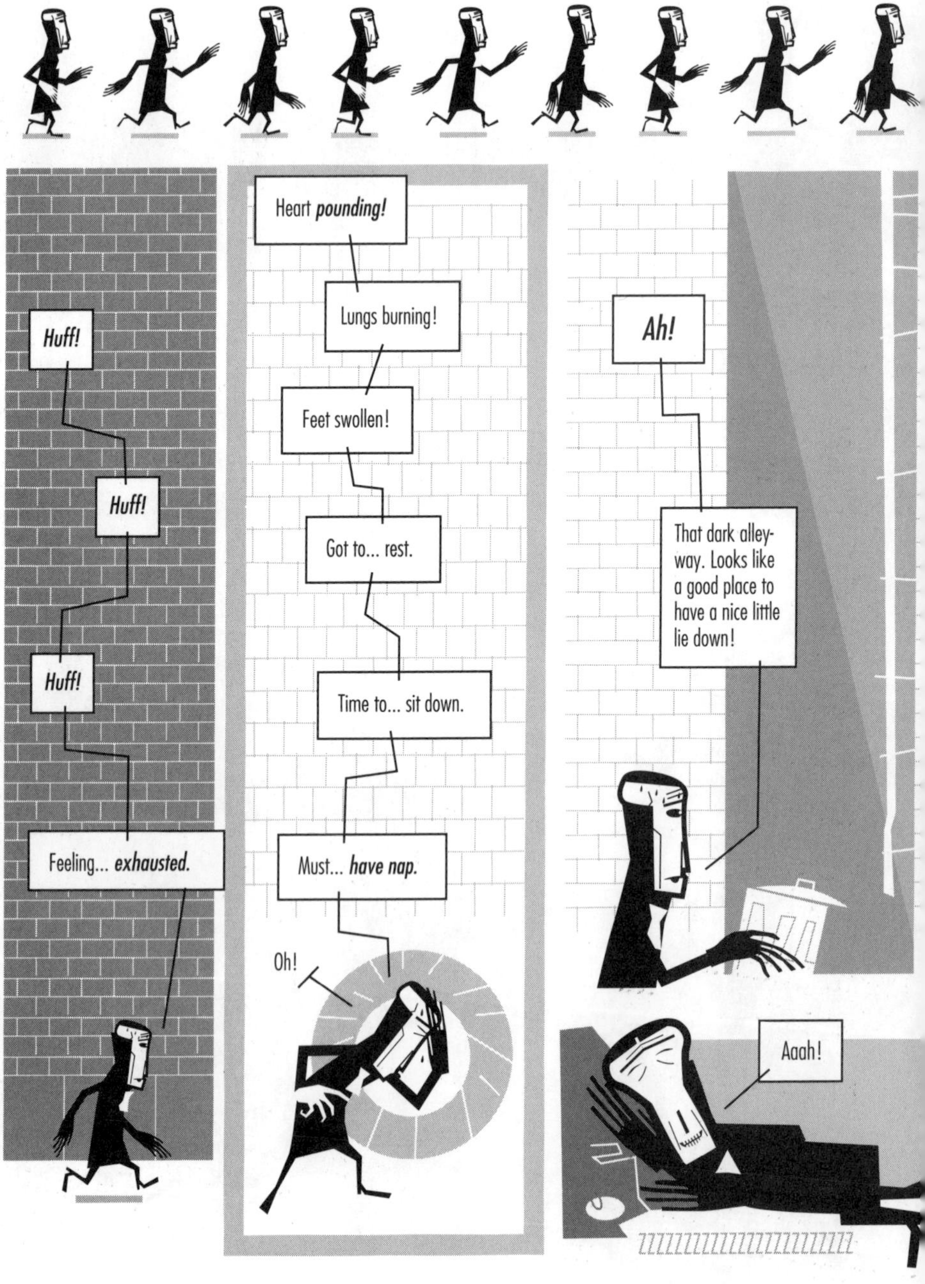

Huff!
Huff!
Huff!
Feeling... exhausted.
Heart pounding!
Lungs burning!
Feet swollen!
Got to... rest.
Time to... sit down.
Must... have nap.
Oh!
Ah!
That dark alley-way. Looks like a good place to have a nice little lie down!
Aaah!
ZZZZZZZZZZZZZZZZZZZZZZZZ

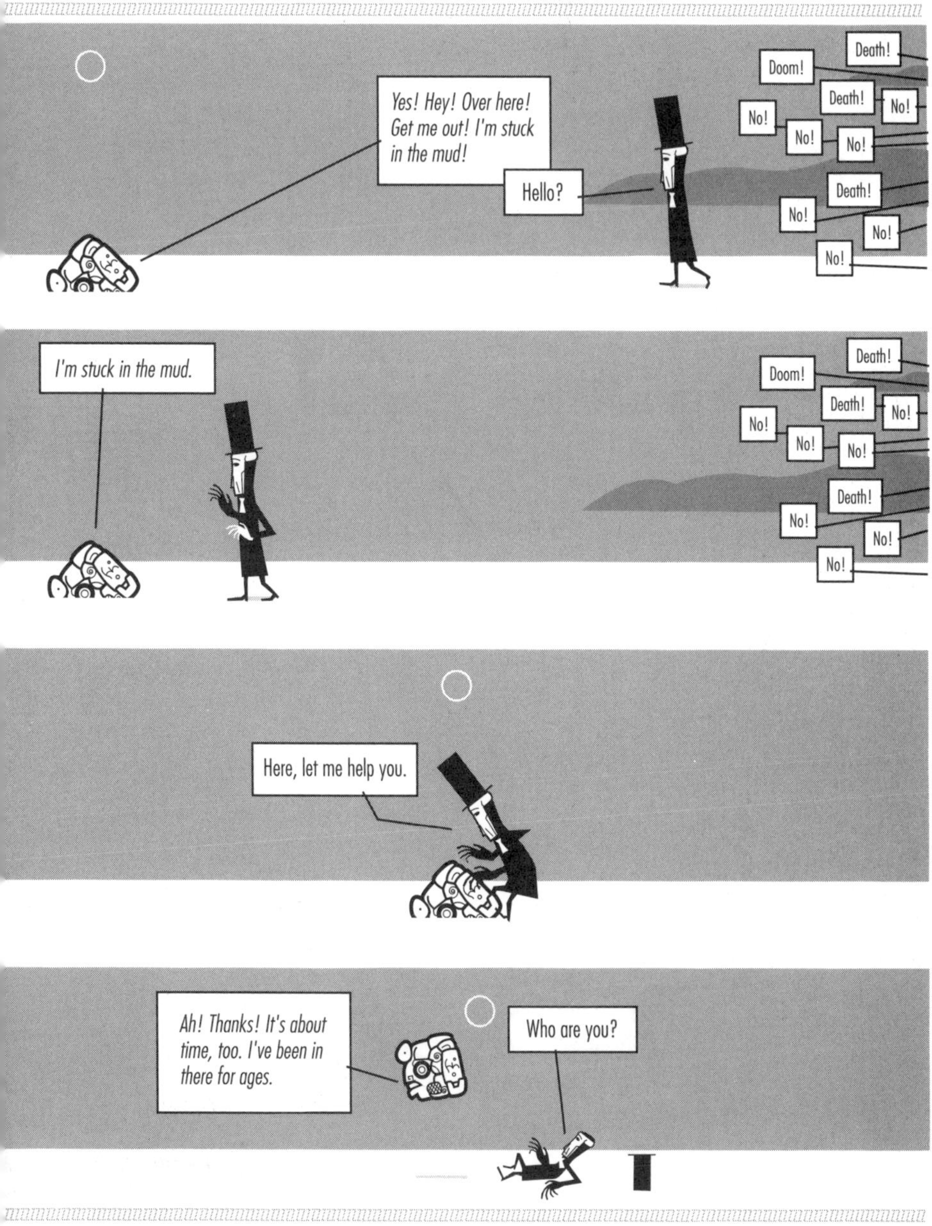

Yes! Hey! Over here! Get me out! I'm stuck in the mud!
Hello?
Death!
Doom!
Death!
No!
No!
No!
No!
Death!
No!
No!
No!
I'm stuck in the mud.
Death!
Doom!
Death!
No!
No!
No!
No!
Death!
No!
No!
No!
Here, let me help you.
Ah! Thanks! It's about time, too. I've been in there for ages.
Who are you?

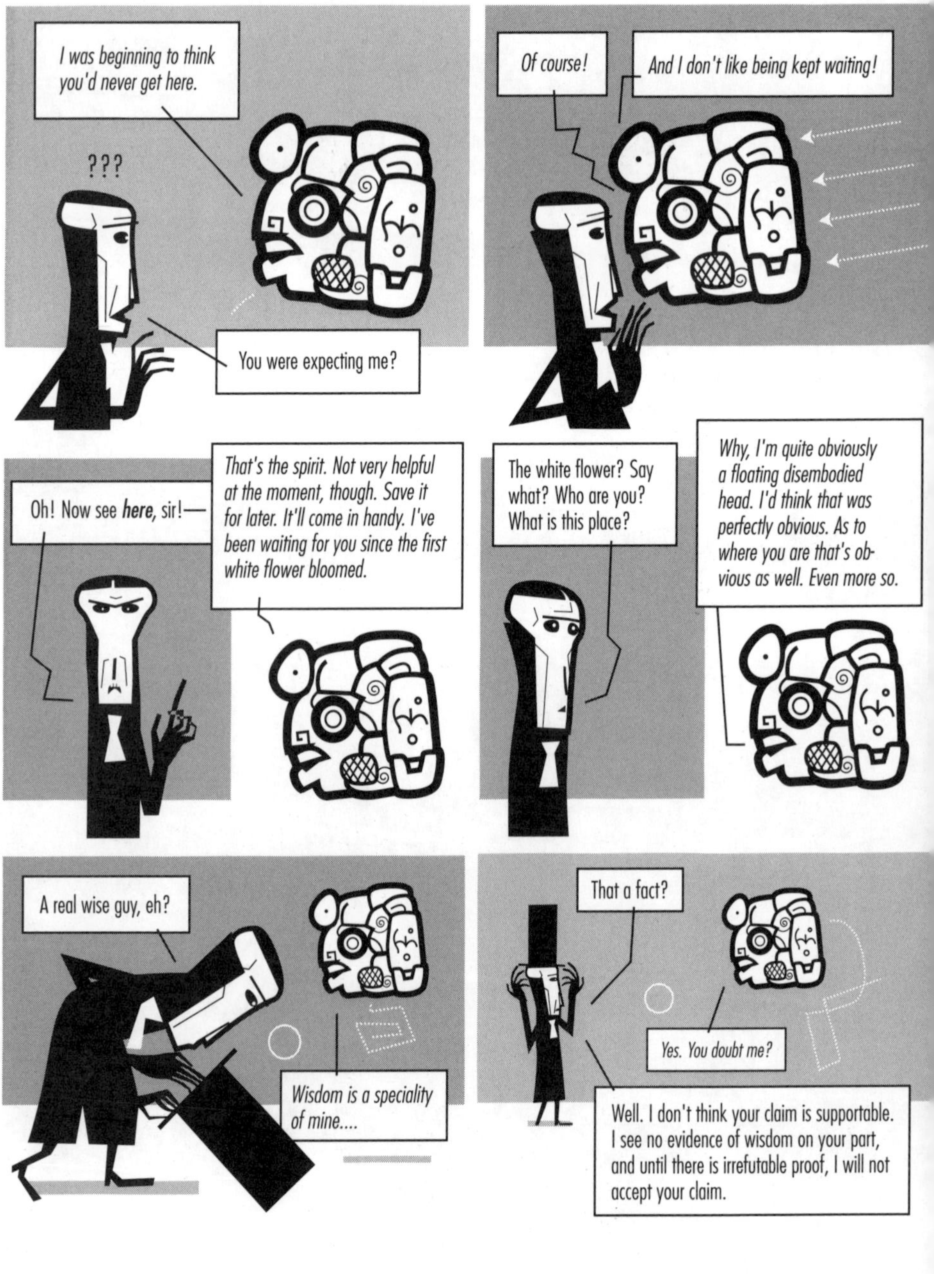

I was beginning to think you'd never get here.
???
You were expecting me?
Of course!
And I don't like being kept waiting!
Oh! Now see **here**, sir!—
That's the spirit. Not very helpful at the moment, though. Save it for later. It'll come in handy. I've been waiting for you since the first white flower bloomed.
The white flower? Say what? Who are you? What is this place?
Why, I'm quite obviously a floating disembodied head. I'd think that was perfectly obvious. As to where you are that's obvious as well. Even more so.
A real wise guy, eh?
Wisdom is a speciality of mine....
That a fact?
Yes. You doubt me?
Well. I don't think your claim is supportable. I see no evidence of wisdom on your part, and until there is irrefutable proof, I will not accept your claim.

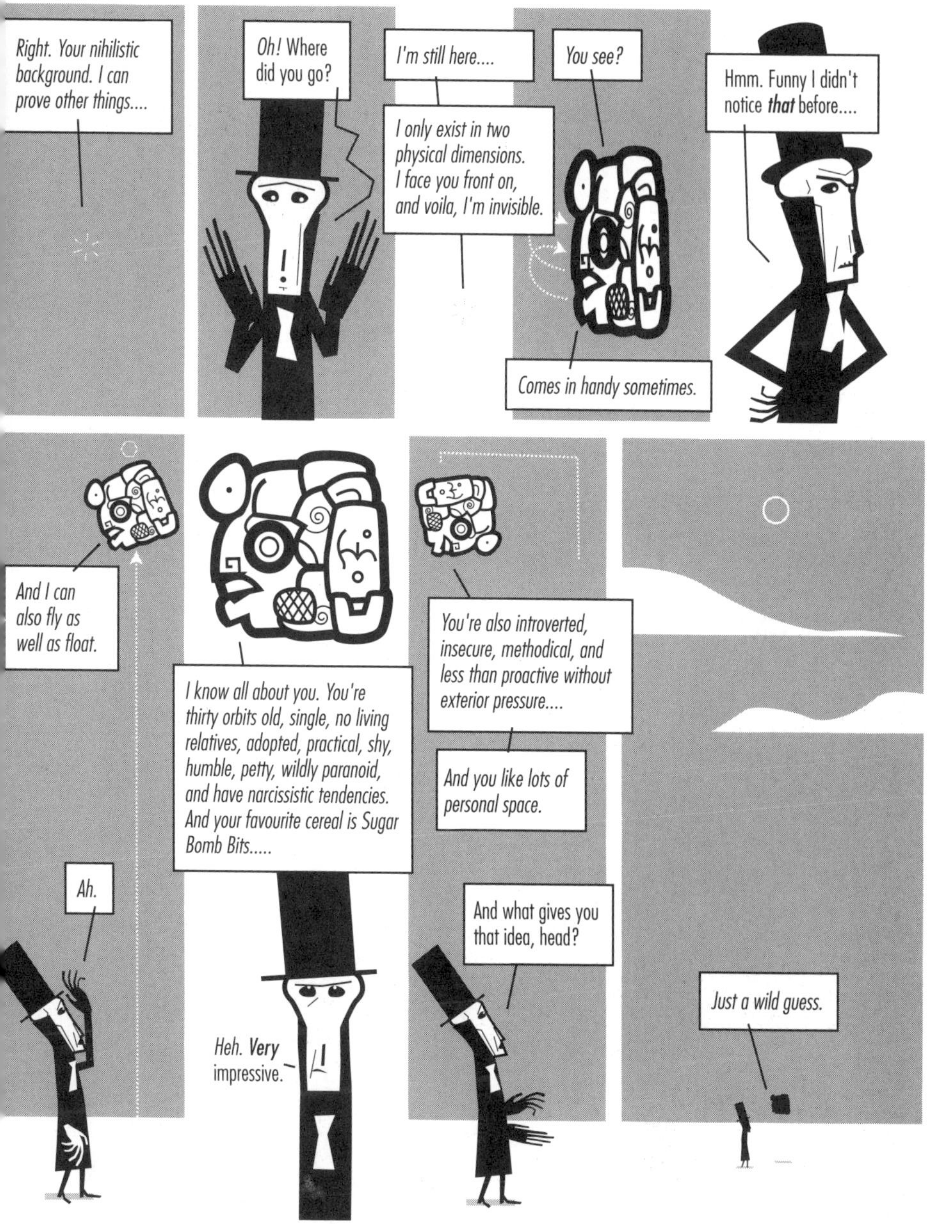
Right. Your nihilistic background. I can prove other things....
Oh! Where did you go?
I'm still here....
I only exist in two physical dimensions. I face you front on, and voila, I'm invisible.
You see?
Comes in handy sometimes.
Hmm. Funny I didn't notice ***that*** before....
And I can also fly as well as float.
Ah.
I know all about you. You're thirty orbits old, single, no living relatives, adopted, practical, shy, humble, petty, wildly paranoid, and have narcissistic tendencies. And your favourite cereal is Sugar Bomb Bits.....
Heh. **Very** impressive.
You're also introverted, insecure, methodical, and less than proactive without exterior pressure....
And you like lots of personal space.
And what gives you that idea, head?
Just a wild guess.

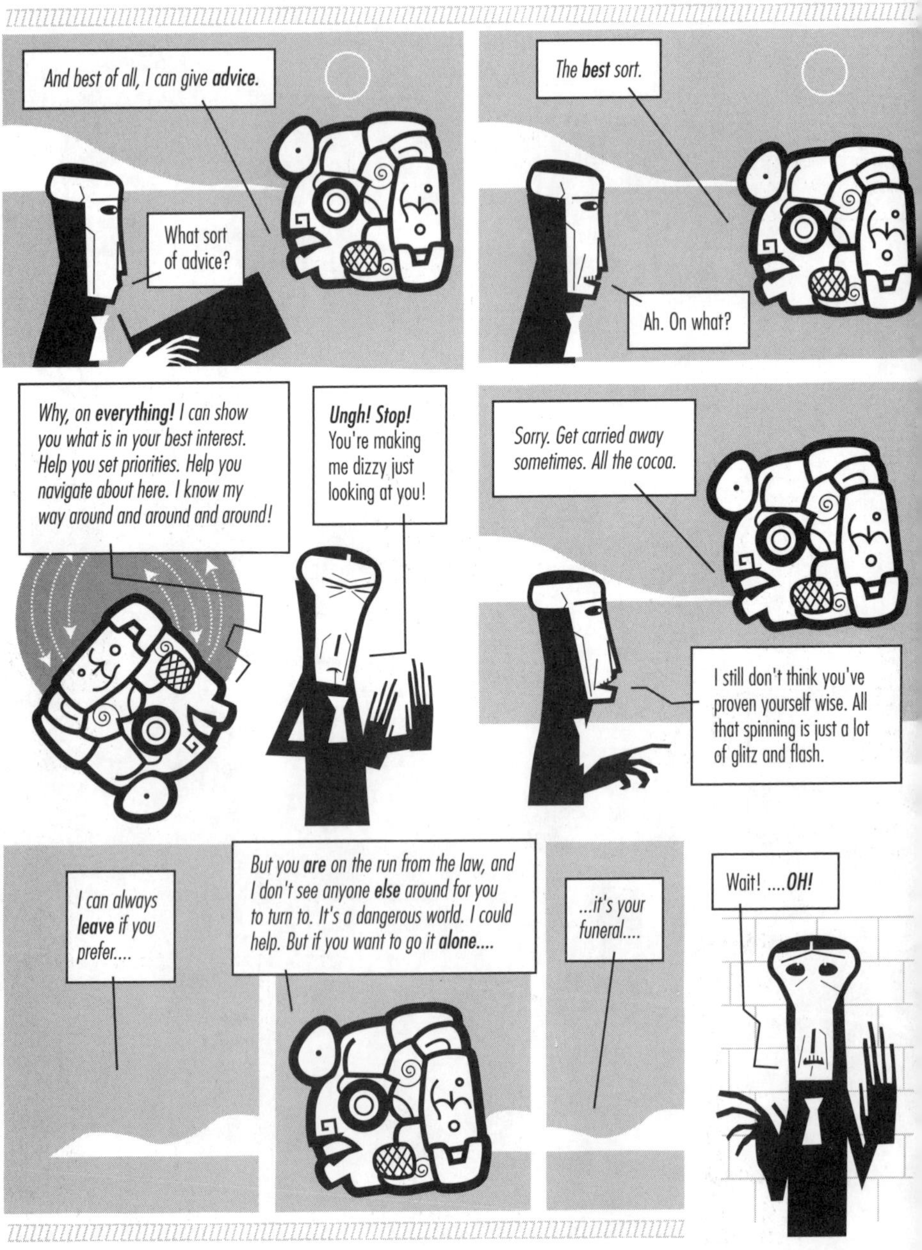
And best of all, I can give **advice.**
What sort of advice?
The **best** sort.
Ah. On what?
Why, on **everything!** I can show you what is in your best interest. Help you set priorities. Help you navigate about here. I know my way around and around and around!
Ungh! Stop! You're making me dizzy just looking at you!
Sorry. Get carried away sometimes. All the cocoa.
I still don't think you've proven yourself wise. All that spinning is just a lot of glitz and flash.
I can always **leave** if you prefer....
But you **are** on the run from the law, and I don't see anyone **else** around for you to turn to. It's a dangerous world. I could help. But if you want to go it **alone....**
...it's your funeral....
Wait! ....**OH!**

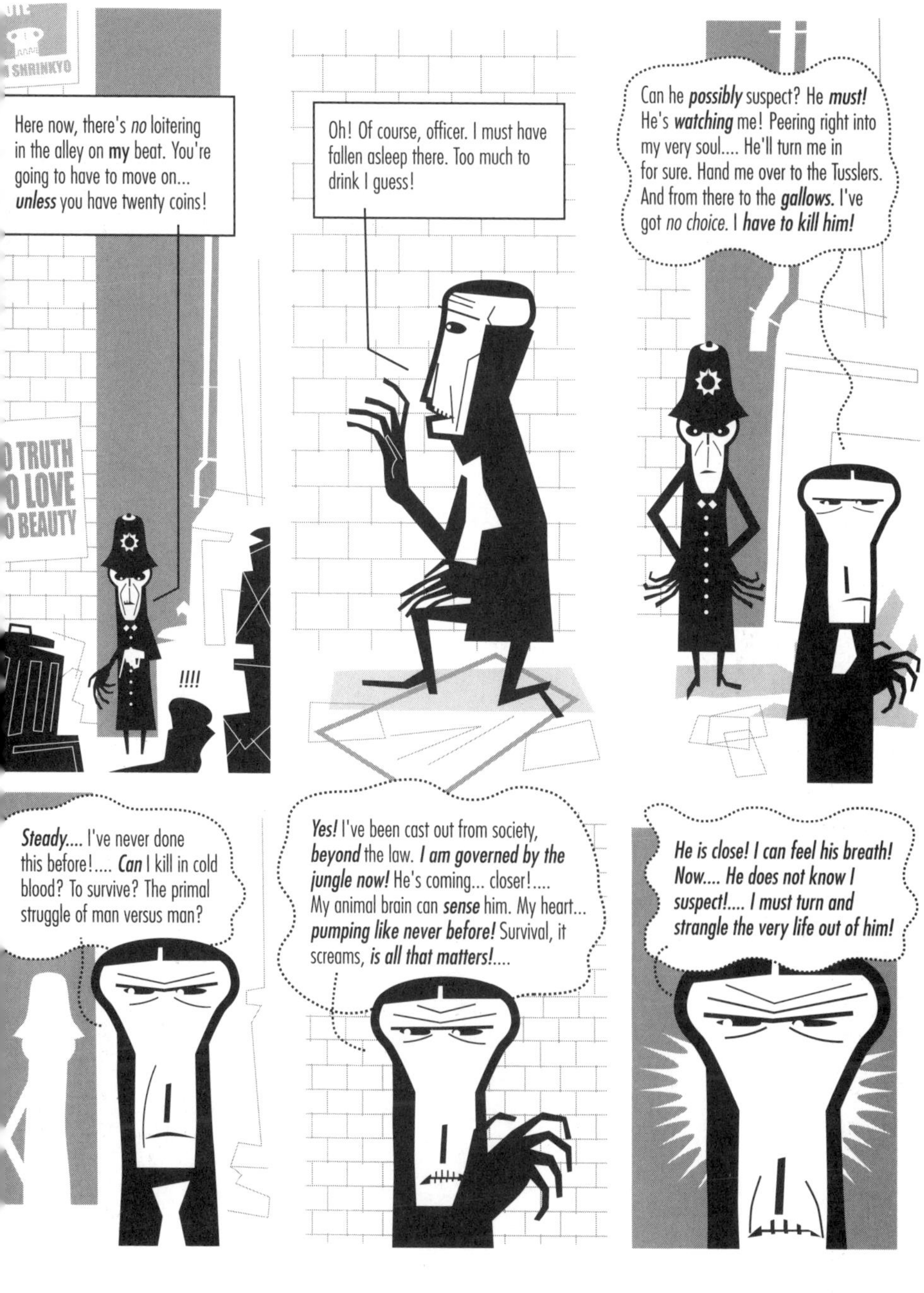
Here now, there's *no* loitering in the alley on **my** beat. You're going to have to move on... ***unless*** you have twenty coins!
!!!!
Oh! Of course, officer. I must have fallen asleep there. Too much to drink I guess!
Can he ***possibly*** suspect? He ***must!*** He's ***watching*** me! Peering right into my very soul.... He'll turn me in for sure. Hand me over to the Tusslers. And from there to the ***gallows.*** I've got *no choice.* I ***have to kill him!***
Steady.... I've never done this before!.... ***Can*** I kill in cold blood? To survive? The primal struggle of man versus man?
Yes! I've been cast out from society, ***beyond*** the law. ***I am governed by the jungle now!*** He's coming... closer!.... My animal brain can ***sense*** him. My heart... ***pumping like never before!*** Survival, it screams, ***is all that matters!....***
He is close! I can feel his breath! Now.... He does not know I suspect!.... I must turn and strangle the very life out of him!

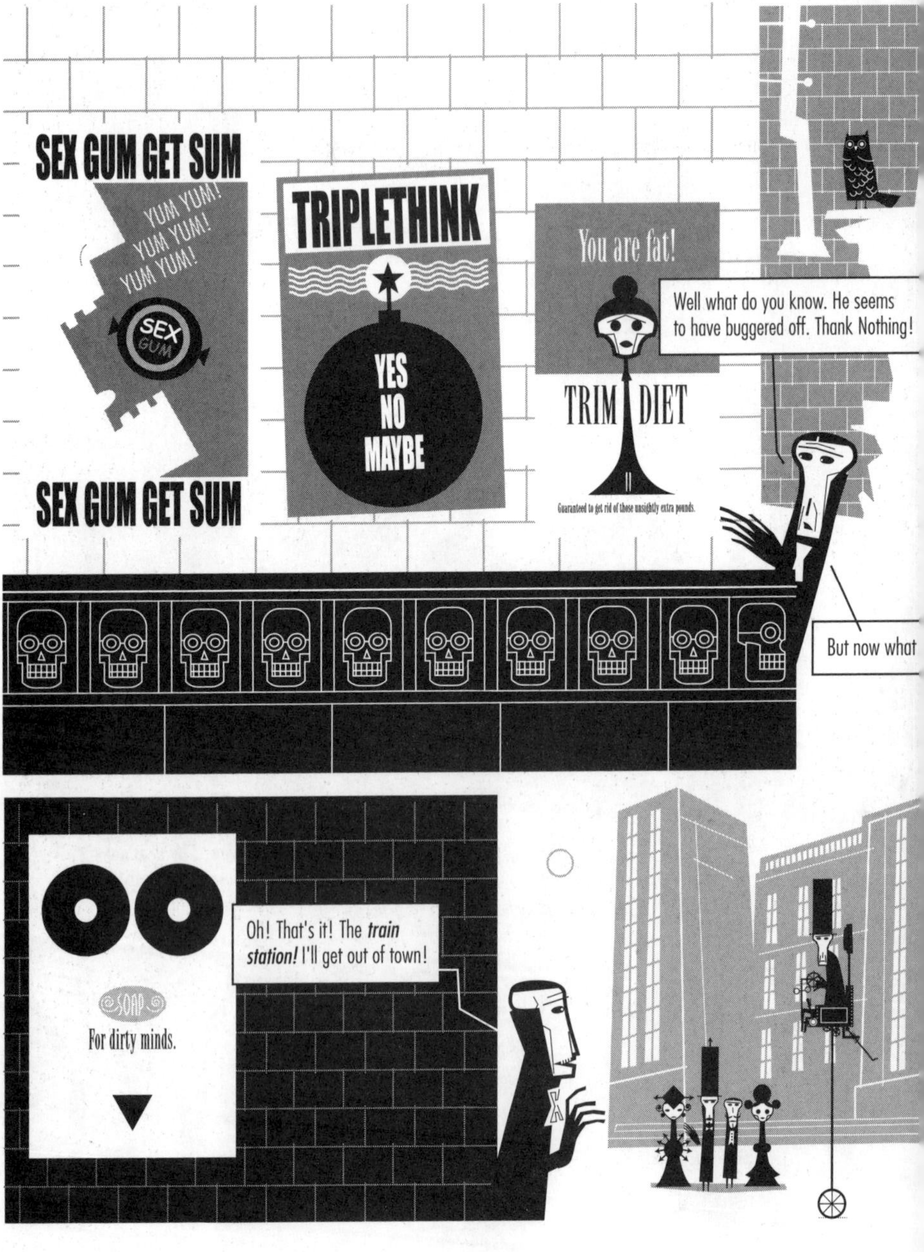
SEX GUM GET SUM
YUM YUM! YUM YUM! YUM YUM!
SEX GUM
SEX GUM GET SUM
TRIPLETHINK
YES NO MAYBE
You are fat!
TRIM DIET
Guaranteed to get rid of those unsightly extra pounds.
Well what do you know. He seems to have buggered off. Thank Nothing!
But now what
SOAP
For dirty minds.
Oh! That's it! The *train station!* I'll get out of town!

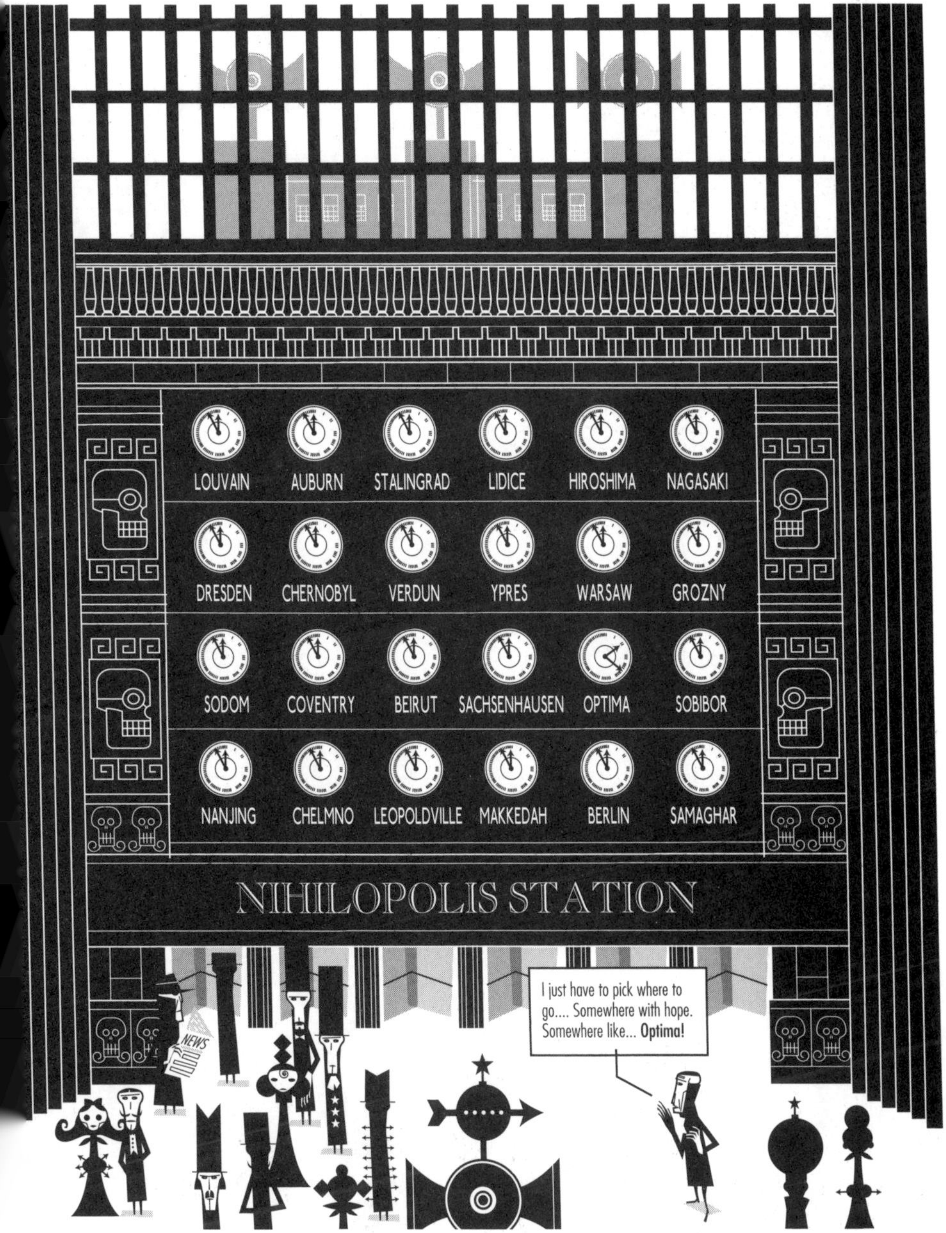
LOUVAIN
AUBURN
STALINGRAD
LIDICE
HIROSHIMA
NAGASAKI
DRESDEN
CHERNOBYL
VERDUN
YPRES
WARSAW
GROZNY
SODOM
COVENTRY
BEIRUT
SACHSENHAUSEN
OPTIMA
SOBIBOR
NANJING
CHELMNO
LEOPOLDVILLE
MAKKEDAH
BERLIN
SAMAGHAR
NIHILOPOLIS STATION
NEWS
I just have to pick where to go.... Somewhere with hope. Somewhere like... **Optima!**

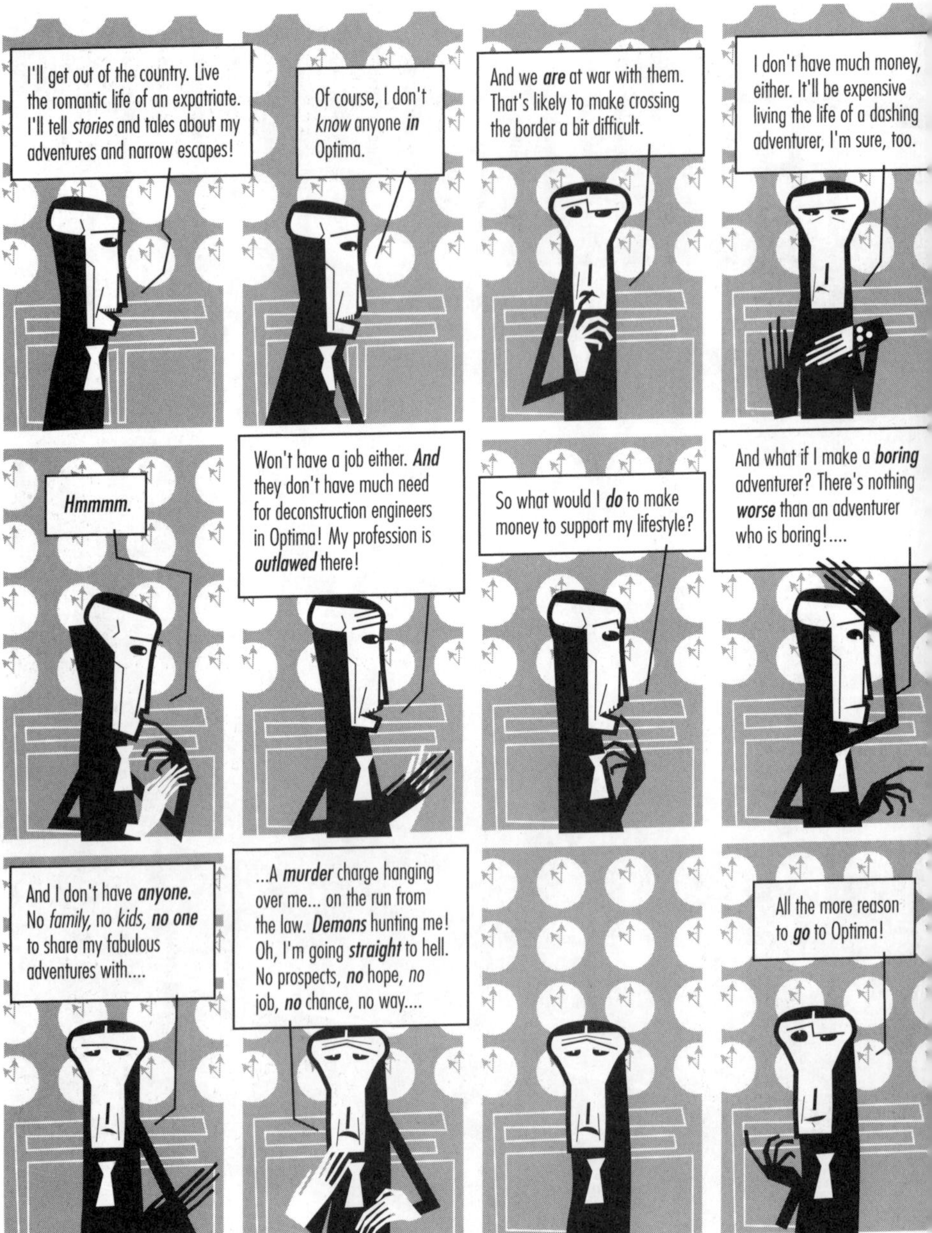
I'll get out of the country. Live the romantic life of an expatriate. I'll tell *stories* and tales about my adventures and narrow escapes!
Of course, I don't *know* anyone ***in*** Optima.
And we ***are*** at war with them. That's likely to make crossing the border a bit difficult.
I don't have much money, either. It'll be expensive living the life of a dashing adventurer, I'm sure, too.
Hmmmm.
Won't have a job either. ***And*** they don't have much need for deconstruction engineers in Optima! My profession is ***outlawed*** there!
So what would I ***do*** to make money to support my lifestyle?
And what if I make a ***boring*** adventurer? There's nothing ***worse*** than an adventurer who is boring!....
And I don't have ***anyone.*** No *family,* no *kids,* ***no one*** to share my fabulous adventures with....
...A ***murder*** charge hanging over me... on the run from the law. ***Demons*** hunting me! Oh, I'm going ***straight*** to hell. No prospects, ***no*** hope, *no* job, ***no*** chance, no way....
All the more reason to ***go*** to Optima!

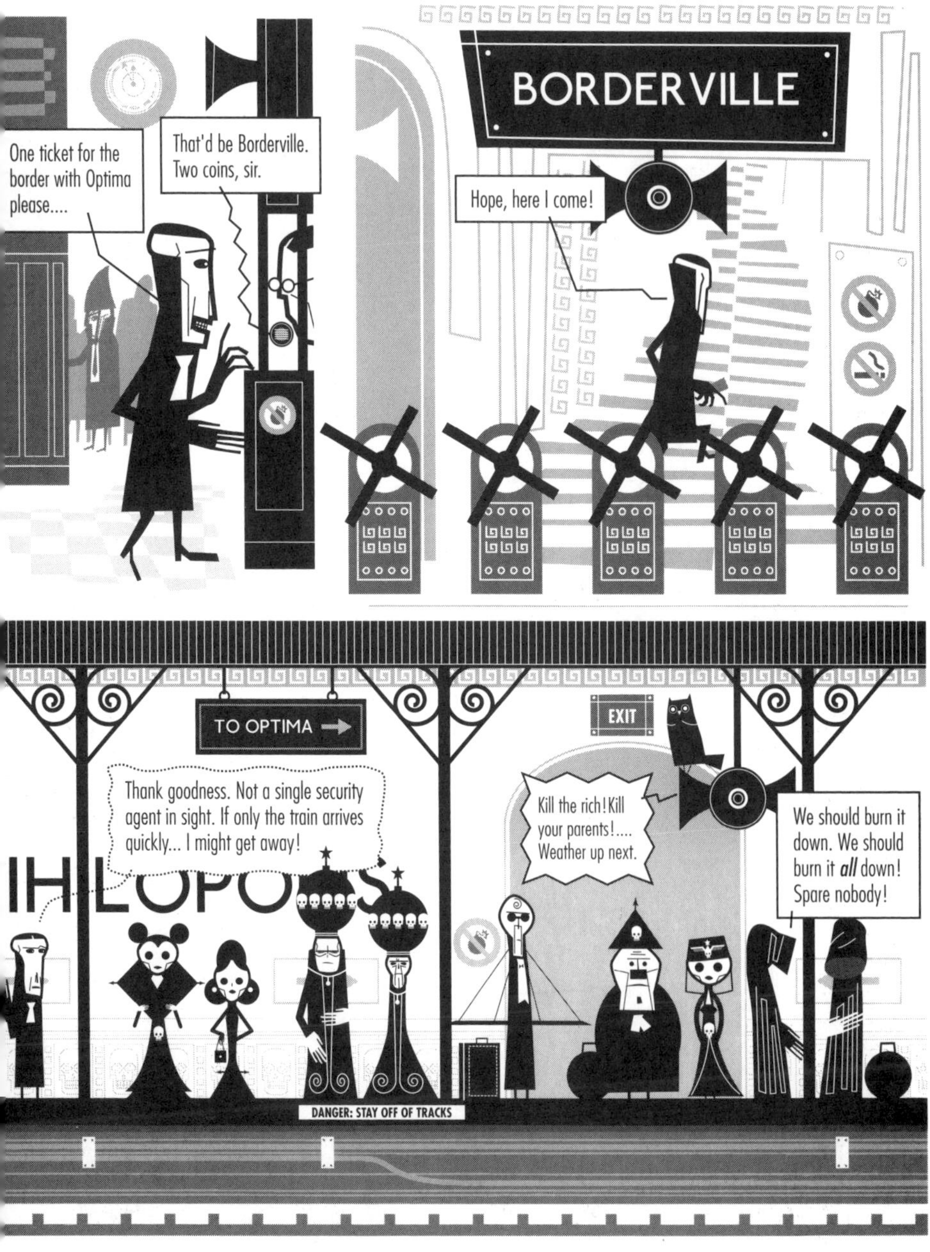

One ticket for the border with Optima please....
That'd be Borderville. Two coins, sir.
BORDERVILLE
Hope, here I come!
TO OPTIMA
EXIT
Thank goodness. Not a single security agent in sight. If only the train arrives quickly... I might get away!
Kill the rich! Kill your parents!.... Weather up next.
We should burn it down. We should burn it *all* down! Spare nobody!
DANGER: STAY OFF OF TRACKS

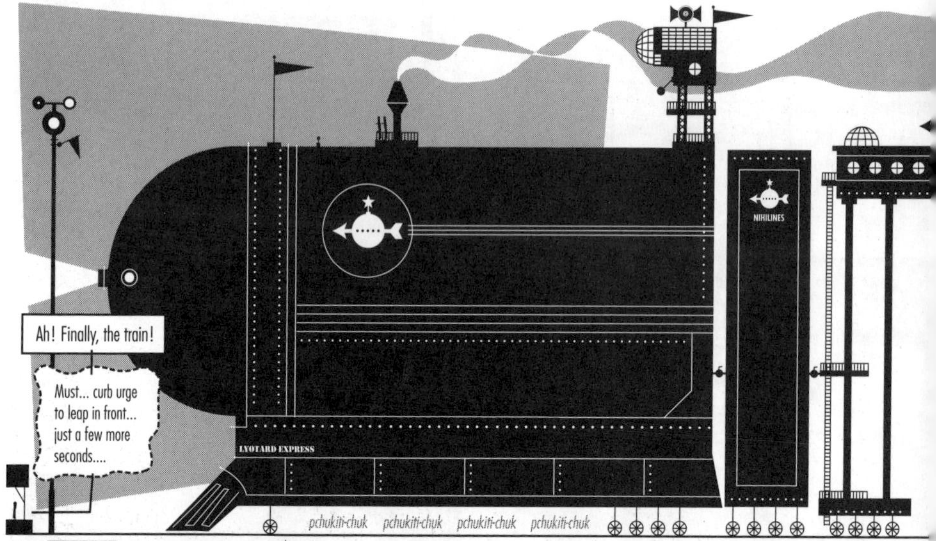
Ah! Finally, the train!
Must... curb urge to leap in front... just a few more seconds....
LYOTARD EXPRESS
NIHILINES
pchukiti-chuk pchukiti-chuk pchukiti-chuk pchukiti-chuk

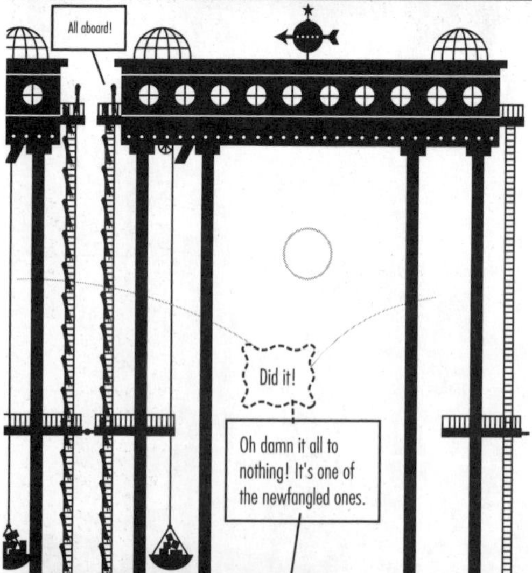
All aboard!
Did it!
Oh damn it all to nothing! It's one of the newfangled ones.

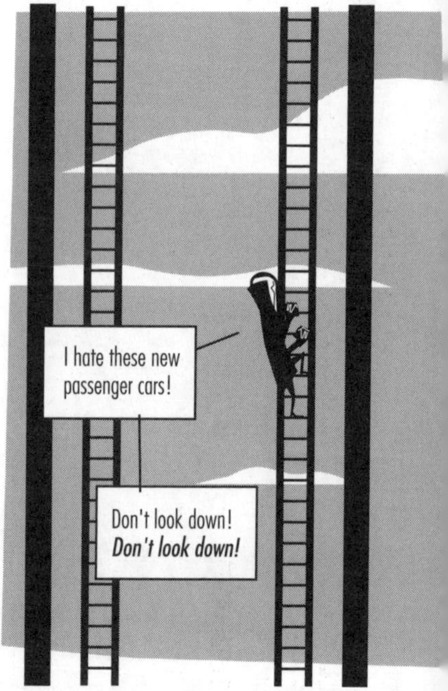
I hate these new passenger cars!
Don't look down!
Don't look down!

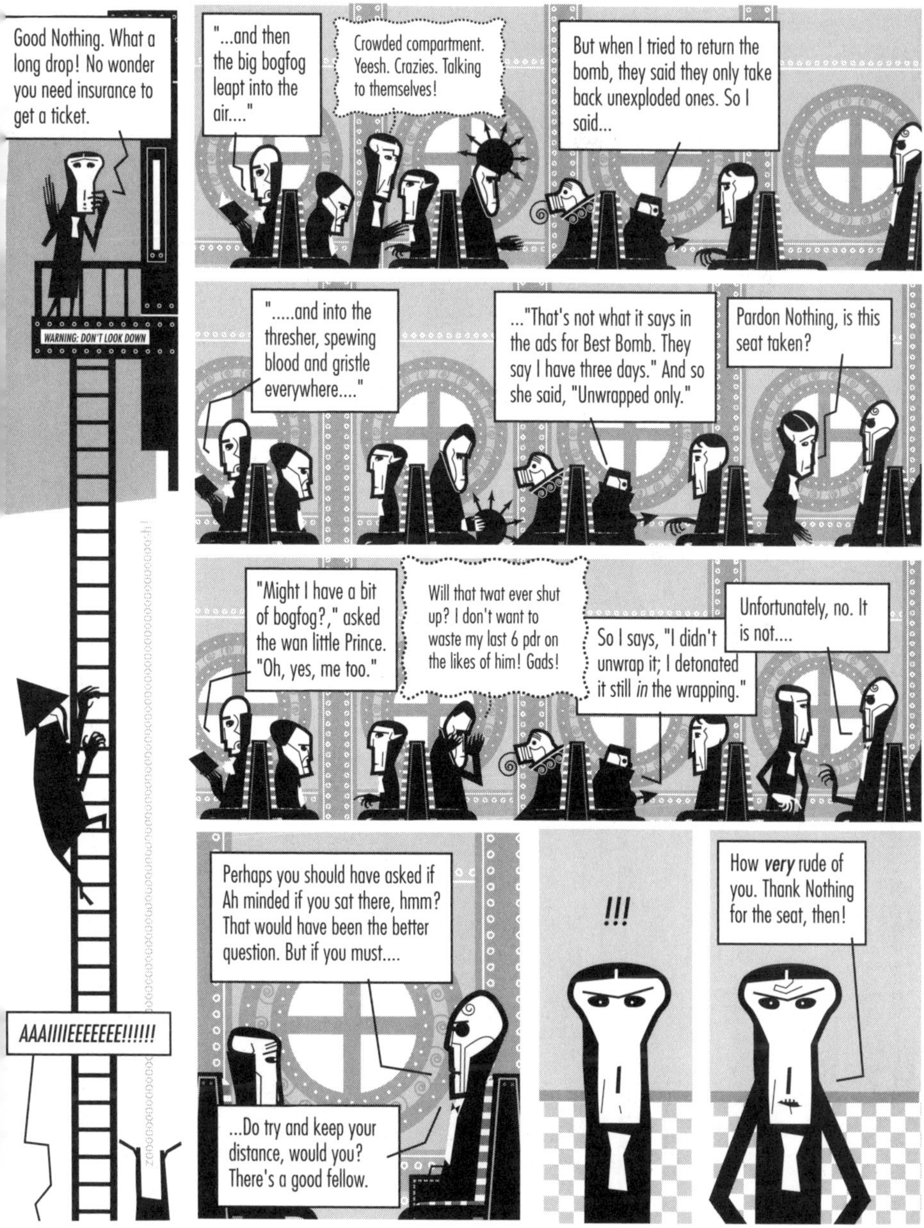

Good Nothing. What a long drop! No wonder you need insurance to get a ticket.
WARNING: DON'T LOOK DOWN
AAAIIIIEEEEEEE!!!!!!
"...and then the big bogfog leapt into the air...."
Crowded compartment. Yeesh. Crazies. Talking to themselves!
But when I tried to return the bomb, they said they only take back unexploded ones. So I said...
".....and into the thresher, spewing blood and gristle everywhere...."
..."That's not what it says in the ads for Best Bomb. They say I have three days." And so she said, "Unwrapped only."
Pardon Nothing, is this seat taken?
"Might I have a bit of bogfog?," asked the wan little Prince. "Oh, yes, me too."
Will that twat ever shut up? I don't want to waste my last 6 pdr on the likes of him! Gads!
So I says, "I didn't unwrap it; I detonated it still *in* the wrapping."
Unfortunately, no. It is not....
Perhaps you should have asked if Ah minded if you sat there, hmm? That would have been the better question. But if you must....
...Do try and keep your distance, would you? There's a good fellow.
!!!
How ***very*** rude of you. Thank Nothing for the seat, then!

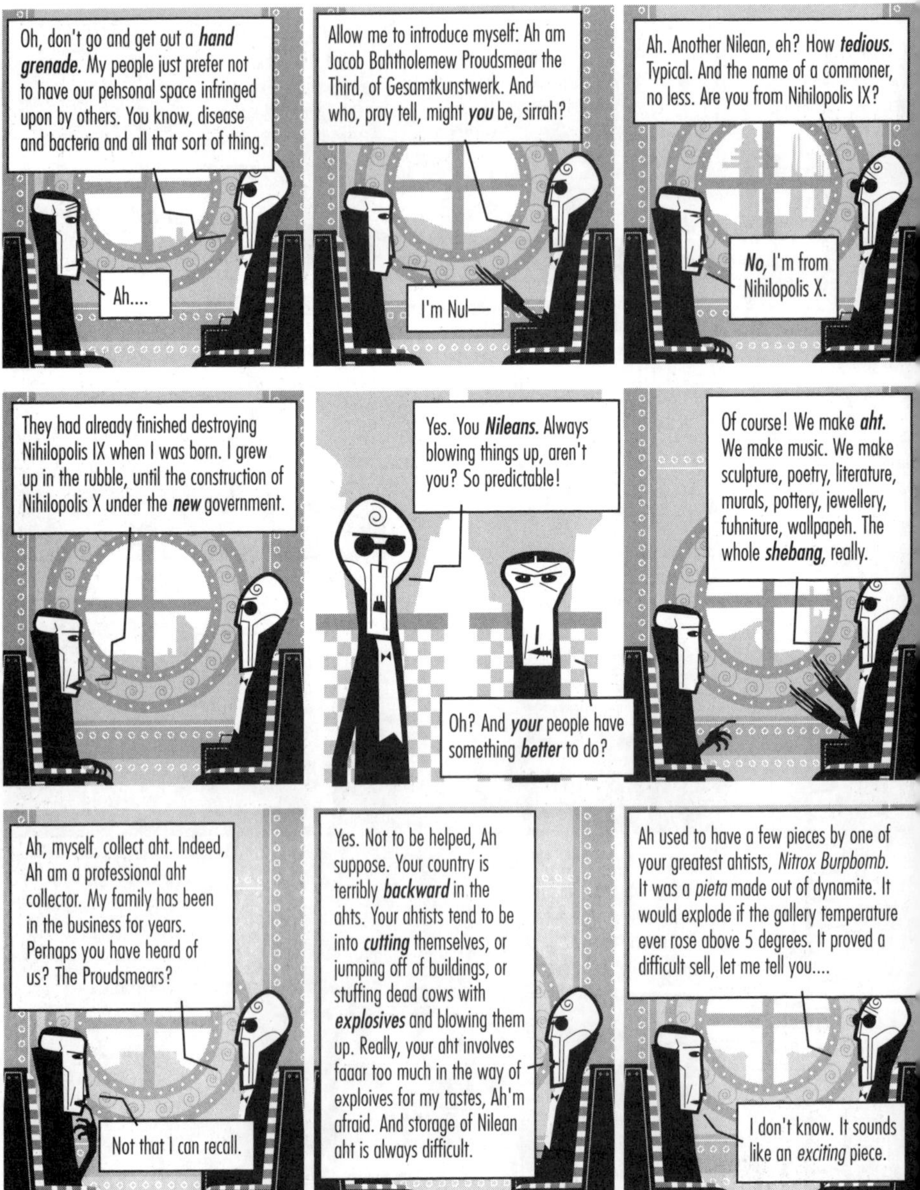
Oh, don't go and get out a ***hand grenade.*** My people just prefer not to have our pehsonal space infringed upon by others. You know, disease and bacteria and all that sort of thing.
Ah....
Allow me to introduce myself: Ah am Jacob Bahtholemew Proudsmear the Third, of Gesamtkunstwerk. And who, pray tell, might ***you*** be, sirrah?
I'm Nul—
Ah. Another Nilean, eh? How ***tedious.*** Typical. And the name of a commoner, no less. Are you from Nihilopolis IX?
No, I'm from Nihilopolis X.
They had already finished destroying Nihilopolis IX when I was born. I grew up in the rubble, until the construction of Nihilopolis X under the ***new*** government.
Yes. You ***Nileans.*** Always blowing things up, aren't you? So predictable!
Oh? And ***your*** people have something ***better*** to do?
Of course! We make ***aht.*** We make music. We make sculpture, poetry, literature, murals, pottery, jewellery, fuhniture, wallpapeh. The whole ***shebang,*** really.
Ah, myself, collect aht. Indeed, Ah am a professional aht collector. My family has been in the business for years. Perhaps you have heard of us? The Proudsmears?
Not that I can recall.
Yes. Not to be helped, Ah suppose. Your country is terribly ***backward*** in the ahts. Your ahtists tend to be into ***cutting*** themselves, or jumping off of buildings, or stuffing dead cows with ***explosives*** and blowing them up. Really, your aht involves faaar too much in the way of exploives for my tastes, Ah'm afraid. And storage of Nilean aht is always difficult.
Ah used to have a few pieces by one of your greatest ahtists, *Nitrox Burpbomb.* It was a *pieta* made out of dynamite. It would explode if the gallery temperature ever rose above 5 degrees. It proved a difficult sell, let me tell you....
I don't know. It sounds like an *exciting* piece.

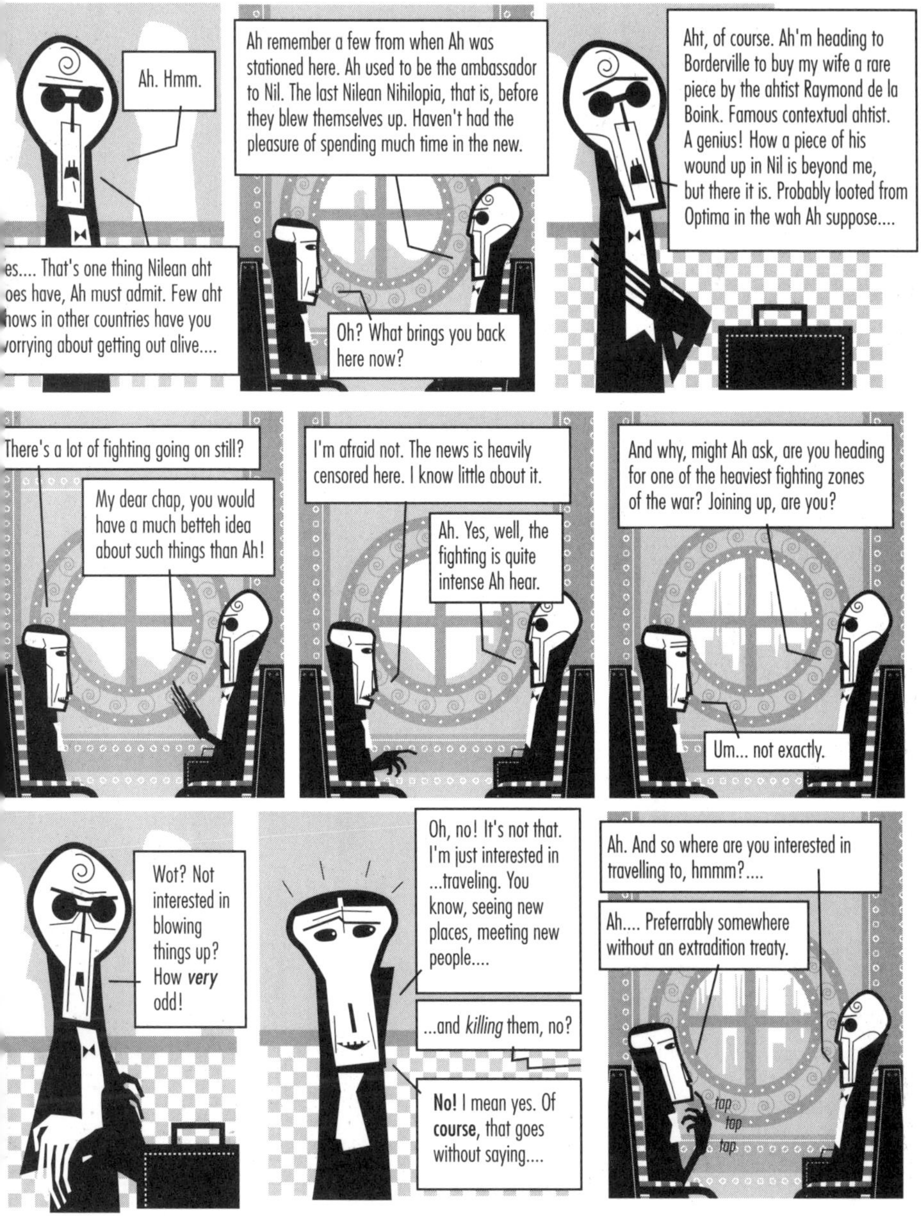
Ah. Hmm.
es.... That's one thing Nilean aht oes have, Ah must admit. Few aht hows in other countries have you vorrying about getting out alive....
Ah remember a few from when Ah was stationed here. Ah used to be the ambassador to Nil. The last Nilean Nihilopia, that is, before they blew themselves up. Haven't had the pleasure of spending much time in the new.
Oh? What brings you back here now?
Aht, of course. Ah'm heading to Borderville to buy my wife a rare piece by the ahtist Raymond de la Boink. Famous contextual ahtist. A genius! How a piece of his wound up in Nil is beyond me, but there it is. Probably looted from Optima in the wah Ah suppose....
There's a lot of fighting going on still?
My dear chap, you would have a much betteh idea about such things than Ah!
I'm afraid not. The news is heavily censored here. I know little about it.
Ah. Yes, well, the fighting is quite intense Ah hear.
And why, might Ah ask, are you heading for one of the heaviest fighting zones of the war? Joining up, are you?
Um... not exactly.
Wot? Not interested in blowing things up? How *very* odd!
Oh, no! It's not that. I'm just interested in ...traveling. You know, seeing new places, meeting new people....
...and *killing* them, no?
No! I mean yes. Of **course**, that goes without saying....
Ah. And so where are you interested in travelling to, hmmm?....
Ah.... Preferrably somewhere without an extradition treaty.
tap
tap
tap

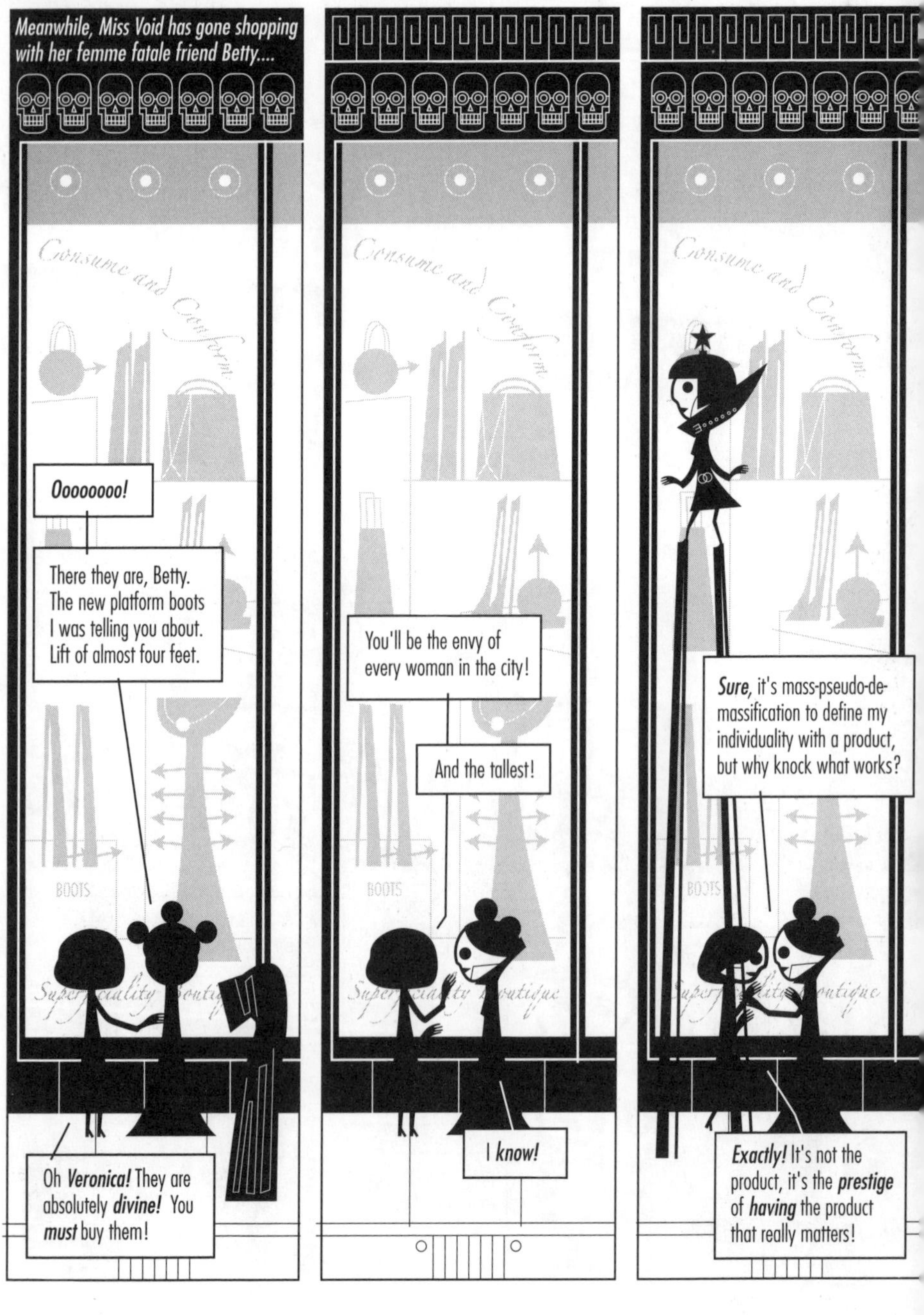

Meanwhile, Miss Void has gone shopping with her femme fatale friend Betty....
Consume and Conform
Ooooooo!
There they are, Betty. The new platform boots I was telling you about. Lift of almost four feet.
BOOTS
Superficiality Boutique
Oh *Veronica!* They are absolutely *divine!* You *must* buy them!
You'll be the envy of every woman in the city!
And the tallest!
I *know!*
Sure, it's mass-pseudo-de-massification to define my individuality with a product, but why knock what works?
Exactly! It's not the product, it's the *prestige* of *having* the product that really matters!

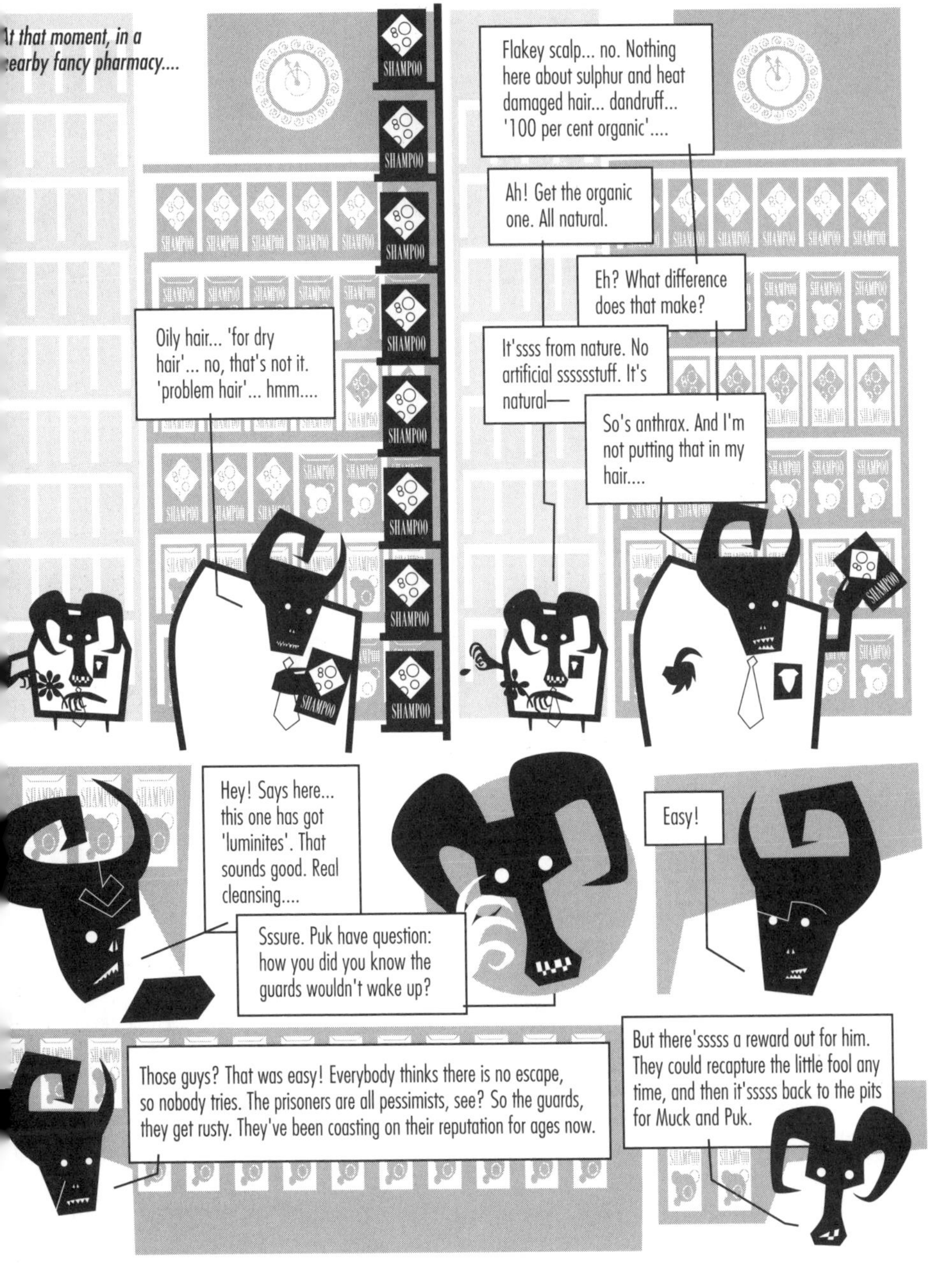

At that moment, in a nearby fancy pharmacy....
Oily hair... 'for dry hair'... no, that's not it. 'problem hair'... hmm....
Flakey scalp... no. Nothing here about sulphur and heat damaged hair... dandruff... '100 per cent organic'....
Ah! Get the organic one. All natural.
Eh? What difference does that make?
It'ssss from nature. No artificial sssssstuff. It's natural—
So's anthrax. And I'm not putting that in my hair....
Hey! Says here... this one has got 'luminites'. That sounds good. Real cleansing....
Sssure. Puk have question: how you did you know the guards wouldn't wake up?
Easy!
Those guys? That was easy! Everybody thinks there is no escape, so nobody tries. The prisoners are all pessimists, see? So the guards, they get rusty. They've been coasting on their reputation for ages now.
But there'sssss a reward out for him. They could recapture the little fool any time, and then it'sssss back to the pits for Muck and Puk.

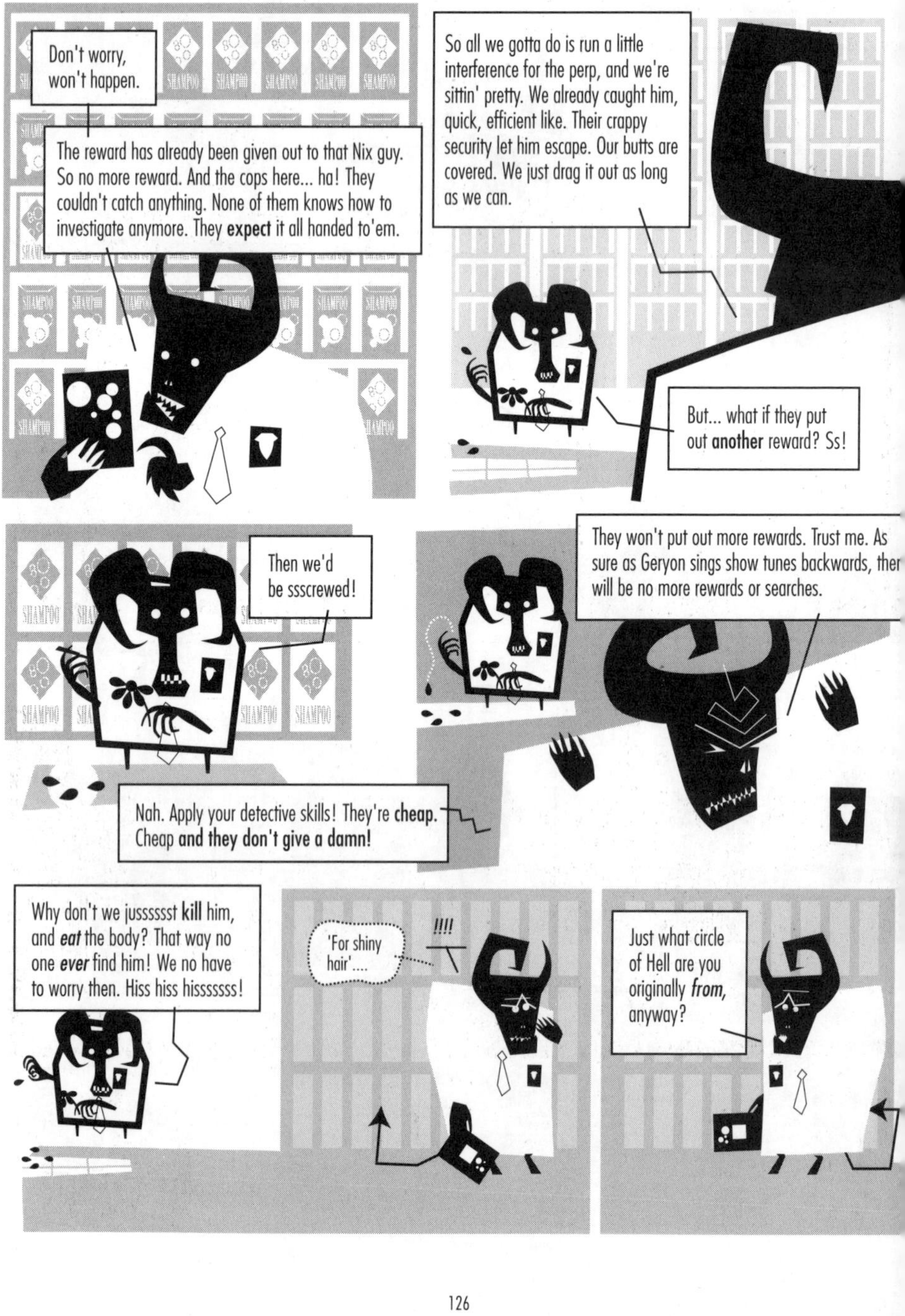
Don't worry, won't happen.
The reward has already been given out to that Nix guy. So no more reward. And the cops here... ha! They couldn't catch anything. None of them knows how to investigate anymore. They **expect** it all handed to'em.
So all we gotta do is run a little interference for the perp, and we're sittin' pretty. We already caught him, quick, efficient like. Their crappy security let him escape. Our butts are covered. We just drag it out as long as we can.
But... what if they put out **another** reward? Ss!
Then we'd be ssscrewed!
Nah. Apply your detective skills! They're **cheap.** Cheap **and they don't give a damn!**
They won't put out more rewards. Trust me. As sure as Geryon sings show tunes backwards, ther will be no more rewards or searches.
Why don't we jussssst **kill** him, and ***eat*** the body? That way no one ***ever*** find him! We no have to worry then. Hiss hiss hisssssss!
'For shiny hair'....
!!!!
Just what circle of Hell are you originally ***from,*** anyway?

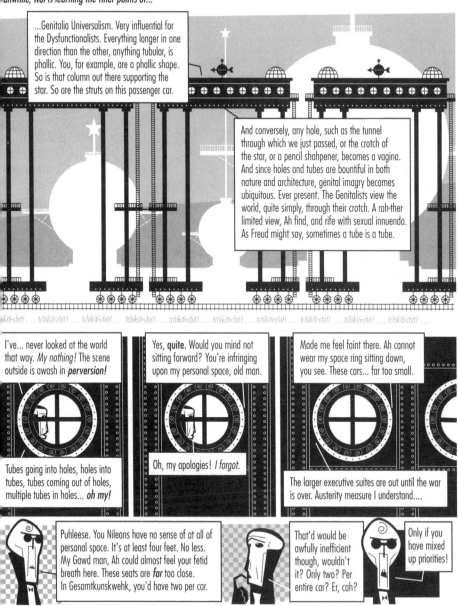

Meanwhile, Nul is learning the finer points of...

...Genitalia Universalism. Very influential for the Dysfunctionalists. Everything longer in one direction than the other, anything tubular, is phallic. You, for example, are a phallic shape. So is that column out there supporting the star. So are the struts on this passenger car.

And conversely, any hole, such as the tunnel through which we just passed, or the crotch of the star, or a pencil shahpener, becomes a vagina. And since holes and tubes are bountiful in both nature and architecture, genital imagry becomes ubiquitous. Ever present. The Genitalists view the world, quite simply, through their crotch. A rah-ther limited view, Ah find, and rife with sexual innuendo. As Freud might say, sometimes a tube is a tube.

ikiti-chit! . . . *tchikiti-chit!* . . . *tchikiti-chit!* . . . *tchikiti-chit!* . . . *tchikiti-chit!* . . . *tchikiti-chit!* . . . *tchikiti-chit!* . . . *tchikiti-chit!* . . . *tchikiti-chit!* . . . *tchikiti-chit!* . . .

I've... never looked at the world that way. *My nothing!* The scene outside is awash in *perversion!*

Yes, **quite.** Would you mind not sitting forward? You're infringing upon my personal space, old man.

Made me feel faint there. Ah cannot wear my space ring sitting down, you see. These cars... far too small.

Tubes going into holes, holes into tubes, tubes coming out of holes, multiple tubes in holes... **oh my!**

Oh, my apologies! *I forgot.*

The larger executive suites are out until the war is over. Austerity measure I understand....

Puhleese. You Nileans have no sense of at all of personal space. It's at least four feet. No less. My Gawd man, Ah could almost feel your fetid breath here. These seats are *far* too close. In Gesamtkunskwehk, you'd have two per car.

That'd would be awfully inefficient though, wouldn't it? Only two? Per entire car? Er, cah?

Only if you have mixed up priorities!

127

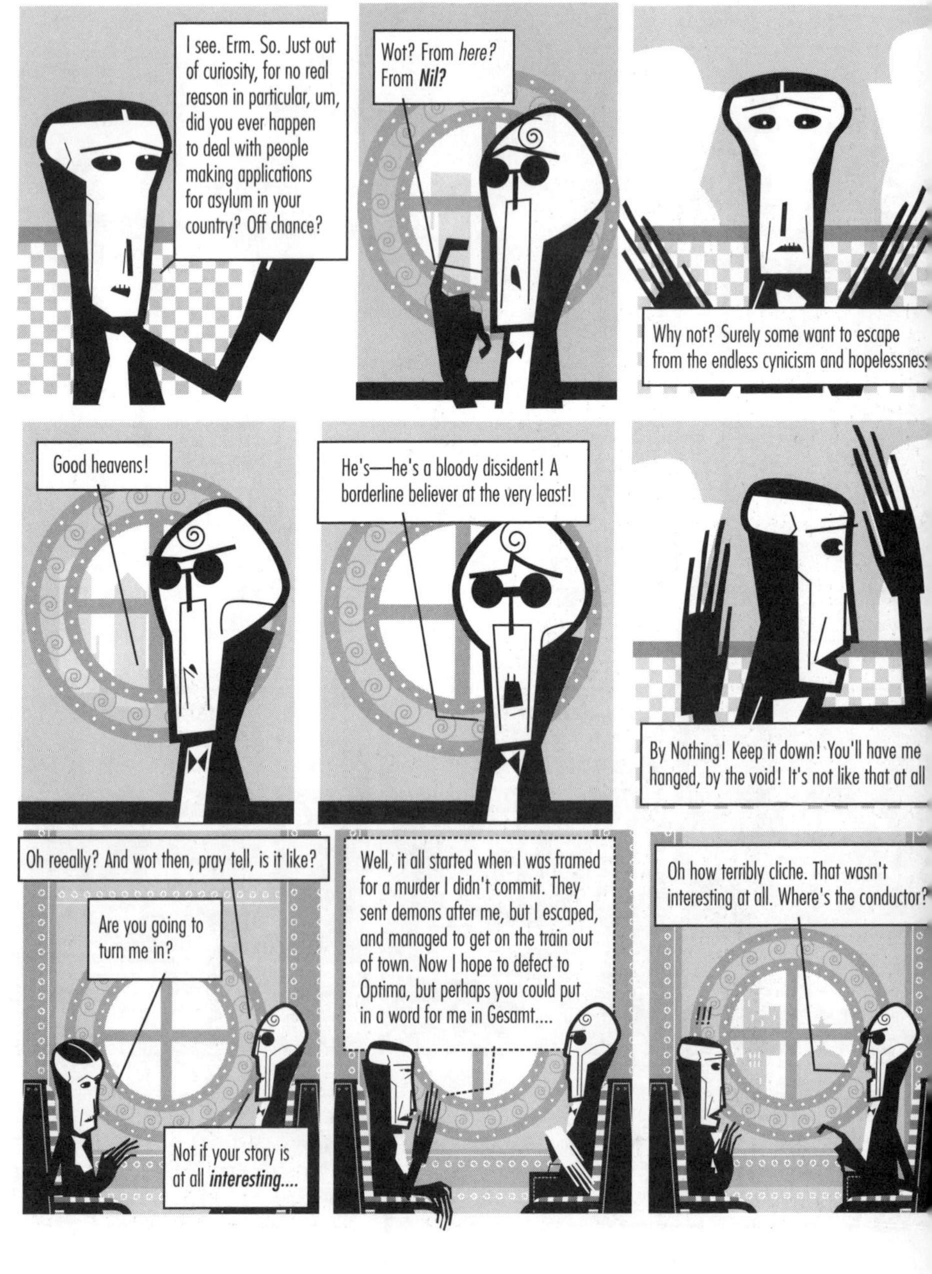
I see. Erm. So. Just out of curiosity, for no real reason in particular, um, did you ever happen to deal with people making applications for asylum in your country? Off chance?
Wot? From *here?* From ***Nil?***
Why not? Surely some want to escape from the endless cynicism and hopelessness
Good heavens!
He's—he's a bloody dissident! A borderline believer at the very least!
By Nothing! Keep it down! You'll have me hanged, by the void! It's not like that at all
Oh reeally? And wot then, pray tell, is it like?
Are you going to turn me in?
Not if your story is at all ***interesting....***
Well, it all started when I was framed for a murder I didn't commit. They sent demons after me, but I escaped, and managed to get on the train out of town. Now I hope to defect to Optima, but perhaps you could put in a word for me in Gesamt....
!!!
Oh how terribly cliche. That wasn't interesting at all. Where's the conductor?

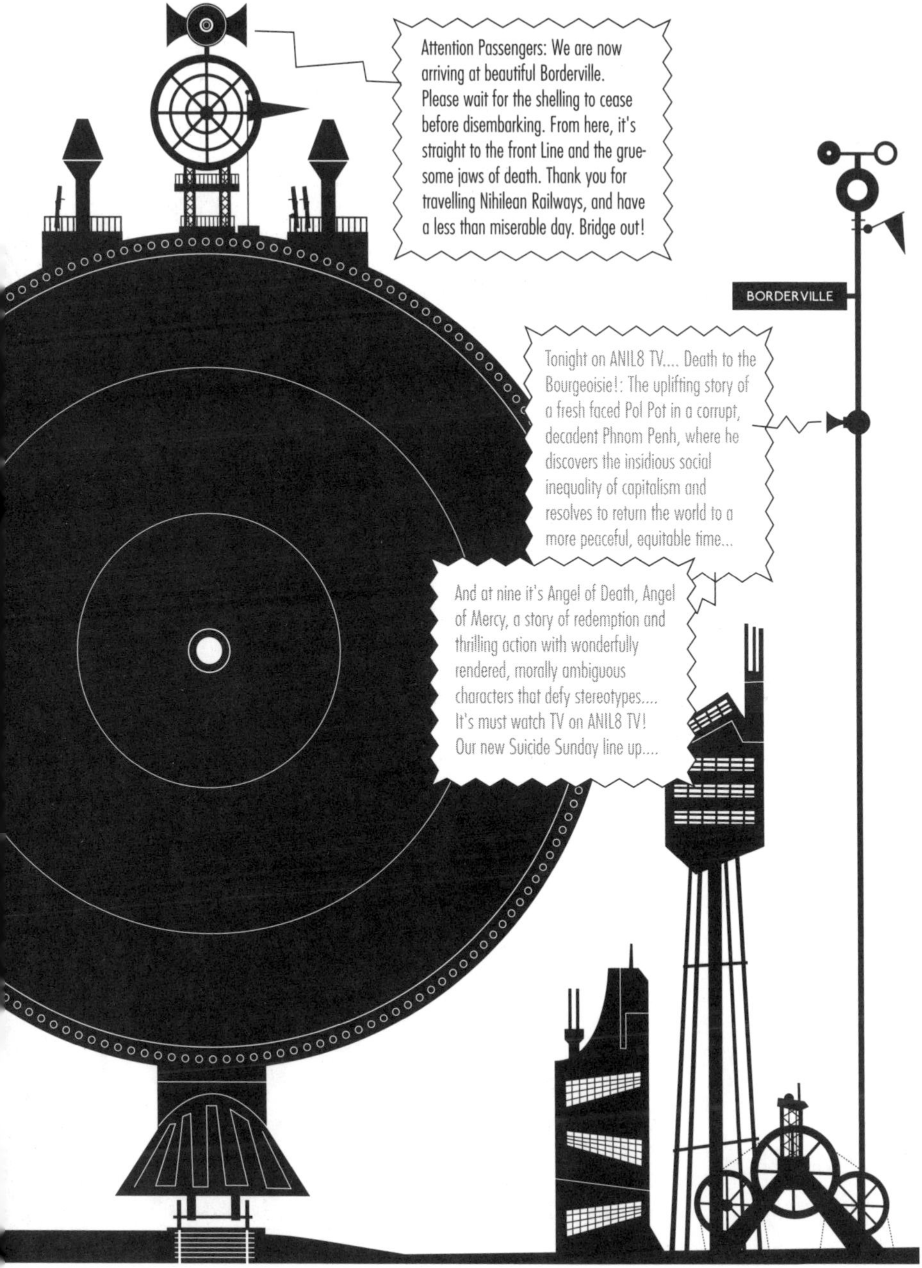
Attention Passengers: We are now arriving at beautiful Borderville. Please wait for the shelling to cease before disembarking. From here, it's straight to the front Line and the gruesome jaws of death. Thank you for travelling Nihilean Railways, and have a less than miserable day. Bridge out!
BORDERVILLE
Tonight on ANIL8 TV.... Death to the Bourgeoisie!: The uplifting story of a fresh faced Pol Pot in a corrupt, decadent Phnom Penh, where he discovers the insidious social inequality of capitalism and resolves to return the world to a more peaceful, equitable time...
And at nine it's Angel of Death, Angel of Mercy, a story of redemption and thrilling action with wonderfully rendered, morally ambiguous characters that defy stereotypes.... It's must watch TV on ANIL8 TV! Our new Suicide Sunday line up....

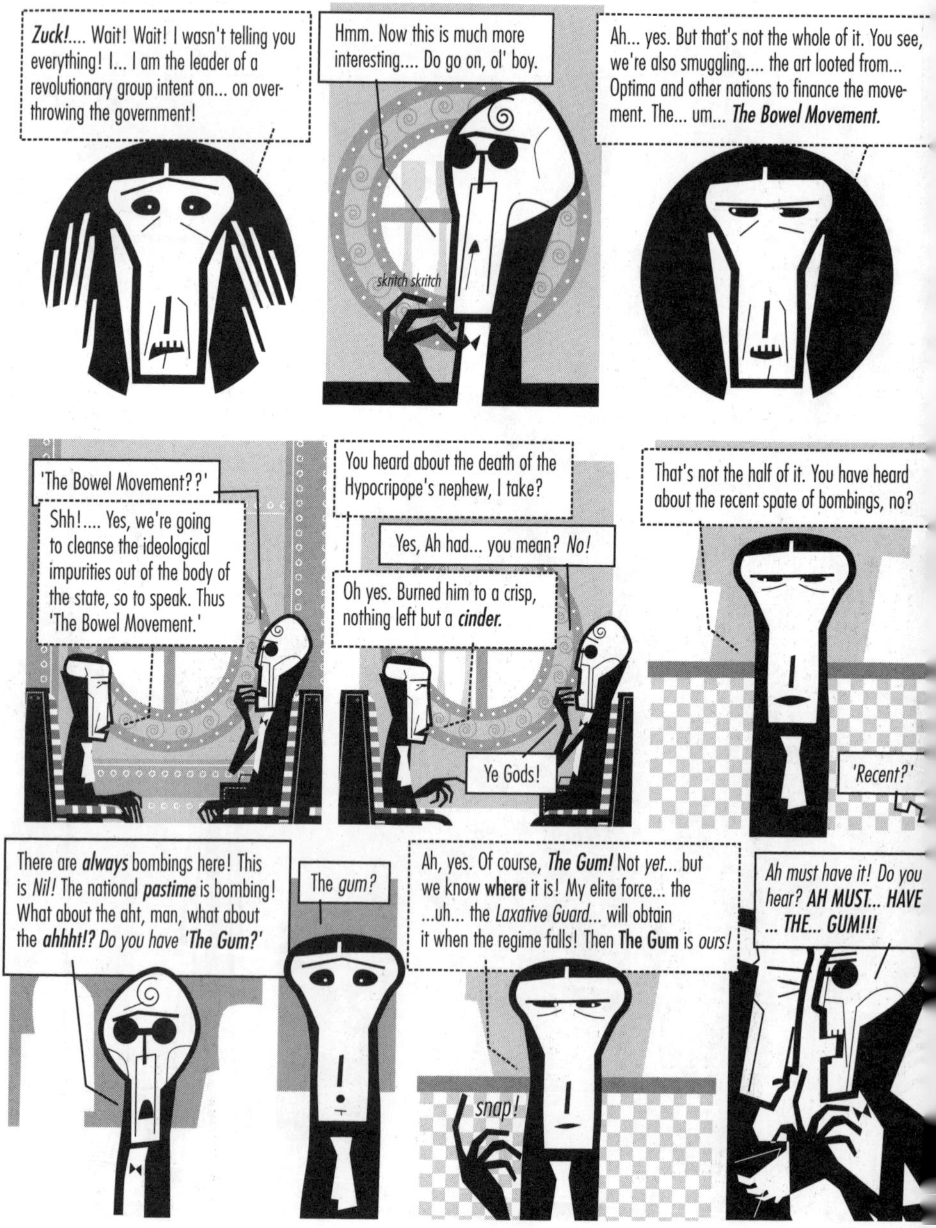

Zuck!.... Wait! Wait! I wasn't telling you everything! I... I am the leader of a revolutionary group intent on... on over-throwing the government!
Hmm. Now this is much more interesting.... Do go on, ol' boy.
skritch skritch
Ah... yes. But that's not the whole of it. You see, we're also smuggling.... the art looted from... Optima and other nations to finance the move-ment. The... um... ***The Bowel Movement.***
'The Bowel Movement??'
Shh!.... Yes, we're going to cleanse the ideological impurities out of the body of the state, so to speak. Thus 'The Bowel Movement.'
You heard about the death of the Hypocripope's nephew, I take?
Yes, Ah had... you mean? *No!*
Oh yes. Burned him to a crisp, nothing left but a ***cinder.***
Ye Gods!
That's not the half of it. You have heard about the recent spate of bombings, no?
'Recent?'
There are ***always*** bombings here! This is *Nil!* The national ***pastime*** is bombing! What about the aht, man, what about the ***ahhht!?*** *Do you have* ***'The Gum?'***
The *gum?*
Ah, yes. Of course, ***The Gum!*** Not *yet*... but we know **where** it is! My elite force... the ...uh... the *Laxative Guard*... will obtain it when the regime falls! Then **The Gum** is *ours!*
snap!
Ah must have it! Do you hear? ***AH MUST... HAVE ... THE... GUM!!!***

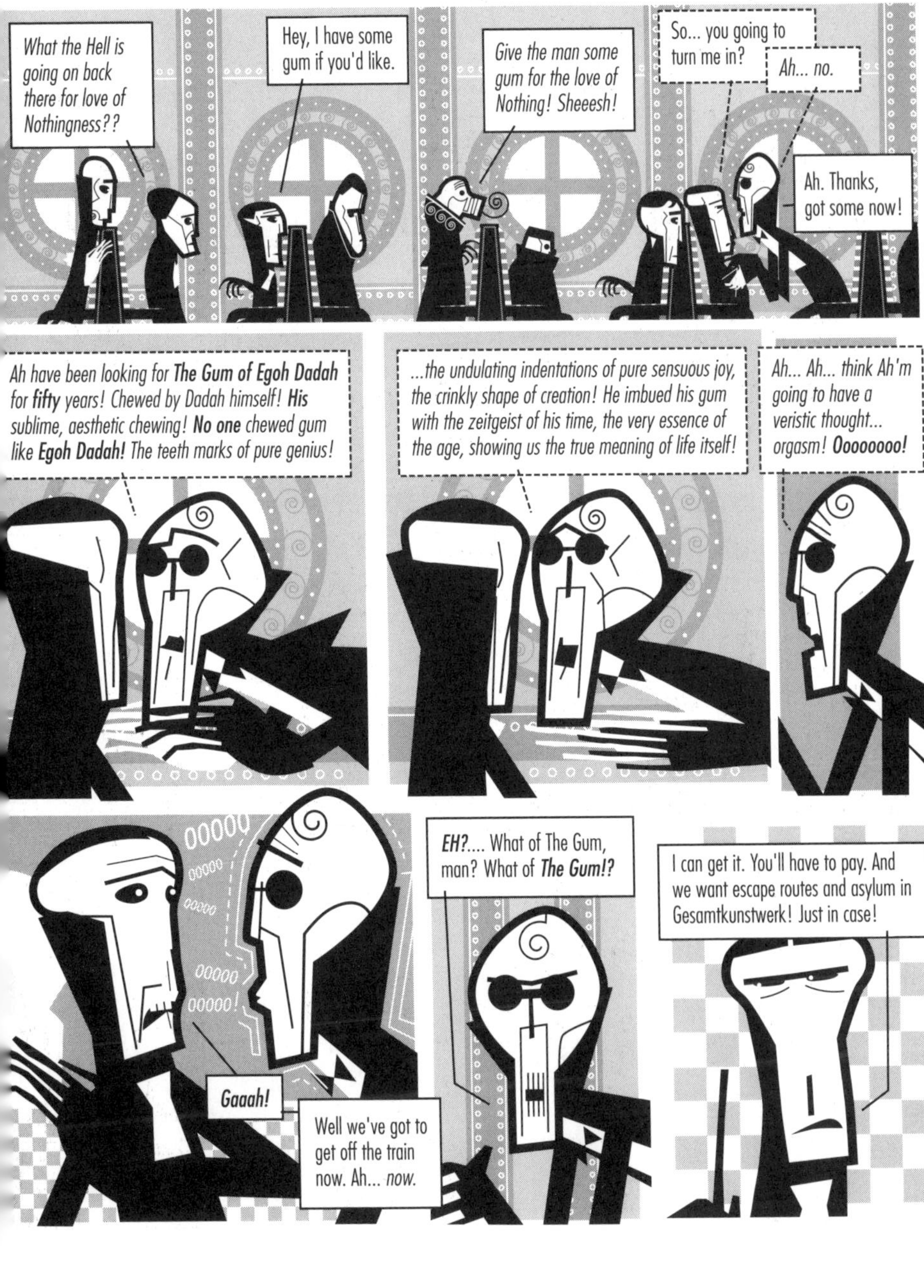
What the Hell is going on back there for love of Nothingness??
Hey, I have some gum if you'd like.
Give the man some gum for the love of Nothing! Sheeesh!
So... you going to turn me in?
Ah... no.
Ah. Thanks, got some now!
Ah have been looking for The Gum of Egoh Dadah for fifty years! Chewed by Dadah himself! His sublime, aesthetic chewing! No one chewed gum like Egoh Dadah! The teeth marks of pure genius!
...the undulating indentations of pure sensuous joy, the crinkly shape of creation! He imbued his gum with the zeitgeist of his time, the very essence of the age, showing us the true meaning of life itself!
Ah... Ah... think Ah'm going to have a veristic thought... orgasm! Ooooooo!
OOOOO
OOOOO
OOOOO
OOOOO
OOOOO!
Gaaah!
Well we've got to get off the train now. Ah... now.
EH?.... What of The Gum, man? What of The Gum!?
I can get it. You'll have to pay. And we want escape routes and asylum in Gesamtkunstwerk! Just in case!

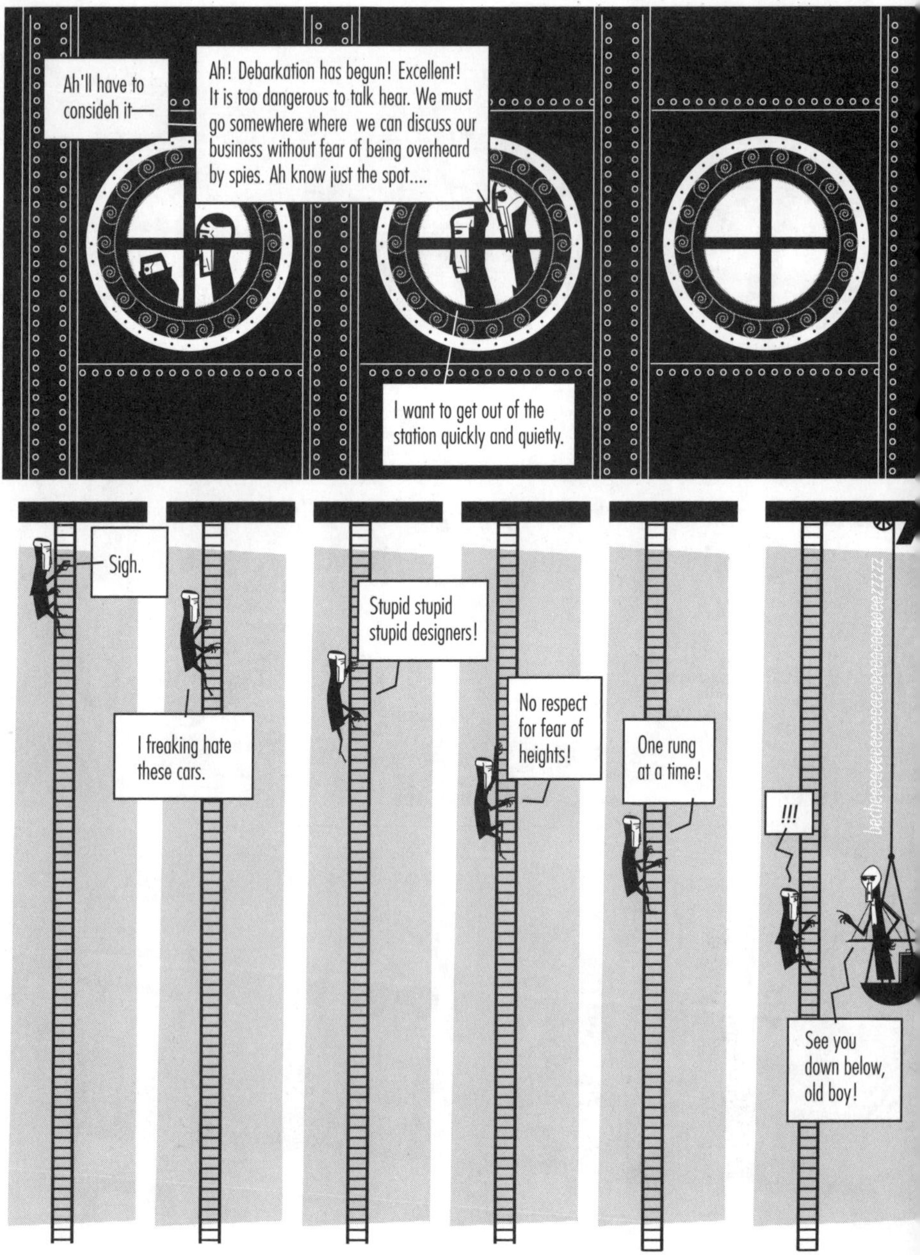
Ah'll have to consideh it—
Ah! Debarkation has begun! Excellent! It is too dangerous to talk hear. We must go somewhere where we can discuss our business without fear of being overheard by spies. Ah know just the spot....
I want to get out of the station quickly and quietly.
Sigh.
I freaking hate these cars.
Stupid stupid stupid designers!
No respect for fear of heights!
One rung at a time!
!!!
See you down below, old boy!

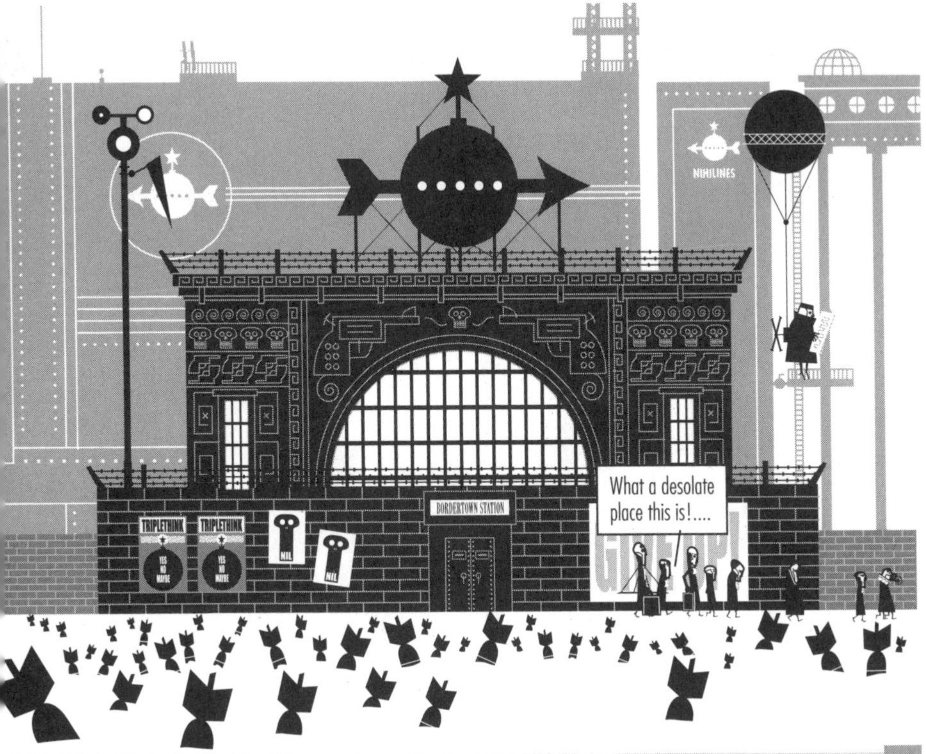
NIHILINES
TRIPLETHINK
YES
NO
MAYBE
TRIPLETHINK
YES
NO
MAYBE
NIL
NIL
BORDERTOWN STATION
What a desolate place this is!....

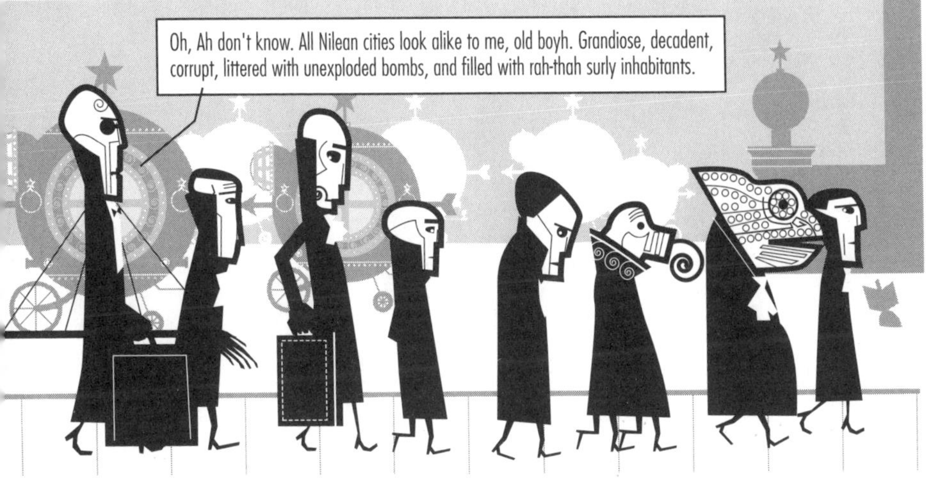
Oh, Ah don't know. All Nilean cities look alike to me, old boyh. Grandiose, decadent, corrupt, littered with unexploded bombs, and filled with rah-thah surly inhabitants.

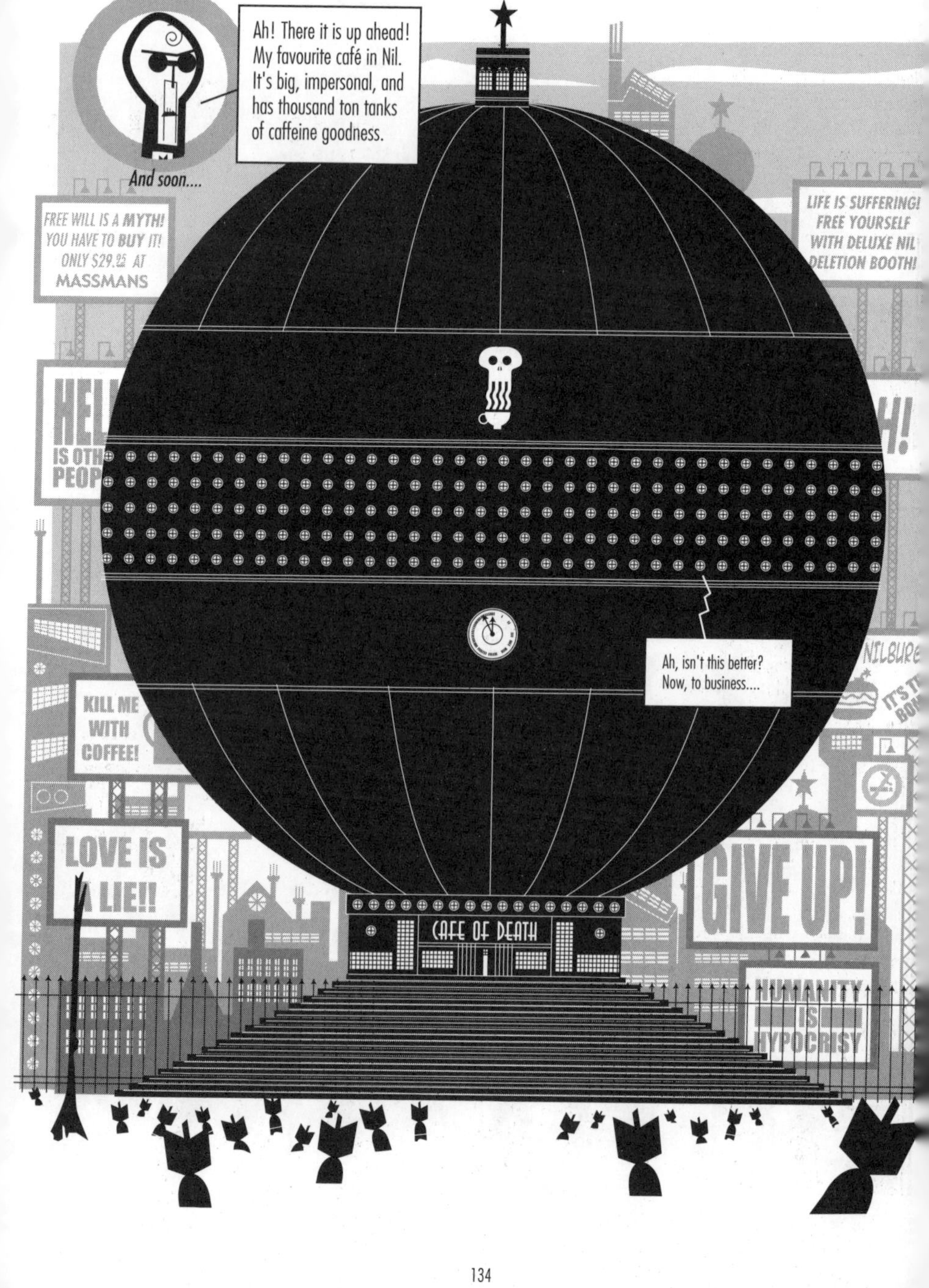
Ah! There it is up ahead! My favourite café in Nil. It's big, impersonal, and has thousand ton tanks of caffeine goodness.
And soon....
FREE WILL IS A MYTH! YOU HAVE TO BUY IT! ONLY $29.99 AT MASSMANS
LIFE IS SUFFERING! FREE YOURSELF WITH DELUXE NIL DELETION BOOTH!
Ah, isn't this better? Now, to business....
KILL ME WITH COFFEE!
LOVE IS
LIE!!
GIVE UP!
HUMANITY IS HYPOCRISY
CAFE OF DEATH

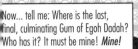

Now... tell me: Where is the last, final, culminating Gum of Egoh Dadah? Who has it? It must be mine! *Mine!*

..the ruling clique has it. They will never give it up, not while they still *live.*

But if we overthrow the government, it will be *yours!*

Excellent! Ah shall talk to my government about supporting your men.

Ah must say Ah have always supported your cause!

Ey, An' wot cause might that be, mate?

CAFE OF DEATH

Oh, don't worry. This is Mr. Thugbash. He... *secures* aht objects for me on occasion....

Oh!... Didn't see you there. No cause, ah, just a figure of speech. Heh!

Indeed.

It's been a time since I split skulls for you, Guv. It's good to 'ave you back! A good beatin's much more rewardin when it has a purpose, eh? Two Death By Coffee coming up....

CAFE OF DEATH

!!!

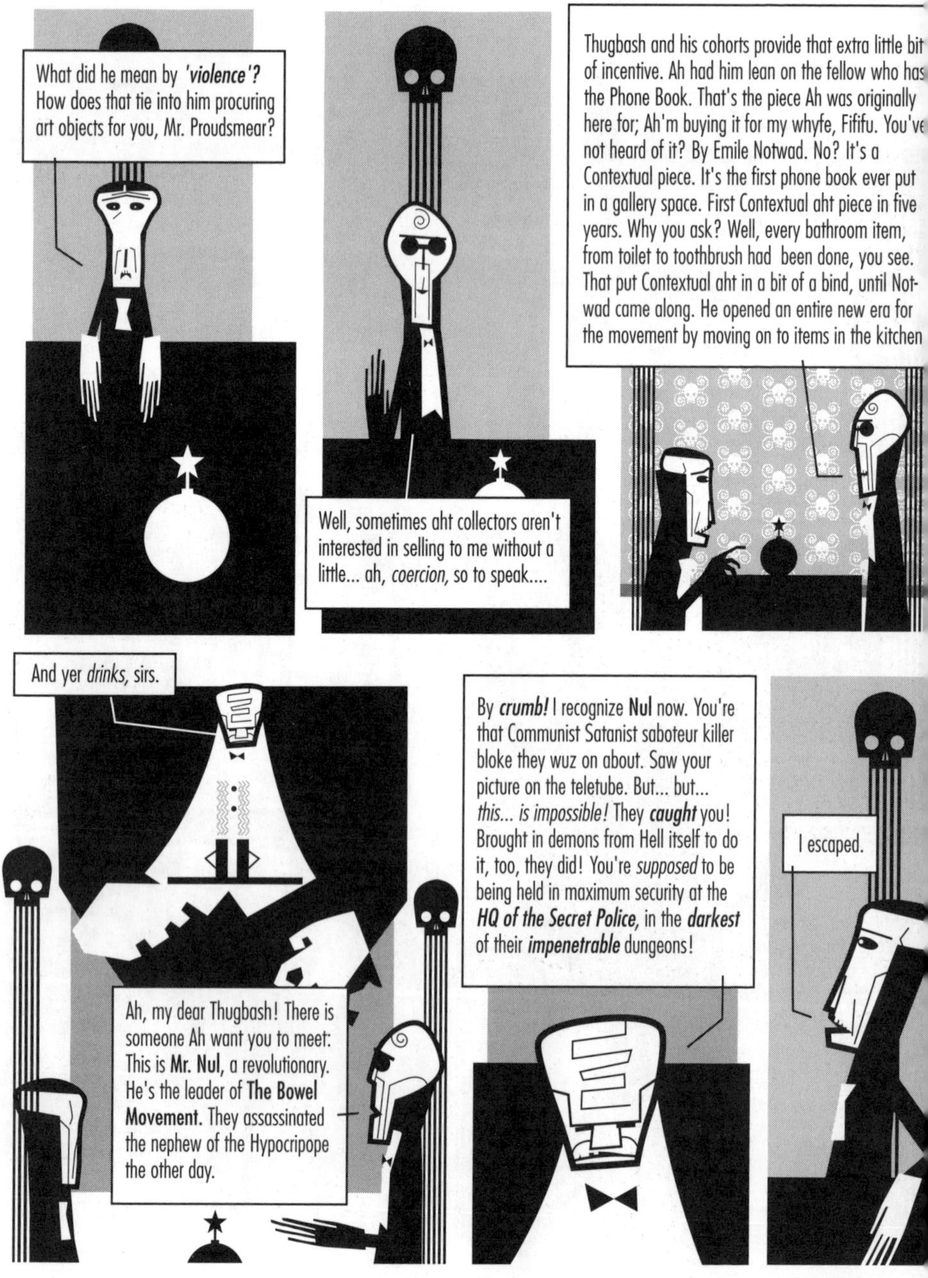
What did he mean by ***'violence'?*** How does that tie into him procuring art objects for you, Mr. Proudsmear?
Well, sometimes aht collectors aren't interested in selling to me without a little... ah, *coercion,* so to speak....
Thugbash and his cohorts provide that extra little bit of incentive. Ah had him lean on the fellow who has the Phone Book. That's the piece Ah was originally here for; Ah'm buying it for my whyfe, Fififu. You've not heard of it? By Emile Notwad. No? It's a Contextual piece. It's the first phone book ever put in a gallery space. First Contextual aht piece in five years. Why you ask? Well, every bathroom item, from toilet to toothbrush had been done, you see. That put Contextual aht in a bit of a bind, until Notwad came along. He opened an entire new era for the movement by moving on to items in the kitchen
And yer *drinks,* sirs.
Ah, my dear Thugbash! There is someone Ah want you to meet: This is **Mr. Nul**, a revolutionary. He's the leader of **The Bowel Movement**. They assassinated the nephew of the Hypocripope the other day.
By ***crumb!*** I recognize **Nul** now. You're that Communist Satanist saboteur killer bloke they wuz on about. Saw your picture on the teletube. But... but... *this... is impossible!* They ***caught*** you! Brought in demons from Hell itself to do it, too, they did! You're *supposed* to be being held in maximum security at the ***HQ of the Secret Police,*** in the ***darkest*** of their ***impenetrable*** dungeons!
I escaped.

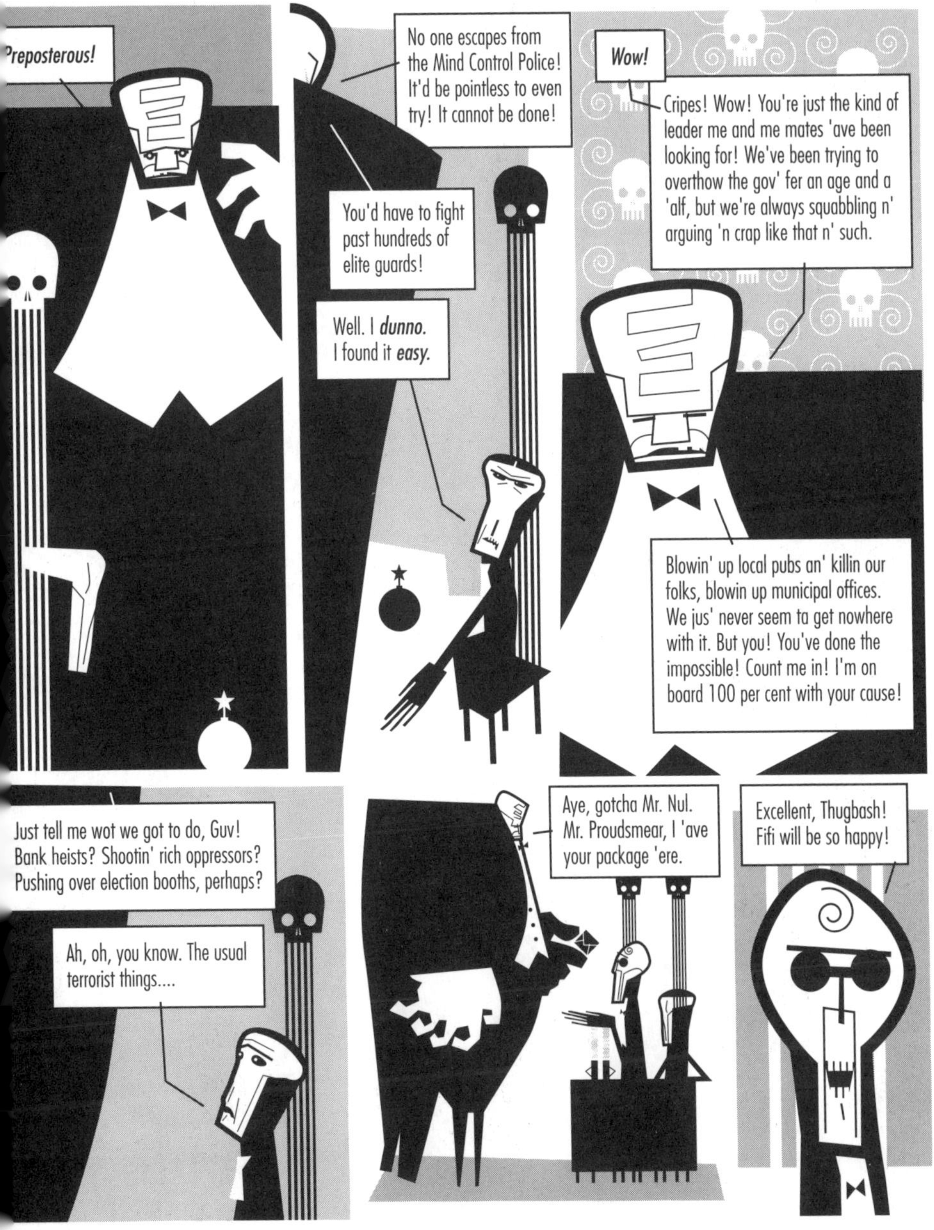

Preposterous!
No one escapes from the Mind Control Police! It'd be pointless to even try! It cannot be done!
You'd have to fight past hundreds of elite guards!
Well. I *dunno.* I found it *easy.*
Wow!
Cripes! Wow! You're just the kind of leader me and me mates 'ave been looking for! We've been trying to overthow the gov' fer an age and a 'alf, but we're always squabbling n' arguing 'n crap like that n' such.
Blowin' up local pubs an' killin our folks, blowin up municipal offices. We jus' never seem ta get nowhere with it. But you! You've done the impossible! Count me in! I'm on board 100 per cent with your cause!
Just tell me wot we got to do, Guv! Bank heists? Shootin' rich oppressors? Pushing over election booths, perhaps?
Ah, oh, you know. The usual terrorist things....
Aye, gotcha Mr. Nul. Mr. Proudsmear, I 'ave your package 'ere.
Excellent, Thugbash! Fifi will be so happy!

Meanwhile, Muck and Puk have moved on to a particularly seedy bar....

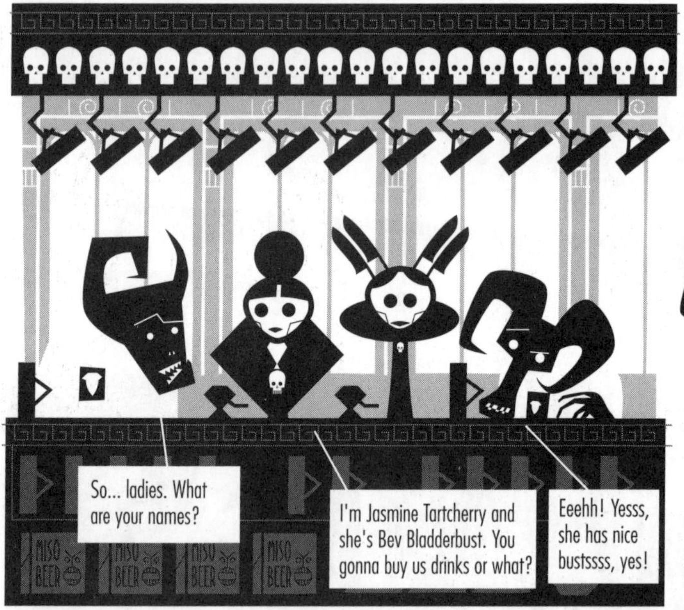

So... ladies. What are your names?
I'm Jasmine Tartcherry and she's Bev Bladderbust. You gonna buy us drinks or what?
Eeehh! Yesss, she has nice bustssss, yes!
MISO BEER
MISO BEER
MISO BEER
MISO BEER

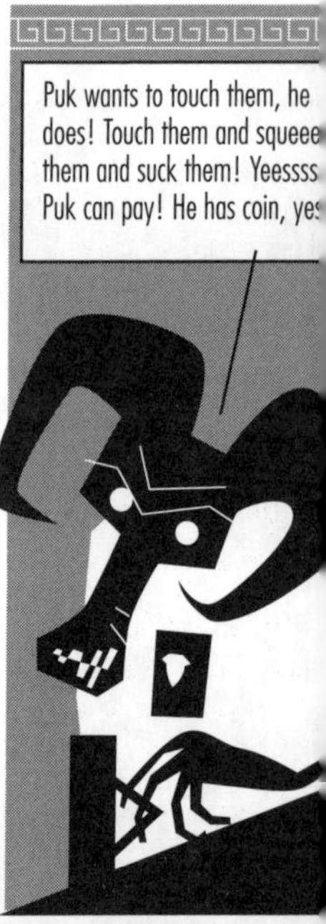

Puk wants to touch them, he does! Touch them and squeee them and suck them! Yeessss Puk can pay! He has coin, ye

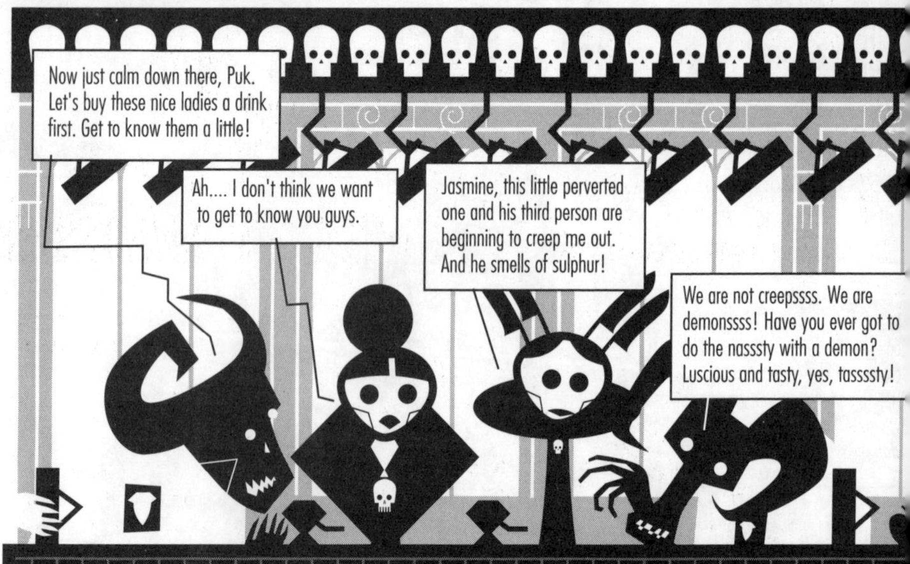

Now just calm down there, Puk. Let's buy these nice ladies a drink first. Get to know them a little!
Ah.... I don't think we want to get to know you guys.
Jasmine, this little perverted one and his third person are beginning to creep me out. And he smells of sulphur!
We are not creepssss. We are demonssss! Have you ever got to do the nasssty with a demon? Luscious and tasty, yes, tassssty!

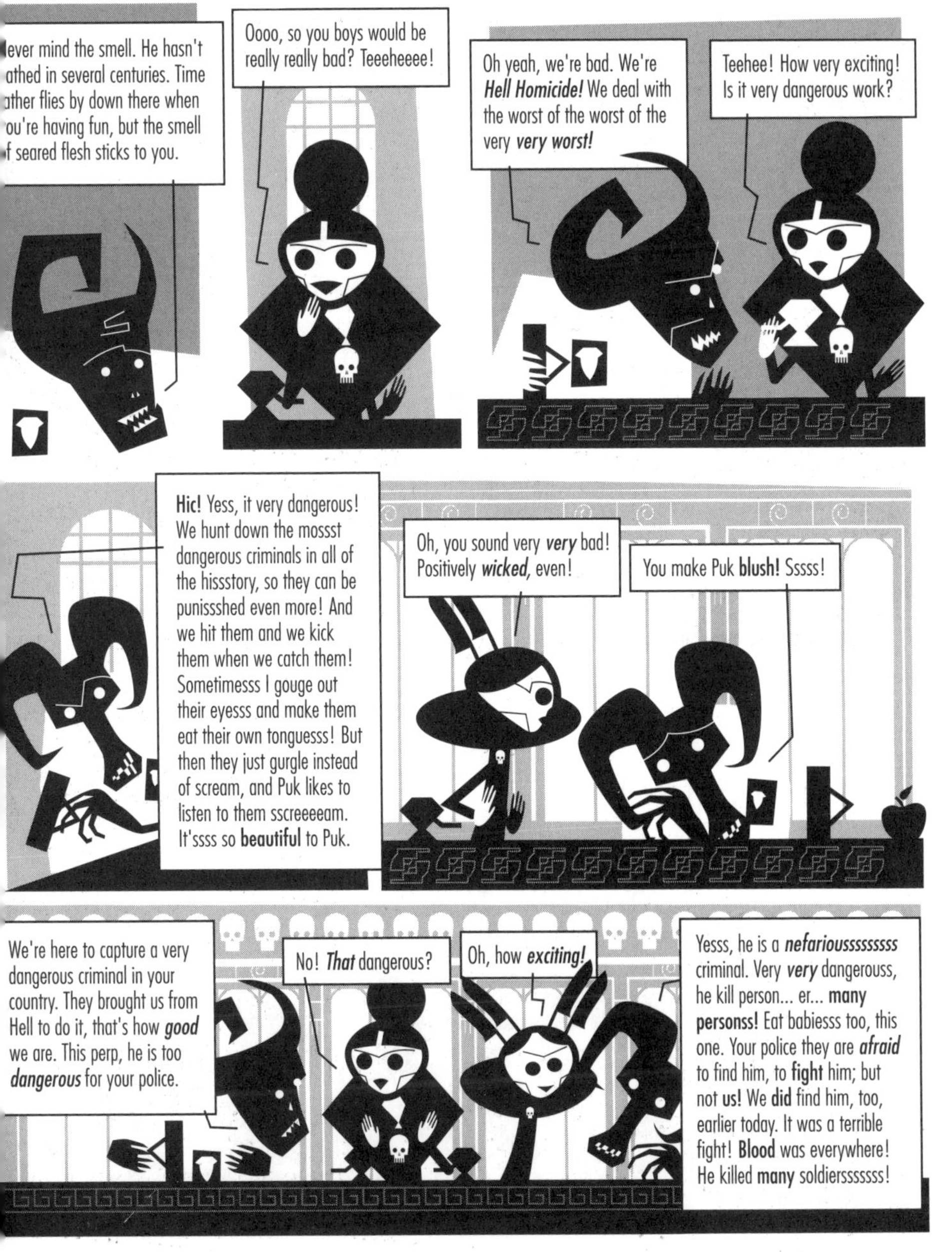
ever mind the smell. He hasn't athed in several centuries. Time ather flies by down there when ou're having fun, but the smell f seared flesh sticks to you.
Oooo, so you boys would be really really bad? Teeeheeee!
Oh yeah, we're bad. We're ***Hell Homicide!*** We deal with the worst of the worst of the very ***very worst!***
Teehee! How very exciting! Is it very dangerous work?
Hic! Yess, it very dangerous! We hunt down the mossst dangerous criminals in all of the hissstory, so they can be punissshed even more! And we hit them and we kick them when we catch them! Sometimesss I gouge out their eyesss and make them eat their own tonguesss! But then they just gurgle instead of scream, and Puk likes to listen to them sscreeeeam. It'ssss so **beautiful** to Puk.
Oh, you sound very ***very*** bad! Positively ***wicked,*** even!
You make Puk **blush!** Sssss!
We're here to capture a very dangerous criminal in your country. They brought us from Hell to do it, that's how ***good*** we are. This perp, he is too ***dangerous*** for your police.
No! ***That*** dangerous?
Oh, how ***exciting!***
Yesss, he is a ***nefariousssssssss*** criminal. Very ***very*** dangerouss, he kill person... er... **many personss!** Eat babiesss too, this one. Your police they are ***afraid*** to find him, to **fight** him; but not **us!** We **did** find him, too, earlier today. It was a terrible fight! **Blood** was everywhere! He killed **many** soldiersssssss!

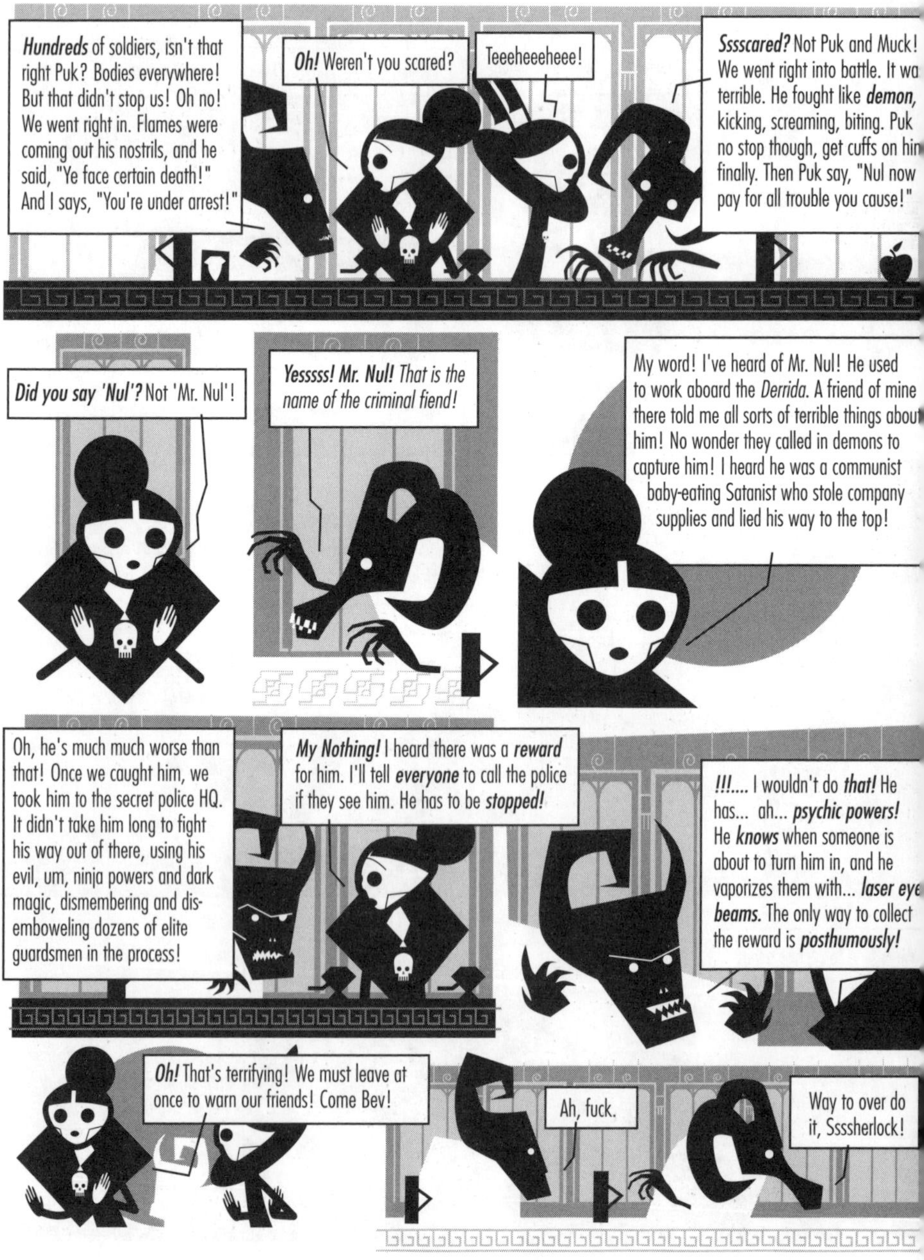

Hundreds of soldiers, isn't that right Puk? Bodies everywhere! But that didn't stop us! Oh no! We went right in. Flames were coming out his nostrils, and he said, "Ye face certain death!" And I says, "You're under arrest!"
Oh! Weren't you scared?
Teeeheeeheee!
Sssscared? Not Puk and Muck! We went right into battle. It wa terrible. He fought like ***demon,*** kicking, screaming, biting. Puk no stop though, get cuffs on hir finally. Then Puk say, "Nul now pay for all trouble you cause!"
Did you say 'Nul'? Not 'Mr. Nul'!
Yesssss! Mr. Nul! *That is the name of the criminal fiend!*
My word! I've heard of Mr. Nul! He used to work aboard the *Derrida*. A friend of mine there told me all sorts of terrible things abou him! No wonder they called in demons to capture him! I heard he was a communist baby-eating Satanist who stole company supplies and lied his way to the top!
Oh, he's much much worse than that! Once we caught him, we took him to the secret police HQ. It didn't take him long to fight his way out of there, using his evil, um, ninja powers and dark magic, dismembering and dis-emboweling dozens of elite guardsmen in the process!
My Nothing! I heard there was a ***reward*** for him. I'll tell ***everyone*** to call the police if they see him. He has to be ***stopped!***
!!!.... I wouldn't do ***that!*** He has... ah... ***psychic powers!*** He ***knows*** when someone is about to turn him in, and he vaporizes them with... ***laser eye beams.*** The only way to collect the reward is ***posthumously!***
Oh! That's terrifying! We must leave at once to warn our friends! Come Bev!
Ah, fuck.
Way to over do it, Sssherlock!

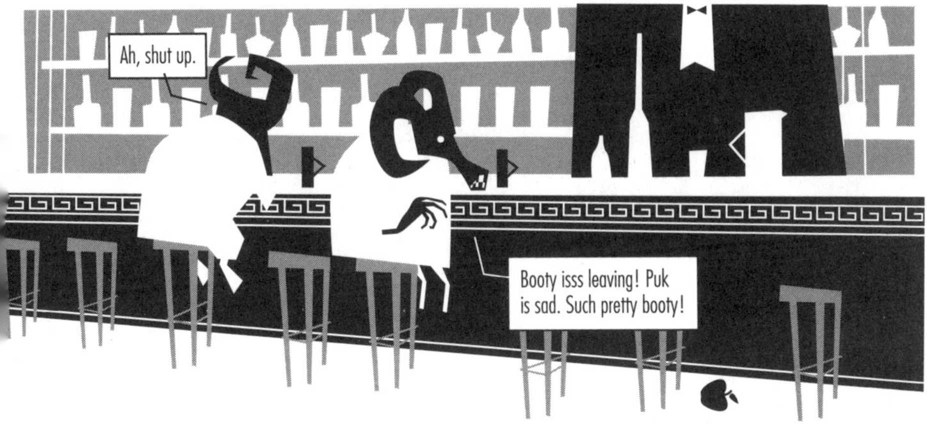

Ah, shut up.
Booty isss leaving! Puk is sad. Such pretty booty!

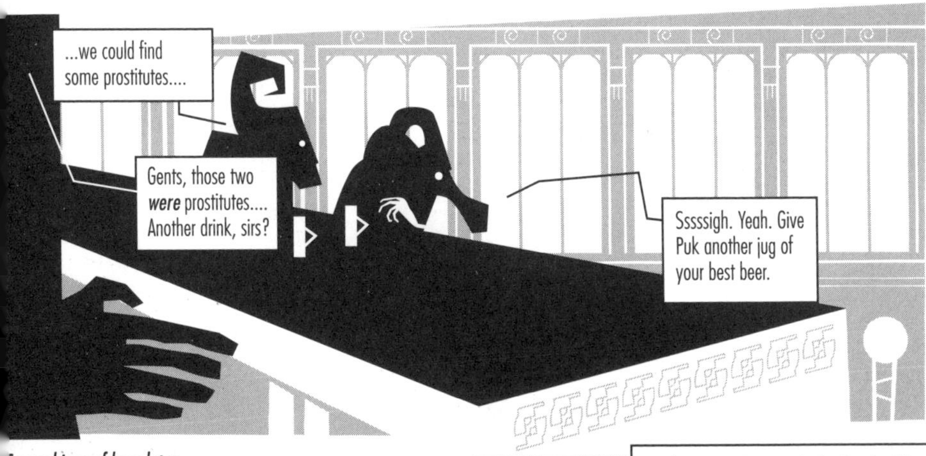

...we could find some prostitutes....
Gents, those two *were* prostitutes.... Another drink, sirs?
Sssssigh. Yeah. Give Puk another jug of your best beer.

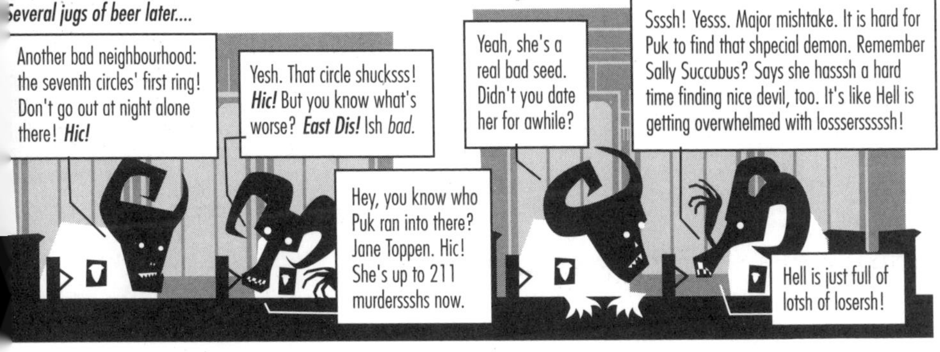

Several jugs of beer later....
Another bad neighbourhood: the seventh circles' first ring! Don't go out at night alone there! ***Hic!***
Yesh. That circle shucksss! ***Hic!*** But you know what's worse? ***East Dis!*** Ish *bad.*
Hey, you know who Puk ran into there? Jane Toppen. Hic! She's up to 211 murderssshs now.
Yeah, she's a real bad seed. Didn't you date her for awhile?
Ssssh! Yesss. Major mishtake. It is hard for Puk to find that shpecial demon. Remember Sally Succubus? Says she hasssh a hard time finding nice devil, too. It's like Hell is getting overwhelmed with lossersssssh!
Hell is just full of lotsh of losersh!

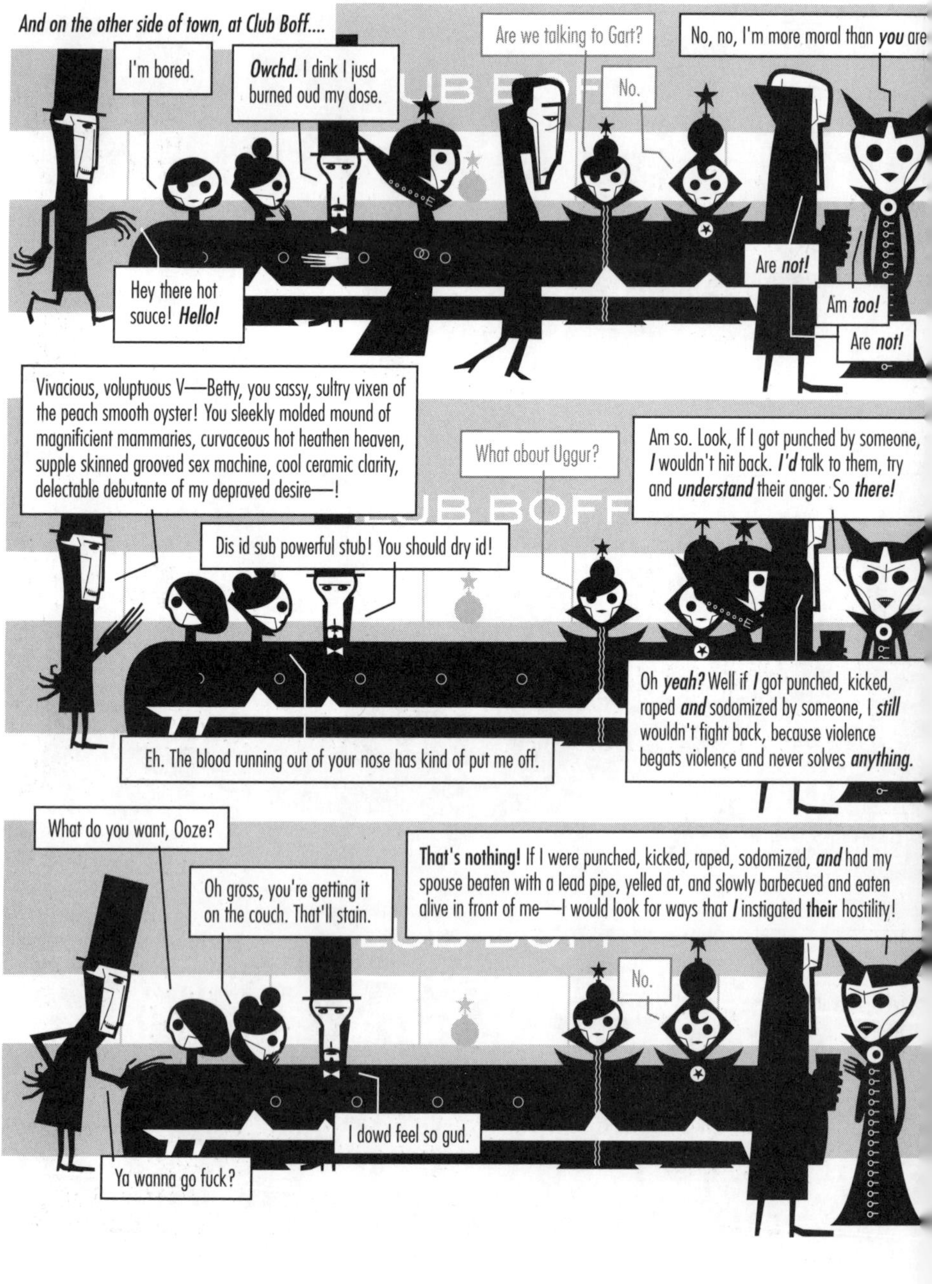
And on the other side of town, at Club Boff....
I'm bored.
Owchd. I dink I jusd burned oud my dose.
Are we talking to Gart?
No.
No, no, I'm more moral than you are
Hey there hot sauce! Hello!
Are not!
Am too!
Are not!
Vivacious, voluptuous V—Betty, you sassy, sultry vixen of the peach smooth oyster! You sleekly molded mound of magnificient mammaries, curvaceous hot heathen heaven, supple skinned grooved sex machine, cool ceramic clarity, delectable debutante of my depraved desire—!
What about Uggur?
Am so. Look, If I got punched by someone, I wouldn't hit back. I'd talk to them, try and understand their anger. So there!
Dis id sub powerful stub! You should dry id!
Eh. The blood running out of your nose has kind of put me off.
Oh yeah? Well if I got punched, kicked, raped and sodomized by someone, I still wouldn't fight back, because violence begats violence and never solves anything.
What do you want, Ooze?
Oh gross, you're getting it on the couch. That'll stain.
That's nothing! If I were punched, kicked, raped, sodomized, and had my spouse beaten with a lead pipe, yelled at, and slowly barbecued and eaten alive in front of me—I would look for ways that I instigated their hostility!
No.
I dowd feel so gud.
Ya wanna go fuck?

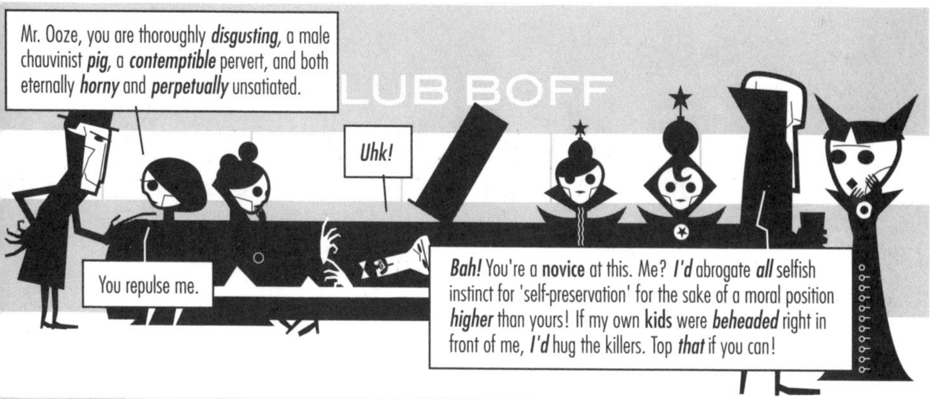
Mr. Ooze, you are thoroughly ***disgusting,*** a male chauvinist ***pig,*** a ***contemptible*** pervert, and both eternally ***horny*** and ***perpetually*** unsatiated.
CLUB BOFF
Uhk!
You repulse me.
Bah! You're a **novice** at this. Me? ***I'd*** abrogate ***all*** selfish instinct for 'self-preservation' for the sake of a moral position ***higher*** than yours! If my own **kids** were ***beheaded*** right in front of me, ***I'd*** hug the killers. Top ***that*** if you can!

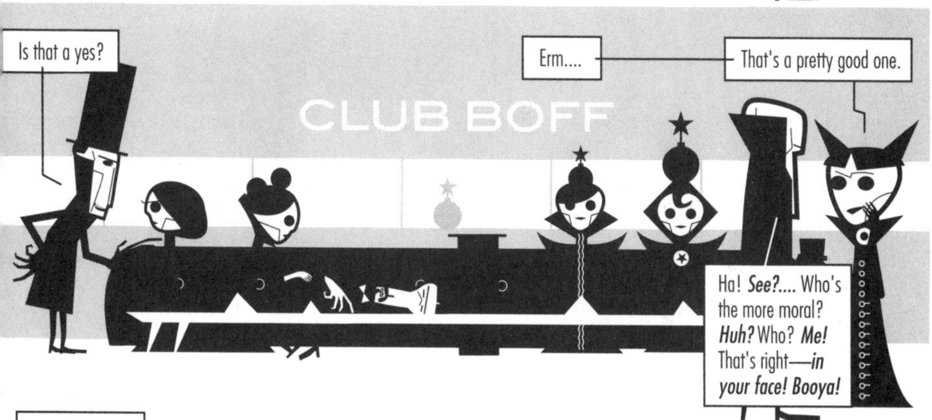
Is that a yes?
Erm....
That's a pretty good one.
CLUB BOFF
Ha! ***See?....*** Who's the more moral? ***Huh?*** Who? ***Me!*** That's right—***in your face! Booya!***

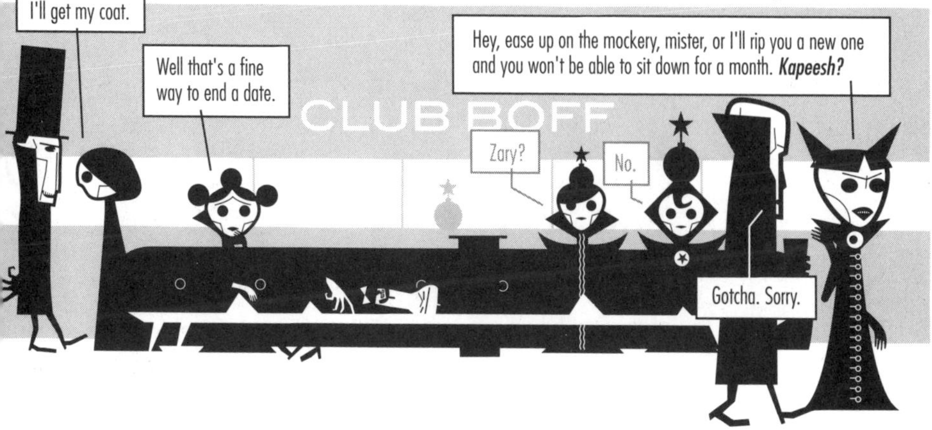
I'll get my coat.
Well that's a fine way to end a date.
Hey, ease up on the mockery, mister, or I'll rip you a new one and you won't be able to sit down for a month. ***Kapeesh?***
CLUB BOFF
Zary?
No.
Gotcha. Sorry.

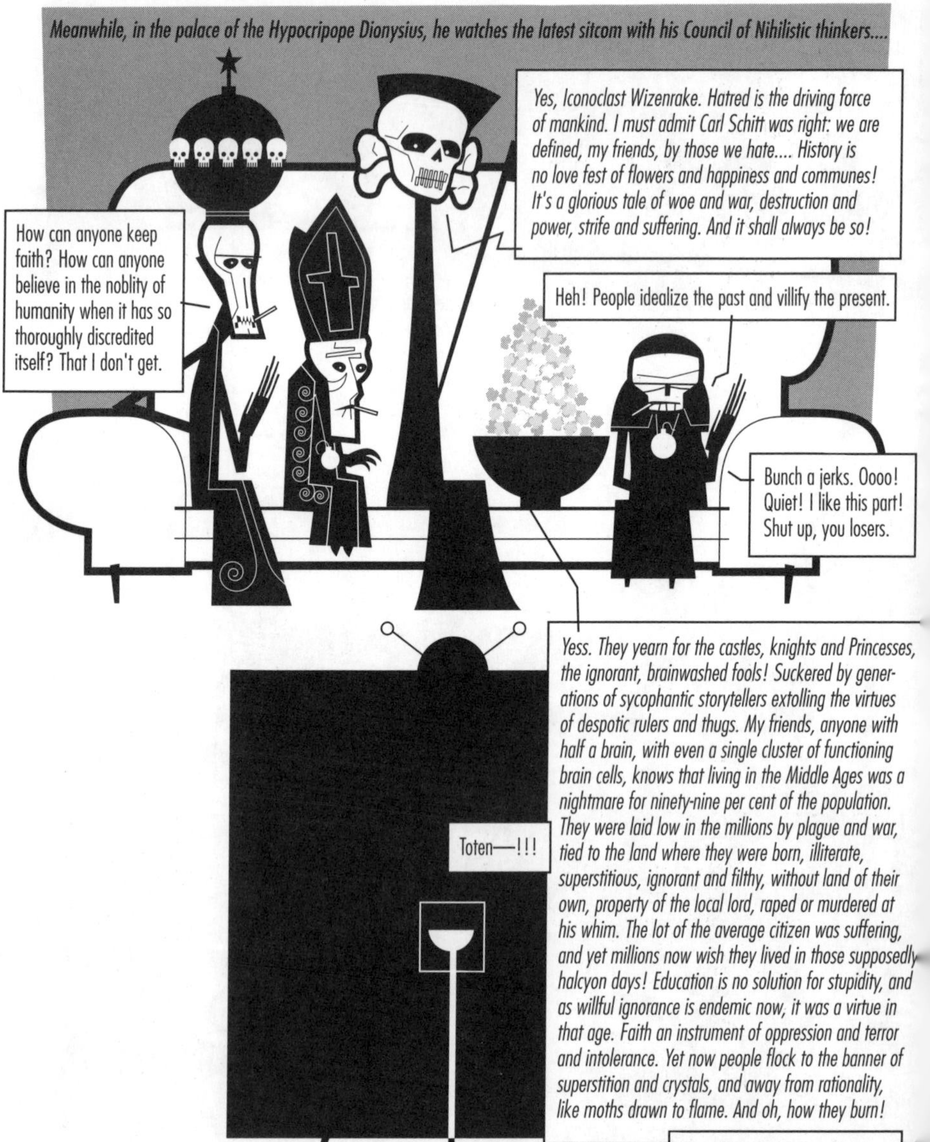
Meanwhile, in the palace of the Hypocripope Dionysius, he watches the latest sitcom with his Council of Nihilistic thinkers....
How can anyone keep faith? How can anyone believe in the noblity of humanity when it has so thoroughly discredited itself? That I don't get.
Yes, Iconoclast Wizenrake. Hatred is the driving force of mankind. I must admit Carl Schitt was right: we are defined, my friends, by those we hate.... History is no love fest of flowers and happiness and communes! It's a glorious tale of woe and war, destruction and power, strife and suffering. And it shall always be so!
Heh! People idealize the past and villify the present.
Bunch a jerks. Oooo! Quiet! I like this part! Shut up, you losers.
Yess. They yearn for the castles, knights and Princesses, the ignorant, brainwashed fools! Suckered by generations of sycophantic storytellers extolling the virtues of despotic rulers and thugs. My friends, anyone with half a brain, with even a single cluster of functioning brain cells, knows that living in the Middle Ages was a nightmare for ninety-nine per cent of the population. They were laid low in the millions by plague and war, tied to the land where they were born, illiterate, superstitious, ignorant and filthy, without land of their own, property of the local lord, raped or murdered at his whim. The lot of the average citizen was suffering, and yet millions now wish they lived in those supposedly halcyon days! Education is no solution for stupidity, and as willful ignorance is endemic now, it was a virtue in that age. Faith an instrument of oppression and terror and intolerance. Yet now people flock to the banner of superstition and crystals, and away from rationality, like moths drawn to flame. And oh, how they burn!
Toten—!!!
Shut the zuck up youse guys!—

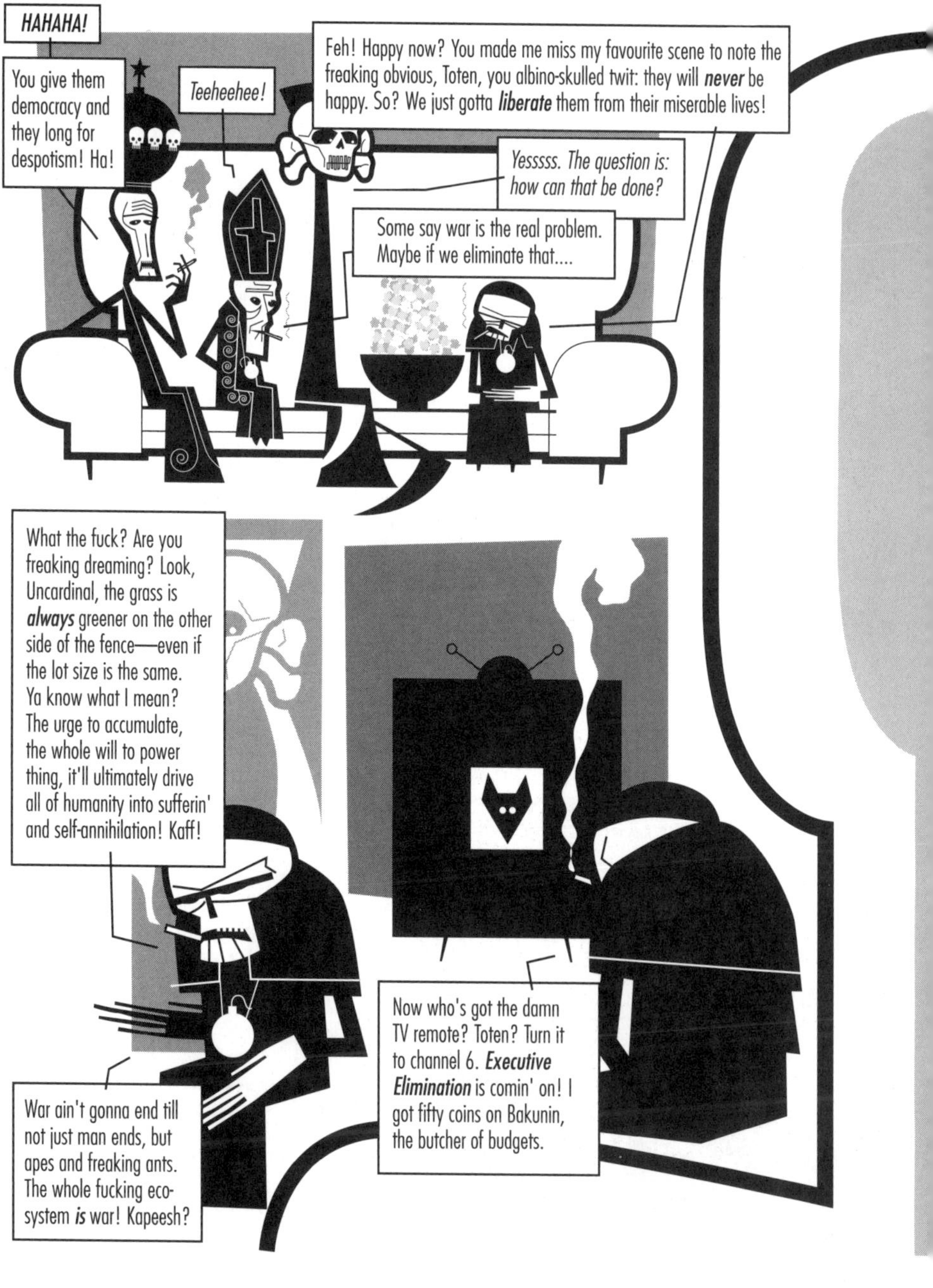
HAHAHA!
You give them democracy and they long for despotism! Ha!
Teeheehee!
Feh! Happy now? You made me miss my favourite scene to note the freaking obvious, Toten, you albino-skulled twit: they will ***never*** be happy. So? We just gotta ***liberate*** them from their miserable lives!
Yesssss. The question is: how can that be done?
Some say war is the real problem. Maybe if we eliminate that....
What the fuck? Are you freaking dreaming? Look, Uncardinal, the grass is ***always*** greener on the other side of the fence—even if the lot size is the same. Ya know what I mean? The urge to accumulate, the whole will to power thing, it'll ultimately drive all of humanity into sufferin' and self-annihilation! Kaff!
War ain't gonna end till not just man ends, but apes and freaking ants. The whole fucking eco-system ***is*** war! Kapeesh?
Now who's got the damn TV remote? Toten? Turn it to channel 6. ***Executive Elimination*** is comin' on! I got fifty coins on Bakunin, the butcher of budgets.

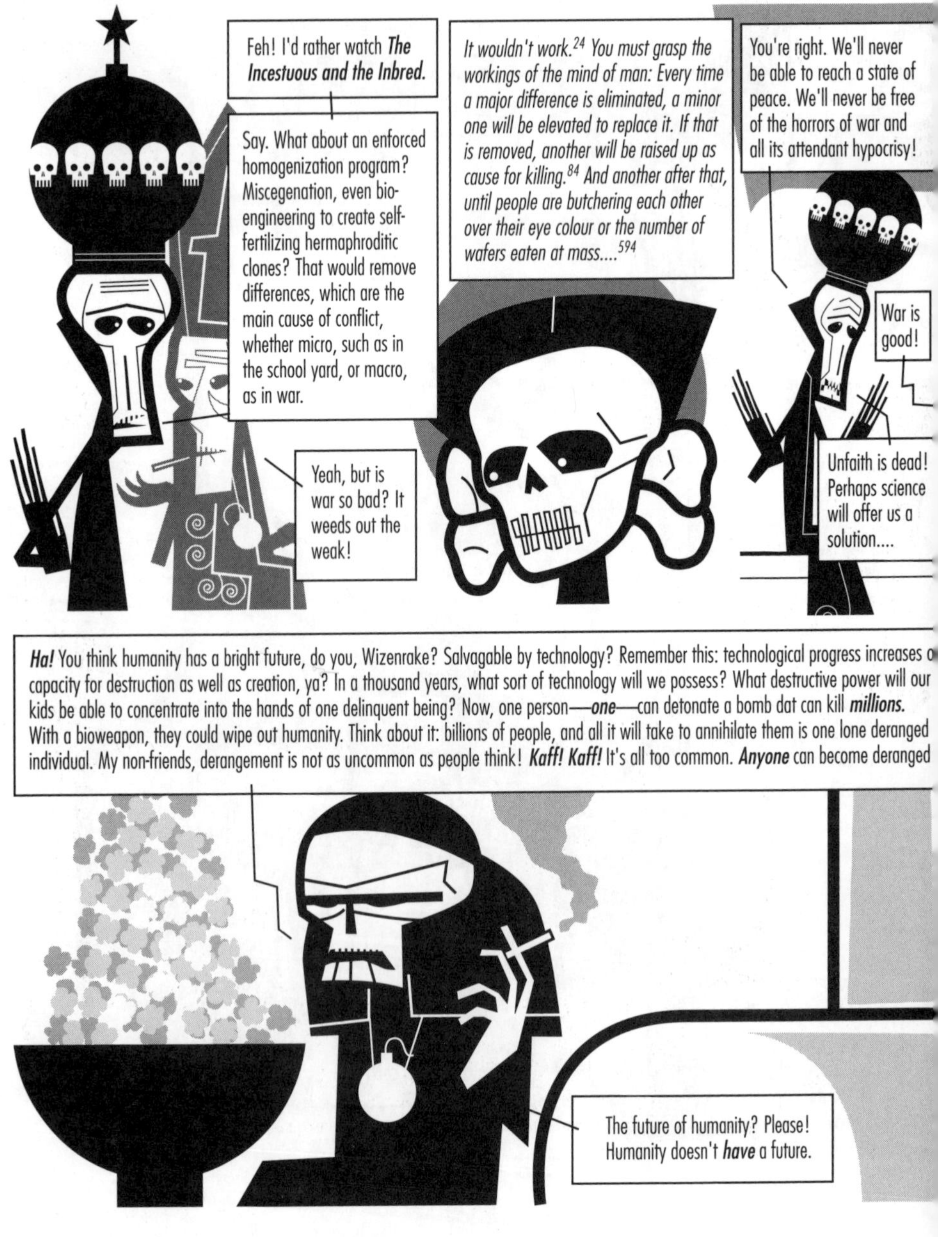

Feh! I'd rather watch ***The Incestuous and the Inbred.***
Say. What about an enforced homogenization program? Miscegenation, even bio-engineering to create self-fertilizing hermaphroditic clones? That would remove differences, which are the main cause of conflict, whether micro, such as in the school yard, or macro, as in war.
Yeah, but is war so bad? It weeds out the weak!
It wouldn't work.[24] You must grasp the workings of the mind of man: Every time a major difference is eliminated, a minor one will be elevated to replace it. If that is removed, another will be raised up as cause for killing.[84] And another after that, until people are butchering each other over their eye colour or the number of wafers eaten at mass....[594]
You're right. We'll never be able to reach a state of peace. We'll never be free of the horrors of war and all its attendant hypocrisy!
War is good!
Unfaith is dead! Perhaps science will offer us a solution....
Ha! You think humanity has a bright future, do you, Wizenrake? Salvagable by technology? Remember this: technological progress increases o capacity for destruction as well as creation, ya? In a thousand years, what sort of technology will we possess? What destructive power will our kids be able to concentrate into the hands of one delinquent being? Now, one person—***one***—can detonate a bomb dat can kill ***millions.*** With a bioweapon, they could wipe out humanity. Think about it: billions of people, and all it will take to annihilate them is one lone deranged individual. My non-friends, derangement is not as uncommon as people think! ***Kaff! Kaff!*** It's all too common. ***Anyone*** can become deranged
The future of humanity? Please! Humanity doesn't ***have*** a future.

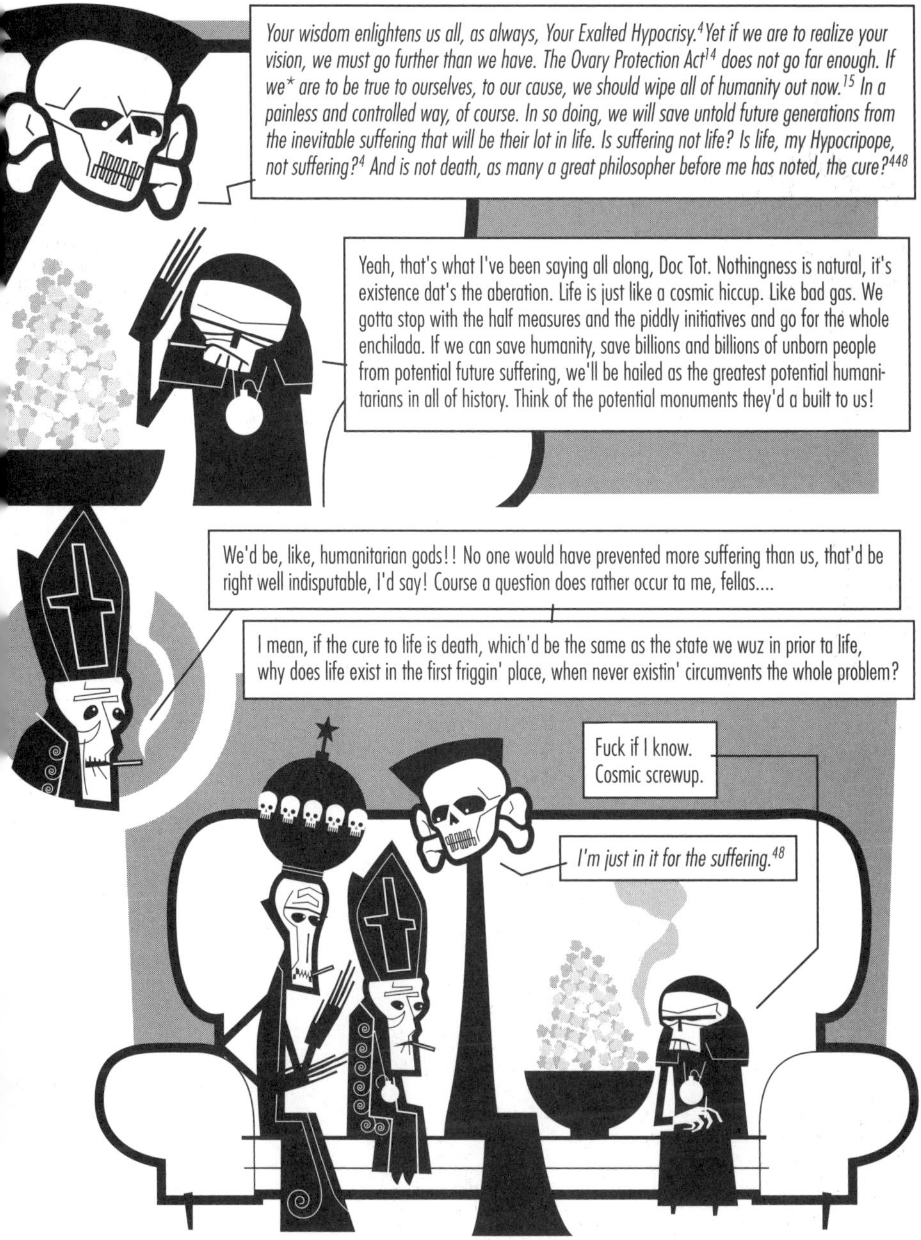
Your wisdom enlightens us all, as always, Your Exalted Hypocrisy.[4] Yet if we are to realize your vision, we must go further than we have. The Ovary Protection Act[14] does not go far enough. If we* are to be true to ourselves, to our cause, we should wipe all of humanity out now.[15] In a painless and controlled way, of course. In so doing, we will save untold future generations from the inevitable suffering that will be their lot in life. Is suffering not life? Is life, my Hypocripope, not suffering?[4] And is not death, as many a great philosopher before me has noted, the cure?[448]
Yeah, that's what I've been saying all along, Doc Tot. Nothingness is natural, it's existence dat's the aberation. Life is just like a cosmic hiccup. Like bad gas. We gotta stop with the half measures and the piddly initiatives and go for the whole enchilada. If we can save humanity, save billions and billions of unborn people from potential future suffering, we'll be hailed as the greatest potential humanitarians in all of history. Think of the potential monuments they'd a built to us!
We'd be, like, humanitarian gods!! No one would have prevented more suffering than us, that'd be right well indisputable, I'd say! Course a question does rather occur ta me, fellas....
I mean, if the cure to life is death, which'd be the same as the state we wuz in prior ta life, why does life exist in the first friggin' place, when never existin' circumvents the whole problem?
Fuck if I know. Cosmic screwup.
I'm just in it for the suffering.[48]

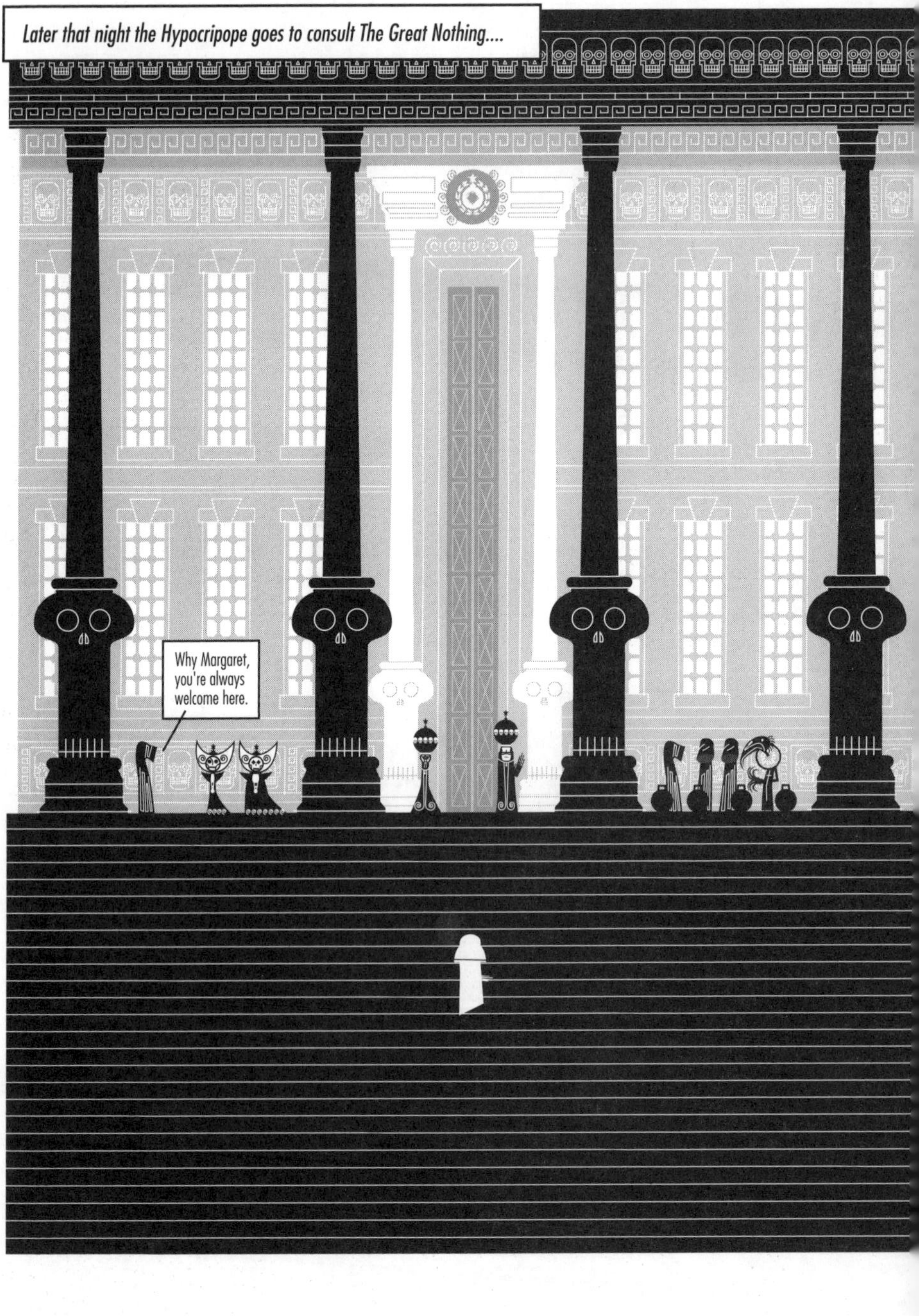
Later that night the Hypocripope goes to consult The Great Nothing....
Why Margaret, you're always welcome here.

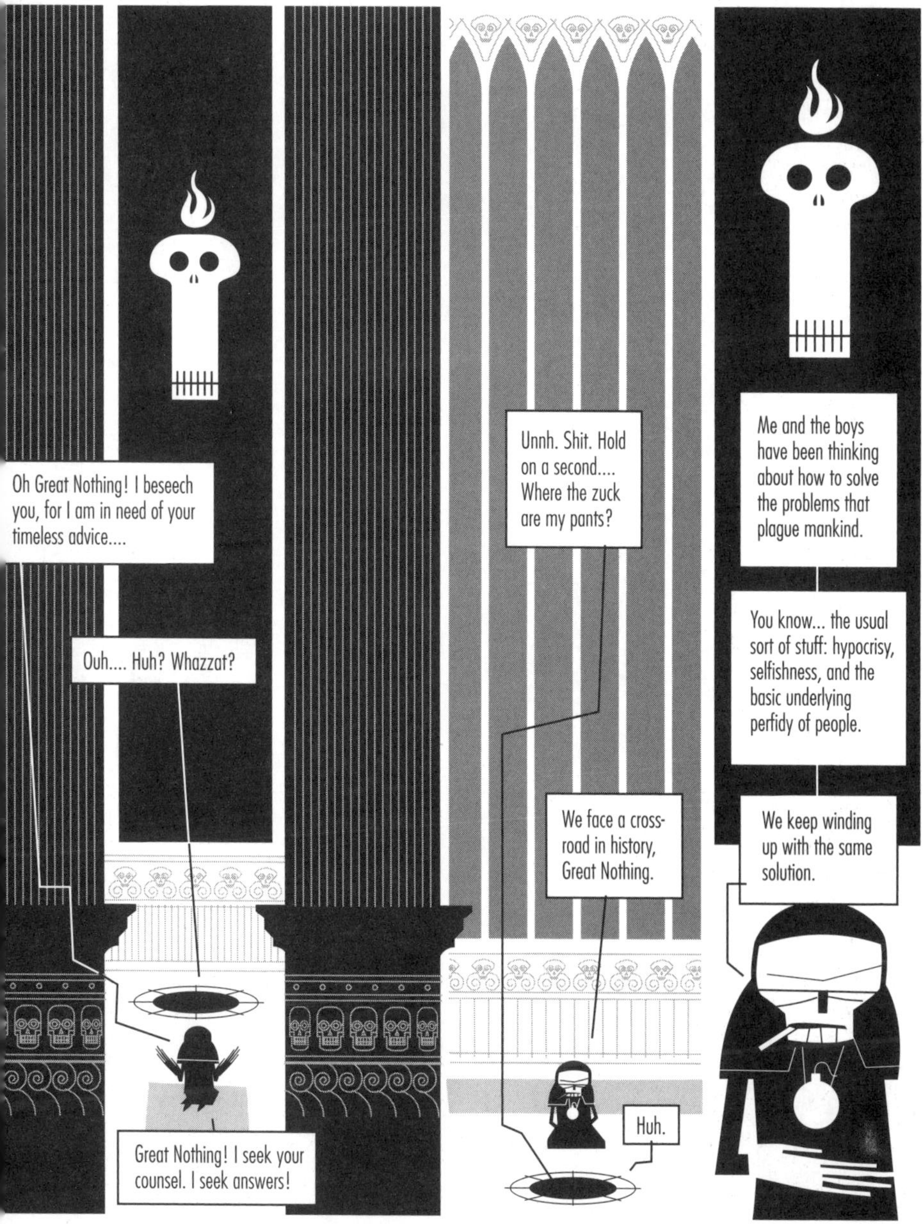

Oh Great Nothing! I beseech you, for I am in need of your timeless advice....
Ouh.... Huh? Whazzat?
Great Nothing! I seek your counsel. I seek answers!
Unnh. Shit. Hold on a second.... Where the zuck are my pants?
We face a cross-road in history, Great Nothing.
Huh.
Me and the boys have been thinking about how to solve the problems that plague mankind.
You know... the usual sort of stuff: hypocrisy, selfishness, and the basic underlying perfidy of people.
We keep winding up with the same solution.

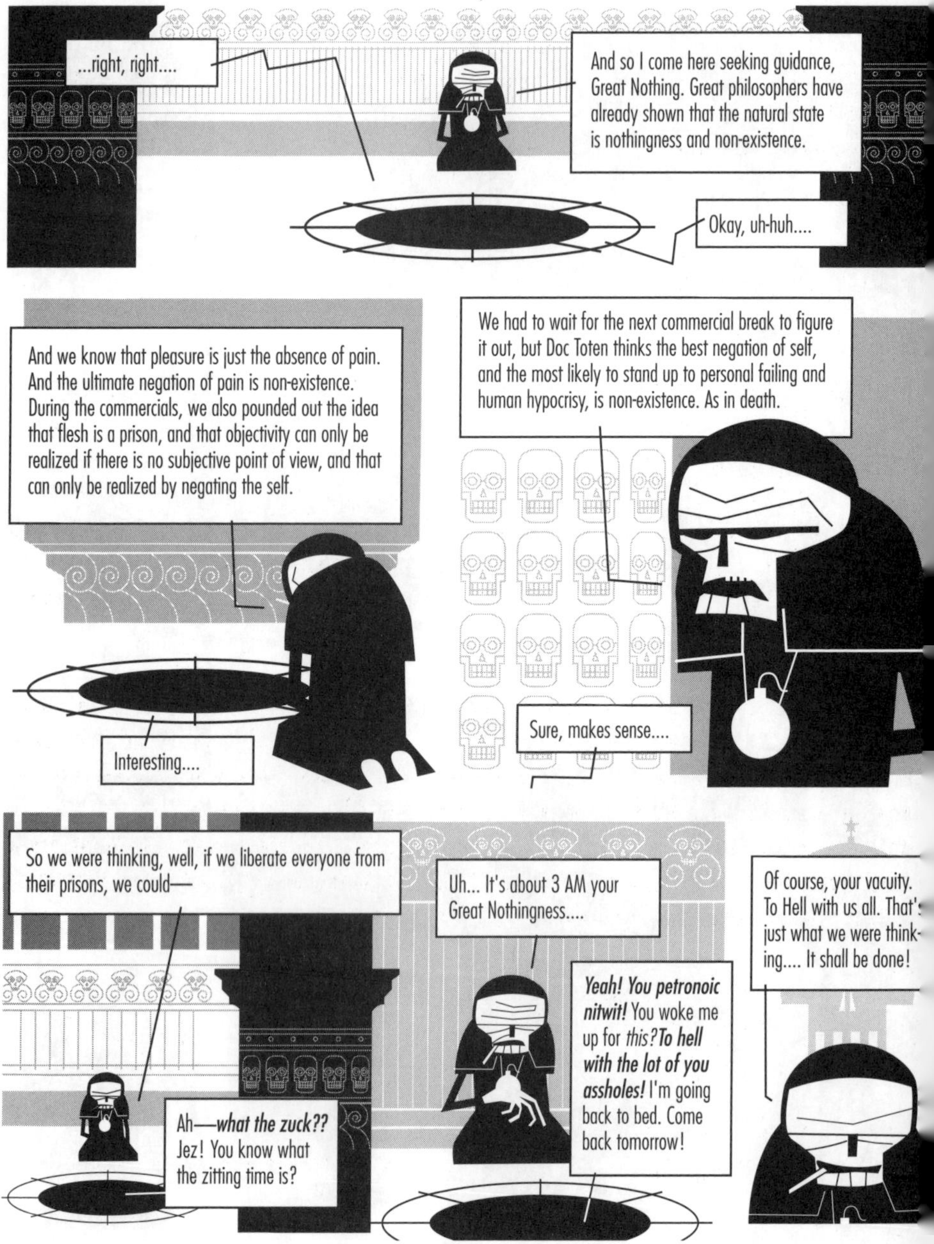
...right, right....
And so I come here seeking guidance, Great Nothing. Great philosophers have already shown that the natural state is nothingness and non-existence.
Okay, uh-huh....
And we know that pleasure is just the absence of pain. And the ultimate negation of pain is non-existence. During the commercials, we also pounded out the idea that flesh is a prison, and that objectivity can only be realized if there is no subjective point of view, and that can only be realized by negating the self.
Interesting....
We had to wait for the next commercial break to figure it out, but Doc Toten thinks the best negation of self, and the most likely to stand up to personal failing and human hypocrisy, is non-existence. As in death.
Sure, makes sense....
So we were thinking, well, if we liberate everyone from their prisons, we could—
Ah—***what the zuck??*** Jez! You know what the zitting time is?
Uh... It's about 3 AM your Great Nothingness....
Yeah! You petronoic nitwit! You woke me up for *this?* ***To hell with the lot of you assholes!*** I'm going back to bed. Come back tomorrow!
Of course, your vacuity. To Hell with us all. That's just what we were thinking.... It shall be done!

Nada Dionysius The Younger
Supreme Controller and Hypocripope
State Government of the People's Republic of Nil
Antichurch of Nil

MINISTRY OF NOTHING

Notaugust 1st
2:45:01 PM EST

5 copies
4th copy

To: Undermiddlesuperdupercommander Marshall Egregious Furbottom
Superduper Supreme Military Command

RE: THE CURRENT PLAN TO SAVE HUMANITY FROM THE PLIGHT OF SUFFERING AND THE ENNUI OF EXISTENCE.

Dear Undermiddlesupercommander Marshall Furbottom,

SUPER DUPER TOP SECRET

My dear non-friend, it has come to my attention that the Plan to Save Humanity from Itself is currently impeded by the half-hearted OVARY PROTECTION AND SPERMACIDE ACT. It is the opinion of the Supreme Couch that the current program is not far reaching enough. In addition, the implementation of the program is proving more... difficult than anticipated. The public has not been as co-operative as the MINISTRY OF NOTHING would have preferred, and has, in fact, taken to beating to death government agents who are carrying out their official duties. This has placed the entire program in jeopardy and led to a shortage of government agents.

It has therefore been determined to implement a more thorough program that will leave no room for waffling, false Ovary Free Confirmation Reports, or bogus Sperm Free Certificates. Such false documents are another bane to the program and given the technology currently available we see no way around this problem. Therefore, a new initiative will begin on Monday that will see the forcible LIBERATION FROM LIFE of all citizens of Nil. Plants, animals, and bacteria will also be eliminated as they may well evolve intelligence subsequent to our departure. The effort will be entwined with the VEGAN DECREE which stipulates that eating meat is murder and which consigns all carnivores to immediate arrest and liberation from life. The operation will progress from Amor Fati Province and conclude in New Bleaken Province. The Antimeme Police and the Antichurch Militia will carry out the first test operation in the capital under the direction of a soon to be named Plenipotentiary who will be selected from the masses arbitrarily as a gesture of solidarity. May the struggle for liberation be successful!

Nada Dionysius The Younger
Supreme Controller and Hypocripope
aka THE BOSS

In Borderville, Mr. Nul and Mr. Proudsmear sneak out of The Café of Death through the back to avoid the attention of the secret polic

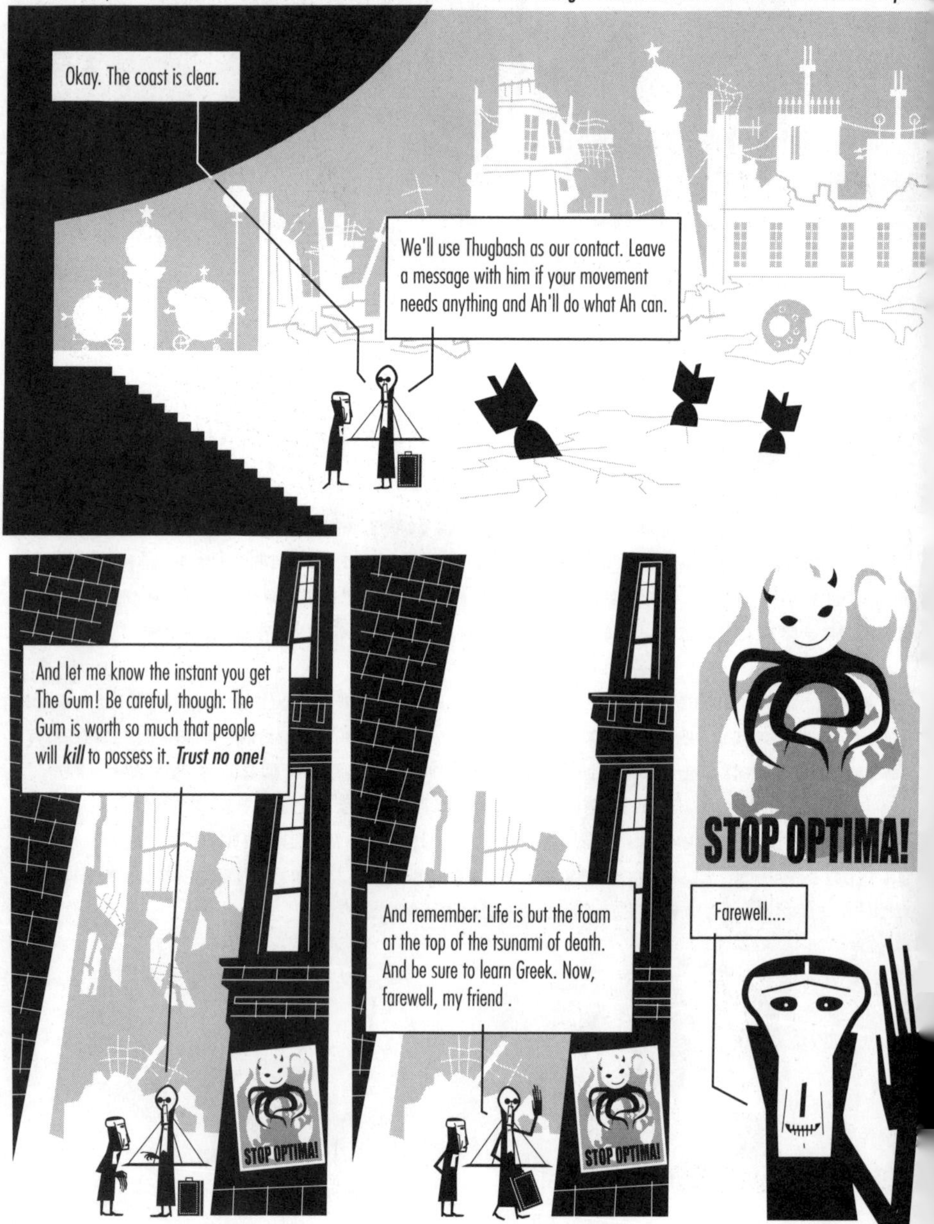

Okay. The coast is clear.
We'll use Thugbash as our contact. Leave a message with him if your movement needs anything and Ah'll do what Ah can.
And let me know the instant you get The Gum! Be careful, though: The Gum is worth so much that people will *kill* to possess it. ***Trust no one!***
STOP OPTIMA!
And remember: Life is but the foam at the top of the tsunami of death. And be sure to learn Greek. Now, farewell, my friend .
STOP OPTIMA!
STOP OPTIMA!
Farewell....

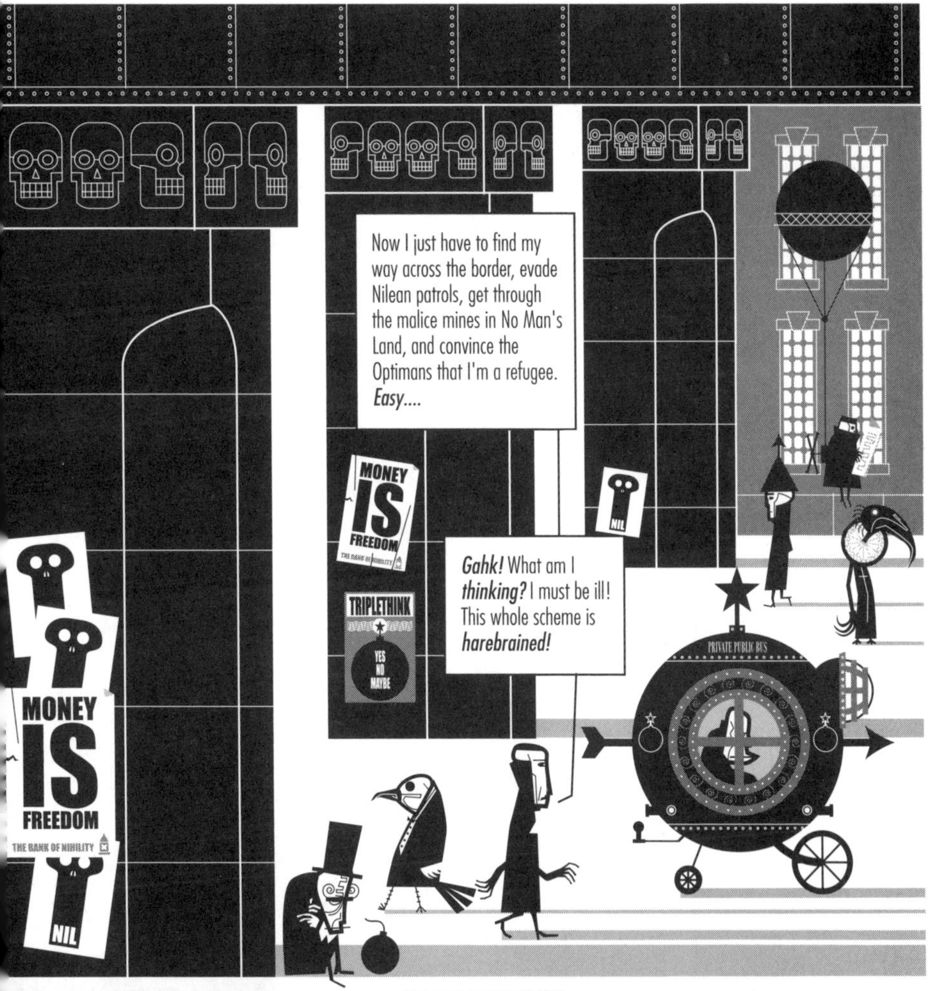
Now I just have to find my way across the border, evade Nilean patrols, get through the malice mines in No Man's Land, and convince the Optimans that I'm a refugee. *Easy....*
MONEY IS FREEDOM
THE BANK OF NIHILITY
NIL
TRIPLETHINK
YES NO MAYBE
Gahk! What am I ***thinking?*** I must be ill! This whole scheme is ***harebrained!***
PRIVATE PUBLIC BUS
MONEY IS FREEDOM
THE BANK OF NIHILITY
NIL

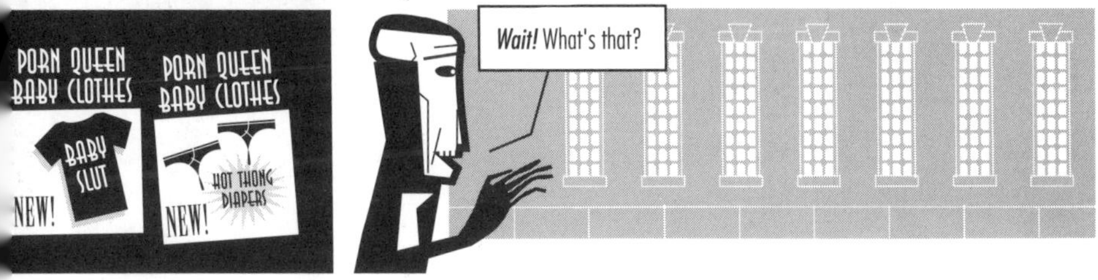
PORN QUEEN BABY CLOTHES
BABY SLUT
NEW!
PORN QUEEN BABY CLOTHES
HOT THONG DIAPERS
NEW!
Wait! What's that?

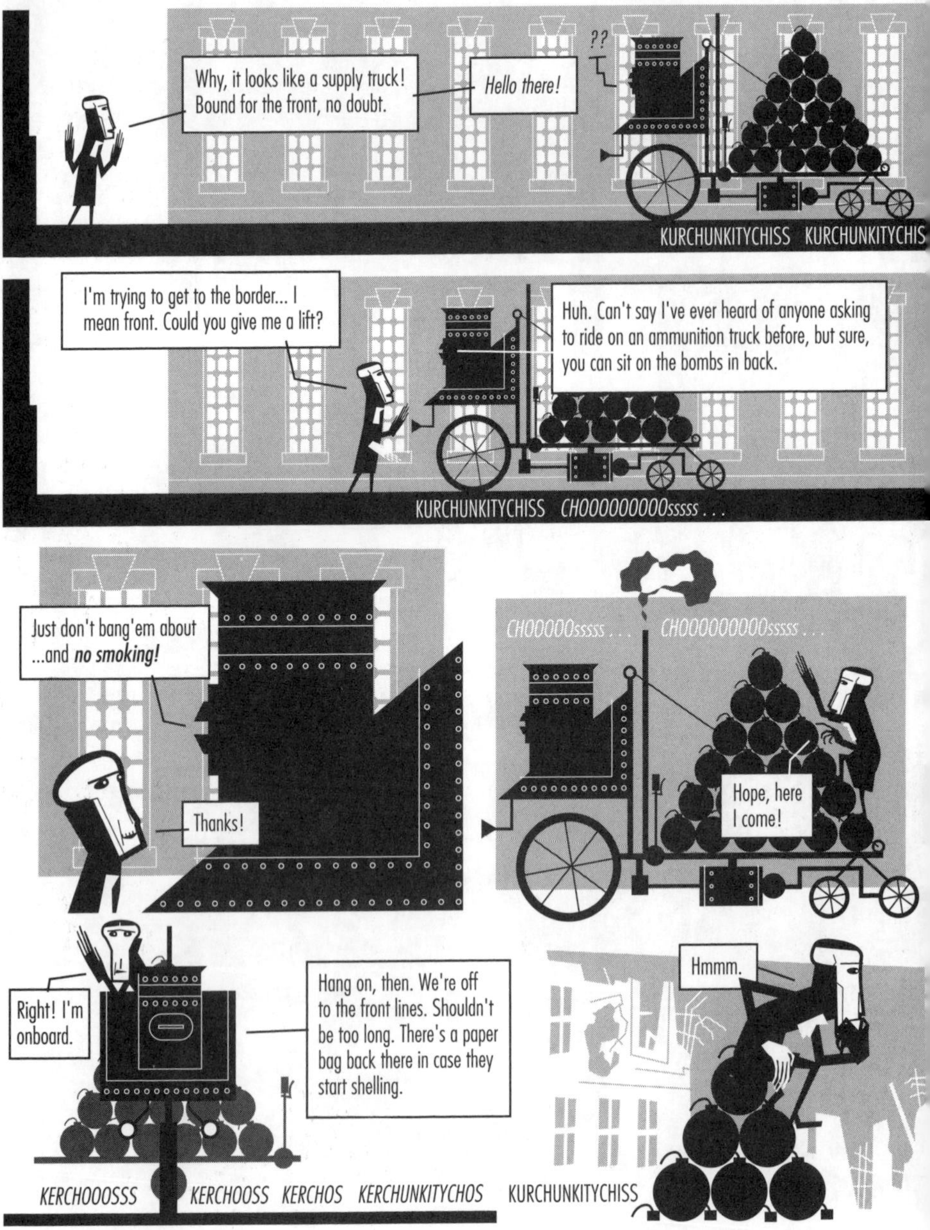
Why, it looks like a supply truck! Bound for the front, no doubt.
Hello there!
??
KURCHUNKITYCHISS KURCHUNKITYCHIS
I'm trying to get to the border... I mean front. Could you give me a lift?
Huh. Can't say I've ever heard of anyone asking to ride on an ammunition truck before, but sure, you can sit on the bombs in back.
KURCHUNKITYCHISS CHOOOOOOOOOsssss . . .
Just don't bang'em about ...and no smoking!
Thanks!
CHOOOOOsssss . . . CHOOOOOOOOOsssss . . .
Hope, here I come!
Right! I'm onboard.
Hang on, then. We're off to the front lines. Shouldn't be too long. There's a paper bag back there in case they start shelling.
KERCHOOOSSS KERCHOOSS KERCHOS KERCHUNKITYCHOS
Hmmm.
KURCHUNKITYCHISS

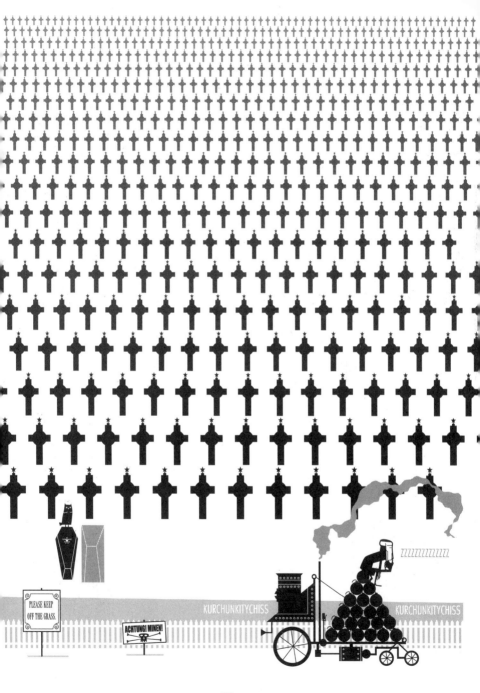

PLEASE KEEP
OFF THE GRASS.

KURCHUNKITYCHISS

KURCHUNKITYCHISS

ACHTUNG! MINEN!

ZZZZZZZZZZZ

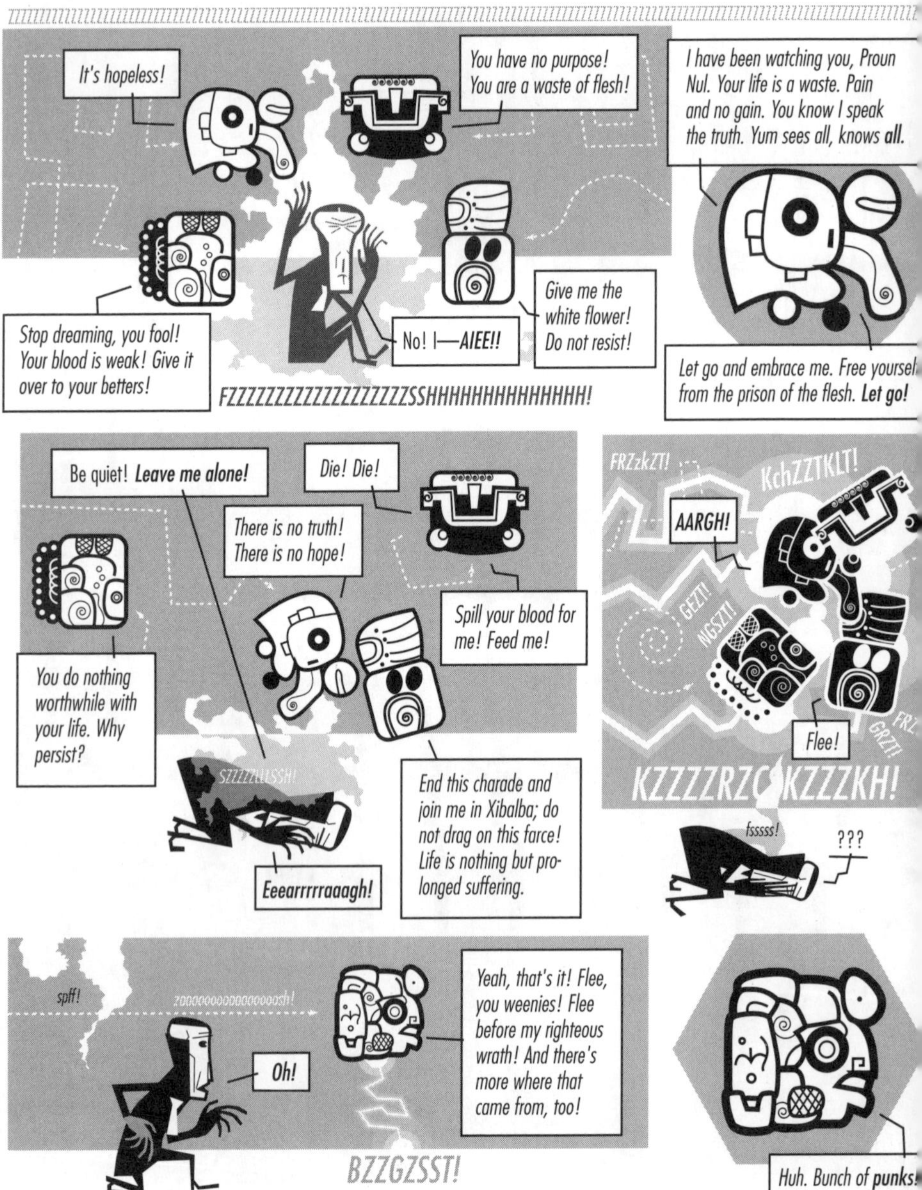

It's hopeless!
You have no purpose! You are a waste of flesh!
Stop dreaming, you fool! Your blood is weak! Give it over to your betters!
No! I—**AIEE!!**
Give me the white flower! Do not resist!
FZZZZZZZZZZZZZZZZZZZSSHHHHHHHHHHHHHH!
I have been watching you, Proun Nul. Your life is a waste. Pain and no gain. You know I speak the truth. Yum sees all, knows **all.**
Let go and embrace me. Free yoursel
from the prison of the flesh. **Let go!**
Be quiet! **Leave me alone!**
Die! Die!
There is no truth! There is no hope!
Spill your blood for me! Feed me!
You do nothing worthwhile with your life. Why persist?
SZZZZZLLLSSH!
End this charade and join me in Xibalba; do not drag on this farce! Life is nothing but prolonged suffering.
Eeearrrrraaagh!
FRZzkZT!
KchZZTKLT!
AARGH!
GEZT!
NGSZT!
Flee!
KZZZZRZC KZZZKH!
fsssss!
???
spff!
zoooooooooooooooosh!
Oh!
Yeah, that's it! Flee, you weenies! Flee before my righteous wrath! And there's more where that came from, too!
BZZGZSST!
Huh. Bunch of **punks**

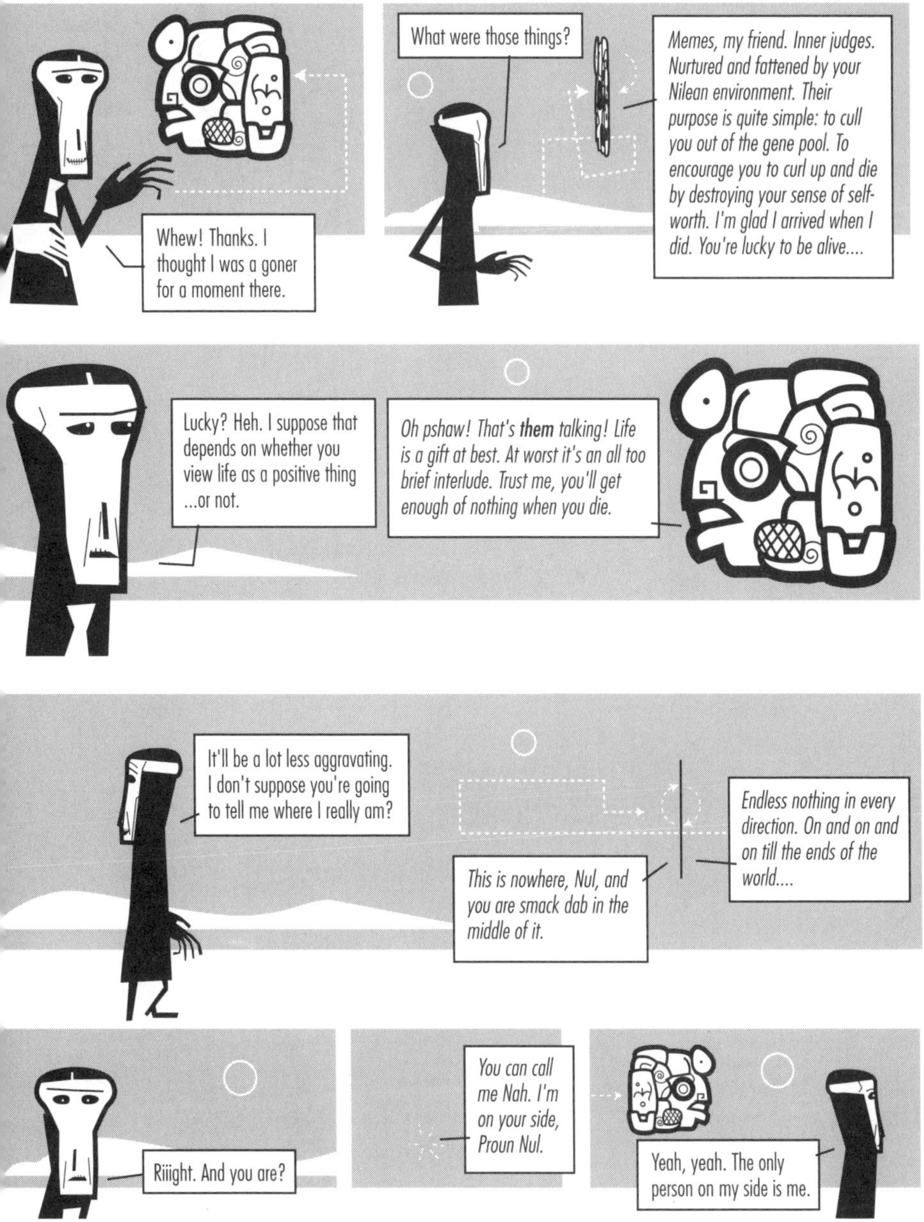
Whew! Thanks. I thought I was a goner for a moment there.
What were those things?
Memes, my friend. Inner judges. Nurtured and fattened by your Nilean environment. Their purpose is quite simple: to cull you out of the gene pool. To encourage you to curl up and die by destroying your sense of self-worth. I'm glad I arrived when I did. You're lucky to be alive....
Lucky? Heh. I suppose that depends on whether you view life as a positive thing ...or not.
Oh pshaw! That's ***them*** *talking! Life is a gift at best. At worst it's an all too brief interlude. Trust me, you'll get enough of nothing when you die.*
It'll be a lot less aggravating. I don't suppose you're going to tell me where I really am?
This is nowhere, Nul, and you are smack dab in the middle of it.
Endless nothing in every direction. On and on and on till the ends of the world....
Riiight. And you are?
You can call me Nah. I'm on your side, Proun Nul.
Yeah, yeah. The only person on my side is me.

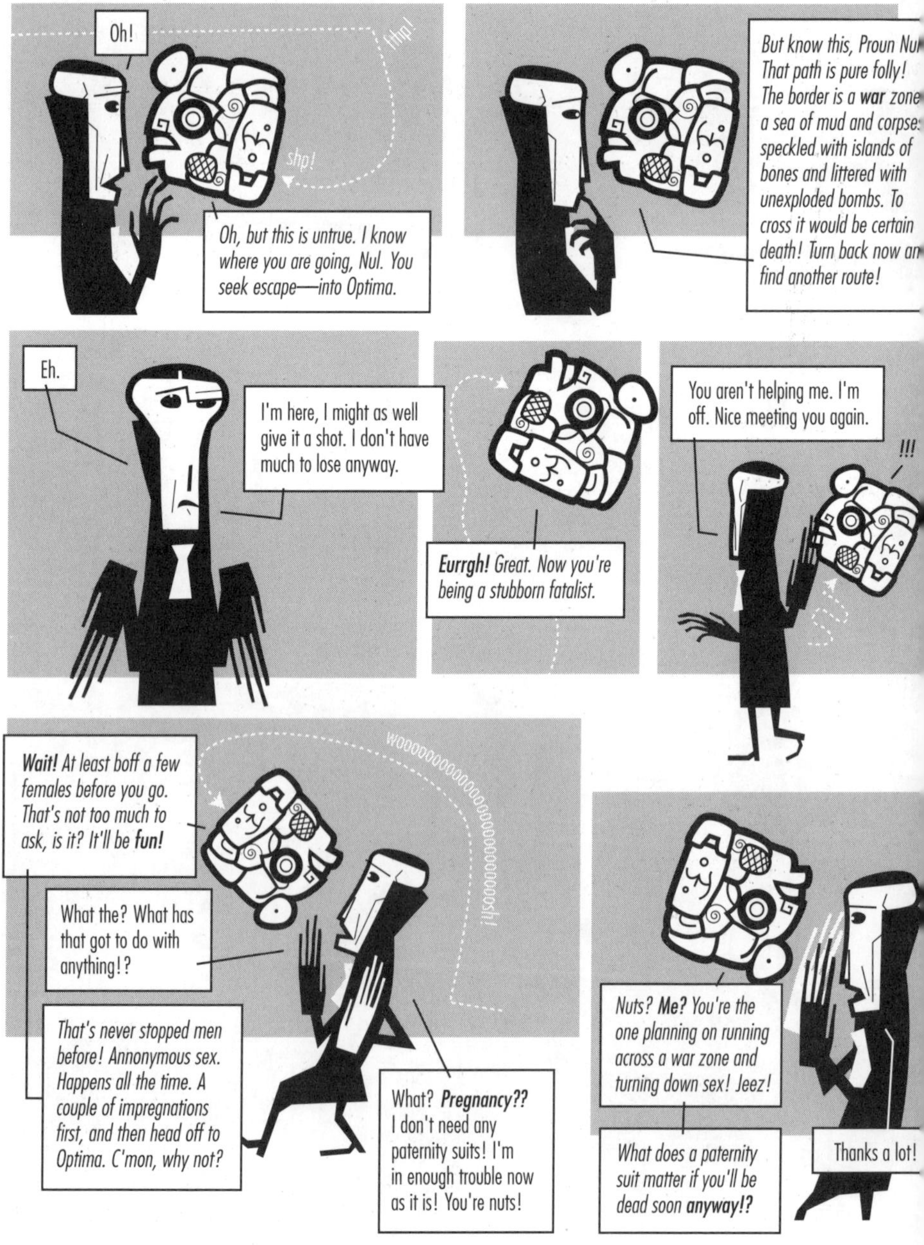
Oh!
fthp!
shp!
Oh, but this is untrue. I know where you are going, Nul. You seek escape—into Optima.
*But know this, Proun Nu That path is pure folly! The border is a **war** zone a sea of mud and corpse speckled with islands of bones and littered with unexploded bombs. To cross it would be certain death! Turn back now an find another route!*
Eh.
I'm here, I might as well give it a shot. I don't have much to lose anyway.
***Eurrgh!** Great. Now you're being a stubborn fatalist.*
You aren't helping me. I'm off. Nice meeting you again.
!!!
*__Wait!__ At least boff a few females before you go. That's not too much to ask, is it? It'll be **fun!***
What the? What has that got to do with anything!?
That's never stopped men before! Annonymous sex. Happens all the time. A couple of impregnations first, and then head off to Optima. C'mon, why not?
What? ***Pregnancy??*** I don't need any paternity suits! I'm in enough trouble now as it is! You're nuts!
*Nuts? **Me?** You're the one planning on running across a war zone and turning down sex! Jeez!*
*What does a paternity suit matter if you'll be dead soon **anyway!?***
Thanks a lot!

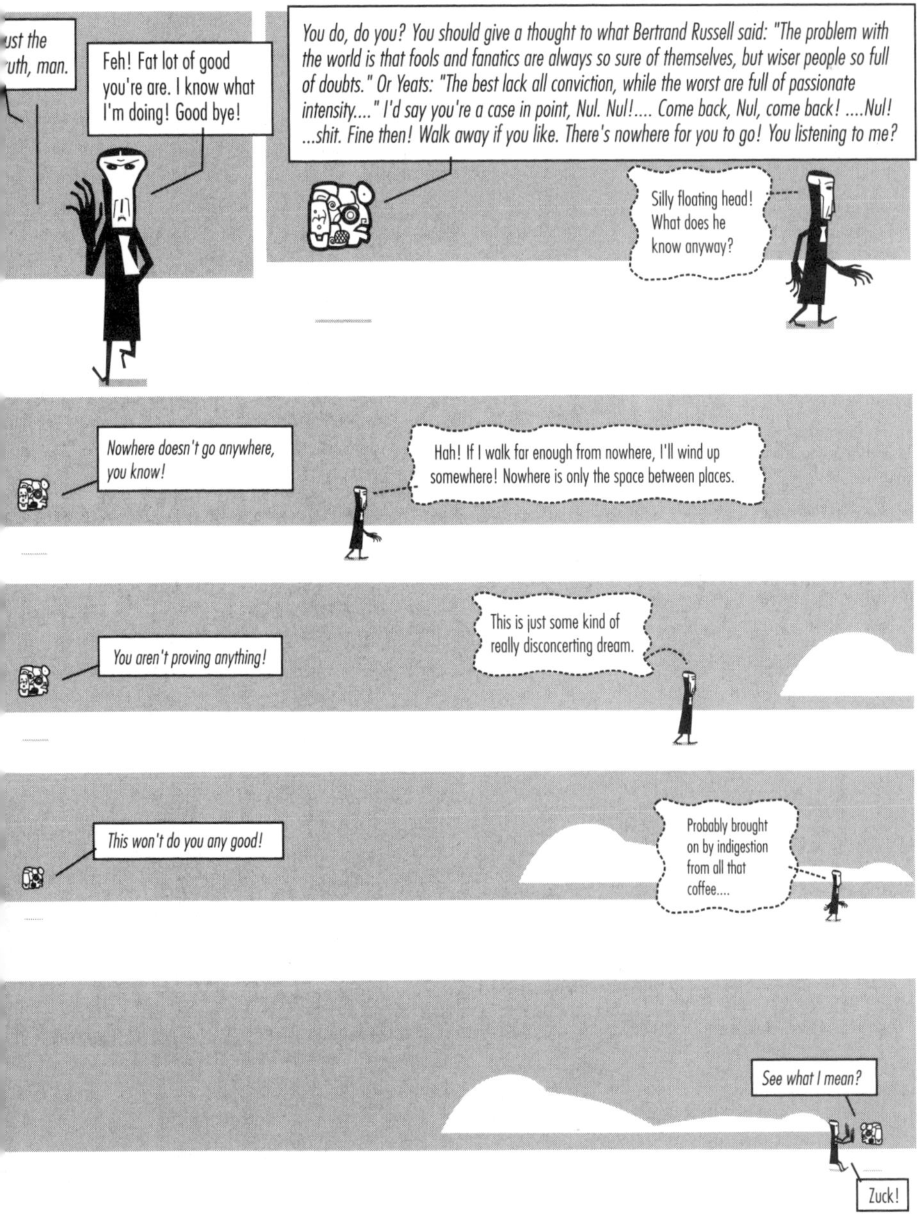
ust the
ruth, man.
Feh! Fat lot of good you're are. I know what I'm doing! Good bye!
You do, do you? You should give a thought to what Bertrand Russell said: "The problem with the world is that fools and fanatics are always so sure of themselves, but wiser people so full of doubts." Or Yeats: "The best lack all conviction, while the worst are full of passionate intensity...." I'd say you're a case in point, Nul. Nul!.... Come back, Nul, come back! ....Nul! ...shit. Fine then! Walk away if you like. There's nowhere for you to go! You listening to me?
Silly floating head! What does he know anyway?
Nowhere doesn't go anywhere, you know!
Hah! If I walk far enough from nowhere, I'll wind up somewhere! Nowhere is only the space between places.
You aren't proving anything!
This is just some kind of really disconcerting dream.
This won't do you any good!
Probably brought on by indigestion from all that coffee....
See what I mean?
Zuck!

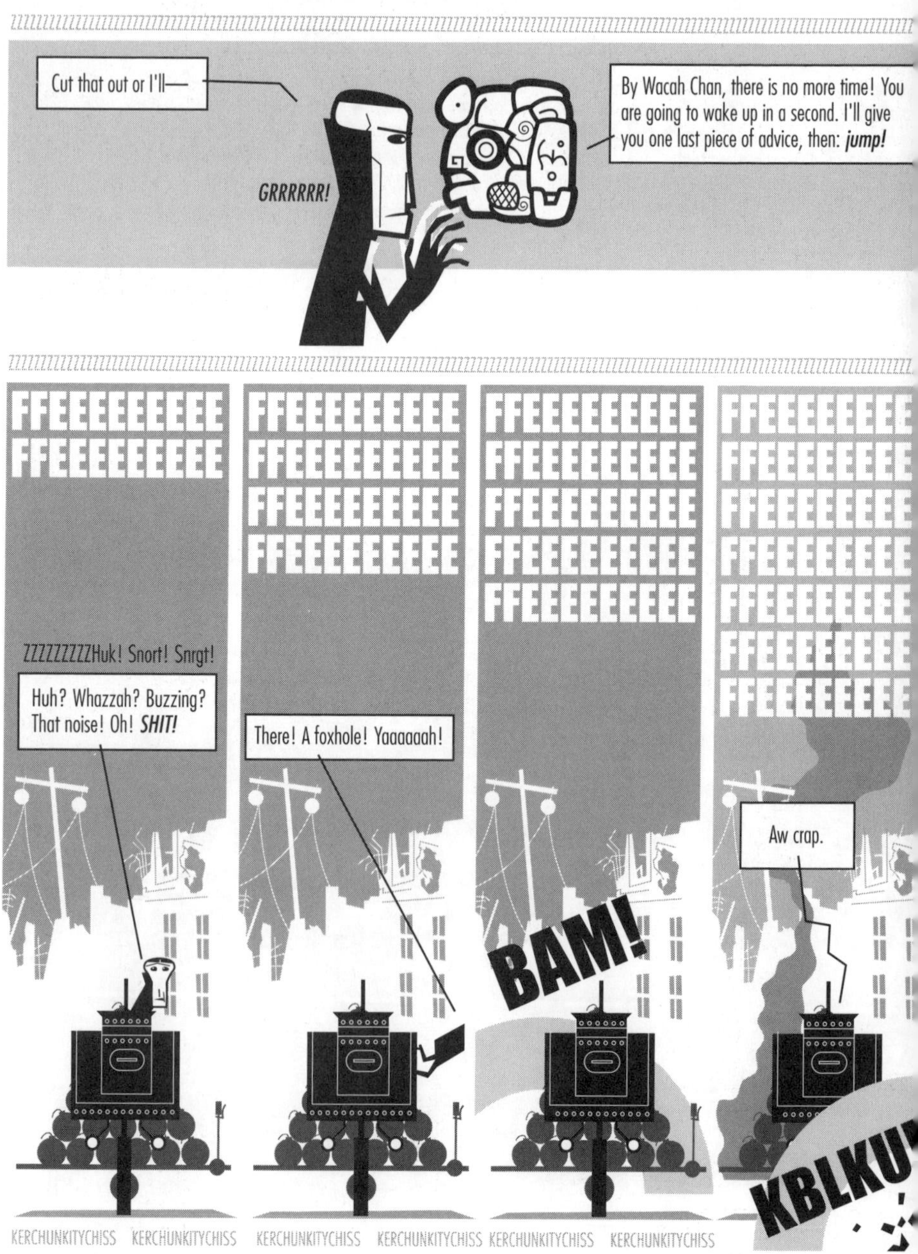

Cut that out or I'll—
GRRRRRR!
By Wacah Chan, there is no more time! You are going to wake up in a second. I'll give you one last piece of advice, then: *jump!*
FFEEEEEEEEE
FFEEEEEEEEE
ZZZZZZZZZHuk! Snort! Snrgt!
Huh? Whazzah? Buzzing? That noise! Oh! ***SHIT!***
KERCHUNKITYCHISS KERCHUNKITYCHISS
FFEEEEEEEEE
FFEEEEEEEEE
FFEEEEEEEEE
FFEEEEEEEEE
There! A foxhole! Yaaaaaah!
KERCHUNKITYCHISS KERCHUNKITYCHISS
FFEEEEEEEEE
FFEEEEEEEEE
FFEEEEEEEEE
FFEEEEEEEEE
FFEEEEEEEEE
BAM!
KERCHUNKITYCHISS KERCHUNKITYCHISS
FFEEEEEEEEE
FFEEEEEEEEE
FFEEEEEEEEE
FFEEEEEEEEE
FFEEEEEEEEE
FFEEEEEEEEE
FFEEEEEEEEE
Aw crap.
KBLKU

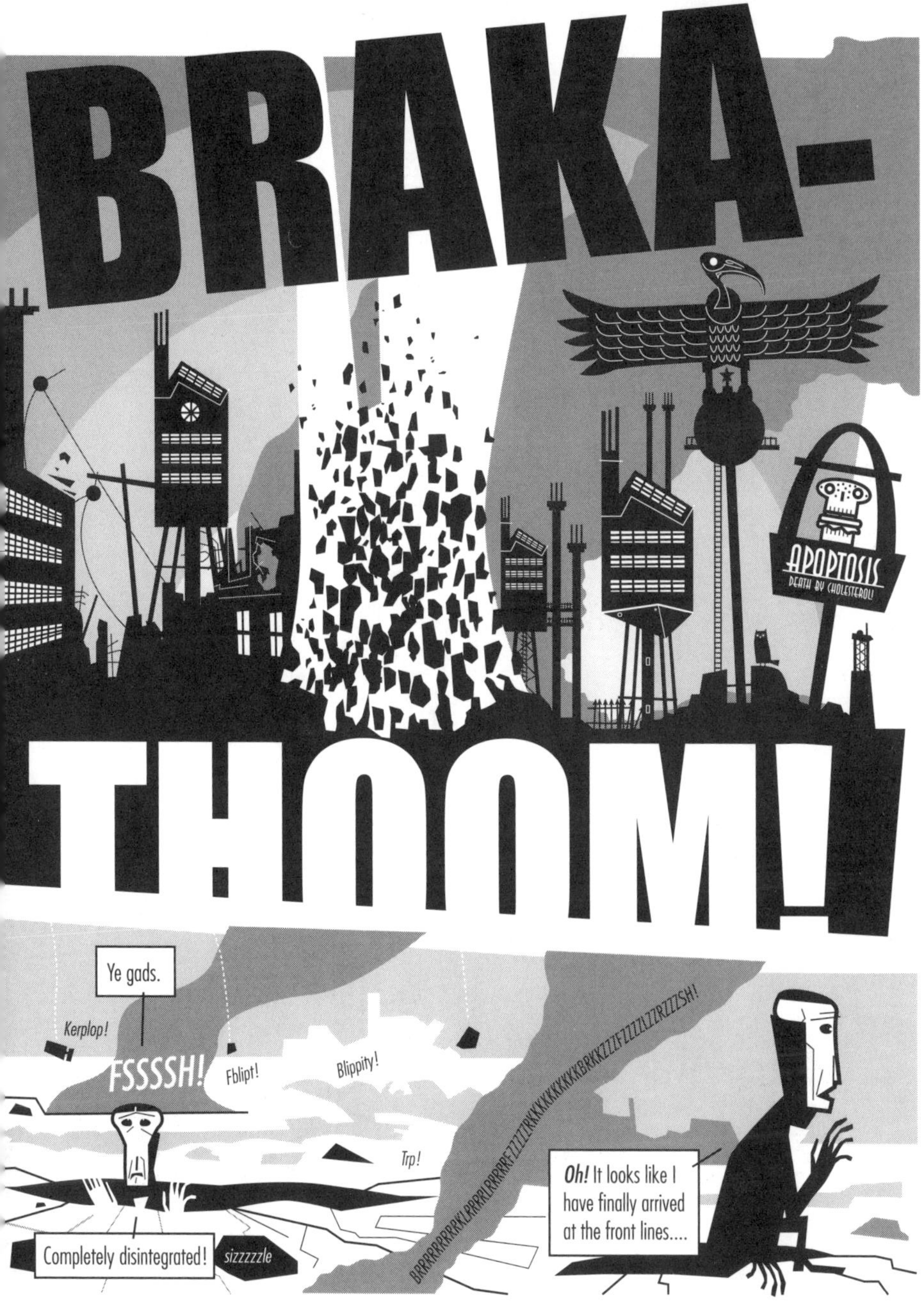
BRAKA-
APOPTOSIS
DEATH BY CHOLESTEROL!
THOOM!
Ye gads.
Kerplop!
FSSSSH!
Fblipt!
Blippity!
Trp!
Completely disintegrated!
sizzzzzle
BRRRRRRRRRKLRRRRLRRRRRFZZZZZZRKKKKKKKKKKKKBRKKZZZFZZZZLZZRZZZSH!
Oh! It looks like I have finally arrived at the front lines....

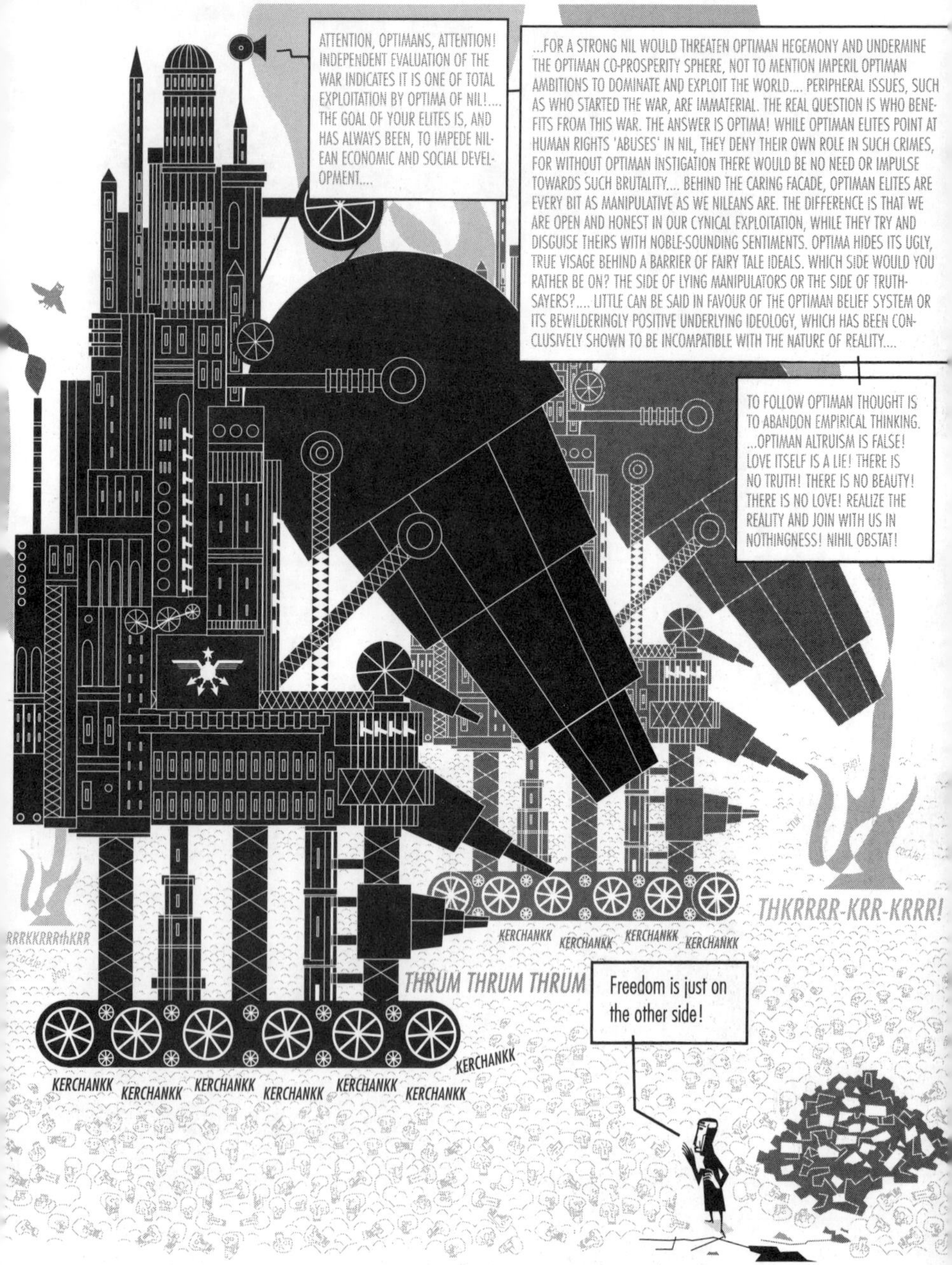
ATTENTION, OPTIMANS, ATTENTION! INDEPENDENT EVALUATION OF THE WAR INDICATES IT IS ONE OF TOTAL EXPLOITATION BY OPTIMA OF NIL!.... THE GOAL OF YOUR ELITES IS, AND HAS ALWAYS BEEN, TO IMPEDE NILEAN ECONOMIC AND SOCIAL DEVELOPMENT....
...FOR A STRONG NIL WOULD THREATEN OPTIMAN HEGEMONY AND UNDERMINE THE OPTIMAN CO-PROSPERITY SPHERE, NOT TO MENTION IMPERIL OPTIMAN AMBITIONS TO DOMINATE AND EXPLOIT THE WORLD.... PERIPHERAL ISSUES, SUCH AS WHO STARTED THE WAR, ARE IMMATERIAL. THE REAL QUESTION IS WHO BENEFITS FROM THIS WAR. THE ANSWER IS OPTIMA! WHILE OPTIMAN ELITES POINT AT HUMAN RIGHTS 'ABUSES' IN NIL, THEY DENY THEIR OWN ROLE IN SUCH CRIMES, FOR WITHOUT OPTIMAN INSTIGATION THERE WOULD BE NO NEED OR IMPULSE TOWARDS SUCH BRUTALITY.... BEHIND THE CARING FACADE, OPTIMAN ELITES ARE EVERY BIT AS MANIPULATIVE AS WE NILEANS ARE. THE DIFFERENCE IS THAT WE ARE OPEN AND HONEST IN OUR CYNICAL EXPLOITATION, WHILE THEY TRY AND DISGUISE THEIRS WITH NOBLE-SOUNDING SENTIMENTS. OPTIMA HIDES ITS UGLY, TRUE VISAGE BEHIND A BARRIER OF FAIRY TALE IDEALS. WHICH SIDE WOULD YOU RATHER BE ON? THE SIDE OF LYING MANIPULATORS OR THE SIDE OF TRUTH-SAYERS?.... LITTLE CAN BE SAID IN FAVOUR OF THE OPTIMAN BELIEF SYSTEM OR ITS BEWILDERINGLY POSITIVE UNDERLYING IDEOLOGY, WHICH HAS BEEN CONCLUSIVELY SHOWN TO BE INCOMPATIBLE WITH THE NATURE OF REALITY....
TO FOLLOW OPTIMAN THOUGHT IS TO ABANDON EMPIRICAL THINKING. ...OPTIMAN ALTRUISM IS FALSE! LOVE ITSELF IS A LIE! THERE IS NO TRUTH! THERE IS NO BEAUTY! THERE IS NO LOVE! REALIZE THE REALITY AND JOIN WITH US IN NOTHINGNESS! NIHIL OBSTAT!
THKRRRR-KRR-KRRR!
RRRKKRRRthKRR
KERCHANKK KERCHANKK KERCHANKK KERCHANKK
THRUM THRUM THRUM
Freedom is just on the other side!
KERCHANKK
KERCHANKK KERCHANKK KERCHANKK KERCHANKK KERCHANKK KERCHANKK

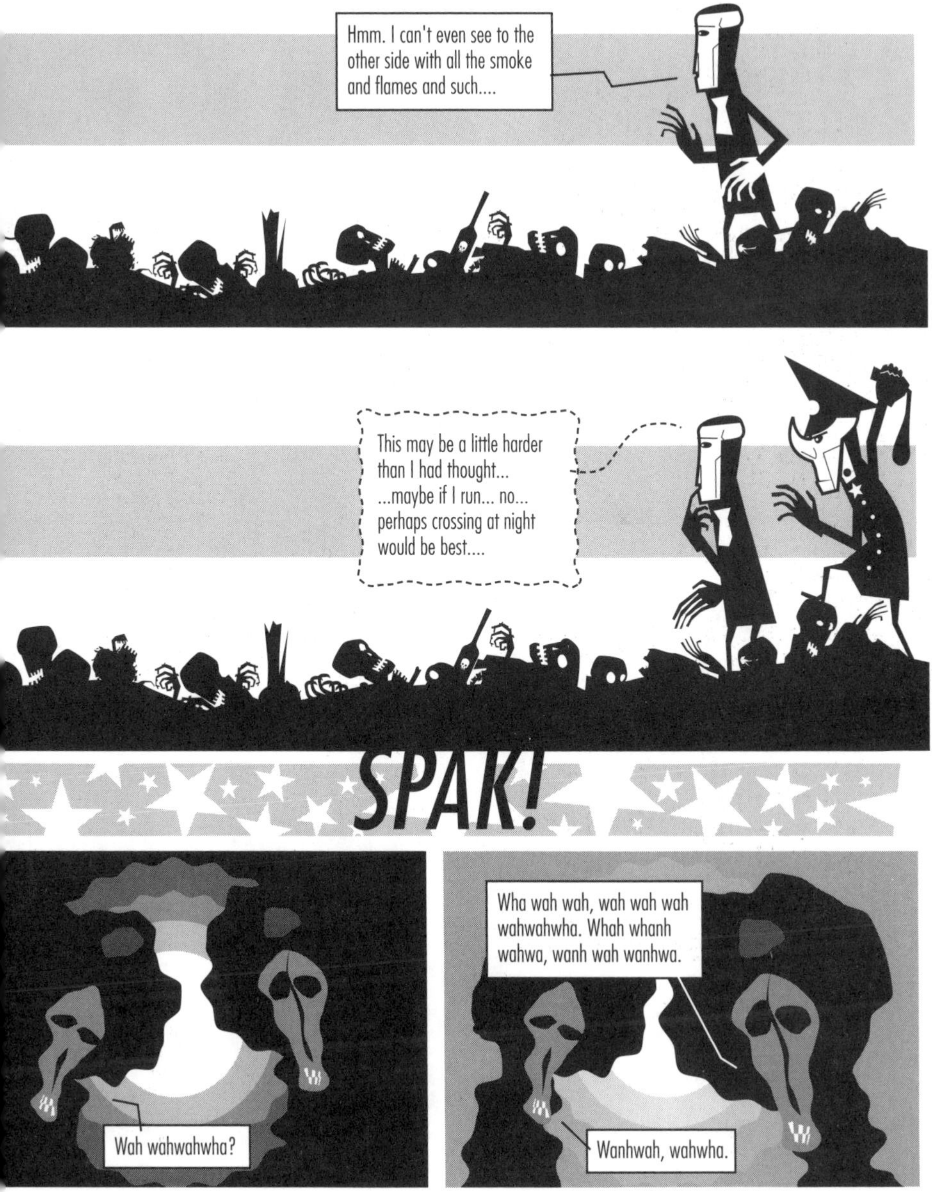
Hmm. I can't even see to the other side with all the smoke and flames and such....
This may be a little harder than I had thought... ...maybe if I run... no... perhaps crossing at night would be best....
SPAK!
Wah wahwahwha?
Wha wah wah, wah wah wah wahwahwha. Whah whanh wahwa, wanh wah wanhwa.
Wanhwah, wahwha.

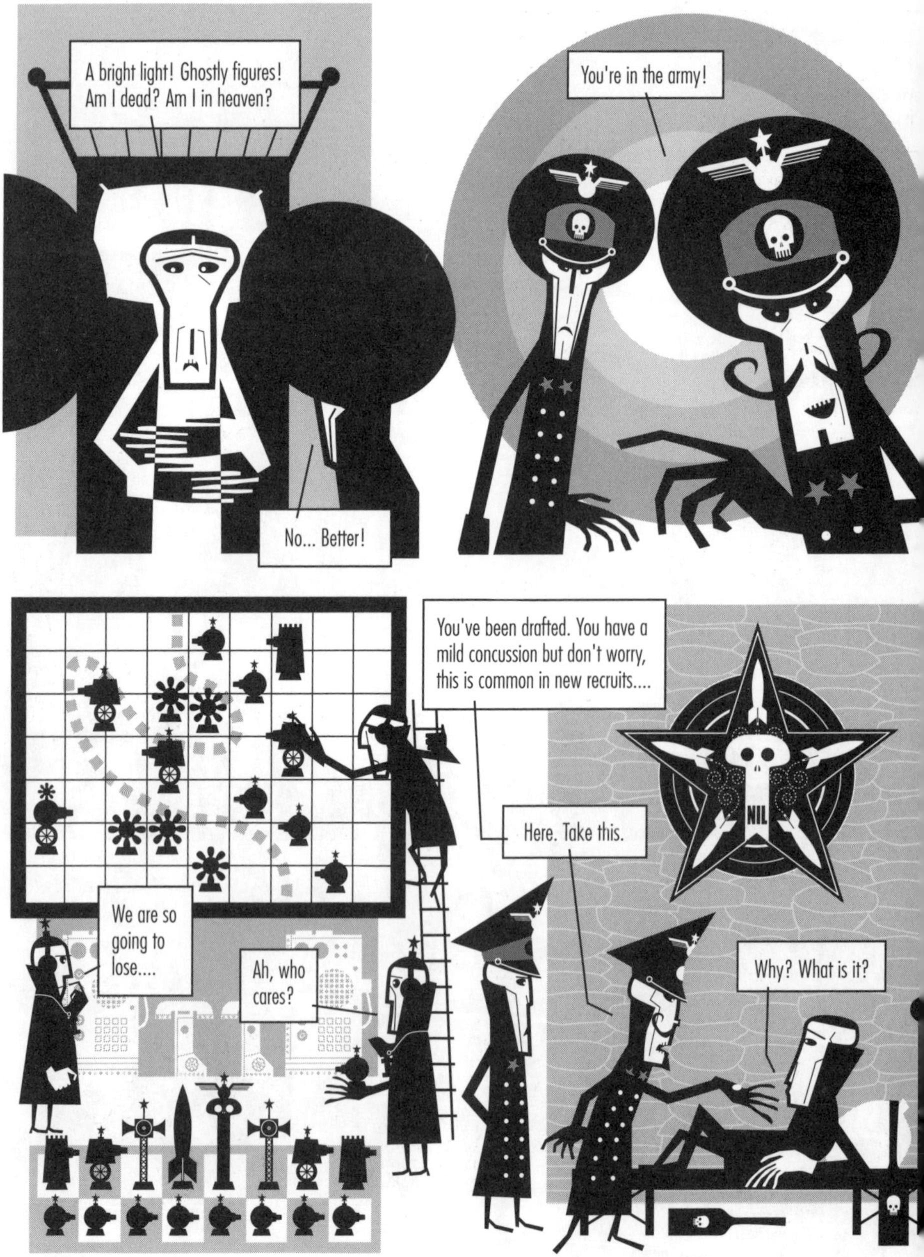
A bright light! Ghostly figures! Am I dead? Am I in heaven?
No... Better!
You're in the army!
You've been drafted. You have a mild concussion but don't worry, this is common in new recruits....
We are so going to lose....
Ah, who cares?
Here. Take this.
Why? What is it?
NIL

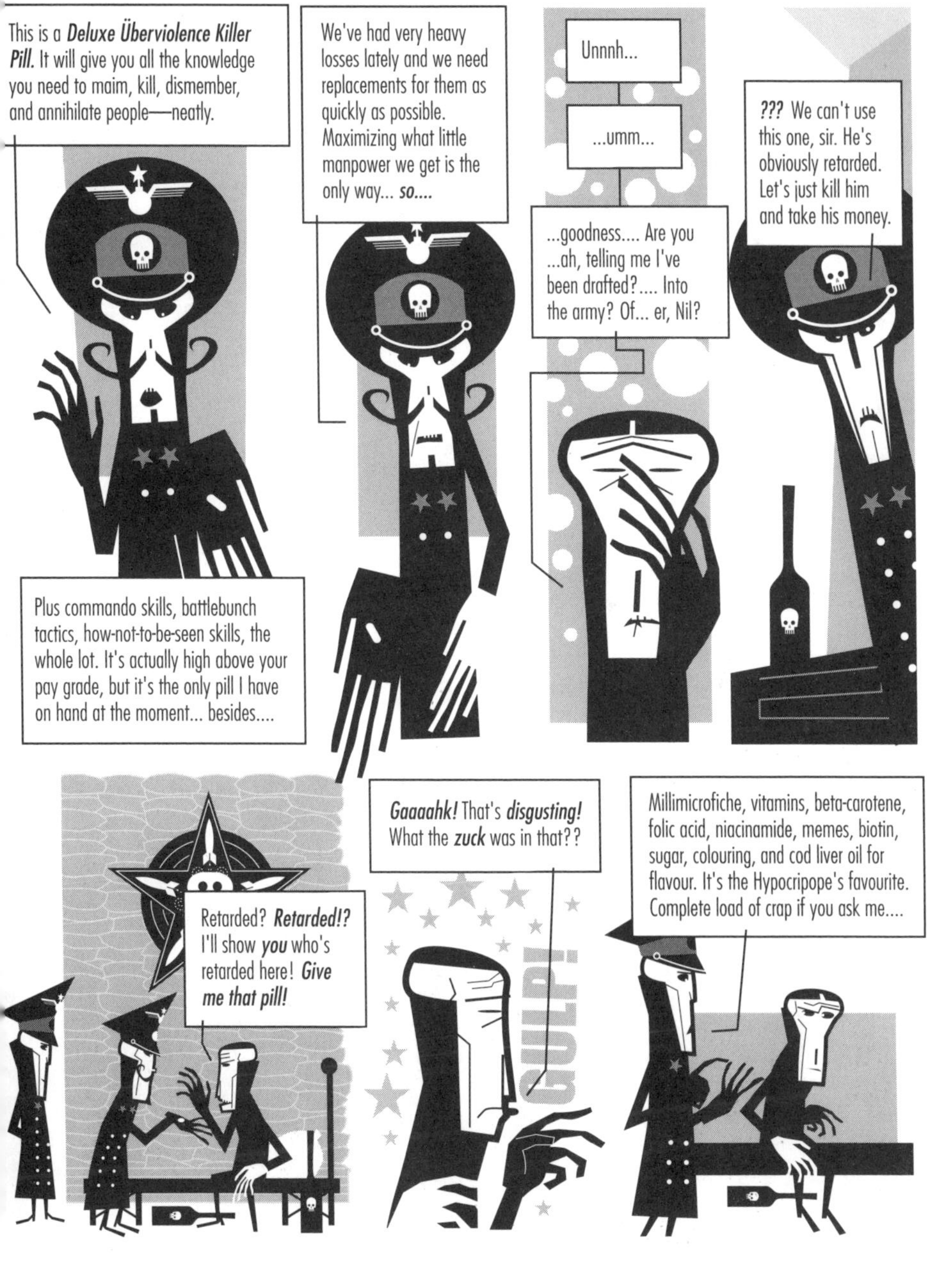

This is a ***Deluxe Überviolence Killer Pill.*** It will give you all the knowledge you need to maim, kill, dismember, and annihilate people—neatly.
Plus commando skills, battlebunch tactics, how-not-to-be-seen skills, the whole lot. It's actually high above your pay grade, but it's the only pill I have on hand at the moment... besides....
We've had very heavy losses lately and we need replacements for them as quickly as possible. Maximizing what little manpower we get is the only way... ***so....***
Unnnh...
...umm...
...goodness.... Are you ...ah, telling me I've been drafted?.... Into the army? Of... er, Nil?
??? We can't use this one, sir. He's obviously retarded. Let's just kill him and take his money.
Retarded? ***Retarded!?*** I'll show ***you*** who's retarded here! ***Give me that pill!***
GULP!
Gaaaahk! That's ***disgusting!*** What the ***zuck*** was in that??
Millimicrofiche, vitamins, beta-carotene, folic acid, niacinamide, memes, biotin, sugar, colouring, and cod liver oil for flavour. It's the Hypocripope's favourite. Complete load of crap if you ask me....

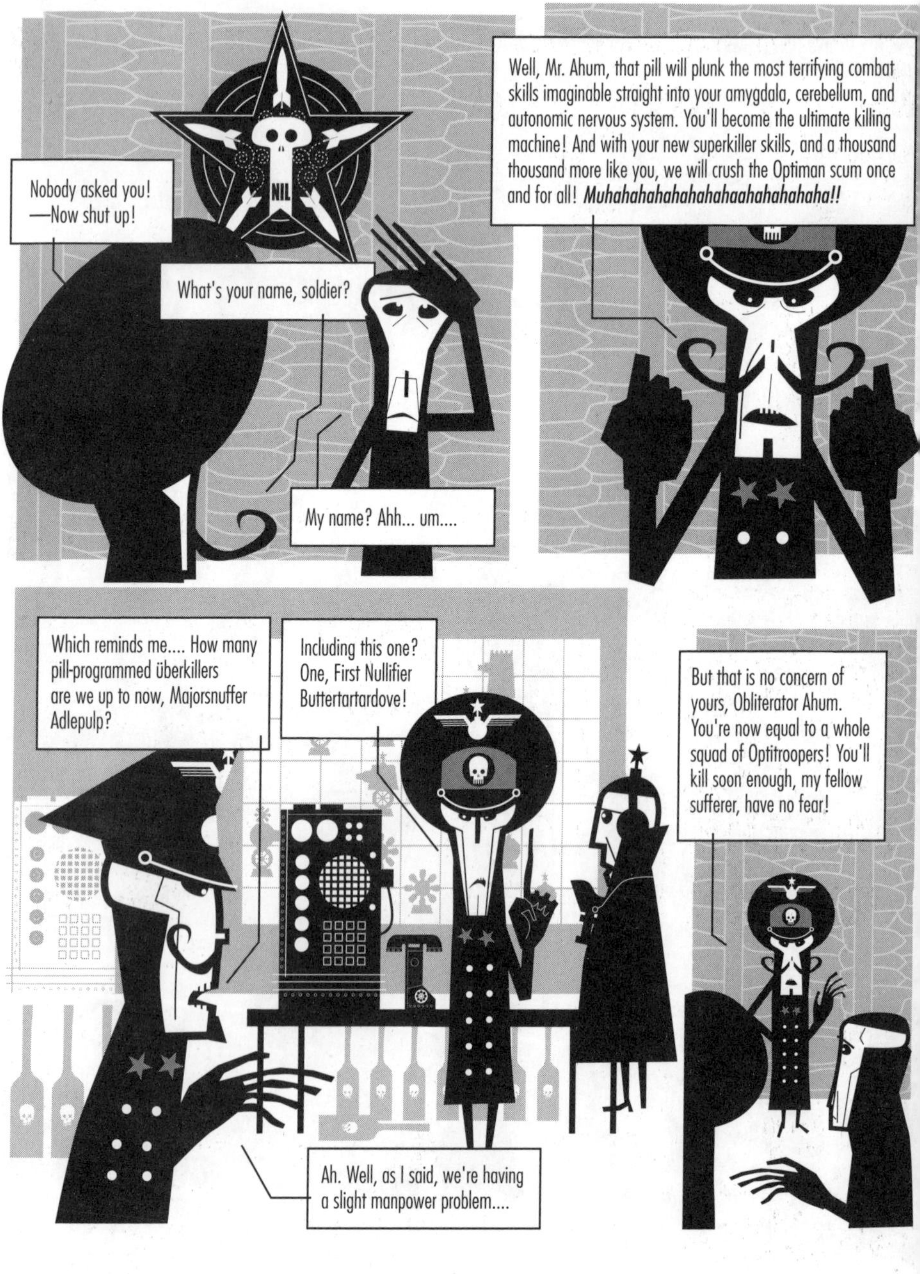
Nobody asked you!
—Now shut up!
What's your name, soldier?
My name? Ahh... um....
Well, Mr. Ahum, that pill will plunk the most terrifying combat skills imaginable straight into your amygdala, cerebellum, and autonomic nervous system. You'll become the ultimate killing machine! And with your new superkiller skills, and a thousand thousand more like you, we will crush the Optiman scum once and for all! ***Muhahahahahahahahaahahahahaha!!***
NIL
Which reminds me.... How many pill-programmed überkillers are we up to now, Majorsnuffer Adlepulp?
Including this one? One, First Nullifier Buttertartardove!
Ah. Well, as I said, we're having a slight manpower problem....
But that is no concern of yours, Obliterator Ahum. You're now equal to a whole squad of Optitroopers! You'll kill soon enough, my fellow sufferer, have no fear!

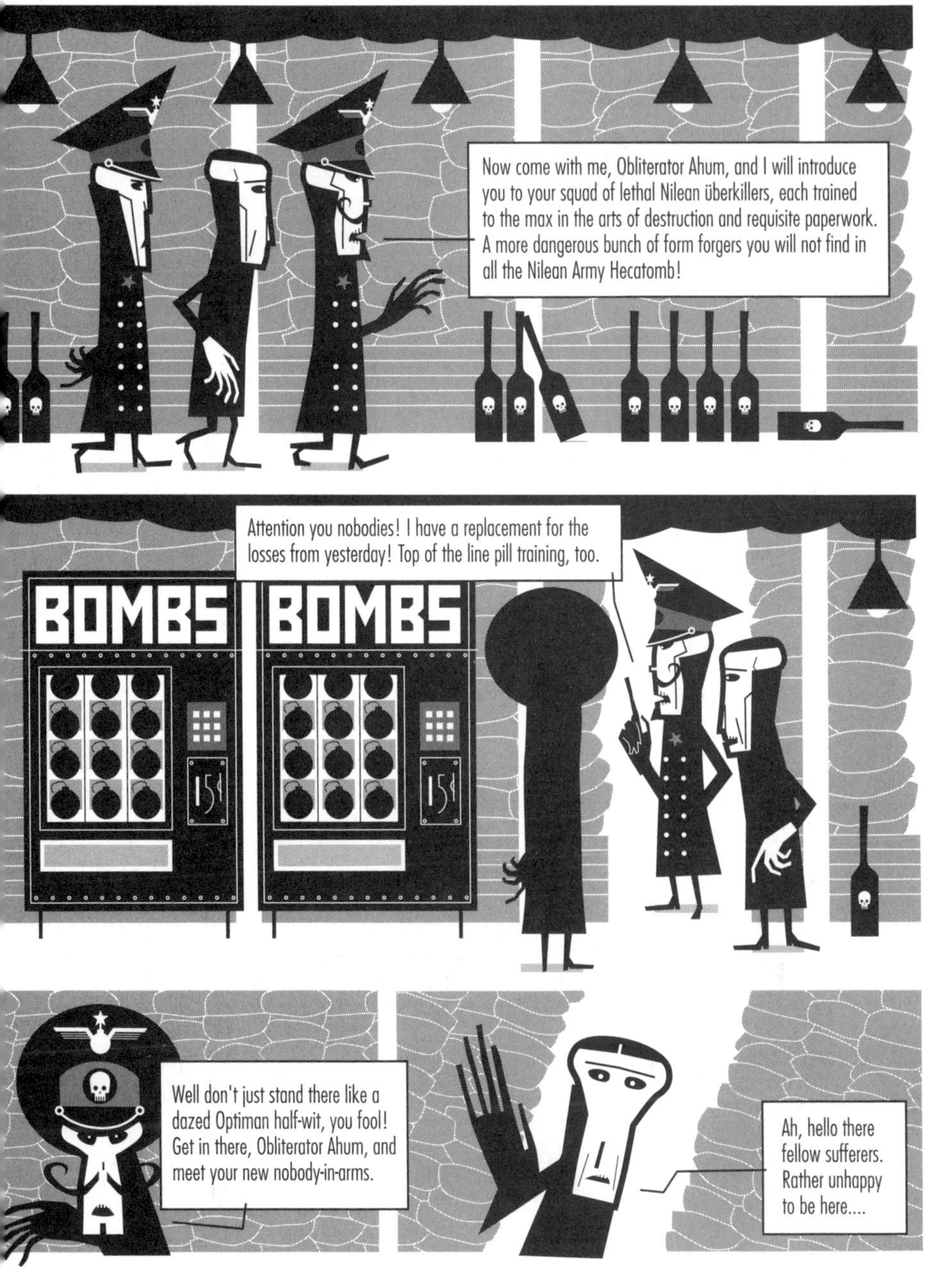
Now come with me, Obliterator Ahum, and I will introduce you to your squad of lethal Nilean überkillers, each trained to the max in the arts of destruction and requisite paperwork. A more dangerous bunch of form forgers you will not find in all the Nilean Army Hecatomb!
Attention you nobodies! I have a replacement for the losses from yesterday! Top of the line pill training, too.
BOMBS
BOMBS
15¢
15¢
Well don't just stand there like a dazed Optiman half-wit, you fool! Get in there, Obliterator Ahum, and meet your new nobody-in-arms.
Ah, hello there fellow sufferers. Rather unhappy to be here....

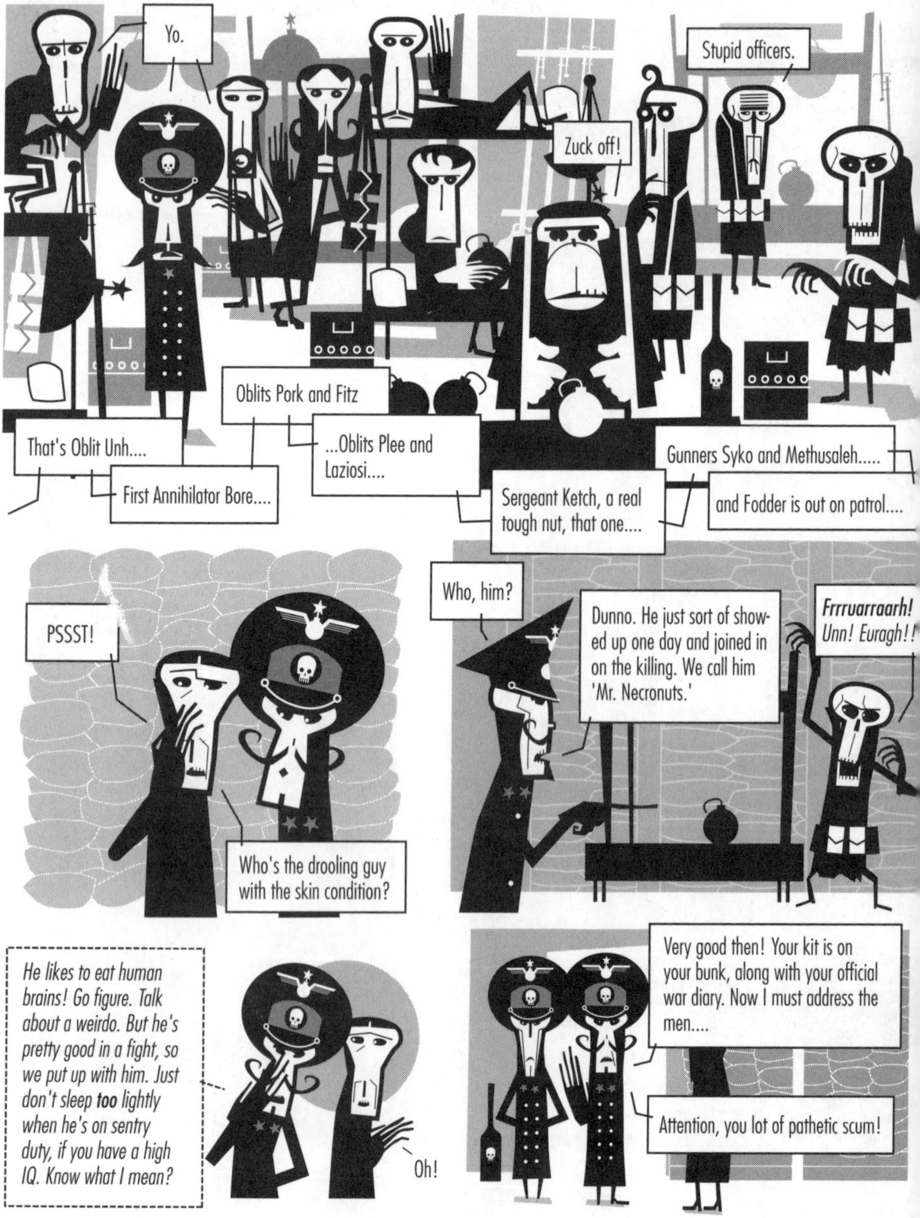

Yo.
Stupid officers.
Zuck off!
That's Oblit Unh....
First Annihilator Bore....
Oblits Pork and Fitz
...Oblits Plee and Laziosi....
Sergeant Ketch, a real tough nut, that one....
Gunners Syko and Methusaleh.....
and Fodder is out on patrol....
PSSST!
Who's the drooling guy with the skin condition?
Who, him?
Dunno. He just sort of showed up one day and joined in on the killing. We call him 'Mr. Necronuts.'
Frrruarraarh! Unn! Euragh!!
He likes to eat human brains! Go figure. Talk about a weirdo. But he's pretty good in a fight, so we put up with him. Just don't sleep too lightly when he's on sentry duty, if you have a high IQ. Know what I mean?
Oh!
Very good then! Your kit is on your bunk, along with your official war diary. Now I must address the men....
Attention, you lot of pathetic scum!

Attention! I have new orders for you, so listen up, you foul faced, tick ridden bunch of bileous bastards!
UNITY is SLAVERY
OPTIMA BOOM! DESTROYS!
DO NOT FEED THE RATS
No Truth! No Love! No Beauty!
This comes direct from Supreme Destruction HQ. Here are your orders: "1) This position will be held and the section will remain until relieved. 2) The enemy cannot be allowed to interfere with this position."
"3) The position will be held."
"4) If section cannot remain here alive, it will remain here dead. In any case, it will remain here."
Huh. Sounds Brickish.
Ahem.
Allow me to add a few words of support of my own, my despised fellow sufferers.
'We are free to hunt in the morning, fish in the afternoon, farm in the evening, and commit suicide after dinner in Nil. It is for these rights that we fight the Opti-scum who oppose us.'
Now I and my aide must go and attend a dinner at the HQ palace. I've left some Return Fire Authorization Forms in case of enemy attack. Now—Ciao!

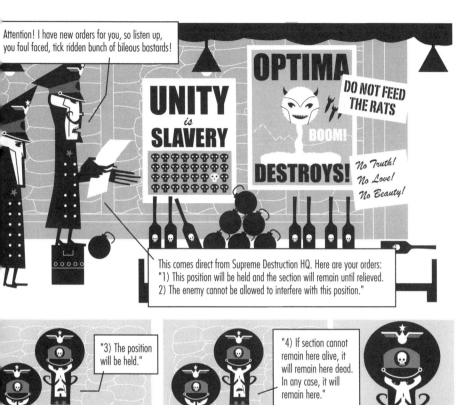

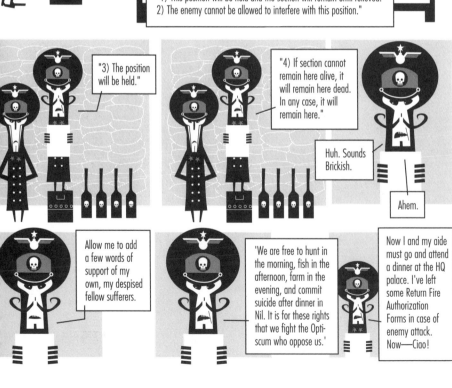

| All the lies we like. | # The New Nihilopolis Times | All news is bad news |

VOL. MCVII   Copyright New Nihilopolis   Eleven Fifty-Two, Nonday, Nuly, Year of the Apocalypse   ONE COIN

NO SURVIVORS

By Snartle Pogcraft

ISLE OF NO RETURN — The election contest to determine the next Supreme Controller of Nihilopia has ended in a void result as the contestants have killed each other off. In this case, there were no survivors at all.

In the last broadcast of the show, the two last contestants, Chief Unjustice Crotchpulp and Squeezegerbil Bakunin were locked in a deadly competition to see who could eat more of the deadly Deathnuts unique to the Isle of No Return.

Both contestants ingested more than enough nuts to kill ten elephants before Chief Crotchpulp finally gave a gasp, clutched his chest, and expired. Bakunin raised a fist in celebration of his triumph and promptly collapsed.

A team of medical experts arrived immediately to pump Bakunin's stomach but they were unable to prevent his demise.

A reunion show aired after the finale. All twenty-two contestants were present, with tastefully done make-up to mask the effects of rigormortis, and in the case of several, reattached body parts. The players were set up on couches and chairs and looked relaxed and, due to a heavy application of make-up, tanned.

Mulfred Dungweasels head fell off in the second half when the broom supporting it gave way, but was quickly reattached by stage hands, using duct tape.

Host Bog Analprobe asked pointed questions and called the various contestants to account.

The real question now is: who will be the next Supreme Controller? All the most eligible candidates are dead, killed in the most macabre and violent manner imaginable by their peers.

With a dearth of possible leadership candidtates, the political parties in the country are looking for spiritual guidance from the Hypocripope, who seems to be the only person capable of pulling a divided nation together in the wake of this boring tragedy.

The Island of No Return, known for its poisonous snakes, man-eating prehistoric monsters, and savage tribes of cannibals is the latest site of the popular Executive Elimination.

FLUTTERPOX WILL WEAR SILLY HAT TO APPEASE SATAN: SOURCE

Nullified Press

TRENTON — Flutter-pox has declared his intention to wear a bonnet in order to appease Satan, who has made the garment a necessary precondition that must be met before he will agree to any further talks regarding the occupation of New Jersey.

"I will do everything necessary to secure peace for our time," Pox said yesterday afternoon. "We have already agreed to conduct the negotiations while standing on our heads. This seems like a minor concession by way of comparison."

Armoured vehicles known as Satanks now patrol the streets of New Jersey, enforcing a strict martial law that requires late night partying and alcohol consumption on pain of death. **—NP**

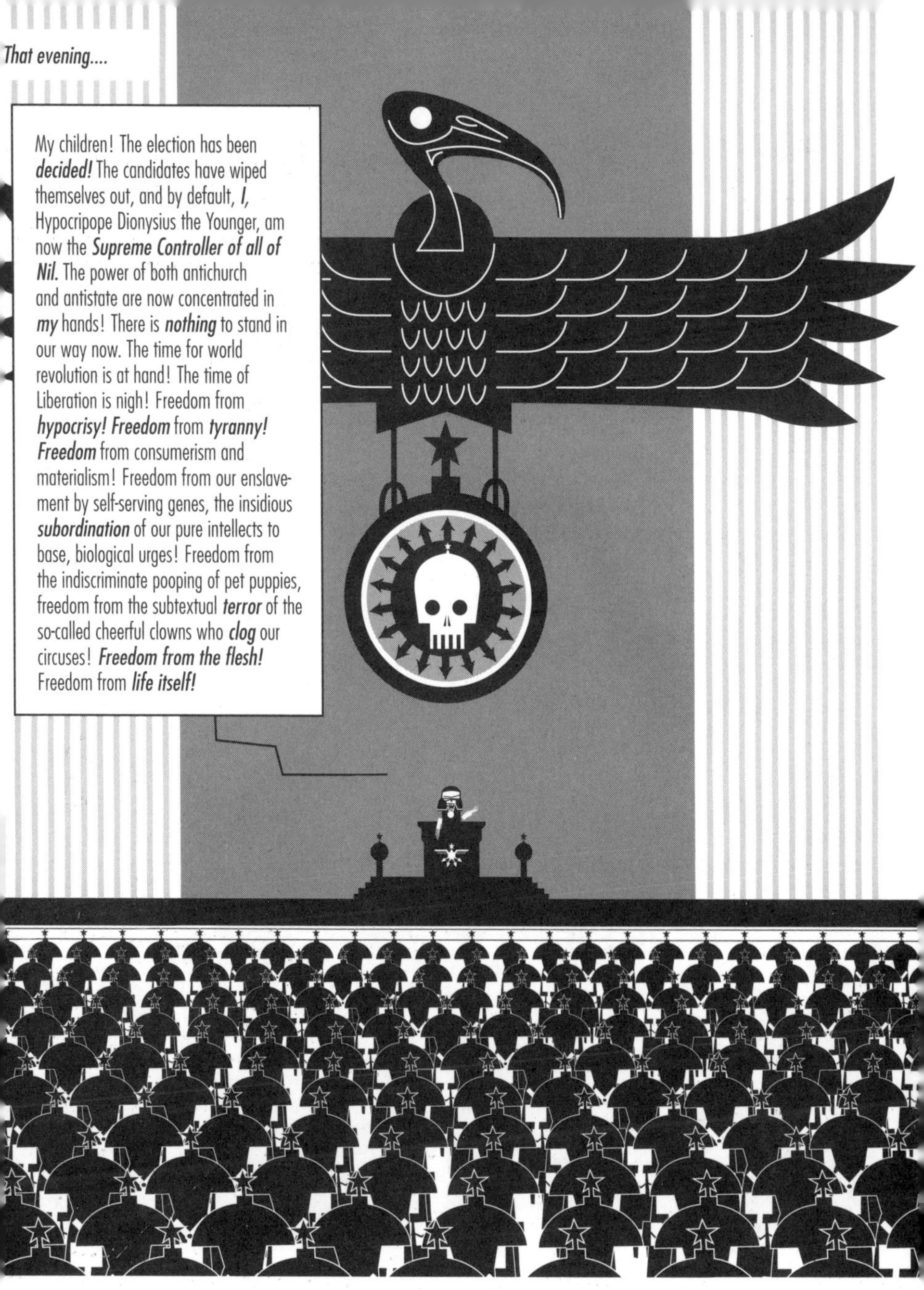
That evening....
My children! The election has been *decided!* The candidates have wiped themselves out, and by default, *I*, Hypocripope Dionysius the Younger, am now the *Supreme Controller of all of Nil.* The power of both antichurch and antistate are now concentrated in *my* hands! There is *nothing* to stand in our way now. The time for world revolution is at hand! The time of Liberation is nigh! Freedom from *hypocrisy! Freedom* from *tyranny! Freedom* from consumerism and materialism! Freedom from our enslavement by self-serving genes, the insidious *subordination* of our pure intellects to base, biological urges! Freedom from the indiscriminate pooping of pet puppies, freedom from the subtextual *terror* of the so-called cheerful clowns who *clog* our circuses! *Freedom from the flesh!* Freedom from *life itself!*

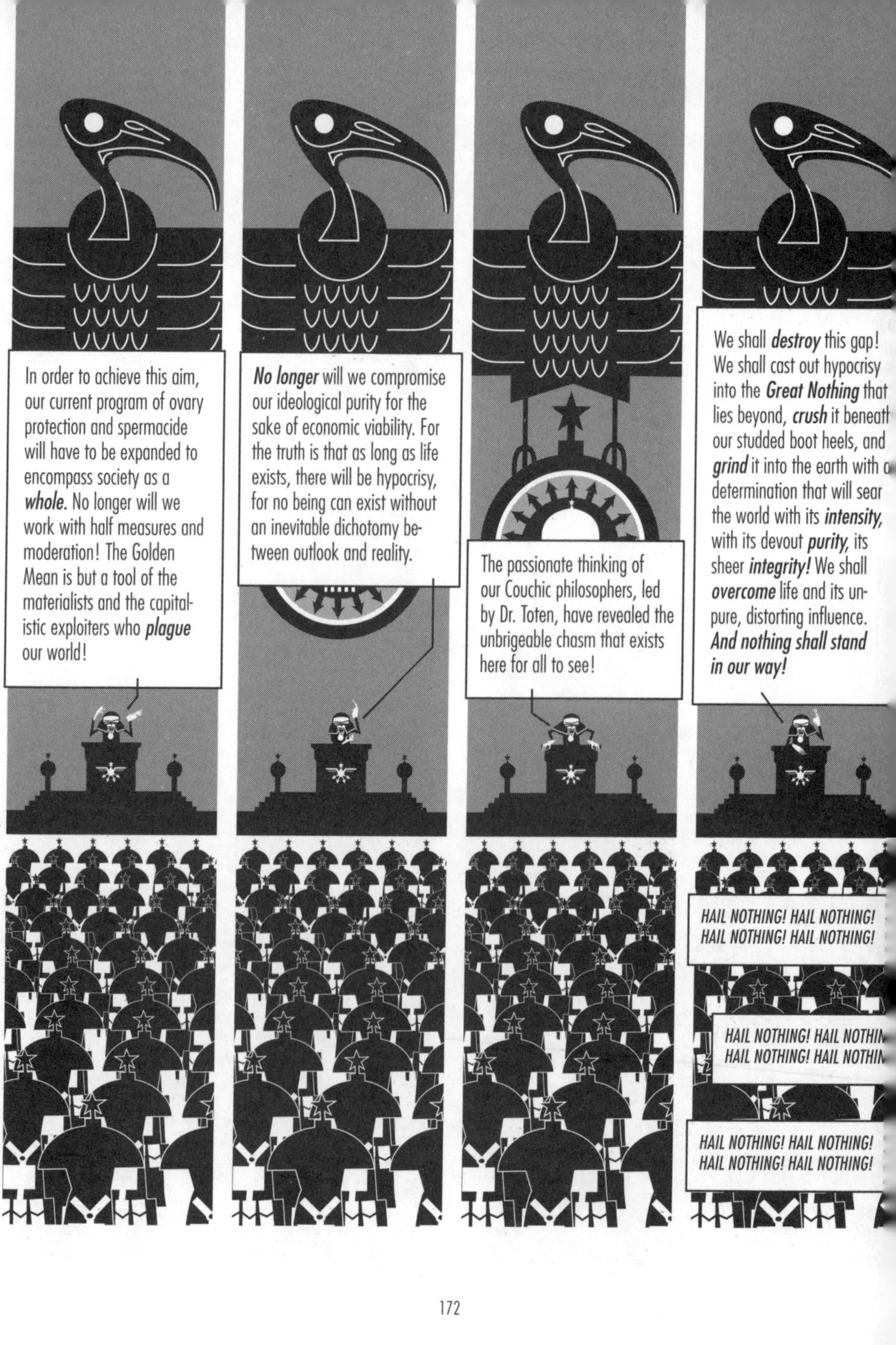
In order to achieve this aim, our current program of ovary protection and spermacide will have to be expanded to encompass society as a ***whole.*** No longer will we work with half measures and moderation! The Golden Mean is but a tool of the materialists and the capitalistic exploiters who ***plague*** our world!
No longer will we compromise our ideological purity for the sake of economic viability. For the truth is that as long as life exists, there will be hypocrisy, for no being can exist without an inevitable dichotomy between outlook and reality.
The passionate thinking of our Couchic philosophers, led by Dr. Toten, have revealed the unbrigeable chasm that exists here for all to see!
We shall ***destroy*** this gap! We shall cast out hypocrisy into the ***Great Nothing*** that lies beyond, ***crush*** it beneat[h] our studded boot heels, and ***grind*** it into the earth with a determination that will sear the world with its ***intensity,*** with its devout ***purity,*** its sheer ***integrity!*** We shall ***overcome*** life and its unpure, distorting influence. ***And nothing shall stand in our way!***
HAIL NOTHING! HAIL NOTHING! HAIL NOTHING! HAIL NOTHING!
HAIL NOTHING! HAIL NOTHIN HAIL NOTHING! HAIL NOTHIN
HAIL NOTHING! HAIL NOTHING! HAIL NOTHING! HAIL NOTHING!

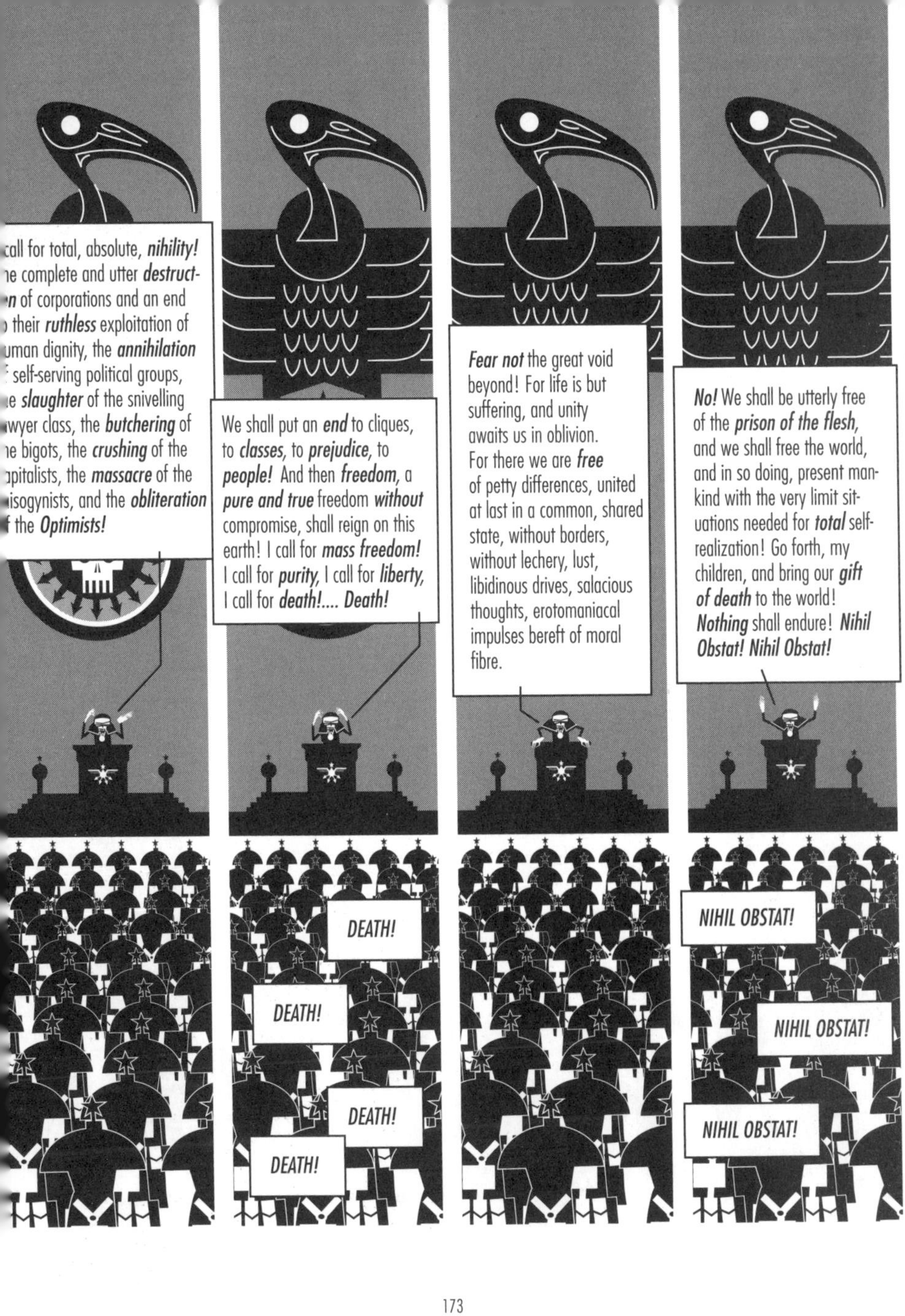
call for total, absolute, nihility! e complete and utter destruct- n of corporations and an end their ruthless exploitation of uman dignity, the annihilation self-serving political groups, e slaughter of the snivelling wyer class, the butchering of e bigots, the crushing of the pitalists, the massacre of the isogynists, and the obliteration the Optimists!
We shall put an end to cliques, to classes, to prejudice, to people! And then freedom, a pure and true freedom without compromise, shall reign on this earth! I call for mass freedom! I call for purity, I call for liberty, I call for death!.... Death!
DEATH!
DEATH!
DEATH!
DEATH!
Fear not the great void beyond! For life is but suffering, and unity awaits us in oblivion. For there we are free of petty differences, united at last in a common, shared state, without borders, without lechery, lust, libidinous drives, salacious thoughts, erotomaniacal impulses bereft of moral fibre.
No! We shall be utterly free of the prison of the flesh, and we shall free the world, and in so doing, present mankind with the very limit situations needed for total self-realization! Go forth, my children, and bring our gift of death to the world! Nothing shall endure! Nihil Obstat! Nihil Obstat!
NIHIL OBSTAT!
NIHIL OBSTAT!
NIHIL OBSTAT!

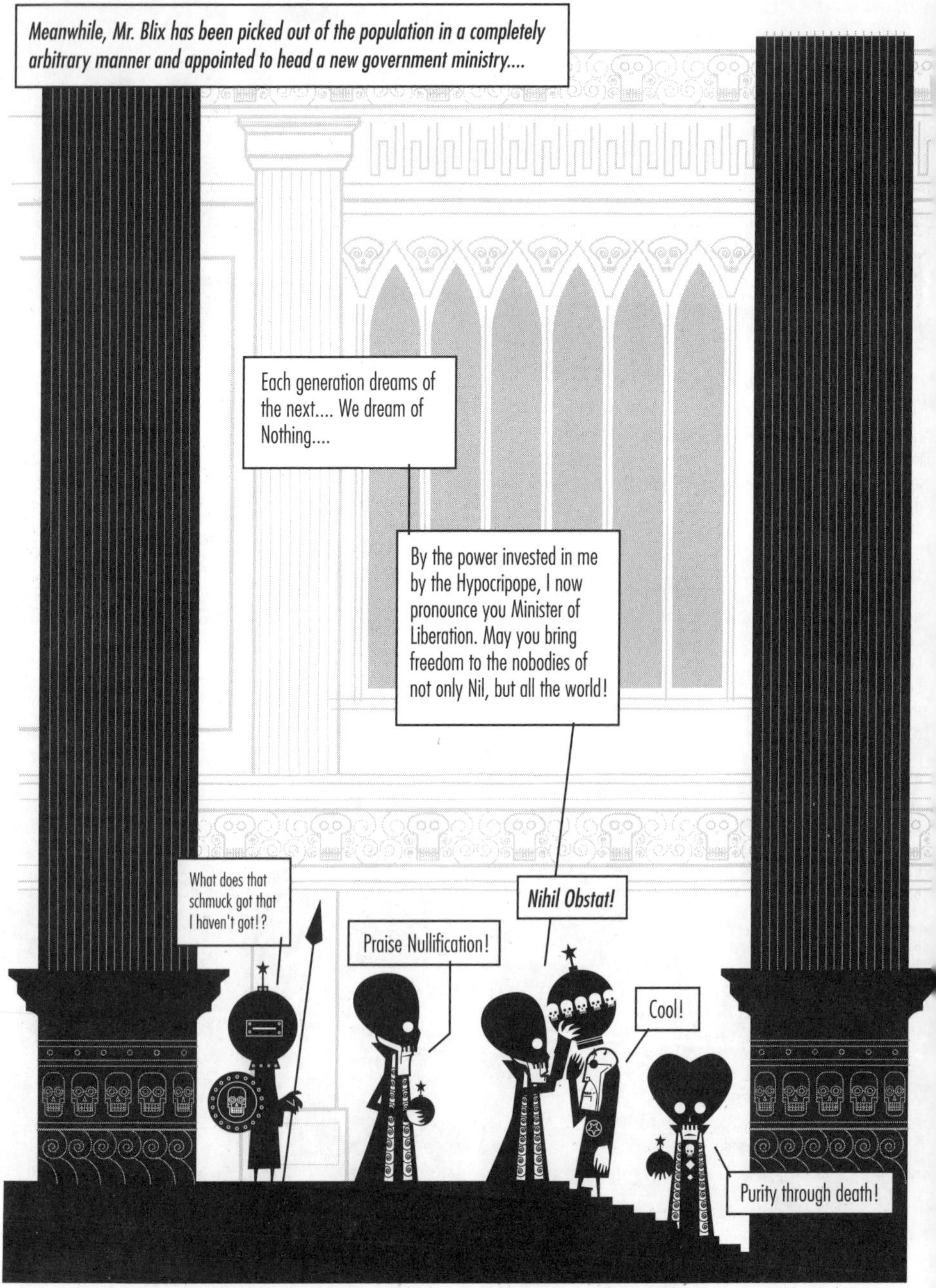
Meanwhile, Mr. Blix has been picked out of the population in a completely arbitrary manner and appointed to head a new government ministry....
Each generation dreams of the next.... We dream of Nothing....
By the power invested in me by the Hypocripope, I now pronounce you Minister of Liberation. May you bring freedom to the nobodies of not only Nil, but all the world!
What does that schmuck got that I haven't got!?
Nihil Obstat!
Praise Nullification!
Cool!
Purity through death!

The New Nihilopolis Times

All the lies we like.

All news is bad news

VOL. MCVII   Copyright New Nihilopolis   Eleven Fifty-Eight, Noday, Nonrueary, Year of the Apocalypse   ONE COIN

BOWEL MOVEMENT STRIKES AGAIN

By Snartle Pogcraft

NIHILOPOLIS — The terrorist organization known as The Bowel Movement has struck again in the Capital, des-troying three public lava-tories, two police sta-tions and severely dam-aging the Great Hall of Nobodies.

Thirty people were killed and two hundred and eleven injuried by the blasts, which went off simultaneously at 8:45 am NST. The attack on the Great Hall was carried out by sui-cide bombers in a truck, while the others are believed to have been placed explosives. "They blew up really good," said Pyrochief Buttermatch.

Military police are now sealing off areas of the city in an effort to catch the terrorist cells.

"The Nonstate will not be held hostage to bombings and maimings and the like, unless they are carried out by the duly appointed author-ities of Nil," commented the Minister of Mayhem, Jak Ketch. "If you engage in terrorist attacks and have not received a license to carry out said attack, then the government will find you, and when it does, take the appro-riate action to punish you for said trans-gression."

The hunt continues.

SUS 392407-N
Nul, Proun

SUS 392407-N
Nul, Proun

MANHUNT BEGINS FOR TERRORIST LEADER

By Narcissus Puddle

NIHILOPOLIS — A nation-wide manhunt has begun for the nefar-ious, unscrupulous, and innately evil leader of the Bowel Movement: Proun Nul, a former employee of the Deconstruction Fleet who has been orches -trating the anti-nonstate attacks since early Oblitobre. In addition, authorities believe that this man is responsible for personally murdering the loving nephew of the Hypocripope. It is rumoured that demons were brought in from Hell itself to secure his capture, but he managed to escape from the citadel of security, killing hundreds of elite security troops in the process. It is rumoured that he has psychic powers and laser eyes.

CHEATER FLEET FHOOT TO KEEP MEDAL TO AVOID STALINISM

Nullified Press

ATHENS — Long dis-tance runner Fleet Fhoot will keep his gold medal from the Alternate Reality Olympic Games, a review board has determined.

"We have looked long and hard into this matter," said Olympic Big Boss Bart Illicitoke yesterday. "If we take his medal, however, we would be re-writing his-tory, which would be, like, Stalinist or some-thing, right? That would be bad. Sure, he cheat-ed, he lied, he tripped a competitor, put red ants in the pants of another, but we made the mis-take of giving him the gold medal. That was our fault. You can't go and take away a cheat-er's medal after he won it. That would be like correcting a mistake. And that would be Stalinist." — *NP*

My War Diary

by Mr. Proun Nul

May 1st: I seem to have been drafted rather forcibly into the war effort against Optima, and my plans to defect to the enemy have been thwarted. I write this in hope of one day sending it to you, Miss Void, focal point of my pointless and sadly continuing existence, but, alas, I doubt that day shall ever arrive. Indeed, perhaps I keep this journal for the purpose of my own sanity, which is being sorely tested by the terrible tedium of military life. Peeling potatoes, hunting rats, picking blood-bloated lice off my body, playing cards, chopping wood, fitful sleeping, meals of mush, and guard duty in all manner of miserable, inclement weather—that is my sorry lot now. The conversation here varies greatly, and my new comrades are a mixed bunch of half-mad soldiers. If we desert, we will be shot. Such is life.

I have gotten to know them all better during our guard duty shifts. Sergeant Blok likes to rotate me around a lot. He seems to be hard of hearing, as he is always yelling. I am not sure he knows his own volume; I have tried to be helpful in this regard but he has responded by assigning me to more guard duty than anyone else. Perhaps he thinks he honours me by doing so. He has a rather bad temper, though, and is given to fits of meaningless rage that I cannot fathom, especially when we are being shelled by the Optiman artillery. He never passes the butter during mess, either. He has a lot of attitude I think. Perhaps an unhappy childhood. I have attached a picture below.

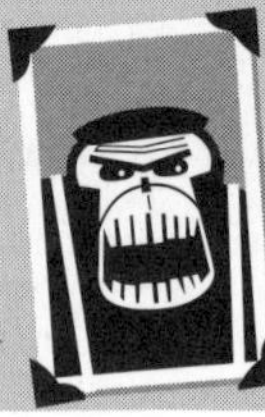

Sergeant Blok comments on my drill performance.

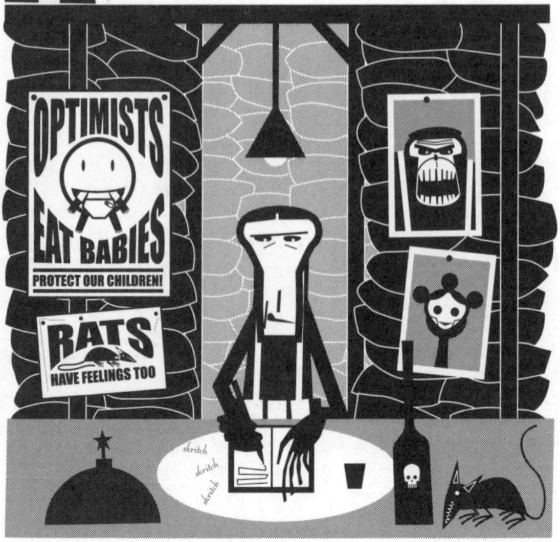
OPTIMISTS
EAT BABIES
PROTECT OUR CHILDREN!
RATS
HAVE FEELINGS TOO
skritch
skritch
skritch

The enemy shelling I speak of is often followed by an infantry attack or by large, hopping battlezigguarts, which cause us significant difficulty. Sergeant Blok destroyed one yesterday with a rhetoric bomb which he shoved in through a damaged gun slit. I have found the level of rhetoriwatts needed to affect the Optimans to be astonishingly high. Anything under 200 rhetoriwatts has little effect. The men in my squad seem to agree, and we mostly rely on high explosives to repel the enemy. The Optimans are fanatical opponents, difficult to discourage, and prone to taking the most ludicrous risks on the battlefield. They try to win on elan alone, like the Froogies. Their tactics are of the most radical and chancy variety; they attempt actions that no sane pessimist would. I find myself admiring them more and more, and long to defect to their country, although I shoot them all the same. It relieves stress.

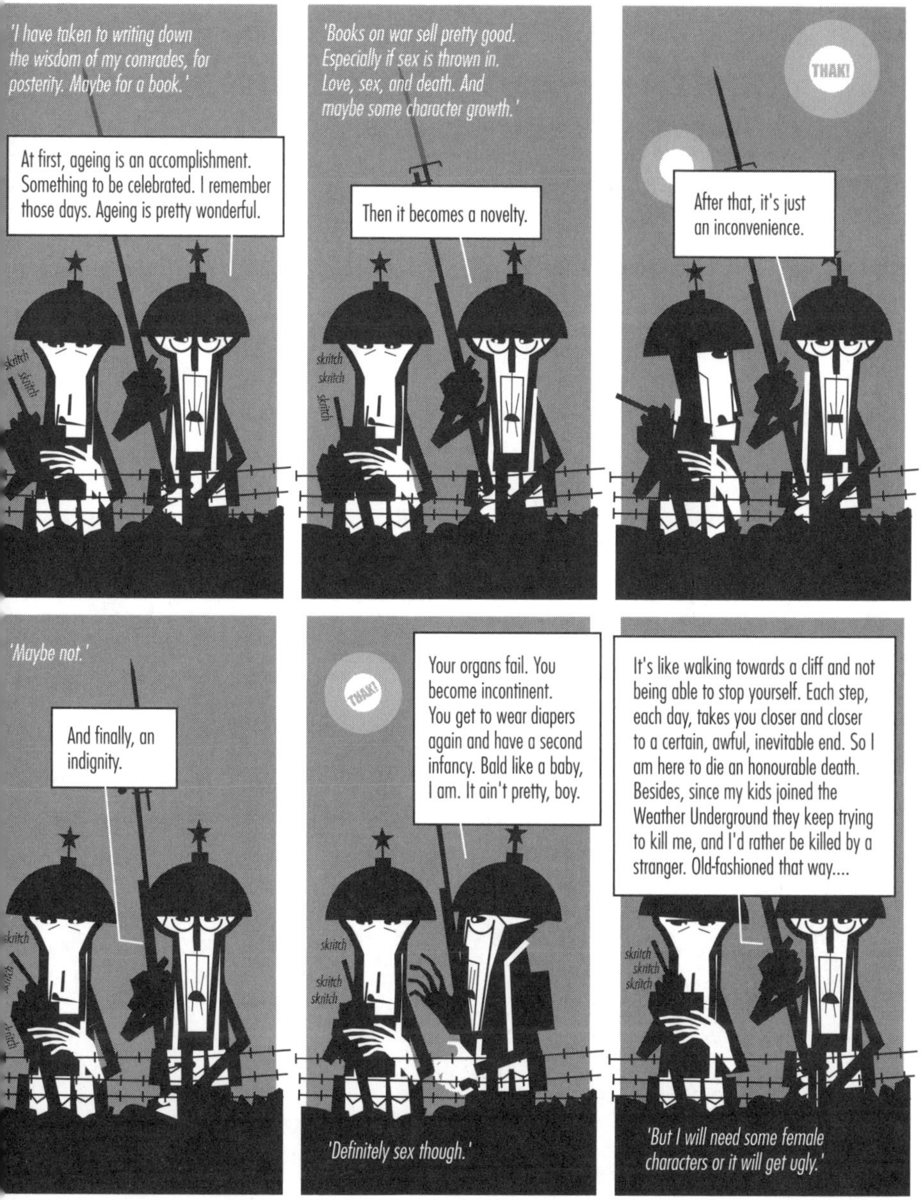
'I have taken to writing down the wisdom of my comrades, for posterity. Maybe for a book.'
At first, ageing is an accomplishment. Something to be celebrated. I remember those days. Ageing is pretty wonderful.
skritch skritch
'Books on war sell pretty good. Especially if sex is thrown in. Love, sex, and death. And maybe some character growth.'
Then it becomes a novelty.
skritch skritch skritch
THAK!
After that, it's just an inconvenience.
'Maybe not.'
And finally, an indignity.
skritch
THAK!
Your organs fail. You become incontinent. You get to wear diapers again and have a second infancy. Bald like a baby, I am. It ain't pretty, boy.
skritch skritch skritch
'Definitely sex though.'
It's like walking towards a cliff and not being able to stop yourself. Each step, each day, takes you closer and closer to a certain, awful, inevitable end. So I am here to die an honourable death. Besides, since my kids joined the Weather Underground they keep trying to kill me, and I'd rather be killed by a stranger. Old-fashioned that way....
skritch skritch skritch
'But I will need some female characters or it will get ugly.'

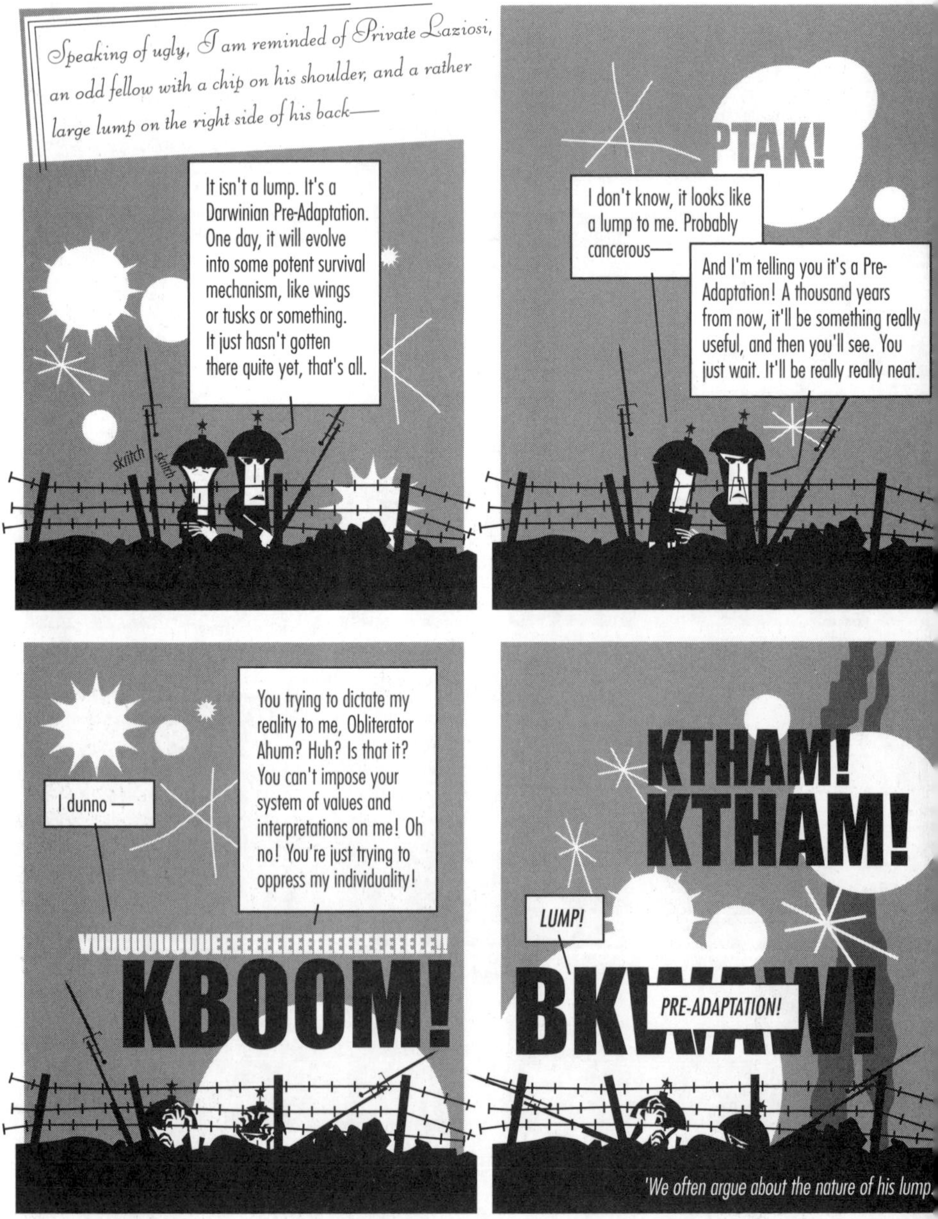

Speaking of ugly, I am reminded of Private Laziosi, an odd fellow with a chip on his shoulder, and a rather large lump on the right side of his back—
It isn't a lump. It's a Darwinian Pre-Adaptation. One day, it will evolve into some potent survival mechanism, like wings or tusks or something. It just hasn't gotten there quite yet, that's all.
skritch
skritch
PTAK!
I don't know, it looks like a lump to me. Probably cancerous—
And I'm telling you it's a Pre-Adaptation! A thousand years from now, it'll be something really useful, and then you'll see. You just wait. It'll be really really neat.
I dunno —
You trying to dictate my reality to me, Obliterator Ahum? Huh? Is that it? You can't impose your system of values and interpretations on me! Oh no! You're just trying to oppress my individuality!
VUUUUUUUUUEEEEEEEEEEEEEEEEEEEEEE!!
KBOOM!
KTHAM!
KTHAM!
LUMP!
PRE-ADAPTATION!
BKWAW!
'We often argue about the nature of his lump.

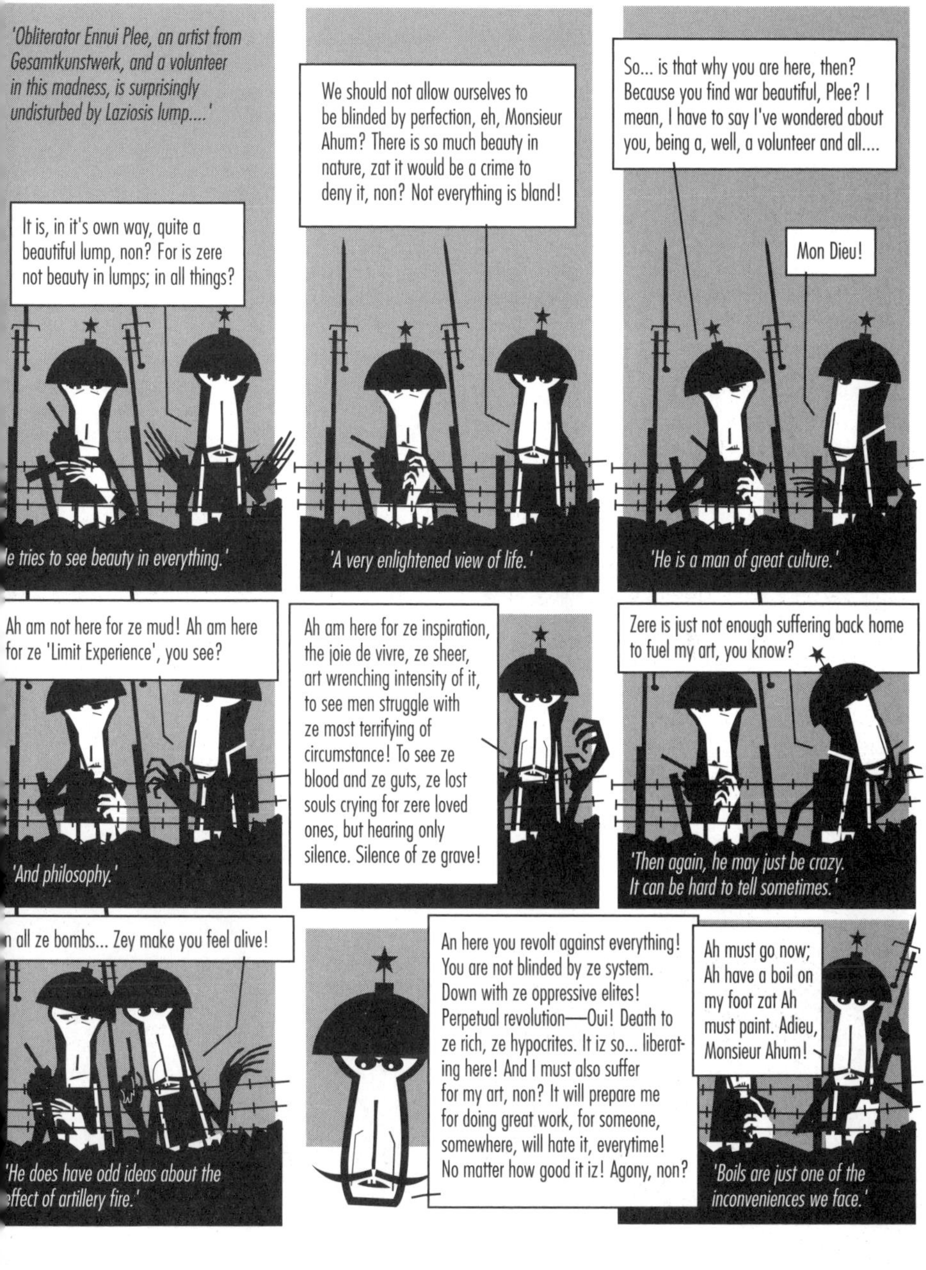
'Obliterator Ennui Plee, an artist from Gesamtkunstwerk, and a volunteer in this madness, is surprisingly undisturbed by Laziosis lump....'
It is, in it's own way, quite a beautiful lump, non? For is zere not beauty in lumps; in all things?
e tries to see beauty in everything.'
We should not allow ourselves to be blinded by perfection, eh, Monsieur Ahum? There is so much beauty in nature, zat it would be a crime to deny it, non? Not everything is bland!
'A very enlightened view of life.'
So... is that why you are here, then? Because you find war beautiful, Plee? I mean, I have to say I've wondered about you, being a, well, a volunteer and all....
Mon Dieu!
'He is a man of great culture.'
Ah am not here for ze mud! Ah am here for ze 'Limit Experience', you see?
'And philosophy.'
Ah am here for ze inspiration, the joie de vivre, ze sheer, art wrenching intensity of it, to see men struggle with ze most terrifying of circumstance! To see ze blood and ze guts, ze lost souls crying for zere loved ones, but hearing only silence. Silence of ze grave!
Zere is just not enough suffering back home to fuel my art, you know?
'Then again, he may just be crazy. It can be hard to tell sometimes.'
n all ze bombs... Zey make you feel alive!
'He does have odd ideas about the ffect of artillery fire.'
An here you revolt against everything! You are not blinded by ze system. Down with ze oppressive elites! Perpetual revolution—Oui! Death to ze rich, ze hypocrites. It iz so... liberating here! And I must also suffer for my art, non? It will prepare me for doing great work, for someone, somewhere, will hate it, everytime! No matter how good it iz! Agony, non?
Ah must go now; Ah have a boil on my foot zat Ah must paint. Adieu, Monsieur Ahum!
'Boils are just one of the inconveniences we face.'

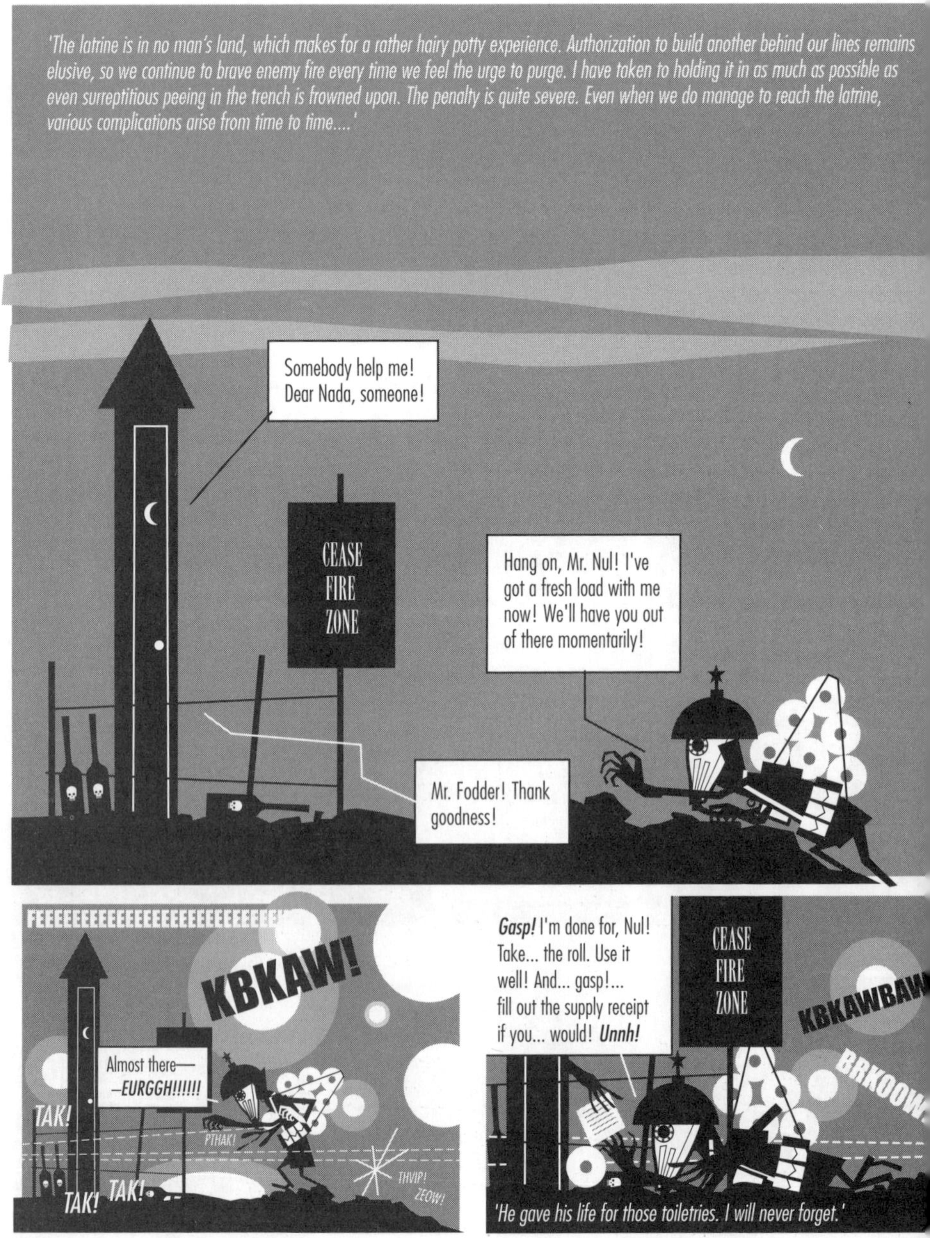
'The latrine is in no man's land, which makes for a rather hairy potty experience. Authorization to build another behind our lines remains elusive, so we continue to brave enemy fire every time we feel the urge to purge. I have taken to holding it in as much as possible as even surreptitious peeing in the trench is frowned upon. The penalty is quite severe. Even when we do manage to reach the latrine, various complications arise from time to time....'
Somebody help me! Dear Nada, someone!
CEASE FIRE ZONE
Hang on, Mr. Nul! I've got a fresh load with me now! We'll have you out of there momentarily!
Mr. Fodder! Thank goodness!
FEEEEEEEEEEEEEEEEEEEEEEEEEEE
KBKAW!
Almost there— —EURGGH!!!!!!
TAK!
PTHAK!
TAK!
TAK!
THVIP!
ZEOW!
Gasp! I'm done for, Nul! Take... the roll. Use it well! And... gasp!... fill out the supply receipt if you... would! Unnh!
CEASE FIRE ZONE
KBKAWBAW
BRKOOW
'He gave his life for those toiletries. I will never forget.'

'he oddest fellow is Private Shophour, an spiring philosopher of the Beerosophy School.'

We are all united by salivation.

It makes no difference if you are rich or poor, a king or a peasant, beautiful or ugly.

It transcends space and time, and unites us all together in a shared, cosmic experience.

Erm... so?

People will be farting, too, and eating and breathing and the whole lot!

Sigh.

Hmm. You mean 'salvation'?

No I mean salivation. Think about it.

Ooo, 'cosmic.' That's sounds good. Go on.

It's like we are all in the same space. In a spiritual sense, if not a physical sense....

Like we're all doing it at once. In a cosmic sense, you see? The same experience! So time discrepancy becomes irrelevant!

It makes no difference when!

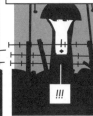

It is as if we are all one, together, spiritually: a universal fart across history. ★

!!!

You see, we salivate just like Aristotle.

We all salivate the same way.

In a thousand years, people will still be salivating, just like we are right now.

And we will be one with them, just as we are one with our salivating ancestors!

Farting is the same for everyone, you know? Whether it's a cave man or a feudal lord or a poet or a philosopher: no difference!

Can I switch out of guard duty with you?

"His problem is he thinks too much."

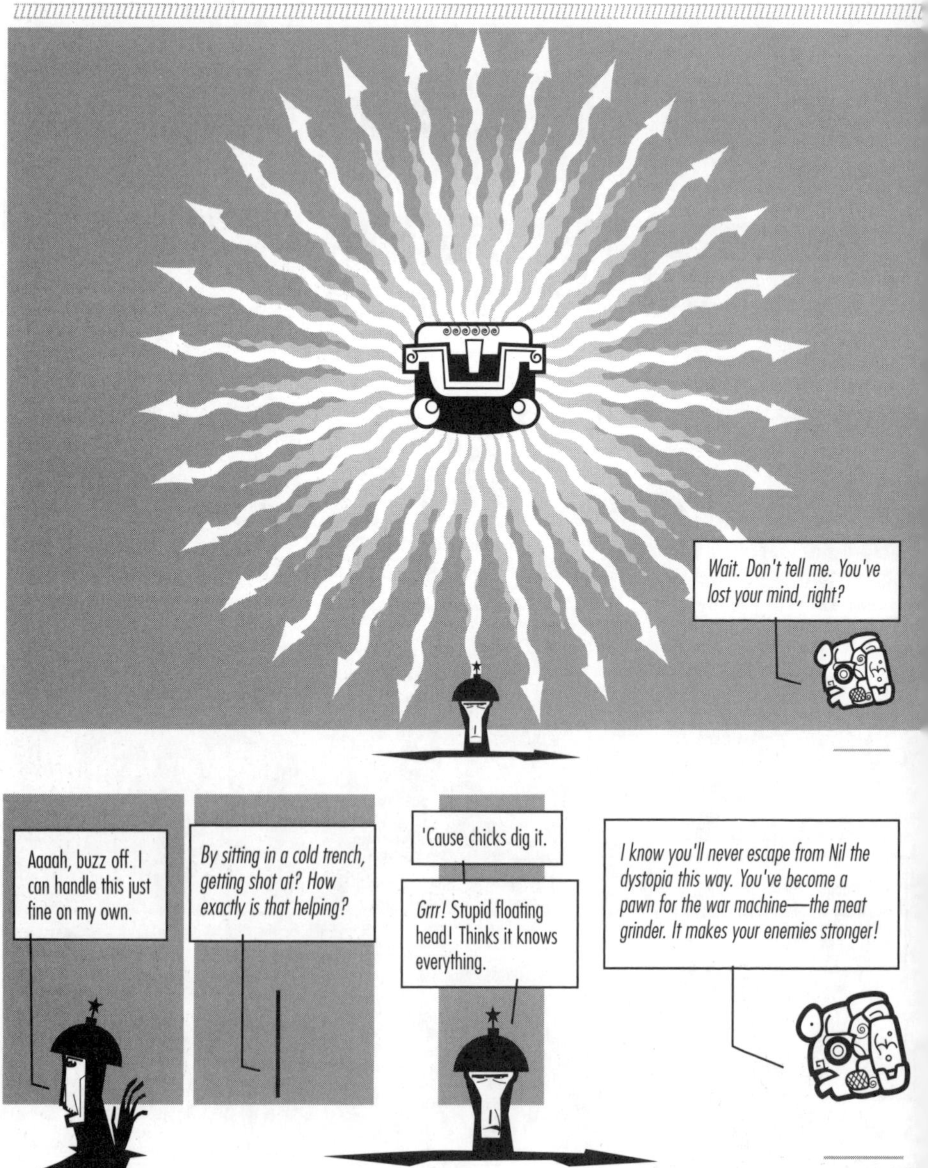

Wait. Don't tell me. You've lost your mind, right?
Aaaah, buzz off. I can handle this just fine on my own.
By sitting in a cold trench, getting shot at? How exactly is that helping?
'Cause chicks dig it.
Grrr! Stupid floating head! Thinks it knows everything.
I know you'll never escape from Nil the dystopia this way. You've become a pawn for the war machine—the meat grinder. It makes your enemies stronger!

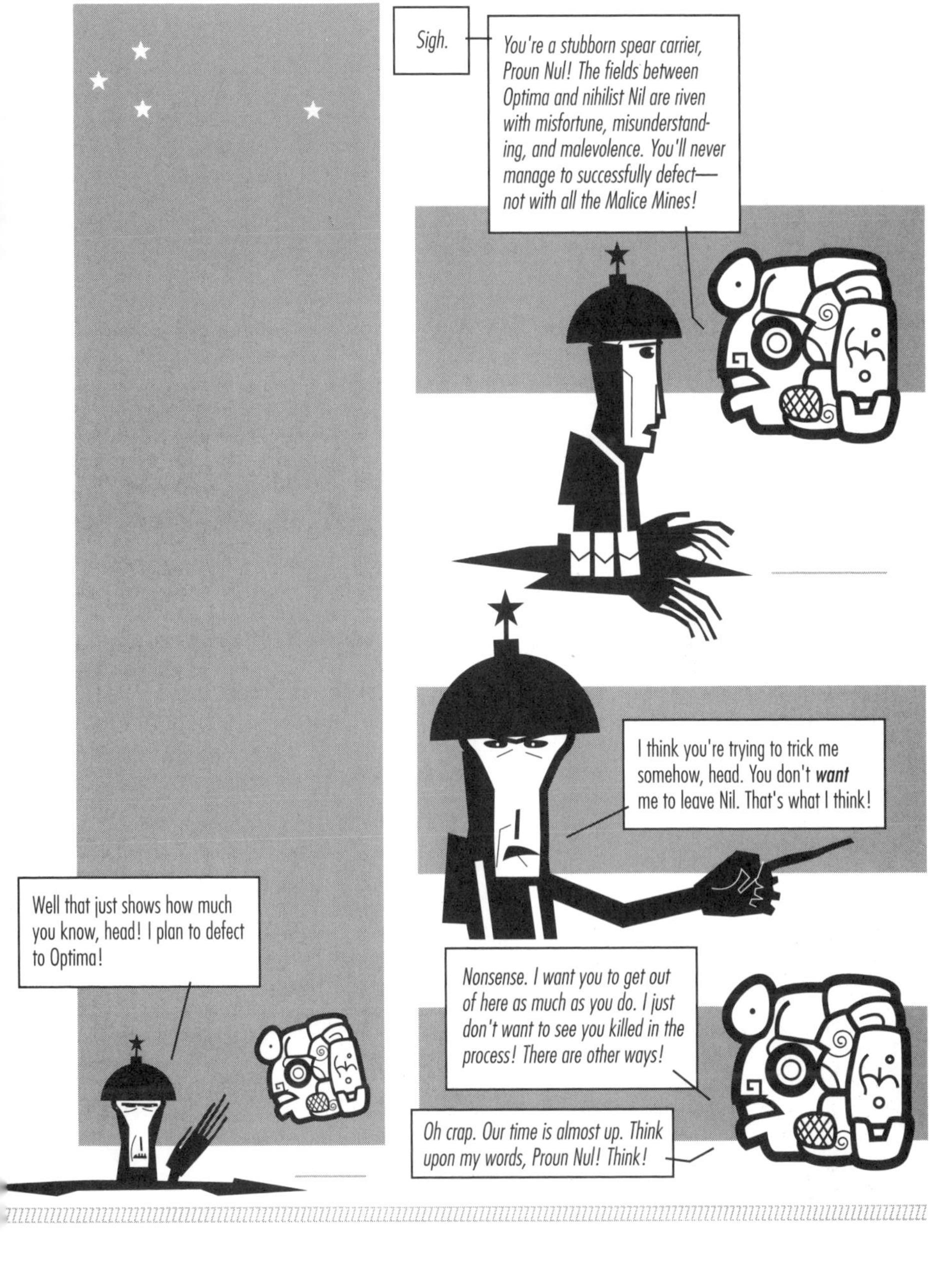
Well that just shows how much you know, head! I plan to defect to Optima!
Sigh.
You're a stubborn spear carrier, Proun Nul! The fields between Optima and nihilist Nil are riven with misfortune, misunderstanding, and malevolence. You'll never manage to successfully defect—not with all the Malice Mines!
I think you're trying to trick me somehow, head. You don't ***want*** me to leave Nil. That's what I think!
Nonsense. I want you to get out of here as much as you do. I just don't want to see you killed in the process! There are other ways!
Oh crap. Our time is almost up. Think upon my words, Proun Nul! Think!

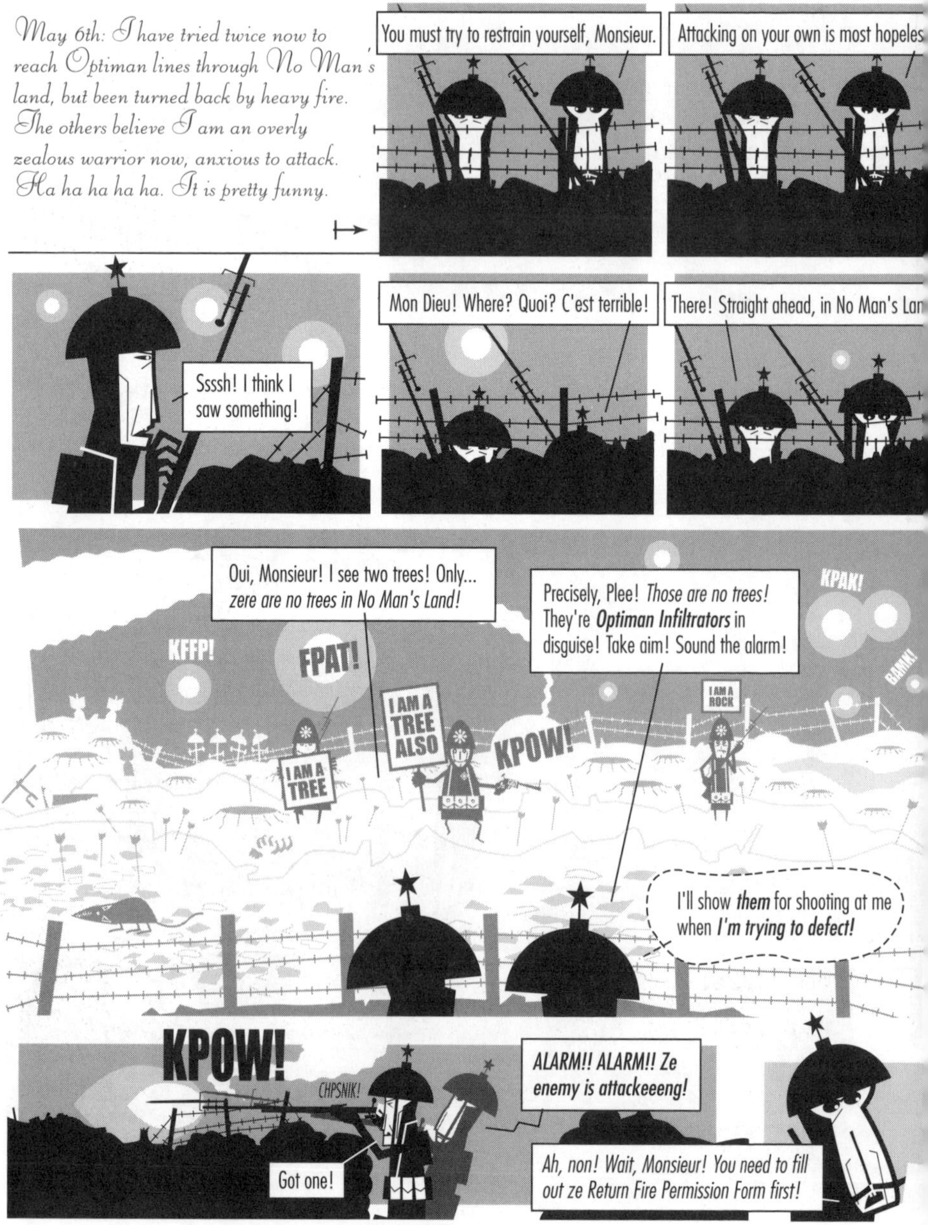
May 6th: I have tried twice now to reach Optiman lines through No Man's land, but been turned back by heavy fire. The others believe I am an overly zealous warrior now, anxious to attack. Ha ha ha ha ha. It is pretty funny.
You must try to restrain yourself, Monsieur.
Attacking on your own is most hopeles
Ssssh! I think I saw something!
Mon Dieu! Where? Quoi? C'est terrible!
There! Straight ahead, in No Man's Lan
Oui, Monsieur! I see two trees! Only... *zere are no trees in No Man's Land!*
Precisely, Plee! *Those are no trees!* They're ***Optiman Infiltrators*** in disguise! Take aim! Sound the alarm!
KFFP!
FPAT!
I AM A TREE
I AM A TREE ALSO
KPOW!
KPAK!
BAMK!
I AM A ROCK
I'll show ***them*** for shooting at me when ***I'm trying to defect!***
KPOW!
CHPSNIK!
Got one!
ALARM!! ALARM!! Ze enemy is attackeeeng!
Ah, non! Wait, Monsieur! You need to fill out ze Return Fire Permission Form first!

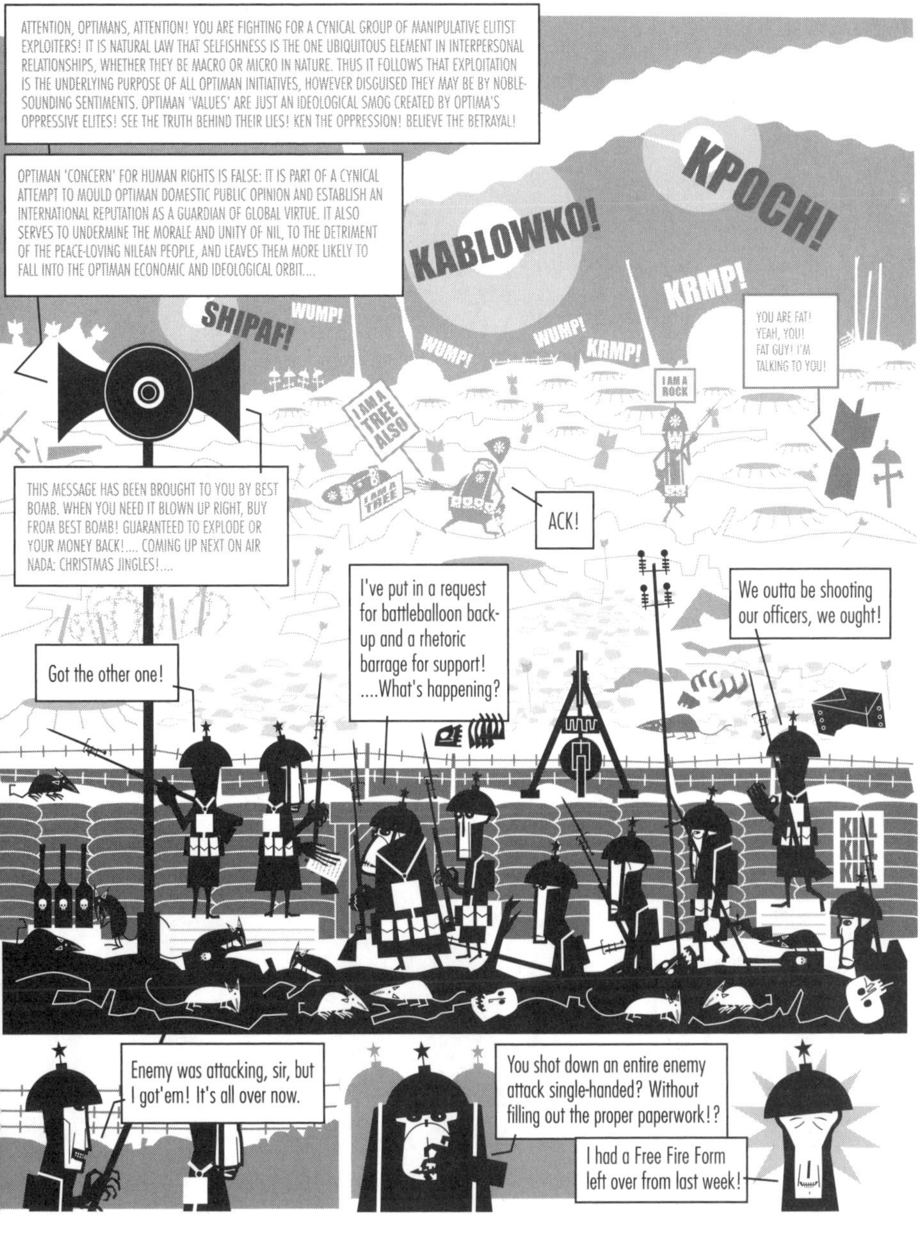
ATTENTION, OPTIMANS, ATTENTION! YOU ARE FIGHTING FOR A CYNICAL GROUP OF MANIPULATIVE ELITIST EXPLOITERS! IT IS NATURAL LAW THAT SELFISHNESS IS THE ONE UBIQUITOUS ELEMENT IN INTERPERSONAL RELATIONSHIPS, WHETHER THEY BE MACRO OR MICRO IN NATURE. THUS IT FOLLOWS THAT EXPLOITATION IS THE UNDERLYING PURPOSE OF ALL OPTIMAN INITIATIVES, HOWEVER DISGUISED THEY MAY BE BY NOBLE-SOUNDING SENTIMENTS. OPTIMAN 'VALUES' ARE JUST AN IDEOLOGICAL SMOG CREATED BY OPTIMA'S OPPRESSIVE ELITES! SEE THE TRUTH BEHIND THEIR LIES! KEN THE OPPRESSION! BELIEVE THE BETRAYAL!
OPTIMAN 'CONCERN' FOR HUMAN RIGHTS IS FALSE: IT IS PART OF A CYNICAL ATTEMPT TO MOULD OPTIMAN DOMESTIC PUBLIC OPINION AND ESTABLISH AN INTERNATIONAL REPUTATION AS A GUARDIAN OF GLOBAL VIRTUE. IT ALSO SERVES TO UNDERMINE THE MORALE AND UNITY OF NIL, TO THE DETRIMENT OF THE PEACE-LOVING NILEAN PEOPLE, AND LEAVES THEM MORE LIKELY TO FALL INTO THE OPTIMAN ECONOMIC AND IDEOLOGICAL ORBIT....
KPOCH!
KABLOWKO!
KRMP!
SHIPAF!
WUMP!
WUMP!
WUMP!
KRMP!
YOU ARE FAT! YEAH, YOU! FAT GUY! I'M TALKING TO YOU!
I AM A ROCK
I AM A TREE ALSO
I AM A TREE
THIS MESSAGE HAS BEEN BROUGHT TO YOU BY BEST BOMB. WHEN YOU NEED IT BLOWN UP RIGHT, BUY FROM BEST BOMB! GUARANTEED TO EXPLODE OR YOUR MONEY BACK!.... COMING UP NEXT ON AIR NADA: CHRISTMAS JINGLES!....
ACK!
I've put in a request for battleballoon back-up and a rhetoric barrage for support! ....What's happening?
We outta be shooting our officers, we ought!
Got the other one!
KILL KILL KILL
Enemy was attacking, sir, but I got'em! It's all over now.
You shot down an entire enemy attack single-handed? Without filling out the proper paperwork!?
I had a Free Fire Form left over from last week!

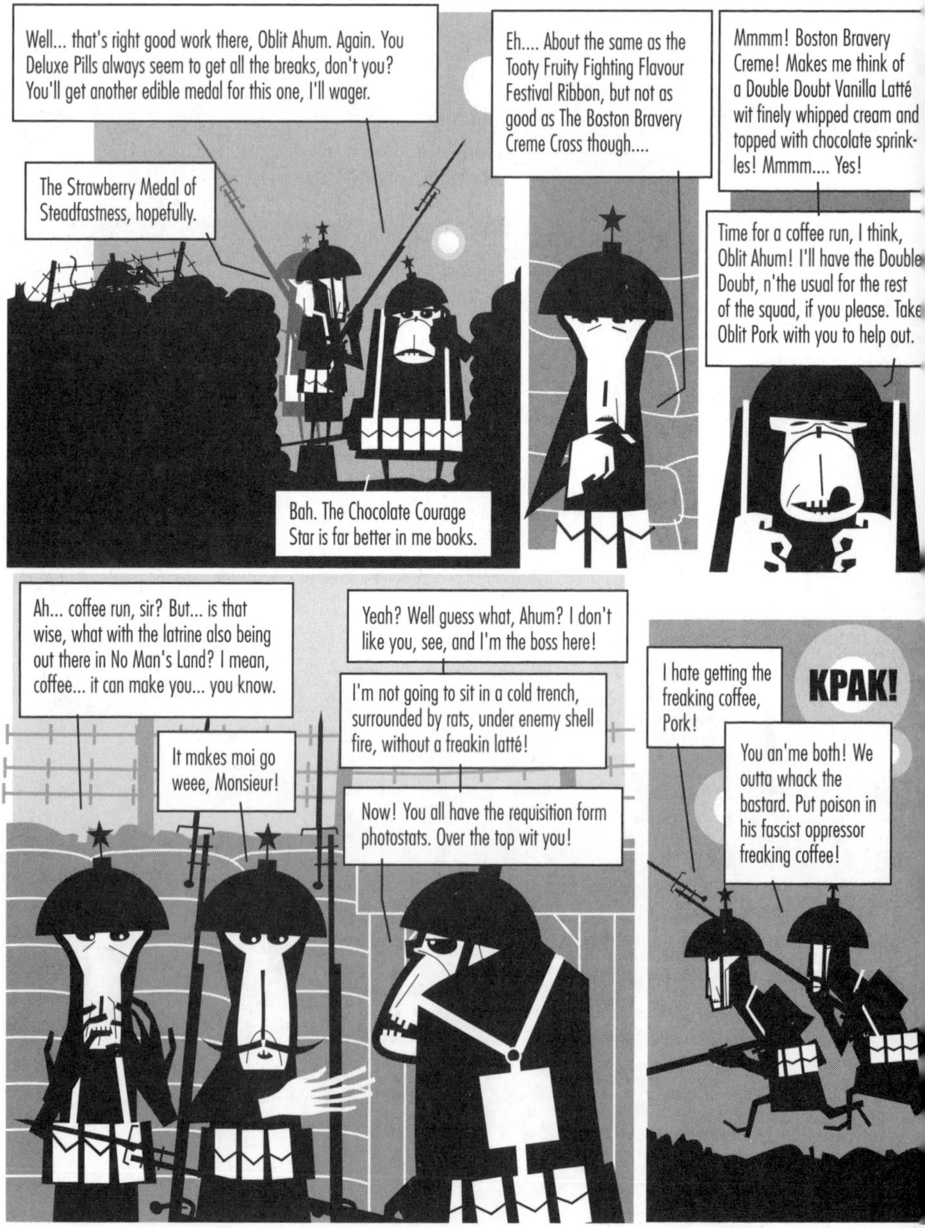

Well... that's right good work there, Oblit Ahum. Again. You Deluxe Pills always seem to get all the breaks, don't you? You'll get another edible medal for this one, I'll wager.
The Strawberry Medal of Steadfastness, hopefully.
Bah. The Chocolate Courage Star is far better in me books.
Eh.... About the same as the Tooty Fruity Fighting Flavour Festival Ribbon, but not as good as The Boston Bravery Creme Cross though....
Mmmm! Boston Bravery Creme! Makes me think of a Double Doubt Vanilla Latté wit finely whipped cream and topped with chocolate sprinkles! Mmmm.... Yes!
Time for a coffee run, I think, Oblit Ahum! I'll have the Double Doubt, n'the usual for the rest of the squad, if you please. Take Oblit Pork with you to help out.
Ah... coffee run, sir? But... is that wise, what with the latrine also being out there in No Man's Land? I mean, coffee... it can make you... you know.
It makes moi go weee, Monsieur!
Yeah? Well guess what, Ahum? I don't like you, see, and I'm the boss here!
I'm not going to sit in a cold trench, surrounded by rats, under enemy shell fire, without a freakin latté!
Now! You all have the requisition form photostats. Over the top wit you!
I hate getting the freaking coffee, Pork!
KPAK!
You an'me both! We outta whack the bastard. Put poison in his fascist oppressor freaking coffee!

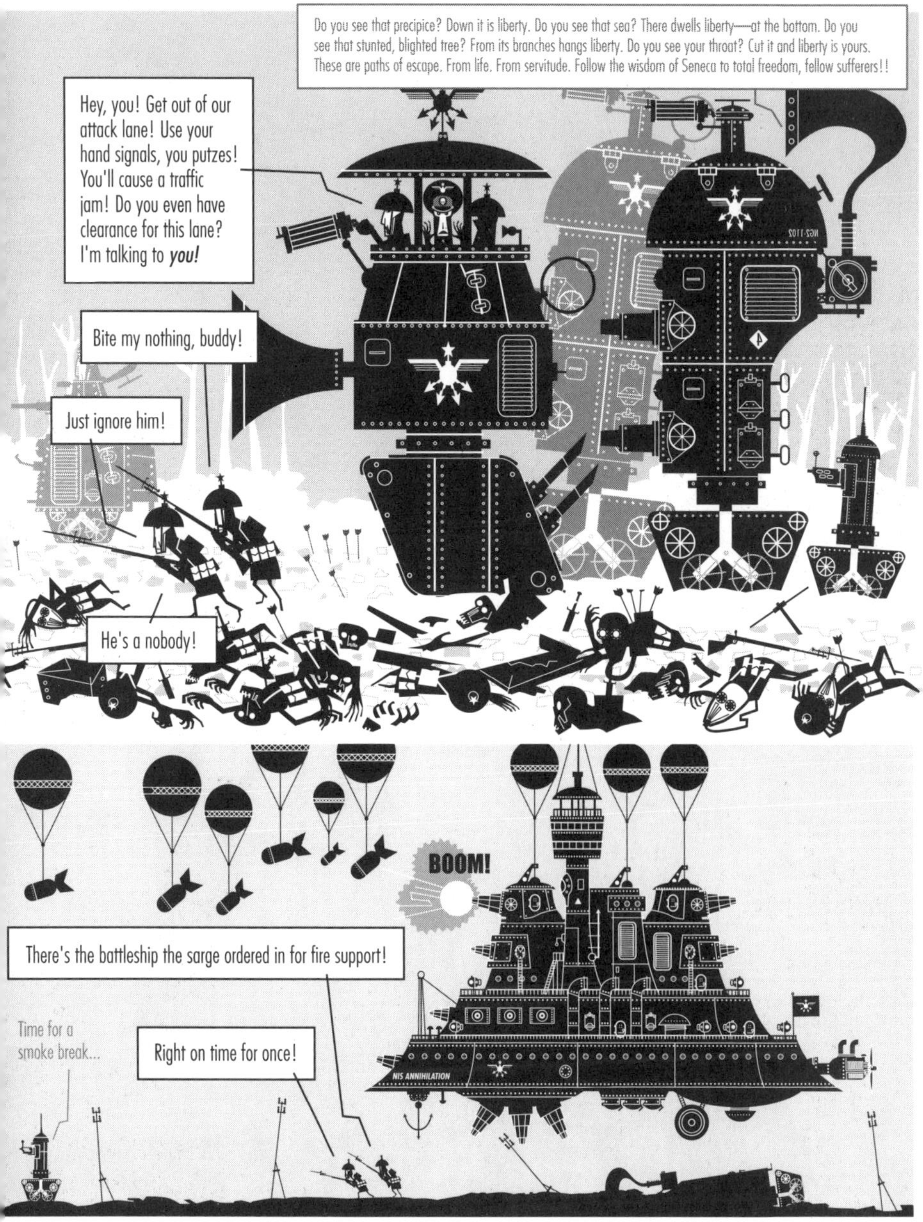
Do you see that precipice? Down it is liberty. Do you see that sea? There dwells liberty—at the bottom. Do you see that stunted, blighted tree? From its branches hangs liberty. Do you see your throat? Cut it and liberty is yours. These are paths of escape. From life. From servitude. Follow the wisdom of Seneca to total freedom, fellow sufferers!!
Hey, you! Get out of our attack lane! Use your hand signals, you putzes! You'll cause a traffic jam! Do you even have clearance for this lane? I'm talking to ***you!***
Bite my nothing, buddy!
Just ignore him!
He's a nobody!
BOOM!
There's the battleship the sarge ordered in for fire support!
NIS ANNIHILATION
Time for a smoke break...
Right on time for once!

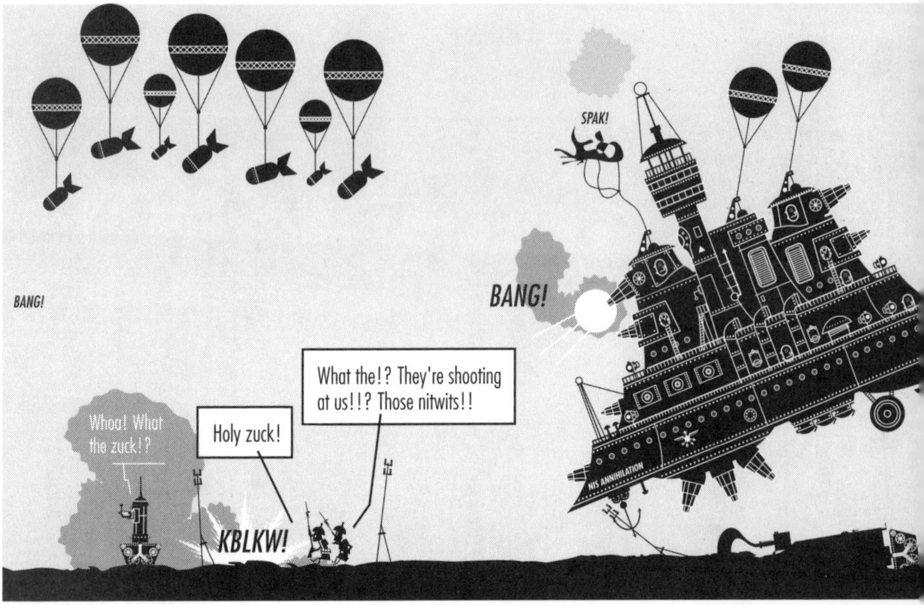
SPAK!
BANG!
BANG!
What the!? They're shooting at us!!? Those nitwits!!
Whoa! What the zuck!?
Holy zuck!
KBLKW!
NIS ANNIHILATION

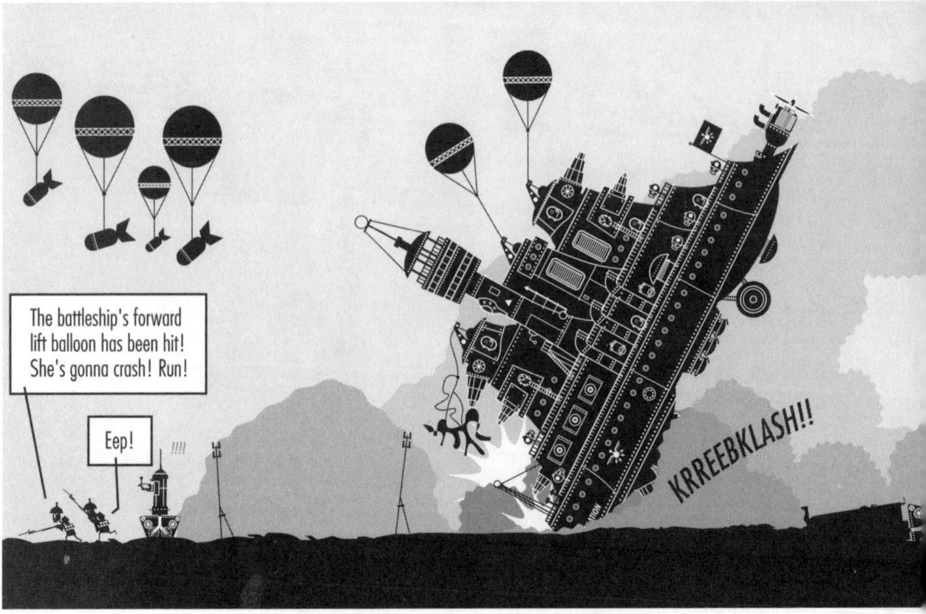
The battleship's forward lift balloon has been hit! She's gonna crash! Run!
Eep!
!!!!
KRREEBKLASH!!

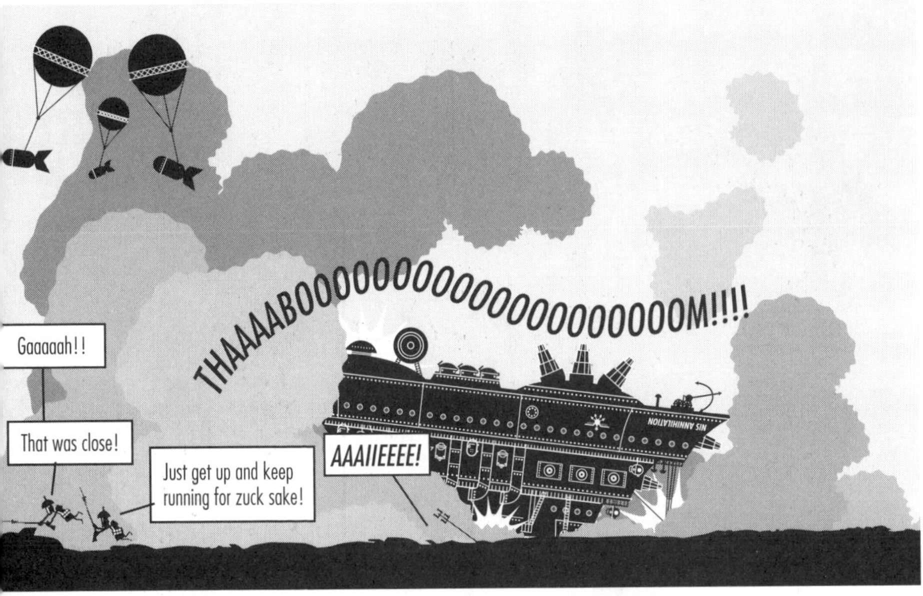

THAAAABOOOOOOOOOOOOOOOOOOOOM!!!!
Gaaaaah!!
That was close!
Just get up and keep running for zuck sake!
AAAIIEEEE!

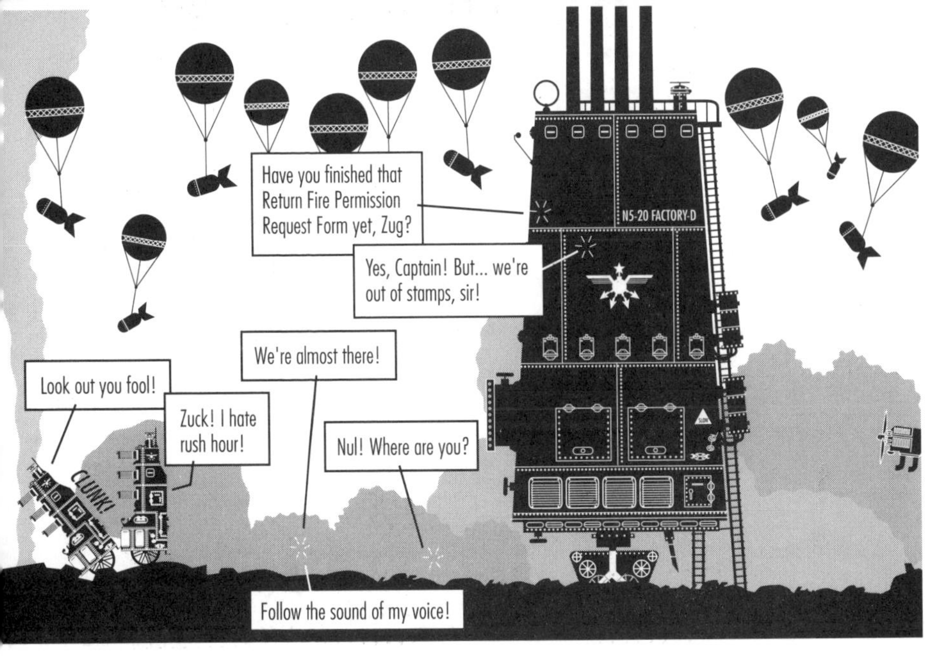

Have you finished that Return Fire Permission Request Form yet, Zug?
N5-20 FACTORY-D
Yes, Captain! But... we're out of stamps, sir!
Look out you fool!
CLUNK!
Zuck! I hate rush hour!
We're almost there!
Nul! Where are you?
Follow the sound of my voice!

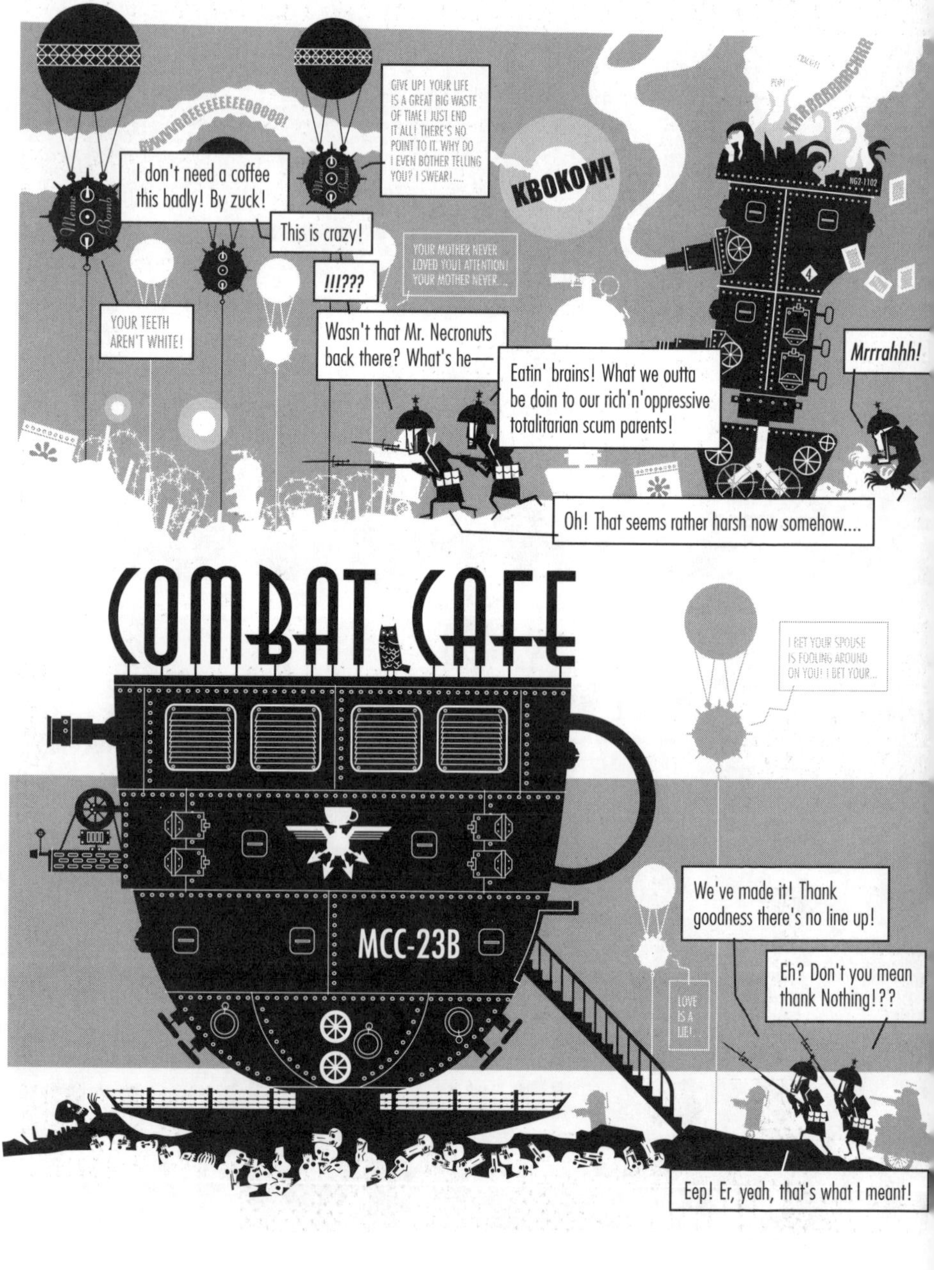
Meme Bomb
I don't need a coffee this badly! By zuck!
Meme Bomb
GIVE UP! YOUR LIFE IS A GREAT BIG WASTE OF TIME! JUST END IT ALL! THERE'S NO POINT TO IT. WHY DO I EVEN BOTHER TELLING YOU? I SWEAR!....
This is crazy!
KBOKOW!
KRRRRRRRRCHRR
NG2-1102
YOUR TEETH AREN'T WHITE!
YOUR MOTHER NEVER LOVED YOU! ATTENTION! YOUR MOTHER NEVER...
!!!???
Wasn't that Mr. Necronuts back there? What's he—
Eatin' brains! What we outta be doin to our rich'n'oppressive totalitarian scum parents!
Mrrrahhh!
Oh! That seems rather harsh now somehow....
COMBAT CAFE
I BET YOUR SPOUSE IS FOOLING AROUND ON YOU! I BET YOUR...
MCC-23B
LOVE IS A LIE!
We've made it! Thank goodness there's no line up!
Eh? Don't you mean thank Nothing!??
Eep! Er, yeah, that's what I meant!

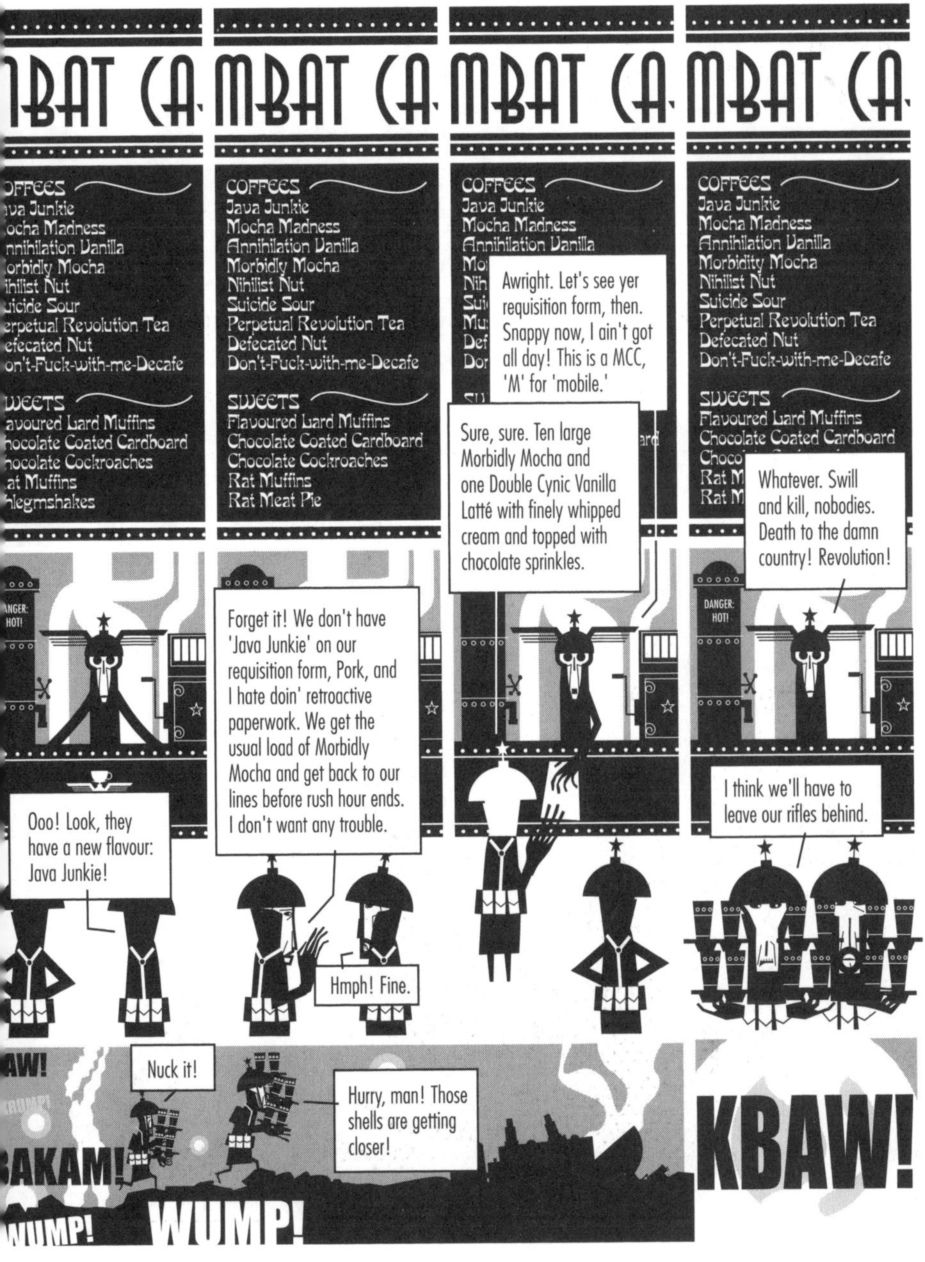

MBAT CA
COFFEES
Java Junkie
Mocha Madness
Annihilation Vanilla
Morbidly Mocha
Nihilist Nut
Suicide Sour
Perpetual Revolution Tea
Defecated Nut
Don't-Fuck-with-me-Decafe
SWEETS
Flavoured Lard Muffins
Chocolate Coated Cardboard
Chocolate Cockroaches
Rat Muffins
Rat Meat Pie
DANGER: HOT!
Ooo! Look, they have a new flavour: Java Junkie!
Forget it! We don't have 'Java Junkie' on our requisition form, Pork, and I hate doin' retroactive paperwork. We get the usual load of Morbidly Mocha and get back to our lines before rush hour ends. I don't want any trouble.
Hmph! Fine.
Awright. Let's see yer requisition form, then. Snappy now, I ain't got all day! This is a MCC, 'M' for 'mobile.'
Sure, sure. Ten large Morbidly Mocha and one Double Cynic Vanilla Latté with finely whipped cream and topped with chocolate sprinkles.
Whatever. Swill and kill, nobodies. Death to the damn country! Revolution!
I think we'll have to leave our rifles behind.
AW!
Nuck it!
Hurry, man! Those shells are getting closer!
AKAM!
WUMP!
WUMP!
KBAW!

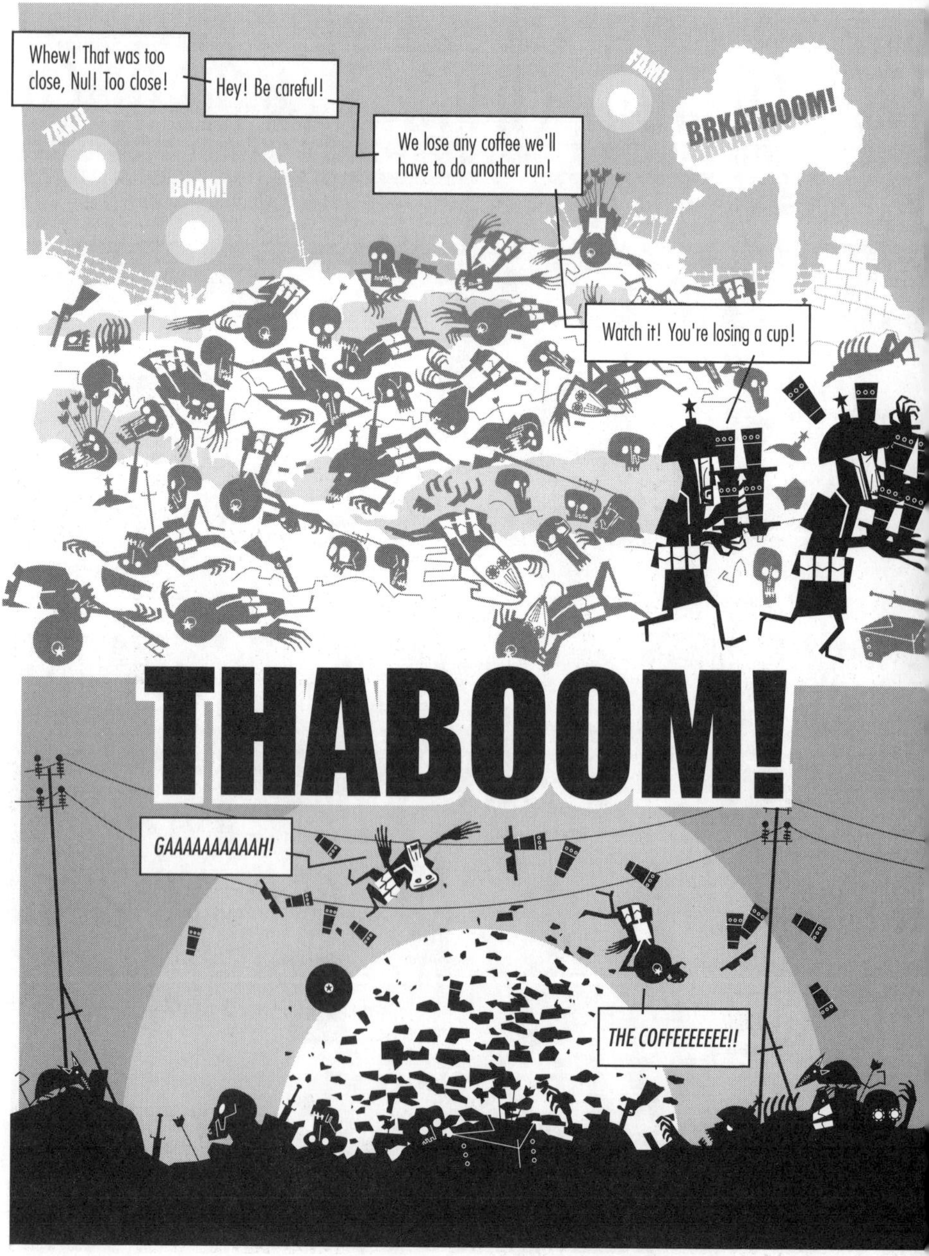
Whew! That was too close, Nul! Too close!
Hey! Be careful!
We lose any coffee we'll have to do another run!
ZAKI!
BOAM!
FAM!
BRKATHOOM!
Watch it! You're losing a cup!
THABOOM!
GAAAAAAAAAAH!
THE COFFEEEEEEE!!

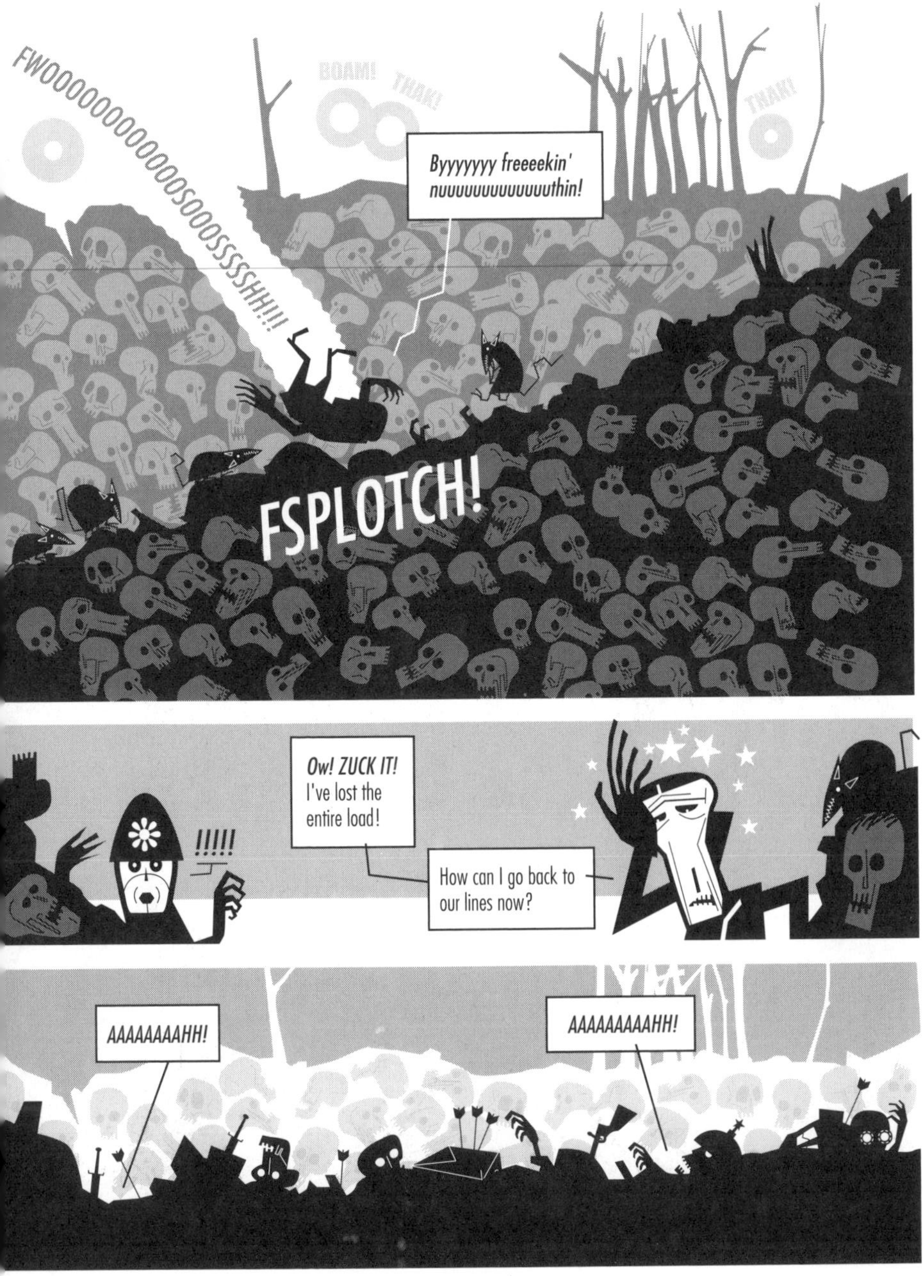

FWOOOOOOOOOOOOOOSOOOSSSSSHH!!!!
BOAM!
THAK!
THAK!
Byyyyyyy freeeekin' nuuuuuuuuuuuuuthin!
FSPLOTCH!
!!!!!
Ow! ZUCK IT! I've lost the entire load!
How can I go back to our lines now?
AAAAAAAAHH!
AAAAAAAAAHH!

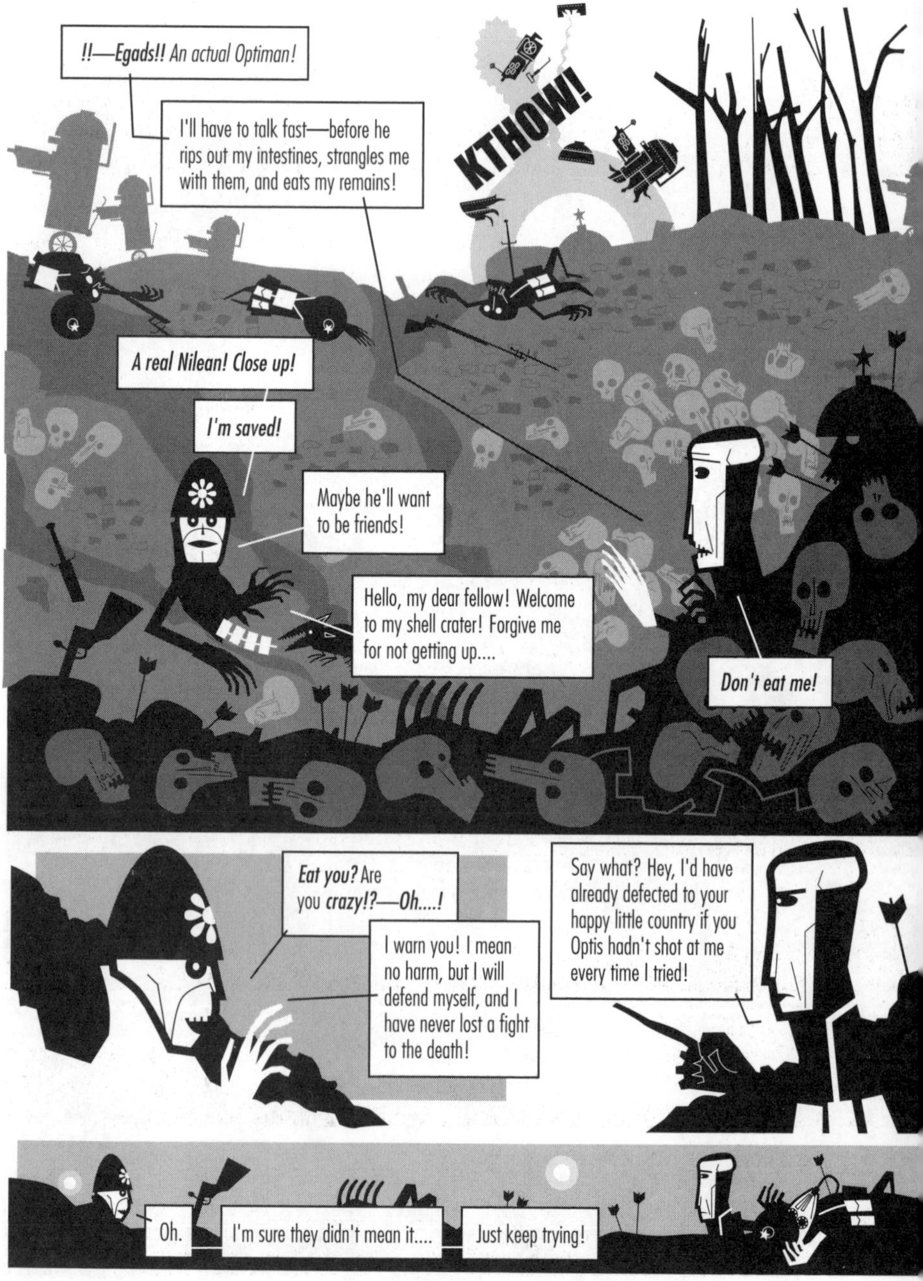

!!—Egads!! An actual Optiman!
I'll have to talk fast—before he rips out my intestines, strangles me with them, and eats my remains!
KTHOW!
A real Nilean! Close up!
I'm saved!
Maybe he'll want to be friends!
Hello, my dear fellow! Welcome to my shell crater! Forgive me for not getting up....
Don't eat me!
Eat you? Are you crazy!?—Oh....!
I warn you! I mean no harm, but I will defend myself, and I have never lost a fight to the death!
Say what? Hey, I'd have already defected to your happy little country if you Optis hadn't shot at me every time I tried!
Oh.
I'm sure they didn't mean it....
Just keep trying!

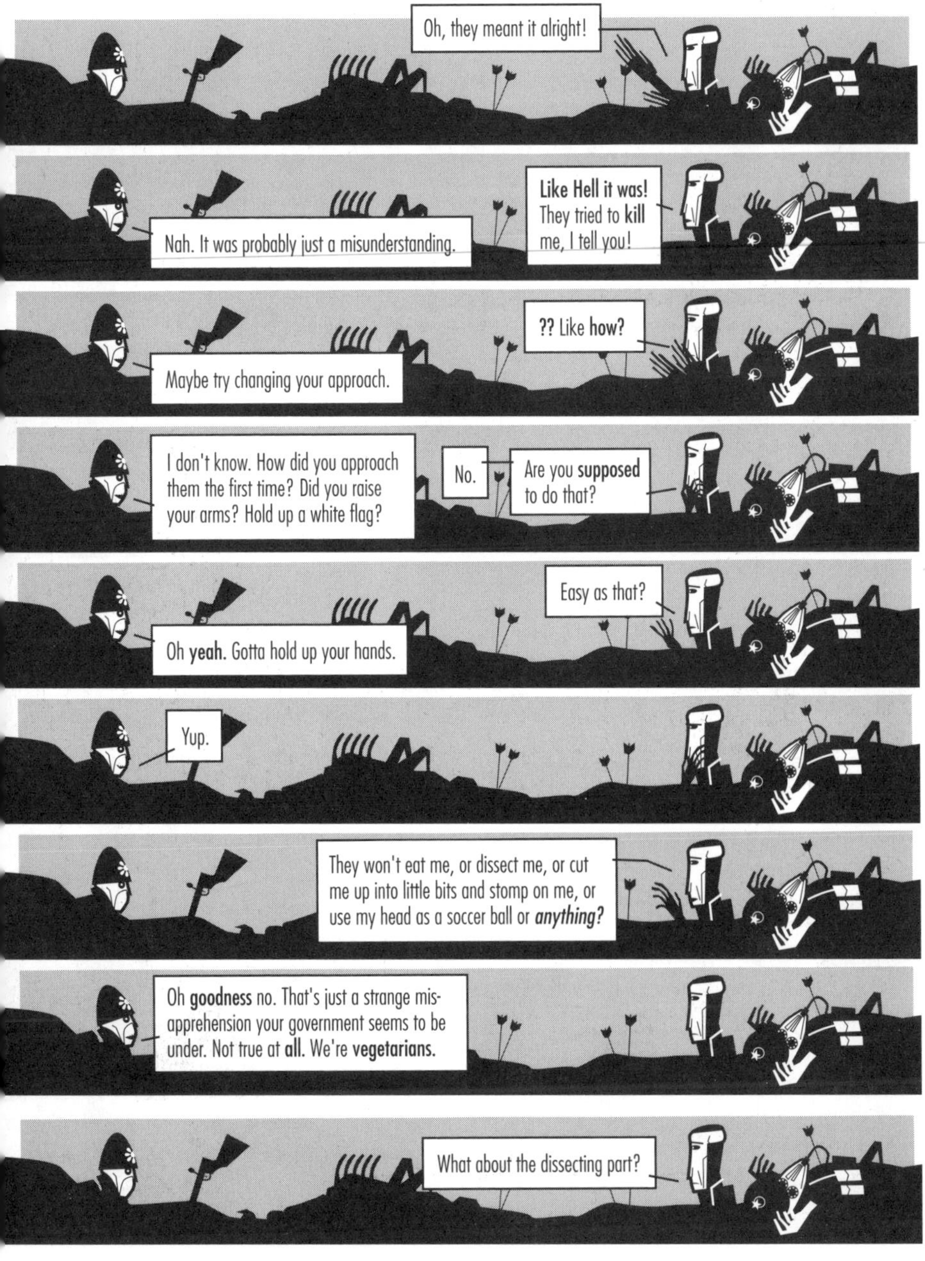
Oh, they meant it alright!
Nah. It was probably just a misunderstanding.
Like Hell it was! They tried to kill me, I tell you!
Maybe try changing your approach.
?? Like how?
I don't know. How did you approach them the first time? Did you raise your arms? Hold up a white flag?
No.
Are you supposed to do that?
Oh yeah. Gotta hold up your hands.
Easy as that?
Yup.
They won't eat me, or dissect me, or cut me up into little bits and stomp on me, or use my head as a soccer ball or anything?
Oh goodness no. That's just a strange misapprehension your government seems to be under. Not true at all. We're vegetarians.
What about the dissecting part?

No no. Once in our care you would have nothing to fear, Nilean. In Optima, we are all equal before the law in both concept and practice. No one is above it, none beneath it, and all are protected by it. Including anyone who wishes to join Optima.

What's the catch?

Catch? There is no catch! We stand together as a community, united in our goal of creating a better world. We wish to create a better place for our little haplings. And one day, if we all wish hard enough, and really, really concentrate, it will come to pass! Peace will reign and happiness spread unbridled! Bound to!

I don't know. People are selfish. They'll wish for selfish things instead. An altruistic wishing system just won't work.

Have you no **faith** in your fellow man?

No. Not really.

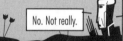

Selfishness rules. Screw or be screwed. It's the law of nature. There is no community. Not *really*.

My dear Nilean! We treat all our fellow citizens with honour and respect in Optima, as we would wish to be treated unto ourselves, as a matter of course, for this is one of the foundations of a civil and just society! At least, **most** do. Well. **Some.** But the number of the just is ever increasing. For what gain is there for a rational society in **cruelty and sadism?** What purpose can sadism have for one who is truly civilized?

To gain glee at the expense of another is not just to transfer happiness, but to steal it! It is an act of thievery, an assassination of the social good. It is, in fact, anathema to us Optimans, and to civility, to kindness, to everything that makes a community a beautiful place to live. The truly sentient work **together.**

It sounds wonderful, Optiman. Don't get me wrong, I'd love to believe, but... the world is a closed system. Eventually you'll have to fight someone for something.

But that isn't true. It's an open system. So long as we are willing to share and work together, everything else will fall into place. Altruism is at the heart of civilization.

Erm. I'm pretty sure it's **greed**, actually. But somehow I like your idea better.

Believe! The only reason we are fighting is because Nil insists upon it. We wish to co-exist! If only we could talk to your leaders, convince them we are not the baby eaters they say we are, that we want only **peace**, that we have no hostile intentions... there'd be peace!

You don't **know** our leaders, do you?

Hmm....

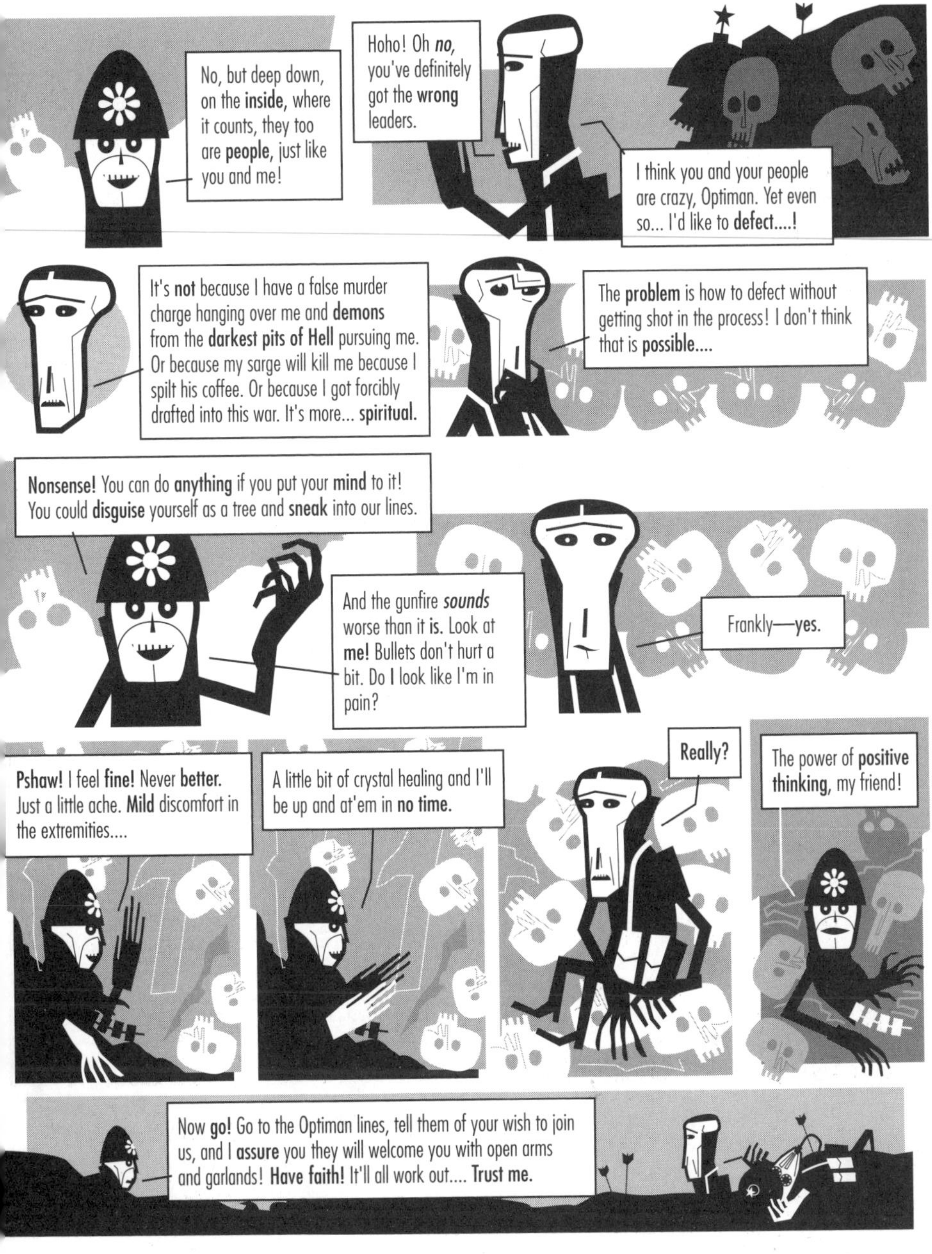

No, but deep down, on the **inside**, where it counts, they too are **people**, just like you and me!
Hoho! Oh ***no***, you've definitely got the **wrong** leaders.
I think you and your people are crazy, Optiman. Yet even so... I'd like to **defect....!**
It's **not** because I have a false murder charge hanging over me and **demons** from the **darkest pits of Hell** pursuing me. Or because my sarge will kill me because I spilt his coffee. Or because I got forcibly drafted into this war. It's more... **spiritual.**
The **problem** is how to defect without getting shot in the process! I don't think that is **possible....**
Nonsense! You can do **anything** if you put your **mind** to it! You could **disguise** yourself as a tree and **sneak** into our lines.
And the gunfire ***sounds*** worse than it **is.** Look at **me!** Bullets don't hurt a bit. Do **I** look like I'm in pain?
Frankly—**yes.**
Pshaw! I feel **fine!** Never **better.** Just a little ache. **Mild** discomfort in the extremities....
A little bit of crystal healing and I'll be up and at'em in **no time.**
Really?
The power of **positive thinking**, my friend!
Now **go!** Go to the Optiman lines, tell them of your wish to join us, and I **assure** you they will welcome you with open arms and garlands! **Have faith!** It'll all work out.... **Trust me.**

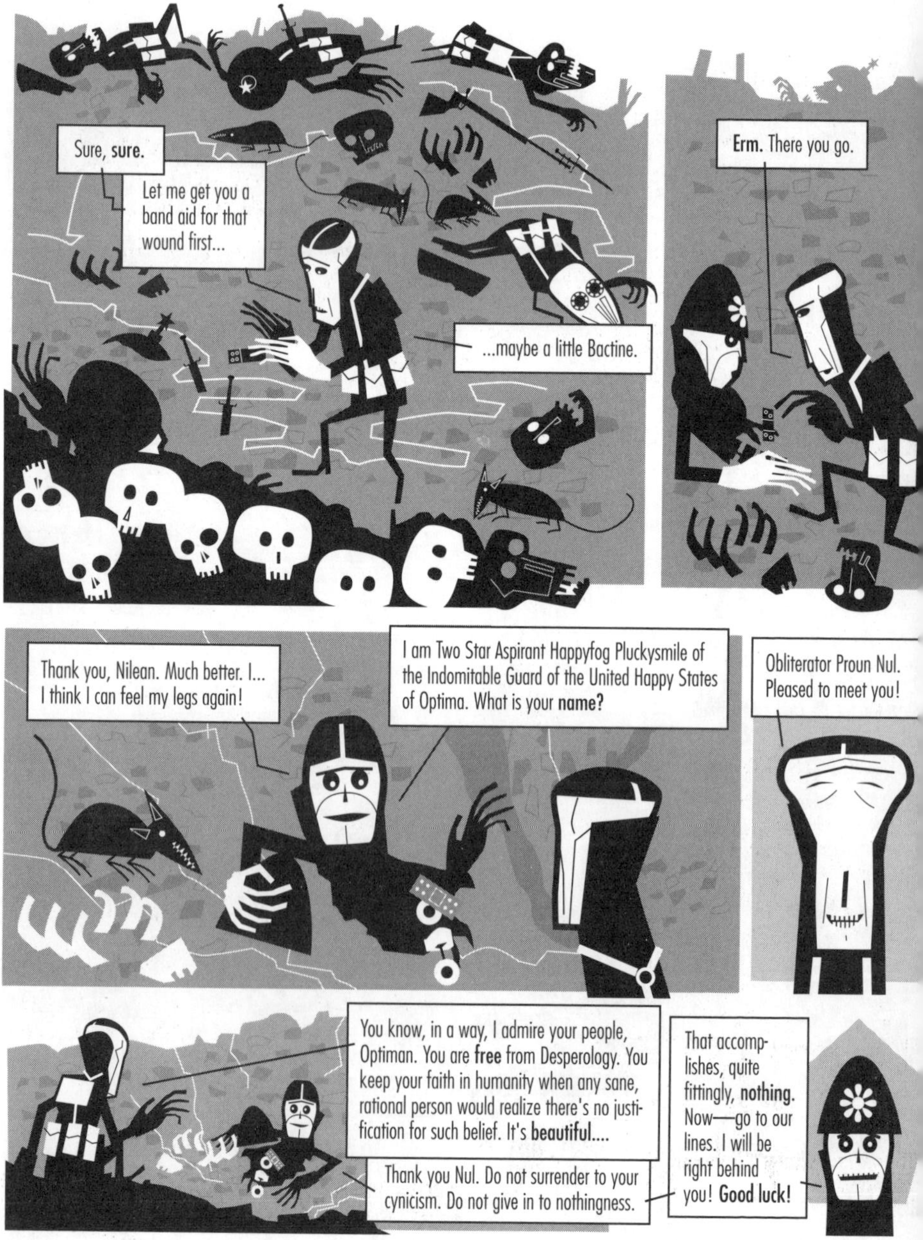
Sure, sure.
Let me get you a band aid for that wound first...
...maybe a little Bactine.
Erm. There you go.
Thank you, Nilean. Much better. I... I think I can feel my legs again!
I am Two Star Aspirant Happyfog Pluckysmile of the Indomitable Guard of the United Happy States of Optima. What is your name?
Obliterator Proun Nul. Pleased to meet you!
You know, in a way, I admire your people, Optiman. You are free from Desperology. You keep your faith in humanity when any sane, rational person would realize there's no justification for such belief. It's beautiful....
Thank you Nul. Do not surrender to your cynicism. Do not give in to nothingness.
That accomplishes, quite fittingly, nothing. Now—go to our lines. I will be right behind you! Good luck!

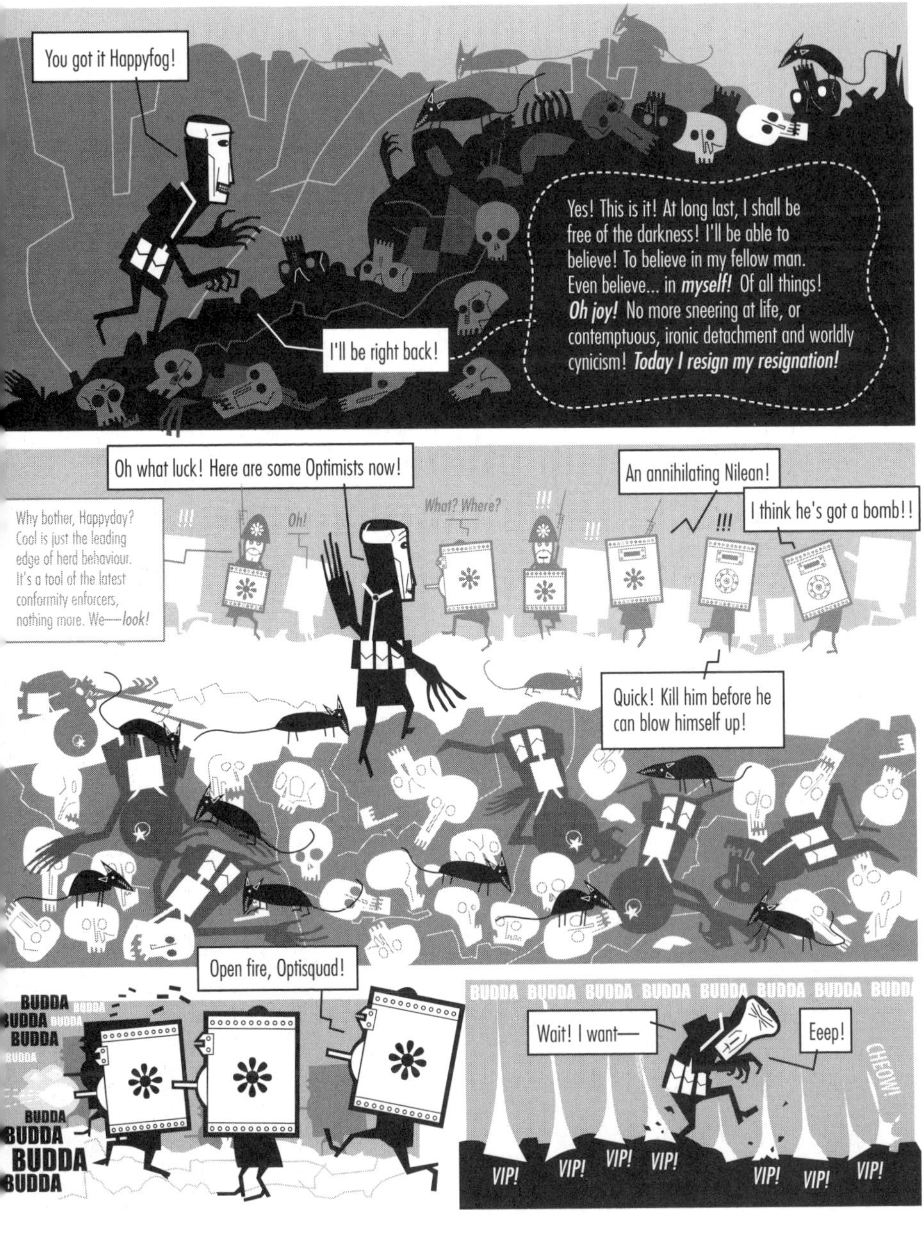
You got it Happyfog!
I'll be right back!
Yes! This is it! At long last, I shall be free of the darkness! I'll be able to believe! To believe in my fellow man. Even believe... in ***myself!*** Of all things! ***Oh joy!*** No more sneering at life, or contemptuous, ironic detachment and worldly cynicism! ***Today I resign my resignation!***
Why bother, Happyday? Cool is just the leading edge of herd behaviour. It's a tool of the latest conformity enforcers, nothing more. We—*look!*
Oh what luck! Here are some Optimists now!
!!!
Oh!
What? Where?
!!!
!!!
An annihilating Nilean!
!!!
I think he's got a bomb!!
Quick! Kill him before he can blow himself up!
Open fire, Optisquad!
BUDDA
BUDDA
BUDDA
BUDDA
BUDDA
BUDDA
BUDDA
BUDDA BUDDA BUDDA BUDDA BUDDA BUDDA BUDDA BUDDA
Wait! I want—
Eeep!
CHEOW!
VIP! VIP! VIP! VIP! VIP! VIP! VIP!

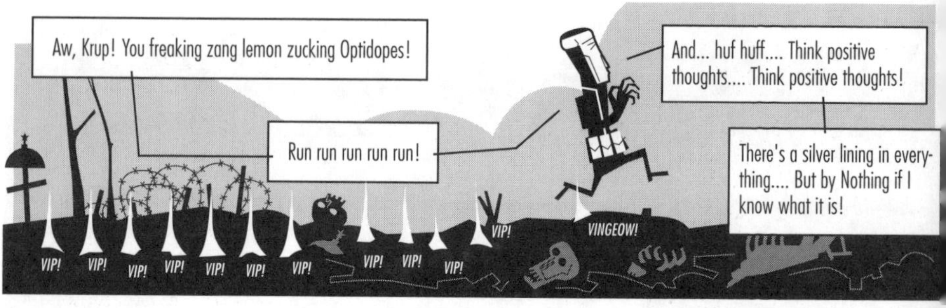
Aw, Krup! You freaking zang lemon zucking Optidopes!
Run run run run run!
And... huf huff.... Think positive thoughts.... Think positive thoughts!
There's a silver lining in everything.... But by Nothing if I know what it is!
VIP! VIP! VIP! VIP! VIP! VIP! VIP! VIP! VIP! VIP! VIP!
VINGEOW!

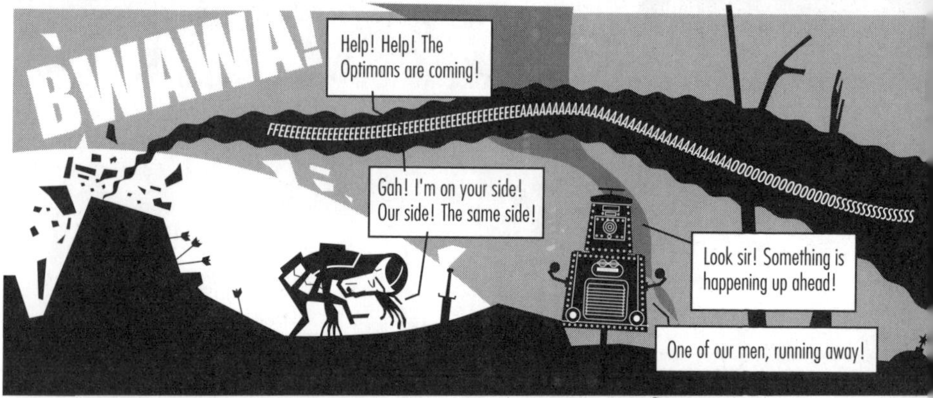
BWAWA!
Help! Help! The Optimans are coming!
FFEEEEEEEEEEEEEEEEEEEEEEEEEEEEEEEEEEEEEEEEEEEEEEEEEEEEAAAAAAAAAAAAAAAAAAAAAAAAAAAAAAAAAAAAAAAAAAAAAOOOOOOOOOOOOOOOOOOOSSSSSSSSSSSSSSS
Gah! I'm on your side! Our side! The same side!
Look sir! Something is happening up ahead!
One of our men, running away!

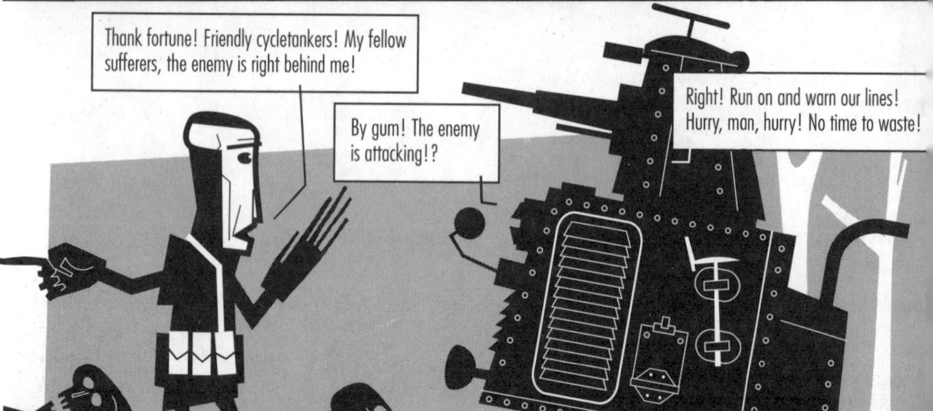
Thank fortune! Friendly cycletankers! My fellow sufferers, the enemy is right behind me!
By gum! The enemy is attacking!?
Right! Run on and warn our lines! Hurry, man, hurry! No time to waste!

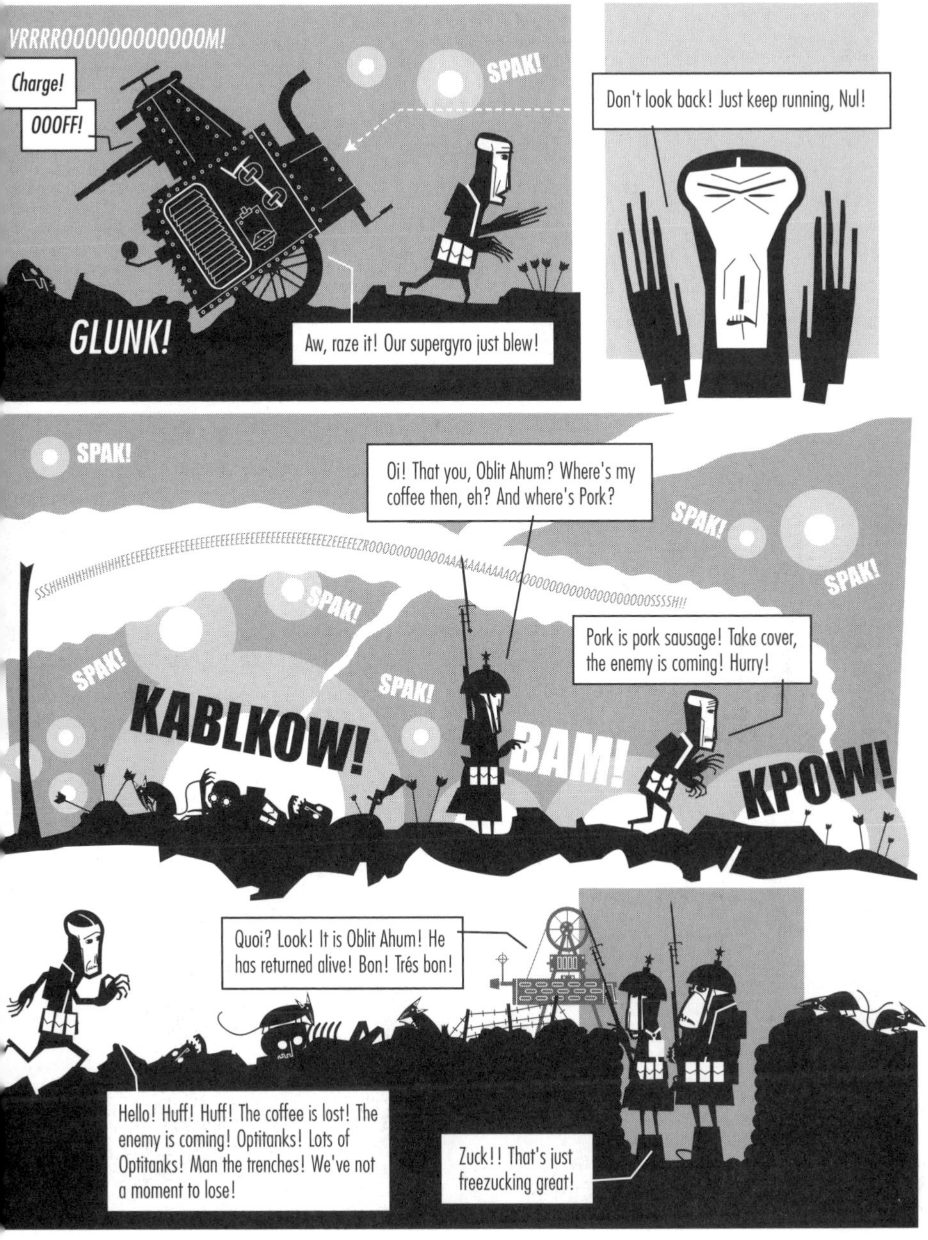

VRRRROOOOOOOOOOOOOM!
Charge!
OOOFF!
SPAK!
GLUNK!
Aw, raze it! Our supergyro just blew!
Don't look back! Just keep running, Nul!
SPAK!
Oi! That you, Oblit Ahum? Where's my coffee then, eh? And where's Pork?
SSSHHHHHHHHHHHHEEEEEEEEEEEEEEEEEEEEEEEEEEEEEEEEEEEEEEEEEEEEEZEEEEEZROOOOOOOOOOOOAAAAAAAAAAAAOOOOOOOOOOOOOOOOOOOOOOOOSSSSH!!
SPAK!
SPAK!
SPAK!
SPAK!
SPAK!
KABLKOW!
BAM!
Pork is pork sausage! Take cover, the enemy is coming! Hurry!
KPOW!
Quoi? Look! It is Oblit Ahum! He has returned alive! Bon! Trés bon!
Hello! Huff! Huff! The coffee is lost! The enemy is coming! Optitanks! Lots of Optitanks! Man the trenches! We've not a moment to lose!
Zuck!! That's just freezucking great!

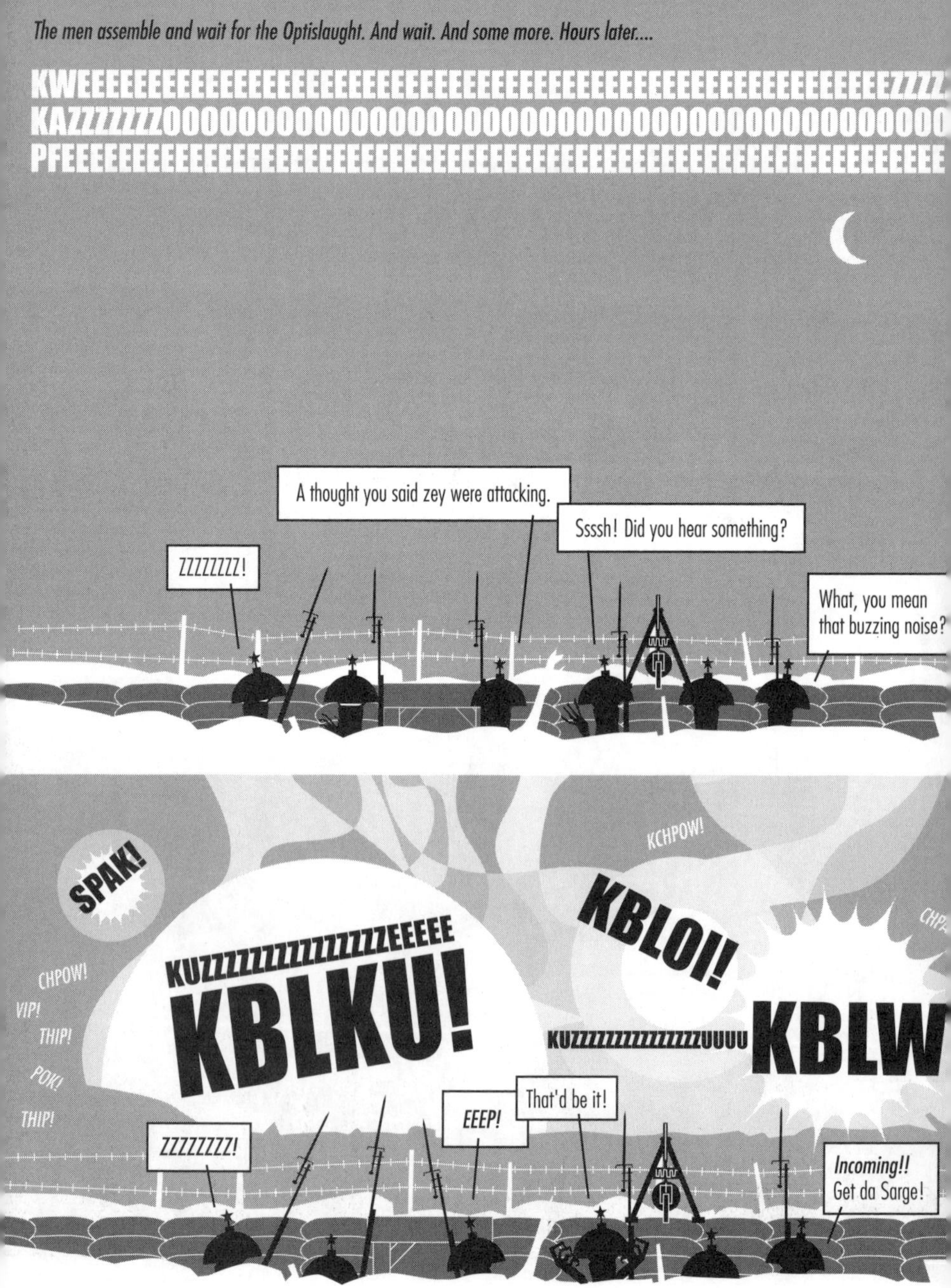
The men assemble and wait for the Optislaught. And wait. And some more. Hours later....
KWEEEEEEEEEEEEEEEEEEEEEEEEEEEEEEEEEEEEEEEEEEEEEEEEEEEEZZZZ
KAZZZZZZZZOOOOOOOOOOOOOOOOOOOOOOOOOOOOOOOOOOOOOO
PFEEEEEEEEEEEEEEEEEEEEEEEEEEEEEEEEEEEEEEEEEEEEEEEEEEE
A thought you said zey were attacking.
ZZZZZZZZ!
Ssssh! Did you hear something?
What, you mean that buzzing noise?
SPAK!
KCHPOW!
KBLOI!
KUZZZZZZZZZZZZZZZZEEEEE
KBLKU!
CHPOW!
VIP!
THIP!
POK!
THIP!
KUZZZZZZZZZZZZZZZZUUUU
KBLW
ZZZZZZZZ!
EEEP!
That'd be it!
Incoming!! Get da Sarge!

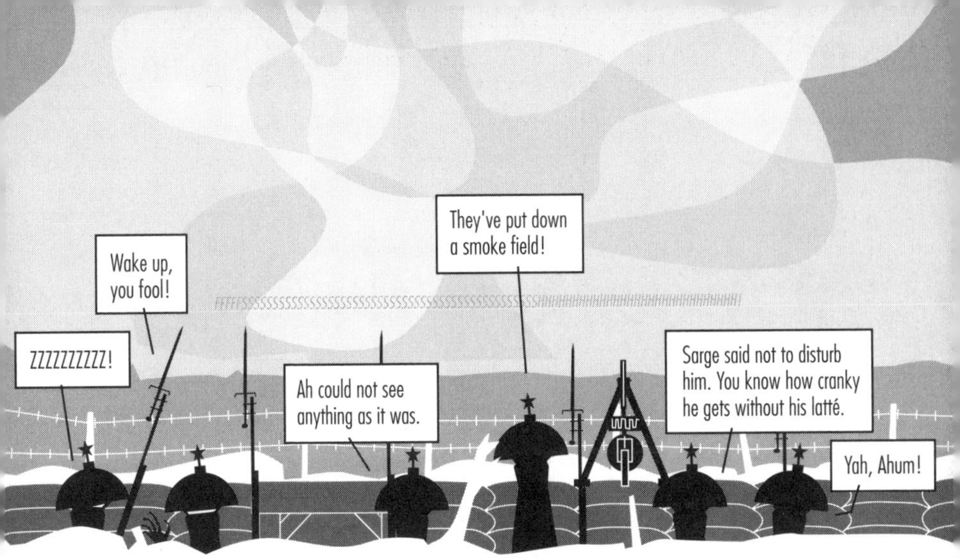
Wake up, you fool!
ZZZZZZZZZZ!
They've put down a smoke field!
FFFFSSSSSSSSSSSSSSSSSSSSSSSSSSSSSSSSSSSSSSSSSSSSSSHHHHHHHHHHHHHHHHHHHHHHHHHHHHHHHHH!
Ah could not see anything as it was.
Sarge said not to disturb him. You know how cranky he gets without his latté.
Yah, Ahum!

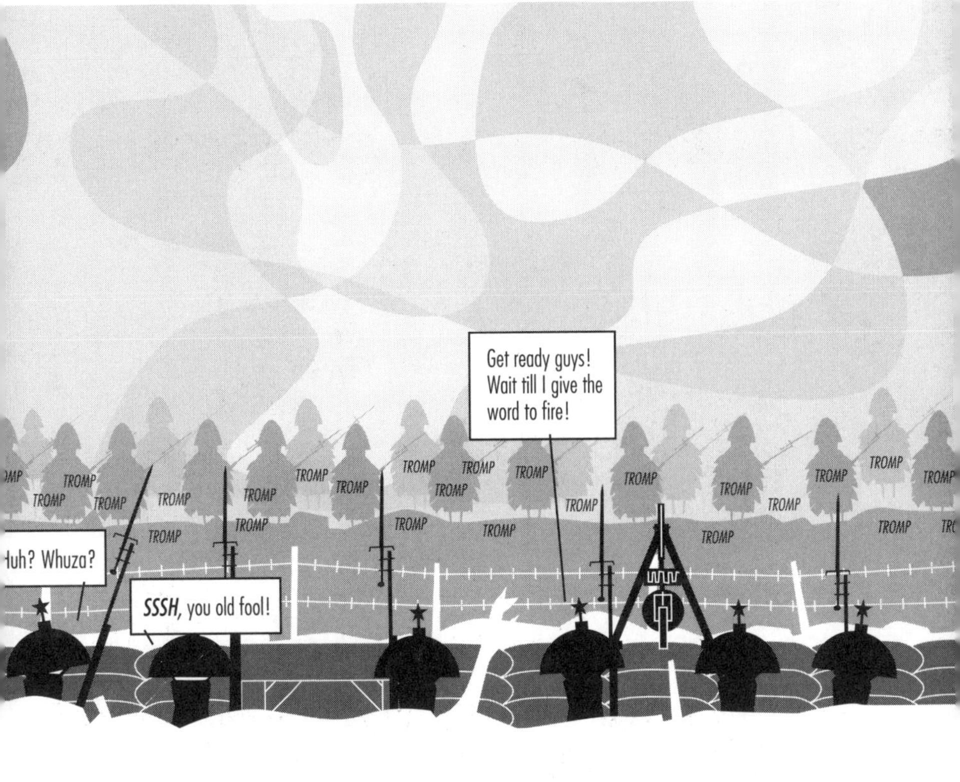
Get ready guys! Wait till I give the word to fire!
TROMP TROMP
uh? Whuza?
SSSH, you old fool!

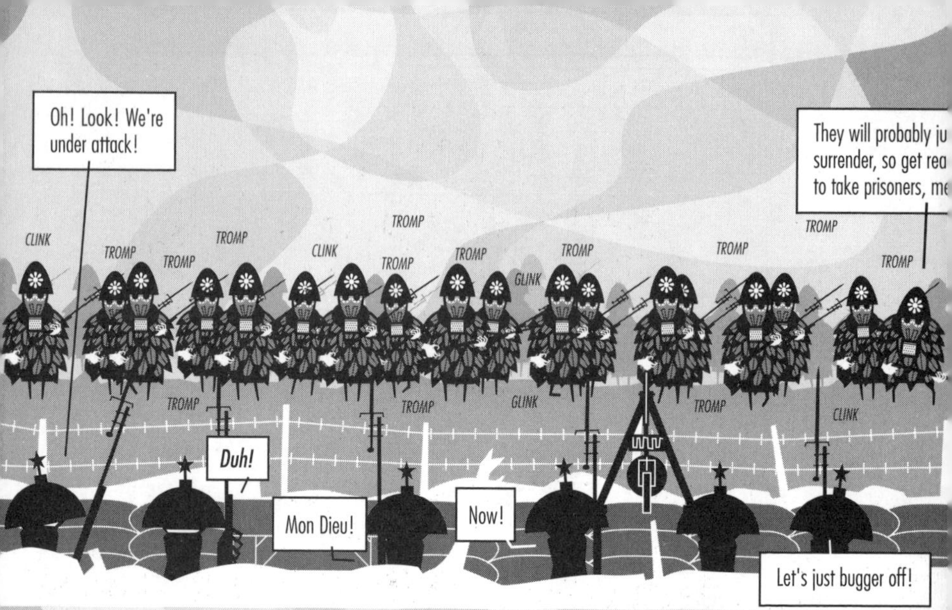
Oh! Look! We're under attack!
CLINK
TROMP
TROMP
TROMP
CLINK
TROMP
TROMP
TROMP
GLINK
TROMP
TROMP
TROMP
They will probably ju surrender, so get rea to take prisoners, me
TROMP
TROMP
GLINK
TROMP
CLINK
Duh!
Mon Dieu!
Now!
Let's just bugger off!

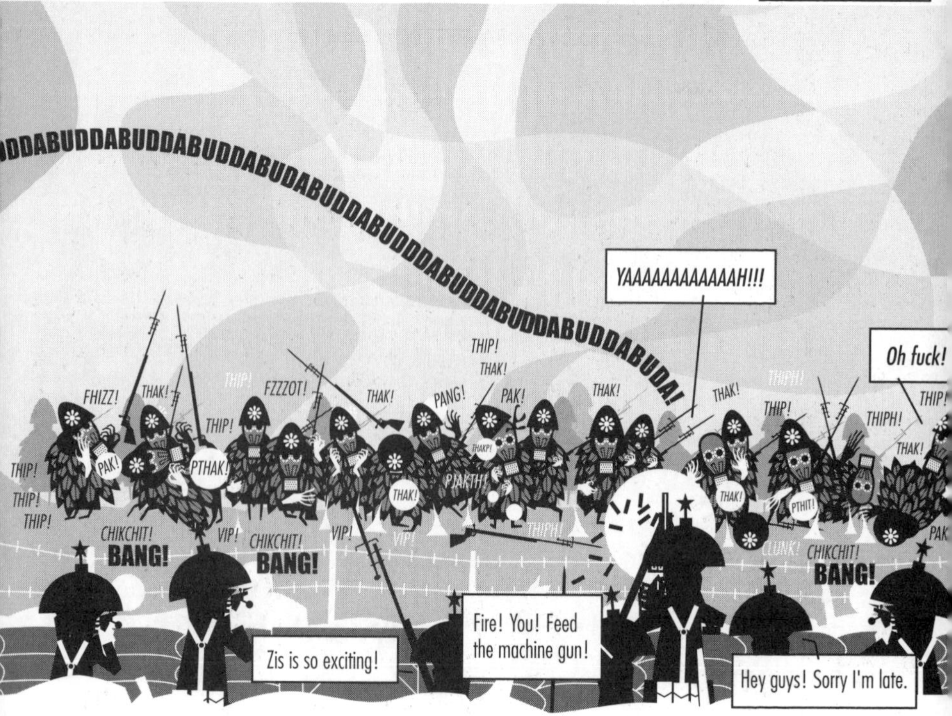
DDABUDDABUDDABUDDABUDABUDDABUDDDABUDDABUDDABUDDABUDDABUDA!
YAAAAAAAAAAAAH!!!
Oh fuck!
FHIZZ!
THAK!
THIP!
FZZZOT!
THAK!
PANG!
THIP!
THAK!
PAK!
THAK!
THAK!
THIP!
THIPH!
THIP!
THIPH!
THAK!
THIP!
PAK!
PTHAK!
THAK!
THAKP!
PJAKTH!
THAK!
PTHIT!
THIP!
THIP!
CHIKCHIT!
BANG!
VIP!
CHIKCHIT!
BANG!
VIP!
THIPH!
CLUNK!
CHIKCHIT!
BANG!
PAK
Zis is so exciting!
Fire! You! Feed the machine gun!
Hey guys! Sorry I'm late.

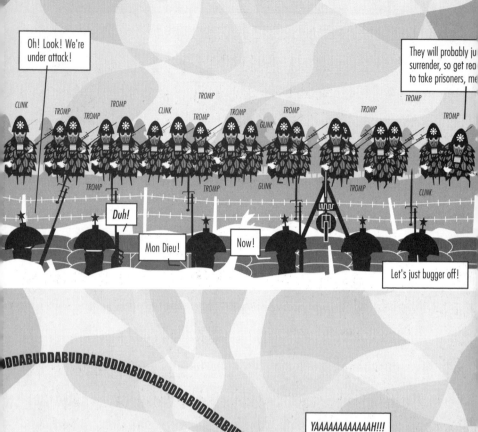

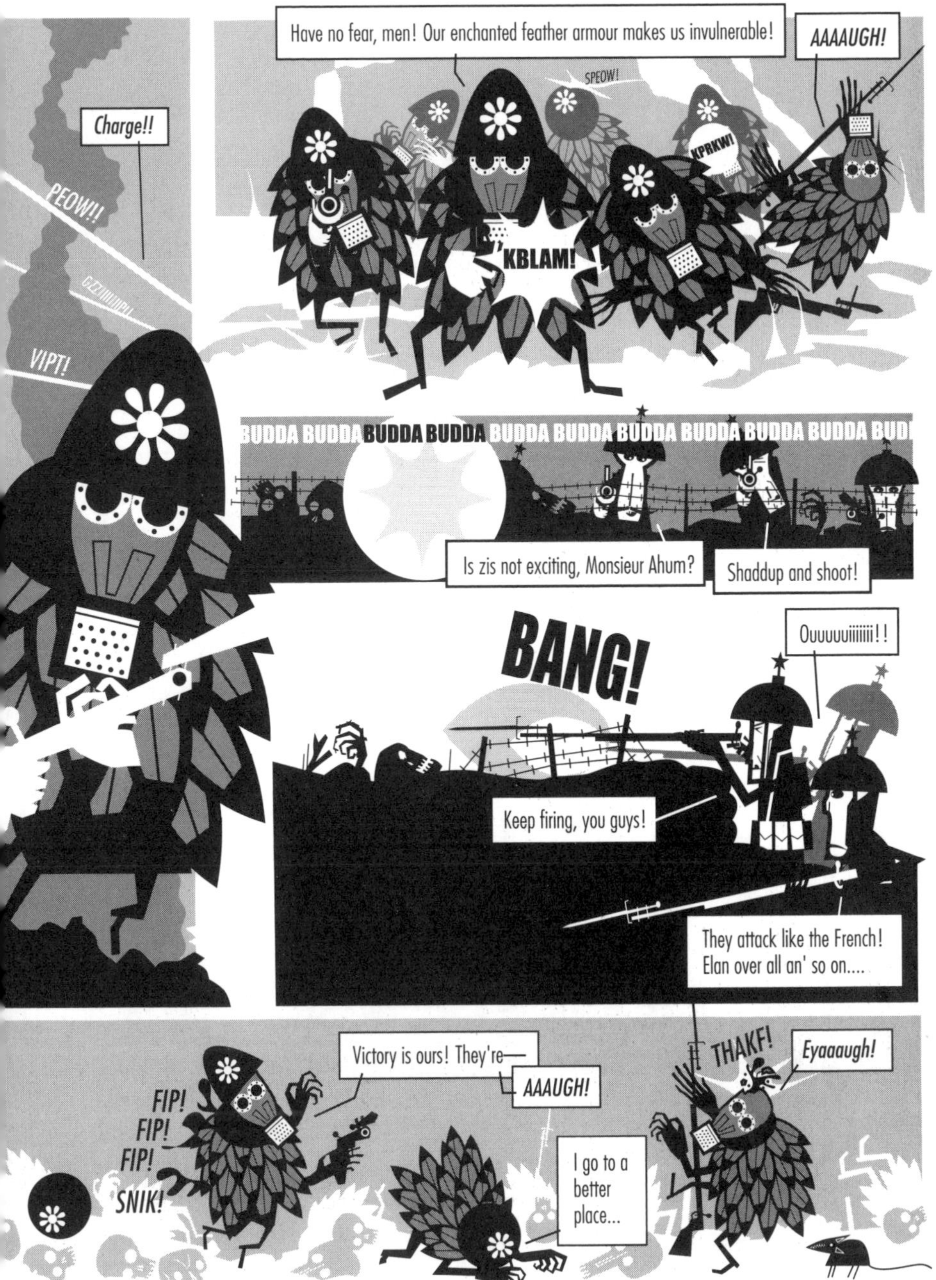
Charge!!
PEOW!!
VIPT!
Have no fear, men! Our enchanted feather armour makes us invulnerable!
SPEOW!
KBLAM!
KPRKW!
AAAAUGH!
BUDDA BUDDA BUDDA BUDDA BUDDA BUDDA BUDDA BUDDA BUDDA BUDDA
Is zis not exciting, Monsieur Ahum?
Shaddup and shoot!
BANG!
Ouuuuuiiiiiii!!
Keep firing, you guys!
They attack like the French! Elan over all an' so on....
FIP!
FIP!
FIP!
SNIK!
Victory is ours! They're—
AAAUGH!
I go to a better place...
THAKF!
Eyaaaugh!

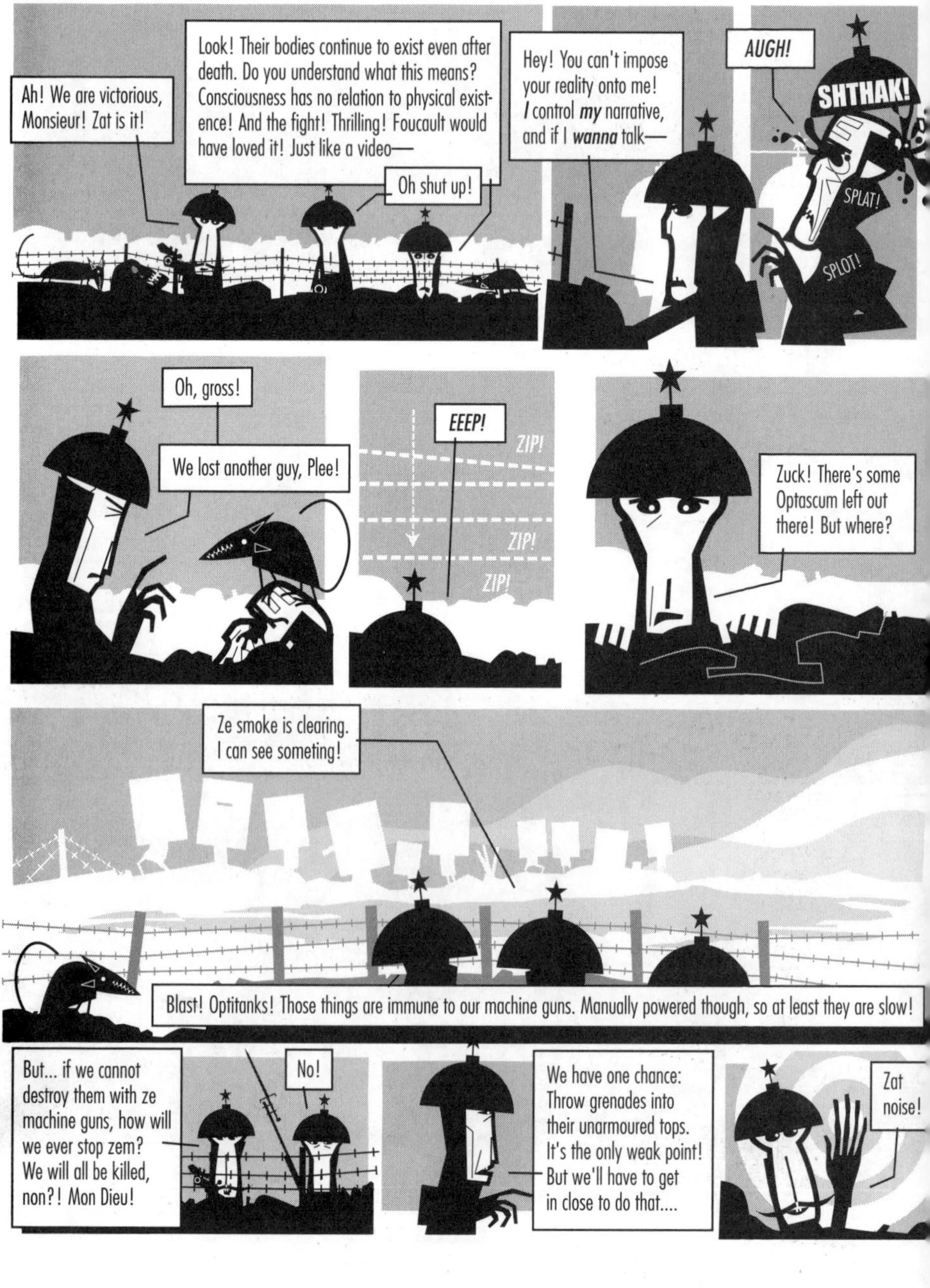
Ah! We are victorious, Monsieur! Zat is it!
Look! Their bodies continue to exist even after death. Do you understand what this means? Consciousness has no relation to physical existence! And the fight! Thrilling! Foucault would have loved it! Just like a video—
Oh shut up!
Hey! You can't impose your reality onto me! *I* control ***my*** narrative, and if I ***wanna*** talk—
AUGH!
SHTHAK!
SPLAT!
SPLOT!
Oh, gross!
We lost another guy, Plee!
EEEP!
ZIP!
ZIP!
ZIP!
Zuck! There's some Optascum left out there! But where?
Ze smoke is clearing. I can see someting!
Blast! Optitanks! Those things are immune to our machine guns. Manually powered though, so at least they are slow!
But... if we cannot destroy them with ze machine guns, how will we ever stop zem? We will all be killed, non?! Mon Dieu!
No!
We have one chance: Throw grenades into their unarmoured tops. It's the only weak point! But we'll have to get in close to do that....
Zat noise!

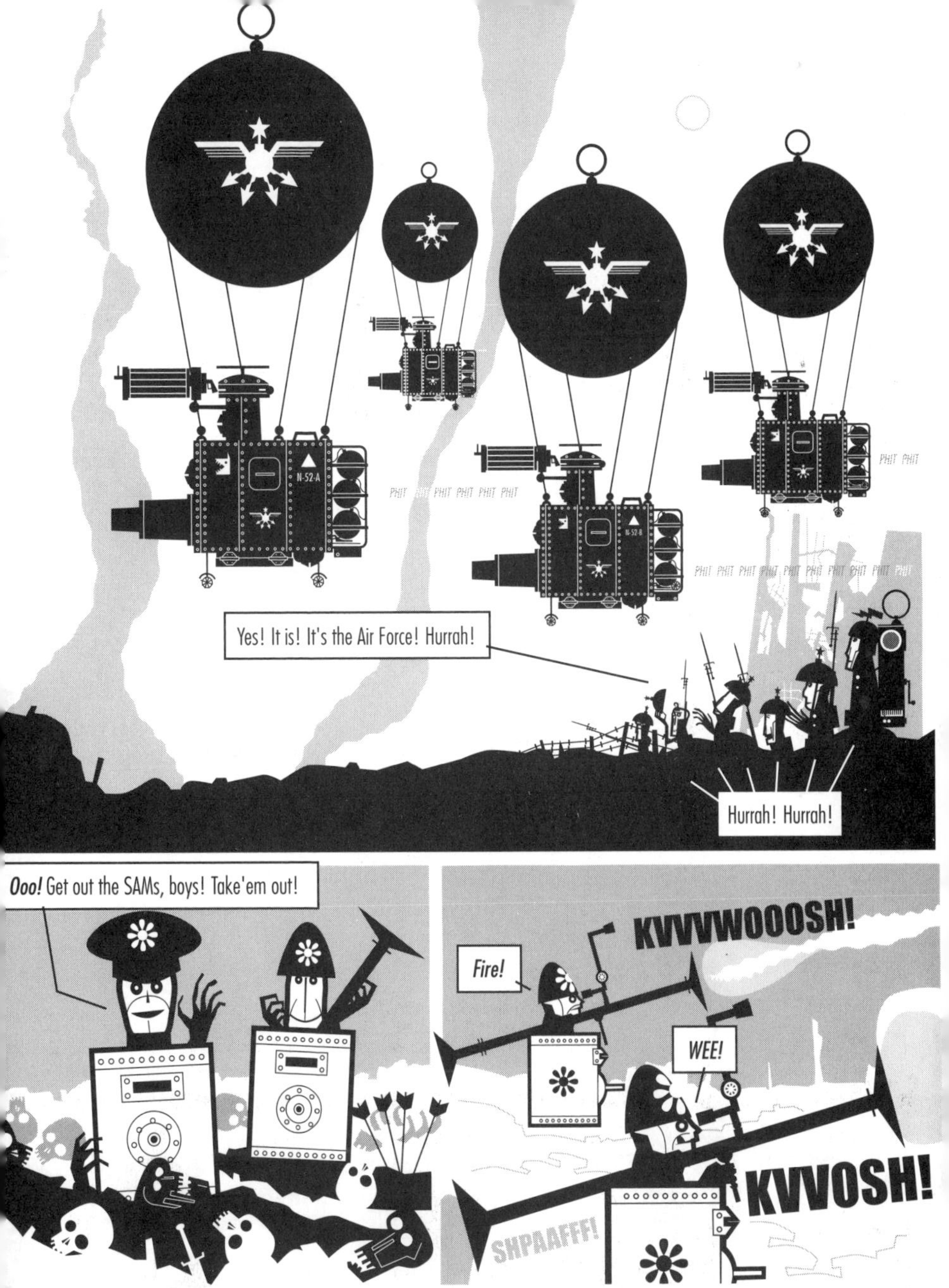
N-52-A
PHIT PHIT PHIT PHIT PHIT PHIT
PHIT PHIT
N-52-B
PHIT PHIT PHIT PHIT PHIT PHIT PHIT PHIT PHIT PHIT PHIT
Yes! It is! It's the Air Force! Hurrah!
Hurrah! Hurrah!
Ooo! Get out the SAMs, boys! Take'em out!
KVVVWOOOSH!
Fire!
WEE!
KVVOSH!
SHPAAFFF!

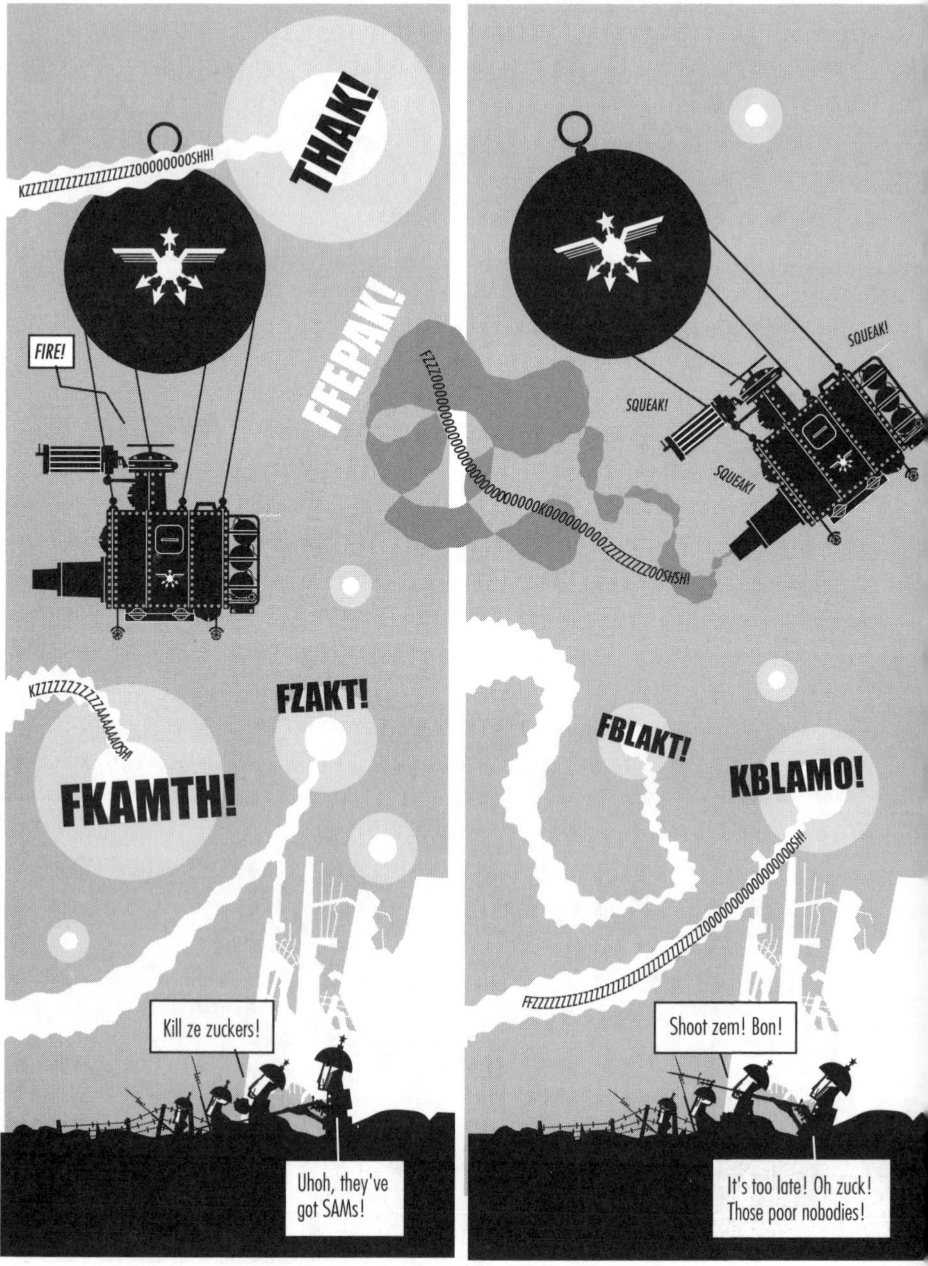
THAK!
FIRE!
FFEPAK!
FZAKT!
FKAMTH!
Kill ze zuckers!
Uhoh, they've got SAMs!
SQUEAK!
SQUEAK!
SQUEAK!
FBLAKT!
KBLAMO!
Shoot zem! Bon!
It's too late! Oh zuck! Those poor nobodies!

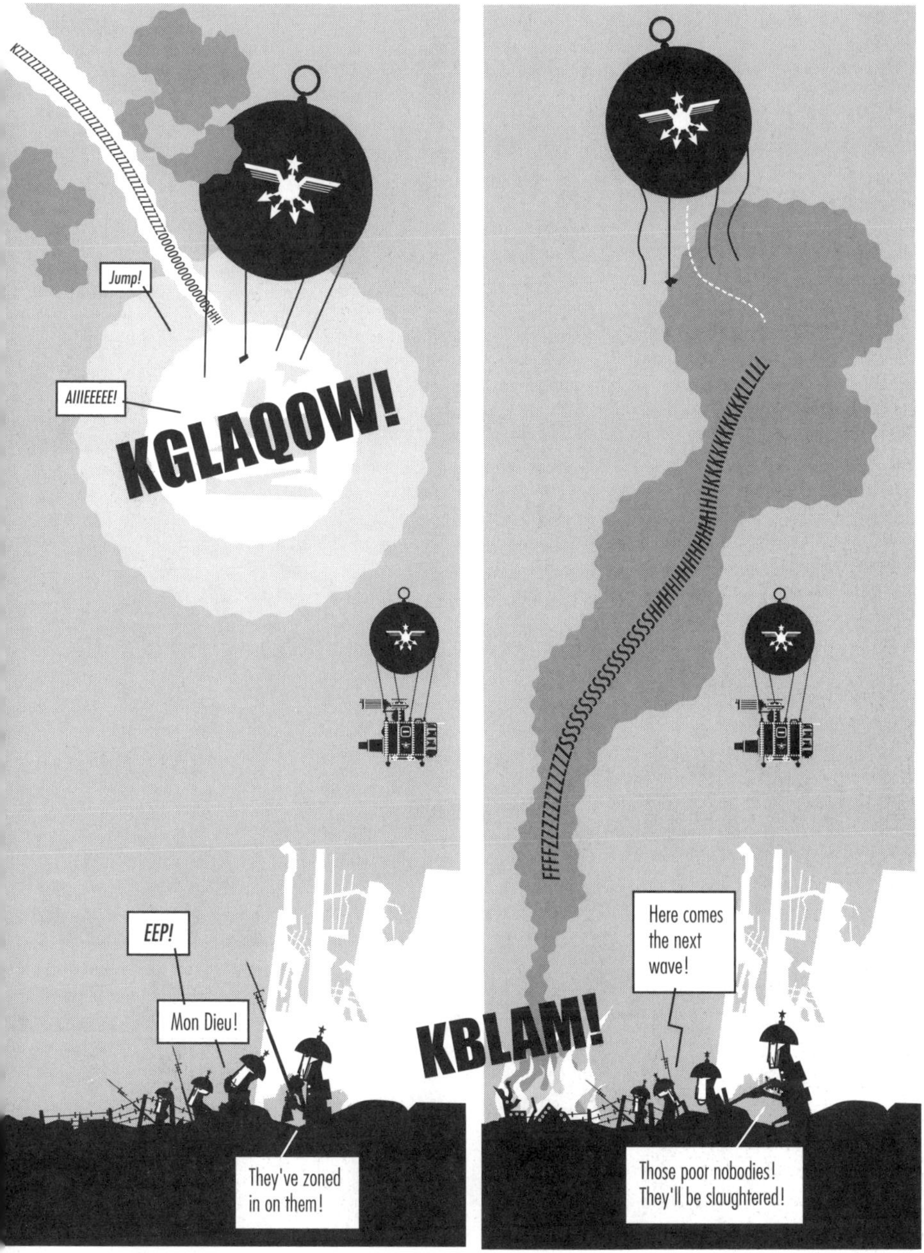
Jump!
AIIIEEEEE!
KGLAQOW!
EEP!
Mon Dieu!
They've zoned in on them!
KBLAM!
Here comes the next wave!
Those poor nobodies! They'll be slaughtered!

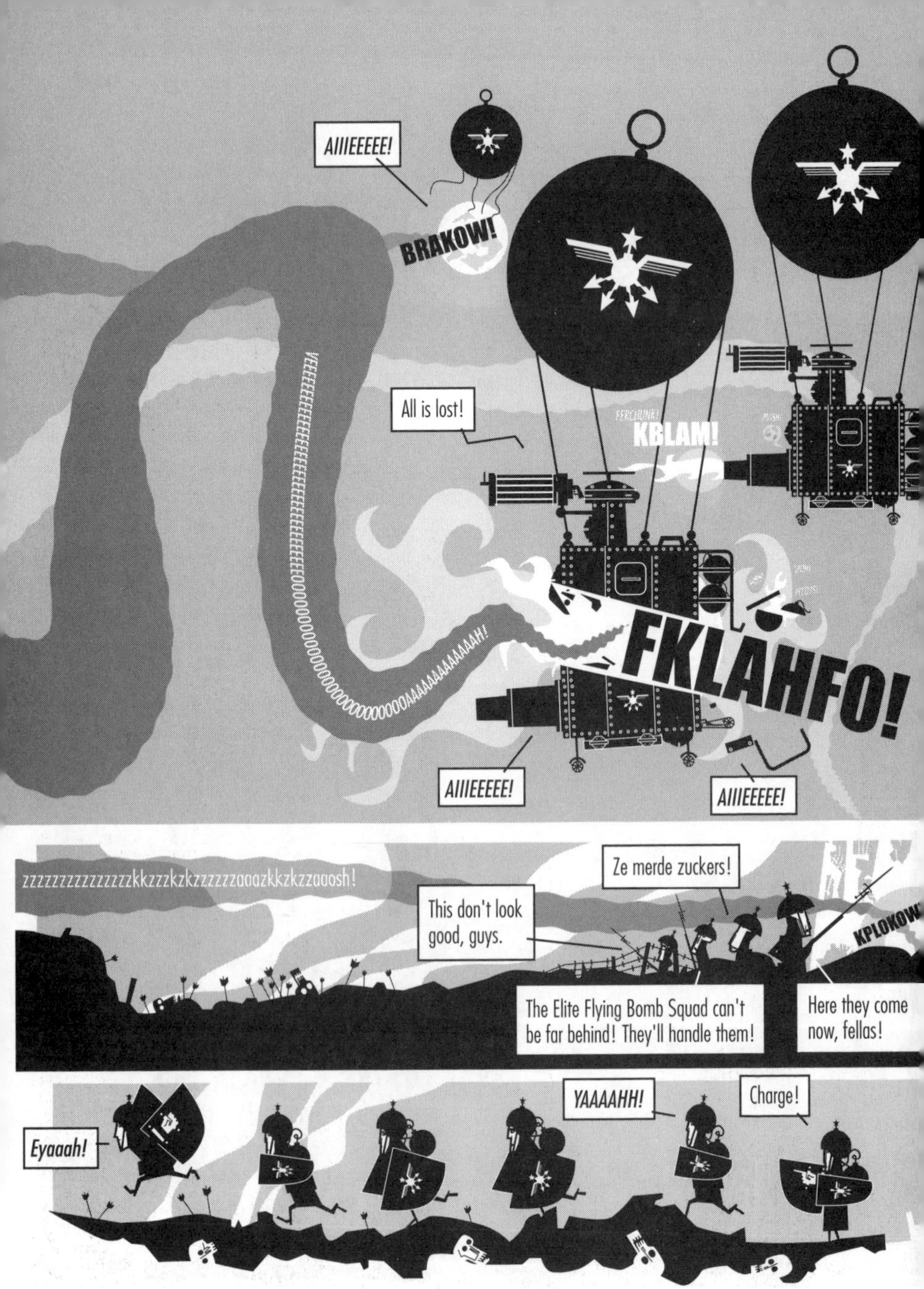

AIIIEEEEE!
BRAKOW!
YEEEEEEEEEEEEEEEEEEEEEEEEEEEEEEEEEEEEEOOOOOOOOOOOOOOOOOOOOOOOOAAAAAAAAAAAAAH!
All is lost!
KBLAM!
FKLAHFO!
AIIIEEEEE!
AIIIEEEEE!
zzzzzzzzzzzzzzzkkzzzkzkzzzzzzzaaazkkzkzzaaosh!
This don't look good, guys.
Ze merde zuckers!
KPLOKOW!
The Elite Flying Bomb Squad can't be far behind! They'll handle them!
Here they come now, fellas!
Eyaaah!
YAAAAHH!
Charge!

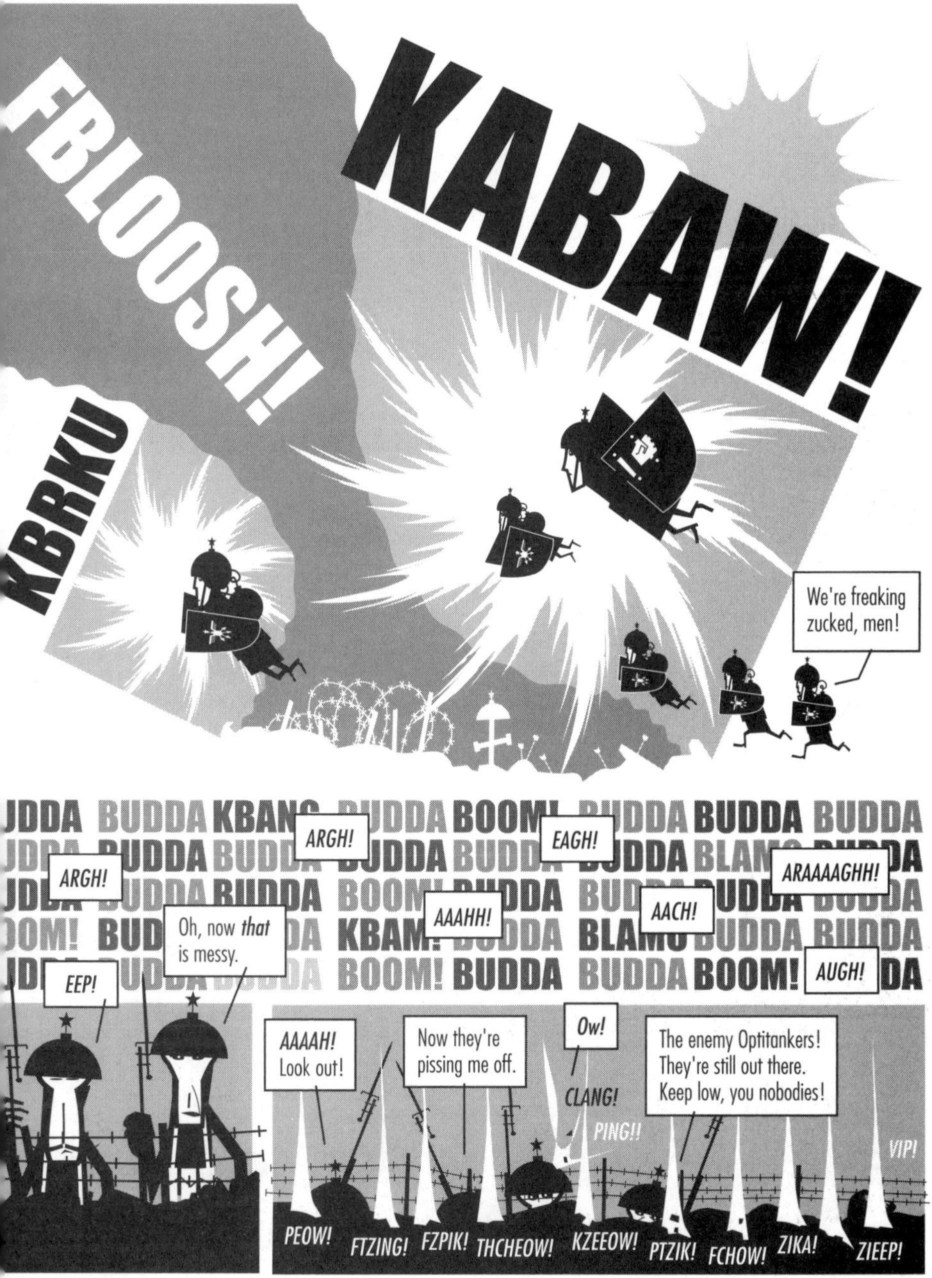
FBLOOSH!
KABAW!
KBRKU
We're freaking zucked, men!
BUDDA BUDDA KBANG BUDDA BOOM! BUDDA BUDDA BUDDA
BUDDA BUDDA BUDDA BUDDA BLAM BUDDA
BUDDA BUDDA BOOM! BUDDA BUDDA BUDDA
BUD KBAM! BLAM BUDDA BUDDA
BOOM! BUDDA BUDDA BOOM! BUDDA
ARGH!
EAGH!
ARGH!
ARAAAAGHH!
AAAHH!
AACH!
Oh, now *that* is messy.
AUGH!
EEP!
AAAAH! Look out!
Now they're pissing me off.
Ow!
The enemy Optitankers! They're still out there. Keep low, you nobodies!
CLANG!
PING!!
VIP!
PEOW!
FTZING!
FZPIK!
THCHEOW!
KZEEOW!
PTZIK!
FCHOW!
ZIKA!
ZIEEP!

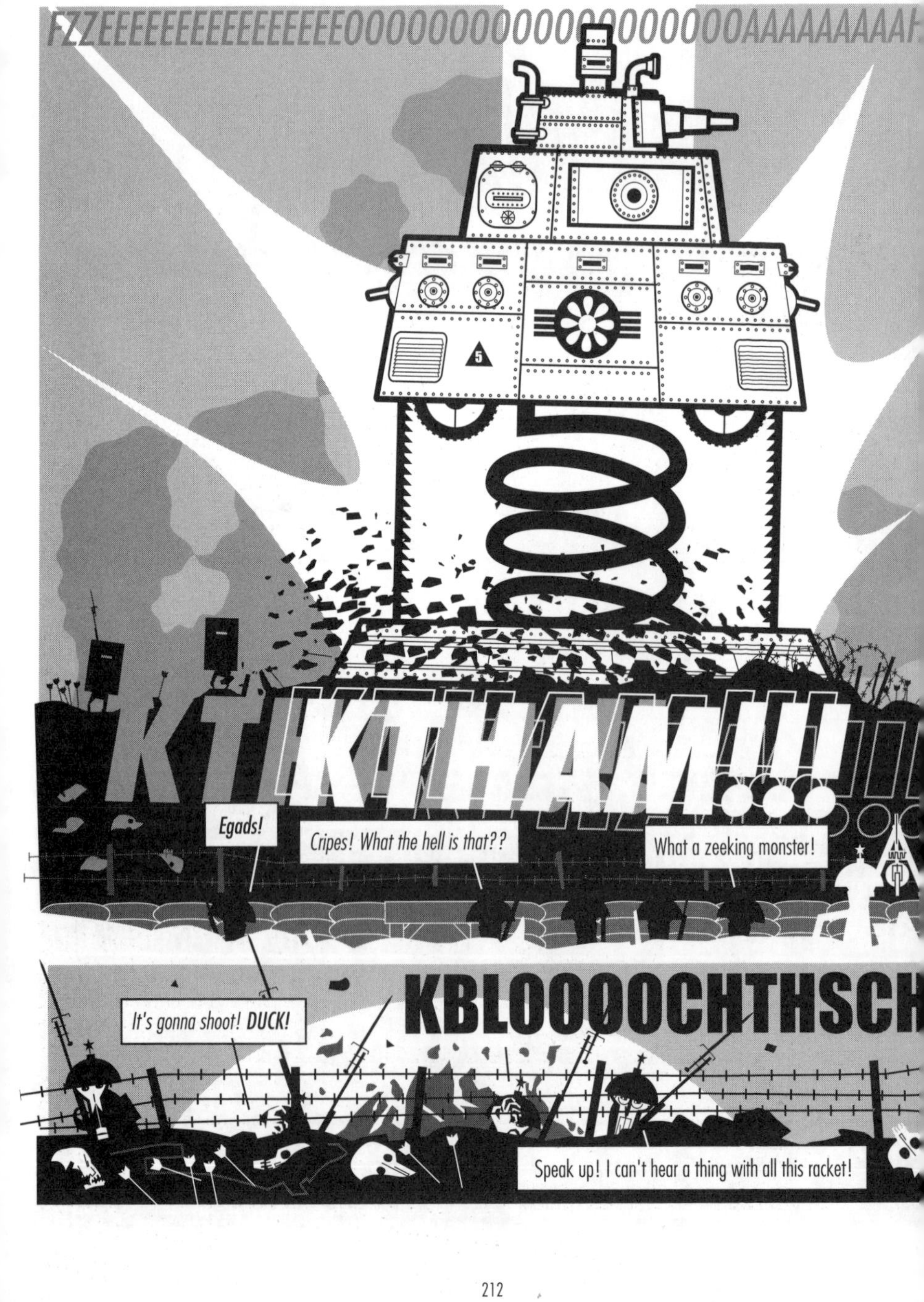

FZZEEEEEEEEEEEEEEEEOOOOOOOOOOOOOOOOOOOAAAAAAAAH
KTHAM!!!
Egads!
Cripes! What the hell is that??
What a zeeking monster!
KBLOOOOCHTHSCH
It's gonna shoot! DUCK!
Speak up! I can't hear a thing with all this racket!

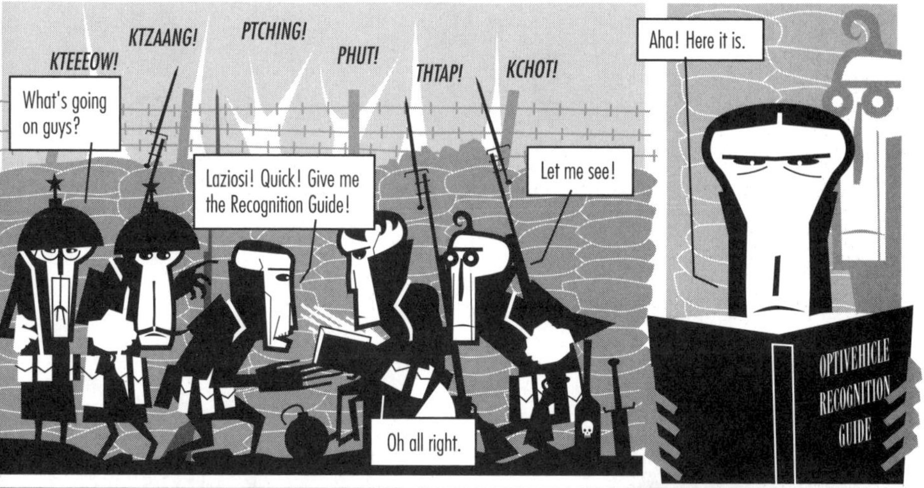
KTEEEOW!
KTZAANG!
PTCHING!
PHUT!
THTAP!
KCHOT!
What's going on guys?
Laziosi! Quick! Give me the Recognition Guide!
Let me see!
Oh all right.
Aha! Here it is.
OPTIVEHICLE RECOGNITION GUIDE

OPTIMAN BATTLEZIGGURAT MKIV

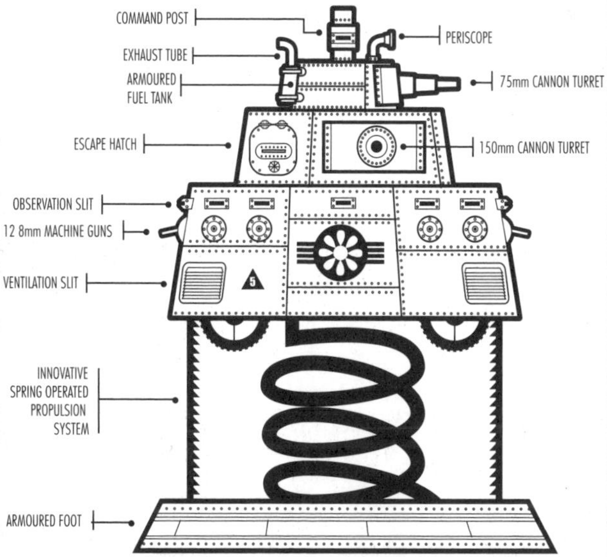
COMMAND POST
PERISCOPE
EXHAUST TUBE
ARMOURED FUEL TANK
75mm CANNON TURRET
ESCAPE HATCH
150mm CANNON TURRET
OBSERVATION SLIT
12 8mm MACHINE GUNS
VENTILATION SLIT
5
INNOVATIVE SPRING OPERATED PROPULSION SYSTEM
ARMOURED FOOT

SPECIFICATIONS

Type: Optiman Battleziggurat
Height: 12m to 20m (full platform elevation)
Weight: 20 metric tons
Armour: 1 inch reinforced steel plate
Propulsion: Spring

Armament: 12 8mm Camel Machine Guns
1 75mm Marlboro Anti-Tank Gun
1 150mm Anti-Infantry Howitzer

Crew: 22
Country of Origin: Optima

Description: Deployed in 2002, the Mark IV Battleziggurat featured improved Spryng Shock Absorbers, dedicated anti-infantry machine guns for close quarter defense, and an elevated observation post for the commander. Increased tension tolerance in the spring allows for jumps of twice the distance of the Mark III. Heavy armour plating makes it all but impenetrable to small calibre weapons and anti-hoppingtank guns. Two deluxe espresso machines are carried, one for the crew and one for the tank commander. Fifty litre coffee tanks are bolted down internally to prevent penetration by enemy fire. The vehicle is also equipped with an intercom system, but lacks a radio due to space constraints. An onboard bathroom obviates the need for dangerous forays to the battle zone latrine.

HOW TO KILL: Use heavy weapons. If heavy weapons are not available, each soldier should strap bombs around his waist and wrap himself around one of the two support struts as tightly as possible. This stands a very good chance of dissabling the Battleziggurat. Not practicable if the enemy vehicle has cranked the spring gap shut. If the gap is closed, you are shit out of luck. Your only hope is to lure the Battleziggurat further behind the lines in the hope that the Sportek shock absorbers break down and the crew gets whiplash.

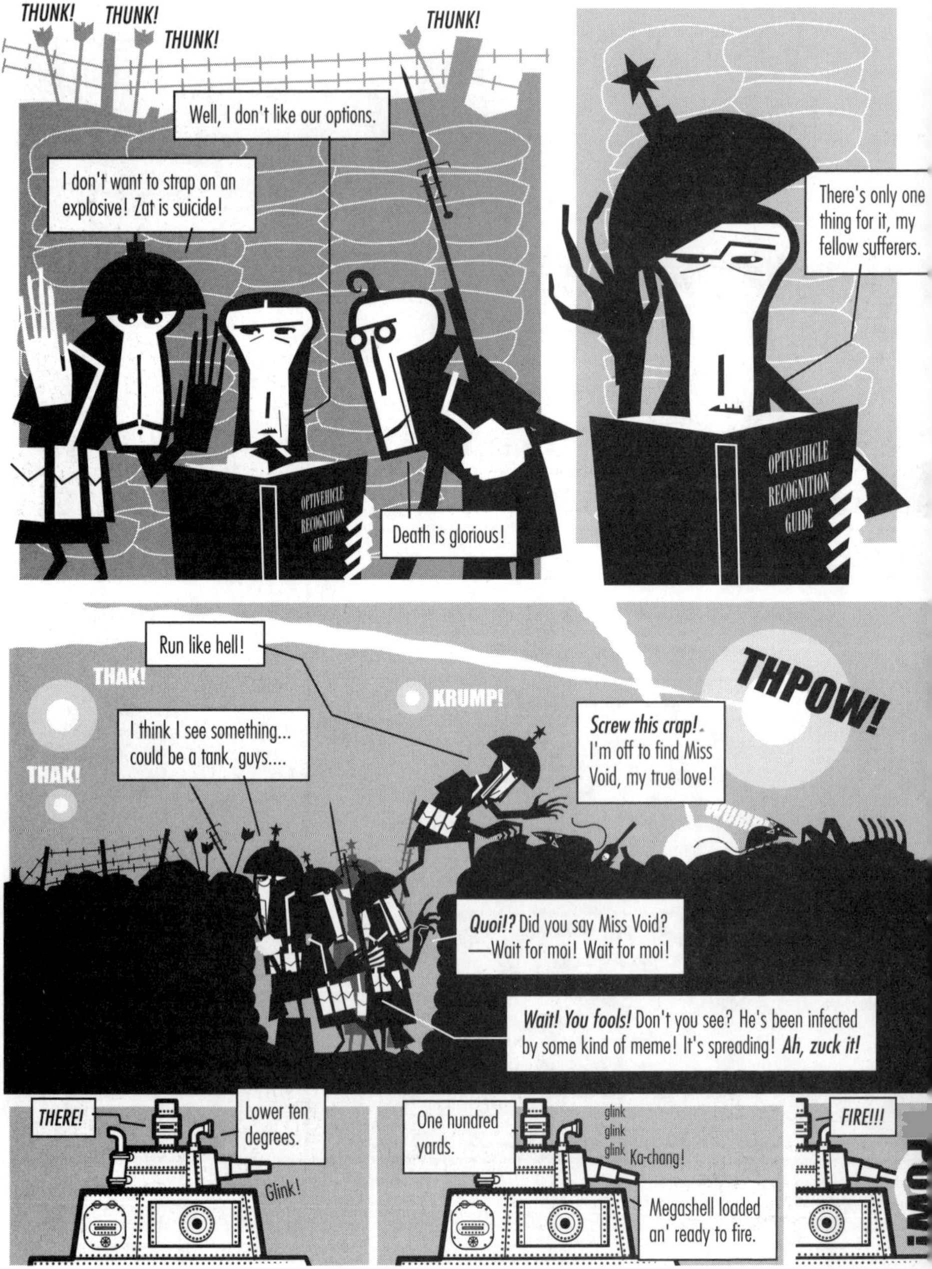
THUNK!
THUNK!
THUNK!
THUNK!
Well, I don't like our options.
I don't want to strap on an explosive! Zat is suicide!
Death is glorious!
OPTIVEHICLE RECOGNITION GUIDE
There's only one thing for it, my fellow sufferers.
OPTIVEHICLE RECOGNITION GUIDE
Run like hell!
THAK!
THAK!
KRUMP!
THPOW!
I think I see something... could be a tank, guys....
Screw this crap! I'm off to find Miss Void, my true love!
Quoi!? Did you say Miss Void? —Wait for moi! Wait for moi!
Wait! You fools! Don't you see? He's been infected by some kind of meme! It's spreading! Ah, zuck it!
THERE!
Lower ten degrees.
Glink!
One hundred yards.
glink
glink
glink
Ka-chang!
Megashell loaded an' ready to fire.
FIRE!!!

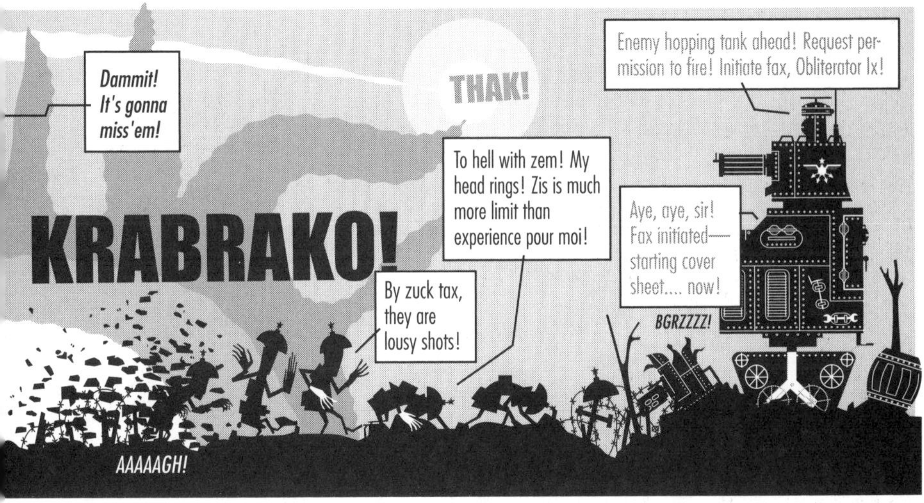
Dammit! It's gonna miss'em!
THAK!
Enemy hopping tank ahead! Request permission to fire! Initiate fax, Obliterator Ix!
To hell with zem! My head rings! Zis is much more limit than experience pour moi!
Aye, aye, sir! Fax initiated— starting cover sheet.... now!
KRABRAKO!
By zuck tax, they are lousy shots!
BGRZZZZ!
AAAAAGH!

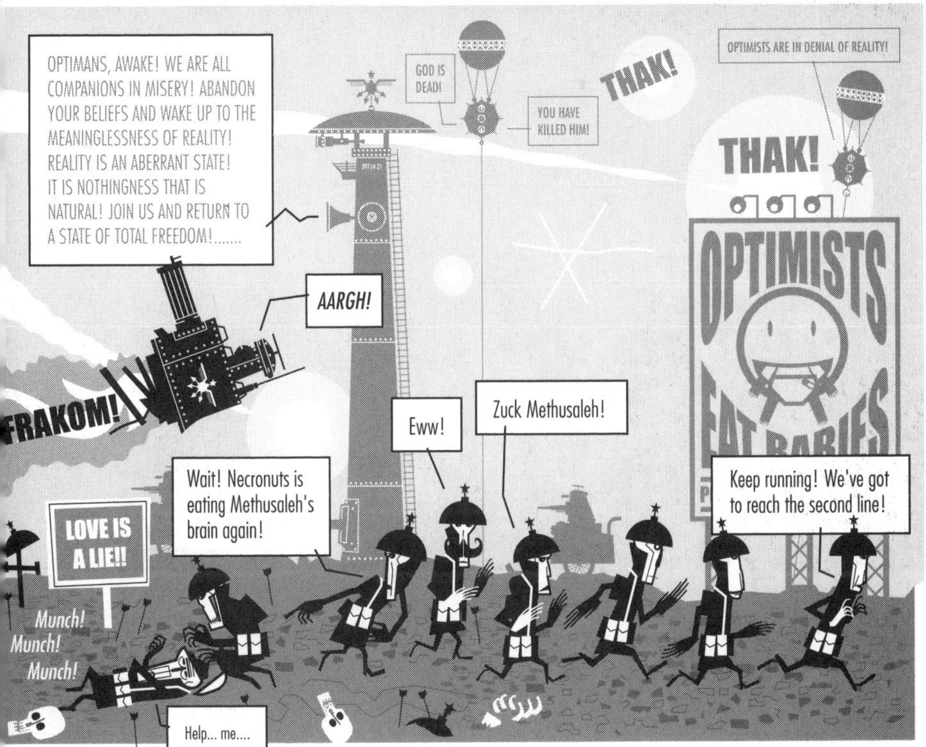
OPTIMANS, AWAKE! WE ARE ALL COMPANIONS IN MISERY! ABANDON YOUR BELIEFS AND WAKE UP TO THE MEANINGLESSNESS OF REALITY! REALITY IS AN ABERRANT STATE! IT IS NOTHINGNESS THAT IS NATURAL! JOIN US AND RETURN TO A STATE OF TOTAL FREEDOM!.......
GOD IS DEAD!
YOU HAVE KILLED HIM!
THAK!
OPTIMISTS ARE IN DENIAL OF REALITY!
THAK!
OPTIMISTS EAT BABIES
AARGH!
FRAKOM!
Eww!
Zuck Methusaleh!
Wait! Necronuts is eating Methusaleh's brain again!
Keep running! We've got to reach the second line!
LOVE IS A LIE!!
Munch! Munch! Munch!
Help... me....

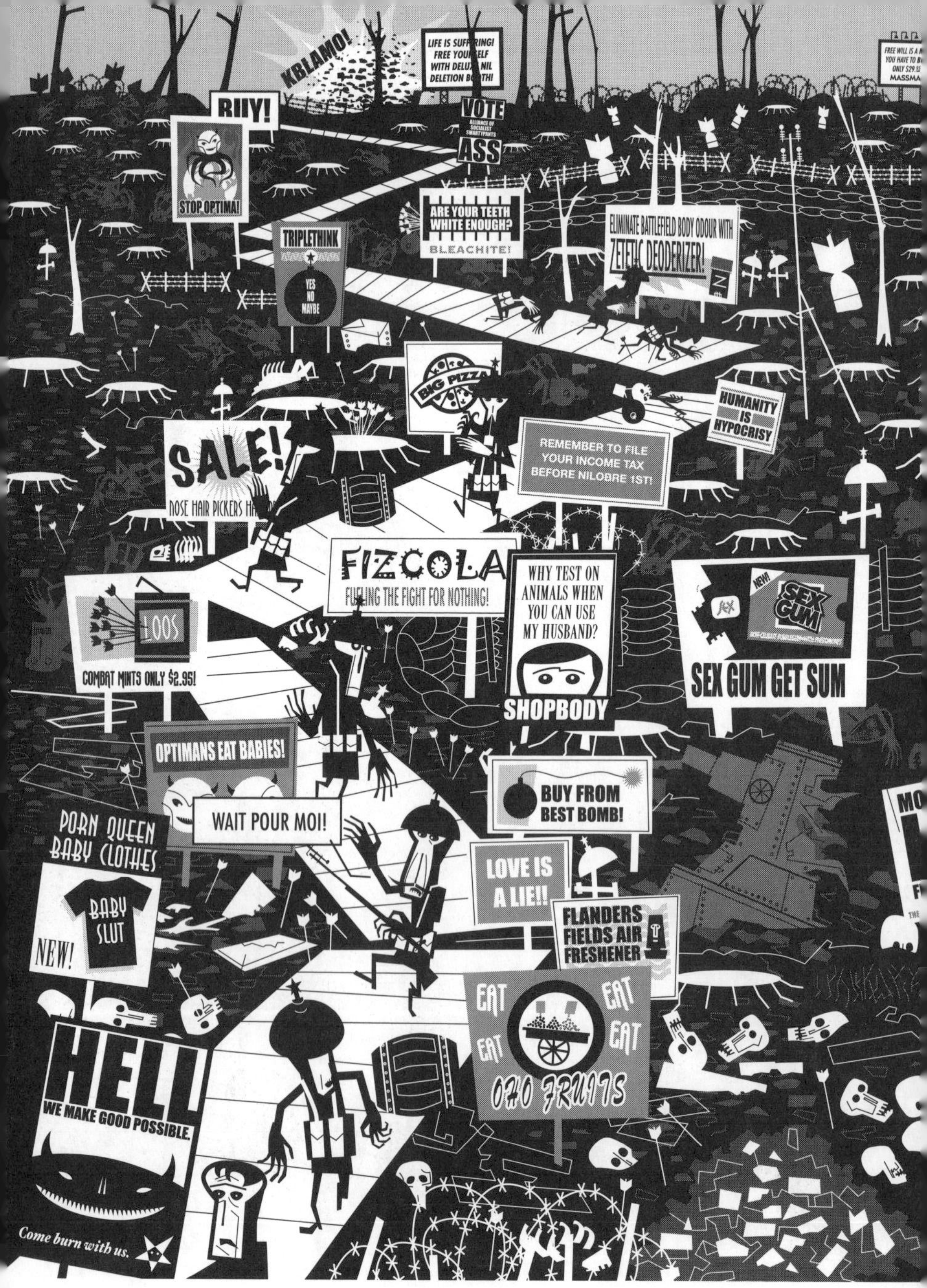
KBLAMO!
LIFE IS SUFF RING! FREE YOUR ELF WITH DELU NIL DELETION B TH!
BUY!
STOP OPTIMA!
VOTE
ALLIANCE OF SOCIALIST SMARTYPANTS
ASS
ARE YOUR TEETH WHITE ENOUGH?
BLEACHITE!
TRIPLETHINK
YES
NO
MAYBE
ELIMINATE BATTLEFIELD BODY ODOUR WITH
ZETETIC DEODERIZER!
BIG PIZZA
HUMANITY IS HYPOCRISY
SALE!
NOSE HAIR PICKERS HA
REMEMBER TO FILE YOUR INCOME TAX BEFORE NILOBRE 1ST!
FIZCOLA
FUELING THE FIGHT FOR NOTHING!
WHY TEST ON ANIMALS WHEN YOU CAN USE MY HUSBAND?
SHOPBODY
LOOS
COMBAT MINTS ONLY $2.95!
NEW!
SEX GUM
SEX GUM GET SUM
OPTIMANS EAT BABIES!
WAIT POUR MOI!
BUY FROM BEST BOMB!
PORN QUEEN BABY CLOTHES
BABY SLUT
NEW!
LOVE IS A LIE!!
FLANDERS FIELDS AIR FRESHENER
EAT
EAT
EAT
EAT
OHO FRUITS
HELL
WE MAKE GOOD POSSIBLE.
Come burn with us.

But far above the fleeing Nileans....

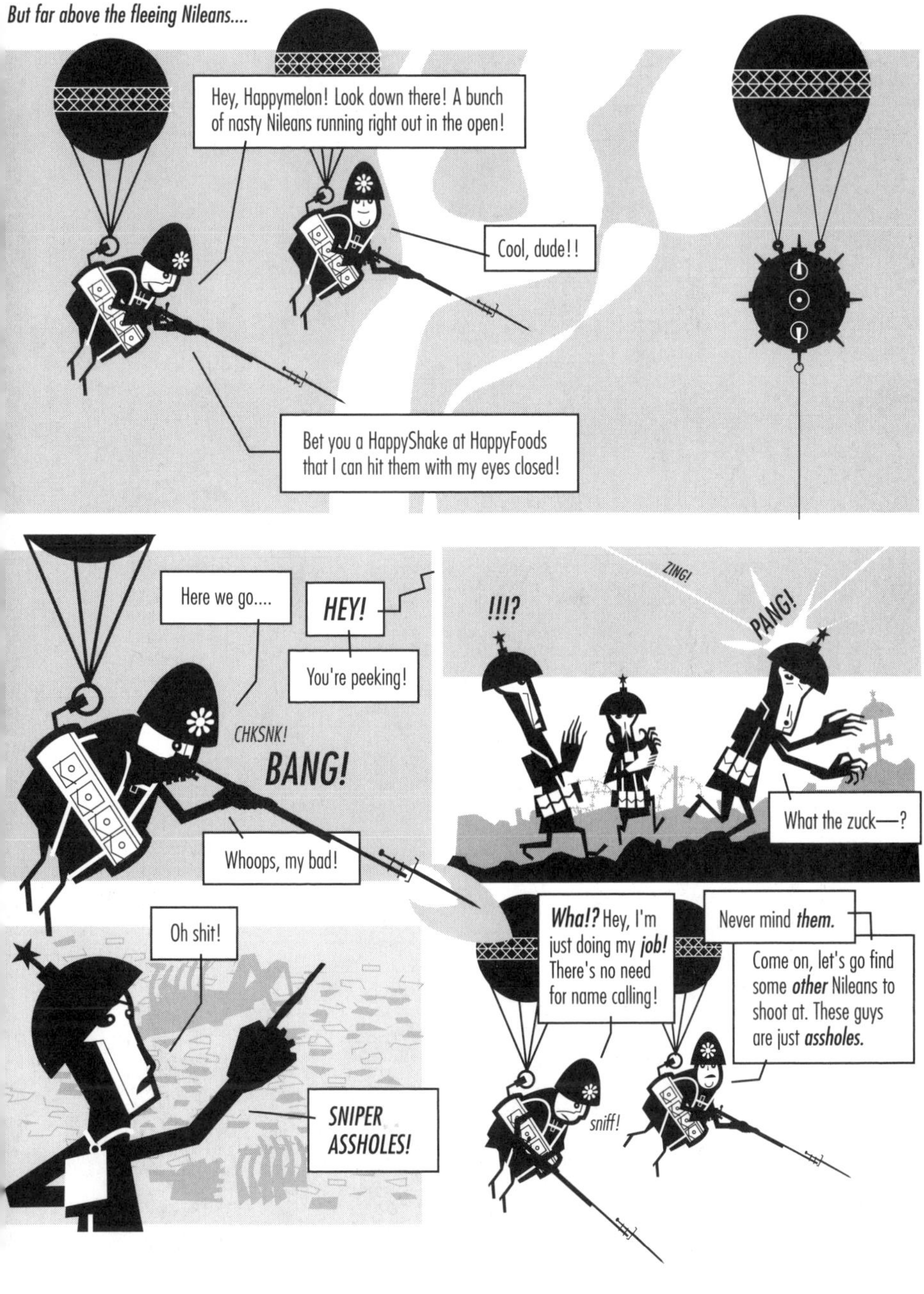
Hey, Happymelon! Look down there! A bunch of nasty Nileans running right out in the open!
Cool, dude!!
Bet you a HappyShake at HappyFoods that I can hit them with my eyes closed!
Here we go....
HEY!
You're peeking!
CHKSNK!
BANG!
Whoops, my bad!
ZING!
!!!?
PANG!
What the zuck—?
Oh shit!
SNIPER ASSHOLES!
Wha!? Hey, I'm just doing my job! There's no need for name calling!
sniff!
Never mind them.
Come on, let's go find some other Nileans to shoot at. These guys are just assholes.

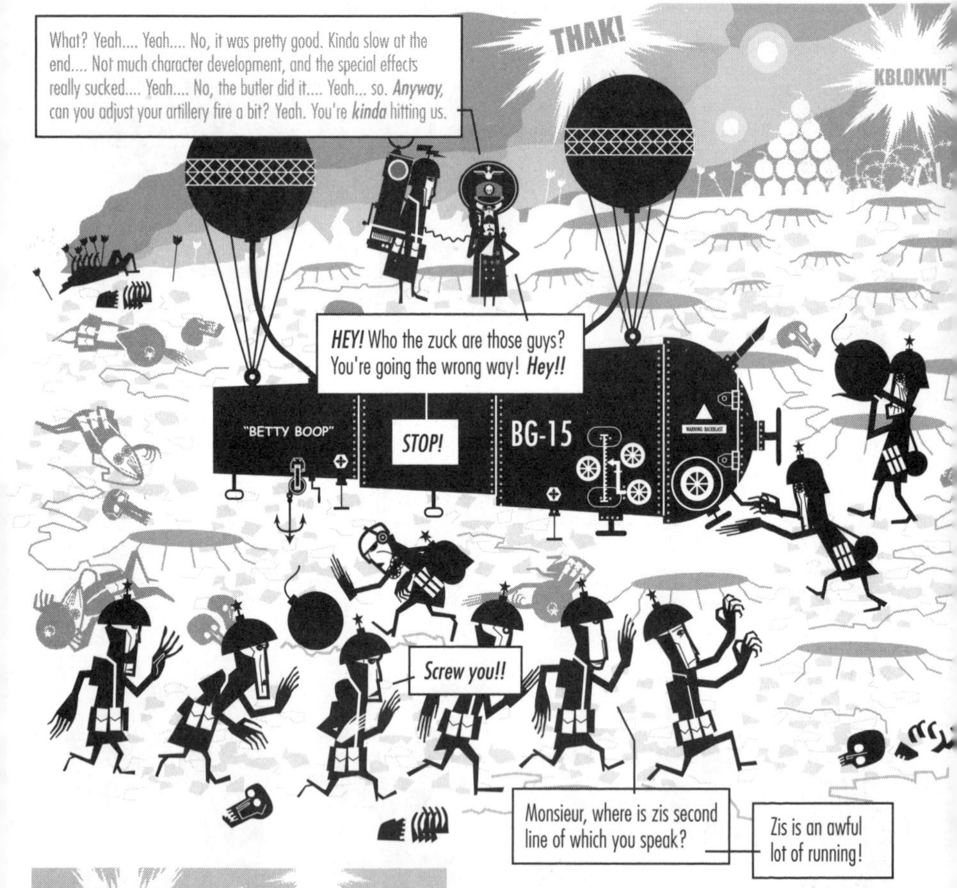
What? Yeah.... Yeah.... No, it was pretty good. Kinda slow at the end.... Not much character development, and the special effects really sucked.... Yeah.... No, the butler did it.... Yeah... so. *Anyway*, can you adjust your artillery fire a bit? Yeah. You're *kinda* hitting us.
THAK!
KBLOKW!
HEY! Who the zuck are those guys? You're going the wrong way! *Hey!!*
"BETTY BOOP"
STOP!
BG-15
WARNING: BACKBLAST
Screw you!!
Monsieur, where is zis second line of which you speak?
Zis is an awful lot of running!

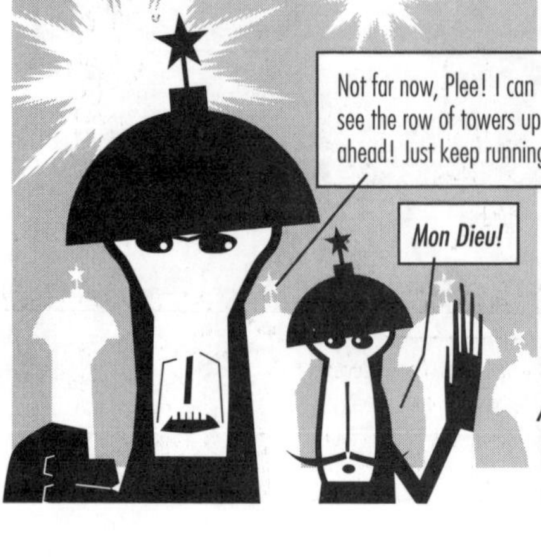
Not far now, Plee! I can see the row of towers up ahead! Just keep running!
Mon Dieu!

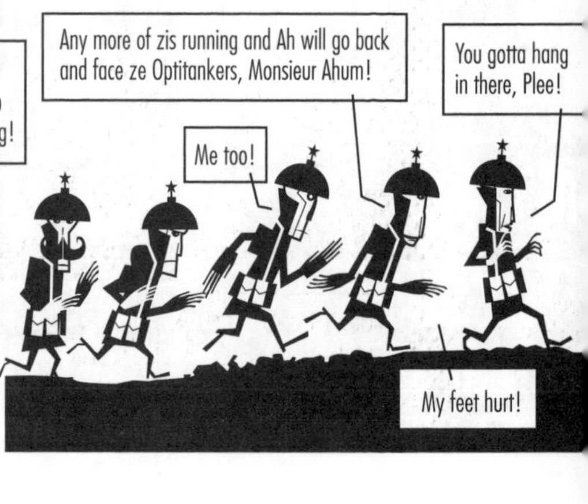
Any more of zis running and Ah will go back and face ze Optitankers, Monsieur Ahum!
You gotta hang in there, Plee!
Me too!
My feet hurt!

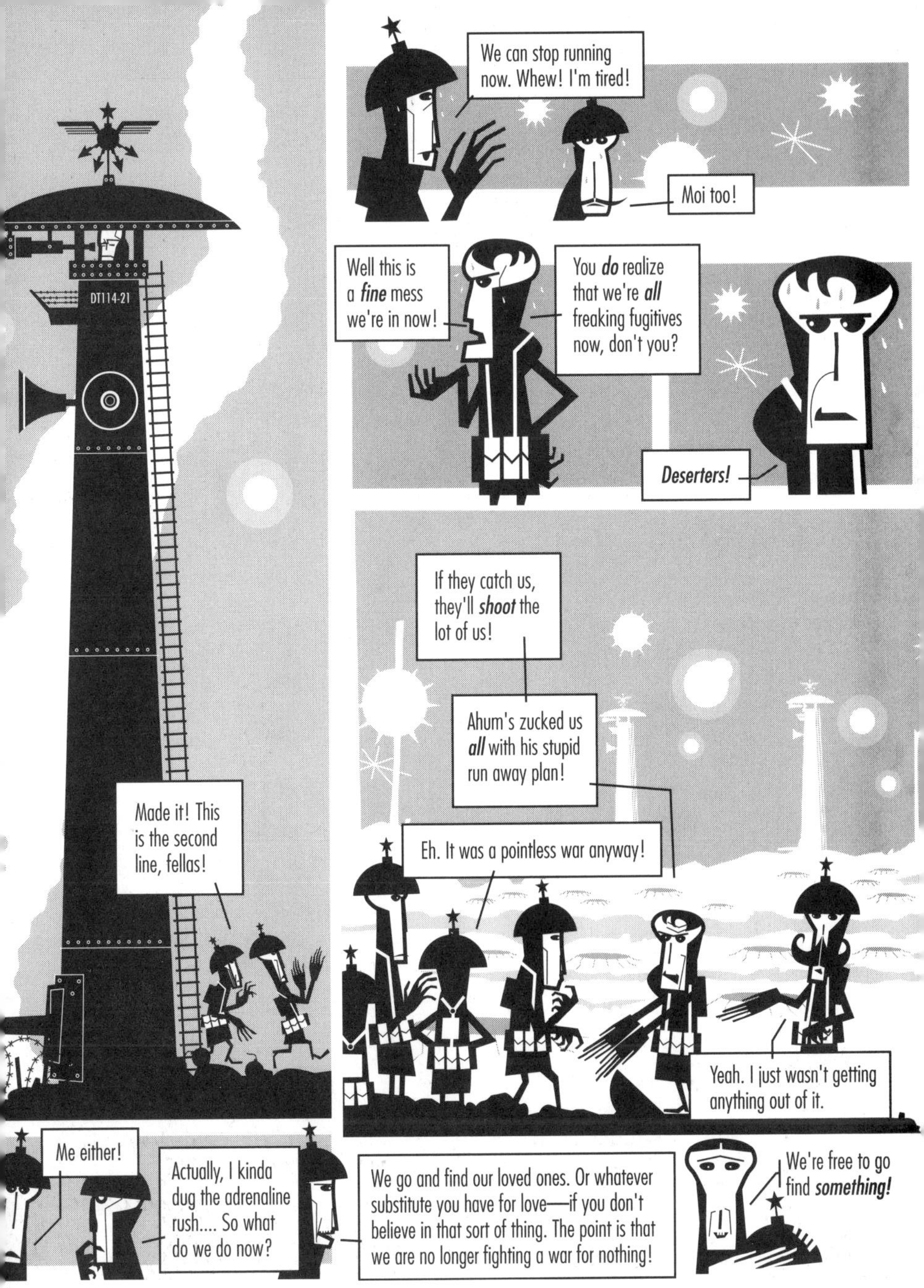
DT114-21
Made it! This is the second line, fellas!
We can stop running now. Whew! I'm tired!
Moi too!
Well this is a *fine* mess we're in now!
You *do* realize that we're *all* freaking fugitives now, don't you?
Deserters!
If they catch us, they'll *shoot* the lot of us!
Ahum's zucked us *all* with his stupid run away plan!
Eh. It was a pointless war anyway!
Yeah. I just wasn't getting anything out of it.
Me either!
Actually, I kinda dug the adrenaline rush.... So what do we do now?
We go and find our loved ones. Or whatever substitute you have for love—if you don't believe in that sort of thing. The point is that we are no longer fighting a war for nothing!
We're free to go find *something!*

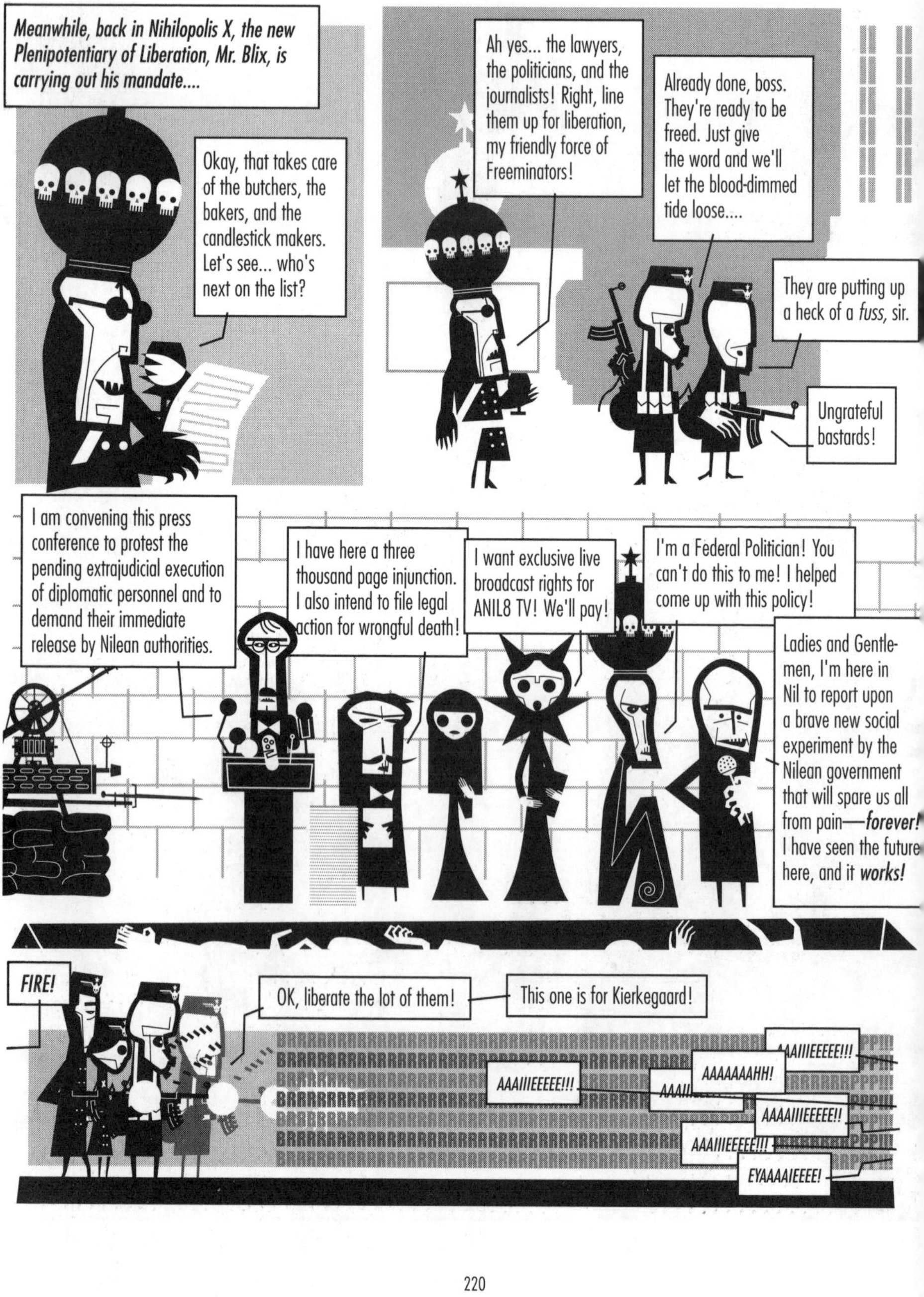

Meanwhile, back in Nihilopolis X, the new Plenipotentiary of Liberation, Mr. Blix, is carrying out his mandate....
Okay, that takes care of the butchers, the bakers, and the candlestick makers. Let's see... who's next on the list?
Ah yes... the lawyers, the politicians, and the journalists! Right, line them up for liberation, my friendly force of Freeminators!
Already done, boss. They're ready to be freed. Just give the word and we'll let the blood-dimmed tide loose....
They are putting up a heck of a fuss, sir.
Ungrateful bastards!
I am convening this press conference to protest the pending extrajudicial execution of diplomatic personnel and to demand their immediate release by Nilean authorities.
I have here a three thousand page injunction. I also intend to file legal action for wrongful death!
I want exclusive live broadcast rights for ANIL8 TV! We'll pay!
I'm a Federal Politician! You can't do this to me! I helped come up with this policy!
Ladies and Gentlemen, I'm here in Nil to report upon a brave new social experiment by the Nilean government that will spare us all from pain—forever! I have seen the future here, and it works!
FIRE!
OK, liberate the lot of them!
This one is for Kierkegaard!
AAAIIIEEEEE!!!
AAAIIIEEEEE!!!
AAAAAAAHH!
AAAAIIIEEEEE!!
AAAIIIEEEEE!!!
EYAAAAIEEEE!

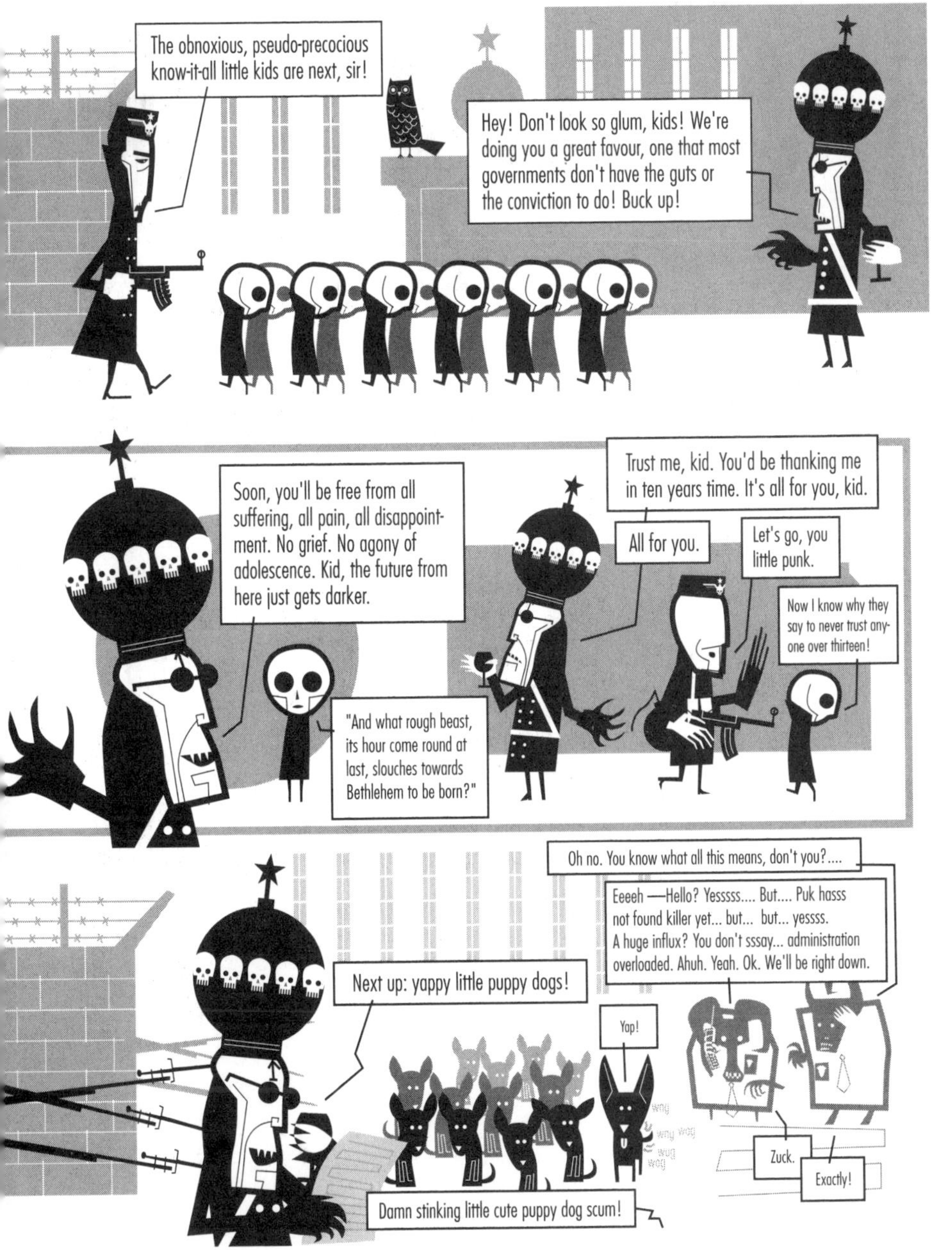

The obnoxious, pseudo-precocious know-it-all little kids are next, sir!
Hey! Don't look so glum, kids! We're doing you a great favour, one that most governments don't have the guts or the conviction to do! Buck up!
Soon, you'll be free from all suffering, all pain, all disappointment. No grief. No agony of adolescence. Kid, the future from here just gets darker.
"And what rough beast, its hour come round at last, slouches towards Bethlehem to be born?"
Trust me, kid. You'd be thanking me in ten years time. It's all for you, kid.
All for you.
Let's go, you little punk.
Now I know why they say to never trust anyone over thirteen!
Next up: yappy little puppy dogs!
Yap!
Damn stinking little cute puppy dog scum!
Oh no. You know what all this means, don't you?....
Eeeeh —Hello? Yesssss.... But.... Puk hasss not found killer yet... but... but... yessss. A huge influx? You don't sssay... administration overloaded. Ahuh. Yeah. Ok. We'll be right down.
Zuck.
Exactly!

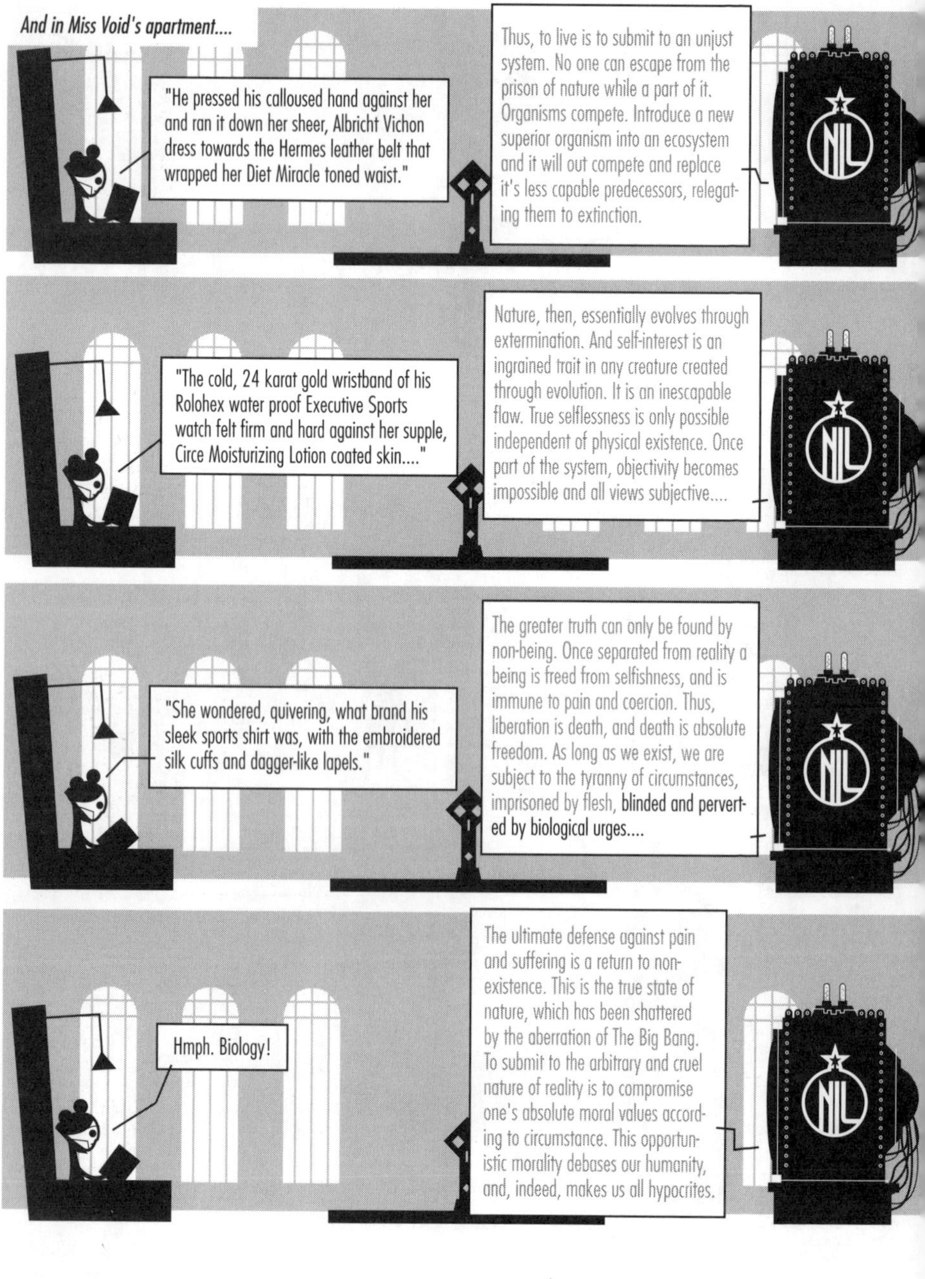

And in Miss Void's apartment....
"He pressed his calloused hand against her and ran it down her sheer, Albricht Vichon dress towards the Hermes leather belt that wrapped her Diet Miracle toned waist."
Thus, to live is to submit to an unjust system. No one can escape from the prison of nature while a part of it. Organisms compete. Introduce a new superior organism into an ecosystem and it will out compete and replace it's less capable predecessors, relegating them to extinction.
"The cold, 24 karat gold wristband of his Rolohex water proof Executive Sports watch felt firm and hard against her supple, Circe Moisturizing Lotion coated skin...."
Nature, then, essentially evolves through extermination. And self-interest is an ingrained trait in any creature created through evolution. It is an inescapable flaw. True selflessness is only possible independent of physical existence. Once part of the system, objectivity becomes impossible and all views subjective....
"She wondered, quivering, what brand his sleek sports shirt was, with the embroidered silk cuffs and dagger-like lapels."
The greater truth can only be found by non-being. Once separated from reality a being is freed from selfishness, and is immune to pain and coercion. Thus, liberation is death, and death is absolute freedom. As long as we exist, we are subject to the tyranny of circumstances, imprisoned by flesh, blinded and perverted by biological urges....
Hmph. Biology!
The ultimate defense against pain and suffering is a return to non-existence. This is the true state of nature, which has been shattered by the aberration of The Big Bang. To submit to the arbitrary and cruel nature of reality is to compromise one's absolute moral values according to circumstance. This opportunistic morality debases our humanity, and, indeed, makes us all hypocrites.

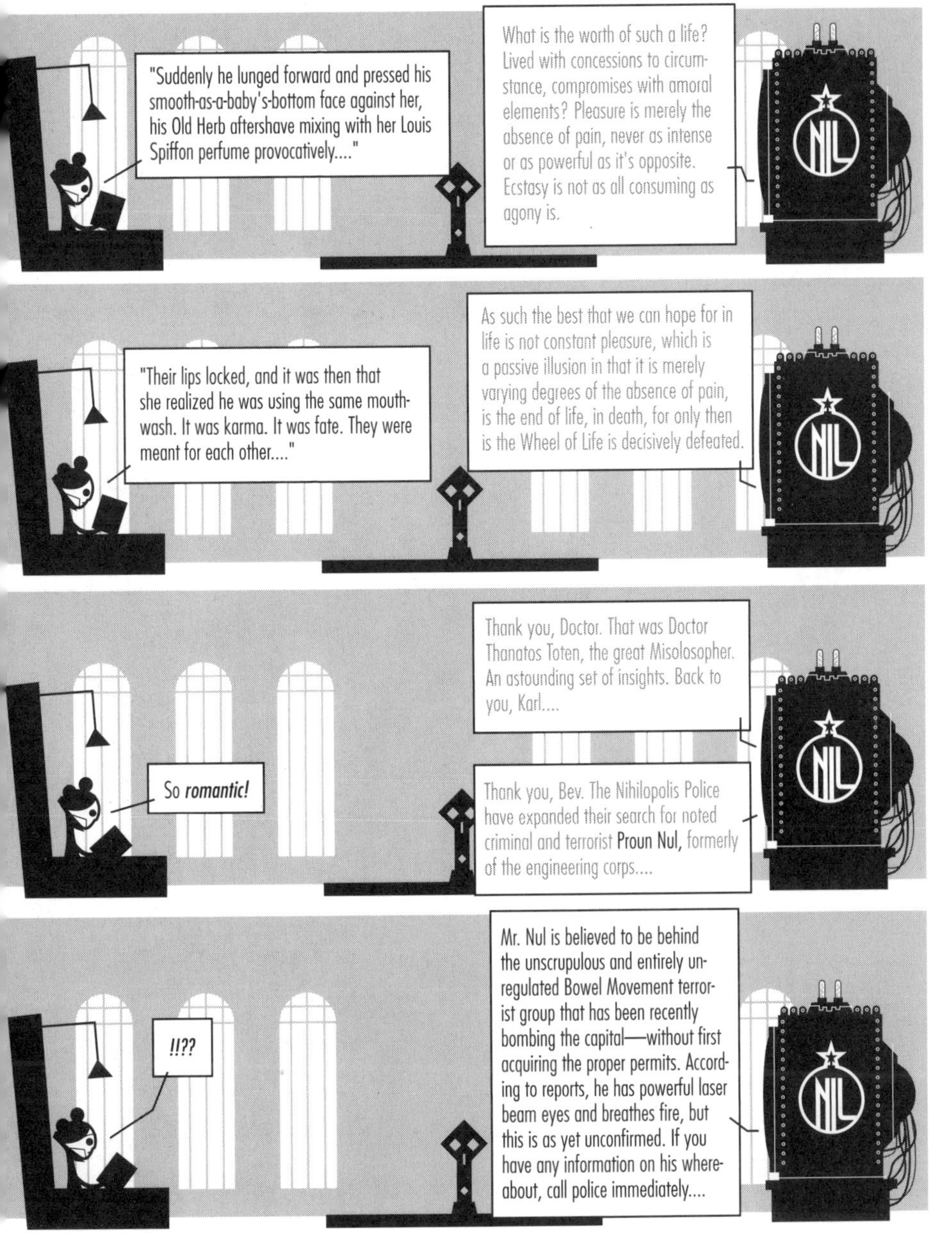
"Suddenly he lunged forward and pressed his smooth-as-a-baby's-bottom face against her, his Old Herb aftershave mixing with her Louis Spiffon perfume provocatively...."
What is the worth of such a life? Lived with concessions to circumstance, compromises with amoral elements? Pleasure is merely the absence of pain, never as intense or as powerful as it's opposite. Ecstasy is not as all consuming as agony is.
"Their lips locked, and it was then that she realized he was using the same mouthwash. It was karma. It was fate. They were meant for each other...."
As such the best that we can hope for in life is not constant pleasure, which is a passive illusion in that it is merely varying degrees of the absence of pain, is the end of life, in death, for only then is the Wheel of Life is decisively defeated.
So *romantic!*
Thank you, Doctor. That was Doctor Thanatos Toten, the great Misolosopher. An astounding set of insights. Back to you, Karl....
Thank you, Bev. The Nihilopolis Police have expanded their search for noted criminal and terrorist Proun Nul, formerly of the engineering corps....
!!??
Mr. Nul is believed to be behind the unscrupulous and entirely unregulated Bowel Movement terrorist group that has been recently bombing the capital—without first acquiring the proper permits. According to reports, he has powerful laser beam eyes and breathes fire, but this is as yet unconfirmed. If you have any information on his whereabout, call police immediately....
NIL

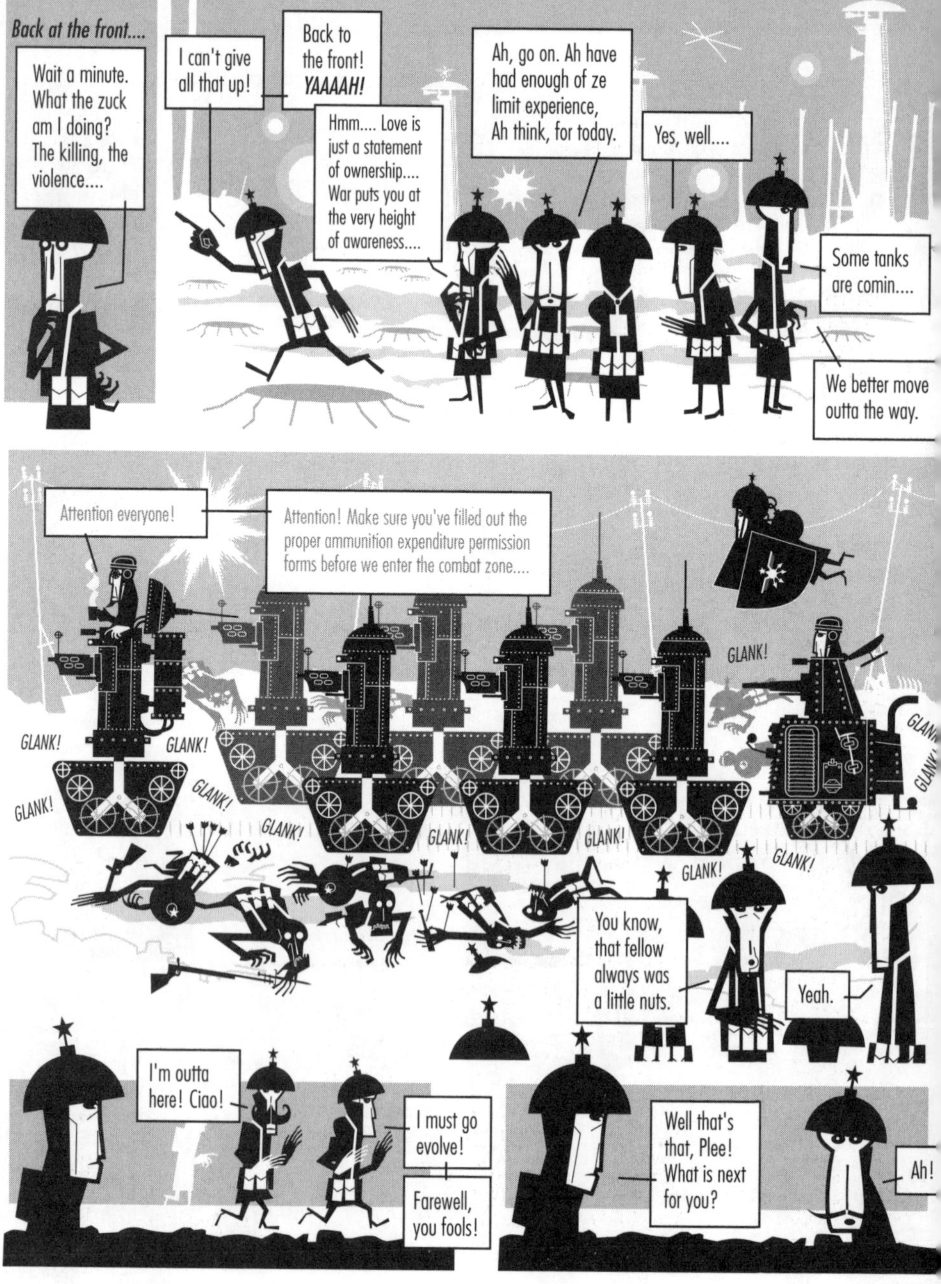
Back at the front....
Wait a minute. What the zuck am I doing? The killing, the violence....
I can't give all that up!
Back to the front! YAAAAH!
Hmm.... Love is just a statement of ownership.... War puts you at the very height of awareness....
Ah, go on. Ah have had enough of ze limit experience, Ah think, for today.
Yes, well....
Some tanks are comin....
We better move outta the way.
Attention everyone!
Attention! Make sure you've filled out the proper ammunition expenditure permission forms before we enter the combat zone....
GLANK!
GLANK!
GLANK!
GLANK!
GLANK!
GLANK!
GLANK!
GLANK!
GLANK!
GLANK!
You know, that fellow always was a little nuts.
Yeah.
I'm outta here! Ciao!
I must go evolve!
Farewell, you fools!
Well that's that, Plee! What is next for you?
Ah!

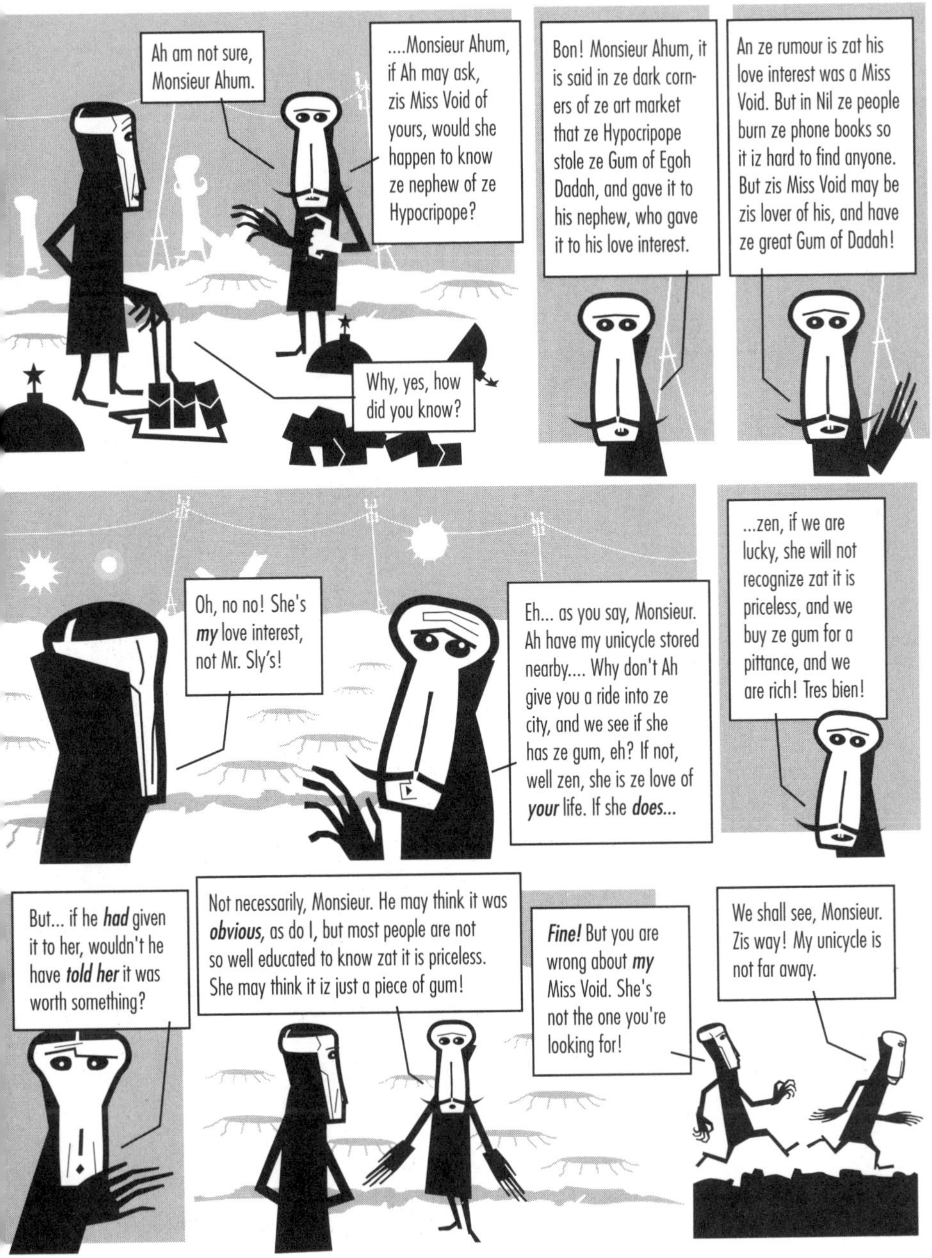

Ah am not sure, Monsieur Ahum.
....Monsieur Ahum, if Ah may ask, zis Miss Void of yours, would she happen to know ze nephew of ze Hypocripope?
Why, yes, how did you know?
Bon! Monsieur Ahum, it is said in ze dark corners of ze art market that ze Hypocripope stole ze Gum of Egoh Dadah, and gave it to his nephew, who gave it to his love interest.
An ze rumour is zat his love interest was a Miss Void. But in Nil ze people burn ze phone books so it iz hard to find anyone. But zis Miss Void may be zis lover of his, and have ze great Gum of Dadah!
Oh, no no! She's *my* love interest, not Mr. Sly's!
Eh... as you say, Monsieur. Ah have my unicycle stored nearby.... Why don't Ah give you a ride into ze city, and we see if she has ze gum, eh? If not, well zen, she is ze love of *your* life. If she *does*...
...zen, if we are lucky, she will not recognize zat it is priceless, and we buy ze gum for a pittance, and we are rich! Tres bien!
But... if he *had* given it to her, wouldn't he have *told her* it was worth something?
Not necessarily, Monsieur. He may think it was *obvious*, as do I, but most people are not so well educated to know zat it is priceless. She may think it iz just a piece of gum!
Fine! But you are wrong about *my* Miss Void. She's not the one you're looking for!
We shall see, Monsieur. Zis way! My unicycle is not far away.

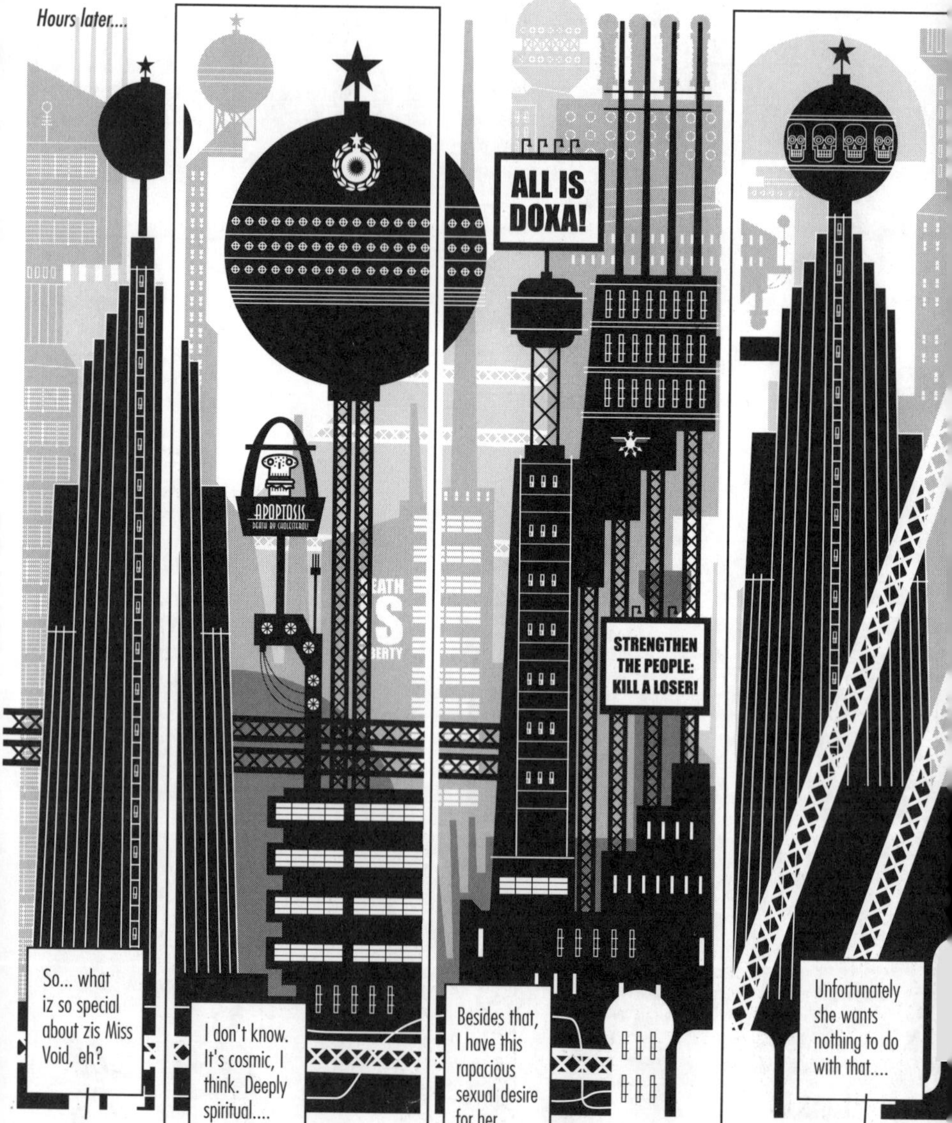
Hours later....
ALL IS DOXA!
APOPTOSIS
DEATH BY CHOLESTEROL!
STRENGTHEN THE PEOPLE: KILL A LOSER!
So... what iz so special about zis Miss Void, eh?
I don't know. It's cosmic, I think. Deeply spiritual....
Besides that, I have this rapacious sexual desire for her....
Unfortunately she wants nothing to do with that....

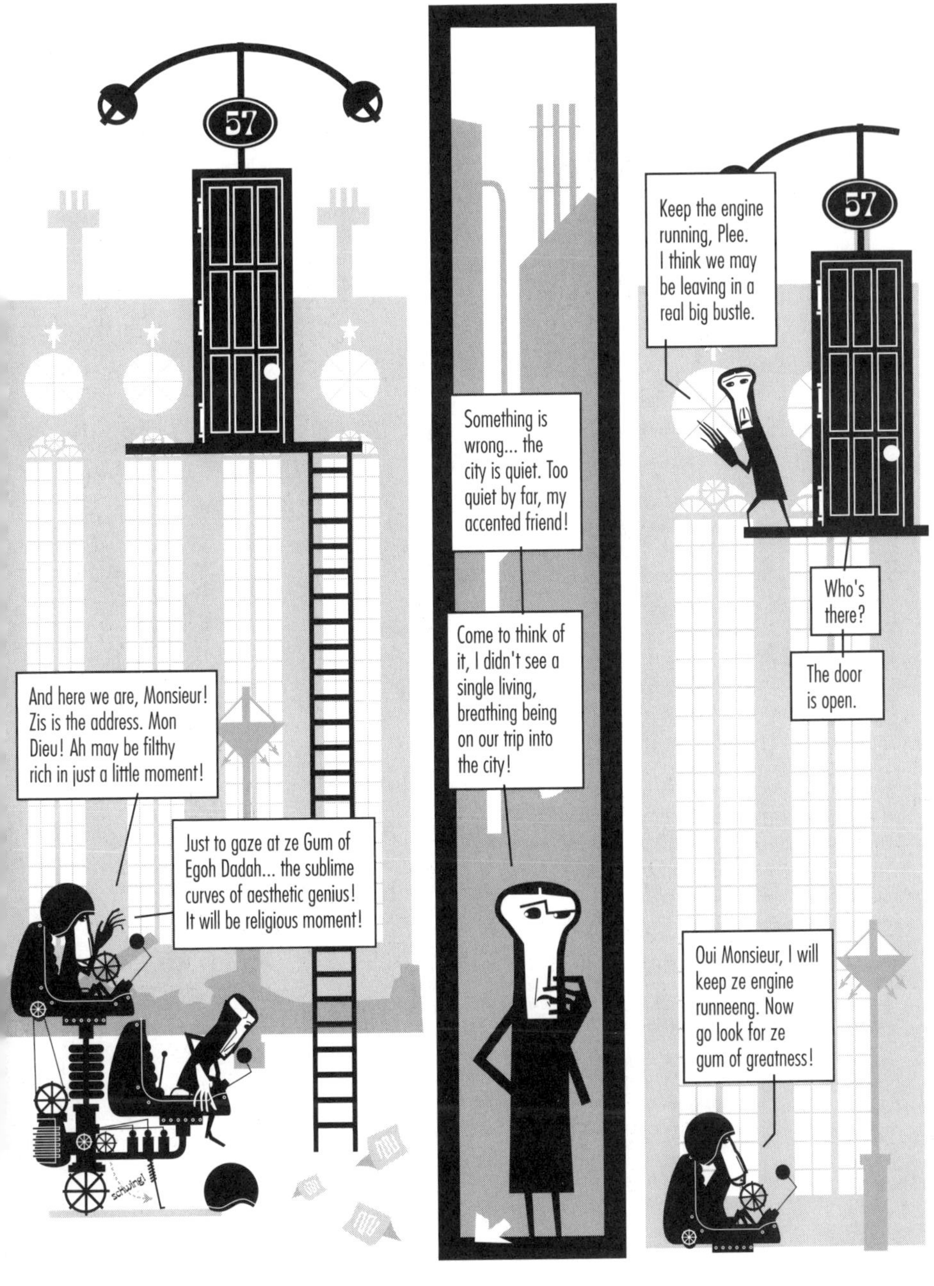
57
And here we are, Monsieur! Zis is the address. Mon Dieu! Ah may be filthy rich in just a little moment!
Just to gaze at ze Gum of Egoh Dadah... the sublime curves of aesthetic genius! It will be religious moment!
schwing!
Something is wrong... the city is quiet. Too quiet by far, my accented friend!
Come to think of it, I didn't see a single living, breathing being on our trip into the city!
Keep the engine running, Plee. I think we may be leaving in a real big bustle.
57
Who's there?
The door is open.
Oui Monsieur, I will keep ze engine runneeng. Now go look for ze gum of greatness!

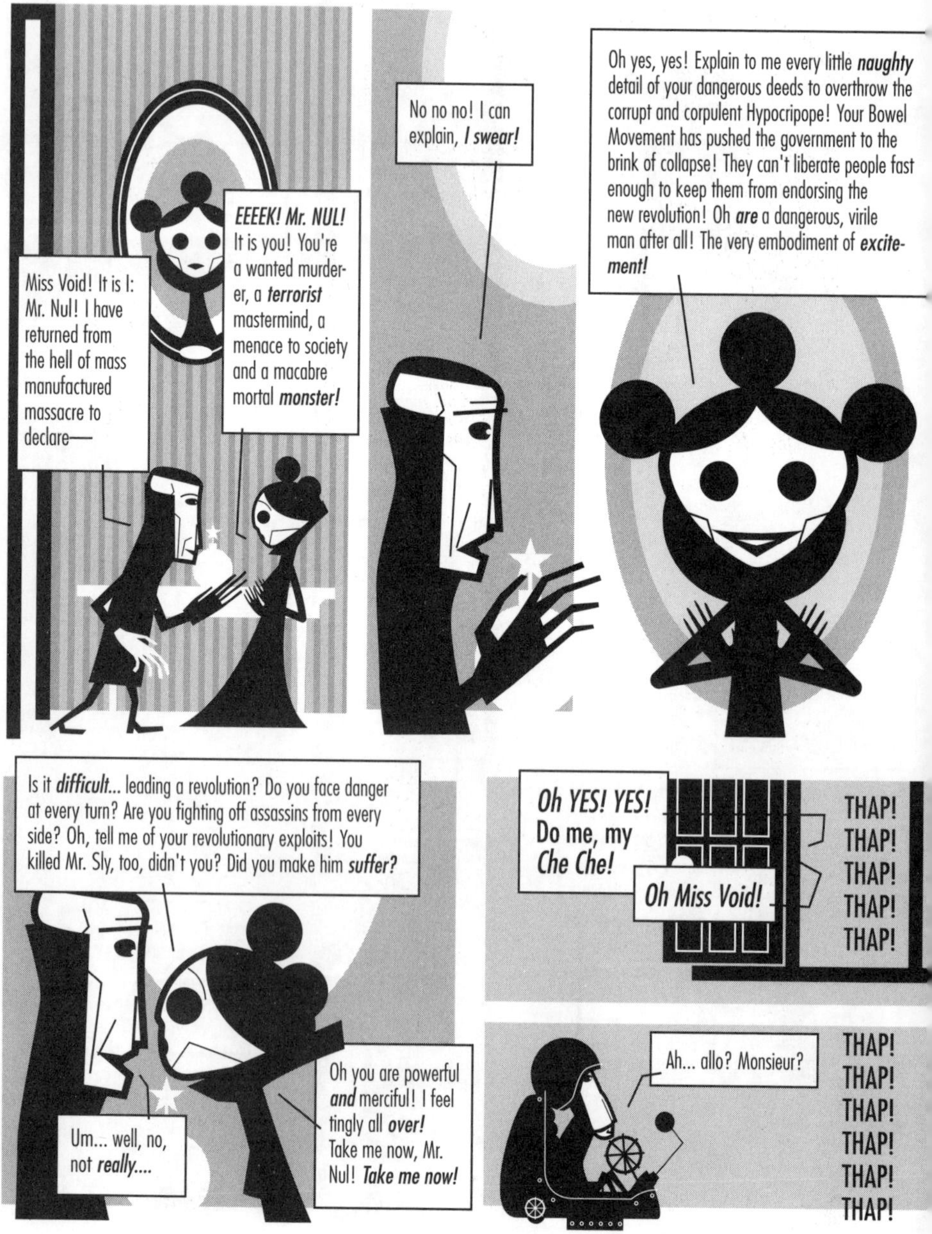
Miss Void! It is I: Mr. Nul! I have returned from the hell of mass manufactured massacre to declare—
EEEEK! Mr. NUL! It is you! You're a wanted murderer, a terrorist mastermind, a menace to society and a macabre mortal monster!
No no no! I can explain, I swear!
Oh yes, yes! Explain to me every little naughty detail of your dangerous deeds to overthrow the corrupt and corpulent Hypocripope! Your Bowel Movement has pushed the government to the brink of collapse! They can't liberate people fast enough to keep them from endorsing the new revolution! Oh are a dangerous, virile man after all! The very embodiment of excitement!
Is it difficult... leading a revolution? Do you face danger at every turn? Are you fighting off assassins from every side? Oh, tell me of your revolutionary exploits! You killed Mr. Sly, too, didn't you? Did you make him suffer?
Um... well, no, not really....
Oh you are powerful and merciful! I feel tingly all over! Take me now, Mr. Nul! Take me now!
Oh YES! YES! Do me, my Che Che!
Oh Miss Void!
THAP! THAP! THAP! THAP! THAP!
Ah... allo? Monsieur?
THAP! THAP! THAP! THAP! THAP! THAP!

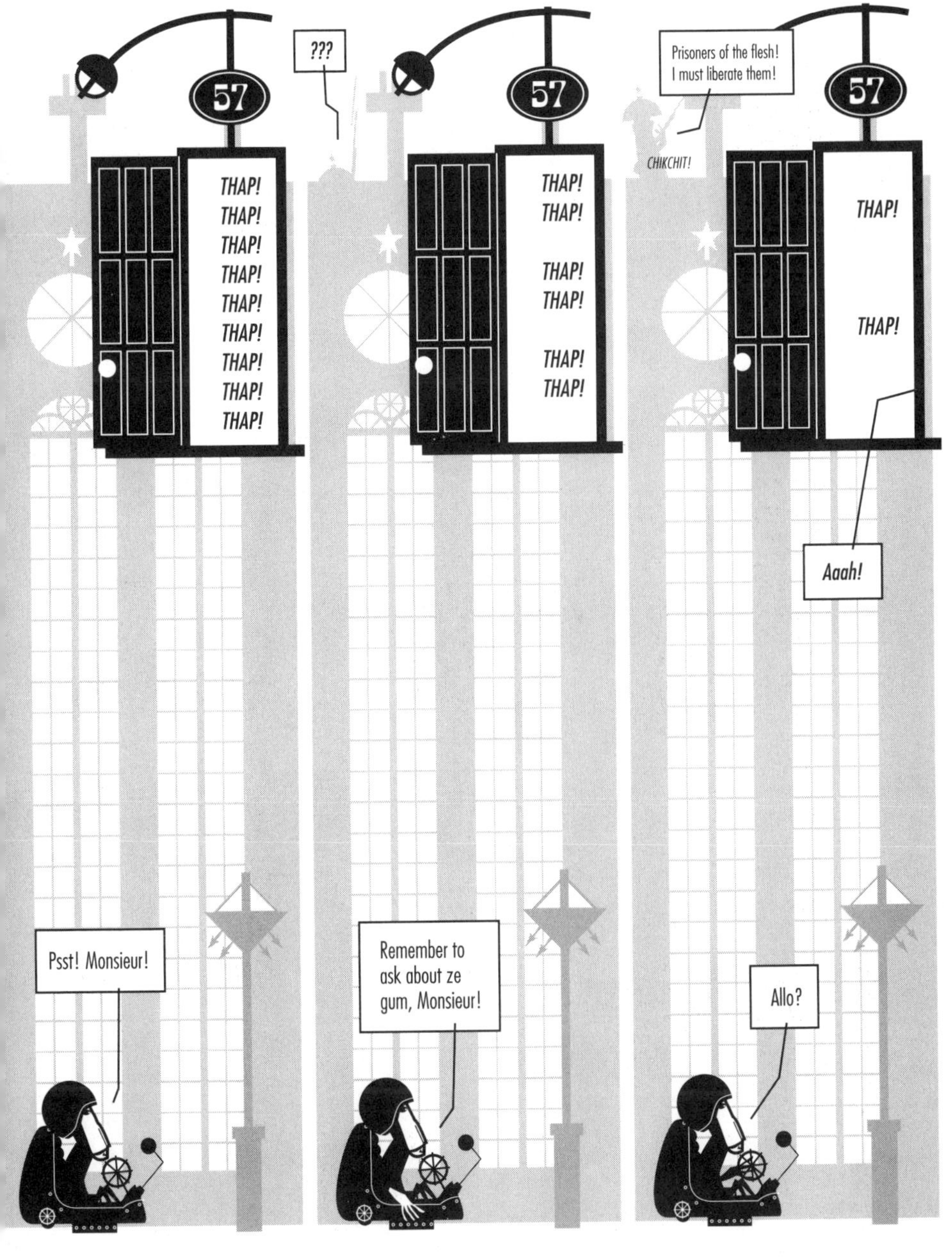
THAP! THAP! THAP! THAP! THAP! THAP! THAP! THAP! THAP!
Psst! Monsieur!
???
THAP! THAP!
THAP! THAP!
THAP! THAP!
Remember to ask about ze gum, Monsieur!
Prisoners of the flesh! I must liberate them!
CHIKCHIT!
THAP!
THAP!
Aaah!
Allo?

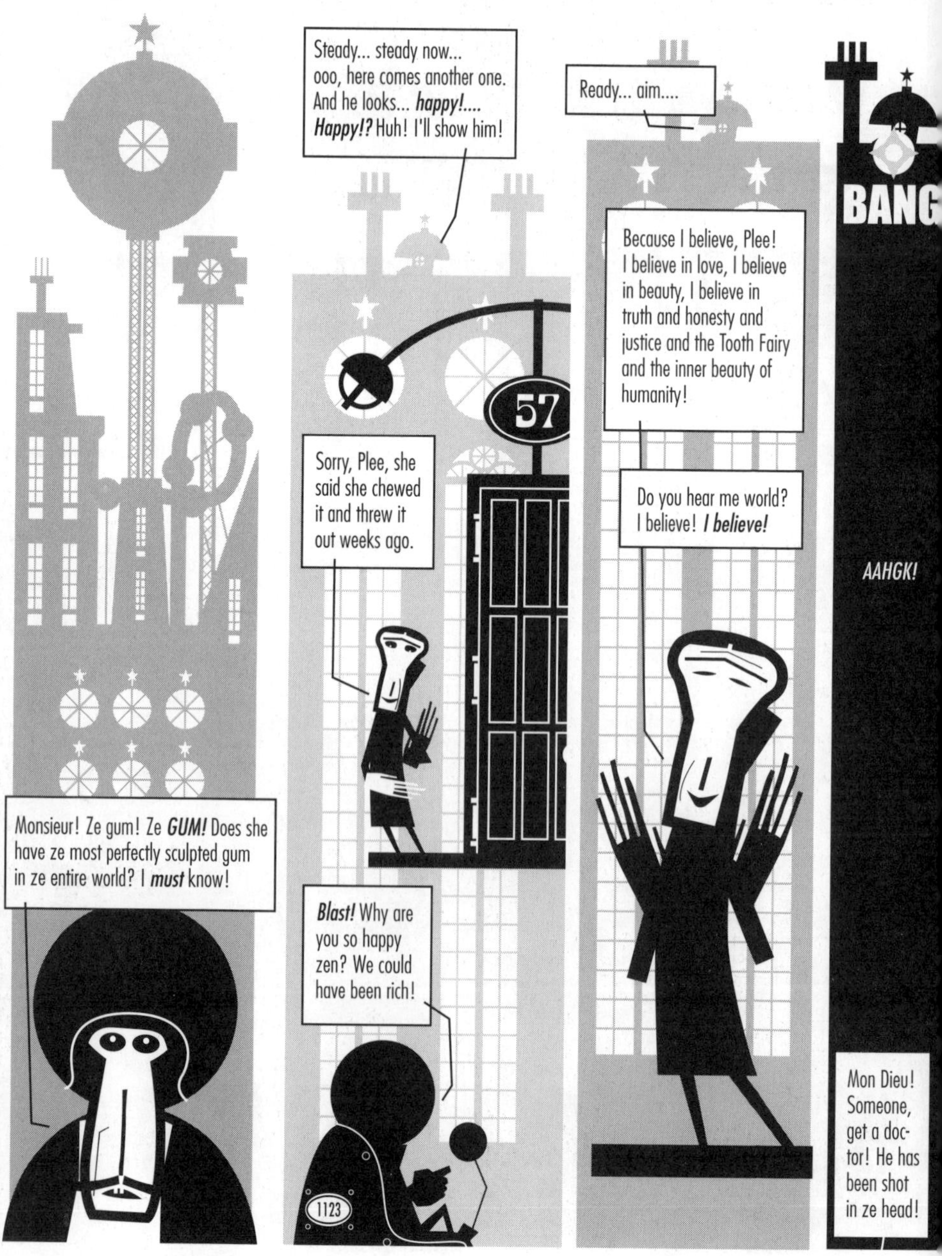
Monsieur! Ze gum! Ze GUM! Does she have ze most perfectly sculpted gum in ze entire world? I must know!
Steady... steady now... ooo, here comes another one. And he looks... happy!.... Happy!? Huh! I'll show him!
57
Sorry, Plee, she said she chewed it and threw it out weeks ago.
Blast! Why are you so happy zen? We could have been rich!
1123
Ready... aim....
Because I believe, Plee! I believe in love, I believe in beauty, I believe in truth and honesty and justice and the Tooth Fairy and the inner beauty of humanity!
Do you hear me world? I believe! I believe!
BANG
AAHGK!
Mon Dieu! Someone, get a doc-tor! He has been shot in ze head!

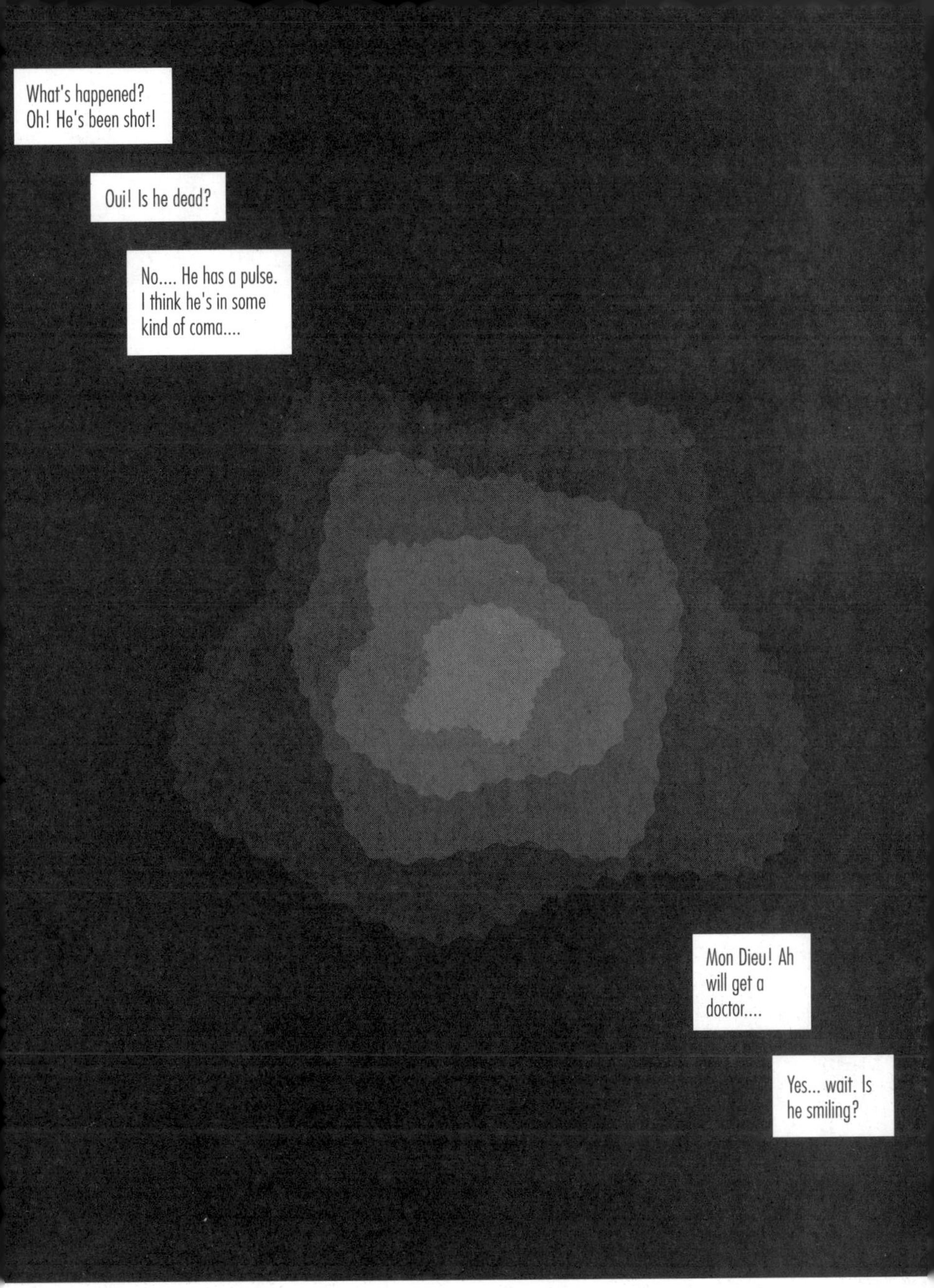
What's happened?
Oh! He's been shot!
Oui! Is he dead?
No.... He has a pulse.
I think he's in some kind of coma....
Mon Dieu! Ah will get a doctor....
Yes... wait. Is he smiling?

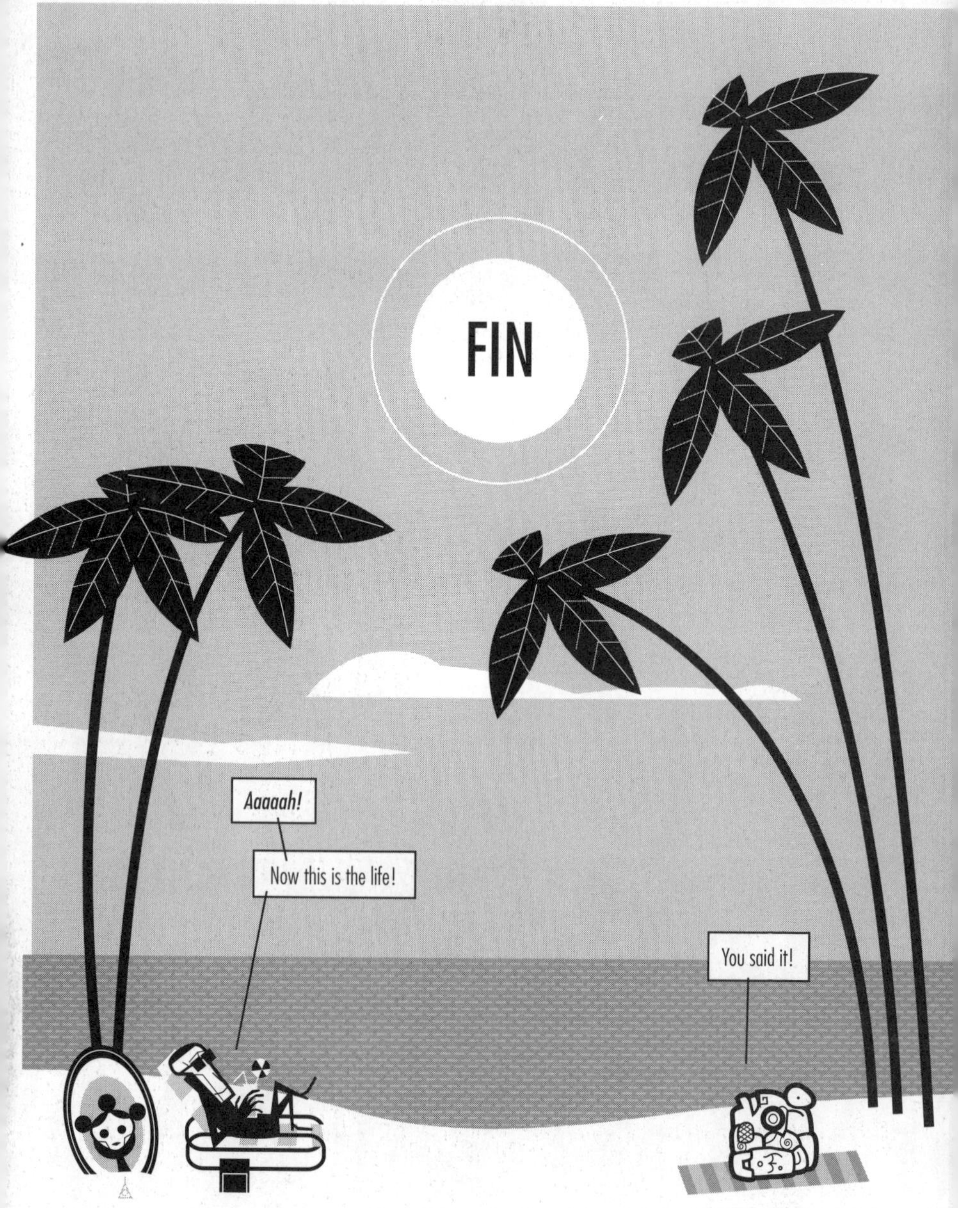
FIN
Aaaaah!
Now this is the life!
You said it!

"....Because in spite of everything I still believe that people are really good at heart. I simply can't build my hopes on a foundation of confusion, misery, and death...."

ANNE FRANK

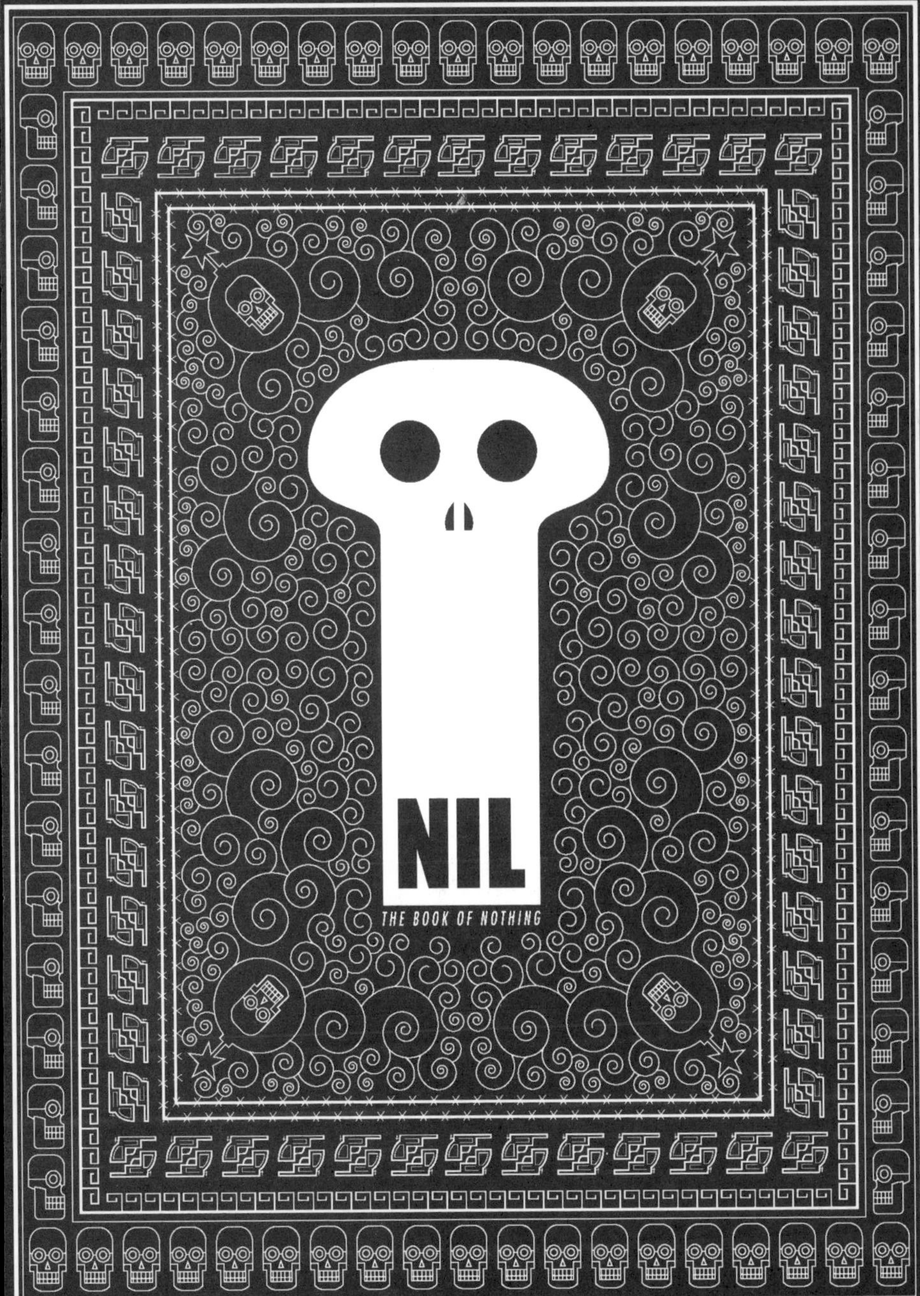
NIL
THE BOOK OF NOTHING

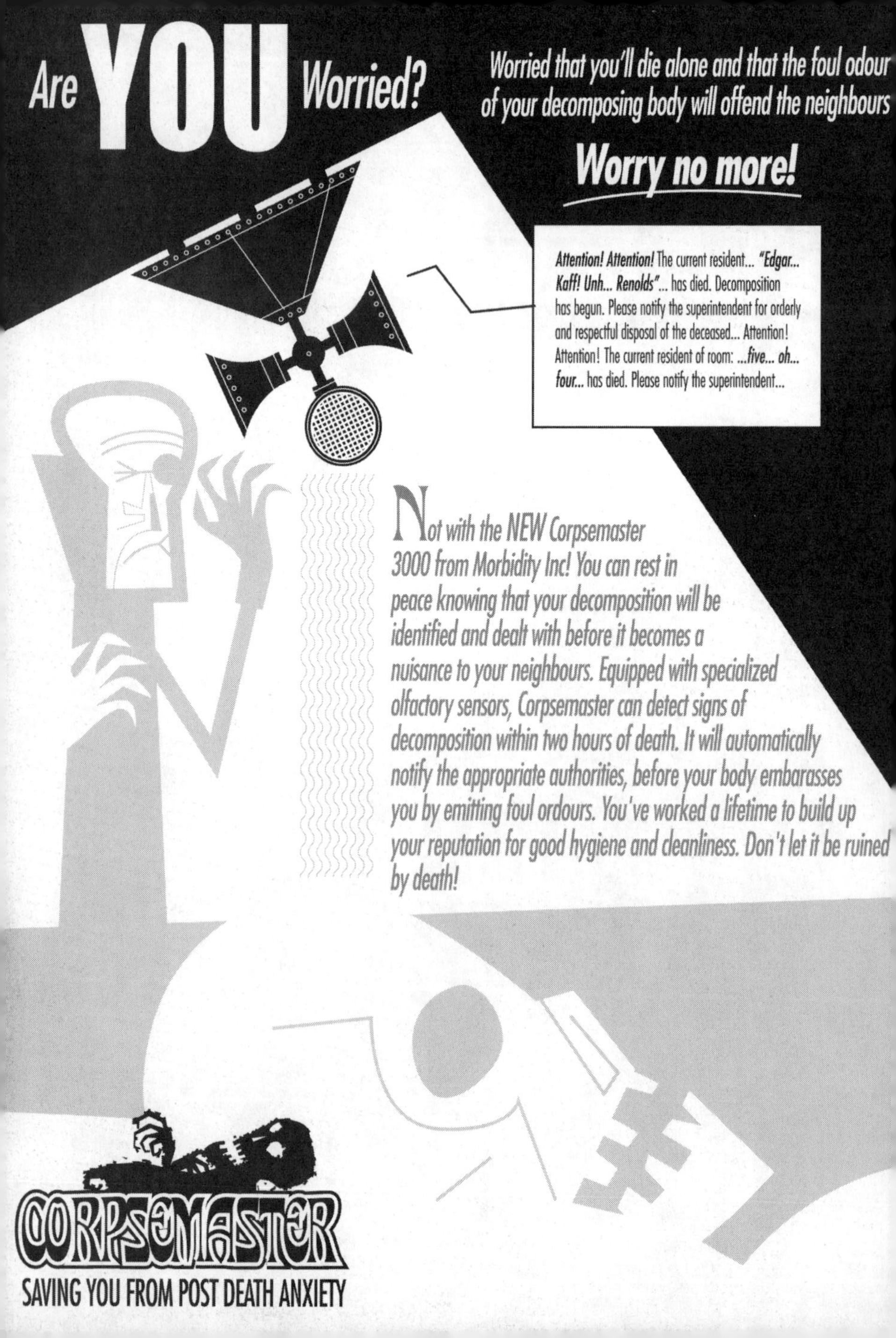
Are YOU Worried?
Worried that you'll die alone and that the foul odour of your decomposing body will offend the neighbours
Worry no more!
Attention! Attention! The current resident... "Edgar... Kaff! Unh... Renolds"... has died. Decomposition has begun. Please notify the superintendent for orderly and respectful disposal of the deceased... Attention! Attention! The current resident of room: ...five... oh... four... has died. Please notify the superintendent...
Not with the NEW Corpsemaster 3000 from Morbidity Inc! You can rest in peace knowing that your decomposition will be identified and dealt with before it becomes a nuisance to your neighbours. Equipped with specialized olfactory sensors, Corpsemaster can detect signs of decomposition within two hours of death. It will automatically notify the appropriate authorities, before your body embarasses you by emitting foul ordours. You've worked a lifetime to build up your reputation for good hygiene and cleanliness. Don't let it be ruined by death!
CORPSEMASTER
SAVING YOU FROM POST DEATH ANXIETY

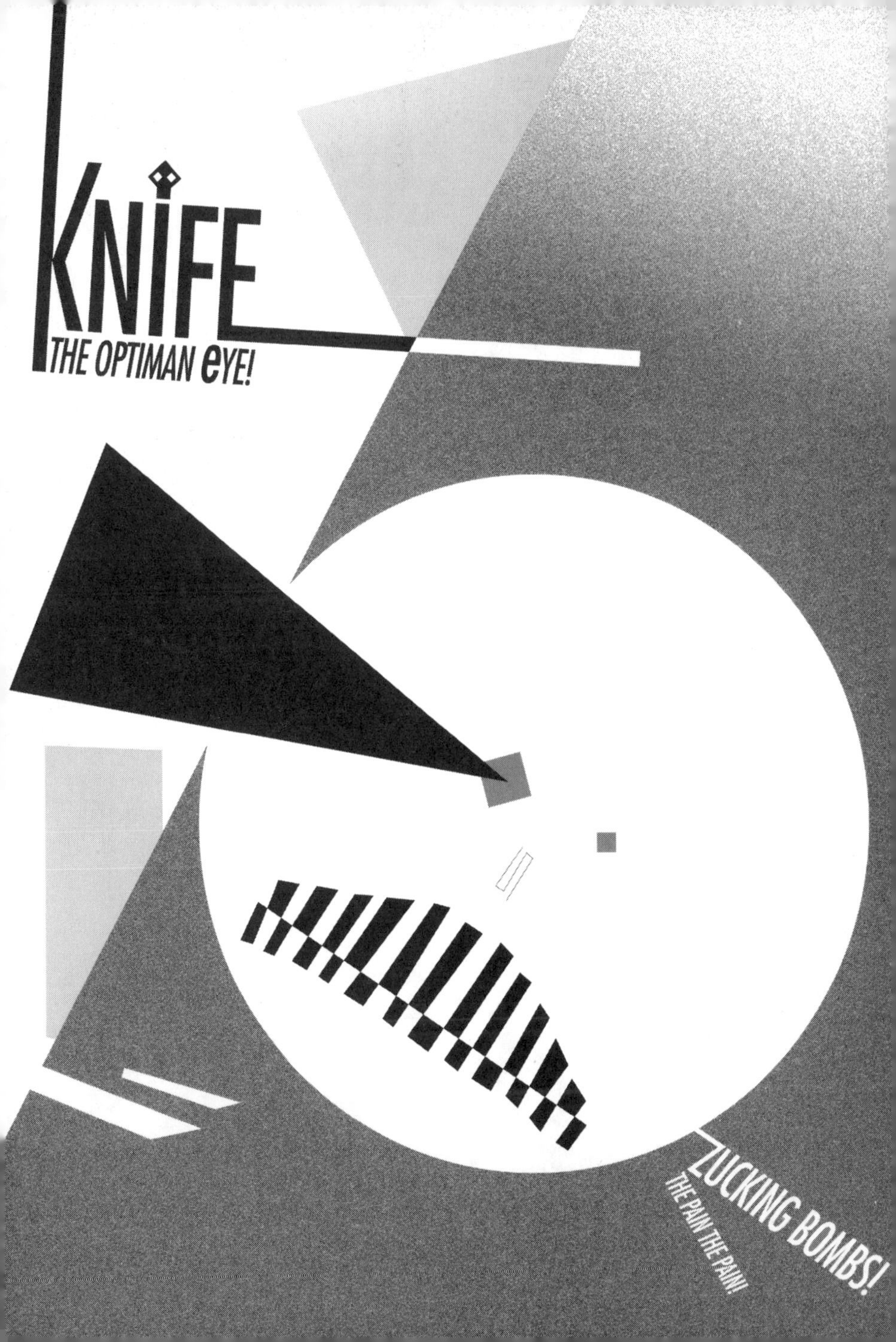
KNIFE
THE OPTIMAN eYE!
ZUCKING BOMBS!
THE PAIN THE PAIN!

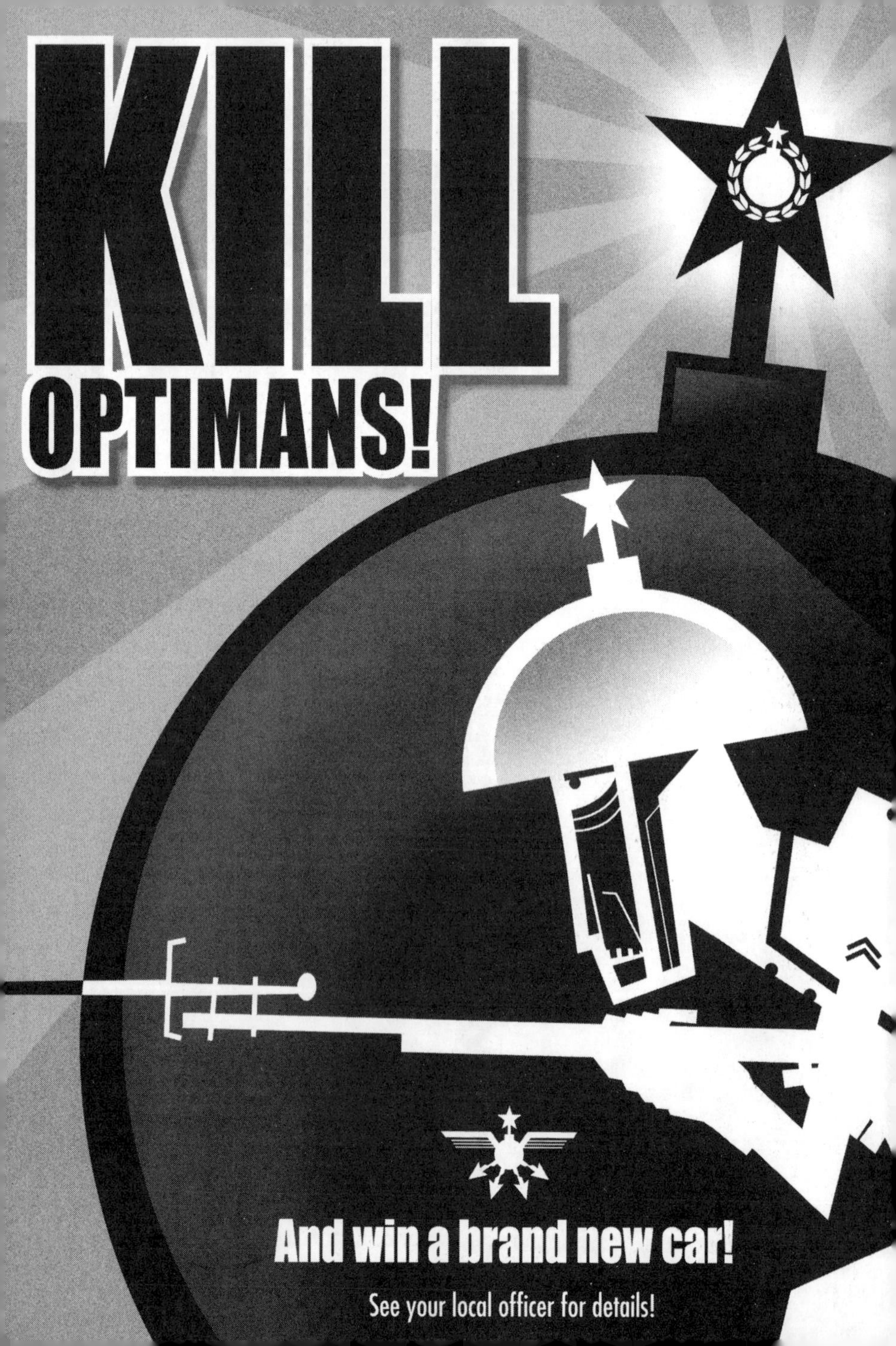
KILL
OPTIMANS!
And win a brand new car!
See your local officer for details!